Jonas & Kovner's

HEALTH CARE DELIVERY IN THE UNITED STATES

10th Edition

Anthony R. Kovner, PhD, is professor of health care management at New York University's Robert F. Wagner Graduate School of Public Service. His research interests include evidence-based management, nonprofit governance, clinician leadership, and hospital service lines in geriatrics. He has been a senior manager in two hospitals, a nursing home, a group practice, a neighborhood health center, and a senior consultant for a large industrial union. Professor Kovner has written 11 books and 91 peer-reviewed articles, book chapters, and case studies. His newest texts include *Evidence-Based Management in Health Care,* with Richard D'Aquila and David Fine (2009), and *Health Care Management: Cases, Readings and Commentary,* with Ann McAlearney and Duncan Neuhauser, 9th edition (2009). He has been an editor or coeditor for several editions of *Health Care Delivery in the United States.* He has consulted with the New York-Presbyterian health system (nurse leadership), Robert Wood Johnson Foundation (swing beds), the WK Kellogg Foundation (clinician management education), Montefiore Medical Center (clinician management education), and the American Academy of Orthopaedics (governance). He was a Lutheran Medical Center board member for 26 years. He directs the NYU/Wagner Executive MPA for Nurse Leaders. Professor Kovner received his PhD in public administration from the University of Pittsburgh.

James R. Knickman, PhD, is the president and chief executive officer of New York State Health Foundation (NYSHF), a private philanthropy that has a mission to improve public health and health care delivery in New York state. The Foundation supports innovative organizations working to improve the health of New Yorkers through systems reform, improvements in access to health care, and improvements in the quality of public health and medical care. Prior to joining NYSHealth, Dr. Knickman was vice president of research and evaluation at Robert Wood Johnson Foundation. He also was a faculty member at the New York University Robert F. Wagner Graduate School of Public Service for 16 years. He has served as chair of the Robert Wood Johnson University Hospital board and as board member of Academy Health. He is on the editorial boards for the *Milbank Quarterly* and *Inquiry* and has published widely on topics related to the financing and organization of health care services. Dr. Knickman received his PhD in public policy analysis from the University of Pennsylvania.

Jonas & Kovner's

HEALTH CARE DELIVERY IN THE UNITED STATES

10th Edition

Anthony R. Kovner, PhD
James R. Knickman, PhD
Editors

Victoria D. Weisfeld, MPH
Managing Editor

Steven Jonas, MD, MPH, MS, FNYAS
Founding Editor

SPRINGER PUBLISHING COMPANY
NEW YORK

Springer Publishing Company, LLC
11 West 42nd Street
New York, NY 10036
www.springerpub.com

Acquisitions Editor: Sheri W. Sussman
Senior Production Editor: Diane Davis
Composition: Absolute Service, Inc.; Matt Gardner, Project Manager
Cover Design: Mimi Flow

ISBN: 978-0-8261-0687-2 (paper)
ISBN: 978-0-8261-0892-0 (cloth)
E-book ISBN: 978-0-8261-0688-9

Supplementary electronic instructors' materials are available to qualified instructors. Please email: textbook@springerpub.com to request these files.

11 12 13 14 15/5 4 3 2 1

The author and the publisher of this work have made every effort to use sources believed to be reliable to provide information that is accurate and compatible with the standards generally accepted at the time of publication. Because medical science is continually advancing, our knowledge base continues to expand. Therefore, as new information becomes available, changes in procedures become necessary. We recommend that the reader always consult current research and specific institutional policies before performing any clinical procedure. The author and publisher shall not be liable for any special, consequential, or exemplary damages resulting, in whole or in part, from the readers' use of, or reliance on, the information contained in this book. The publisher has no responsibility for the persistence or accuracy of URLs for external or third-party Internet Web sites referred to in this publication and does not guarantee that any content on such Web sites is, or will remain, accurate or appropriate.

Library of Congress Cataloging-in-Publication Data
Jonas & Kovner's health care delivery in the United States / Anthony R. Kovner, James R. Knickman, editors ; Victoria D. Weisfeld, managing editor ; Steven Jonas, founding editor. -- 10th ed.
      p. ; cm.
    Jonas and Kovner's health care delivery in the United States
    Health care delivery in the United States
    Includes bibliographical references and index.
    ISBN 978-0-8261-0892-0 (cloth) -- ISBN 978-0-8261-0687-2 (pbk.) -- ISBN 978-0-8261-0688-9 (e-book)
    1. Medical care--United States. I. Kovner, Anthony R. II. Knickman, James. III. Jonas, Steven. IV. Title: Jonas and Kovner's health care delivery in the United States. V. Title: Health care delivery in the United States.
    [DNLM: 1. Delivery of Health Care--United States. 2. Health Policy--United States. 3. Health Services--United States. 4. Quality of Health Care--United States. W 84 AA1]
    RA395.A3H395 2011
    362.10973--dc22
                                          2011014223

Printed in the United States of America by Bang Printing

BRIEF CONTENTS

CONTENTS

Part I: Health Policy

Part IV. Support for Medical Care Delivery

14 GOVERNANCE, MANAGEMENT, AND ACCOUNTABILITY   *299*

Anthony R. Kovner

15 HEALTH WORKFORCE   *315*

Richard Scheffler and Joanne Spetz

16 HEALTH INFORMATION TECHNOLOGY   *331*

Roger Kropf

LIST OF TABLES AND FIGURES

Chapter 5

Chapter 6

Chapter 7

Chapter 8

Chapter 9

Chapter 10

Chapter 11

Chapter 15

FOREWORD

In the beginning—that is in the mid-1970s—there was nothing like this book. It was then that our group of young health policy analysts came together to produce the first edition of *Health Care Delivery in the United States,* published by Springer Publishing Company in 1977. None of us, or any of our predecessors who had ever taught about the U.S. health care system to students had had a textbook to use. We all came in with stacks of reprints to hand out. But folks did not publish articles with titles like "Hospitals," "Government," "Financing," and so on and so forth, describing the basics of each sector of the health care delivery system. So we set out to create such a book. And here we are at its 10th edition. What a special anniversary! It's one that none of us could have foreseen back then.

Each of us had a major focus on the structure and function of one or more of the different sectors of the U.S. health care delivery system. We had a common perspective in terms of our values: first and foremost, the system's primary functions should be to take care of sick people and try to help the healthy stay well. Other considerations, such as making profits, gaining and maintaining power, and earning prestige, should all be secondary.

We established a firm rule for the text—the bulk of it was to be descriptive. Surely we would discuss policy options—recognizing that all policy discussions are informed by the points of view of the discussants. But in the book those discussions would be treated as condiments. The meat and potatoes—nowadays, the fish, poultry, and vegetables—would be description. Perhaps the most important feature of the successive editions—first under my leadership, then under Dr. Kovner's alone, then with me back in an editor's chair, then with Dr. Kovner joined by Dr. Knickman—is that that rule has been consistently followed. Policy questions are raised and answered in the book. The separation between policy analysis and description is kept clear. Because although even "pure" description is informed by a point of view, one can still be reasonably objective in providing it. Therefore, before any attempts can be made to consider what, if anything, needs to be done, and how it should be done, the "what" and the objective "why's," in terms of health and sickness—how people are cared for and not cared for, and how that care is paid for and not paid for, must first to be understood.

To appreciate the importance of understanding the what and the why before policy recommendations are made, one only has to examine those recommendations currently on the political front burners. Few of them appear to be informed by any in-depth understanding of what our system is all about, in all of its complexity. Unfortunately, these comments apply equally to a number of the main features of the Patient Protection and Affordable Care Act of 2010.

The second major feature of the book is that the book has never had a rigid format. Over the years, we editors have always been open to new ideas about how to present the material, new features that ought to be added, and old features that should be condensed or even eliminated. And so, recent editions discussed features such as: a consideration of public health services and their importance; a consideration of health-related behavior and the enormous impact it has on the structure, function, and cost of the delivery system; growing interest on the part of the editors, as in the public and profession at large, on exploring the issue of quality of care; and the specific role in determining the structure and function of the U.S. health care system that is played by pharmaceuticals and the industry that produces them. Continuity and change. We established that twosome as principles to guide us at the beginning, and they have remained with the book ever since.

Third in the list of major features of this book that have been maintained over the years has been the continuing freshening of the authorship by bringing new voices on board, which again this time has been done for a number of the chapters. Fourth has been the orientation of the book to compatibility with the computer age—something not even contemplated by most of us back in the 1970s. So, continuity and change, tradition coupled with new ideas and approaches have marked the march of our book over the past 30-plus years. I am so proud to continue to have my name associated with it.

Finally, let me add a personal note. Tony Kovner and I have known each other for more than 50 years. We first met socially, through a mutual friend. In the mid-60s, we had our first professional contact. We both worked at the ground-breaking Gouverneur Ambulatory Care Center of the New York City Health Services Administration. I was a preventive medicine resident with the New York City Health Department. Tony for a time was the acting director, on loan from the Beth Israel Hospital. We next became associated in the mid-1980s when I was preparing the 3rd edition of this book, and I felt that I needed new blood to take over my Hospitals chapter. Tony by that time had become the director of the program in Health Policy and Management at New York University. He was in the process of taking the program from its very early stages of formation to its present preeminence. And so, when it came time to create the 4th edition, and my own attention was being turned toward writing on sports, weight management, and regular exercise for the general public, I turned to Tony as my first choice to take over the book's editorship. Was I gratified when he said "yes"! He was kind enough to invite me to come back to the book as an active editor for the 6th and 7th editions. Then, when I stepped down from active participation in the book for a second time, he was smart enough to ask Jim Knickman to join him.

And so, Tony and I have been friends and colleagues for many years. Making this relationship even more special than it would have been had we shared only a mutual interest in bettering the health and health care of the people of the United States, is our mutual support for a special four of New York's professional sports teams: the Mets, the Knicks, the Rangers, and last, but certainly not least, the Giants. Regardless of what was happening with us, to the U.S. health care delivery system, and to our book, we could always have fun discussing the ups and downs of our favorites. Tony—it has been such a pleasure to work with you for lo these many years and an honor to have my name up there with yours on the masthead of this book. Let us hope that it will be many more years before our run together is over.

Steven Jonas, MD, MPH, MS, FNYAS
Stony Brook, NY

ACKNOWLEDGMENTS

The editors would like to express our deep appreciation to the team of people who put this book together at a time of rapid changes. After our conception of the book, we were fortunate to have an outstanding roster of experts in many health fields agree to do the actual work of writing chapters! Our managing editor, Victoria Weisfeld, edited all the chapters—even ours—and prepared the charts chapter. We also owe a debt of gratitude to Sheri Sussman for much aid and good advice on behalf of Springer Publishing Company. We appreciate her—and Springer's—belief in us and in *Health Care Delivery in the United States* through our many editions. Thanks, too, to Steve Jonas who originated this book and has been a cheerleader as well as an author, including writing the generous foreword to this 10th edition.

And, finally, we must express our appreciation and admiration to our current and former chapter authors—some of whom have written for multiple editions—for their insights, inspiration, and shared commitment to improving the health of the American people.

Gerard F. Anderson
David Banta
Nancy R. Barhydt-Wezenaar
Lynne Barton
John Billings
Charles Brecher
Carol S. Brewer
Joel C. Cantor
Carol A. Caronna
Elaine F. Cassidy
Carol S. Chang
Mary Ann Chiasson
Carolyn Clancy
Chelsea Clinton
Michael Enright
Penny Hollander Feldman
Steven A. Finkler
Bianca Frogner
Ron Geigle
Thomas E. Getzen
Marc N. Gourevitch
Michal D. Gursen
Ruth S. Hanft
Paul Hofmann
Susan D. Horn
Kelly A. Hunt

Kelli A. Hurdle
Steven Jonas
Gary Kalkut
James R. Knickman
Lorrin Koran
Christine Kovner
Roger Kropf
Robert S. Lawrence
Jessica Leight
Laura C. Leviton
Jane Levitt
Robert Lloyd
John R. Lumpkin
Carol McCarthy
Douglas McCarthy
Andrew P. Mezey
Pamela Nadash
Jennifer Nelson
Michael Ong
C. Tracy Orleans
David A. Pearson
Carol Raphael
Lesley Reis
Scott D. Rhodes
Hila Richardson
Barbara Rimer

Victor G. Rodwin
Stephen N. Rosenberg
Thomas C. Rosenthal
Pamela Russo
Edward S. Salzberg
Amir Satvat
Richard Scheffler
Dena J. Seiden
Steven S Sharfstein
Helen L. Smits
Michael Sparer
JoAnn Spetz

Anne N. Stoline
Robin J. Strongin
Jo-Ann L. Thorpe
Kenneth E. Thorpe
Bonnie J. Wakefield
Douglas S. Wakefield
Hugh Waters
Victoria D. Weisfeld
Beth C. Weitzman
Terrie T. Wetle
Herbert P. White
Victoria A. Wicks

In addition, we would like to recognize individuals and organizations who have made particularly valuable contributions to this edition:

Amy A. Lee for research assistance in preparing Chapter 3, "Health Care Financing."

Anne-Marie Audet, MD, MSc, and other current and former colleagues of Douglas McCarthy at The Commonwealth Fund who gave advice and contributed to previous publications from which Chapter 10, "Integrative Models and Performance," is adapted in part. The views presented there are those of the author, Douglas McCarthy, and not necessarily those of The Commonwealth Fund or its directors, officers, or staff.

Finally, Chapter 12, "Health Care Costs and Value," is partially based on Chapter 17 of the 9th edition of this text, which was authored by Thomas Getzen, PhD, and Steven Finkler, PhD, portions of which have been retained in this 10th edition.

ORGANIZATION OF THIS BOOK

This is the 10th edition of *Jonas & Kovner's Health Care Delivery in the United States*, which, although its title has evolved in the last 35 years, has stayed true to its original purpose: helping instructors and students better understand the complicated, expensive, and ever-changing U.S. health care delivery system.

The recent national debates that led to the 2010 health care reform legislation, the Patient Protection and Affordable Care Act, provided disturbing and irrefutable evidence of how far short that understanding falls—not only for the average American, but for our political leaders, the news media, and others who shape public opinion. Health care is a substantial part of the nation's economy and employment and important for those reasons alone. And, the manner in which health care services are delivered will affect all of us and our families at many points in our lives, for better or for worse. A more vital and dynamic area for study is difficult to imagine.

This text is divided into several sections—health policy, population health, medical care delivery, support for medical care delivery, and the future of health care delivery—in order to provide some coherence to this broad terrain.

In addition to the text, the editors have compiled an online Instructor's Guide, which includes a variety of background materials teachers will find useful in guiding class discussion, offering students additional resources, and class projects. We encourage instructors to communicate with us about this edition, so that we may make the 11th edition even more useful to you. Please submit any comments or questions directly to Tony Kovner and he will get back to you. You can find us at HCDUS10@newassoc.com.

As always, we appreciate your suggestions.

Anthony R. Kovner, PhD

James R. Knickman, PhD

Note to Readers: Data in the chapters, tables, and figures in this book are the most recent available at the time the authors prepared them. Often, government sources, especially, update important health information annually. You may be able to find more recent data by searching online for the most recent edition of the same publication cited herein.

CONTRIBUTORS

Gerard F. Anderson, PhD, is a professor of health policy and management and professor of international health at the Johns Hopkins University Bloomberg School of Public Health, professor of medicine at the Johns Hopkins University School of Medicine, director of the Johns Hopkins Center for Hospital Finance and Management, and co-director of the Johns Hopkins Program for Medical Technology and Practice Assessment. Dr. Anderson is currently conducting research on chronic conditions, comparative insurance systems in developing countries, medical education, health care payment reform, and technology diffusion. He has directed reviews of health systems for the World Bank and USAID in multiple countries. He has authored two books on health care payment policy, published over 200 peer reviewed articles, testified in Congress almost 50 times as an individual witness, and serves on multiple editorial committees. Prior to his arrival at Johns Hopkins, Dr. Anderson held various positions in the Office of the Secretary, U.S. Department of Health and Human Services, where he helped to develop Medicare prospective payment legislation.

John Billings, JD, is Associate Professor of Health Policy and Public Service at NYU Wagner Graduate School of Public Service, and he is currently director of the school's Health Policy and Management Program. Professor Billings is principal investigator on numerous projects to assess the performance of the safety net for vulnerable populations and to understand the nature and extent of barriers to optimal health for vulnerable populations. Much of his work has involved analysis of patterns of hospital admission and emergency room visits as a mechanism to evaluate access barriers to outpatient care and to assess the performance of the ambulatory care delivery system. He has also examined the characteristics of high-cost Medicaid patients to help in designing interventions to improve care and outcomes for these patients. As a founding member of the Foundation for Informed Decision-Making, Professor Billings is helping to provide patients with a clearer mechanism for understanding and making informed decisions about a variety of available treatments.

Joel C. Cantor, ScD, directs the Center for State Health Policy and is professor of public policy at Rutgers University. Dr. Cantor's research focuses on issues of health care coverage, financing, and delivery. His recent work includes studies of health insurance market regulation, state health system performance, and access to care for low income and minority populations. Dr. Cantor is a frequent advisor on health policy matters to New Jersey state government. He has published widely in the health policy and health services research literature and is a member of the editorial board of *Inquiry*. He currently leads several studies of policies requiring insurance companies to extend dependent coverage to young adults and strategies to improve health care delivery in low income urban areas. Prior to joining the Rutgers faculty in 1999, Dr. Cantor served as director of research at the United Hospital Fund of New York and director of evaluation research at Robert Wood Johnson Foundation. He received his doctorate in health policy and management from the Johns Hopkins University School of Public Health in 1988.

Carol A. Caronna, PhD, is an associate professor of sociology in the Department of Sociology, Anthropology, and Criminal Justice at Towson University. She currently serves on the editorial board of the *Journal of Health and Social Behavior* and is a past officer of the Medical Sociology section of the American Sociology Association. Her work focuses on health care organizations and institutions, with specific emphases on the evolution of health policy, the changing identity of health maintenance organizations, and entrepreneurship in the nonprofit sector. She has contributed to research methodology volumes, including *The SAGE Handbook of Qualitative Methods in Health Research* (2010). She is a coauthor of *Institutional Change and Healthcare Organizations: From Professional Dominance to Managed Care* and has published in numerous sociology journals. She received her PhD in sociology from Stanford University and, from 2000 to 2002, was a Robert Wood Johnson Scholar in Health Policy Research at the University of California, Berkeley, School of Public Health.

Elaine F. Cassidy, PhD, is a research and evaluation consultant at the OMG Center for Collaborative Learning, where she manages projects related to child and adolescent health promotion. Prior to joining OMG, she served as a program officer in research and evaluation at Robert Wood Johnson Foundation, where she oversaw research and evaluation activities for the Vulnerable Populations portfolio. Her work and professional interests focus primarily on child and adolescent health and risk behavior, violence prevention, and school-based interventions, primarily for young people living in low income, urban environments. She is a trained school psychologist and mental health clinician who has provided therapeutic care to children and families in school, outpatient, and acute partial hospitalization settings. She holds an MSEd in psychological services from the University of Pennsylvania and a PhD in school, community, and child-clinical psychology from the University of Pennsylvania.

Carol S. Chang, MPH, MPA, is the regional senior program director of Programs and Services at the American Red Cross of Central New Jersey. She oversees American Red Cross Emergency Services, Community Services, and Health and Safety Services programs across the Central New Jersey region. She was previously a program officer in the Research and Evaluation Unit at Robert Wood Johnson Foundation, where she worked on public health evaluations and developed initiatives with partner organizations to establish performance measures and benchmarks to improve public health agency performance and accountability. She also co-managed The Robert Wood Johnson Health and Society Scholars Program, a post-doctoral fellows program designed to build the nation's capacity for research, leadership, and action to address the broad range of factors affecting the health of populations. Prior to her work at Robert Wood Johnson Foundation, she worked with CARE-International on emergency programs in Latin America, Asia, and Africa.

Carolyn M. Clancy, MD, is director of the federal Agency for Healthcare Research and Quality (AHRQ) and former director of AHRQ's Center for Outcomes and Effectiveness Research. Dr. Clancy, a general internist and health services researcher, is a graduate of Boston College and the University of Massachusetts Medical School. Following clinical training in internal medicine, she was a Henry J. Kaiser Family Foundation Fellow at the University of Pennsylvania. She holds an academic appointment at the George Washington University School of Medicine and serves as senior associate editor for the journal *Health Services Research*. She serves on multiple editorial boards, is a member of the Institute of Medicine, and was elected a Master of the American College of Physicians in 2004. In 2009, she was awarded the William B. Graham Prize for Health Services Research. Dr. Clancy's major research interests include improving health care quality and patient safety and reducing disparities in care associated with race, ethnicity, gender, income, and education. As director of AHRQ, she launched the first annual report to Congress on health care disparities and health care quality.

Chelsea Clinton, MPH, MPhil, is currently a doctoral candidate at New York University's Robert F. Wagner Graduate School of Public Service. She previously worked as an analyst for a financial services firm and an engagement manager at McKinsey and Company, both in New York.

Bianca K. Frogner, PhD, is an assistant professor in the Health Services Management and Leadership Department in the School of Public Health and Health Services at The George Washington University. Dr. Frogner has coauthored articles published in *Health Affairs* comparing health spending in industrialized countries. She is currently engaged in a project with the Kaiser Family Foundation to examine the health and economic impacts of U.S. global health investments using economic models. She is a consultant for the World Bank with a focus on provider, patient, and household surveys to evaluate the Ukrainian health system. Prior to her appointment at George Washington, Dr. Frogner was a postdoctoral fellow at the University of Illinois at Chicago School of Public Health. Dr. Frogner received a PhD from the Johns Hopkins Bloomberg School of Public Health in the Health Policy and Management Department with a concentration in Health Economics.

Steven Jonas, MD, MPH, MS, FNYAS, is professor of Preventive Medicine, School of Medicine and Professor, Graduate Program in Public Health, at Stony Brook University (NY). He is an elected Fellow of the New York Academy of Sciences, the Royal Society of Medicine (London), the American College of Preventive Medicine, the New York Academy of Medicine, and the American Public Health Association. He is editor-in-chief of the *American Medical Athletics Association Journal*. He is the recipient of the Duncan Clark Career Achievement Award of the Association for Prevention Teaching and Research (2006) and the Distinguished Alumnus Award of the Yale University School of Public Health (2010). Over the course of an academic career that began in 1969, his research has focused on health care delivery systems analysis, preventive medicine and public health, and personal health and wellness. He has authored, coauthored, edited, and coedited more than 30 books and published more than 135 papers in scientific journals, as well as numerous articles in the popular literature. In the mid-1970s he created *Health Care Delivery in the United States*.

Roger Kropf, PhD, is a professor in the Health Policy and Management Program at New York University's Robert F. Wagner Graduate School of Public Service. Dr. Kropf is the author of two books on the application of information systems to health care management. *Strategic Analysis for Hospital Management* was written with James Greenberg, PhD, and published by Aspen Systems in 1984. *Service Excellence in Health Care through the Use of Computers* was published by the American College of Healthcare Executives in 1990. His most recent book is *Making Information Technology Work: Maximizing the Benefits for*

Health Care Organizations, written with Guy Scalzi and published by AHA Press in 2007. He teaches graduate and executive education courses on information technology. More information on his work can be found at his Web site, www.nyu.edu/classes/kropf.

Jessica Leight, PhD, MPhil, is a third-year PhD candidate in economics at the Massachusetts Institute of Technology. Ms. Leight specializes in development economics, political economy, and health economics. Recently, Ms. Leight received a $1 million grant, as a co-principal investigator, to research maternal mortality in Nigeria. She previously received an MPhil in economics with distinction from Oxford University in 2008 as a Rhodes Scholar, receiving the George Webb Medley prize for excellence in the degree. Previous publications have included two Harvard Business School case studies, an article in the *Journal of Latin American Studies,* and a recent retrospective of public choice theory published in the volume *Government and Markets: Toward a New Theory of Regulation.*

Laura C. Leviton, PhD, is special advisor for evaluation at Robert Wood Johnson Foundation, Princeton, New Jersey. She has been with the foundation since 1999, overseeing more than 60 national and local evaluations. She was formerly a professor at two schools of public health, where she collaborated on the first randomized experiment on HIV prevention, and later on two large place-based randomized experiments on improving medical practices. She received the 1993 award from the American Psychological Association for Distinguished Contributions to Psychology in the Public Interest. She has served on two Institute of Medicine committees and was appointed by the secretary of DHHS to CDC's National Advisory Committee on HIV and STD Prevention. Dr. Leviton was president of the American Evaluation Association in 2000 and has coauthored two books: *Foundations of Program Evaluation* and *Confronting Public Health Risks.* She received her PhD in social psychology from the University of Kansas and postdoctoral training in research methodology and evaluation at Northwestern University.

Robert Lloyd, MA, PhD, is executive director of performance improvement for the Institute for Healthcare Improvement (IHI). Dr. Lloyd provides leadership in the areas of performance improvement strategies, statistical process control methods, development of strategic dashboards, and quality improvement training. He serves as faculty for various IHI initiatives and demonstration projects in the United States and abroad. Before joining IHI, Dr. Lloyd was corporate director of Quality Resource Services for Advocate Health Care (Oak Brook, Ill.) and senior director of Quality Measurement for Lutheran General Health System (Park Ridge, IL). He directed the American Hospital Association's Quality Measurement and Management Project (QMMP). Dr. Lloyd holds a master's degree in regional planning and a doctorate in rural sociology, both from Penn State University. He has served as faculty for the Harvard School of Public Health, the American College of Healthcare Executives, the American Society for Quality (ASQ), The Joint Commission, and numerous other organizations. He is coauthor of *Measuring Quality Improvement in Healthcare: A Guide to Statistical Process Control Applications,* and his most recent book is *Quality Health Care: A Guide to Developing and Using Indicators,* published March 2004.

Douglas McCarthy, MBA, is president of Issues Research, Inc., in Durango, Colorado. As a senior research advisor to The Commonwealth Fund, he coauthors National and State Scorecards on Health System Performance, conducts case-study research on high-performing health care organizations and initiatives, and is a contributing editor to the newsletter *Quality Matters*. His 25-year career has spanned research, policy, operations, and consulting roles for government, corporate, academic, and philanthropic organizations. *A Chartbook on the Quality of Health Care in the United States*, coauthored with Sheila Leatherman, was named by AcademyHealth as one of 20 core books in the field of health outcomes. He is a past research director for UnitedHealth Group's Center for Health Care Policy and Evaluation. He received a master's degree in health care management from the University of Connecticut. During 1996–97, he was a public policy fellow at the Humphrey Institute of Public Affairs at the University of Minnesota.

Michael K. Ong, MD, PhD, is an assistant professor in the Division of General Internal Medicine and Health Services Research at UCLA's David Geffen School of Medicine. Dr. Ong received his medical degree from the UC San Diego and a PhD in Health Services and Policy Analysis from the UC Berkeley. He completed the Primary Care Internal Medicine residency at the UC San Francisco and a VA Ambulatory Care Fellowship with the Center for Primary Care and Outcomes Research at Stanford University. He is currently a faculty scholar in the Robert Wood Johnson Foundation Physician Faculty Scholars Program. His research focuses on improving the delivery of appropriate and efficient health care by general internal medicine physicians, particularly with respect to hospital-based care, mental health, and smoking cessation. His recent research has focused on heart failure patients hospitalized at the five University of California Medical Centers and Cedars-Sinai Medical Center to better understand the wide variation in resource use they report. He also chairs the State of California Tobacco Education and Research Oversight Committee, which oversees the California Tobacco Control Program.

C. Tracy Orleans, PhD, is the senior scientist and distinguished fellow at Robert Wood Johnson Foundation (RWJF). She has led or co-led the Foundation's public policy and health care system-based grant-making in the areas of tobacco control, physical activity promotion, childhood obesity prevention, and chronic disease management. She has led Foundation working groups on tobacco, chronic disease, and health and behavior and has developed and led numerous RWJF national research initiatives in these areas, as well as substance abuse policy research, active living, healthy eating research, and teen obesity. A clinical health psychologist with a strong public health orientation, Dr. Orleans has authored or coauthored more than 225 publications, served on numerous journal editorial boards, national scientific panels, and advisory groups, including for the Institute of Medicine, National Commission on Prevention Priorities, and U.S. Preventive Services Task Force, Community Preventive Services Task Force, and as president of the Society of Behavioral Medicine. She is an elected member of the Academy of Behavioral Medicine Research and a recipient of the John Slade Tobacco Research Policy Award of the Society for Research on Nicotine and Tobacco and the Distinguished Scientist Award of the Society of Behavioral Medicine.

Scott D. Rhodes, PhD, MPH, CHES, is a behavioral scientist, whose research focuses on the integration of community development, community-campus partnerships, and health promotion and disease prevention in both rural and urban communities. He is an associate professor in the Department of Social Sciences and Health Policy, Wake Forest University School of Medicine in Winston-Salem, North Carolina. His research explores sexual health, HIV and sexually transmitted disease prevention, obesity prevention, and other health disparities among vulnerable populations. Dr. Rhodes has broad experience in quantitative and qualitative data collection and analysis techniques; the design, implementation, and evaluation of multiple-level interventions for improved health outcomes; community-capacity development; community-based participatory research; exploratory evaluation; the application of behavioral theory; community-campus partnerships; PhotoVoice as a method for participatory action research; lay health advisor intervention approaches; the exploration of socio-cultural determinants of health; and internet research, including data collection, intervention delivery, and evaluation.

Pamela G. Russo, MD, MPH, is a senior program officer at Robert Wood Johnson Foundation (RWJF), Princeton, New Jersey. She was recruited to RWJF to lead the Population Health: Science and Policy team in 2000. Prior to RWJF, she was an associate professor of Medicine, director of the Clinical Outcomes Section, and program co-director for the Master's Program and Fellowship in Clinical Epidemiology and Health Services Research at the Cornell University Medical Center in New York City. Dr. Russo earned her BS from Harvard College, with a major in the History and Philosophy of Science; her MPH in epidemiology from the University of California, Berkeley, School of Public Health; and her MD from the University of California, San Francisco. She completed a residency in general internal medicine at the Hospital of the University of Pennsylvania and a combined clinical epidemiology and rheumatology fellowship at Cornell and the Hospital of Special Surgery.

Amir Satvat, MPA, is a second-year MBA/MB candidate in health care management and biotechnology at the University of Pennsylvania's Wharton School and Schools of Engineering and Arts and Sciences, respectively. Currently, Mr. Satvat is a teaching and research assistant in the Health Care Management department. He is coauthor with Professor Lawton Burns, head of the Wharton Health Care Management Department, of a book on organizational change in health care institutions (forthcoming). At Wharton, he received a Kaiser Foundation Scholarship (twice), the Ford Motor Company Fellowship for research on emerging technologies, and an award in the Walmart Better Living Business Plan Challenge. Mr. Satvat earned his MPA in health policy and management at New York University, where he was one of eight national finalists for the Roback Scholarship, the top national prize for policy studies. Previously, Mr. Satvat worked at Goldman Sachs as a health care investment banking analyst, where he completed the $9B UnitedHealth/PacifiCare acquisition. Finally, Mr. Satvat's paper on a theory for a Board Rotation Principle for corporate governance, co-written with Mark Rogers, Oxford University, was published in the *Monash Business Review*.

Richard M. Scheffler, PhD, is distinguished professor of Health Economics and Public Policy at the School of Public Health and the Goldman School of Public Policy at the University of California, Berkeley. He also holds the chair in Healthcare Markets and Consumer Welfare endowed by the Office of the Attorney General for the State of California. Professor Scheffler is director of The Global Center for Health Economics and Policy Research as well as director of The Nicholas C. Petris Center on Health Care Markets and Consumer Welfare. He has been a Rockefeller and a Fulbright Scholar and served as president of the International Health Economists Association 4th Congress in 2004. Professor Scheffler has published more than 150 papers and edited and written six books, including his most recent, *Is There a Doctor in the House? Market Signals and Tomorrow's Supply of*

Doctors, published by Stanford University Press, September 2008. He has conducted a recent review on Pay For Performance in Health for the World Health Organization and the OECD.

Michael S. Sparer, PhD, JD, is professor and chair in the Department of Health Policy and Management at the Mailman School of Public Health at Columbia University. Professor Sparer studies and writes about the politics of health care, with a particular emphasis on the health insurance and health delivery systems for low income populations, and the ways in which inter-governmental relations influence policy. He is a two-time winner of the Mailman School's Student Government Association Teacher of the Year Award, as well as the recipient of a 2010 Columbia University Presidential Award for Outstanding Teaching. Professor Sparer spent 7 years as a litigator for the New York City Law Department, specializing in inter-governmental social welfare litigation. After leaving the practice of law, Sparer obtained a PhD in Political Science from Brandeis University. Sparer is a former editor of the *Journal of Health Politics, Policy and Law*, and the author of *Medicaid and the Limits of State Health Reform*, as well as numerous articles and book chapters.

Joanne Spetz, PhD, is a professor in the Departments of Community Health Systems and Social and Behavioral Sciences at the UCSF School of Nursing. She also is a faculty researcher at the UCSF Center for the Health Professions. She has led national and state surveys of registered nurses and nursing schools, evaluations of programs to expand the supply of nurses, research on the effects of health information technologies in hospitals, studies of hospital industry structure, and analysis of the effects of minimum nurse staffing regulations on patients and hospitals. Joanne was a member of the National Commission on VA Nursing and is an advisor to the Institute of Medicine Initiative on the Future of Nursing. She frequently provides testimony and technical assistance to state and federal agencies and policymakers. She has taught quantitative research methods for doctoral students and financial management and health economics for master's students in nursing administration and public health.

Hugh R. Waters, PhD, is a health economist and associate professor of Health Policy and Management at the Johns Hopkins Bloomberg School of Public Health. Dr. Waters has 22 years' experience working with public health programs and has worked extensively as a consultant with the World Bank, World Health Organization, and other international organizations. His areas of expertise are: (1) health insurance and health financing reforms; (2) evaluation of the effects of health financing mechanisms on access, equity, and quality; and (3) economic evaluation of public health policies and programs.

Victoria D. Weisfeld, MPH, has combined her academic training in public health and journalism in a career devoted to helping health care organizations plan and implement strategic communications programs. Major employers were Robert Wood Johnson Foundation, Princeton, and the Institute of Medicine, Washington, DC, where, in 1978, she co-wrote the first draft of *Healthy People*. Since 2005, she has been a principal in NEW Associates, LLC, a communications company she owns with her husband. Their clients include foundations, think tanks, and other nonprofit organizations. Sample projects: writing the report of the President's Commission on Care for America's Returning Wounded Warriors; editing more than 45 Brookings scholar papers on diverse national and international issues for the 2008 presidential campaign; white papers on nursing investment opportunities for two Blues plans; and contributing to several major Institute of Medicine reports. She served as managing editor of *Health Care Delivery in the United States* for editions 9 and 10.

Herbert White, MBA, has more than 26 years of health care finance experience. He is currently the associate vice president of Finance for Temple University Health System. Mr. White is a board member of Core Solutions, Inc., a behavioral health software solutions firm. He is also a member of Temple University Health System's Finance and Investment Committee and Health Partners of Philadelphia's Finance and Audit Committee. He received a bachelor of science in Accounting from La Salle University and a master's degree in Business Administration (Finance) from Temple University's Fox School of Business. He is a fellow in the Healthcare Financial Management Association (HFMA) and has received HFMA's Reeves and Follmer awards.

Jonas & Kovner's

HEALTH CARE DELIVERY IN THE UNITED STATES

10th Edition

Health Policy

I

The first step in the policy making process is to understand the current system and how it affects patients, providers, and the overall economy, and the next step is pointing out the problems and challenges the health system faces. In Chapter 1, Tony Kovner and Jim Knickman describe the influence of the U.S. health care system on our lives, its defining characteristics, and the issues and concerns facing leaders and stakeholders. They specify who the leading stakeholders are and how their interests differ—from government; to pharmaceutical and insurance companies; to doctors, nurses and hospitals; to taxpayers and patients. Because issues take on different meanings when viewed by different stakeholders, it is extraordinarily difficult to make and implement fair and effective health care policy.

The 11 key charts that Victoria Weisfeld presents in Chapter 1A provide useful background on the health care system, including the history and breadth of federal activity in health matters. Charts illustrate issues touched on throughout the book—the supply of hospitals and doctors, costs, quality, and so on—and introduce the theme of geographic variation.

Michael Sparer focuses on the role of government in the U.S. health system in Chapter 2 on health policy and health reform, devoting a significant part of the chapter to the passage of health reform—the Patient Protection and Affordable Care Act (ACA)—in 2010. Sparer describes the achievements and limitations of the ACA and indicates the agenda going forward as the legislation is inevitably amended and shaped by its implementation. Sparer goes on to discuss the many roles of government in health care as payer, regulator, and provider of health care.

In Chapter 3, Jim Knickman explains how health care is paid for in the United States. Observers generally agree that our $2.3 trillion annual investment in the health sector has not been as effective as it should be in actually improving Americans' health and that we need to obtain more value for this enormous expenditure. Knickman explains how health insurance works, how reimbursement approaches impact costs, and how health reform is intended to affect financial incentives. He concludes that aligning financial incentives to promote efficient investment of resources is the key to reducing future health care costs.

Bianca Frogner, Hugh Waters, and Gerry Anderson conclude Part I with a chapter comparing the U.S. health system with those of selected other nations. Part of the tremendous pressure to contain U.S. health care costs is the recognition that, relative to other developed countries, the United States spends at least twice as much on health care per person, but does not achieve better health results. The authors describe a few chief organizational models used by other nations and how each is addressing universal challenges—containing costs, population aging, increasing chronic disease rates, care coordination, and quality improvement.

THE CURRENT U.S. HEALTH CARE SYSTEM

Anthony R. Kovner and James R. Knickman

KEY WORDS

quality
acess
health insurance
health care delivery
public health
financing

health care costs
healthy behavior
health workforce
stakeholders
performance

LEARNING OBJECTIVES

- Understand the importance of health and health care to American life
- Analyze defining characteristics of the U.S. health care system
- Identify major issues and concerns with the current system
- Identify different stakeholders in the health care system and the constraints and opportunities facing leaders of change
- Understand the importance of engagement at the ground level

TOPICAL OUTLINE

- The importance of health and health care to American life
- Defining characteristics of the U.S. health care system
- Major issues and concerns facing the health sector
- Constraints and opportunities for change
- Engagement at the ground level

In this first chapter of the 10th edition of *Health Care Delivery in the United States*, we present an overview of the U.S. health care system. Why and how do we organize health care the way that we do? What are the key problems and current issues in health care delivery? What is the role of the individuals and of providers in improving health care delivery and Americans' health? What are the constraints and opportunities leaders face in trying to standardize **quality** outcomes, contain increases in health care costs, and improve **access** to health care? Many of these vital questions are discussed in detail in subsequent chapters of this volume and we hope you find them challenging and germane to the health care stories that you read about not only at the national level, but also in the communities where you work, live, and go to school.

The Importance of Health and Health Care to American Life

The health care enterprise is one of the most important parts of the U.S. social system and of our economic system as well. Good health care is an essential foundation for being able to function in society and to enjoy life. People view health and health care quite differently depending on whether they are sick or well or whether they have adequate **health insurance**. Millions of Americans work in **health care delivery** and the health care industry is the largest employer in many American cities. The incomes of many people—not just health care professionals, but also suppliers of equipment, pharmaceuticals, and supplies; a large part of the construction industry; and an array of supporting personnel such as kitchen workers, drivers, delivery workers, computer specialists, accountants, lawyers, maintenance personnel, laundry workers, security staff—rely on the continued economic vitality of this key sector.

Defining Characteristics of the U.S. Health Care System

The word "system" implies a purposeful and contained universe, with constituent parts all working together. This hardly describes the American health care system, which can more accurately be defined as a "situation," "an "environment," or an "enterprise." The key idea here is the concept of a boundary line that separates what is "health" from what is "non-health." Building cars and attending grade school is "not health," whereas living in a nursing home and planning for health services *is* "health."

Of course there are shades of gray. For example, is "health education" in grade schools part of "health" or part of "education"? Our view is that we don't have a "health care system." Rather we have many health care systems that, when put into the same framework, constitute a "system" for the purpose of studying health care, rather than for the purpose of organizing and delivering health care services.

> *A first defining characteristic of the health care enterprise is the line between activities directed at keeping people healthy and those directed at restoring health once a disease or injury occurs.*

A first defining characteristic of the health care enterprise is the line between activities directed at keeping people healthy and those directed at restoring health once a disease or injury occurs. Keeping people healthy is the business of the **public health** system, activities associated with behavioral health, and actions associated with our social system. Public health includes activities to protect the environment, making sure water supplies, restaurants, and food supplies are safe, and providing preventive health services, such as vaccinations. Behavioral health helps people make better choices to improve or protect health—for example, not smoking, eating well, exercising, and reducing stress. Our social system creates the environment that supports healthy living. For example, making sure healthy food and safe places to be physically active are available in every community is part of our social policy. Similarly, being poor is perhaps the single largest determinant of health status; how we distribute income in America is part of social policy.

Once people become sick, the medical care sector delivers a wide variety of services and interventions to restore health and functioning. In general, changing an individual's behavior has much greater impact on health and mortality than does medical care. Despite excellent research documenting the importance of healthy lifestyles and healthy communities, as a country, we spend nine times more on medical care than on public and behavioral health. And, many communities do not have environments that encourage healthy lifestyles.

Additional defining features of the U.S. health care system include:

- *The importance of institutions in delivering care.* These include hospitals, nursing homes, community health centers, physician practices, and public health departments.
- *The role of professionals in running the system.* These include physicians, nurses, managers, policy advocates, researchers, technicians of many types, and those directing technology and pharmaceuticals businesses.
- *Medical technology, electronic communication, and new drugs that fuel changes in health care delivery.* New techniques in imaging, electronic communication, pharmaceuticals, and surgical procedures are remarkable and expensive ways of improving health care.
- *Tension between "the free market" and "government control."* This tension shapes America's culture. Relative to citizens of other countries and among ourselves, Americans differ more over whether health care, or certain health care services, are goods or rights. And part of the equation are nonprofit health care services, which make up an important part of the health sector. For example, most community hospitals are not-for-profit and nongovernmental.
- *The dysfunctional financing and payment system.* The **financing** and payment system is dysfunctional for all parties to it—providers, payers, patients, pharmaceutical companies, all of whom feel it either (a) costs too much or (b) brings too little revenue. How we pay health care providers does not provide adequate incentives to emphasize quality, value, and efficiency.

These defining characteristics make the health care system an important part of American life for consumers, taxpayers, and providers of care. Addressing the challenges of this health care enterprise is worth the best effort and thinking of tomorrow's health care managers and policy makers.

> *Addressing the challenges of this health care enterprise is worth the best effort and thinking of tomorrow's health care managers and policy makers.*

Major Issues and Concerns Facing the Health Sector

The defining characteristics of the health care sector listed suggest the key challenges that have been the focus of health care leaders' attention in recent years. Six of the most important are:

- *Improving quality:* Reliable studies indicate that between 44,000 and 98,000 Americans die each year because of medical errors. Other well-regarded studies show that fewer than half of people with costly and debilitating mental health or substance abuse problems, asthma, or diabetes receive care known to be effective.

- *Improving access and coverage:* Some 50.7 million Americans lacked insurance coverage in 2009 and millions more had inadequate coverage. The 2010 health reform law is expected to insure 32 million of these. Even if the new law accomplishes its goal, nearly 20 million people will continue to lack insurance coverage, including many recent or undocumented immigrants. Lack of coverage is a peculiarly American problem. Why are we different from all other developed countries in this regard? Even when Americans have insurance coverage, access to health care is not always assured. Many rural areas have shortages of doctors, dentists, and other health professionals. Many doctors refuse to treat patients who have Medicaid—or even Medicare—coverage.

- *Slowing the growth of health care costs:* **Health care costs** are the product of price of services multiplied by the volume of services. Health care costs are growing much more rapidly than the rest of the economy. The choices payers can make to contain health care costs include: not paying for services that are not medically effective or capping what providers are paid for them. For example, payers might limit payments for individual procedures or negotiate capitation rates at current amounts for large populations of insured people.

- *Encouraging healthy behavior:* **Healthy behavior** can help people avoid disease and injury or prevent disease or disability from worsening. Unfortunately, for millions of Americans, leading healthy lives is not a high enough priority. The first step in efforts to improve healthy behavior is to make sure every community has an environment that supports healthy lifestyles, including access to healthy food and safe places for being physically active. Changing behavior also can be influenced either by limiting choices, such as what children are served in grade school cafeterias, or by penalizing unhealthy behavior, for example, by taxing sugar-laden soft drinks.

- *Improving the public health system:* The public health system provides the infrastructure undergirding the health care delivery system. Largely a state-organized system of state and local health departments, these agencies monitor the health of the people in the state, provide public health services, and regulate health care providers. The effectiveness and funding of state health departments (and the municipal and county health departments within them) is widely variable.

- *Improving the coordination, transparency, and accountability of local systems of care:* Problems of quality, cost, and access are largely attributable to the fragmentation and lack of coordination within the system. This lack of coordination exists within health care organizations as well as between them. It is affected by a lack of integrated and electronic record systems, but also by cultural traditions of independence. Each doctor practices independently and usually each hospital does, too. Little attention is paid to all the services that a patient may need to get well or return to functioning if they are found outside the walls of the doctor's office or the hospital.

> *Problems of quality, cost, and access are largely attributable to the fragmentation and lack of coordination within the system.*

There are many other issues and concerns in health care delivery, such as addressing inequalities in health status among various income groups, social classes, and ethnic groups, or shortages in the **health workforce**, particularly in primary care. But many of these issues and concerns would be substantially ameliorated if there were progress in dealing with the Big Six issues cited. For example, improvements in quality and coordination would reduce inequalities on health status among various groups.

Constraints and Opportunities for Change

STAKEHOLDERS WHO CONSTRAIN OR PROPEL CHANGE

Stakeholders with interests in health care delivery include:

- *Consumers and taxpayers.* Typically those who need medical care want more of it and more choice regarding how they get it, whereas taxpayers who are healthy are more likely to urge health care cost containment.
- *Doctors, nurses, hospitals, and other health providers.* All those who work in the health sector want to receive higher incomes for their work. All are in favor of improving the quality of care but they typically disagree as to how this may best be accomplished.
- *Pharmaceutical, insurance, and other for-profit companies.* These firms want to sell more of their product and increase their profits.
- *Payers and organizations that regulate or accredit health care providers.* These organizations want to slow the growth of costs, improve quality, and improve access. But they are not certain of the best ways to do this and may disagree with each other, as well as with the representatives of stakeholders whom they are regulating and accrediting. For example, government may wish to limit amounts paid to patients suffering from medical malpractice. Opinions vary as to the best method to do this. Should it be, for example, by capping awards, forcing medical arbitration, capping what attorneys can collect, or other measures?

Changes are constrained by forces operating at local, state, and national levels.

THE NEED FOR BETTER INFORMATION

Part of the problem is that we lack scientific explanations for the results of various suggested interventions. For example, what would happen if the federal government no longer supported doctors' medical education and the services provided by resident physicians? Would that raise or lower the cost and quality of hospital care? To find out, do we conduct pilot demonstrations and evaluate the results? Where does the money come from to fund that research? And, how do policy makers and practitioners behave in the absence of these answers?

Opportunities exist for better (as well as worse) **performance** in all six key challenge areas. Some of the best results have been generated by accountable health care systems, many of them large, covering millions of Americans, such as Kaiser-Permanente, Mayo Clinic, Cleveland Clinic, Geisinger Health System, the Veterans Health Administration, Partners Health Care, and others. They have been able to improve quality, encourage healthy behavior, and improve the coordination, transparency, and accountability of health care delivery.

Other stakeholders can claim improvements, too. So have some locales. The Anesthesiology Professional Society has greatly improved outcomes from surgery. Medical technology companies have standardized higher quality outcomes with robotic surgery. New drugs have helped to improve patient outcomes in heart disease and cancer. Government regulation has controlled the increase in hospital costs in Maryland. Local legislation against smoking has decreased smoking death rates in New York City.

Leadership counts. There is no substitute for better data produced by better research to justify the results of medical and management interventions and for better leadership to use that data to communicate and persuade effectively, in order to remove obstacles to implementation.

Engagement at the Ground Level

Today's health care system challenges are exciting, especially as new possibilities open up with the implementation of the 2010 health reform law. The editors have enjoyed the privilege of working for many years as part of numerous efforts to improve health care in the United States. We remain optimistic that pragmatism, flexibility, consensus-building, and attention to objective, high-quality evidence can bring about positive change. We remain stimulated by the challenges and pleased that our choice of careers has allowed us to contribute to maintaining a viable and effective health care system for all Americans.

Certainly, we have observed that best practices are now being used to improve health care and health across a wide range of health care delivery settings in the United States and worldwide. But we need to speed the process of getting more parts of the system— including more professionals and more of our population—engaged in best practices. Our text gives readers the motivation, the information, and some of the skills to do so.

In the future, the U.S. health care delivery system will see improvements if committed and informed Americans choose to enter the field. We hope this book acquaints future leaders with not just the challenges, but also the promise of our nation's health care system and inspires them to help create what all Americans have always wanted our health system to be—the best in the world.

DISCUSSION QUESTIONS

1. What is the real and perceived performance of the U.S. health care system? Are the views different among patients, providers, payers, and policy makers? Why or why not?
2. Why does the United States spend so much money on health care?
3. Why aren't Americans healthier and how might the health system make them so?

CASE STUDY

You have an analyst's position in the Department of Health and Human Services. The 2010 health reform law is expected to increase insurance coverage for a significant number of Americans. But many problems in the health care system remain unresolved. Write a one-page memorandum to your new supervisor describing what you believe are the most important of these, saying why they are important and suggesting how they might be approached.

AN OVERVIEW IN CHARTS

Victoria D. Weisfeld

TOPICAL OUTLINE
- "Get government out of my health care!"
- The department of health and human services
- Health-related responsibilities of other federal entities
- The U.S. hospital and physician supply
- Costs of care
- Where the money comes from
- Health care quality
- Satisfaction with care
- The health care workforce

"Get Government Out of My Health Care!"

The futility of this theme, which emerged during the acrimonious 2009–2010 public debate about national health care reform, arises from the fact that government is already much too embedded in our nation's health care system—indeed, it presides over what few aspects of it that can really be called a "system"—to extricate itself from the health care business. Through its policies and programs, government has essentially made our nation's health care system what it is today, for good and bad.

The federal government affects all aspects of health care at the national, state, and local levels through: *public health programs* that affect and protect every citizen; *service delivery programs* for Americans who have disabilities or who are low income, migrant workers, certain minorities (American Indians, Alaska Natives, Native Hawaiians), members of the military, and the elderly; *training programs* and support for health professions students; efforts to create healthier and safer *environments*; *research* on new ways of preventing and treating diseases and providing more efficient services; and the huge *payment programs*, such as Medicare, Medicaid, and Children's Health Insurance Program (CHIP).

The Department of Health and Human Services (DHHS) is the principal federal agency in health-related matters. DHHS has 11 operating divisions—many quite well known—that manage its major responsibilities and account for most of its budget (Table 1A.1).

TABLE 1A.1

President's FY2011 Budget for Principal Agencies of the Department of Health and Human Services (in millions of dollars)

Agency	Amount	Agency	Amount
Centers for Medicare and Medicaid Services	763,290	Food and Drug Administration	4,033
Administration for Children and Families	57,897	Substance Abuse and Mental Health Services Administration	3,541
National Institutes of Health	32,255	Administration on Aging	1,625
Health Resources and Services Administration	7,635	Agency for Healthcare Research and Quality	611[a]
Centers for Disease Control and Prevention	6,342	Office of the National Coordinator for Health Information Technology	78
Indian Health Service	4,556	Office of Civil Rights[b]	44

Note. [a]Since 2002, AHRQ has not had its own budget allocation and has been funded by other Public Health Service (PHS) agencies through the PHS evaluation set-aside.
[b]Office of Civil Rights is not an operating division, but, as the entity responsible for enforcing privacy policies under the Health Insurance Portability and Accountability Act (HIPAA), plays an important role in the health care system.
Source: U.S., Department of Health and Human Services. (2010). Advancing the health, safety, and well-being of our people. FY 2011 President's Budget for HHS. Retrieved June 14, 2010, from http://dhhs.gov/asfr/ob/docbudget/index.html#Brief; U.S., Government Printing Office. (2010). Budget of the United States Government: Department of Health and Human Services. Retrieved June 14, 2010, from http://www.gpoaccess.gov/usbudget/fy11/index.html

But not all health programs are housed within DHHS. Over the years, as we have learned more about the many factors that affect health and disease, nearly every other cabinet department has acquired some health-related responsibilities. Coordination of the many moving parts inside DHHS and across departments is not always easy. For example, responsibility for food safety is shared by the Food and Drug Administration (FDA), the U.S. Department of Agriculture's Food Safety and Inspection Service (FSIS), and at least 13 other agencies. The two principal agencies—FDA and FSIS—do not share resources and no single agency has the ultimate authority for the nation's total food supply (U.S., Government Accountability Office, 2008).

The Department of Health and Human Services

The federal government has been involved in health affairs since the late 1700s (Figure 1A.1). DHHS is the largest federal department after the Department of Defense, with a requested 2011 budget of more than $900 million. The accompanying timeline uses agencies' *current* names, many of which have changed numerous times as their roles evolved. The years tell when the agency or its principal predecessor began; a second year indicates a major reorganization.

The $30 billion a year National Institutes of Health began as a one-room disease research laboratory on Staten Island.

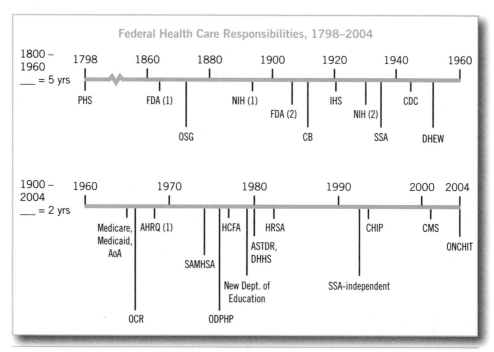

FIGURE 1A.1
Growth in federal health care responsibilities, 1798–2004.

- The **U.S. Public Health Service** (1798), which first served sick and disabled seamen, now encompasses:
  1. The **Food and Drug Administration (FDA)** (1862; 1906) today is charged with assuring the safety of most of the U.S. food supply; all drugs and related products; medical equipment and devices that emit radiation, including microwave ovens; animal drugs and feed; and cosmetics.
  2. The **National Institutes of Health (NIH)** (1887; 1930), which comprises 27 institutes and centers, is the world's premier medical research organization. NIH supports research projects at more than 3,000 research facilities worldwide.
  3. The **Indian Health Service (IHS)** (1921) provides health services to federally recognized American Indian and Alaska Native tribes.
  4. The **Centers for Disease Control and Prevention (CDC)** (1946) develops and implements disease prevention and control, environmental health, and health promotion/health education activities. It also maintains the nation's health statistics.
  5. The **Substance Abuse and Mental Health Services Administration (SAMHSA)** (1974) supports prevention and treatment programs and monitors the extent of substance abuse in American society.
  6. The CDC director administers the **Agency for Toxic Substances Disease Registry (ATSDR)** (1980), which assesses risks from toxins and helps prevent exposure to hazardous substances.
  7. The **Health Resources and Services Administration (HRSA)** (1982) funds health professions education programs, provides student financial support, and administers programs offering health care for uninsured, isolated, or medically vulnerable people.
  8. The **Agency for Healthcare Research and Quality (AHRQ)** (1989) supports research on health care systems and quality of care.

- The ***Office of the Surgeon General*** of the United States (1871). Appointed by the president, the surgeon general's primary duty is to provide leadership and authoritative, science-based recommendations about the public's health.
- The roots of the ***Administration for Children and Families (ACF)*** began with the ***Children's Bureau (CB)*** (1912). Today ACF promotes the economic and social well-being of children, families, and communities, including through programs like Temporary Assistance for Needy Families (TANF) and Head Start.
- ***Administration on Aging (AoA)*** (1965) activities promote health and successful aging.
- *Healthy People 2020* is the most recent in a series of reports from the ***Office of Disease Prevention and Health Promotion (ODPHP)*** (1976) that set scientifically sound, consensus-based health objectives for the nation.
- The ***Centers for Medicare and Medicaid Services (CMS)*** (which began in 1977 as the Health Care Financing Administration) reimburse health care services provided by nongovernmental facilities and health care professionals (mostly doctors). Medicare mainly serves the elderly and some people with disabilities, Medicaid serves low income Americans, and the Children's Health Insurance Program (CHIP) (1997) covers low income children not poor enough for Medicaid. CMS reimbursement policies are a significant factor shaping the U.S. health care system and the services it provides.
- The ***Office of the National Coordinator for Health Information Technology (ONCHIT)*** (2004) promotes widespread national adoption of health information technology and health information exchanges, as a way to improve health care.

Health-Related Responsibilities of Other Federal Entities

A comprehensive view of what makes a person healthy includes not just physical health, but mental, emotional, and spiritual health as well. A "healthy" person is able to be an effective student, a productive worker, a supportive family member, and a contributing member of the community and society.

Not surprisingly, a large number of societal sectors have an interest in keeping people healthy and protecting them from harm. These sectors are represented in the several federal departments. For example:

- The Labor Department protects worker safety through the Occupational Safety and Health Administration
- The Department of Defense provides medical care to ill and injured service members, with the goal of returning them to their units
- The Veterans Administration provides a range of health and rehabilitative services to former service members
- The Department of Justice's crime prevention activities protect citizens from violence
- The Department of Housing and Urban Development is concerned with healthy homes and controlling lead hazards

Table 1A.2 lists many of the areas and programs within almost every corner of the government—some that might initially appear far afield from health—that are involved in Americans' health and safety. Clearly, getting government out of the health and health care business is not nearly as simple as it may sound.

TABLE 1A.2

Responsibility for Health Is Shared by Many U.S. Government Departments and Agencies

Social Security Administration
- Disability benefits
- Retiree income benefits

Department of Labor
- Occupational Safety and Health Administration
- Mine Safety and Health Administration
- Employee Benefits Security Administration
- Administers the Family Medical Leave Act
- Bureau of Labor Statistics (health care workforce data)

Department of Homeland Security
- Programs to address safety threats, including from biological, chemical, and nuclear weapons
- Combats illegal drugs as part of border protection and other activities
- Disaster response and recovery
- Includes an Office of Health Affairs
- Insurance benefits for immigrants

Department of Defense
- Military medicine programs of the Armed Services
- TRICARE: an insurance program covering 9.6 million active duty and retired military personnel family members and survivors
- Active efforts to prevent traumatic brain injury and posttraumatic stress disorder

Department of Veterans Affairs
- Hospitals and health care facilities that provide comprehensive care to more than 5.5 million veterans

Department of Agriculture
- Center for Nutrition Policy and Promotion
- Animal and Plant Health Inspection Service
- Emergency preparedness and response

Department of Justice
- Crime prevention, drug control, and public safety
- Office of Violence Against Women
- Bureau of Alcohol, Tobacco, Firearms and Explosives
- Drug Enforcement Administration

Department of Energy
- Health and safety programs, especially nuclear related

Department of Housing and Urban Development
- Green homes and communities programs for healthy environments
- Healthy homes initiatives
- Lead hazard control

Department of Transportation
- National Highway Transportation Safety Administration
- Federal Aviation Administration
- Safety programs for autos, trucks, rail, and air travel

Department of Education
- Special education and rehabilitative services
- Violence, alcohol, and drug prevention on college campuses
- Safe and drug-free schools

Department of Commerce
- U.S. Census and special studies of uninsured, etc.

Environmental Protection Agency
- Protects people from risks
- Safeguard air, water, and land

(continued)

TABLE 1A.2

Responsibility for Health Is Shared by Many U.S. Government Departments and Agencies *(continued)*

Department of State
● Office of International Health Affairs
● Office of Global AIDS Coordinator

Agency for International Development (Global Health)

U.S. Chemical Safety Board

Consumer Product Safety Commission

Drug Enforcement Administration

Medicare Payment Advisory Commission

National AIDS Policy Office

National Bipartisan Commission on the Future of Medicare

National Council on Disability

Office of National Drug Control Policy

Uniformed Services University for the Health Sciences

The U.S. Hospital and Physician Supply

The density of major health care resources—most notably hospital beds and physicians—varies markedly across the United States. Where there are the most people, you would expect to find the most doctors and larger, more numerous hospitals. But resource distribution is not solely dependent on population. In fact, much research over the past 30 years has shown that—regardless of age, race, gender, income, and illness patterns of the population—different regions of the United States simply have a much greater intensity of health resources than others (Skinner & Fisher, 2010).

Americans living in areas with fewer hospital beds and doctors do receive fewer health care services. However, the most intriguing aspect of these research findings is that health outcomes in these regions, including death rates, are at least as good as—and often better than—those found in areas rich in health care resources.

The United States spends more on hospital and physician services than any other component of health care expenditures. Of the 2008 total spent on health ($2.34 trillion), more than 30% went to hospitals and 21% to physician services (Hartman et al., 2010). Doctors have a greater impact on health spending than that figure suggests, of course, because they generally order the hospitalizations and home health services, prescribe the medications, and authorize many other health services.

HOSPITALS

Across the nation, some geographic areas have more than twice the number of hospital beds per 1,000 residents than do others, based on 2006 data (Figure 1A.2). This holds true even after demographic factors are taken into account. Particularly well-resourced areas were Jackson and Gulfport, Mississippi. Each had 4.44 hospital beds for every 1,000 residents. By contrast, San Mateo and San Luis Obispo Counties in California had only 1.45 hospital beds for every 1,000 residents (Goodman, Fisher, & Bronner, 2009). The medical community in these two areas clearly practices medicine very differently, with the Mississippi doctors relying heavily on inpatient care.

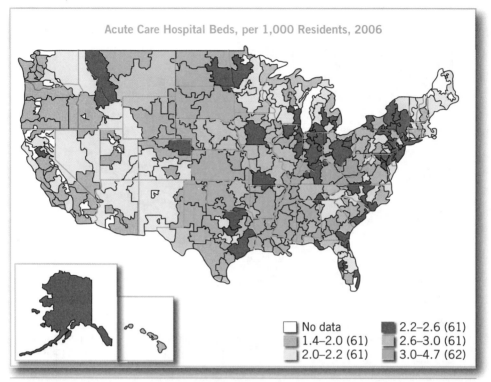

FIGURE 1A.2

Acute care hospital beds per 1,000 residents, 2006.
Source: The Dartmouth Atlas of Health Care (http://www.dartmouthatlas.org), copyright the Trustees of Dartmouth College.

In the 1970s, there was a nationwide effort to eliminate unnecessary hospital beds—so-called "over-bedding"—because it was assumed that "an existing bed is a filled bed," and that taking care of people in hospitals who didn't absolutely need to be there was an unnecessarily high cost way to deliver care.

At the same time, hospitals moved many activities into outpatient settings. Technological developments made outpatient surgery, diagnostic centers, and dialysis treatments possible and popular. Financial pressures from the federal government encouraged this trend. Medicare developed a payment system that pays hospitals a fixed fee for a particular diagnosis, which encouraged earlier discharges.

As a result of such factors, the number of hospitals and hospital beds declined, but who goes to the hospital, when, and why depends almost exclusively on doctors.

PHYSICIANS

As with hospital beds, the supply of doctors also varies across regions. This is true both for primary care physicians (family physicians, general internists, pediatricians, and OB-GYNs) and for specialists and subspecialists (cardiologists, pulmonologists, nephrologists, and so on) (Figure 1A.3).

Primary care physicians should be patients' source of ongoing wellness care and first contact in case of problems (see Chapter 9), and some regions have more than 2.5 times

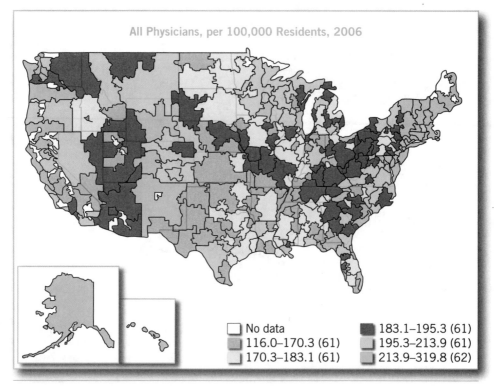

All Physicians, per 100,000 Residents, 2006

☐ No data	■ 183.1–195.3 (61)
■ 116.0–170.3 (61)	■ 195.3–213.9 (61)
■ 170.3–183.1 (61)	■ 213.9–319.8 (62)

FIGURE 1A.3

All physicians per 100,000 residents, 2006.
Source: The Dartmouth Atlas of Health Care (http://www.dartmouthatlas.org), copyright the Trustees of Dartmouth College.

as many of them as do others. San Francisco has the highest rate (117 primary care physicians per 100,000 residents) and other cities with high rates are Lebanon, New Hampshire, and Washington, D.C. The lowest rates were found in several Texas towns, with Odessa the lowest at 43.9, followed by McAllen at 45.1.

Specialist physicians generally provide more complex—and costly—services. Other countries encourage citizens to rely on primary physicians for most of their care and to use specialists sparingly. However, in the United States, we do the opposite. Not only is this an expensive way to obtain care, it produces worse health outcomes. Some evidence suggests that a population's health outcomes, including death rates, improve as the number of primary care physicians increases (Starfield, Shi, Grover, & Macinko, 2005a; Starfield, Shi, & Macinko, 2005b).

In the United States, high rates of specialists are found in densely urban areas—White Plains, New York, for example, has 215 specialists for every 100,000 people. Washington, D.C., Manhattan, San Francisco, and Boston also have high rates of specialists. The lowest rate is found in McAllen, Texas (68.3). Other cities with low rates are Harlingen, Texas; Tupelo, Mississippi; Sioux City, Iowa; and Aurora, Illinois. (Chapters 8 and 9 further discuss the problem of a primary care/specialist physician imbalance.)

Over the past few decades, the pendulum of health policy experts' opinion has swung wildly between "too many doctors" and fears of a looming physician shortage. With recent health care reform set to provide health insurance for millions more Americans, we have recently reentered a pending shortage phase. This is interesting, given that the above threefold difference in physician supply apparently comes with no health penalty for the low supply regions. Moreover, "higher physician supply *per se* offers little benefit in population health or in patients' satisfaction with access and with the care received" (Goodman, Fisher, & Bronner, 2009, pp. 12–15).

Costs of Care

In 2008, total U.S. health care costs were $2.3 trillion—$7,681 per person (Hartman et al., 2010). To understand how dramatic this growth has been over the last few decades, compare the 2008 per capita costs to the $356 per person spent on health care in 1970. Although the growth rate in expenditures declined in 2008, attributable in large part to the national recession, in earlier years of this century the annual growth in health costs was typically above 6%.

Experts differ about the significance of the rising costs of entitlement programs (Medicare, Medicaid, and Social Security) to the U.S. economy in the long term, but it is clear that health care costs are constraining growth in other areas. For many years, workers have traded wage increases for more generous health benefits; high costs of employee and retiree health benefits limit corporate expansion and the global price competitiveness of U.S. products and state budgets, which by law must be balanced, strain under the burden of Medicaid payments and employee health insurance obligations.

When you look at health care expenditures *per capita* (Figure 1A.4), you can see that Texas, California, and Georgia were among the lower groups of states in terms of spending per resident. Their large *total* expenditures are driven more by population size than generous health programs. Northeast states (plus Alaska) generally spent the most, per resident, with the District of Columbia a complete outlier at $8,295.

It also may be useful to note the costs of treating specific disease. In 2007, on average—and variation is clearly enormous—caring for a cancer patient cost about $40,000, for a person with heart disease treatment was $26,000, and for a person with a mental illness it was $11,000. These figures include hospitalizations, doctor visits, and other resources used (U.S., DHHS, Agency for Health Care Research & Quality, 2007).

Where the Money Comes From

The nation's $2.3 trillion in national health expenditures comes from numerous sources: private funds (private health insurance and out-of-pocket payments, plus some smaller sources) and public funds—federal, state, and local (Figure 1A.5).

In 2007, 54% of total national health expenditures came from private sources. Not surprisingly, in recent years, health care costs paid out-of-pocket have increased between 4% and 5% a year, whereas household income grew at about half that rate. U.S. households spent almost 6% of their income on health care in 2008 (Hartman et al., 2010). In total, these payments amounted to some $269 million in 2007. By contrast, private insurance expenditures in 2007 were $775 million.

In the U.S. Constitution, states are given responsibility for health matters, but, especially with the advent of Medicare and Medicaid (the cost of which is shared with states), the federal government dominates the public sector's expenditures on health. The federal share accounts for a third of total expenditures, whereas state and local governments are responsible for less than 13%.

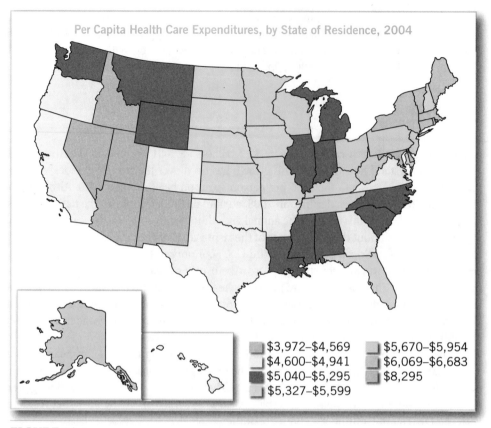

FIGURE 1A.4

Per capita health care expenditures, by state of residence, 2004.

Source: Kaiser Family Foundation. *State health facts. Health care expenditures, per capita, by state of residence, 2004.* Retrieved June 1, 2010, from http://www.statehealthfacts.org. This information was reprinted with permission from the Henry J. Kaiser Family Foundation, a nonprofit private operating foundation, based in Menlo Park, California, dedicated to producing and communicating the best possible analysis and information on health issues.

FIGURE 1A.5

Percent of funds contributing to national health expenditures, by source, 2007.

Source: Hartman, M., Martin, M., McDonnell, P., Catlin, A., & the National Health Expenditure Accounts Team. (2009). National health spending in 2007: Slower drug spending contributes to lowest rate of overall growth since 1998. *Health Affairs, 28,* 246–261.

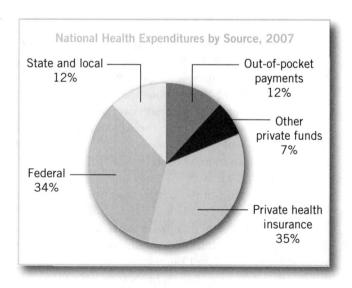

Health Care Quality

UNDERLYING PROBLEMS

In one sense, Americans might not care how much the country spends on health care, if only they were receiving good value for dollars spent. The technical quality of U.S. health care, especially for people who are acutely ill, can be excellent. The United States has among the world's most advanced science, equipment, techniques, facilities, and training for dealing with complex and life-threatening illnesses and injuries.

But these are rare, compared to the everyday situations that affect the most people—people with chronic diseases, mental disorders, substance abuse, behavioral health problems, and end-of-life issues. These people have found the system faltering, fragmented, and frustrating (Chapters 7 and 9).

Blinded by the "best in the world" mythology, health care leaders and professionals have been slow to examine underlying factors in professional training and health care system performance that determine how—and how well—care is delivered (Figure 1A.6).

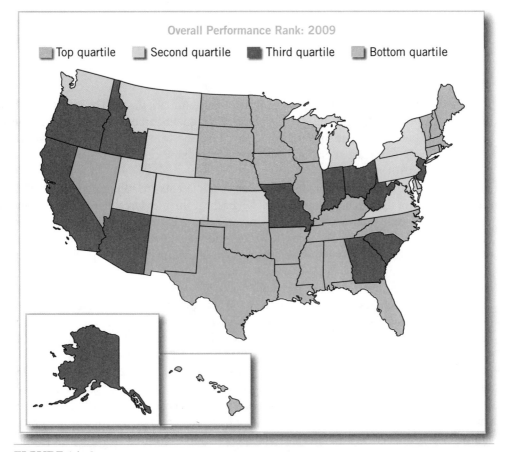

FIGURE 1A.6

Overall performance ranking of U.S. states, based on 38 indicators of access, quality, costs, and health outcomes.

Source: McCarthy, D., How, S.K.H., Schoen, C., Cantor, J.C., & Belloff, D. (2009). *Aiming higher: Results from a state scorecard on health system performance, 2009.* Retrieved March 15, 2010, from http://www.commonwealthfund.org/ Content/Publications/ Fund-Reports/2009/Oct/2009-State-Scorecard.aspx?page=all. Reprinted with permission.

Not until two landmark Institute of Medicine reports, published in 2000 and 2001, did these issues begin to be aired. The first report addressed patient safety and suggested that, every year in U.S. hospitals, 44,000 Americans die—and hundreds of thousands more are injured—as a result of medical errors. It called on doctors and hospitals to stop blaming these deaths on individual carelessness, but to probe for systems problems that create the opportunities for errors—like amputating the wrong limb, medication mix ups, or hospital-acquired infections.

The 2001 report laid out a roadmap to achieve greater quality in the health care system as a whole. It called for changes to assure that care is safe, effective, patient-centered, timely, efficient, and equitable.

So, how are we doing? According to The Joint Commission—the principal organization that accredits U.S. hospitals—the past 7 years have seen "steady improvement" in hospital care for heart attacks, heart failure, and pneumonia. Other sources confirm this (McCarthy et al., 2009). But gaps remain.

Hospital safety itself remains a problem. Health Grades, Inc., an independent health care ratings organization, reports that in the 3 years of 2006 to 2008, nearly a million hospital patient-safety incidents occurred among Medicare patients (the group for whom the best data are available), resulting in almost 100,000 deaths and $9 billion in costs.

IMPACTS ON INDIVIDUALS

Too often, necessity demands that quality improvements (or lack thereof) be assessed with measures that look at discrete, measurable pieces of the quality problem—for example, the percentage of pneumonia patients in the intensive care unit who receive antibiotics within 24 hours or whether heart attack patients received smoking cessation advice (The Joint Commission, 2010).

Efforts to combine measures for specific types of patients are still more an art than a science—how are they weighted, for example? Each of the measures that has been constructed by multiple quality improvement organizations is important, but they do not necessarily add up to a better experience for the individual patient, worried more about the totality of care received and how well the parts of the health care system are integrated, coordinated, and informed.

An overall measure of health care quality is Commonwealth Fund's "Healthy Lives" measure, which includes indicators that measure "the degree to which a state's residents enjoy long and healthy lives, as well as factors such as smoking and obesity that affect health and longevity." Comparing the map of overall quality against that of the extent to which a state's residents enjoy "healthy lives" (Figure 1A.7) shows some, but not complete similarity—indicating there is more to health than the presence of high-quality health care.

Finally, throughout this section, we've examined the great geographic variability in many aspects of health care. On this topic, we have barely scratched the surface. Variability, in and of itself, is a marker of poor quality care. All things being equal, people should pretty much receive the same intensity of care from one place to another. But, in the United States, either some people are receiving too much or others are receiving too little, or both. Despite all the talk about "health care systems," health care in the United States, in many respects, remains a cottage industry.

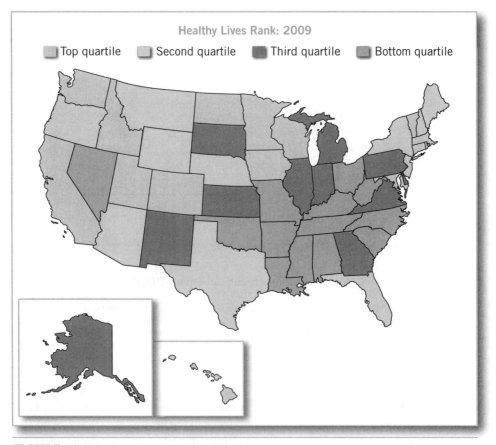

FIGURE 1A.7
Achieving long and healthy lives.
Source: McCarthy, D., How, S.K.H., Schoen, C., Cantor, J.C., & Belloff, D. (2009). *Aiming higher: Results from a state scorecard on health system performance, 2009.* Retrieved September 9, 2010, from http://www .commonwealthfund.org/Content/Charts/Report/Aiming-Higher-2009-Results-from-a-State-Scorecard-on-Health-System-Performance/State-Ranking-on-Healthy-Lives-Dimension.aspx. Reprinted with permission.

Satisfaction With Care

For many years, public opinion polling has made it clear that Americans are unhappy with the U.S. health care system. A June 2010 Harris poll, which rated 16 different aspects of American life, found "the health care system" fourth from the bottom, with only a third of respondents rated it excellent (6%) or pretty good (27%). By contrast, 29% rated it poor and 39% rated it only fair. The only social institutions that fared worse were the public schools, the economic system, and, perhaps not surprising, considering the rancor among the political parties at that time, the political system (The Harris Poll, 2010).

Americans commonly express negative opinions of broad institutions such as "public schools," while believing their *local* public schools are fine. In health care, responses indicate, in essence, "the health system is a mess, but I like my doctor." That pattern is repeated in international surveys. U.S. respondents are somewhat more likely than residents in 29 other countries (members of the Organisation for Economic Co-operation

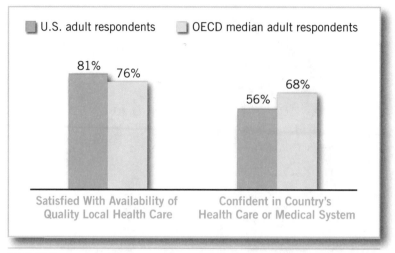

FIGURE 1A.8

Satisfaction with local and national health care among OECD countries.
Note: Data collected between 2006 and 2008.
Source: Khoury, C. & Brown, I.T. (2009. Among OECD nations, U.S. lags in personal health: Not feeling health benefits of high spending. Accessed September 9, 2010, from http://www.gallup.com/poll/117205/americans-not-feeling-health-benefits-high-spending.aspx. Reprinted with permission from Gallup World Poll.

and Development [OECD]) to say they are satisfied with the availability of quality health care locally, but much more likely to lack confidence in the health care system (Khoury & Brown, 2009). The opinion of both U.S. and international respondents drops when considering the national versus the local health care system, but U.S. respondents' drops much more (Figure 1A.8).

People in other nations also dislike aspects of their health systems, but to a far lesser degree than U.S. residents. The OECD compiled a number of surveys documenting the high proportion (82%) of Americans who, in 2007, believed the country's health care system needed to have fundamental changes (48%) or to be completely rebuilt (34%) (OECD, 2009). This was a much higher percentage compared to residents of Australia, Canada, Germany, the Netherlands, New Zealand, and the United Kingdom (see Chapter 4).

Almost always, the more a country spends on health care, the more satisfied residents are with their *personal* health. In this regard, the United States is a unique case. Despite the substantially larger amounts spent on health care in the United States, Americans fall somewhere in the middle, compared to residents of the 29 other OECD countries, with respect to their satisfaction with personal health (Khoury & Brown, 2009).

Satisfaction reflects not just actual experiences, but how these experiences measure up to expectations. Americans low rate of health care literacy—and tendency to expect miracle cures—means many people may enter into a health care encounter with unrealistic expectations. For example, cardiopulmonary resuscitation (CPR) on television usually ends with a healthy looking individual sitting up in bed. In fact, CPR is often performed on the elderly, where the result can be broken ribs and other problems, and fewer than 1 in 5 CPR patients survives to be discharged from the hospital (Ramenofsky & Weissman, 2007).

The Health Care Workforce

Of the 145 million civilians employed in the United States in 2008, more than 1 in 10 (just over 15 million) were employed in health services—in places such as offices of health care practitioners, clinics, hospitals, outpatient and home health services, nursing homes, and residential care. The largest group of these workers—some 6.2 million, or 41%—worked in hospitals.

These diverse worksites employ a wide variety of health care professionals—not just doctors, dentists, and nurses, but a wide range of technicians, pharmacists, aides, counselors and administrative personnel (Table 1A.3).

According to the federal Bureau of Labor Statistics, the future outlook for health care jobs is excellent. The sector will generate an estimated 3.2 million new jobs by 2018—more than any other industry. As Table 1A.3 shows, even the estimates for the slowest growing occupational categories indicate an increase of at least 9%. And, the outlook for physician assistants—who, along with advanced practices nurses can help make up shortages in the primary care workforce (see Chapter 15)—indicates 41% growth.

In fact, 10 of the 20 fastest growing occupations are related to health care. These jobs result from growth in the sector (more demand) and the high average age of individuals in a number of professions, who are likely to retire (reduced supply).

TABLE 1A.3

Prospects for Growth in the U.S. Health Care Workforce, 2008–2018

Occupation	Employment, 2008		Percent Change, 2008–2018
	Number	Percent	
All occupations	14,336.0	100.0	22.5
Management, business, and financial occupations	614.6	4.3	16.8
Professional and related occupations	6,283.9	43.8	22.5
• Counselors	171.3	1.2	22.6
• Social workers	206.7	1.4	19.5
• Dietitians and nutritionists	35.5	0.3	9.8
• Pharmacists	67.5	0.5	14.0
• Physicians and surgeons	512.5	3.6	26.0
• Physician assistants	66.2	0.5	41.3
• Registered nurses	2,192.4	15.3	23.4
• Clinical laboratory technologists and technicians	278.8	1.9	14.0
• Emergency medical technicians and paramedics	142.1	1.0	9.2
• Licensed practical and licensed vocational nurses	619.1	4.3	21.9
Office and administrative support occupations	2,540.3	17.7	19.7
• Billing and posting clerks and machine operators	194.8	1.4	19.7
• Receptionists and information clerks	386.3	2.7	16.1
• Secretaries and administrative assistants	770.7	5.4	26.5

Note: Columns may not add to total due to omission of occupations with small employment.
Source: U.S., Department of Labor. Bureau of Labor Statistics. (2010). *National employment matrix, 2008–18.* Retrieved September 16, 2010, from http://www.bls.gov/oco/cg/cgs035.htm.

REFERENCES

Goodman, D. C., Fisher, E. S., & Bronner, K. K. (2009). *Hospital and physician capacity update*. Lebanon, NH: The Dartmouth Institute.

The Harris Poll. (2010, June 8). *What we love and hate about America*. Retrieved September 9, 2010, from http://www.harrisinteractive.com/NewsRoom/HarrisPolls/tabid/447/mid/1508/articleId/405/ctl/ReadCustom%20Default/Default.aspx

Hartman, M., Martin, A., Nuccio, O., Catlin, A., & the National Health Expenditure Accounts Team. (2010). Health spending growth at a historic low in 2008. *Health Affairs, 29*, 147–155.

Institute of Medicine. (2000). *To err is human: Building a safer health system*. Washington, D.C.: National Academy Press.

Institute of Medicine. (2001). *Crossing the quality chasm: A new health system for the 21st century*. Washington, D.C.: National Academy Press.

The Joint Commission. (2010). *Improving America's hospitals: The Joint Commission's annual report on quality and safety*. Retrieved June 15, 2010, from http://www.jointcommission.org/library/annual_report.

Khoury, C. & Brown, I. T. (2009). Among OECD nations, U.S. lags in personal health: Not feeling health benefits of high spending. Retrieved September 9, 2010, from http://www.gallup.com/poll/117205/americans-not-feeling-health-benefits-high-spending.aspx

McCarthy, D., How, S. K. H., Schoen, C., Cantor, J. C., & Belloff, D. (2009). *Aiming higher: results from a state scorecard on health system performance, 2009*. Retrieved March 15, 2010, from http://www.commonwealthfund.org/Content/Publications/Fund-Reports/2009/Oct/2009-State-Scorecard.aspx?page=all

Organisation for Economic Co-operation and Development (OECD). (2009). Public's satisfaction with health care system, selected European and non-European countries, 1988–2007. Retrieved June 15, 2010, from http://www.ecosante.fr/OCDEENG/65.html

Ramenofsky, D. H., & Weissman, D. E. (2007). CPR survival in the hospital setting. Fast facts and concepts, #179. Retrieved September 16, 2010, from http://www.eperc.mcw.edu/fastfact/ff_179.htm

Skinner, J., & Fisher, E. S. (2010). Reflections on geographic variations in U.S. health care. Retrieved June 15, 2010, from http://www.dartmouthatlas.org/

Starfield, B., Shi, L., Grover, A., & Macinko, J. (2005a). The effects of specialist supply on populations' health: Assessing the evidence. *Health Affairs Web Exclusive, W5*, 97–107.

Starfield, B., Shi, L., & Macinko, J. (2005b). Contribution of primary care to health systems and health. *Milbank Quarterly, 83*, 457–502.

U.S., Department of Health and Human Services (DHHS), Agency for Healthcare Research & Quality. (2007). Table 3a. Mean expenses per person with care for selected conditions by type of service: United States, 2007. *Medical Expenditure Panel Survey*. Retrieved September 16, 2010, from http://www.meps.ahrq.gov/mepsweb/data_stats/tables_compendia_hh_interactive.jsp?_SERVICE=MEPSSocket0&_PROGRAM=MEPSPGM.TC.SAS&File=HCFY2007&Table=HCFY2007_CNDXP_CA&_Debug=

U.S., Government Accountability Office. (2008). *Federal oversight of food safety: FDA's Food Protection Plan proposes positive first steps, but capacity to carry them out is critical*. GAO-08-435T. Washington, D.C.: Author.

2

HEALTH POLICY AND HEALTH REFORM

Michael S. Sparer

KEY WORDS

patient protection and affordable care act
(ACA)
medicaid
medicare

children's health insurance program (CHIP)
employee retirement income security act
(ERISA)

LEARNING OBJECTIVES

- Review the evolution of government's role in the U.S. health care system
- Describe the roles of federal, state, and local government in the U.S. health care system
- Explore key issues on the government's health policy agenda, including the enactment and implementation of the Patient Protection and Affordable Care Act of 2010

TOPICAL OUTLINE

- The government as payer: the health insurance safety net
- The government as regulator
- The government as health care provider
- Key issues on the U.S. health care agenda

Government is deeply entrenched in every aspect of the U.S. health care system (see Chapter 1A, Charts). The federal government provides tax incentives to encourage employers to offer health insurance to their employees; provides health insurance to the poor, the aged, and the disabled; operates health care facilities for veterans; and supports the training of doctors and other health professionals. State governments administer and help pay for Medicaid, license health care providers, and operate facilities for the mentally ill and developmentally disabled. Local governments own and operate public hospitals and public health clinics and develop and enforce public health codes.

With the enactment of the **Patient Protection and Affordable Care Act of 2010 (ACA)**, government's role is about to expand dramatically, especially when it comes to insurance coverage. Some of the new provisions take effect soon: young adults will be able to stay on their parents' private health insurance policies until they turn 26 years old, private insurers will be prohibited from discriminating against children with preexisting health conditions, and thousands of adults with such preexisting conditions will be able to buy affordable coverage through newly created "high-risk" insurance pools.

As of 2014, even more significant new initiatives go into effect. Federal law will require nearly all Americans to have some form of health insurance (or pay a penalty through the tax code). Private insurance companies will need to comply with a host of new federal rules and regulations. Large employers who do not provide adequate insurance coverage for their employees will be penalized. There will be an additional 16 to 18 million persons enrolled in state Medicaid programs. Millions more will receive public subsidies that will enable them to afford private coverage purchased through newly created, state-administered insurance pools.

The goal of this chapter is to provide an overview of government's role in the health care system. The chapter is divided into three sections. First is a discussion of government as a payer for health care services. The theme is that government provides health insurance to many of those who are not covered by the employer-sponsored private health insurance system, while also subsidizing (directly or indirectly) a growing portion of the cost of private coverage. Second is a summary of government as regulator of the health care system. The focus is on state and federal efforts to enact patient protection legislation. Third is a discussion of government as a provider of health care. The section reviews health systems operated by the three levels of government: the Veterans Administration (VA) facilities run by the federal government, the institutions for the mentally ill operated by the states, and the public hospitals and public health clinics owned and administered by local governments.

The Government as Payer: The Health Insurance Safety Net

For much of U.S. history, the national government and the states were minor players in the nation's health and welfare systems. The social welfare system was shaped instead by the principles that governed the English poor law system. Social welfare programs were a local responsibility and assistance was provided only to those who were outside the labor force through no fault of their own (the "deserving poor"). National welfare programs were considered unwise and perhaps even unconstitutional. The main exception was the Civil War pension program, which provided federal funds to Union veterans, but even this initiative was administered and implemented at the local level.

Lacking federal or state leadership (and dollars), local governments tried to provide a social and medical safety net. The most common approach was to establish almshouses (or shelters) for indigent aged and disabled people. A medical clinic often provided health care to almshouse residents. These clinics eventually evolved into public hospitals, offering services to the poor without charge. Generally speaking, however, the clinics (and hospitals) provided poor-quality care and were avoided by people who had any alternative. Similarly, the few private hospitals then in operation were charitable facilities that served only the poor and the disabled. These hospitals, like their public counterparts, represented only a small and rather disreputable portion of the nation's health care system.

Most 19th-century Americans received health care in their homes, often from family members who relied on traditional healing techniques. At the same time, an assortment of health care providers—physicians, midwives, medicine salesmen, herbalists, homeopaths, and faith healers—offered their services as well. Generally speaking, these practitioners charged low fees, which families paid out-of-pocket, much as they would for other commodities.

As the 19th century drew to a close, two developments fundamentally changed the U.S. health care marketplace. First, allopathic physicians (MDs) won the battle for primacy among medical providers. Americans increasingly recognized that medicine was a science and believed that medical doctors were the most scientific and best able to deliver high-quality care. The status and prestige accorded to MD-physicians grew, while the role of alternative medicine providers declined.

The emergence of a physician-dominated health care system was accompanied by a second pivotal factor—the dramatic growth in the size and the status of the U.S. hospital industry. Indeed, the nation's stock of hospitals grew from fewer than 200 in 1873 to 4,000 (with 35,500 beds) in 1900, to nearly 7,000 (with 922,000 beds) by 1930 (Annas, Law, Rosenblatt, & Wing, 1990).

This growth was prompted by several factors. Advances in medical technology (antiseptics, anesthesia, X rays) encouraged wealthier people to use hospitals, eliminating much of their prior social stigma. The number of nurses expanded dramatically, as nurses evolved from domestics to trained professionals, and hospital-based nurses worked hard to improve hospitals' hygiene. The growing urbanization and industrialization of American life produced an increasingly rootless society, less able to rely on families to care for their sick at home. Finally, the medical education system began to require internships and residencies in hospitals as part of physician training, which put a cadre of trained doctors working full-time in these facilities.

As the hospital industry grew, so too did the costs of care. By the mid-1920s, there was growing recognition that middle income Americans needed help in financing the rising costs of hospital care and increasingly high tech medicine. The onset of the Great Depression made the situation more problematic, as hospital occupancy rates plummeted and numerous facilities went bankrupt. In response to this crisis, the hospital industry created Blue Cross, for-profit insurers soon followed Blue Cross into the health business, and the nation's private health insurance industry began to emerge.

The health insurance industry then received a major boost from the federal government, first during World War II, when federal policy makers excluded most employer-sponsored health insurance from wage and price controls, and then in the early 1950s when federal officials ruled that premiums paid by employers would not be considered income to the employee (a tax exclusion that now costs the federal government over $250 billion a year). By the mid-1950s, employer-sponsored private insurance was on its way to becoming the vehicle through which most Americans could afford the rising cost of health care (see Chapter 3 for more on the early history of private health insurance).

At the same time, the demonstrable advances in medical technology after World War II engendered confidence that the medical system would in time conquer nearly all forms of disease. This perception prompted the federal government (through the National Institutes of Health) to funnel billions of dollars to academic medical researchers. And, with federal dollars so readily available, medical schools soon emphasized research, and medical students increasingly chose research careers. Around the same time, Congress enacted the Hill-Burton Program, which provided federal funds to stimulate hospital construction and modernization. The policy assumption was that all Americans should have access to the increasingly sophisticated medical care rendered in state-of-the-art hospital facilities.

Even with the growing employer-sponsored health insurance system, it was soon clear that large portions of the population would not easily have access to such coverage, or to the benefits of the new medical advances. Left out of these new systems were the retired elderly, the disabled, the unemployed, the self-employed, the part-time worker, and most of those who worked for small businesses.

> *Sixty years ago, President Harry Truman posited that health insurance was part of the Fair Deal all Americans are entitled to.*

To be sure, for many years, liberal politicians had argued without success in favor of government-sponsored health insurance that would replace the employer-sponsored private system and would cover all Americans. President Harry Truman posited that health insurance is part of the Fair Deal all Americans are entitled to. However, neither Truman nor his liberal predecessors ever came close to overcoming the strong opposition to national health insurance from doctors, businessmen, and others who viewed it as un-American and socialistic. And, in the doctors' case, they feared a government program would lead to greater oversight, requirements to serve indigent patients, and reduced income potential.

By 1949, mainstream Democrats had abandoned their visions of universal insurance and proposed instead that the Social Security (retirement) system be expanded to provide hospital insurance for the aged, reasoning that the elderly were a sympathetic and deserving group, and hospital care was the most costly sector of the health care system.

Conservatives opposed the plan, arguing that it would give free coverage to many people who were neither poor nor particularly needy. They argued instead that government's role is to provide a safety net to the deserving poor who are unable to access employer-sponsored coverage. The result was an amendment to the Social Security Act in 1950 that, for the first time, provided federal funds to states willing to pay health care providers to care for welfare recipients. Interestingly, this "welfare medicine" approach passed with bipartisan support (Sparer, 1996). For liberals, this was an acceptable, albeit inadequate, first step, but at least some poor people finally could obtain services. Conservatives went along, because a medical safety net for the poor would undermine arguments for a more comprehensive health insurance program and because responsibility for the program was delegated to state officials.

In 1960, newly elected President John F. Kennedy revived the effort to enact hospital insurance for the aged. Congress responded by enacting the Kerr-Mills Program. This program distributed federal funds to states that were willing to pay health care providers to care for the indigent aged, expanding the welfare medicine model. Congress later opened the program to covering the indigent disabled. These initiatives again deflected support from the president's broader social insurance proposal.

The political dynamic evolved considerably by 1965. President Lyndon B. Johnson and the Democrats controlling Congress were enacting various laws designed to turn the United States into a "Great Society." This seemed an opportune time to renew the effort to enact national health insurance. Even longtime opponents of health insurance expansions expected Congress to enact a plan far more comprehensive than Kerr-Mills. President Johnson followed the path set by Truman and Kennedy and again proposed hospital insurance for the aged. At the same time, various Republican legislators, citing the nation's oversupply of hospitals, and desiring to return to a physician-centered delivery system, recommended that Congress enact physician insurance for the aged. And the American Medical Association (AMA), hoping once again to scuttle the social insurance model, urged Congress simply to expand Kerr-Mills.

As Congress debated these various proposals, President Johnson (working behind the scenes) convinced Congressman Wilbur Mills, powerful chair of the House Ways and

Means Committee and an aspiring presidential candidate, to demand that his colleagues enact all three expansion initiatives (Blumenthal & Morone, 2009). The president's proposal for hospital insurance for the aged became Medicare Part A; the Republican proposal for physician insurance for the aged became Medicare Part B. The AMA's effort to expand Kerr-Mills became Medicaid. These government programs, for the first time, became a true health insurance safety net for Americans without employer-sponsored coverage (Marmor, 2000).

MEDICAID

Medicaid is not a single national program, but a collection of 50 state-administered programs, each providing health insurance to low-income state residents, but with differing eligibility rules, benefits, and payment schedules. Each state initiative is governed by various federal guidelines and the federal government contributes between 50% and 78% of its cost (the poorer the state, the larger the federal contribution). In 2007, the various Medicaid programs covered roughly 58 million Americans at an annual cost of just under $339 billion (Kaiser Family Foundation, 2010a).

Given Medicaid's decentralized structure, state officials have considerable discretion. One not-surprising result is that states such as New York have more generous eligibility criteria than do poorer states like Alabama or Mississippi. Interestingly, however, there are stark contrasts even among the larger states. In FY2007, New York, for example, spent $8,450 per Medicaid enrollee, whereas California spent only $3,168 (Kaiser Family Foundation, 2010b). During the late 1980s, Congress began imposing rules designed to increase state coverage. In 1988, it required states to cover pregnant women and infants with a family income below 100% of the poverty line. Previously, states typically covered this group only if family income was around 50% of the poverty level.

The next year, Congress required states to cover pregnant women and children under age 7 whose family income was below 133% of the poverty level. Then, in 1990, Congress required states to phase in coverage for all children younger than 19 with family income below 100% of the poverty level. As a result of these mandates, the number of children on Medicaid nearly doubled between 1987 and 1995, and the total number of recipients increased from roughly 26 million to nearly 40 million. Medicaid expansions had become the federal government's main strategy for reducing the ranks of the uninsured.

Concomitantly, Medicaid's annual price tag grew from $57.5 billion in 1988 to $157.3 billion in 1995. State officials blamed this increase on the federal mandates. Federal regulators disputed the claim and suggested that the states themselves were largely responsible for the increase, citing accounting techniques through which states shifted state-funded programs into their Medicaid budget so they could draw down additional federal dollars. This argument produced significant intergovernmental tension (Holahan & Liska, 1997).

During the early 1990s, President Clinton, a former state governor and a critic of Medicaid mandates, stopped considering Medicaid the linchpin in efforts to reduce the number of uninsured. Recognizing that many uninsured people are in families where the husband or wife works full- or part-time, he proposed instead to require that employers offer health insurance to their employees. The Clinton administration's proposal for national health insurance failed, but the shift away from federal Medicaid mandates persisted. Instead, federal officials became more lenient in approving state requests for waivers from federal Medicaid rules, giving states additional flexibility and autonomy.

Two trends dominated Medicaid policy during most of the 1990s. First, states used their expanded discretion to encourage or require recipients to enroll in managed care delivery systems. Between 1987 and 1998, the percentage of enrollees in Medicaid managed care increased from less than 5% to more than 50%, from fewer than 1 million people to more than 20 million. Second, growth in the number of Medicaid enrollees ended and a slow decline began. The most convincing explanation for the decline was federal welfare reform, enacted in 1996. Before then, people receiving Aid to Families with Dependent Children (welfare) were automatically enrolled in Medicaid. Thereafter, welfare recipients needed to apply separately for Medicaid, as did those no longer entitled to welfare but still eligible for Medicaid. Millions did not know they were Medicaid-eligible, the states set steep administrative hurdles that deterred others from applying, and still others were dissuaded by the stigma attached to receiving public assistance. For all of these reasons, between 1995 and 1997, the number of adult Medicaid recipients declined 5.5% and the number of child recipients declined 1.4%.

During the late 1990s, state and federal officials undertook a major effort to increase Medicaid enrollment. One strategy was to simplify the eligibility process (shortened application forms, mail-in applications, and more eligibility-determination sites). A second strategy was to simplify eligibility rules (eliminating assets tests and ensuring 12 months of continuous eligibility). A third strategy was to expand outreach and education, by increasing marketing activities and encouraging community-based institutions to educate and enroll their constituents. These efforts succeeded. Beginning in mid-1998, Medicaid enrollment began to increase again, a trend that has continued into 2010.

The growth in enrollment, along with higher costs for prescription drugs, services for people with disabilities, and long-term care, has led to escalating Medicaid costs and, for some years, states' Medicaid expenditures have exceeded what they spend on education. At the same time, state tax revenues declined precipitously in the late 2000s. The ensuing budget crises prompted Medicaid cost-containment efforts in every state. The most popular option was an effort to control the rising cost of pharmaceuticals, either through leveraged buying (purchasing pools) or limits on access (formularies). Other Medicaid cost-containment strategies have included freezing or cutting provider reimbursement, reducing benefits (such as dental and home care), cutting eligibility, increasing co-pays, and expanding disease management initiatives.

MEDICARE

Like Medicaid, **Medicare** was enacted in 1965 to provide health insurance to segments of the population not generally covered by the mainstream employer-sponsored health insurance system. And like Medicaid, Medicare has become a major part of the nation's health care system, providing insurance coverage to 38 million persons over the age of 65 and to just over 8 million of the young disabled population, at a total annual cost of more than $509 billion (Kaiser Family Foundation, 2010c).

In other respects, however, Medicare differs significantly from its sister program. Medicare is a social insurance program, providing benefits to the aged and the disabled regardless of income, whereas Medicaid is a welfare initiative, offering coverage only to those with limited income. Medicare is administered by federal officials and the private insurers they hire to perform particular tasks, whereas Medicaid is administered by the states following federal guidance. Medicare is funded primarily by the federal government (plus beneficiary co-payments and deductibles), whereas Medicaid is funded by the federal government and the states without any beneficiary contribution. Medicare has a relatively limited benefit package that excludes much preventive care, long-term care, and, until 2006, prescription drugs outside of the hospital and the oncologist's office, whereas Medicaid offers a far more generous array of benefits.

For the first 30 years of its existence, Medicare had two separate parts, each with different funding sources and eligibility requirements. *Medicare Part A* covers inpatient hospital care. It is financed by a 2.9% payroll tax (1.45% paid by the employer and 1.45% paid by the employee), the FICA deduction that appears on an employee's pay stub. All beneficiaries automatically receive Part A coverage. *Medicare Part B*, in contrast, is a voluntary program, providing coverage for outpatient care for beneficiaries who choose to pay a $110 monthly premium (individuals with annual income over $85,000 pay a higher, income-based premium). Some 95% of Medicare beneficiaries choose to enroll in Part B. The balance of the Part B bill is paid by general federal revenues.

Prior to 1994, the revenue contributed to the Part A Trust Fund exceeded the program's expenses and the fund built up a significant surplus. Beginning in 1994, expenses began to exceed revenue, the surplus was used to pay bills, and it began to shrink. Alarmed Medicare experts predicted that the surplus would be gone by the early 2000s, that the Trust Fund would be unable to pay its bills, and that Medicare would slide into bankruptcy. In response to this crisis, Congress in 1997 enacted a broad effort to reduce Medicare costs, mainly by cutting provider reimbursement.

The 1997 legislation also created a new program, known as *Medicare Part C*, which offers beneficiaries the option of enrolling in a private, "Medicare Advantage" plan. Part C plans typically are structured as health maintenance organizations or preferred provider organizations. Although they offer all of the physician and hospital benefits of Parts A and B, and often additional benefits, enrollees are limited in the choice of physicians and hospitals they may use. Enrollees still pay their monthly Medicare Part B premium and may have an additional premium for their plan's extra benefits. The Medicare managed care initiative has had only moderate success, enrolling about 22% of Medicare beneficiaries, as of 2010 (Kaiser Family Foundation, 2010d). Yet, the effort to cut Medicare spending was remarkably successful. In 1998, Medicare spending declined for the first time in the program's 33-year history.

The rapid shift in the economics of Medicare prompted an equally rapid change in its politics

The rapid shift in the economics of Medicare prompted an equally rapid change in its politics (Oberlander, 2003). No longer were politicians claiming that the program was about to go bankrupt. No longer was there talk of greedy providers overcharging and generating excess profits. No longer was there an intense effort to enroll beneficiaries in managed care. There were instead three competing views about how to respond. One camp emphasized the need to undo some of the cuts in provider reimbursement, another focused on the importance of expanding the benefits package, and still another argued against new spending measures, whether on behalf of providers or beneficiaries. This last group—the fiscal conservatives—proposed that any surplus remain in the Trust Fund to be used in years to come.

Faced with these options, Congress chose in 1999 to undo some of the cuts in provider reimbursement. Provider organizations argued that the prior cuts were unnecessarily endangering the financial health of thousands of doctors and hospitals. Even supporters of the cuts conceded that the extent of the reductions was far greater than expected. As a result, Congress reduced the impact of the cuts by $16 billion over the following 5 years and $27 billion over the following 10 years. In 2000, Congress passed another giveback initiative, this time delivering to providers $35 billion over 5 years and $85 billion over 10 years.

Following the provider giveback legislation, newly elected President George Bush and Congress took up the issue of prescription drug coverage and enacted Medicare Part D. Under this legislation, beneficiaries can receive outpatient drug coverage through a managed care plan or, if they wish to stay in fee-for-service Medicare, through a private prescription drug plan. In most communities, seniors can choose between dozens of plans, some of which offer limited coverage for a small monthly premium, whereas others offer more generous benefits for a higher premium. The average monthly premium nationwide is $32, in exchange for which the beneficiary has a $310 deductible, after which the plan pays 75% of drug costs up to $2,830 and 95% of the costs beyond $4,550 (the beneficiary pays 100% of the costs between $2,830 and $4,550—the so-called "donut hole," which is slowly being phased out as part of the 2010 health reform legislation).

The Medicare drug legislation was extraordinarily controversial and partisan. President Bush and leading Republicans maintained that the legislation, expected to cost $410 billion over its first 10 years, was the largest public insurance expansion since Medicare was first enacted and that it would provide significant coverage to millions of seniors. Leading Democrats, while supporting the goals of the legislation, complained that the initiative gave too little to needy seniors and too much to health maintenance organizations, big business, and the pharmaceutical industry.

The prescription drug plan was designed, in part, to revive the effort to encourage beneficiaries to enroll in managed care. Medicare managed care enrollment had been sagging largely because of declining health plan interest. In 1998, for example, more than 6 million Medicare beneficiaries were enrolled in 346 health plans. By early 2004, only 4.6 million were enrolled in 145 plans (Kaiser Family Foundation, 2004). Health plans said the main reason they exited the program was inadequate reimbursement. However, several studies suggested that Medicare was actually losing money on the managed care initiative because its capitation rates were set high, based on the health care experience of the average client in a particular community, whereas the typical managed care enrollee was healthier and less costly than average (Kaiser Family Foundation, 2004).

In an effort to reverse the decline in health plan participation and to advance the goals of privatization and competition, the Bush administration proposed that the new drug benefit be delivered exclusively by managed care plans. Although the legislation as enacted does not go so far, it does dramatically increase health plan capitation rates in an effort to encourage plans to get back in the game. In 2004, for example, average monthly capitation rates increased almost 11% and, in some communities, rates went up more than 40%. As a result, plans began aggressively marketing to beneficiaries and, as noted, by mid-2010, there were just under 11 million Medicare Advantage enrollees (Kaiser Family Foundation, 2010d).

RECENT EFFORTS TO HELP THE UNINSURED

Over the last decade, the number of Americans without health insurance has grown from roughly 40 million to approximately 50.7 million—more than 16% of the nation's population. Millions more Americans are underinsured, with high out-of-pocket medical expenses and, often, considerable medical debt. Most of the uninsured (more than

80%) are in families with a full- or part-time worker and most of these workers are self-employed or employed by small businesses. States with a strong unionized industrial and manufacturing base are likely to have fewer uninsured, whereas states with large numbers of immigrants and a service-based economy are likely to have more. In Iowa, Massachusetts, and Wisconsin, for example, less than 10% of the population is uninsured; whereas in California, Louisiana, and Texas, the percentage hovers between 20% and 25%.

Rather remarkably, the dramatic increase in the nation's uninsured population began in the mid-1990s—an era of unprecedented economic growth, low unemployment, and relatively small rises in health care costs; it then accelerated during the economic downturn of the early 2000s. Much of the increase in the uninsured population also occurred during a time when the Medicaid rolls were expanding dramatically. The best explanation for the rise in the number of uninsured is the decline in the number of Americans with employer-sponsored private health insurance. Between 1977 and 2004, the percentage of Americans under age 65 with employer-sponsored coverage dropped from 66% to 61% (Clemens-Cope, Garrett, & Hoffman, 2006).

The decline in employer-sponsored coverage is due to several factors. Many employers have increased the share of the bill that the employee must pay, prompting some employees to abandon their coverage. Other employers are eliminating coverage for spouses and children or phasing out retiree health coverage. Still others are hiring more part-time workers and outside contractors, thereby avoiding the need to offer health insurance. At the same time, much of the recent job growth is in the service and small business sectors of the economy. These jobs are notoriously low-paying and rarely provide health insurance.

In response to these trends and to media and political attention to the problems of the uninsured, state and federal officials tried during the early 1990s to enact new coverage programs (Brown & Sparer, 2001; Sparer, 2003). These proposals generally sought to require employers to provide health insurance to their employees and to use public dollars as a safety net for those outside the labor market. The idea was to retain and reinvigorate the employer-sponsored health insurance system. By the mid-1990s, however, the various employer mandate proposals, including the plan proposed by President Bill Clinton, had disappeared, defeated by vehement opposition from the business community. Business opponents argued that the mandate would be too costly and would force employers to eliminate jobs.

Following the collapse of the employer mandate strategy, policy makers (especially at the state level) enacted a host of efforts designed to make health insurance more available and more affordable in the small group and individual insurance markets (see Chapter 8). These reforms focused on three structural problems in the health care system:

1. Employers in the small business community often cannot afford to provide health insurance to their employees. These employers lack the market clout to negotiate a good deal, particularly given the high administrative costs associated with insuring a small group.
2. People who are self-employed or employees of small businesses generally earn too little to purchase health insurance in the individual market.
3. People with a high risk of catastrophic medical costs are often excluded from the individual insurance market, regardless of their ability to pay.

Many of the state initiatives required insurers to guarantee coverage to segments of the small business community. Others encouraged small businesses to join state-run or state-administered purchasing alliances. Still others allowed insurers to sell no-frills insurance policies, presumably at a lower cost than the more comprehensive packages states often require. Taken together, however, the various state mandates have had only a modest impact on the number of uninsured (Robert Wood Johnson Foundation, 2007), while generating significant political controversy, especially from healthy younger workers who complain about paying higher rates to subsidize the older and the sicker and from insurance companies threatening to exit reform-minded states.

By the late 1990s, state and federal policy makers had shifted their focus away from the insurance reforms that had been disappointing up to that point and toward programs that expanded health insurance for children. Several factors explained the trend. Children are considered a deserving group; there is bipartisan agreement that youngsters should not go without health care services because their parents cannot afford to pay; and children are a relatively low-cost population to insure. In 1993, for example, the average child on Medicaid cost just under $1,000, whereas the typical elderly recipient cost more than $9,200 and disabled recipients' costs averaged just under $8,000. (By 2007, the comparable figures were $2,135 for children; $12,499 for the elderly; and $14,481 for people with disabilities.)

Child health initiatives are consistent with the political agendas of both Republicans and Democrats. Republicans, along with many moderate Democrats, support insurance expansions as a counterbalance to other social welfare cutbacks. For example, families that move from welfare to work continue to need help obtaining health insurance for their children. At the same time, liberal Democrats, still reeling from the defeat of national health insurance proposals, saw health insurance for children as an incremental step on the path to universal health coverage.

Given this bipartisan support, Congress enacted the State **Children's Health Insurance Program** (SCHIP, changed to **CHIP** in 2009). States can use CHIP funds to liberalize their Medicaid eligibility rules, to develop a separate state program, or to create a combination of the two. The main advantage to using CHIP funds to expand Medicaid is administrative simplicity for both the client and the state. This is especially so for families in which some children are eligible for Medicaid and others for CHIP. At the same time, there are several advantages to creating a separate state program:

- Enrollment can be suspended when the dollars are spent, unlike with Medicaid, which is an entitlement program.
- The state has more discretion when developing the benefits package.
- It can impose co-payments and premiums, which generally are not allowed under Medicaid.
- Beneficiaries and providers may be more likely to participate because the new program lacks the stigma associated with Medicaid.

By all accounts, early efforts to enroll children into SCHIP were disappointing. By the end of 1999, roughly 1.5 million youngsters were enrolled in the program, far fewer than predicted. The low enrollment was due to several factors. Large numbers of eligible families did not know they were eligible. Others were deterred by the complicated application processes. Still others were dissuaded by the stigma often associated with government insurance programs. And the premiums and other cost-sharing requirements clearly discouraged others. As a result, by the end of 2000, 38 states had not spent their full allotment of federal SCHIP dollars. Funds not expended in these states were reallocated to the dozen other participating states.

Beginning in early 2000, however, SCHIP enrollment began to rise significantly. By the end of the year, roughly 3.3 million children were enrolled—nearly double the number from the prior year—and, by 2005, there were more than 4 million enrollees. Policy makers attribute the turnaround to improved outreach and education initiatives and to simplified processes for eligibility and enrollment.

As program enrollment grew, bipartisan support began to fade. The political battling was particularly intense during the effort to reauthorize the program in 2007. Congressional Democrats proposed significantly increased funding so as to expand enrollment even further. President Bush and many congressional Republicans opposed the expansion, arguing that expanding enrollment to more middle class families would undermine the nation's private insurance system, because employers would drop private coverage for children eligible for the expanded public program. The political battling continued during the last year of the Bush administration, as the president twice vetoed reauthorization legislation. When President Obama took office, in late January 2009, one of his first priorities was to sign legislation reauthorizing and expanding the program. He did so on February 4, 2009. As a result, CHIP enrollment continues to increase.

> *Despite the growth in public insurance programs like Medicaid and CHIP, the number of uninsured keeps rising, leading to an ongoing debate over whether and how government should aid this population.*

Despite the growth in public insurance programs like Medicaid and CHIP, the number of uninsured keeps rising, leading to an ongoing debate over whether and how government should aid this population. This debate returned to the national agenda during the 2008 presidential campaign, as several Democratic candidates proposed federal legislation to dramatically reduce the number of uninsured, whereas their Republican counterparts challenged such proposals as both unwise and counterproductive. Following the election of Barack Obama and a strong Democratic majority in both the Senate and the House of Representatives, the nation engaged in a fierce and partisan debate over the merits of health reform, a debate that culminated in the enactment of the ACA of 2010.

THE ACA AND THE UNINSURED

Early in his administration, President Obama decided to push hard for comprehensive health reform legislation. The goals were to: (1) reduce dramatically the number of uninsured; (2) pay for such coverage without adding to the nation's budget deficit; (3) slow the rising cost of health care more generally; and (4) encourage a more efficient and higher-value health care delivery system. The president understood, however, that the politics of health reform would be contentious and difficult. Health care is a $2.6 trillion industry and interest groups (insurers, pharmaceutical companies, employers, hospitals, doctors) would vigorously resist proposals that threatened their share of these dollars.

In addition, reform opponents can (and do) characterize comprehensive health reform initiatives as "socialistic" and contrary to our political culture, arguing instead for more incremental reforms that focus on notions of personal responsibility rather than social solidarity or equity. Finally, America's political institutions are designed to make it difficult to enact major new legislation, as the various checks and balances at the heart of American government provide numerous veto points for those opposed to reform.

In this context, President Obama needed to develop a strategy to overcome the interest group, ideological, and institutional obstacles to reform. By mid-2009, he had developed his strategy. First, he declared health reform to be his top domestic priority (doable during a recession only by declaring that fixing the economy required fixing the health care system). Second, he urged that health reform be enacted during the first year of his term, recognizing that delay was the enemy of reform. Third, he delegated the task of developing a health reform plan to congressional leaders, eschewing the White House–centered approach that ran aground in the Clinton administration, hoping instead to persuade the leadership (especially the Democratic leadership) to be fully invested in the reform initiative. Finally, he encouraged administration officials to negotiate with key interest groups, emphasizing the need to compromise and build incrementally off the current system.

After months of partisan politicking and various unexpected political hurdles (such as the election of Scott Brown to the seat of the recently deceased Ted Kennedy, which meant the Democrats no longer had a 60-vote filibuster-proof Senate majority), Congress enacted the Patient Protection and Affordable Care Act of 2010. The legislation is long and complex and covers nearly every aspect of the nation's health care system. At its core, however, is an ambitious effort to provide insurance coverage to more than 32 million of the currently uninsured. The ACA accomplishes this with five key initiatives, most of which take effect in 2014:

1. Federal law will require nearly all Americans to have some form of health insurance or pay a penalty through the tax code.
2. State Medicaid programs will be required to provide coverage to all persons (and their dependents) with incomes below 133% of the federal poverty level. As a result, an additional 16 to 18 million people are expected to enroll in Medicaid over the next several years.
3. Each state will be required to create a so-called "insurance exchange," a vehicle through which the uninsured and the small-business community can presumably purchase more affordable private coverage. The federal government will then provide subsidies to persons with incomes up to 400% of the federal poverty level to help them afford the more reasonably priced coverage. This initiative is expected to result in private coverage for another 16 to 18 million of the currently uninsured.
4. Employers with more than 50 employees will be required to either provide coverage to their employees or to pay a financial penalty to the federal government.
5. Private insurance companies will need to comply with a host of federal regulations that seek to eliminate the practice of discriminating against persons with preexisting conditions or who are otherwise likely to incur high medical costs.

The Government as Regulator

One of the key issues in contemporary health politics is the extent to which the states and the federal government should regulate the private health insurance industry. In the late 1990s, for example, 35 states enacted laws designed to protect patients enrolled in private plans. During that same period, both the U.S. Senate and the House of Representatives passed their own versions of a "managed care bill of rights," although the effort to resolve differences between the two bills became a bitter partisan stalemate.

The focus on patient protection during this period was prompted by a consumer backlash against managed care. Interestingly, that legislation, if enacted, would have represented an important policy shift, because the federal government has, until enactment of the ACA, exercised very little oversight of the health insurance industry. At the same time, state legislators, while more accustomed to regulating private insurers (as well as other sectors of the health care industry), complained that their efforts are undermined by a federal pension law (the **Employee Retirement Income Security Act [ERISA]**) that restricts states' authority to regulate health plans. These officials urged Congress to repeal or amend ERISA and thereby allow the states far greater autonomy.

States have traditionally dominated regulation of all aspects of the nation's health care system. States supervise the nation's system of medical education, license health care professionals, and oversee the quality of care delivered by health care providers. States administer workers' compensation systems, which provide benefits to workers injured on the job, and states govern consumer-protection efforts, such as those that hold providers accountable through, for example, medical malpractice litigation. Beginning in the 1920s, the states also began to regulate the nation's private health insurance system, establishing capitalization and reserve requirements, regulating marketing and enrollment activities, and (in some states) establishing the rates paid by insurers to various providers, especially hospitals.

Prior to the 1960s, state insurance departments rarely exercised their regulatory power, imposing few substantive requirements on insurance companies. Liberal critics complained that the relationships among providers, insurers, and regulators were far too cozy. Providers—especially hospitals—charged high rates and insurers paid the bill with few questions asked, regulators did little to make sure that insurance companies were adequately capitalized, and they did even less to guarantee that clients were treated fairly. In response, several states imposed new administrative requirements, most of which dealt with health plans' finances, benefit packages, and marketing practices. In the mid-1960s, for example, New York regulated hospital reimbursement rates. About the same time, states also imposed tougher capitalization and reserve requirements.

Over the next two decades, states required insurers to cover certain medical services— from mental health to chiropractor visits—in every insurance package they issued. Indeed, there are now more than 1,000 of these benefit mandates. For example, 40 states require that insurers cover alcohol treatment services, 39 require coverage for mammography, and 29 require mental health coverage.

The states' ability to regulate health insurers was constrained in 1974, when Congress enacted ERISA. ERISA was intended primarily to prevent unfair denial of pensions to employees. But the law also contains a provision that prohibits states from regulating employee benefit programs unless the regulation is part of the "traditional" state regulation of insurance, a provision that has led to endless confusion, controversy, and litigation.

Consider, for example, the convoluted legal reasoning that governs state efforts to require insurers to cover certain medical services. The courts have ruled that these laws apply to coverage provided by a traditional insurance company (like Blue Cross or Prudential), but not by a company that self-insures (i.e., bears the risk of employee medical costs itself, hiring insurers simply to process claims and manage utilization). Following the same reasoning, the courts have held that companies that self-insure are exempt from state capitalization and reserve requirements, state taxes imposed on insurers, and all other state regulations. Thus, self-insured plans do not have to comply with state laws that provide patient protections—for example, appeals processes when care is denied, access to the hospital emergency room or certain medical specialists, or bans on censoring what doctors can say to their patients.

To be sure, companies that self-insure are required to adhere to *federal* regulatory requirements; ERISA simply exempts them from state regulation. But prior to 2010, federal officials generally steered clear of imposing any such requirements. As a result, self-insured companies were more or less unregulated. The states cannot regulate them and the federal government rarely did. Not surprisingly, this legal quirk provided a strong incentive for firms to self-insure. By the mid-1990s, more than 70% of large firms offered self-insured plans to their employees (Dranove, 2000) and more than 56 million Americans were covered by self-insured health plans.

ERISA also makes it extremely difficult for subscribers to sue their health plan. Consider, for example, the situation in which an individual claims she was injured when her health plan wrongfully refused to authorize needed care. The woman seeks to sue the health plan for negligence. Prior to ERISA, she could have initiated such a lawsuit in state court and demanded damages to cover the cost of the denied services, as well as compensation for the injury and the unnecessary pain and suffering endured. She might also have won punitive damages (intended to punish the health plan for its wrongful behavior). But, because of ERISA, the woman cannot bring her case to state court, with few exceptions (unless she is a government employee, is in a government-funded health plan, or buys health insurance in the non-group market). She must instead proceed in federal court under a very different set of rules and protections. Yet, in her federal action, the most the woman could recover would be the cost of the wrongfully denied care; she could not win compensation for pain and suffering, nor could she exact punitive damages.[1]

Until recently, ERISA also was viewed as a barrier to suits against health plans for poor care delivered by an affiliated doctor. During the late 1990s, however, several states, led by Texas, enacted laws designed to overcome this barrier and to permit such cases to proceed in state court. The courts have consistently distinguished these "poor quality of care" cases from "wrongful denial of care" cases and so far have permitted them to proceed. Patients' right to sue their managed care plan thus depends on the source of their health insurance and the nature of the claim. In June 2004, the Supreme Court upheld this unwieldy and unfair set of rules, deciding that only Congress could remedy the inequity and that it could do so only by amending ERISA. (*Aetna Health, Inc.,* vs. *Davila,* 542 US 200, 2004).

The regulatory vacuum became especially controversial during the mid-1990s as a consumer backlash arose against much of the managed care industry. Congress was pressured either to amend ERISA and allow state regulation of the self-insured or to enact federal consumer protection legislation. Several relatively incremental pieces of legislation followed, such as a federal law modeled after state laws guaranteeing new mothers the right to spend at least 48 hours in the hospital following the birth of a child, and the Health

---

[1]The impact of the ERISA barrier is also illustrated by the case of *Goodrich* vs. *Aetna.* Mr. Goodrich was a government prosecutor in California suffering from stomach cancer, whose request for surgical relief was wrongfully denied and delayed (even though Aetna's own doctors were in favor of the procedure). After Goodrich died, his estate brought a lawsuit in state court seeking damages for the wrongful denial of care. The jury awarded his estate $4.5 million in actual compensatory damages and $116 million in punitive damages (Johnston, 1999). Had Goodrich not worked for state government, his estate would have had to proceed in federal court and could have collected a maximum of roughly $400,000 (the cost of the surgical procedure).

Insurance Portability and Accountability Act (1996), which sought to make health insurance more available to the self-employed and to those who work in small companies.

> *The political logjam broke in 2010 with the enactment of health reform (ACA),*
> *which for the first time imposes comprehensive federal oversight over*
> *the private health insurance industry.*

More ambitious efforts consistently failed, however, for more than a decade, until the political logjam broke in 2010 with the enactment of health reform (ACA), which for the first time imposes comprehensive federal oversight over the private health insurance industry. For example, health plans are no longer able to deny coverage to children based on a preexisting condition, young adults can now stay on their parents' coverage until age 26, and health plans in the large group market must spend at least 85% of their revenue on patient care (and plans in the small group and individual markets must spend at least 80%). Moreover, when the new law is fully implemented in 2014, health plans will not be able to deny coverage to anyone based on a preexisting condition, there will be no lifetime limits on coverage, and health plans will not be able to charge higher premiums based on health status or gender.

The Government as Health Care Provider

Each of the three levels of government owns and operates large numbers of health care institutions. For example, the federal government provides care to veterans through the massive Department of Veterans Affairs health care system, the Veterans Health Administration (VHA); the states care for mentally ill and developmentally disabled individuals in both large institutional facilities as well as smaller group homes; and local governments own and operate acute care hospitals and public health clinics that provide a medical safety net for the poor and the uninsured (see Chapter 6).

THE VETERANS HEALTH ADMINISTRATION

The VHA is required to offer health care to eligible veterans, their dependents, and their survivors. Approximately 70 million Americans currently are eligible for these services (25 million veterans and 45 million dependents or survivors) (Oliver, 2007). To serve this population, the VHA owns and operates 153 medical centers, 788 outpatient clinics, and 232 counseling centers (VHA, 2010). Approximately $41 billion was appropriated for VHA activities for FY2010 (VHA, 2010).

The VHA system is an integral part of the nation's system of medical education. Nationally, 107 medical schools and 55 dental schools use VHA facilities to train students and residents. Indeed, more than 50% of the nation's physicians have received part of their education and training in the VHA system.

In recent years, the VHA system has engaged in a wide-ranging initiative to improve the quality of care provided in its facilities. It created the National Center for Patient Safety (NCPS) to lead efforts to reduce the number of medical errors. The NCPS program is considered so innovative and important that it was recently a finalist in the Innovations in American Government Program sponsored by the Ford Foundation and the Kennedy School of Government at Harvard University.

The issue of medical errors received national attention when the Institute of Medicine (IOM) reported that an estimated 44,000 to 98,000 Americans die each year because of medical errors and pointed to the importance of *systems* problems in these high rates. Prior to the IOM analysis, much of the usual effort to reduce medical errors focused on individual wrongdoing: if only Dr. Jones had operated on the correct leg or if only Nurse Smith had given the right medication. Hospitals and other providers' responses to medical errors were to attempt to identify and punish the "culprit," whereas policy makers pressed for a practitioner data bank that would list providers guilty of errors.

VHA's NCPS takes a different approach. It focuses on finding the root cause of the error, a much more effective strategy for preventing future errors. For example, if a medication error is due to unclear labeling of drugs, it is better to fix the label than punish the individual who misread it. In the NCPS system, health care staff members are encouraged to report "close calls" as well as "adverse events." In the past, no one was likely to report or investigate such near-misses. The nurse would be too embarrassed and the system too uninterested. Taking a cue from the airline industry, where the culture of safety is especially strong, the goal now is to encourage near-miss reports, by ensuring that they are completely confidential. A small team then seeks out the root cause of the problem and a plan of action is created to make a similar error less likely in the future.

A major strategy in VHA quality improvement efforts has been widespread implementation of information technology. Over the past few years, it has spent hundreds of millions of dollars on an electronic medical records system, bar-coded medication administration, and computerized physician order entry. One result is that, in August 2005, after Hurricane Katrina, the VHA could quickly retrieve the health records for Gulf Coast evacuees scattered around the country, whereas the civilian health system remained in chaos for weeks and months (Markle Foundation et al., 2006). Relaxed eligibility requirements combined with a growing reputation for quality care has increased demand for VHA services.

STATE FACILITIES FOR THE MENTALLY ILL

Prior to the 1860s, government's role in caring for the mentally ill was handled locally, part of the safety net provided to the so-called deserving poor. Many mentally ill people never came to the attention of public authorities, because families, embarrassed by the presence of a mentally ill relative, kept them at home, out of sight, in sometimes appalling conditions. Perhaps the most common strategy utilized by county governments was to house the indigent insane in almshouses or shelters for the poor. Many of the severely mentally ill were locked in local jails. But, by the mid-19th century, several countries had established hospitals for mentally ill people, although little treatment was offered even in the best of them. The goals were to warehouse mentally ill people and separate them from the rest of society.

Dorothea Dix and other reformers slowly persuaded nearly every state legislature to assume responsibility for people with mental illnesses and to construct state hospitals for their care. State mental hospitals generally were located in remote rural communities. Reformers believed that patients were more likely to improve in a quiet and serene environment, which accorded with communities' desire to put the mentally ill "out of mind, out of sight." State mental hospitals were extraordinarily large, some with as many as 2,000 patients. In 1920, the nation's 521 state hospitals had an average bed capacity of 567. In contrast, the nation's 4,013 general hospitals at that time had an average bed capacity of only 78 (Starr, 1982).

By the turn of the 20th century, state governments had emerged as the primary providers of care for people with mental illnesses and behavioral disorders. Behavioral health became the only health problem with a separately financed and managed treatment system, and state governments assumed responsibility for the entire system (Hogan, 1999). The system grew exponentially, as county governments transferred many noncriminal people—and the costs of caring for them—such as the old and the senile, to state facilities. By 1959, roughly 559,000 patients were housed in state mental hospitals across the country (Katz, 1989).

Beginning in the 1960s, a new generation of reformers challenged the conditions in many state institutions. They contended that patients were warehoused rather than treated, were kept isolated from families and friends, and often were brutalized by staff or other patients. At the same time, medical researchers were developing a host of new drugs that enabled large numbers of patients to cope more successfully in the community. Perhaps most important, the federal government began funding community-based mental health services, while restricting federal funding for inpatient psychiatric services. Medicaid, for example, prohibited coverage for inpatient care in psychiatric institutions for people between the ages of 22 and 64, while providing coverage for a host of mental health services provided in community settings. Similarly, Congress provided direct funding to help establish a system of community mental health centers.

For all of these reasons, state governments began a massive effort to discharge patients from state hospitals and to divert others from admission. This policy, however, has not been a complete success. Although people with mental illness are no longer subjected to overcrowded and poor-quality institutions, large numbers of them cannot find housing or services in the community and end up homeless and inadequately treated. State officials' most popular strategy for addressing these new problems is to delegate responsibility for the indigent mentally ill to managed care plans specializing in behavioral health. It remains to be seen whether the managed care revolution will solve the long neglect of our mentally ill citizens, yet it is quite clear that state governments will continue to have the overall responsibility for their care.

LOCAL GOVERNMENT AND THE SAFETY NET FOR THE POOR

Scattered throughout the United States are more than 1,500 public general hospitals, nearly all of which are owned and operated by local governments. More than two-thirds are small (fewer than 200 beds), located in rural communities, and have low occupancy rates (generally well below 50%). Many urban public hospitals, in contrast, are quite large and have high occupancy rates. For example, the 100 largest urban public hospitals average nearly 600 beds and have an occupancy rate of roughly 80%. Indeed, the average big-city public hospital is three times the size of the typical, non–government-owned facility, has four times as many inpatient admissions, provides five times as many outpatient clinic visits, and delivers seven times as many babies.

Public hospitals, both large and small, treat a disproportionately high percentage of the poor and uninsured. In 2008, for example, the 89 members of the National Association of Public Hospitals (NAPH, whose members are generally the largest of the public facilities) provided 19% of the nation's uncompensated hospital care, even though they account for only 2% of the nation's acute care hospitals (NAPH, 2009). Moreover, roughly two-thirds of the revenue received by these hospitals comes either from public insurance programs or from state and local governments. Generally, public institutions are "providers of last resort," treating the homeless mentally ill, the babies addicted to cocaine, and the victims of violence.

> *Generally, public institutions are "providers of last resort," treating the homeless mentally ill, the babies addicted to cocaine, and the victims of violence.*

Local governments also fund and administer more than 3,000 public health departments. Each of these departments makes an effort, at least to some degree, to assess the public health needs of the community, develop policies that address those needs, and assure that primary and preventive health services are available to all.

Key Issues on the U.S. Health Care Agenda

Health care policy makers currently are grappling with a host of difficult issues, ranging from reorganizing health care delivery to slowing the rising costs of health care to developing a long-term care system that is responsive to the growing number of senior citizens.

Over the next several years, each of these issues will be addressed most directly as part of the effort to implement the health reform legislation enacted in early 2010. By all accounts, this legislation has the potential to dramatically change the nation's health care system. It will presumably enable more than 32 million of the currently uninsured to obtain public or private coverage, with the cost of such coverage paid for by a combination of tax increases and Medicare reimbursement cuts. The legislation also contains a plethora of other provisions, including:

(a) an additional $11 billion in federal funding for community health centers;
(b) a new entity (called the Patient Centered Outcomes Research Institute) designed to encourage research into the comparative effectiveness of new drugs, medical devices, and care management programs;
(c) pilot programs to implement alternatives to medical malpractice litigation;
(d) a host of new prevention, public health, and wellness programs; and
(e) pilot programs to test new payment (and cost-containment) methodologies and care delivery approaches.

Most of the reform legislation is to be phased in over the next 4 years. The task of implementation will be enormous. State governments will need to expand their Medicaid programs dramatically (and find health care providers willing to serve the new enrollees). States also need to create brand new "insurance exchanges." Federal officials need to promulgate thousands of new regulations that will govern the changing insurance industry, as well as create new institutions (such as the new Medicare Independent Payment Advisory Board), implement contentious reimbursement cuts, and develop, implement, and evaluate a host of payment and delivery reform pilot programs.

Implementation could also be slowed (or even stopped) by the courts, as states and private litigants have already commenced numerous lawsuits, challenging different parts of the bill, most notably the requirement that all Americans have health insurance and the mandated expansions to the Medicaid program.

Making things even more difficult is the sheer complexity of the reform legislation and the fact that most Americans do not have a good understanding of how the health care system works, how the new legislation will affect them, which provisions will be implemented when, and how the expanding system will be financed. The confusion is likely to grow even more pronounced during the 2010 and 2012 elections, as President Obama and the Democrats tout the legislation as their primary legislative accomplishment, while their Republican counterparts cite the legislation as one of the administration's key blunders and as evidence of a federal government attempting to take over the health care industry.

In the end, the 2010 debate over health reform was (and is) largely about the role of government in the U.S. health care system. The ACA goes a long way toward expanding the scope of government's role, especially that of the federal government, but the debate over the extent of that role will surely continue.

DISCUSSION QUESTIONS

1. Should the government play such a key role in aiding the uninsured, or should market forces reign supreme?
2. How should government finance its efforts to aid the uninsured?
3. How much control should government have over the private health insurance industry?
4. What is the right division of labor between the different branches of government, the private sector, and the individual consumer?

CASE STUDIES

CASE STUDY #1

You are the Medicaid director of a large Western state. Your governor has required you to slow the state's rising Medicaid bill. The following are your main options; what are the pros and cons of each?
- Convince the legislature to cut the eligibility levels
- Impose administrative burdens making it more difficult to apply for coverage
- Cut benefits
- Cut reimbursement
- Cut pharmaceutical costs
- Reduce fraud and abuse
- Impose co-pays
- Encourage more managed care
- Cut long-term care costs
- Other?

CASE STUDY #2

You are a staffer for the federal secretary of Health and Human Services. The secretary has asked for a memorandum that sets forth the key issues involved in implementing the Patient Protection and Affordable Care Act of 2010 (ACA). The ACA imposes enormous administrative burdens on both federal and state officials. This is one of the reasons that much of the law will not be fully implemented until 2014.

Start your effort to respond to this assignment by listing at least three tasks immediately before the Department, as well as the key issues involved in each task.

CASE STUDY #3

You are the president of a public hospital in Los Angeles. The mayor has asked whether the new health reform legislation will enable the city to reduce its annual appropriation to the hospital. Your assignment is to write a memorandum to the mayor on this topic, setting forth the pros and cons of the legislation, as well as whether the time is right for a cut in local funding.

REFERENCES

Annas, G., Law, S., Rosenblatt, R., & Wing, K. (1990). *American health law*. Boston: Little, Brown & Co.

Blumenthal, D., & Morone, J. (2009). *The heart of power: health and politics in the oval office*. Berkeley, CA: University of California Press.

Brown, L. D., & Sparer, M. S. (2001). Window shopping: State health reform politics in the 1990s. *Health Affairs, 20,* 50–67.

Clemens-Cope, L., Garrett, B., & Hoffman, C. (2006). *Changes in employee health insurance coverage, 2001–2005*. Washington, D.C.: Kaiser Commission on Medicaid and the Uninsured.

Dranove, D. (2000). *The economic evolution of American health care*. Princeton, NJ: Princeton University Press.

Hogan, M. (1999). Public sector mental health care: New challenges. *Health Affairs, 18,* 106–111.

Holahan, J., & Liska, D. (1997). The slowdown in Medicaid growth: Will it continue? *Health Affairs, 16,* 157–163.

Johnston, D. (1999, January 21). $116 million punitive award against Aetna. *New York Times*, p. Cl.

Kaiser Family Foundation. (2010a). *The Medicaid program at a glance*. Menlo Park, CA: Author.

Kaiser Family Foundation. (2010b). *Medicaid Payments per Enrollee, FY2007*. Retrieved July 27, 2010, from http://www.statehealthfacts.org/comparemaptable.jsp?ind=183&cat=4

Kaiser Family Foundation. (2010c). *Medicare at a glance*. Menlo Park, CA: Author.

Kaiser Family Foundation. (2010d). State Health Facts. *Medicare*. Calculated from 2010 data on total Medicare enrollment and Medicare Advantage Enrollment. Data retrieved July 27, 2010, from http://www.statehealthfacts.org/comparecat.jsp?cat=6&rgn=6&rgn=1

Kaiser Family Foundation. (2004). *Medicare advantage fact sheet*. Menlo Park, CA: Author.

Katz, M. (1989). *The undeserving poor*. New York: Pantheon Books.

Markle Foundation, American Medical Association, Gold Standard, RxHub, & SureScripts. (2006). *Lessons from KatrinaHealth*. Retrieved July 27, 2010, from katrinahealth.org/katrinahealth.final.pdf

Marmor, T. (2000). *The politics of Medicare* (2nd ed.). New York: Aldine de Gruyter.

National Association of Public Hospitals. (2009). *2008 annual survey underscores the key role of the nation's safety net hospitals and health systems.* Washington, D.C.: Author.

Oberlander, J. (2003). *The political life of Medicare.* Chicago, IL: University of Chicago Press.

Oliver, A. (2007). The Veterans Health Administration: an American success story? *The Milbank Quarterly, 85.* Retrieved July 27, 2010, from http://www.milbank.org/quarterly/8501feat.html

Robert Wood Johnson Foundation. (2007). *The state of the states.* Princeton, NJ: Author. Retrieved July 27, 2010, from http://www.rwjf.org/files/publications/bther/StateoftheStates2007.pdf

Sparer, M. S. (2003). Leading the health policy orchestra: The need for an intergovernmental partnership. *Journal of Health Politics, Policy and Law, 28,* 245–270.

Sparer, M. S. (1996). *Medicaid and the limits of state health reform.* Philadelphia: Temple University Press.

Starr, P. (1982). *The social transformation of American medicine.* New York: Basic Books.

U.S., Department of Veterans Affairs. Veterans Health Administration. (2010). *VA benefits and health care utilization.* Fact sheet. Retrieved July 27, 2010, from http://www1.va.gov/vetdata/

3

HEALTH CARE FINANCING

James R. Knickman

James R. Knickman

KEY WORDS

public insurance

private insurance

safety-net provider

payer mix

individual insurance market

health maintenance organizations (HMOs)

preferred provider organizations (PPOs)

accountable care organizations (ACOs)

consumer-driven health care

diagnosis-related groups (DRGs)

bundled payments

LEARNING OBJECTIVES

- Understand U.S. health care spending over time
- Describe major sources of health care spending
- Understand the major categories of services purchased
- Differentiate between public and private spending and purchasing in addition to the categories of health plan types within the public and private systems
- Explain how 2010 federal health reform legislation is expected to change the health care financing system
- Describe the major reimbursement mechanisms for health care services
- Understand current policy issues in health care financing

TOPICAL OUTLINE

- General overview of health care financing
- What the money buys and where it comes from
- How health insurance works
- How health reform may affect the financing system
- Reimbursement approaches
- Current policy issues in financing

T he issue of how we pay for health care services dominated the pubic policy agenda during the first 2 years of the Obama administration. One of the most ambitious pieces of social legislation ever was signed into law on March 23, 2010. The Patient Protection and Affordable Care Act should result in an additional 32 million Americans becoming insured for health care. In addition, the new law, when and if fully implemented, would have a substantial impact on how much we spend on health care in the United States and all aspects of how we pay for it.

No matter what type of role an individual plays in the American health care system, the complex way that we pay for health services influences what is done and how it is done. Almost every aspect of how we organize health care services and how we manage them is shaped by how they are paid for. And, most attempts to improve quality or to shift resources from one type of health care to another (e.g., from hospital care to primary care or from acute care services to preventive services) also are shaped by how these services are funded.

General Overview of Health Care Financing

What do we mean by the "financing of health care"? This overall question includes not only how we pay for care, but also who pays for care, how transactions between users and providers are handled, and how many total dollars are spent on care. If we think of health care as a service that people need to purchase in an economic sense, we find that the approach used to purchase this service is far different than the typical approach for purchasing other kinds of services or commodities in our economy.

For most goods and services, we use a simple payment system: if you want the item, you pay money for it directly. Suppliers of goods and services set prices they think make sense, and if purchasers are willing to pay the price (sometimes they can haggle a bit) the transaction happens, and the consumer buys the service. In the U.S. market-based economy, the consumer needs only to have enough money to make the purchase and the transaction occurs with little intervention from the government or anybody else.

But health care is not a normal commodity or service because of two features: (1) need for health care varies starkly from one individual to another (20% of Americans use 80% of all health care dollars expended in any given year); and (2) the cost of health care is very high, and many people just could not afford it if they had to pay cash each time they needed a service. A typical 5-day stay in a hospital could cost well over $5,000 in 2011. An MRI to diagnose the presence of a tumor can easily cost well over $2,000.

To overcome the obstacle of high costs, the United States has developed an insurance system where we collectively pay for services. Put most simply, we pool our risks for needing health care. Each individual in essence pays an insurance company the average annual costs of health care (plus administrative fees and a profit margin); when these premiums are pooled across a population of people (often employees of a company), there is enough money to pay the expenses of the minority of people who need costly health care. Most of the time, people pay for health insurance but never use any or many of the dollars they put into the pool. But, in a year when they have high health care needs, they benefit by being able to tap many more resources from the insurance pool than they contributed.

This description greatly oversimplifies how the financing system really works across a range of dimensions. In fact:

1. There are many types of insurance; some are publicly paid for through taxes, whereas others are paid by employers, and yet others are paid by individuals directly.
2. Insurance does not pay for the entire costs of an individual's health care. Usually, insurance pays only a share of the costs while the individual pays the rest. How this co-payment arrangement is structured varies greatly from insurance plan to insurance plan and can be quite complex.
3. Once insurance is involved in the transaction between a service provider and a user of the service, there have to be rules regarding which services the insurer will pay and how much it will pay for them. These insurance reimbursement rules also can become incredibly complex and confusing.
4. When people do not directly and fully pay for services, economists worry that they will use more services than they need or that a provider will deliver more care than needed. An insurance system must create incentives to avoid overuse and oversupply, or system-wide expenditures could skyrocket.

The U.S. health care financing system has evolved continuously since World War II, when the first health insurance products began to be marketed. In the 1960s, wide-scale **public insurance** programs were enacted: Medicare, which is insurance for the elderly and the permanently disabled, and Medicaid, which is an insurance-type system for low income Americans (see Chapter 2).

The U.S. system of financing health care is quite distinct from that used in other developed nations (see Chapter 4). Most other developed countries have a system that involves a set of services that every citizen is entitled to that is paid by the central government. In these situations, **private insurance** companies either help manage the government-financed system or offer supplementary or alternative coverage.

The emergence of insurance in the United States occurred just as new, more effective types of health care technology and practices were being developed. The combination of insurance and rapidly expanding clinical advances led to an expenditure explosion in the 1970s, which has continued rather steadily ever since. In 1970, U.S. health expenditures totaled $74.9 billion and represented 7.2% percent of the nation's gross domestic product (GDP) (i.e., 7.2% of all goods and services purchased in our economy were health-related). By 2019, health expenditures are expected to reach nearly $4.5 trillion, or 19.3% of GDP, with no clear path to slowing their growth (see Table 3.1 and Figure 3.1).

This chapter provides an introduction to how the American health financing system works. It considers what types of care are paid for, how individuals go about paying for care, and how providers are paid. The chapter also explains the types of insurance and how each works, how the 2010 federal health reform would change financing, how reimbursement systems have evolved for paying providers and creating incentives for quality and efficiency, and finally, emerging approaches for limiting the growth of health expenditures in the years to come.

TABLE 3.1

U.S. National Health Expenditures (in billions of dollars), Selected Categories and Years, 1970–2019

Type of Expenditure	Actual				Projected			
	1970	2000	2005	2008	2009	2010	2014	2019
Total national health expenditures	$74.9	$1,309.4	$1,987.7	$2,338.7	$2,472.2	$2,569.6	$3,225.3	$4,482.7
Total of all personal health care	63.2	1,135.3	1,661.4	1,952.3	2,068.3	2,141.7	2,677.1	3,709.0
• Hospital care	27.6	413.2	611.6	718.4	760.6	788.9	996.3	1,374.5
• Physician and clinical services	14.0	290.3	421.2	496.2	527.6	535.8	646.8	882.0
• Prescription drugs	5.5	121.5	200.7	234.1	246.3	260.1	322.1	457.8
Program administration and net cost of private health insurance	2.8	80.3	143.0	159.6	162.8	172.6	225.1	320.3

Source: 2005–2015 data are from U.S., Centers for Medicare & Medicaid Services, Office of the Actuary. 2007. Retrieved April 5, 2007, from http://www.cms.hhs.gov/NationalHealthExpendData/downloads/proj2006.pdf; 1970 and 2000 data are from Levit, K., Smith, C., Cowan, C., Sensenig, A., Catlin, A., 7 the Health Accounts Team. (2004). Health spending rebound continues in 2002. *Health Affairs, 23*, 147–159.

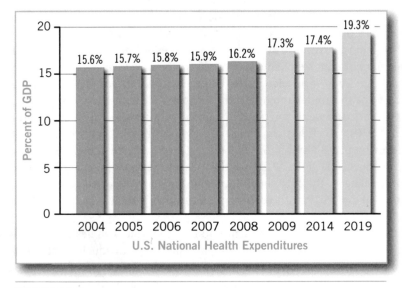

FIGURE 3.1

U.S. national health expenditures as a share of Gross Domestic Product (GDP), 2004–2019.
Source: U.S. Centers for Medicare and Medicaid Services. (2009). *National Health Expenditure Projections 2009–2019.* Washington, D.C.: Author.

What the Money Buys and Where It Comes From

If we consider all types of expenditures in the health system, the total national bill in 2009 is expected to be $2.6 trillion dollars. The overwhelming share of this money ($2.1 trillion, or 84%) will pay for personal health care services to individuals, whereas the balance will pay for public health services, research, and administrative costs associated with running the delivery and financing system (see Table 3.1). Among personal health care services, 81% of expenditures will focus on four types of care: hospital care (the largest type by far), physician and other clinical services, nursing home care, and prescription drugs.

HOW INDIVIDUALS PAY FOR HEALTH CARE

To start, we should go back to basics and consider how individuals pay for health care when they become ill or injured. In essence, there are two main ways the transaction for a service happens: either through a person's insurance coverage or out-of-pocket from income or savings. If the person is uninsured and has no money, there is a third option: they can attempt to obtain the service free, as a charity case, through a **"safety-net provider."** States have various laws about when providers must give charity care and the insurance system—especially public insurance—gives providers some money to help reimburse them for the charity care they deliver.

When people have either a public or private insurance policy, they usually can receive services after showing their insurance card. The provider then bills the insurance company directly. However, if a person's insurance will pay for only part of the bill, the individual is usually responsible for paying the balance at the time services are delivered.

HOW PROVIDERS ARE PAID FOR HEALTH SERVICES THEY DELIVER

Again, starting with basics, providers are paid from the same three sources that individuals tap into: public or private insurance programs, cash payments from individuals, or various sources of indirect payments from insurers or government to help pay for charity care.

The sources of provider payments vary greatly depending on where the provider is located and what types of patients are served. Consider the examples of three New York City hospitals:

- Montefiore Medical Center, a private hospital serving a broad range of people in the North Bronx,
- New York University Medical Center, a very specialized mid-Manhattan hospital, closely linked to a medical school and serving many relatively wealthy people, and
- Lincoln Hospital, a public safety-net hospital in the South Bronx that serves mostly low income residents.

Lincoln Hospital receives a very small percentage of its revenues from private insurance programs, but a large share from the Medicaid program, which covers low income patients (see Table 3.2). Lincoln, compared to most hospitals, also receives a relatively large amount of money from safety-net programs that help pay for charity care but a relatively small amount from Medicare.

Montefiore Medical Center, by contrast, also receives a relatively low share of its revenue from private insurance programs because a large number of Bronx residents do not work for employers that offer insurance coverage and cannot afford to buy it on their own. But

TABLE 3.2

Hospital Sources of Revenue

	Vulnerable Community: *Montefiore*	Wealthier Community: *NYU*	Public Hospital: *Lincoln*	Daily Rate Compared to Average Costs (AC)
Medicare	40%	29%	20%	Daily Rate = AC
Private insurance	23%	65%	5%	Daily Rate > AC
Medicaid	36%	5%	52%	Daily Rate < AC
Charity care/self-pay	1%	1%	23%	Daily Rate < AC

Source: Commission on Health Care Facilities in the 21st Century. *Final Report.* Available at: http://www.nyhealthcarecommission.org

Montefiore has large numbers of elderly Medicare and Medicaid patients, and a smaller share of patients who seek charity care than does Lincoln. In fact, patients covered by public insurance programs (Medicare and Medicaid) represent 76% of all admissions at Montefiore.

New York University Medical Center has a distinctly different **payer mix** than the other two: 65% of its revenues come from private insurance, whereas just 35% comes from the other three types of payers combined.

These differences in payer mix have very large implications for the financial health of these three hospitals. Private insurers and Medicare tend to pay relatively good rates for each day of hospital care, whereas Medicaid and charity care tends to pay much lower rates. This means that NYU receives much more revenue per day to cover its costs than do Montefiore or Lincoln, and Montefiore has a healthier payer mix than Lincoln Hospital, which serves the most vulnerable of the population.

> *The ability to provide good care depends on the mix of patients (and insurance plans) the hospital serves and its ability to negotiate good rates with each type of payer.*

The source of insurance for the patients that tend to use a specific hospital has much more to do with the financial health of the institution than the quality of its care or the complexity of the services that it must provide. This makes the challenge of managing different types of hospitals a complex one. The ability to provide good care depends on the mix of patients (and insurance plans) the hospital serves and its ability to negotiate good rates with each type of payer.

How Health Insurance Works

A range of insurance types covers different subsets of the American population. The first key differentiation among them is *public programs* vs. *privately sponsored insurance products*.

Public insurance programs include Medicare for the elderly and disabled, Medicaid for low income individuals, other insurance systems for low income individuals, such as the Children's Health Insurance Program (CHIP), which covers children not eligible for Medicaid. Other types of public insurance programs cover veterans, public employees, members of the armed services and their families, and American Indians.

Private insurance coverage varies depending on who pays for it. Small employers can purchase coverage for their workers through commercial companies (such as Blue Cross plans, or insurance companies like United Health Care, Aetna, or Kaiser Permanente).

Individuals who work for employers that offer no coverage or who are self-employed or unemployed also may buy insurance through commercial companies. Large employers can either buy coverage from commercial companies, as above, or they can "self-insure." They often can save substantial costs by self-insuring, which they are able to do because they have so many employees that the risks balance out. Even when employers do self-insure, they usually engage a commercial insurance company to manage their plan and enforce its rules.

PUBLICLY FINANCED PROGRAMS

Medicaid

Medicaid originally was designed to assist recipients of public assistance—primarily single-parent families and low income people who are aged, blind, and disabled. Over the years, Medicaid has expanded to include additional groups and now covers poor children, their parents, pregnant women, the disabled, and very poor adults (including those 65 and older). Much public attention is given to Medicaid's role in covering children's care, but in reality, nearly 70% of its expenditures are for long-term care for the one-quarter of enrollees who are elderly or disabled (Figure 3.2).

Medicaid is administered by the states, and both the state and federal governments finance the program. Except for minimum mandatory benefits, the federal government gives states flexibility in implementing and administering Medicaid to best meet the needs of their residents. As a result, there are many seemingly arbitrary differences in eligibility and benefits across states. For example, in 2008, 14 states offering CHIP included the same dental benefits as Medicaid, whereas other states provided limited benefits similar to those of private insurance, including seven that put an upper limit on annual dental expenditures or limited the number of annual dental services (Kaiser Commission on Medicaid and the Uninsured, 2008).

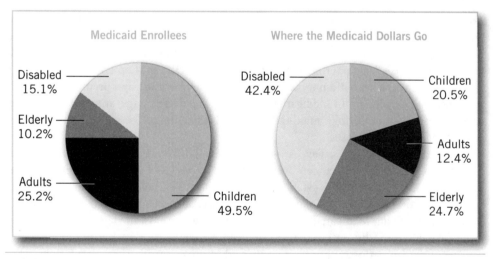

FIGURE 3.2

Medicaid enrollments and expenditures, FY2007.
Source: Kaiser Family Foundation. State Health Facts. *Medicaid enrollment: Distribution of Medicaid enrollees by enrollment group, FY 2007.* Retrieved August 4, 2010 from http://www.statehealthfacts.org/comparemaptable. jsp?ind=200&cat=4; Kaiser Family Foundation. State Health Facts. *Medicaid spending: Payments by enrollment, FY 2007.* Retrieved August 4, 2010, from http://www.statehealthfacts.org/comparemaptable.jsp?ind=858&cat=4. This information was reprinted with permission from the Henry J. Kaiser Family Foundation, a nonprofit private operating foundation, based in Menlo Park, California, dedicated to producing and communicating the best possible analysis and information on health issues.

Rocky economic times often cause states to tighten Medicaid eligibility, enrollment standards, and benefits in order to reduce their outlays. Recently, California proposed to reduce the number of residents eligible for CHIP and eliminate the vision coverage benefit, whereas Arizona and South Carolina have imposed either a freeze or a cap on CHIP enrollment (Kaiser Commission on Medicaid and the Uninsured, 2010). Already, federal rules Medicaid place tight restrictions on coverage for immigrant families. Even *legal immigrants* must wait 5 years before becoming Medicaid-eligible.

A major change in Medicaid occurred when it adopted a managed care approach in the early 1990s, but a number of problems undermined the hoped-for savings. Medicaid already paid providers rates below (sometimes significantly below) commercial levels and could not easily reduce them further. Additional reductions would have squeezed safety-net providers that largely depend on Medicaid revenues, jeopardizing their financial viability and, while managed care enrollment campaigns were targeted at low income women and children, most Medicaid spending is for the elderly and disabled (Hurley & Somers, 2003). Congress made another significant change in 1996, when welfare reform legislation for the first time de-linked welfare and Medicaid. Previously, people eligible for cash assistance were automatically eligible for Medicaid. The impact of this change was to reduce the number of people eligible for Medicaid in many states because Medicaid eligibility levels could be set lower than welfare eligibility levels (Ellwood & Ku, 1998).

The 2010 federal health reform law will expand state Medicaid programs substantially because it will set minimum eligibility levels in states at 133% of the federal poverty line. As described later in this chapter, the new law is expected to enable some 32 million more Americans to obtain health insurance by 2014, with approximately half of the newly insured covered by an expanded Medicaid program, whereas the balance would be covered by subsidized private insurance policies.

Medicare

Administered by the federal government, Medicare originally targeted people 65 and over, but was quickly expanded to cover people with disabilities and severe kidney disease. To qualify, an individual has to be a U.S. resident for a specified number of years and pay the Social Security/Medicare payroll tax for at least 10 years. The entitlement was expanded in 1972 to allow people who did not meet the latter requirement to pay a premium for coverage. Although enrollment in Medicare has doubled since its passage, annual expenditures have increased about 40-fold, making the federal government the nation's single largest payer of health care expenses.

Medicare has two parts: Part A, which is hospital insurance, and Part B, which is supplemental medical insurance covering physician services and outpatient care. The Balanced Budget Act of 1997 established the Medicare+Choice program, designed to build on existing Medicare managed care programs and expand options under Part B. In addition to giving Medicare beneficiaries more plan options, the law was supposed to bring savings. Ironically, enrollment in Medicare managed care was more rapid prior to passage of the legislation, although it continued to grow steadily until about 1999. After that, it declined for several reasons. First, a natural market phenomenon occurred—many managed care plans ceased offering Medicare+Choice because they could not or did not want to compete. At the same time, the government reduced payments, forcing seniors to pay higher premiums and out-of-pocket costs. Eventually, many managed care operators found the program unprofitable and pulled out of it entirely (Gold, 2001). In the 1980s and 1990s, Medicare experienced a series of changes to its payment mechanisms, which show up as dips in the overall growth rate of national health expenditures. In the 1980s, Medicare started paying hospitals under a prospective payment system; by the 1990s, it had started paying physicians differently, too. The only other major change to the program before 2004 was the Medicare Catastrophic Coverage Act (1998), repealed within 2 years of passage because it was unpopular with seniors and interest groups.

The Catastrophic Coverage Act repeal and the Clinton Health Reform debacle of the early 1990s curbed the political appetite for Medicare reform for a number of years. The issue finally came back when George W. Bush included a promise to add drug coverage to Medicare in his 2000 presidential campaign. This time the political stars were aligned and Congress passed and the president signed into law the Medicare Modernization Act in December 2003.

A key difference between the unpopular Catastrophic Coverage Act and the drug coverage act is that the former involved mandated payments by elders whereas the latter was paid for with general tax revenues. The 2010 national health reform legislation will face the challenge of gaining acceptance of nonelders, many of whom will be required to pay for at least part of newly mandated private health insurance coverage.

Other Public Programs

In addition to Medicaid and Medicare, the United States has a patchwork of government health care programs for special populations—active duty and retired military personnel and their families, American Indians, and injured and disabled workers.

Historically, most health care needs of active duty military personnel have been handled in military facilities, where retirees and families also could receive free treatment on a space-available basis. Defense Department spending on medical care more than doubled from 1988 to 2005, rising from $14.6 billion to $49 billion.

The Veterans Health Administration operates the largest integrated health care system in the United States, providing primary care, specialized care, and related medical and social support services to U.S. veterans and their dependents.

In 1921, the Snyder Act established a program of health services for American Indians, known today as the Indian Health Service and administered by the Department of Health and Human Services. Eligible are members of federally recognized Indian tribes and their descendants. The program's budget is approximately $3 to $4 billion annually and it serves approximately 1.9 million of the nation's estimated 3.3 million American Indians and Alaska Natives (U.S. Department of Health and Human Services, 2010).

Workers' compensation is an insurance system intended to protect workers against the costs of medical care and loss of income resulting from work-related injuries and, in some cases, illnesses. Underlying workers' compensation is the premise that all job-related injuries, regardless of fault, are the result of the risks of employment and the employer and employee should share the burden of loss. Workers' compensation programs are operated by the states, each with its own authorizing legislation and requirements. The first such law was enacted in New York in 1910; by 1948, all states had a workers' compensation program.

PRIVATELY FINANCED HEALTH CARE

The private share of health care expenditures has been declining since the 1960s, as Medicare, Medicaid, and other public sources of payments have increased. In 2008, the private share of U.S. health care spending was 53% or $1.2 trillion, paid out-of-pocket by individuals and various third-parties. Third-party payers—mostly insurance companies— accounted for $783 billion of these private dollars.

Employer-Based Insurance

During the Great Depression, hospitals found that most Americans could not afford to pay their bills. The hospital industry, through the American Hospital Association, supported the growth of the first major health insurers: the Blue Cross plans in each state that pay for hospital care and the Blue Shield plans that pay for physician and other outpatient services. Over time these nonprofit insurers had to compete with for-profit insurance companies that emerged during World War II, when unions began fighting for medical insurance to be part of employee benefits packages.

Growth in the health insurance market was a byproduct of wartime wage and price controls; because wages couldn't be increased, enhanced benefits packages were one way unions and employees could obtain increased compensation. Growth accelerated following a decision by the Internal Revenue Service that employers could take a tax deduction for the cost of employee health insurance. The growing costs of health care would have led to increased private or public insurance coverage eventually.

Over the next several decades, the employer-based health insurance system became increasingly entrenched. By the end of 2002, more than 64% of Americans received health insurance through their employer (Glied & Boirzi, 2004). Since then, the percentage of Americans obtaining employer-based health insurance has slowly, but steadily, decreased, reaching 61% in 2008.

The Individual Insurance Market

Although employer-based insurance dominates the private health insurance sector, a significant number of people must arrange and pay for health insurance on their own. The Employee Benefit Research Institute found that, in 2008, although more than 160 million nonelderly Americans were covered by employment-based health benefits, about 16 million purchased coverage for themselves and family members in the **individual insurance market** (Fronstin, 2009).

When people work for employers that do not offer insurance, or are between jobs, or are self-employed, they must rely on the individual insurance market, where premiums are high and benefits less than generous. Employers can secure better, lower cost coverage for several reasons: employed individuals tend to be in better health, reducing the risk and thus the cost to the insurer; risk can be spread across the group; and marketing and administrative costs are lower. The type of insurance employers offer varies by the size of the workforce.

As described later in this chapter, the 2010 Patient Protection and Affordable Care Act will offer substantial subsidies for many Americans to purchase insurance as individuals. As many as 16 million people uninsured in 2010 may be able to purchase subsidized private insurance after the law is fully implemented in 2014.

COBRA

The Consolidated Omnibus Budget Reconciliation Act (COBRA) of 1985 attempted to reduce gaps in insurance coverage for individuals between jobs. It requires employers to extend health insurance benefits to former employees for up to 18 months. Depending on qualifying circumstances, coverage may be extended for a spouse or dependent children for up to 36 months. Employees generally pay the entire premium for the coverage. Although the cost of COBRA coverage may be high, it is still much less expensive than comparable coverage purchased in the individual market.

MANAGED CARE

The biggest change in the privately financed portion of the U.S. health care system over the last three decades is the shift toward various forms of managed care. This shift began in the late 1980s and took hold by the mid-1990s. Large businesses steered this shift, in an attempt to reduce their health insurance costs.

Health Maintenance Organizations

Managed care plans structure and reimburse care differently than conventional insurance does. Very strict managed care plans, like **health maintenance organizations (HMOs)**, use *capitated payments* and control which providers participate in their network. Capitated payments are fixed annual payments for each person for whom the provider is responsible to provide care, regardless of the amount and kinds of services eventually needed. HMOs also require primary care physicians to be gatekeepers to other types of services, by requiring referrals for diagnostic tests and specialty care.

> *The theory was that capitation would encourage providers to think more carefully about the necessity of costly tests and procedures and discourage unnecessary referrals to expensive specialists.*

The theory was that capitation would encourage providers to think more carefully about the necessity of costly tests and procedures and discourage unnecessary referrals to expensive specialists. Despite capitation's limits on reimbursement, providers were expected to participate because they would have a "captive audience" of patients—in other words, they could make up any reimbursement shortfall by having increased numbers of patients. For patients, in return for giving up the freedom to use whichever physician or hospital they chose, care would be more organized and specialist and primary care more effectively coordinated.

HMOs generally act as both the insurer and the provider of services. However, HMOs use a range of approaches to actually providing services. Some employ physicians and own hospitals, whereas others contract with networks of physicians and develop contracts with local hospitals. The best known HMO, Kaiser Permanente, uses a defined network of physicians and owns its hospitals.

Managed care was very effective in reducing costs during the mid-to-late 1990s. But, consumers had begun to loathe this type of insurance product. They perceived many HMO features as overly restrictive. They wanted to choose their own physicians, resented specialty care gatekeeping and other HMO "hassle factors," and demanded more plan options. They complained loudly to employers, who eventually moved toward offering less tightly controlled plans, which also were not capitated for providers. This trend was in stark contrast to Medicaid managed care, which nationwide enrolls about two-thirds of Medicaid recipients into capitated programs, in order to control spending.

Today, most consumers do not choose to enroll in HMO plans. Only in California and, to a lesser extent, the other West Coast states, do HMOs represent a significant share of the insurance and service delivery market. And, in many areas of the country—including most of the Eastern half—HMO penetration is minimal.

Preferred Provider Organizations

At the "liberal" end of the managed care spectrum are the rapidly growing **preferred provider organizations (PPOs)**, which negotiate discounts with a list of physicians that they encourage plan members to use, for which they are rewarded with lower out-of-pocket costs (deductibles, co-pays, and co-insurance). Patients who use an out-of-network provider often must pay the difference between the insurer's reimbursement rate and whatever the physician charges.

Accountable Care Organizations

Despite the dislike of managed care in the 1990s, the 2010 national health reform law and many private insurers are again promoting a version of managed care called **accountable care organizations (ACOs)** (described later in this chapter; see also Chapters 8, 9, and 10). Why the reconsideration? Quickly rising health costs and the prospects of sharply rising direct co-payments (deductibles and coinsurance) suggest that consumers may be more amenable to trading freedom of provider choice for more coordination of care and lower co-payments. Additionally, there is now some evidence that organizations, such as the Geisinger Health System in Pennsylvania (which acts somewhat like an ACO), offer a more comprehensive, organized, and integrated experience for patients that is seen as favorable to consumers and effective at improving quality.

Consumer-Driven Health Care and High Deductibles

An approach to financing that focuses on making consumers sense "price signals" when they purchase health care is often called "**consumer-driven health care**." This approach generally involves setting a large deductible before individuals receive insurance benefits. Sometimes costs of care during a deductible period can be paid by a savings account that employers or employees can set up for health-related costs.

In many ways, consumer-driven health care—which puts individuals at risk to pay the bulk of everyday health care and pharmaceutical needs—offers a stark alternative to the managed care option. People have very free choice but face sizable personal financial risk. This financial risk is particularly difficult for people with chronic health conditions.

How Health Reform May Affect the Financing System

The Patient Protection and Affordable Care Act of 2010 (ACA) is expected to have a major impact on the financing of health care, principally by expanding insurance coverage to approximately 32 million of the current 50.7 million uninsured by 2014. If this goal is reached, 95% of all Americans will have health insurance coverage. The federal health reform law will expand coverage in two key ways: expanding Medicaid eligibility and through a blend of subsidies and mandates that encourage the working class to purchase affordable insurance coverage in the private market.

Medicaid eligibility rates will be expanded so that most people who earn less than 133% of the federal poverty level will be covered. Currently, each state sets the upper-bound percentage of poverty for Medicaid eligibility and these percentages vary from 26% in Texas to more than 100% for states such as New York, New Jersey, and Massachusetts. Raising eligibility to 133% of poverty is expected to insure an additional 16 million Americans.

Individuals in families that earn between 133% and 400% of the federal poverty level will receive substantial subsidies to enable them to purchase insurance through an "insurance exchange" that will link private insurance companies to eligible individuals. Unless the subsidy an individual family can receive is too small, the family will be required to purchase insurance and, if it fails to do so, it will have to pay a financial penalty through its federal tax return. Employers with more than 50 employees also will have to pay financial penalties if they fail to offer their employees private insurance. It is expected that 24 million people will purchase subsidized policies through insurance exchanges.

The new law also requires that insurance companies offer insurance to all individuals, even those with existing health care problems. Although insurance premiums may vary due to the insured's age, tobacco use, geographic area, and family composition, insurance companies cannot set premium prices based on health status or gender. Policies must include minimum sets of benefits, in order to assure that they provide adequate financial protection. Insurers also will face limits on how much they can charge for administrative costs.

The new law does not change the overall structure of the health care financing system, which will continue to rely on a blend of private and public insurance plans. Instead, it builds on the existing system. Coverage provisions of the law will be implemented over a 4-year period, with the major insurance expansions occurring in 2014.

The reform law includes a host of provisions that will change reimbursement policies, in order to create incentives for providers to improve the quality of care and the value of health services (described later in this chapter; political aspects of the reform law are discussed in Chapter 2). Many of these proposed changes have the theme of encouraging more resources and more attention to the management of chronic conditions in "health homes," with the goal of better balancing the health system's focus on acute, high-technology services with the need for more efficient clinical management and prevention of chronic medical conditions.

Reimbursement Approaches

HOW DOCTORS ARE PAID

Physician services are a significant component of our national health care bill, accounting for more than one-fifth of all health care spending. Traditionally, physicians have worked for themselves or in group practices, rather than as salaried employees in clinics, hospitals, laboratories, or other sites. This trend is changing, with growing numbers of physicians seeking salaried positions, but even when working under such arrangements, they often are expected to generate their own income. Further, they have a great deal of autonomy in caring for their patients. Their decisions and recommendations have a tremendous impact not only on their own incomes, but, because of the tests they order, drugs they prescribe, treatments they recommend, and referrals they make, they greatly influence the whole of health care spending (see Chapter 9).

The way public and private insurers reimburse physicians for care has changed a great deal in the past two decades. Traditionally, physicians were paid on a fee-for-service basis. They set their price and the patient or insurer paid it. Because insurers simply passed the costs along to employers in the form of higher premiums, which employers in turn built into the price of their products and services, no one had an incentive to keep fees down. Most consumers usually did not pay directly for care, so did not pressure for lower prices, and insurers and employers lacked a framework for intervening. The fee-for-service system is often blamed for some of the rapid health care cost growth on the one hand and for government regulation of Medicare and Medicaid reimbursement rates on the other.

In recent years, net income for primary care doctors and most specialists has grown slowly, if at all, and, in some specialties, incomes have actually decreased. Interestingly, in most areas of the country, physicians have not organized into large group practices, even though this might increase their ability to negotiate higher fees.

GOVERNMENT REGULATION OF PHYSICIAN PAYMENT RATES

The federal Medicare program responded to price inflation in the late 1980s by developing a complicated set of fixed rates for specific physician services. The system, which covered a large number of services, is called the Resource-Based Relative Value Scale (RBRVS) (Hsiao et al., 1988). The rates were determined through detailed research measuring the expected time and other resource inputs that physicians needed to deliver a specific service.

Each state's Medicaid program also developed physician reimbursement rates, generally adopting the federal "take it or leave it" model. The Medicaid rates are often much lower than Medicare rates for the same services, which may result in fewer physicians accepting Medicaid patients. The 2010 federal health reform law mandates that state Medicaid programs raise physician reimbursement rates to at least 60% of the rates paid by Medicare.

HOW HOSPITALS ARE PAID

Approaches to paying hospitals are similar to the approaches used to reimburse physicians. Medicare and Medicaid offer "take it or leave it" rates, often based on complicated formulas, whereas private insurers negotiate rates with hospitals individually. Insurers often permit managed care enrollees to use only certain hospitals. The current system has evolved considerably in recent decades; in the past, insurers, including Medicare, generally paid hospitals whatever they said their costs were, as long as the costs were considered "reasonable." For many years, this unregulated approach fueled hospital cost inflation, especially when medical technology and new treatments began their rapid expansion. Today, many hospitals operate with small margins—many claim with negative margins—and must try to overcome shortfalls in government insurance payments with higher charges to private-paying patients.

DIAGNOSIS-RELATED GROUPS AND PROSPECTIVE PAYMENT

In 1983, the federal government introduced a new hospital reimbursement system that dramatically altered the way it pays for Medicare beneficiaries' hospital care. The **diagnosis-related groups (DRGs)** system set rates prospectively—that is, Medicare said up-front that it would pay a fixed amount for the hospital stay of a patient with a specific diagnosis and no more (with some outlier exceptions), no matter how much the patient's care eventually cost or how long the hospitalization turned out to be. Fixed payments give hospitals a powerful incentive to increase efficiency, minimize unnecessary tests and services, and shorten patients' hospital stays.

A newer approach to payment is the concept of "**bundled payments**," which provide both the physician and the hospital a fixed amount to take care of an episode of care or for a time period of care, in the case of patients with chronic conditions. Various provisions of the 2010 health reform law would encourage use of bundled payments in the health system.

PER DIEM HOSPITAL REIMBURSEMENT

Many private insurers and state Medicaid programs have not adopted the DRG payment approach and instead continue to negotiate per diem (daily) rates for hospital care. Medicaid programs often set their per diem rates prospectively and require hospitals to accept them. Private insurers in most parts of the county negotiate intensively with hospitals over rates.

Insurers and hospitals alike use their market power to influence favorable rates. Insurers—especially if they cover a substantial share of a hospital's potential patient pool—have considerable clout if they can prevent their covered patients from using hospitals with higher rates, whereas hospitals have market power, because many employers will not purchase insurance plans that do not include in their networks popular, highly regarded hospitals.

This negotiation environment more closely mirrors how prices are set in other markets involving large purchasers and producers (e.g., the market linking automobile manufacturers with the many companies that make auto parts). When the market works smoothly, both parties will come to agreements that push efficiency but leave the supplier—in this case, the hospital—with sufficient reimbursements that it can achieve high-quality care and stay financially viable.

Current Policy Issues in Financing

The period between 2011 and 2015 will likely be dominated by attention to implementing the wide-ranging features of the 2010 health care reform law. The law left many details open related to implementation of the insurance expansion and system reform goals. Over time, these will be determined through regulation, by the executive branch of the federal government and by state governments that are responsible for implementing the rules.

Designing insurance exchanges that will link private insurers to individuals who can purchase subsidized insurance policies will be an administrative, information technology, and policy challenge. States need to adapt current state insurance regulations and current Medicaid rules to the requirements of the new law. Expanding coverage to 32 million Americans represents a complex task, both to get the insurance plans in place and then to make sure that the health care delivery system can handle the surge in people who will, for the first time, have a regularized method of paying for services.

> *At least the early implementation of health care reform will take place in a time of great economic difficulty for state and federal government due to the national economic downturn.*

At least the early implementation of health care reform will take place in a time of great economic difficulty for state and federal government due to the national economic downturn. As states face falling tax revenues, they often are cutting reimbursement rates for Medicaid providers at the same time they are expected to expand insurance coverage. The federal government also faces an implementation challenge as a result of large federal budget deficits and partisan differences in assessments of the law's viability. A number of state governors were very unsympathetic to implementing the new law, lawsuits were filed, and Republican members of Congress might attempt to completely revamp the law if they achieve sufficient electoral success before full implementation

Two policy issues are key to the success or failure of implementation: whether the growth of health care expenditures can be constrained; and whether effective "insurance exchanges" can be implemented in all 50 states.

CONSTRAINING THE GROWTH OF HEALTH CARE COSTS

Nothing threatens access to high-quality health care for the average American more than the growth of health care costs over time. In recent years, costs have grown in the neighborhood of 6% per year, whereas overall inflation and economic growth are near zero. The relentless increase in costs either will raise the financial burden facing governments along with the burdens on employers' labor costs or will lead to higher out-of-pocket costs for consumers.

Why is the relentless expansion of expenditures on health care of concern? The main reason is that the costs are largely paid by government and employers. These growing expenditures force higher taxes in the public sector and increased product prices and depressed wages in the private sector. All of these problems are considered bad for our economy. If individuals paid for health care directly, making choices between buying health care versus buying other items, growing health care expenditures would not be seen as so burdensome to the economy.

The high expenditure levels also raise concerns because the United States spends so much more on health care than do other countries (see Chapter 4). Even within the United States, expenditures on health care vary a great deal across communities and states with little to no difference in health outcomes. In fact, low-spending areas often exhibit better health outcomes, even when controlling for population age and other factors.

The very best way to reduce the costs of health care is to keep as many Americans as possible as healthy as possible. Prevention of chronic diseases, such as diabetes, heart disease, or HIV-related illnesses, not only reduces the need for health care but also improves the quality of life for Americans. Prevention often requires improved everyday behavior, in terms of exercise, nutrition, or safe sex, and environmental changes, such as reduced exposure to toxic substances and healthier places to live, work, and play (see Chapters 6 and 7). Explaining to people how they can maintain healthy behavior and change environmental conditions—such as assuring availability of fruits and vegetables and safe places to exercise—all take focus and resources. In essence, cost containment in health care will happen if we can figure out how to invest in healthy lifestyles in ways that lead to long-term financial and health returns.

Unfortunately, it has been difficult to coordinate these investments and their potential benefits: often the costs associated with preventive services are paid by one set of actors but the returns on these investments go to other actors. This means nobody has the financial incentive to make the investments in the first place.

Misaligned financial incentives are present throughout the health system. For example, primary care physicians do not generally have incentives to avoid unnecessary referrals to costly specialists or expensive diagnostic tests. Hospitals traditionally have not had an economic incentive to coordinate posthospital services that would reduce the need to readmit patients.

Many policy experts believe that aligning financial incentives to promote efficient investment of resources is the key to reducing health care costs in the coming years. The federal health reform package includes a wide range of provisions that focus on changing financial incentives to promote both increased efficiency and improved quality of care.

One provision in the new law would fund systems of providers that wish to act as "accountable care organizations" and take various types of capitated payments to coordinate all of the care required by people in the covered group. Because they will receive only this fixed amount, providers will have strong incentives to invest in prevention, wellness, disease management, and various systems that assure the efficient use of health care resources. Other provisions of the law will encourage new approaches to meeting long-term care needs with community-based, rather than institutional, forms of care. And yet other provisions will penalize hospitals that have high rates of readmissions of patients within 30 days of discharge.

A range of demonstration initiatives funded by a new federal center for innovation will experiment with other reimbursement approaches and incentive systems. And, various provisions of the law will work to expand primary care capacity, with the hope that better access to primary care will reduce the need for expensive specialist and hospital care.

IMPLEMENTING EFFECTIVE INSURANCE EXCHANGES

A key feature of the 2010 federal health reform legislation is the creation of insurance exchanges that will offer private insurance policies with premium rates subsidized by federal dollars. Families with incomes below 400% of poverty (in 2010, an income of $88,000 was 400% of the poverty level for a family of four) will be eligible for insurance subsidies on a sliding scale. In addition, everyone will be required to buy some form of insurance policy, as long as at least one offering by a private insurer meets affordability tests for that person or family.

The exchanges are intended to play at least three key roles: calculating the amount of the subsidy for a given family, explaining the features of each private insurance offering, and linking each family to the insurance option the family selects. Exchanges also will most likely determine which insurance offerings meet federal qualifications to be offered on the exchange. And, some states may choose to have their exchanges facilitate enrollment in public insurance plans, such as Medicaid.

These are all difficult roles to play for new organizations with few organizational precedents and significant learning curves. It is the responsibility of resource-strapped state governments to design and operationalize these exchanges by 2014. Complicated consensus-building processes will be necessary that involve insurance companies, consumer groups, and policy makers to accomplish this in a timely way. A large task will be development of new eligibility information systems that can translate income levels into subsidy amounts and verify the accuracy of reported incomes. Most states will need new laws to bring state insurance regulations in line with federal requirements and to set governance rules and financing approaches to pay for the operation of the exchanges.

Perhaps the greatest challenge in establishing the insurance exchanges under health reform will be to assure seamless enrollment.

Perhaps the greatest challenge in establishing the exchanges is to assure seamless enrollment in unsubsidized private policies, subsidized private policies, and the publicly supported Medicaid program. If a family has a change in its income status, it often will have a change in the type of insurance it qualifies for: when incomes exceed 400% of poverty, an unsubsidized policy is required; when incomes are between 133% and 400% of poverty, individuals in most states will be required to purchase a subsidized policy; and when family incomes are less than 133% of poverty, families will be eligible for free Medicaid insurance.

If enrollment and income documentation systems vary from one insurance category to another, many families will have difficulty making transitions among insurance types. In particular, many people who become eligible for Medicaid coverage may fail to comply with complex enrollment processes. A successful integration of differing enrollment requirements could result not only in increased private coverage but also better take-up rates for the Medicaid program. This would represent an impressive achievement for the new reform law.

Conclusion

The new federal health reform law represents the largest change in the nation's health care financing system since the initiation of Medicare and Medicaid in the mid-1960s. It will very likely change reimbursement approaches for nearly all providers of services and dramatically expand the number of Americans with health coverage, if implemented as expected. In addition, it will require many currently uninsured middle income Americans to purchase subsidized private policies.

However, the law will endure only if health care costs can be contained. If they continue to increase year after year—especially at a pace exceeding that of the overall economy— either subsidized insurance will become unaffordable or the federal government will be forced to increase the subsidies. The latter may not be feasible at a time when federal budget deficits already are considered burdensome and state resources to cover Medicaid costs are threatened. Cost increases also will put pressure on reimbursement rates and the generosity of private insurance coverage. This, in turn, will make it increasingly difficult for health care providers to remain financially viable.

One great new hope is that emerging reimbursement reforms and new incentive payment schemes will relatively quickly lower the growth rate of health care costs. We have been through a period of early experimentation with various incentive payment schemes and have many viable approaches to try. But, firm evidence that they will work is not yet available.

Another great hope is that, as a nation, we will make progress on the public health and prevention tasks of helping people live healthier lives and avoid the health and medical care cost consequences of chronic diseases such as diabetes, heart disease, and asthma. The best way to lower the rate of growth of health care costs is to reduce the incidence of chronic disease. Helping people eat better, exercise more, use alcohol responsibly, and avoid the use of tobacco and addicting drugs is crucial both to population health and economic health in our country.

One final challenge for the American health system is to care for the 5% of people living in America who will continue not to have insurance coverage, even if insurance reform is fully and effectively implemented. Our health system will continue to require a safety net for the vulnerable and uninsured. A world of tight reimbursements will make it increasingly difficult for hospitals and other providers to pay for safety net care by shifting dollars from other payers and revenue sources.

What will happen if federal health reform does achieve the anticipated expansions of access and control over the growth in health care costs? One of two radical options will most likely emerge: a collapse of the private approach to health care financing, which would lead to a single-payer public system like those of most other parts of the developed world (see Chapter 4), or the emergence of a two-tiered system of care that maintains access for Americans with comfortable incomes but restricts access for everyone else—a particularly brutal form of rationing. Either option goes against fundamental principles engrained in American history and politics: free enterprise on one hand and equality and equity on the other. The task of implementing a 21st century financing system that will endure needs to engage new thinkers, new leaders, and new researchers who can reinterpret these principles in light of current realities.

DISCUSSION QUESTIONS

1. What complications does our current health financing system cause for providers of care?
2. What complications does our insurance system cause individual consumers?
3. What are some of the promising new approaches to changing our health system so that it has incentives to provide more efficient care?
4. Some people view increases in health care spending as a response to consumer demand, whereas others see these increase as potentially wasteful spending. When other industry sectors assume a rising share of gross domestic product (GDP), it is viewed as a positive development. Should we be concerned about the rising costs of health care and its share of GDP? What types of health care spending might be classified as valuable? Wasteful?

CASE STUDY

Assume you are the chief executive officer of a large technology-intensive hospital in a community of 200,000 people that includes two other smaller community hospitals and a wide range of physicians and other providers working in private practice. Currently, you are paid by Medicare—the federal insurance program for the elderly—a fixed amount for every admission to your hospital, based on the severity of the patient's needs. Physicians and other providers in your community are paid fee-for-service. The federal government has just made an offer to your community that it form an accountable care organization (ACO) that could accept a capitated annual payment for each person eligible for Medicare.

CASE STUDY QUESTIONS

1. How would you go about deciding whether to accept that offer?
2. Would you want to lead that ACO or just be a part of it?
3. Would you argue against accepting the federal offer?
4. If you did want to proceed and even lead the effort to form an ACO, how would you coordinate with the other local hospitals and providers?
5. How might you change the way care currently is organized in your community, given the new financial incentives embedded in a capitated rate?

REFERENCES

Ellwood, M. R., & Ku, L. (1998). Welfare and immigration reforms: Unintended side effects for Medicaid. *Health Affairs, 17*, 137–151.

Fronstin, P. (2009). Sources of health insurance and characteristics of the uninsured: Analysis of the March 2009 Current Population Survey. *Issue Brief 334*. Washington, D.C.: Employee Benefit Research Institute.

Glied, S. A., & Borzi, P. C. (2004). The current state of employer based health care. *Journal of Law, Medicine, and Ethics, 32*, 404–409.

Gold, M. (2001). Medicare+Choice: An interim report card. *Health Affairs, 20*, 120–138.

Hsiao, W. C., Braun, P., Dunn, D., Becker, E. R., Chen, S. P., Couch, N. P., et al. (1988). *A national study of Resource-Based Relative Value Scales for physician services: Final report to the Health Care Financing Administration*. Publication 17-C-98795/1-03. Boston, MA: Harvard School of Public Health.

Hurley, R., & Somers, S. (2003). Medicaid and managed care: A lasting relationship? *Health Affairs, 22*, 77–88.

Kaiser Commission on Medicaid and the Uninsured. (2008). *Filling an urgent need: Improving children's access to dental care in Medicaid and SCHIP*. Retrieved January 18, 2011, from http://www.kff.org/medicaid/7792.cfm

Kaiser Commission on Medicaid and the Uninsured. (2010). *Medicaid's continuing crunch in a recession: A mid-year update for state FY 2010 and preview for FY 2011*. Retrieved January 18, 2011, from http://www.kff.org/medicaid/8049.cfm.

U.S., Department of Health and Human Services. Indian Health Service. (2010). *IHS fact sheets, IHS Year 2010 Profile*. Washington, D.C.: Author.

4

COMPARATIVE HEALTH SYSTEMS

Bianca K. Frogner, Hugh R. Waters, and Gerard F. Anderson

KEY WORDS

purchasing power parity (PPP)
health outcomes
patient satisfaction
Bismarck model
Beveridge model

fee-for-service
capitation
global budget
means tests

LEARNING OBJECTIVES

- Understand the evolution of health care systems among selected OECD countries
- Learn characteristics of four different models of health care systems
- Understand how the U.S. health care system's costs and outcomes compare with those of other OECD countries
- Identify challenges facing each health care system model

TOPICAL OUTLINE

- Basic health care system characteristics
- Health care quality similarities across models
- Evolution of health care systems
- Exploring major health system models
- Common challenges facing systems

Although the focus of this book is the U.S. health care system, it helps to consider the U.S. system in relation to systems in other industrialized countries that have created different ways to finance health care, provide health care services, and monitor access to care and its quality. Costs and outcomes differ across these various systems, and the United States may be able to adapt some of the good ideas from other industrialized countries for itself and learn from their mistakes.

The industrialized countries most commonly used in comparisons of health measures are the 32 countries that make up the Organisation for Economic Co-operation and Development (OECD). By comparing the United States with other OECD countries, policy makers, clinicians, managers, students, and other interested individuals can identify new ways to assess the performance of the U.S. health care system and how it might be more effective in improving the health of the population.

Insights for possible health care system changes can come from comparisons of how countries (1) spend on health care; (2) allocate their health care resources; (3) protect their population from financial risk; (4) ensure access to treatment and prevention services; and (5) provide quality care. A bottom-line comparison suggests that the United States is not receiving adequate value for its enormous health care investments.

Basic Health Care System Characteristics

HEALTH CARE SPENDING

Before taking a trip around the world of health care systems in OECD countries, here are some features of the basic "language" of international comparisons. A starting point is how much money a country spends on health care; one commonly used measure is *total spending*. In 2008, the United States spent $2.3 trillion and projections by the Centers for Medicare and Medicaid Services suggest that spending will increase to more than $4.5 trillion by 2019. However, as an indicator, total health care spending may not be the best comparison measure because countries have different numbers of people, different costs of living, and other factors that can affect total spending.

A better alternative is to compare total health care spending per person (per capita), adjusted to achieve **purchasing power parity**, or **PPP**. Purchasing power parities are used in addition to exchange rates to reflect differences in the cost of acquiring basic goods in a given country. In 2008, the United States had the highest annual health care spending per capita in terms of PPP ($7,538). This is significantly higher than PPP spending in other OECD countries. Spending per capita (PPP) in seven other OECD nations ranged from $3,129 for Great Britain to $4,627 for Switzerland. This trend has persisted for almost four decades.

Economists generally prefer to compare different countries' total spending on health care as a percent of their gross domestic product (GDP). GDP measures the monetary value of all the finished goods and services produced in the country (including private and government expenditures, investments, and so on) over some fixed time period, usually annually. The health care share of GDP has been growing in nearly all OECD countries, with the United States showing some of the most rapid increases. The U.S. share of GDP spent on health care is now 16%, compared to 8.7% in the UK and 11.2% in France, and reflects the priority placed on the health care industry relative to the rest of the economy.

The tradeoff in prioritizing health care over other goods and services (e.g., education or manufacturing) is what economists call the *opportunity cost,* because a dollar spent on health care cannot be spent on something else. The share of GDP dedicated to health care is in part influenced by government decisions to increase/decrease spending in other areas of the economy and, in part, by individuals' demands to consume goods and services in either health care or other areas.

In summary, comparative international data on spending show that the U.S. health care system is the most expensive per capita, U.S. health care spending is growing more rapidly than spending in most other OECD countries, the United States spends the highest percentage of its GDP on health care among all OECD countries, and this higher spending has persisted for the last 40 years.

PRIVATE AND PUBLIC SPENDING

Comparisons of health care spending also can focus on whether the source of the revenue is from public funds (government) or private funds (business, private insurance, or individuals paying for care out-of-pocket). The share of health care spending funded by public sources measures the government's involvement in paying for health care. In recent years among most OECD countries, approximately three-fourths of health care spending was from public funds, whereas the remaining quarter was from private funds.

Private insurance and business play a relatively small role in health care funding in most OECD countries. On average, about a quarter of OECD countries' total health care expenditures come from private sources; in the United States, where business and private insurance play a much larger role, half of the total health care expenditures are from private sources. Among the private sources, on average, 75% came from residents' out-of-pocket payments in OECD countries, mostly for services such as dental care that are not routinely covered by public insurance. Out-of-pocket payments were only 23% of the private sources in the United States in 2008.

HEALTH COVERAGE AND ACCESS

A logical expectation is that additional health care spending within a country translates to additional health care access to its citizens—and, ultimately, better health. There are many different ways to measure access to health care services. One is health insurance coverage. Most OECD countries have achieved universal or near-universal health insurance coverage, in spite of spending much less per capita or as a percent of the GDP than the United States does. The U.S. health reform of 2010 will extend coverage to almost three-quarters of the uninsured, but still will not achieve universal coverage. The most current estimate is that 5 to 6% of the population will remain uninsured.

Two other common measures of access to health care are (1) the availability of health care resources and (2) the rate of utilization of available resources. Consistently, the United States has had fewer health care resources than other OECD countries, with fewer physicians and fewer acute care hospital beds per 1,000 residents. U.S. citizens visit the doctor less often than people in other countries and stay in the hospital for fewer days. These patterns do not say anything about the intensity of the services delivered while in the hospital or during a doctor visit. Due to difficulty in defining intensity accurately across settings, it is unknown whether U.S. patients receive more care during a visit or whether the care delivered was provided more effectively or efficiently in the United States than in other countries.

Low utilization rates and low resource levels are not necessarily bad, if patients can gain access to care when needed. However, among a sample of the general population in OECD countries, the United States had the largest proportion of adults (17%) who reported an extremely or very difficult time seeing a specialist. In all countries, people with lower-than-average income levels reported much more difficulty in seeing a specialist when needed, as compared to people with above-average incomes. This was particularly the case in the United States (Blendon et al., 2002).

In a survey of a sicker population, U.S. adults with at least one chronic disease had slightly better access to specialists than did their counterparts in Australia and Canada, but more difficulty than UK citizens (Blendon, Schoen, DesRoches, Osborn, & Zapert, 2003). Also, U.S. citizens tend to report the shortest wait for specialist care (74% waited fewer than 4 weeks), whereas 42% of Canadians had to wait 2 months or longer.

HEALTH OUTCOMES

Another common assumption is that additional spending on health care may result in better **health outcomes**. Again, the challenge in comparing outcomes across OECD countries is the lack of any universally agreed-upon measures of health outcomes. As a result, there are measures showing that the United States (or some other OECD country) does well and other measures where the United States does poorly.

Perhaps the most widely used measure to compare health care outcomes across nations is life expectancy at birth, which, in the United States, is lower and increasing more slowly than in other OECD countries. Between 1980 and 2008, U.S. life expectancy at birth increased 4.2 years, compared to a median increase of 6.6 years for seven other OECD countries. The only country with slower improvement during this time period was the Netherlands; however, the Netherlands had a life expectancy in 1980 that was 2.2 years longer than that of the United States.

Life expectancy at age 65 is another frequent measure of a population's health status. Again, in the United States, we see lower life expectancy at age 65 for both men and women, compared to other OECD countries. In 1980, U.S. life expectancy among adults at age 65 was relatively good, compared to many other nations. But the rate of improvement slowed over the two decades from 1980 to 2008. This is in spite of nearly universal access to health insurance among Americans over age 65 through Medicare.

Another commonly used measure to compare health status across countries is the infant mortality rate. U.S. infant mortality rates again are improving more slowly than in other OECD countries. Between 1980 and 2008, the U.S. infant mortality rate declined by 47% (from 12.6 to 6.7 deaths per 1,000 live births) whereas each of the other countries saw a decline of more than 50%. A number of studies have attempted to explain the relatively high U.S. infant mortality rates. One explanation could be that the poor performance of the United States is attributable to substantial racial and socioeconomic disparities in infant survival (Singh & Yu, 1995). However, even if white Americans are the focus of the comparison, many other countries have lower overall infant mortality rates than U.S. whites (Braveman, Cubbin, Egerter, Williams & Pamuk, 2010; Singh & Kogan, 2007).

As measures of health care systems' outcomes, life expectancy and infant mortality rates are limited because they reflect the influence of socioeconomic and other factors in addition to the contribution of the health care system.

In summary, on most indicators the United States has not achieved the best health outcomes, compared to other countries, in spite of our high levels of health care spending. Overall, the health status of the U.S. population is in the middle of the OECD countries and, in the last few decades, improving more slowly than are other nations.

Health Care Quality Similarities Across Models

IMPROVING QUALITY OF CARE

Each OECD country is not likely to deliver health care in the same way, but the impacts of these differences are difficult to measure. For example, international comparisons of the quality of health care are limited, but available evidence shows that quality has no clear relation to the level of health care spending or health care system characteristics (Davis et al., 2007; Hussey et al., 2004). Higher quality of care is sometimes equated with new, advanced technologies. The use of advanced technologies may come with a high price tag and estimates are that half of the increase in U.S. health spending can be attributed to new technology.

> *Estimates are that half of the increase in U.S. health spending can be attributed to new technology.*

Relative to other OECD countries, the United States has done well on some quality of care indicators, such as cancer survival rates and screenings, but more poorly on indicators such as immunizations and asthma care (Anderson & Frogner, 2008). While all countries have improved their cancer survival rates, for more than a decade, the United States has had the highest 5-year survival rates for breast and colorectal cancers; however, it does not have the best 5-year survival rate for cervical cancer. The underlying reasons for the variation in survival rates are not entirely certain; perhaps physician practice guidelines of the various countries recommend first screening at different ages, different intervals between screenings, or different treatment practices, whereas patients may have different level of awareness, exposure to public health campaigns, or genetic makeup. Finally, as mentioned, hospital admissions rates for asthma—a highly preventable condition—for people over 15 years old, are highest in the United States, especially among women.

PATIENT SATISFACTION

No country's citizenry is completely satisfied with its health care system. But in most surveys, larger percentages of Americans have expressed serious dissatisfaction with the U.S. system, which in part drove the health reform efforts of 2010 (see, for example, Blendon et al., 2002, 2003). **Patient satisfaction** scores encompass issues such as quality of experience with providers, length of time waiting for care, ability to pay for services, and trust in the medical system.

Citizens in each country mentioned here believe their health care system could use improvement or reform in each of these elements. Surveys conducted over time indicate that most U.S. adults with at least one chronic disease—people who encounter the health care system fairly often—have long wanted fundamental change (46%) or complete rebuilding (33%) of the U.S. system (Blendon et al., 2003). Adults in the Netherlands and France have the highest satisfaction with their health care systems and generally believe they need only minor changes (42% and 41%, respectively) (Schoen, Osborn, How, Doty, & Peugh, 2009). These comparisons need to be viewed carefully because many factors can influence public opinion about health care systems.

Evolution of Health Care Systems

As different countries have progressively modified their health care systems, the four basic health care system models discussed here have evolved to fit the context of each nation. By now, no country has a pure form of any of the four basic models; each has modified its chosen model to meet its own needs.

BISMARCK MODEL

The oldest health care system model—the *social insurance model* or **Bismarck model**—was introduced in 1883 by German Chancellor Otto von Bismarck. In developing the social insurance model, Bismarck was balancing two competing demands: on one hand, German leaders did not want to raise taxes, so a government-financed health care system was not feasible, and, on the other, German workers were concerned about loss of income as they retired or got sick, compounded by the cost of health care.

The Bismarck model is based on a philosophy of national solidarity. Every worker and employer must contribute to the social insurance system commensurate with their income. Multiple funds were created to collect and redistribute these contributions, according to government regulations, in order to cover the costs of illness care. Hence the funds are called *sickness funds*. There are multiple sickness funds in Germany that actually provide the insurance. Initially the sickness funds were tied to the worker's employer or trade union. Today, workers can choose among competing sickness funds.

Bismarck's objective was to offer universal coverage that provided nationally defined benefits, in order to reduce Germans' financial risks from work-related injuries and disability. The model has been modified over time, but the Bismarck model remains the foundation of the German system. Its elements can be found in the health care systems of Japan, France, the Netherlands, and many other countries.

BEVERIDGE MODEL

In 1946, the **Beveridge model** of publicly financed health insurance that provides universal coverage was developed by Sir William Beveridge for the United Kingdom. Its creation followed World War II, when most of the UK's health system was operated by the government to the population's apparent satisfaction, and it became Britain's current National Health Service (NHS).

Rather than the employer/employee-based contribution model developed by Bismarck, the Beveridge model is chiefly characterized by progressive tax-financing (i.e., taxes increase in proportion to increases in income). The British government acts as the single insurer. Variations of the Beveridge model can be seen in New Zealand, Spain, and Scandinavia. The Beveridge model is a government-run, single-payer system.

NATIONAL HEALTH INSURANCE

The Bismarck and Beveridge models have been combined in several countries to create a variety of insurance systems. Canada has adopted one such combination model. Its National Health Insurance (NHI) program differs from the Beveridge model, in that the private sector plays a strong role in providing health care services. The similarity is that the government collects and finances care through a single-payer system, rather than through multiple sickness funds, as under the Bismarck model.

Taiwan and South Korea have achieved universal insurance coverage financed primarily through payroll taxes, cross-subsidized by general government revenues. These systems feature a relatively high degree of private sector involvement in the delivery of health care services, especially outpatient care (Lee, Chun, Lee, & Seo, 2008).

PRIVATE HEALTH INSURANCE

As noted earlier, most OECD countries have a small private health insurance sector. In some countries, private insurers are permitted to compete with the federal government but, in most, there is no direct private sector competition for the government's basic benefits package, and private insurers are limited to insuring for services and amenities, such as a private room, that are not covered by public insurance.

In contrast, the U.S. health care system gives a prominent role to private health insurance. Similar to the Bismarck model, the private health insurance system is financed through employer and employee contributions. However, most private sector insurance is premium-based: that is, insured individuals pay a set amount determined by the insurance company, rather than a percentage of their income determined by the government. In economic terms, the U.S. system is much less progressive because low income individuals pay a higher percentage of their income for health care than do the wealthy.

Switzerland and the Netherlands also have created an important role for private health insurance, but with much greater government regulation than in the United States. Insurance mandates require private insurers to cover specific services, and there is strong government oversight. Some of the changes in the 2010 U.S. health reform legislation are based on Swiss and Dutch models, such as the elimination of preexisting condition exclusion clauses and other practices that allow insurers to drop coverage when an insured individual becomes sick.

Exploring Major Health System Models

Building on the foundations of the history of health systems and their basic characteristics, this section explores how aspects of international health systems operate within the U.S. health care system and discusses the similarities and differences with regard to the major components of a health care system: financing, pooling, provision of services, and regulation.

PRIVATE HEALTH INSURANCE

Financing and Pooling

In the United States, when most individuals enter the workplace, they voluntarily contribute a portion of their pre-tax income, which is added to a contribution by their employer, to purchase health insurance. In other words, employees *pool* their risk among their coworkers with the expectation that only a few employees may be sick and use a significant amount of health care services, whereas most others may use health care very little or not at all. Health insurance companies consider the characteristics of this risk pool and price the employer's insurance plan accordingly.

In the United States, the employee contribution amount varies according to the premium (or price) charged to consumers (employers and employees) and the proportion of that premium that the employer is willing to pay on behalf of the employee. The amount of the premium is negotiated by insurance companies and employers. France and Germany also finance their health care system primarily by voluntary contributions by employers and employees. There, the risk-pooling occurs at the plan level. However, in France and Germany, insurance contributions are a fixed percentage of employees' income.

In return for their employees' financial contributions, large U.S. employers are likely to offer a few different benefit packages, each administered by a private health insurance company. The options within the benefit packages are likely to be chosen by the employer, and many states impose specific minimum coverage requirements. Similarly, federal employees are offered a choice of private health insurance benefit packages through the Federal Employee Health Benefits Program, Programs for active or retired military service members, their families, and surviving family members are offered through the military medical program, TRICARE, and the Veterans Health Administration.

In the Netherlands and Switzerland, people also have a choice of private health insurance companies. However, benefit packages are likely to be more similar and to be regulated by the government. In the United States, workers in small firms are unlikely to have a choice of coverage, but this may change under health reform, because exchanges will be created that will combine individuals and small businesses in a state into one large pool.

In most countries there is no cost-sharing for services covered by government health insurance. U.S. citizens with private health insurance face a variety of cost-sharing requirements: *co-payments* (a fixed amount paid per visit or per procedure), *co-insurance* (requiring them to pay a set percentage of treatment costs, commonly ranging from 5% to 20%), and/or *deductibles* (out-of-pocket payments as high as $2,500 before insurance kicks in), depending on the specific provisions of their health insurance plan. The Medicare program also includes a variety of cost-sharing arrangements.

The Netherlands requires a deductible, but citizens are refunded a standard amount if they incur no health care costs during the year. Or, if their costs were below the standard amount, they receive the difference. Switzerland provides first-dollar coverage (in other words, with *no* deductible) if care is obtained within the patient's residential area.

Provision of Services

In the United States, each private health insurance company negotiates a separate contract with each different health care provider (doctors, hospitals, and others) and, conversely, most health care providers must negotiate rates with multiple insurance companies. Individuals usually must choose providers who have a contract with their insurance company; if they do not, they may have to pay a larger portion—or sometimes all—of the "out-of-network" provider's bill. Americans can choose individual or family coverage, with the latter more expensive. In other countries, family coverage is the norm and, in most countries, only one standard contract exists between the citizens receiving insurance and the public or private insurer.

In two OECD countries that use private health insurance companies to administer benefits, the Netherlands and Switzerland, physicians may negotiate with multiple insurance companies. General practitioners in the Netherlands and all Swiss physicians see patients who are on their practice list, with some allowances for patients to change physicians. In the Netherlands, specialist physicians are almost all based in hospitals and serve patients assigned to their hospital. In these countries, reimbursements paid by private insurers are quite similar across providers.

Countries are exploring a variety of payment options. In the United States, **fee-for-service** (payment for each service rendered) is the typical reimbursement mechanism for preferred provider organizations (PPOs), whereas **capitated** (per person) payments are characteristic of health maintenance organizations (HMOs). The various financing mechanisms allow for different levels of gate-keeping to reduce costs. Some private insurance plans still pay hospitals on a combination of itemized and per-diem (for "hotel" services) charges or, as in Medicare and HMOs, on a fixed-price basis, depending on the patient's diagnosis. In Medicare's case, these set prices are established under the diagnosis related groups, or DRG system. Under this system, whether a patient with pneumonia, say, is hospitalized 2 days or 2 weeks, the hospital receives the same payment. Under recent new legislation, hospitals can be penalized if a patient is rehospitalized too soon after discharge. This latter provision was adopted in order to reduce hospitals' financial incentive to send patients home too quickly, before they are physically ready.

Self-employed physicians in Switzerland contract with private health insurance companies and are paid on a fee-for-service basis for outpatient care, whereas physicians working in hospitals are paid a salary; hospitals receive a daily flat rate per patient. General practitioners in the Netherlands receive capitated payments whereas hospital-based physicians are reimbursed by diagnosis treatment combinations (similar to DRGs). In most publicly funded programs, hospital-based physicians are paid a salary, whereas most community physicians are paid fee-for-service. Hospitals are paid on the basis of budgets, DRGs, and per-diem rates.

> *The private health insurance market in the United States is not as strongly regulated as in most OECD countries, although the 2010 U.S. health reform law is a step in this direction.*

Regulation

The private health insurance market in the United States is not as strongly regulated as in most OECD countries, although the 2010 U.S. health reform law is a step in this direction. Both the Netherlands and Switzerland have defined a basic benefit package to be offered by private health insurance companies in order to reduce disparities in coverage of disadvantaged groups. Also, the financial contribution levels are clearly defined by the government and do not vary by insurance company, as in the United States.

NATIONAL HEALTH INSURANCE PROGRAMS AND THE U.S. MEDICARE PROGRAM

Financing

The federal Medicare program combines the Bismarck and Beveridge models. Financial contributions to Medicare come through payroll taxes collected by the federal government, and all employees must contribute a percentage of their income, which their employer matches. (A common misconception is that people's Medicare contributions are like a savings account that they have "paid in" to. In actuality, Medicare is a pay-as-you-go system, so that people who pay now are supporting elders who need care now, *not* creating a reserve for their own care in the future.) Other parts of Medicare, such as physician services, are financed through general tax revenues. Australia combines a health tax on income and funds from general taxation to finance its NHI. Canada also funds its health system using general taxation, along with extra premiums collected by certain provinces.

Provision of Services

NHI provides universal coverage to all citizens regardless of ability to pay, as is the case in Australia and Canada. Medicare also is a near-universal entitlement for all Americans over 65 and some people with disabilities. The federal government sets reimbursement rates for physicians, hospitals, and other care providers. Most physicians in the United States, Canada, and Australia are in private practice settings (i.e., not government employees) and are reimbursed through fee-for-service arrangements. Most hospitals in Australia are public and receive set payments for patient care, according to the patient's diagnosis; U.S. hospitals receive similar set DRG payments from Medicare. Canadian hospitals are mostly private, not-for-profit; their payment rates are established through prospective budgets set by the provincial governments.

Regulation

Government plays a large role in the operations of NHI programs. The Australian and Canadian governments are deeply involved not only in setting payment rates, but also in defining standard benefit packages and capping excessive treatment costs. Much of the regulatory power is decentralized to the states or provinces. Although physician care is mostly private, these governments regulate the quality of care provided, as well as guarantee access to services. By contrast, Medicare provides less explicit governmental control, given that multiple private health insurance programs also exist in the United States and that health care providers are not required to accept payment from Medicare. In reality, private payers often follow Medicare's lead with respect to major coverage decisions, and providers with a large proportion of Medicare patients cannot easily stop serving this group.

NATIONAL HEALTH SERVICES AND THE U.S. VETERANS HEALTH ADMINISTRATION

Financing

The U.S. Veterans Health Administration (VHA) contains elements of the Beveridge model, as exemplified by the UK's NHS. The NHS is primarily funded through general tax revenues allocated to health care. The VHA also is financed from general tax revenues. When patients visit a health provider in the UK, care is free at the point of delivery, whereas the VHA system requires co-payments for some services and from some veterans.

Provision of Services

Primary care physicians in the NHS are paid from publicly funded primary care trusts that operate at a regional level. UK physicians negotiate payment rates through a combination of salary, fee-for-service, and capitation, depending on their years of experience and setting, with different systems used to pay primary care and hospital doctors. The VHA owns and operates its hospitals and many outpatient services and employs most of the physicians that staff these facilities. Physician services are funded through an annual **global budget** (a lump sum, prospective budget) approved by Congress as part of the overall federal budgeting process. For 2011, the VHA budget for medical care is more than $48 billion.

As in the VHA, UK hospitals are owned by the government; UK hospitals are reimbursed by regional hospital trusts. Some Scandinavian governments own and operate their nations' health facilities and pay their physicians, as does the VHA, although this is changing, with much greater decentralization occurring in these countries.

Regulation

Among the health system models reviewed in this chapter, regulation is the strongest within an NHS model, such as in the UK and the VHA. Both systems have defined benefit packages. The secretary of Veterans Affairs annually reviews the VHA budget to make sure that it is adequate for specific priority populations. Similarly, the central government in the UK's NHS sets separate budgets for primary care trusts and hospital trusts, which are reviewed every 3 years and adjusted based on achievement of nationally set quality measures.

SOCIAL INSURANCE

Elements of the Bismarck-based social insurance model exist in the United States, although with some modifications. In Germany, payroll tax contributions are pooled into the more than 200 not-for-profit, nongovernmental sickness funds described earlier. These funds have many attributes in common with U.S. private insurers. The German government closely regulates the operations of the sickness funds, whereas, in the United States, the federal Department of Labor regulates self-insured companies, whereas state insurance commissioners regulate private insurance.

Germans are allowed to obtain health care from any physician or hospital and care is free at the point of delivery. Associations of German physicians negotiate with sickness funds to determine rates, but global budgets are set per capita. Hospitals in Germany are mostly public, although there is a growing segment of private hospitals that uses a DRG reimbursement model similar to Medicare's.

MEDICAID/CHIP

In the United States, Medicaid and the Children's Health Insurance Program (CHIP), which serve low income Americans, contain elements of several basic health care system models. Funds for Medicaid/CHIP come from state tax revenues, with matching contributions by the federal government. In part, this is similar to the systems in Australia and Canada, which also use a mixed federal and state/provincial funding model. In those two countries, decision making and negotiation of payment rates also take place at the state and province level; similarly, Medicaid/CHIP programs negotiate payment rates with providers, but with some federal oversight. Although a wide range of providers accepts Medicaid/CHIP patients, they are not required to participate in these programs. Similar to the case in many other countries, a person's eligibility for the Medicaid/CHIP program is determined by both federal and state rules. Medicaid/CHIP eligibility criteria are based primarily on income. Such **means tests** are unnecessary in countries with universal coverage, with exceptions for complementary coverage, which is available, for example, to the poor in France.

PRESCRIPTION DRUG PLANS

Coverage plans for prescription drugs share a number of characteristics across health care systems. Although most require a co-payment that includes some element of increased cost-sharing for the costliest drugs (e.g., branded drugs versus generics), each country designs its plan somewhat differently. Although the UK's NHS has co-payments, almost 90% of medications are exempt from them. The Netherlands, Australia, Canada, the UK, and Germany include prescription drug benefits as part of their overall health insurance programs.

Participants in the U.S. Medicare program must enroll in a separate plan (Medicare Part D) to obtain prescription drug coverage. Australia's NHI plan covers about a third of prescription drugs, but Australians need supplementary insurance if they want coverage for medications not on the approved national list. Most countries are adopting some form of comparative effectiveness evaluations to determine the value of new and existing pharmaceuticals.

Common Challenges Facing Systems

SPENDING INCREASES

As noted, the United States has had the world's highest per capita health care spending for more than four decades. Although health care spending has captured a growing share of GDP in all OECD countries, the share devoted to health spending also is largest in the United States, despite all the countries' having started at a similar level nearly 40 years ago (Anderson, Reinhardt, Hussey, & Petrosyan, 2003). The factors frequently listed in the health economics literature that have led to increased spending include:

- Growth of the private health insurance market with increasing administrative complexity;
- Supplier-induced demand, or the ability for physicians to recommend services that may or may not be medically necessary;
- Defensive medicine, or services ordered by health providers primarily to reduce the risk of malpractice law suits;
- Factor productivity, or the ability for health workers to complete more tasks in the same amount of time; and, what is often considered the most significant factor,
- Medical technology, or expensive, advanced capital investments.

AGING POPULATION

The percent of the population over age 65 increased in all OECD countries from 1970 to 2005, on average, by 36%. This increase has been due mainly to a combination of increasing life expectancy and declining fertility rates (Anderson & Hussey, 2000). Aging by itself has not been a major contributor to the rapid growth of health care spending in the United States and has been a somewhat larger factor in other OECD countries (White, 2007). Still, in the long term, increasingly older populations will experience a higher incidence (emerging cases) and prevalence (existing cases) of costly chronic conditions that could increase health care spending.

CHRONIC DISEASE AND COORDINATION OF CARE

Chronic diseases create a growing burden on health care spending in all OECD countries, although data on chronic disease costs are not available for most of them. Within the United States, 85% of health care spending is attributable to people with chronic diseases. Five of the most common chronic diseases (diabetes mellitus, chronic lower respiratory disease, cerebrovascular disease, ischemic heart disease, and cancers) accounted for an estimated 19% to 28% of the increase in overall U.S. health care spending between 1987 and 2000 (Thorpe, Florence, & Joski, 2004). Compared to European countries, the United States has consistently higher prevalence and treatment rates for these diseases (Thorpe, Howard, & Galactionova, 2007).

Compared to European countries, the United States has consistently higher prevalence and treatment rates for serious chronic diseases.

Chronic disease patients often have multiple conditions, see multiple providers, and receive numerous tests, procedures, and medications. Coordination of care for chronic disease patients is a challenge for any country. More centralized health care systems such as the NHS or NHI provide continuity across care settings. Receiving coordinated care within private health insurance plans in the United States remains difficult, due to complex benefit designs and limited networks. The increased use of electronic health records—already widely implemented in other OECD countries as well as in the VHA system—may improve coordination, and thereby improve quality of care and reduce costs (see Chapter 16).

IMPROVING QUALITY

One method to improve quality of care that many countries have adopted is to develop, implement, and enforce national clinical guidelines to guarantee a basic level of quality care. An additional benefit of national guidelines is the reduction in costs because of fewer unnecessary visits, tests, and procedures (see Chapter 13). Another approach to improving quality is to emphasize first improving access to care and health system data, then compare performance with benchmarks for similar countries or across regions of the same country.

Conclusion

This exploration of international health systems demonstrates that the U.S. system shares attributes with systems of many other countries. The existence of multiple payment systems makes the U.S. approach both unique and complex. Health insurance is administered by private insurance companies for U.S. employees, as is the case in the Netherlands or Switzerland. Although U.S. employees generally contribute to the cost of their health premiums, their employers also may contribute, which is the practice in France and Germany. Medicare beneficiaries experience a health system similar to that of Australia or Canada. U.S. military veterans who use the VHA system may feel camaraderie with UK citizens regarding their similar health care experiences. But, even within countries, various microsystems exist that do not always fit neatly into the models presented.

Each health system has pros and cons and it's clear that no one system has found the magic combination that leads to high levels of satisfaction, quality, and value. Lower costs tend to be associated with more centrally administered health systems, due to lower overhead and stronger cost-control measures. The tradeoff is that more decentralized health systems may offer more consumer choice, by relying more heavily on private health insurance options to supplement or cover gaps in benefits.

DISCUSSION QUESTIONS

1. What are the strengths and limitations of having multiple payers versus a single payer?
2. Which health system model would you recommend to low and middle income countries, and why?
3. What are the advantages or disadvantages of having strong government involvement in (a) health care financing, (b) pooling, and (c) provision of health care services?

4. Does having a diversified payment system covering different populations automatically mean lack of equity? Explain why or why not.
5. What are the advantages and disadvantages of collecting health insurance premiums through a payroll deduction compared to financing them through general tax revenues?
6. What health insurance system might work best for a country with a large percentage of the workforce outside the "formal" economic sector, where employees are paid under-the-table and not subject to payroll taxes?
7. What are the incentives, advantages, and disadvantages for insurance systems that pay primary care physicians through capitation compared to fee-for-service?
8. What are the incentives, advantages, and disadvantages for insurance systems that reimburse hospitals through diagnosis related group (DRG) payments, rather than fee-for-service or global budgets?

CASE STUDY

You are a program officer for a major health care foundation that wants to revitalize primary care in the United States. You've been asked to look at the experiences of other countries to see whether the methods and ideas they have used to promote primary care might have application in this country. Here is some of the information you have found.

Spain

Spain's new 1978 Constitution declared health protection and health care to be the right of every citizen and required creation of a "universal, general, and free national health system that guaranteed equal access to preventive, curative, and rehabilitative services" (Borkan, Eaton, Novillo-Ortiz, Corte, & Jadad, 2010).

Compared to the United States, by 2006, Spain had widened the gap in terms of greater life expectancy and lower infant mortality rates, and it had achieved or maintained lower rates of premature death for most major diseases, at an annual cost of less than $2,700 per person, compared to the U.S. per capita rate of almost $7,300.

Spain's rapid accomplishment relied on eight key principles: greatly strengthened primary care, giving citizens a voice in decisions, adopting electronic health records, creating an accessible network of community pharmacies (with medications free to people over 65 and some other groups), regional and local flexibility in implementing national policy, wide adoption of best practices, a systemwide approach that "transcend(s) traditional geographic, sector, and institutional boundaries," and a sustained, bipartisan commitment to achieving the goals of access and quality.

The system is funded through tax dollars. To assure that every citizen has services nearby, the country's 17 autonomous regions and communities are further broken down into health areas, which manage facilities, health services, and benefits for people in a prescribed geographic area, and even further, into "basic health zones" typically organized around a single primary care team and covering 5,000 to 25,000 residents.

Switzerland

In 1996, the Switzerland restructured its health system, in order "to turn the existing system of private voluntary health insurance into . . . a mandatory private social health insurance system" (Cheng, 2010). Today, 84 highly regulated private health insurers, which offer basic benefit packages and supplemental coverage, compete for enrollees. Swiss citizens are required to have the basic package and those who cannot afford it may receive a premium subsidy from the government, but government itself does not offer an insurance plan. Private insurers are not allowed to earn profits on the basic packages they offer, only on supplemental coverage.

Health care providers receive the same reimbursement for basic benefits, regardless of the income level of their patients or whether they are subsidized. Basic benefits cover (1) what a doctor prescribes, (2) pharmaceuticals included in the national formulary, and (3) controversial procedures included on a "positive list" by the national health authority. "Negative lists" contain items excluded from basic benefits.

In the future, Switzerland wants to abandon its fee-for-service system for ambulatory care and move to "integrated care," probably paid for on a capitated basis. Another step needed is to overcome the shortage of primary care physicians, who have long working hours and lower pay than specialists. Still, system leaders have managed to convince the citizenry that health promotion and disease prevention—pillars of primary care—are important parts of a complete health care system. But, says Thomas Zeltner, Switzerland's former health minister, health reform is "a never-ending task" (Cheng, 2010).

CASE STUDY DISCUSSION

Using the brief country descriptions and the other material about international experiences in this chapter:

1. What are alternative ways to use system-wide incentives to encourage delivery of high-quality, prevention-oriented primary care?
2. How might Americans be reoriented to using primary care, rather than costlier specialty services?
3. How does the design of the payment system affect individuals' choice of provider?
4. What appear to be the best ideas from other nations' experiences that could be tested in the United States as ways to increase primary care?
5. If Thomas Zeltner is correct and health reform efforts are never-ending, which of these promising ideas should be the top priority, or tried first?

REFERENCES

Anderson, G. F., & Frogner, B. K. (2008). Health spending in OECD countries: Obtaining value per dollar. *Health Affairs, 27,* 1718–1727.

Anderson, G. F., & Hussey, P. S. (2000). Population aging: A comparison among industrialized countries. *Health Affairs, 19,* 191–203.

Anderson, G. F., Reinhardt, U. E., Hussey, P. S., & Petrosyan, V. (2003). It's the prices, stupid: Why the United States is so different from other countries. *Health Affairs, 22,* 89–105.

Blendon, R. J., Schoen, C., DesRoches, C., Osborn, R., Scoles, K. L., & Zapert, K. (2002). Inequities in health care: A five-country survey. *Health Affairs, 21,* 182–191.

Blendon, R. J., Schoen, C., DesRoches, C., Osborn, R., & Zapert, K. (2003). Common concerns amid diverse systems: Health care experiences in five countries. *Health Affairs, 22,* 106–121.

Borkan, J., Eaton, C. B., Novillo-Ortiz, D., Corte, P. R., & Jadad, A.R. 2010. Renewing Primary Care: Lessons Learned from the Spanish Health Care System. *Health Affairs, 29,* 1432–1441.

Braveman, P. A., Cubbin, C., Egerter, S., Williams, D. R., & Pamuk, E. (2010). Socioeconomic disparities in health in the United States: What the patterns tell us. *American Journal of Public Health, 100,* S186–S196.

Cheng, T.-M. 2010. Understanding the 'Swiss Watch' Function of Switzerland's Health System. *Health Affairs, 29,* 1442–1451.

Davis, K., Schoen, C., Schoenbaum, S. C., Doty, M. M., Holmbren, A. L., Kriss, J. L., & Shea, K. K. (2007). Mirror, mirror on the wall: An international comparison update in the comparative performance of American health care. *The Commonwealth Fund Report, 59.*

Hussey, P. S., Anderson, G. F., Osborn, R., Feek, C., McLaughlin, V., Millar, J., & Epstein, A. (2004). How does the quality of care compare in five countries? *Health Affairs, 23,* 89–99.

Lee, S-Y., Chun, C-B., Lee, Y-G., & Seo, N. K. (2008). The National Health Insurance system as one type of new typology: The case of South Korea and Taiwan. *Health Policy, 85,* 105–113.

Singh, G. K., & Kogan, M. D. (2007). Persistent socioeconomic disparities in infant, neonatal, and postneonatal mortality rates in the United States, 1969–2001. *Pediatrics, 119,* e928–e939.

Singh, G. K., & Yu, S. M. (1995). Infant mortality in the United States: Trends, differentials and projections, 1950 through 2010. *American Journal of Public Health, 85,* 957–964.

Thorpe, K. E., Florence, C. S., & Joski, P. (2004). Which medical conditions account for the rise in health care spending? *Health Affairs,* Web Exclusive 26 August. Retrieved January 23, 2011, from http://content.healthaffairs.org/cgi/content/full/hlthaff.w4.437/DC1

Thorpe, K. E., Howard, D. H., & Galactionova, K. (2007). Differences in disease prevalence as a source of the U.S.-European health care spending gap. *Health Affairs, 26,* w678–686.

White, C. (2007). Health care spending growth: How different is the United States from the rest of the OECD? *Health Affairs, 26,* 154–161.

Population Health

II

The four chapters in Part II discuss the ways people become and stay healthy—or not. The first, Chapter 5, introduces the concept of population health. This is health promotion and disease prevention writ large. Pamela Russo explains that population health is not about the one-on-one interactions people have with their doctors or other care providers. It is about all the steps that can be taken to protect the health of large population groups.

Under the "medical model," a doctor will treat (at great expense) a smoker who develops lung cancer, but the population health approach would try to prevent smoking in the first place, through a multipronged effort at many levels—for example, employer rules against smoking on the job, community laws that prohibit smoking in public places, high state cigarette taxes, and large-scale federal communications campaigns. Population health interventions focus on the root causes of illnesses and injuries—whether social, environmental, or behavioral—and how these causes interact.

In Chapter 6, Laura Leviton and colleagues discuss how the population health approach is institutionalized through the often-invisible actions of public health agencies and programs. She explains how population health is operationalized through the well-defined "core functions" of public health, as they are administered primarily by various levels of government. Some of the key challenges and opportunities for public health in the next few years are described.

A significant root cause of many diseases and injuries is personal behavior. In Chapter 7, Tracy Orleans and Elaine Cassidy describe the importance of behavioral choices in health, paying special attention to efforts to reduce or prevent tobacco use—the case in which research has learned the most about influencing personal behavior. In addition, tobacco use has been the test-bed for learning how best to influence provider behavior, motivating and enabling physicians to offer their patients more effective anti-tobacco strategies.

Chapter 8 returns to a discussion of the familiar territory of doctors, hospitals, and other health care facilities. John Billings and colleagues describe the problem of lack of access to care, particularly as it results from being uninsured, and the effects of lack of access on people's health and the health system itself. With health reform, more Americans will be insured over the next few years and the chapter describes the likely effects that increased coverage will have on the health care system.

POPULATION HEALTH

Pamela Russo

The majority of this book concerns what happens *within* the walls of health care institutions—hospitals, clinics, physician offices, and long-term care facilities. The focus in those chapters is on how health care is delivered, financed, managed, and measured for quality and impact, and how access to appropriate and safe diagnostic and treatment modalities varies across populations. In several chapters, disparities in health care and outcomes are shown to exist between insured, underinsured, and uninsured groups; different races and ethnic groups; rural and urban populations; immigrant groups; and even between men and women.

However, access to high-quality medical care is not the only factor that leads to disparities in *health* between different groups nor are health care and medical services even the most important factors that determine the overall health of a population. This chapter documents the profound influences on health that occur *outside* of the health care system where the vast majority of people—or patients—spend the overwhelming majority of their time.

Whether people live long and healthy lives is largely determined by powerful social factors such as education, income, racial or ethnic group, and the quality of environments where they live, learn, work, and play. In fact, the effects of the systematic differences in *health care* are far smaller than the effects of the nonrandom differences in other determinants of health on a population's overall health outcomes. These influences that are *outside* the health care system greatly influence which groups of people are more likely to become ill in the first place, be injured, or die early. And these influences also help determine people's health care outcomes once they become sick, injured, or disabled.

The Population Health Model

The **population health model** seeks to explain and intervene in the causes of the systematic differences in health between different groups (Kindig & Stoddart, 2003). To do so, it analyzes the patterns or distribution of health between different groups of people in order to identify and understand the factors leading to poorer outcomes. These factors are often described as "upstream" factors, in the sense that they influence health through a series of pathways that may not be immediately visible (see also Chapter 7).

In addition, population health employs an **integrative model**, meaning that different factors are highly likely to intersect and combine to produce good or poor health and should be assessed in combination. Population health scientists use the term **determinants** of health rather than factor or cause, and the term the **multiple determinants** of health to describe five different types of determinants:

1. The social and economic environment—including factors like income, education, employment, social support, and culture
2. The physical environment—including urban design, housing, availability of healthy foods, air and water safety, exposure to environmental toxins
3. Genetics
4. Medical care, including prevention, treatment, and disease management
5. Health-related behavior, such as smoking, exercise, and diet, which in turn is shaped by the preceding determinants

Health is therefore conceptualized as the result of exposure to different patterns of these multiple determinants. Although the determinant categories are listed independently, they have substantial and complex interactions over the life course of an individual or group.

Some health care outcomes can, in turn, affect the determinants; that is, they can have a **reverse causality** impact on determinants. For example, although social determinants like income have an impact on health outcomes, becoming unhealthy also can have a negative impact on income (Kindig & Chin, 2009).

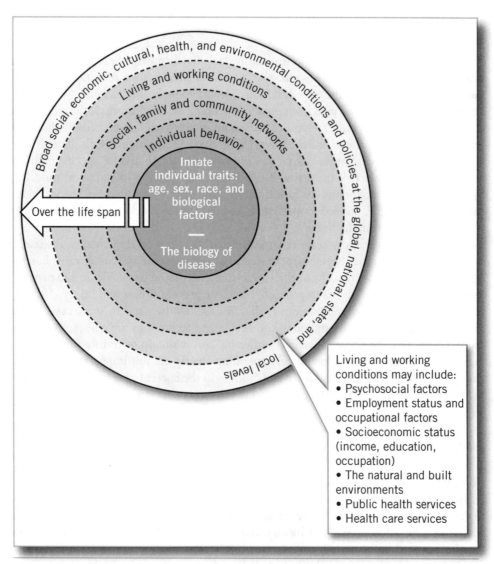

FIGURE 5.1

A guide to thinking about determinants of population health.
Source: Institute of Medicine (2002). *The future of the public's health in the 21ˢᵗ century.* Washington, D.C.: National Academies Press, p. 52. Reproduced with permission from National Academies Press, copyright 2002, National Academy of Sciences.

The population health paradigm is that of a web of causation, in which multiple different influences interact to produce good or poor health (see Figure 5.1). Over the past 40 years, a significant body of knowledge has developed demonstrating the profound effects of multiple determinants from different domains, as well as the interactions among them, their effects at different stages in the life course, from gestation to old age, and their cumulative effects.

The Medical Model

The **medical model**, in contrast, hones in on individuals and focuses on the factors that are more immediately linked to the pathophysiology of a person's disease. It is a reductionist model, in the sense that it searches for the most distal antecedents to poor health outcomes (disease diagnoses or complications), and puts an emphasis on defining the mechanisms at the cellular level that explain how these specific factors produce illness or act as markers of incipient disease. In turn, the therapeutic goal is to find the "silver bullet" that will stop or reverse the illness.

The medical model frames risk factors as working through disease-specific pathways and typically analyzes risk factors as if they were independent in statistical modeling. The medical model does consider how different biological systems within the individual interact—for example, the endocrine system and the cardiovascular system—but the lens remains focused within the body.

Health care is generally reactive—meaning, it responds to abnormality, disease, or injury, and as a result has been characterized as a "sickness care system" (Evans, Barer, & Marmor, 1994). Historically, the health care system has placed less value on and provided less reimbursement for efforts to promote health or prevent illness and injury. Although health care has achieved great strides in diagnosing, treating, and in some cases curing illness and injury—and although new knowledge and technology are constantly increasing the capacity to preserve life, relieve suffering, and maintain or restore function—the inexorable increases in U.S. health care spending clearly are not improving Americans' chances for living long and healthy lives. Children in the current generation are predicted to be the first in American history to have a shorter life expectancy than their parents.

Comparing the Medical and Population Health Models

Consider two examples, obesity and tobacco use, that illustrate the different explanatory and intervention approaches of the medical model versus the population health model. In the medical model, when an obese adolescent visits a health care provider, the provider will likely take a family medical history and a diet and physical activity history. These may be followed by laboratory tests to rule out hormonal or other physiological causes for obesity and to check for diabetes and other consequences of obesity. Interventions are likely to include referrals to nutritionists and recommendations for decreasing calories and increasing physical activity, with regular monitoring. In very serious cases (morbid obesity) or failure to achieve weight loss through these means, the patient may be referred for bariatric surgery.

> *The medical model does not ask* why *an epidemic of obesity has occurred over the past 20 years.*

The medical model does not ask *why* an epidemic of obesity has occurred over the past 20 years, or why there are higher rates of obesity in low income and minority populations, or grapple with the circumstances that make it difficult for many patients to comply with medical recommendations for eating less and exercising more.

In contrast, the population health model has identified a wide variety of causes that have worked synergistically—an unintended conspiracy of causes over time—to produce the epidemic and the differing patterns of obesity observed among population groups. These causes include:

- The higher density of fast food restaurants in low income neighborhoods (which offer high calorie, high fat, low nutrient, super-sized meals at very low prices)
- The presence of vending machines in schools (selling high calorie soft drinks as a source of needed revenue for the schools)
- Subsidized school lunches (containing high caloric and fat content, a result of agricultural policies)
- The decrease in physical education classes and near-elimination of recess periods (due to shrinking school budgets and a narrow focus on meeting academic test score requirements)
- Fewer children and adults walking or bicycling to school or other destinations (due in part to the lack of sidewalks, safe pedestrian crossings, and bicycle lanes)
- Increased busing of students (due to liability concerns)
- In urban, low income neighborhoods, few places to play or walk (due to unsafe playgrounds, crime, and violence)
- A lack of grocery stores with healthy food options, such as fresh fruit and vegetables in many neighborhoods (related to their higher cost and lower profit margins)

These determinants are all in the social and physical environmental domains and they strongly limit people's behavior choices. It is extremely difficult to achieve lasting lifestyle behavior changes in people who *do* have the economic resources to join gyms, have child care while they exercise, and afford healthier food choices. It is almost impossible to achieve such changes among people for whom healthy choices are out of their reach.

In a population health framework, the relevant interventions could include zoning law changes, menu labeling, working with fast food industries to provide healthier but still low-cost menu options, educational policies that encourage healthy food choices and increased physical activity in schools and after school, and so on. Such interventions are not traditionally considered part of the health arena by adherents of the medical model.

Tobacco use offers a second example. In the medical model, the focus is on individual patients who smoke or chew tobacco. The solution is framed in individual terms and is geared toward behavior change through cessation counseling and nicotine replacement options. Success requires having access to providers who support and encourage cessation (see Chapter 7).

In the population health model, the understanding of the problem includes the influences of tobacco production, advertising, distribution, and patterns of use in different groups and the interventions include smoke-free laws, tobacco taxes, and regulation of advertising and marketing. Without doubt, these population-wide policy changes are what have changed U.S. social norms regarding the acceptability of tobacco use and prompted a dramatic decrease in the rate of smoking.

Antitobacco policy changes are usually coupled with increases in access to cessation programs at the community level, such as free quit lines and free nicotine patches, which assist smokers to quit. The population health model also enables targeting policies toward groups with the highest rates of tobacco use and it responds to tobacco industry actions to redirect their advertising from the more affluent smokers who are able to access cessation programs to new, more susceptible markets, including youth, minorities, and people in developing countries (Kreuter & Lezin, 2001).

The Influence of Social Determinants on Health Behavior and Outcomes

The medical model is well accepted and respected by health care providers, laboratory researchers, clinical researchers, and health services researchers. Many people tend to regard medical knowledge as based on the "hard sciences," and thus as having greater likelihood of reflecting the "true" nature of human pathophysiology. The population health model, conversely, requires multiple disciplines to collaborate and integrate different social science concepts, methods, and data sources with those of the biological sciences. Although few people doubt that poverty and lack of education are associated with worse health—as the Australian-born population health researcher John Lynch says, population health is the "science of the bleedin' obvious"—they are not aware of the strength of the scientific basis regarding these effects, **gradients** in effects, the importance of interactions, and the biological pathways. They are even less aware of the most effective public health interventions.

> *Although few people doubt that poverty and lack of education are associated with worse health—as the Australian-born population health researcher John Lynch says, population health is the "science of the bleedin' obvious"—they are not aware of the strength of the scientific basis.*

It comes as a surprise to many users of the medical model that the social science disciplines are just as rigorous, if not more so in their analysis of data, that large longitudinal datasets that are collected under strict criteria, and that these are coupled with work in tightly controlled experimental settings. In fact, significant progress has been made in defining the pathways between the social determinants and health. In other words, how these factors "get under the skin," using a wide variety of methods including animal research; neuroimaging; experimental psychology studies; a variety of stress related physiological phenomena involving the cardiovascular, endocrine, neural, and other systems; and epigenetics (the study of gene-environment interactions).

The following section uses a sample of this body of work to illustrate the history and depth of the evidence. (For a recent, more comprehensive review of the research on the social determinants of health see Adler & Stewart [2010].) The initial work was based on epidemiological findings linking socioeconomic status, defined by either education, income, or occupational status or grade, to morbidity and mortality. One of the earliest studies to demonstrate the importance of social factors on health was Michael Marmot's Whitehall study, a longitudinal study conducted over two decades with results reported throughout the 1970s and 1980s.

The Whitehall study collected extensive information on more than 10,000 British civil servants, from the lowest rung of the income and rank hierarchy to the highest. Marmot found that the likelihood of death was about *three and a half times higher* for those in the lowest status rank (clerical and manual workers) than for those in the highest administrative jobs. Mortality rates increased steadily with every reduction in rank.

Such a steady increase is known as a "gradient" in the population health model and a "dose-response effect" in the medical model, where it is taken as evidence of a robust relationship between causal factor and outcome. None of the workers in this population were actually poor, and none had high exposure to work-related toxins or other risks in the physical environment. All had access to the British National Health System for their health care.

In addition, the same mortality gradient was observed for specific diseases, such as heart disease, stroke, lung cancer, injuries, and suicide. The prevalence of smoking did not explain the gradient, even though people in the lowest ranks were more likely to smoke. The gradient in heart disease mortality continued to be present after adjusting the data for different rates of smoking, high blood pressure, and high cholesterol. In other words, after controlling for the traditional medical model risk factors, the 3:1 difference in death rate by social class, based on occupational rank, could not be explained away.

This led researchers to consider the biological pathways through which differences in social class could influence health outcomes. The study of primates in the wild had shown significant differences between dominant and subordinate males in their endocrine systems' and other physiological responses to stress. Dominant animals rapidly recover normal physiology after stress, but the stress response continues in subordinate animals.

To investigate the relevance of this to Whitehall's civil servants, Marmot and colleagues analyzed blood pressure at work and at home. All ranks showed similarly elevated blood pressure while at work, but blood pressure at home was much lower among people in the top ranks. The researchers concluded that rank correlates directly with a better ability to cope with stress.

Over the past 20 years, further studies on the stress response have rigorously demonstrated its effects on multiple bodily systems in addition to the endocrine system, including the immunological, neural, and cardiovascular systems. These effects have been shown under both laboratory and community situations. A wide variety of stressful stimuli have been studied, including social subordination, lack of job control, discrimination, social isolation, economic insecurity, job loss, bankruptcy, and other situations provoking anxiety. The proposed pathway is that such situations result in greater stress, which leads to biological dysregulation, adverse physiological responses, and a common pathway of pathology, including the onset and progression of diseases.

The concept of **allostatic load**, developed first in animal models by Bruce McEwen (1998), demonstrated the involvement of the hypothalamic-pituitary-adrenal axis and the central role of the brain in animals subjected to stress. This model was then translated to human studies, which first focused on acute stress exposure. However, social disadvantage can result in prolonged stress (also known as toxic stress) and multiple studies of toxic stress have documented negative effects on a variety of biological systems, leading to permanent organ damage.

Scientists increasingly recognize that the mechanisms by which social determinants act depend on the context in which people encounter stressful events. One area of research focuses on "neighborhood effects," which include the interaction of social and physical environmental determinants; for example, the negative interaction between the physical environment (poor housing, areas of crime and violence, lack of stores with healthy foods, and so on) and social determinants related to poverty or discrimination.

Recent U.S. data on the links between social factors and health and the wide variations in health among groups come from the Commission to Build a Healthier America (2009), a national, independent, nonpartisan group of leaders that investigated how factors outside the health care system shape and affect opportunities to live healthy lives. The Commission's team of researchers compared average life expectancy by county and found significant, still-to-be-studied variations. For example, the average life expectancy in Bennett County, South Dakota, is 66.6 years, compared to 81.3 years in nearby Sioux County, Iowa—an almost 15-year difference.

Examination of the relationship between measures of education and income on U.S. life expectancy showed that:

- American college graduates can expect to live at least 5 years longer than Americans who did not complete high school
- Upper middle class Americans can expect to live more than 6 years longer than poor Americans, and this has a significant effect on national life expectancy, given that one-quarter of adults nationwide live in poor or near-poor households (middle income adults are defined as those with incomes of 200 to 399% of the federal poverty level, equal to between $34,340 and $68,680 for a family of 3 in 2007, whereas poor adults are those living at less than the federal poverty level, or $17,170 in 2007 for a family of 3.)
- People with middle class incomes can expect to live shorter lives than those with higher incomes (greater than 400% of FPL) whether or not they have health insurance

The Commission also examined the relationship between health status and educational attainment and racial or ethnic group. The measure of health status was self-reported assessment of one's own health as excellent, very good, good, fair, or poor. Studies have shown that self-reported health status corresponds closely with clinical assessments of overall health made by health professionals. For example, among the adults studied by the Commission's research team, those who reported being in less than very good health had rates of diabetes and cardiovascular disease that were more than five times as high as the rates for adults who reported being in very good or excellent health. Highlights of the results related to education status and race/ethnicity include:

- Overall, 45% of adults ages 25 to 74 reported being in less than very good health, with rates varying among states from 35 to 53%.
- The least educated adults (less than high school graduates) were more than *two to three times* as likely to be in less than very good health than the most educated adults (college graduates). Similar to the Whitehall study, there was a gradient in health by educational level, with the best health status reported by college graduates, followed by those with some college, followed by high school graduates, and finally by those with a less than high school degree.
- Health status also varied across racial or ethnic groups, such that non-Hispanic whites were more likely to be in very good or excellent health than were other groups nationally and in almost every state. In some states, non-Hispanic black and Hispanic adults were *more than twice* as likely as white adults to be in less than very good health.
- Analyzing both social factors together, non-Hispanic whites had better health status than adults in any other racial or ethnic group *at every level* of education. The gradient in health by educational level within each racial or ethnic group is shown in Figure 5.2.

Educational attainment may influence healthy choices and better health via multiple pathways. For example, people with more schooling may have a better understanding of the importance of healthy behavior. Or, higher educational attainment can lead to higher-paying jobs with greater economic security, healthier working conditions, better benefits,

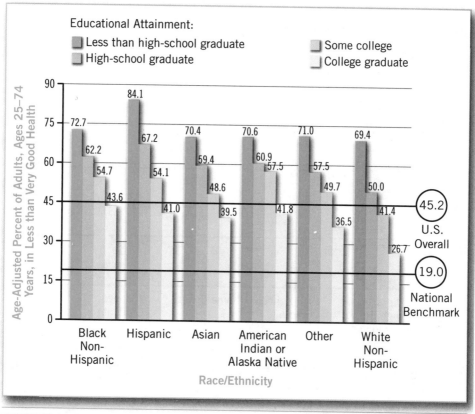

FIGURE 5.2

Gradients within gradients.

Source: RWJF Commission to Build a Healthier America (2009). Retrieved January 23, 2011, from http://www.commissiononhealth.org

and increased ability to purchase more nutritious foods and live in a safe neighborhood with good schools and recreational facilities. Figure 5.3 demonstrates that behavior and education both affect health: at every level of educational attainment, adults who smoke and do not participate in leisure time exercise are less likely to be in very good health than adults who do not smoke and do get exercise.

As in Marmot's analysis of the Whitehall study, it is clear that the effect of socioeconomic factors on health goes beyond simply affecting behavioral choices. Lantz and colleagues (2001) found that four common types of risky behavior (smoking, lack of physical activity, alcohol consumption, and body mass index) had only modest value in predicting functional status and self-rated health in low income populations *after controlling for* socioeconomic factors. They concluded that "risk behaviors are not the dominating mediating mechanism for socioeconomic health differences."

As noted previously, the population health model calls for integration of the multiple determinants of health, with consideration of both negative and positive interactions among different factors. The relationships between socioeconomic status and health are complicated. Clinical researchers increasingly recognize the importance of

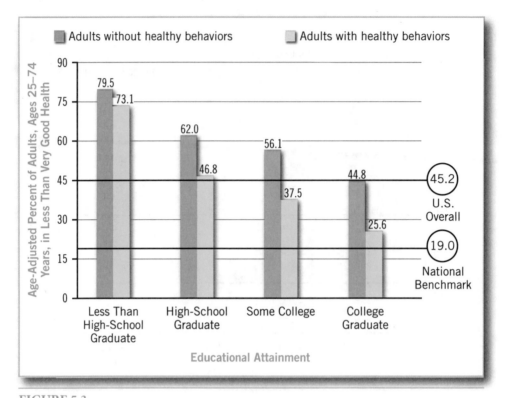

FIGURE 5.3

Health-related behavior and education both affect health.
Source: RWJF Commission to Build a Healthier America (2009). Retrieved January 23, 2011, from
http://www.commissiononhealth.org

socioeconomic status on health outcomes; however, to date, they tend to use simplistic
and inconsistent measures to represent socioeconomic determinants, rather than the more
refined methods developed by population health researchers. Finally, the most persistent
disparities in health between groups clearly involve the intersection of multiple types of
social disadvantages (Adler & Stewart, 2010).

Leading Determinants of Health: Weighting the Different Domains

The five different domains or categories of health determinants, described previously
in this chapter, do not make equal contributions to the health outcomes of populations.
This is not "new news." In the 1970s, Thomas McKeown (1976) concluded that improved
health and longevity in England over the previous 200 years were the result of changes
in food supplies, sanitary conditions, and smaller family sizes, rather than medical interventions. In the United States, John Bunker and colleagues (1995) estimated that during
the 20th century, medical care explained only 5 of the 30-years' increase in life expectancy, and between 1950 and 1990, when many new therapies were developed for infectious diseases and heart disease, medical care accounted for only 3 of the 7 years of life
expectancy increase.

During the 20th century, medical care explained only 5 of the 30-years' increase in life expectancy.

Medical care actually can be responsible for *increasing* mortality rates. A 2000 Institute of Medicine report publicized the startling finding that medical errors accounted for approximately 2% to 4% of U.S. deaths annually (Kohn, Corrigan, & Donaldson, 2000), whereas the U.S. Centers for Disease Control and Prevention (CDC) reported that health care system deficiencies (including access and quality, as well as safety) are responsible for approximately 10% of total mortality.

There was a period of time in the 1990s in which medical scientists expected that genetics could explain much of the variation in health between groups and individuals; however, experience to date has not borne out this belief. Current estimates suggest that, although many diseases have genetic contributors, only about 2% of U.S. deaths can be explained by genetic factors alone. On a population level, multiple studies of immigrants show that the patterns of disease and death change from those of the original country to those of the new country over a fairly short time period—again suggesting that genetics plays a relatively minor role in preventable deaths (Evans et al., 1994).

Health behavior (smoking, physical activity, substance abuse, sexual activity, diet, and so on) is considered a major determinant of health in both the medical and population health models. Analysis of data from 22 European countries showed that variations in health disparities could be attributed to variations in smoking, alcohol consumption, and access to care, but that the patterns of determinants of inequality were different for men and women, by country, and by which outcome was measured (Mackenbach et al., 2008). One thing is clear from the comparison of different types of behavior and outcomes across countries: the United States comes out first for both the prevalence and increasing incidence of obesity.

The best weighting scheme to determine the combined effects of determinants from different domains obviously depends on the health outcome of interest. Some outcomes will be more dependent on certain determinants than on others. Researchers have therefore estimated the relative contributions of the multiple determinants of health through what are called *summary* measures of mortality and morbidity: that is, measures that summarize the length and quality of life. Significant progress has been made in accumulating the empirical data that can yield the best approximations of the relative weights of each domain on summary health outcomes.

McGinnis and Foege (1993) reviewed the relevant literature from 1977 to 1993 to analyze the leading causes of U.S. deaths. Their ground-breaking paper was published in the flagship journal of the medical care model, the *Journal of the American Medical Association*. They concluded that approximately half of all deaths in 1990 were due to key nonmedical care factors, led by tobacco use and followed by diet and physical activity. Based on knowledge available at the time, they looked for the underlying causes of these types of behavior and attempted to attribute them to the various domains (social determinants, physical environment, genetics, etc.).

Ten years later, the Institute of Medicine (2003) revised that figure upward to 70% of all deaths, after reviewing evidence on a broader range of health determinants. The CDC repeated the McGinnis and Foege analysis with updated data and concluded that smoking remained the leading cause for preventable deaths, at approximately 18% of deaths, with poor diet and lack of physical activity a close second at 15.2% (Mokdad, Marks, Stroup, & Gerberding, 2004).

The America's Health Rankings report ranks states in order of health status and uses an expert panel to assign weights to four categories of determinants: behavior at 36% percent, community environment at 25%, public and health policies at 18%, and clinical care, 21% (United Health Foundation, 2007). The main point is that there are many ways to calculate the relative impact of various factors on health and, of them all, medical care is never the most significant.

In February 2010, the first national *County Health Rankings* report was released. This report ranked the overall health of every county within each of the 50 states and reported the contribution of the multiple determinants of health on each county's overall health using a population health framework. That is, health outcomes are viewed as the result of a combined set of factors and these factors are also affected by conditions, policies, and programs in their communities. The report is based on a model that compares overall rankings on health outcomes with rankings on different health factors (see Figure 5.4).

Health outcomes in the *County Health Rankings* represent how healthy a county is. They measure two types of health outcomes: how long people live (mortality) and how healthy people feel while alive (morbidity). The factors affecting health are divided into four categories of determinants and weighted based on analysis of all available data: health behavior has a weight of 30%, clinical care 20%, social and economic factors 40%, and physical environmental factors 10%. There is strong empirical validation for this model, as it explains approximately 70% of the correlation between health factors and health outcomes—an extraordinarily high level of explanation for any medical or population health statistical analysis.

The *County Health Rankings* project also demonstrates the dramatic amount of variation between one county and another in health outcomes and in health determinants. This variation is even greater than the variation in health care expenditures and health outcomes that has been demonstrated over many years by health services researchers. For example, the premature death rate in the least healthy counties was two and a half times greater than in the healthiest counties. Looking at health determinants, the disparities in adult smoking rates ranged from 26% in the least healthy counties to 16% in the healthiest counties; preventable hospital stays were also 1.6 times higher in the least healthy counties; the child poverty rate was 30% in the least healthy counties versus 9% percent in the healthiest county. On average, rural counties were less healthy than urban counties.

The bottom line message of the *County Health Rankings* is that some places are healthy and others are not, so that *where* people live matters to their health. The population health framework enables communities to see which factors are contributing the most to their poor or good health outcomes and thus choose to act to improve the factors affecting health, vitality, and productivity of all community residents.

Health Policy and Returns on Investment

In a rational world, the more that is known about the causes of a problem, the more resources would be allocated toward reducing the (modifiable) causes that contribute the most to the problem. In the United States, two-thirds of what we spend on health care is attributable to diseases that are preventable. Yet, we invest less than 5% of our more than $2 trillion annual spending on health on efforts to prevent illness, whereas 95% goes to direct medical care. The population health model shows that only perhaps 10% to 15% of

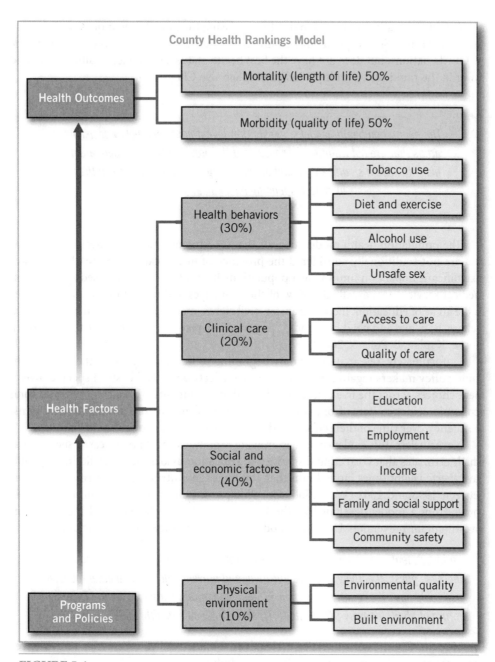

FIGURE 5.4
County health rankings model.
Source: University of Wisconsin Population Health Institute. (2010). County Health Rankings Model.
Madison, Wis.: Author. See also: http://www.countyhealthrankings.org/. Reprinted with permission of the
University of Wisconsin Population Health Institute.

preventable mortality could be avoided by increasing the availability or quality of medical care. The United States spends more on health care than any other country among the 32 OECD nations, but does not have the best health status, and in fact is falling lower and lower in the rankings on multiple indicators (See also Chapter 4).

> *The population health model suggests that investments and policy decisions in areas that are not traditionally considered the province of health care are more likely to have a significant impact on improving a population's health than will increased spending on medical services.*

The population health model suggests that investments and policy decisions in areas that are not traditionally considered the province of health care are more likely to have a significant impact on improving a population's health than will increased spending on medical services. An excellent review of the challenges and impact on health of policies in the areas of education, income transfer, civil rights, macroeconomics and employment, welfare, housing, and neighborhoods is provided in a recent comprehensive text (Schoeni, House, Kaplan, & Pollack, 2008).

Unfortunately, researchers are only beginning to be able to provide the evidence to guide policy makers regarding the comparative effectiveness and costs of specific investment choices across the five categories of health determinants. This lack of cross-sectoral economic evidence stems from complicated issues of interactions among determinants, the latency over time of their effects, and the absence of robust longitudinal data sets.

Nevertheless, this evidence base is growing rapidly, as shown by research such as that which estimates that correcting disparities in education-associated mortality rates would have averted eight times more deaths than improvements attributable to medical advances between 1996 and 2002 (Woolf, Johnson, Phillips, & Philipsen, 2007). Another example comes from a model developed by the Urban Institute, which calculated the return on investment for prevention. Using this model, Trust for America's Health concluded that:

> *an investment of $10 per person per year in proven community-based programs to increase physical activity, improve nutrition, and prevent smoking and other tobacco use could save the country more than $16 billion annually within five years. This is a return of $5.60 for every $1[invested] (Trust for America's Health, 2008).*

In 2009, the Commission to Build a Healthier America delivered a series of evidence-based recommendations to improve health, including:

- Ensure that all children have high quality early developmental services and support
- Redesign and fund the Women, Infants, and Children (WIC) and food stamp programs to increase the availability of nutritious food for low income Americans
- Create public–private partnerships to open and sustain full-service grocery stores in communities without access to healthful foods
- Feed children only healthy foods in schools
- Require all schools (K-12) to include time for all children to be physically active every day
- Become a smoke-free nation

- Ensure that decision makers in all sectors have the evidence they need to build health into public and private policies and practices

The last strategy in the list, which underscores the need to consider the health effects of policies, programs, and projects in other sectors can be achieved through the use of Health Impact Assessments (HIAs) (www.healthimpactproject.org/). HIAs have a long history of use in the same countries that led the way in developing and acting on the population health model. They are increasingly being used in a wide variety of decisions regarding transportation, housing, zoning, and other aspects of the built environment. Now they also are being used to assess the health effects of social policies related to education, labor, natural resources use, and a wide variety of other areas. HIAs provide a framework for analyzing the trade-offs between different outcomes, including health outcomes, to guide the public and its leaders.

The recommendations for improving health that come from a population health model are very different from the technological breakthroughs and "silver bullets" hoped for in the medical model. Population health interventions, with their broad reach across an entire population or community and with their focus on the fundamental causes of illness have the potential to create much greater improvements in the health of Americans than further spending increases for medical services.

Conclusion

The population health model has been accepted and used as a basis for health policy decisions in Europe, Canada, Australia, and New Zealand for almost 20 years, and the World Health Organization Commission on Social Determinants made recommendations for implementation in 2008.

The United States is finally catching up. Recognition of the importance and value of population health research in the United States is demonstrated by numerous types of evidence:

- The very large bibliography of relevant peer-reviewed articles appearing in top U.S. medical and health care journals, as well as books in multiple disciplines
- National Institutes of Health and Centers for Disease Control and Prevention funding of multidisciplinary population health research and intervention programs
- Numerous Institute of Medicine (IOM) review committees and reports on the multiple determinants of health and the 2009 IOM annual meeting dedicated to population health
- Interdisciplinary population health centers and training programs at premier universities across the country
- The MacArthur Network on Socioeconomic Status and Health, a research working group funded by the MacArthur Foundation from 1998 to 2010
- National commissions on population health and prevention, including Robert Wood Johnson Foundation's Commission to Build a Healthier America
- The release of the first national County Health Rankings report based on a multiple determinants of health

As the population health model is increasingly accepted, there is a risk that some groups will co-opt the term "population health" and try to transform it into something more in line with the medical model. This chapter should have made it clear what population health does *not* refer to: it is not a concept related to management of a capitated population in a health care management organization; it is not the patient population of a hospital system or potential patient population in the current framing of nonprofit hospital "community benefits" tax rules; and population health improvement cannot be accomplished by clinical preventive care alone.

There is, however, a great potential for population health strategies to aid medical care providers in improving the outcomes for their patients. As noted previously in the chapter, population health is not only about primary prevention, because the social, behavioral, and environmental determinants of health also strongly affect patients' ability and likelihood to carry out medical care providers' recommendations related to managing or reversing illness and disability.

As envisioned in the 2003 IOM report on the future of the public's health, collaboration among those using the medical and population health models would provide a more coherent national approach to health improvement. Such an approach would include an integrated set of determinants and outcomes and it would result in more strategic planning for the actions best suited for improving the conditions needed for all Americans to have the opportunity to lead healthy lives.

DISCUSSION QUESTIONS

1. The general public equates the word "health" with "health care." Polls asking people about their health typically result in responses about their health care experiences. How would you define health, and how would you assess how healthy a population is if you could ask the people in that population only one question on a survey?
2. Why do some refer to the health care system as "the sickness care system"? Do you agree or disagree?
3. Cross-sectional research shows that, on average, people with disabilities secondary to illness or injury have lower socioeconomic status than people without disabilities. How could longitudinal research help to explain whether this is because people of lower socioeconomic status are at higher risk of developing disabilities, or because disability leads to loss of income and thus lower socioeconomic status? In a population health model, how could lower socioeconomic status increase the risk of disability secondary to illness or injury?
4. The Commission to Build a Healthier America found that non-Hispanic whites were more likely to be in very good or excellent health than were other groups nationally and in almost every state. In addition, non-Hispanic whites had better heath status than adults in any other racial or ethnic group at every level of education, but all groups showed a gradient in health by educational level. What are some of the determinants that are likely contributing to this disparity in health between non-Hispanic whites and other groups after controlling for different educational levels?
5. It is possible that a community's *County Health Rankings* would suggest that the biggest driver of poor health in that community is unemployment. How would you present the case to your nonprofit hospital board that the biggest community benefit contribution the hospital could make would be to join and support an initiative to increase job openings in the community, rather than holding health fairs or offering educational lecture series?

CASE STUDY

Recent data show that that Americans consume, on average, more than three times the recommended level of sodium per day in their food and beverages. High salt intake contributes to high blood pressure and its complications—stroke, heart attack, congestive heart failure, and kidney failure. In fact, thousands of lives could be saved if sodium consumption could be lowered in people with high blood pressure.

CASE STUDY DISCUSSION

1. Contrast how a health care plan might address this problem in its patient population using the medical model versus how a public health official would address this problem using the population health model.

    Hint: Information on managing sodium intake may be found online at, for example, the New York City health department Web site, the CDC Web site, or by searching "sodium intake" or "sodium consumption" and the names of specific countries that have tackled this problem aggressively, notably Finland, the United Kingdom, or Canada.

2. How far can and should governments go in attempting to create a more healthful environment? Intrinsic to many population health policies is the specter of the "nanny state"—in this case, should everyone have to be exposed to lower sodium in their bread, in other common foods, and in restaurants, so as to protect people who have salt-sensitive illnesses? Should manufacturers bear the costs of manufacturing different versions of foods in order to protect the public's health? Should they be required to manufacture healthier foods even if customers prefer the others? Or be liable if they don't?

REFERENCES

Adler, N. E., & Stewart, J., eds. (2010). The biology of disadvantage: socioeconomic status and health. *Annals of the New York Academy of Sciences, vol. 1186.*

Bunker, J. P., Frazier, H. S., & Mosteller, F. (1995). The role of medical care in determining health: creating an inventory of benefits. In B. C. Amick III, S. Levine, A. R. Tarlov, & D. C. Walsh (Eds.), *Society & Health*. New York: Oxford University Press.

Commission to Build a Healthier America. (2009). *Beyond health care: new directions to a healthier America*. Princeton, NJ: Robert Wood Johnson Foundation.

Evans, R. G., Barer, M. L., & Marmor, T. R., eds. (1994). *Why are some people healthy and others not? The Determinants of Health of Populations*. New York: Walter de Gruyter, Inc.

Institute of Medicine. (2003). *The future of the public's health in the 21st century*. Washington, D.C.: National Academies Press.

Kindig, D., & Chin, S. (2009). Achieving 'a culture of health' - what would it mean for costs and our health status? Presentation at Altarum Institute Distinguished Scholars Seminar: *Innovation, Health, and Equity: Taking A Systems Approach to Health and Economic Vitality*. Ann Arbor, MI: Altarum Institute.

Kindig, D., & Stoddart, G. (2003). What is population health? *American Journal of Public Health, 93,* 380–383.

Kohn, L. T., Corrigan, J. M., & Donaldson, M. S., eds. (2000). *To err is human: building a safer health system.* Washington, D.C.: National Academy Press.

Kreuter, M., & Lezin, N. (2001). *Improving everyone's quality of life: A primer on population health.* Seattle, WA: Group Health Community Foundation.

. Lantz, P. M., Lynch, J. W., House, J. S., Lepkowski, J. M., Mero, R. P., Musick, M. A., & Williams, D. R. (2001). Socioeconomic disparities in health change in a longitudinal study of US adults: the role of health-risk behaviors. *Social Science & Medicine, 53,* 29–40.

Mackenbach, J. P., Stirbu, I., Roskam, A-J.R., Schaap, M. M., Menvielle, G., Leinsalu, M., & Kunst, A. E., for the European Union Working Group on Socioeconomic Inequalities in Health. (2008). Socioeconomic inequalities in health in 22 European countries. *New England Journal of Medicine, 358,* 2468–2481.

McEwen, B. (1998). Protective and damaging effects of stress mediators. *New England Journal of Medicine, 338,* 171–178.

McGinnis, J. M., & Foege, W. H. (1993). Actual causes of death in the United States. *Journal of the American Medical Association, 270,* 2207–2212.

McKeown, T. (1976). *The role of medicine: dream, mirage, or nemesis?* London, UK: Nuffield Provincial Hospitals Trust.

Mokdad, A. H., Marks, J. S., Stroup, D. F., & Gerberding, J. L. (2004). Actual causes of death in the United States, 2000. *Journal of the American Medical Association, 291,* 1238–1245. Correction printed in "Letters," from Ali H. Mokdad, (2005). *Journal of the American Medical Association, 293,* 293–294.

Schoeni, R. F., House, J. S., Kaplan, G. A., & Pollack, H. (2008). *Making Americans healthier: social and economic policy as health policy.* New York: Russell Sage Foundation.

Trust for America's Health. (2008). Prevention for a healthier America: Investments in Disease Prevention Yield Significant Savings, Stronger Communities. Retrieved September 1, 2010, from: http://healthyamericans.org/reports/prevention08/

United Health Foundation. (2007). *America's health rankings™: A call to action for people and their communities.* Minnetonka, MN: Author.

Woolf, S. H., Johnson, R. E., Phillips, R. L., Jr., & Philipsen, M. (2007). Giving everyone the health of the educated: an examination of whether social change would save more lives than medical advances. *American Journal of Public Health, 97,* 679–683.

6

PUBLIC HEALTH: POLICY, PRACTICE, AND PERCEPTIONS

Laura C. Leviton, Scott D. Rhodes, and Carol S. Chang

KEY WORDS

nongovernmental organizations	assessment
World Health Organization definition of health	assurance
public interest	policy development
utilitarianism	preemption of law
social justice	categorical funding
disease prevention	essential services
health promotion	public health infrastructure
universal prevention	health impact assessments
targeted prevention	collaborative leadership approach
core functions	

LEARNING OBJECTIVES

- Contrast defining characteristics of public health and curative health care
- Describe state, federal, and local authorities for public health law, regulation, and services
- Identify issues and concerns with the current system
- Identify emerging opportunities to correct the system

TOPICAL OUTLINE

- Who's in charge of public health?
- A healthy population is in the public interest
- Core functions of public health
- Governmental authority and services
- Challenges and opportunities

Who's in Charge of Public Health?

This chapter introduces the policies, programs, and practices that constitute public health in the United States. Public health is defined as "organized community efforts aimed at the prevention of disease and promotion of health" that focus "on society as a whole, the community, and the aim of optimal health status" (Institute of Medicine, 1988). It is the science, practice, and art of protecting and improving the health of populations. Historically, public health emphasized regulating and improving community sanitation and monitoring environmental hazards. Over time it greatly expanded its role in documenting and controlling communicable diseases and encouraging healthful behavior. Most recently public health has looked beyond the health sector to advocate for a broader set of policies that improve and protect health.

We first describe the distinctive goals and characteristics of public health that differentiate it from curative care and we outline the core functions of public health. We then describe the complex network of laws, regulations, authorities, and services involved. State, federal, and local government agencies, often called the *infrastructure*, are legally responsible for the core functions. In addition, a wide variety of other public, private, and nonprofit organizations carry out responsibilities that affect the public's health.

PUBLIC HEALTH EVERY DAY

Public health affects the lives of Americans profoundly, but more often than not it is invisible to them. A thought experiment shows how this works. Imagine waking up and going through your morning routine. You slept 8 hours for a change, because health experts claim that lack of sleep causes stress and other health problems. You wander into the bathroom and brush your teeth—they are still in your mouth thanks to adequate nutrition, the fluoride in your local water supply, and routine dental visits. You rinse your mouth with water that is safe to drink. Before it ever reached your faucet, it was checked for heavy metals such as lead (which causes lower intelligence in children) and chemicals such as polychlorinated biphenyls, which cause cancer. When you flushed the toilet, the waste did not get into the water supply where it could kill you.

You get your children ready for school; so far, they have all survived, never having had measles, diphtheria, polio, or other diseases that killed and maimed so many children in bygone days. The kids' breakfast includes cereal and pure pasteurized milk. (The kids talked you into buying the cereal they saw advertised on television. You looked at the nutritional label and thought the ingredients were okay.) You open the newspaper to see that a new influenza strain is spreading, and the authorities have renewed their advisory for hand-washing and travel precautions. Your sister calls to announce she is going to have a baby! She is able to have children because she never got infected with a sexually transmitted disease, which is one cause of infertility. She is not aware that the toast she is eating is fortified with folic acid, the B vitamin that prevents birth defects.

> *Public health affects the lives of Americans profoundly, but more often than not it is invisible to them.*

The two of you also discuss your father. He needs to have his flu shot right away! The last time he got flu, he went to the hospital with pneumonia and could have died. Both of you are worried about him, because he is overweight, still smokes, and never exercises. Is a heart attack, diabetes, or stroke in his future? The odds are not in Dad's favor. Quit-smoking programs are available in the community without charge, so you agree that Dad's doctor should try suggesting them again. Too bad there are no sidewalks in Dad's neighborhood; he loves to walk, but there is too much traffic. Does the senior center have an exercise program that might appeal to him? You buckle the kids into their safety belts. When you get to your job, you see an updated sign that reads: "607 days without an accident at this worksite."

DIVIDED RESPONSIBILITIES AND ISSUE-SPECIFIC ORGANIZATIONS

The responsibility for public health and the infrastructure to make it work are divided among many agencies across all levels of government and many **nongovernmental organizations**, professional associations, and businesses. In our thought experiment, for example, municipal authorities handle waste water, but the federal government regulates chemicals in the water supply. The federal government recommends physical activity for older adults, but senior centers, YM and YWCAs, private gyms, and city departments of parks and recreation provide opportunities for physical activity. The federal government sets standards for seat belts and air bags, but state laws mandate seat belt use and the penalties for violation, and local police generally enforce the laws.

At least four factors account for the complexity and diffuse responsibility for public health in the United States. The first factor is decentralized government; in the Constitution, states have responsibility for public health except where specified by federal law. How much responsibility the states in turn share with local government varies a great deal and rests with diverse agencies, boards of health, and municipal codes.

Second is the distinctive American tendency, first recognized by Alexis de Tocqueville in the 1830s, to design laws, policies, and organizations that are problem-specific, rather than general. For example, individual diseases receive special legal recognition, and new federal programs are created to deal with them. Diverse federal departments (see Chapter 1A) deal with such health problems as assuring pure food and drugs (FDA and USDA), monitoring and controlling infectious diseases (CDC), providing guidance to prevent chronic diseases (CDC, NIH), improving traffic safety (U.S. Department of Transportation, NHTSA), and assuring a healthy place to work (OSHA, MSHA, NIOSH).

A third distinctively American approach is the heavy reliance on nongovernmental organizations to achieve public health goals. Yet these organizations also tend to be issue-specific. For example, the American Red Cross, American Heart Association, the Planned Parenthood Federation of America, the Environmental Defense Fund, the American Foundation for AIDS Research, and local AIDS service organizations arose to meet specific needs.

The fourth cause of diffused responsibility lies in the broad definition of health goals and debates over what should be done to achieve them. The **World Health Organization**, in its widely cited 1978 **definition**, asserts that **"health is more than the absence of disease, it is "a state of complete mental, physical and social well-being.""** Well-being is achieved, for example, when children perform well in school and do not fear neighborhood violence, when physical and mental functioning is maintained well into old age, and when people have a better quality of life. But where, then, do we draw the line between health goals and other societal goals? Should we draw such a line? Who has responsibility, and for which goals?

A Healthy Population Is in the Public Interest

Two key assumptions distinguish public health from the health care delivery systems discussed elsewhere in this text: (a) a healthy population is in the **public interest**; and (b) working at a societal or community level, we can improve a population's health.

> *Most of the increased life expectancy seen in the 20th century was not accomplished by curative medical care, but by pervasive improvements in sanitation and nutrition—classic public health arenas.*

THE HEALTH OF POPULATIONS

Public health focuses on the *health status of entire populations,* not just individuals. It is concerned with the incidence, prevalence, and distribution of health problems (see Chapter 5). In using these indicators, public health aims to identify health problems and improve or resolve them through action at a community or collective level. This aim is well justified by past successes. Most of the increased life expectancy seen in the 20th century was not accomplished by curative medical care, but by pervasive improvements in sanitation and nutrition—classic public health arenas. In the present day, health still is most strongly determined by behavioral, community, and societal-level forces, not by medical care (see Chapter 7).

Public health takes action on the *health risks of the whole population.* Thus, although physicians address heart health for individual patients, public health efforts attempt to encourage heart health in entire populations by addressing cholesterol, high blood pressure, unhealthy weight, sedentary lifestyle, and smoking (U.S. Department of Health and Human Services [DHHS], 2000). In the same way, laws requiring seat belts (and their enforcement) protect the entire population, because everyone is at risk of a serious traffic accident.

THE PUBLIC INTEREST JUSTIFICATION

Since ancient times, people have taken action to protect themselves when faced with plague, famine, and environmental disaster. Prevention became effective in the 19th century, when bacteriology emerged as a discipline and cities created clean water and sanitation systems. In that era, public health was justified mostly on **utilitarian** grounds: the greatest good for the greatest number. Healthy people were (and are) a more productive workforce and better able to defend the nation (Rosen, 1993). This is still a compelling case: a recent report describes how health issues impair the combat readiness of America's youth (Mission: Readiness, 2010).

However, public health today is also justified as a human right, and public health is seen as a means to achieve **social justice** by addressing social and economic disparities in health. Conservatives challenge this rationale for public health but, in truth, most public health services serve both utilitarian and social justice aims. For example, many local health departments provide medical care to the poor, but these efforts also help produce healthy children, better able to learn, and a healthier workforce. Also, libertarians point out that collective action for community benefit limits individual liberty (Leviton, Needleman, & Shapiro, 1997). Indeed, public health policy and practice usually balance individual freedoms and collective benefits. For example, health departments have police powers to control infectious disease as a "clear and present danger," but they need to do so without appearing to abuse this power.

Finally, some Americans may question whether the government should be involved in public health: can't private health care address these issues? In fact, government services address some important market failures of both curative and preventive care. For example, private physicians greatly under-diagnose dangerous sexually transmitted diseases, and they lack the health department's legal authority to notify and treat sexual partners. As a result, *only* government action can prevent the spread of gonorrhea, HIV, and other sexually transmitted infections (Eng & Butler, 1997).

A COLLECTIVE FOCUS ON PREVENTION AND HEALTH PROMOTION

Prevention

Public health focuses primarily on health promotion and **disease prevention**. Prevention works at a collective level through health education and health promotion, changes in policy or law, and consensus of professional societies about relevant individual prevention efforts. The U.S. Preventive Services Task Force (U.S. Agency for Healthcare Research and Quality, 2009) uses three long-accepted categories to describe the full array of potential preventive interventions:

- *Primary prevention,* helping people avoid the onset of a health condition, including injuries
- *Secondary prevention,* identifying and treating people who have risk factors or preclinical disease
- *Tertiary prevention,* treating people with an established disease, in order to restore their highest functioning, minimize negative impact, and prevent complications

> *Disease prevention and health promotion are rarely completely effective, because there are no "magic bullets" for most health problems.*

These categories, especially tertiary prevention, obviously spill over into individual medical care delivery, but at a systems level, they are public health issues. Providers need guidance and support to carry them out. In Table 6.1 we can see the differences between individual and collective prevention for heart disease and stroke. Notice that successful prevention for an individual (in this case, a person who might have a heart attack or stroke) depends on the widespread availability of prevention services at a *population* level.

TABLE 6.1

Differences Between the Roles of Individual Medical Care and Public Health

	Individual Medical Care	Public Health
Primary prevention	Encourages patients to maintain healthy weight, be physically active, and not smoke	Works to establish bike and walking paths and to eliminate trans fats from foods, offers smoking quit-lines, advocates for smoke-free public spaces and higher cigarette taxes, provides prevention guidelines to medical care providers
Secondary prevention	Regular checkups for detecting and treating high blood pressure, elevated cholesterol, and other risk factors	Mounts public service campaigns about the importance of controlling blood pressure and "knowing your number" for cholesterol, provides guidelines to medical care providers on diagnosis of blood pressure and hypercholesterolemia
Tertiary prevention	Medical treatment to save the heart muscle after a heart attack or to prevent complications from stroke, treatment of atherosclerosis, cardiac rehabilitation, and medication to restore function and prevent recurrence	Provides guidelines to medical care providers, creates widespread awareness of the symptoms of heart attack and stroke and the need to seek help quickly, provides CPR training, provides automated external defibrillators in public places and worksites, establishes effective emergency systems, sponsors patient support groups

Health promotion is defined as "the combination of educational and environmental supports for actions and conditions of living conducive to health" (Green & Kreuter, 1999). Health promotion often focuses on prevalent types of behavior that promote or impair health (see Chapter 7). An important resource for public health, the federal Department of Health and Human Services' guide, *Healthy People,* provides a comprehensive review of priority health risks, effective strategies, and public health focus areas for the nation, each with many specific, but ambitious, objectives. These areas are updated every 10 years, and those for *Healthy People 2020* are presented at http://www.healthypeople.gov. Progress in meeting these objectives has been very uneven (Sondik, Huang, Klein, & Satcher, 2010). Disease prevention and health promotion are rarely completely effective, because there are no "magic bullets" for most health problems. A residual group of people will continue to fall prey to illness and injury. For example, heart attacks still occur, even with all the primary and secondary prevention strategies currently in place.

Universal prevention means that everyone receives an intervention equally, whereas **targeted prevention** involves identifying and serving people at higher risk. When they are possible, universal approaches are often more effective in improving the health of populations. The case of traffic safety illustrates these approaches. People who drive while intoxicated are clearly at high risk of injury, and targeting drunk drivers improves road safety for everyone. However, universal protections, such as seat belts, air bags, and safer vehicles contribute much more to reducing traffic fatalities and injuries, because they help everyone, even those who never encounter a drunk driver (National Highway Traffic Safety Administration, 2010). Combining several strategies can have a cumulative benefit.

Targeted prevention is an important focus for public health when the risk is prevalent and when there are effective means to identify and treat it. For example, a national campaign in the 1970s led to improved identification and treatment of people with high blood pressure. This, in turn, greatly reduced premature death and disability from cardiovascular disease (U.S. Centers for Disease Control and Prevention [CDC], 1999). However, an initial goal was to make sure that providers screened *all* their patients for high blood pressure, a universal strategy with a population focus.

Core Functions of Public Health

DEFINITION OF CORE FUNCTIONS

Public health serves three **core functions** to solve health problems at a population level (Institute of Medicine, 1988). **Assessment** of public health problems involves understanding their prevalence, severity, and causes, using various well-tested statistical tools. Public health agencies have the primary responsibility for surveillance of population health status, monitoring of disease trends, and analysis of the causes of those trends. With the advent of electronic health records, shared databases, and high-speed computing and connectivity, public health assessment is undergoing profound changes. These improvements are needed to respond rapidly to potential bioterrorism, pinpoint and analyze outbreaks of infectious diseases, and contain virulent new infectious diseases, such as H1N1 influenza (Institute of Medicine, 2003). New applications of such tools as geographic information systems (GIS) make it possible to assess local environmental factors that contribute to poor health—for example, mapping healthy food access onto data about obesity and diet-related death rates (Giang, Karpyn, Laurison, Hillier, & Perry, 2008) or using the prevalence of asthma inhaler use in various neighborhoods to pinpoint local situations that are triggers for asthma (http://asthmapolis.com/explore/).

The second core function, **policy development**, is to create and advocate for solutions to achieve public health goals. Formal policy development includes devising laws and regulations to protect the public, as in the case of environmental protection; funding and reimbursement for specific services such as child immunizations; and setting guidelines or standards for services such as laboratory testing for infectious diseases.

The third core function, **assurance**, involves enforcement of policy, as in the case of sanitation inspections of restaurants or safety inspections of nursing homes; ensuring proper implementation of necessary services, as in the supervision of home visits to new mothers in disadvantaged communities; and adequate crisis response, as when public health plays a role in coping with natural disasters. As described here, many public health departments take on a special assurance function—direct health care provider—to assure that indigent Americans receive health care.

In order to fulfill all three core functions, public health organizations are highly dependent on other organizations and individuals. For *assessment*, public health relies on medical care providers, first responders, and others to provide the necessary data on births, deaths, reportable diseases, and environmental hazards. For *policy development* it relies on advocates and policy makers who share a common interest in public health goals. For *assurance* it relies on complementary health care services and voluntary compliance with standards and regulations. Public health organizations do not have the legal authority, financial capability, or personnel to address all health problems by themselves. Realistically, public health agencies need to collaborate with other organizations that have the power and resources to achieve many public health outcomes—for example, in promoting worker safety, assuring safe food, or building bicycle and pedestrian-friendly streets for physical activity.

CORE FUNCTIONS: AN EXAMPLE

The following example, concerning the birth defect spina bifida, illustrates the cyclical problem-solving approach used in public health (see Figure 6.1). Different types of assessment, policy development, and assurance issues emerge during this cycle.

1. ***Define the problem:*** Spina bifida is a neural tube defect that develops in the first 3 to 4 weeks of pregnancy, when the "neural tube" that will form the spine does not close properly. In its most severe form, spina bifida leads to leg paralysis, bowel and bladder control problems, and, without treatment, mental retardation. Spina bifida affects 3.05 out of every 10,000 live births (*Assessment*).
2. ***Identify causes:*** The CDC projects that 50% to 70% of spina bifida cases can be prevented if women take enough folic acid (a B vitamin) before and during pregnancy. Folic acid is most effective in promoting healthy neural tube development when taken before pregnancy and during the critical first weeks. For this reason, CDC recommends that, even before they become pregnant, women take a multivitamin with 400 mg of folic acid every day and eat foods rich in folic acids (*Policy Development*).
3. ***Develop and test interventions:*** Unfortunately, women may not know they are pregnant until it is too late, and the defect has developed. Also, foods that naturally contain folic acid may not be readily available to the poor (*Assessment*). One alternative is to fortify common foods with folic acid (*Policy Development*).
4. ***Implement the interventions:*** Since 1998, the government has required that enriched cereal, pasta, flour, and bread products include folic acid (*Assurance*).

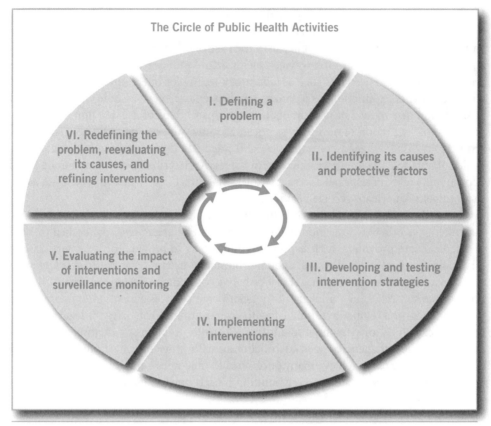

FIGURE 6.1

The circle of public health activities.
Source: U.S., Department of Health and Human Services. (2001, revised January 2007). *The Surgeon General's Call to Action To Prevent and Decrease Overweight and Obesity* (p. 3). Rockville, MD: Author.

5. ***Evaluate their impact:*** Since the fortification requirement began, the rate of spina bifida in the United States has declined by 31% *(Assessment)*.
6. ***Revisit and refine:*** Many scientists believe that the amount of folic acid in grain products is not enough and want to change the regulation to increase it *(Policy Development)*.

Governmental Authority and Services

STATE AUTHORITY FOR PUBLIC HEALTH

State Law

The 10th Amendment to the U.S. Constitution gives states the primary responsibility for public health. The 50 states vary greatly on how they define and delegate public health authority and responsibility. States enacted public health statutes over time to respond to specific diseases or health threats. These laws are fragmented and badly out of date (Gostin, 2000; Institute of Medicine, 2003). For example, some state laws have separate sections for specific communicable diseases, instead of standard approaches to address infectious disease in general. This leaves them with no standards for addressing new infectious diseases. Some state public health statutes do not reflect advances in public health practice and constitutional law, or they neglect important safeguards for privacy and due process and against discrimination. Inconsistencies among states' public health laws create problems when diseases and emergencies cross state lines, as they do in the event of bioterrorism, natural disasters, or pandemic disease.

> *Inconsistencies among states' public health laws create problems when diseases and emergencies cross state lines.*

For these reasons, public health law is reemerging as a powerful force to improve effectiveness. The Model State Public Health Act takes a systematic approach to establishing authority and implementing public health responsibilities. As of 2008, the Model Act was introduced in whole or in part through 134 bills or resolutions in 33 states, of which 49 passed (Centers for Law and the Public's Health, 2008). The Model Act addresses modern surveillance and reporting, investigations of specific outbreaks, testing and screening, immunization, and use of quarantine.

Although the Model Act addresses inconsistencies within a state, other improvements are needed for problems that cross state lines. Currently, the states and localities have mutual aid agreements and laws that permit government personnel to work across state borders during emergencies. However, incompatible state privacy laws could be a serious problem, as they were in the case of Hurricanes Katrina and Rita. In those instances, Gulf Coast residents from at least three states were evacuated to every state of the union, where they were served by emergency personnel brought in from still other states. The DHHS Office of Civil Rights, which administers the Health Insurance Portability and Accountability Act (HIPAA), the nation's primary health information privacy law, has developed a tool to help sort out conflicting privacy standards.

Public health professionals advocate enactment of the Model State Public Health Emergency Powers Act. It aims to ensure timely and effective planning and response to public health emergencies while respecting individual rights. As of 2006, it was introduced in whole or in part through 171 bills or resolutions in 44 states. Thirty-eight states have passed a total of 66 bills or resolutions that include provisions drawn from, or similar to, the Act (Centers for Law and the Public's Health, 2008).

State Health Departments

A state's chief health officer directs the department of public health and may report directly to the governor or to an officer in the governor's cabinet. The health department's position in the chain of command affects the power of its director and the quality of the services it manages. In 2005, 29 state public health departments were freestanding, whereas 21 were bureaus within a larger umbrella department (Beitsch, Brooks, Menachemi, & Libbey, 2006). Umbrella departments combine public health with related programs, such as Medicaid, human services and welfare, mental health and substance abuse, or environmental management. Medicaid and public assistance programs, being among the costliest state programs, tend to garner most of a governor's attention.

The way various health-related programs are organized affects how well public health activities can be coordinated. For example, environmental protection is often located outside the health department, in which case conservation, wilderness preservation, or litigation around toxic spills may head that agency's agenda. This situation often leaves less opportunity for effective interaction with the health department, even though it must monitor potential health consequences of environmental exposures.

INTERGOVERNMENTAL RELATIONS

Federal–State Relations

Although the states have constitutional authority to implement public health, a wide variety of federal programs and laws affect their work. Federal law relating to public health preempts state laws, just as state law preempts local laws. **Preemption** is extremely important to many areas of public health, because the federal government can require minimum protections below which states cannot go—a "floor preemption." For example, the Clean Water Act requires a minimum standard for water in all states, although states are allowed to have more stringent standards. But "ceiling preemption" can pose an obstacle to prevention when states and localities are more aggressive than the federal government. For example, the tobacco industry challenged state and local regulation of tobacco in the courts and this may happen again if local attempts are made to regulate junk food. In our example of birth defects, states could not require more folic acid in foods than required by the federal standard.

The federal agencies working in public health are described in Chapter 1A. States must constantly interact with these federal agencies. For example, DHHS provides substantial support directly to state health departments in the form of block grants for maternal and child health and preventive services and to state agencies for child welfare services, substance abuse, and mental health. The CDC provides grants and cooperative agreements to states, cities, and community-based organizations for HIV prevention, chronic disease control, and in 2010, for improving state and local infrastructure (see later). The U.S. Department of Agriculture (USDA) provides health departments with direct support for food assistance and nutrition education. The Environmental Protection Agency (EPA) provides direct resources to the states for environmental management. Most of these funding streams are **categorical**—that is, the funding is intended for specific categories of people or special purposes. Congress authorizes categorical funding to address a specific health problem, such as preventing AIDS or infant mortality. However, categorical funding limits states' flexibility to deliver a range of relevant services with available resources.

Both the state and federal governments have strengths and resources for public health. States and localities usually understand local problems better and how local conditions affect services. Meanwhile, the federal government has greater resources and scientific expertise for tackling large and complex health threats. The CDC, for example, leads the investigation of serious disease outbreaks, such as H1N1, and makes recommendations for both clinical and community prevention. The federal government also steps in when health threats cross state borders, or when states cannot comply with federal regulations, by offering technical assistance and financial support.

Delegation of State Authority to Local Health Departments

A 2005 survey classified the way that states share power between state and local public health departments (Beitsch et al., 2006). Thirteen states have centralized public health powers with no autonomous local public health departments, only satellite offices around the state. Twenty-one states use a decentralized approach in which the state public health agency does not directly perform public health services and minimally regulates local and municipal services. The state delegates public health authority and direct responsibility to local communities. Often this means that municipalities create a board of health and a local health department. Sixteen states use either a mixed or a shared-authority model, sharing public health functions between state and local governments. The local public health authorities enjoy independence from state control over their assigned responsibilities, but on some matters they must defer to the state department of health.

The National Association of County and City Health Officials Web site (www.naccho.org) offers further detail on the range of organizational arrangements, responsibilities, and authority of local health departments. One reason that state–local health department arrangements are so varied is simply historical. The first public health agencies were formed in the early 1800s and were primarily city-based. Later in the 19th century, state health agencies began to form. Throughout the 20th century, county health departments developed. One can see the effects by comparing older states to states that were admitted to the union more recently: Massachusetts has 351 local boards of health, whereas Oregon has 24 county health departments. Massachusetts is working on consolidation of its health departments as a quality improvement process.

PUBLIC HEALTH SERVICES

Essential Services

State responsibilities for public health generally include disease and injury prevention, sanitation, controlling water and air pollution, vaccination, isolation and quarantine, inspection of commercial and residential premises, food and drinking water standards, extermination of vermin, fluoridation of municipal water supplies, and licensure of physicians and other health care professionals. However, the specific activities and services provided vary widely across states and localities.

In the face of this variation, public health professionals agree that all health departments should provide the 10 **essential services** listed in Table 6.2. The ability of every health department to do so is questionable. Most are seriously understaffed. Staff skills in many local health departments are weak. Large numbers of the most experienced professionals are on the verge of retirement (Gebbie & Turnock, 2006). Health departments have difficulty replacing well-trained personnel, because of a low supply of training slots, as well as low salaries and rural location of many local health departments (U.S., DHHS, Health Resources and Services Administration, 2005). Departments with undertrained staff cannot be expected to establish effective partnerships with other organizations, particularly those in the highly professionalized health care sector. These issues are addressed in the final section.

Public Health Departments as Providers of Last Resort

In the mid-1970s, many state and local health departments shifted resources away from traditional public health initiatives and became direct providers of primary and preventive care for people with limited options for care (Wall, 1998). By the late 1980s, for example, 92% of local health departments were immunizing children, 84% were providing other child health services, and nearly 60% were offering prenatal care services. The emphasis on direct-care services was prompted by the growing number of people without health insurance and by the growing number of communities in which the local health department was the only or at least the primary source of care for the medically indigent. At the

TABLE 6.2

Ten Essential Public Health Services

Assessment
1. Monitor health status to identify community health problems.
2. Diagnose and investigate health problems and health hazards in the community.

Policy Development
3. Inform, educate, and empower people about health issues.
4. Mobilize community partnerships to identify and solve health problems.
5. Develop policies and plans that support individual and community health efforts.

Assurance
6. Enforce laws and regulations that protect health and ensure safety.
7. Link people to needed personal health services and assure the provision of health care when otherwise unavailable.
8. Assure a competent public health and personal health care workforce.
9. Evaluate effectiveness, accessibility, and quality of personal and population-based health services.

Serving All Functions
10. Research for new insights and innovative solutions to health problems.

Source: Abstracted by the author from: Institute of Medicine. (2002). *The future of the public's health in the 21st century.* Washington, D.C.: National Academies Press.

same time, however, the growing emphasis on direct-care services meant fewer resources for activities to improve the health of *populations*. This shift prompted concern among many public health leaders. The public health department seemed to be retreating from its core mission (population-based activities), just as the nation was experiencing an epidemic of public health problems.

The federal health reform law, the Patient Protection and Affordable Care Act of 2010 (ACA), will change this situation over time. The law expands Medicaid coverage and subsidizes health insurance for other poor individuals, who may choose providers other than the health department. At a minimum, the health department will receive more reimbursement for the care of indigent people. The Act also provides a tax benefit to providers working in underserved areas, so the number of providers in such areas may expand and alleviate pressure on health departments. The law reimburses evidence-based preventive services for individuals through Medicare and Medicaid, so health education campaigns and public screenings for disease can become more effective and eventually, less necessary. In addition, however, both the recent stimulus funding (American Recovery and Reinvestment Act of 2009) and the ACA provide substantial funding to better support the prevention services—collective prevention—of health departments and communities. Implementing these activities at scale will be the next big challenge for health departments nationwide.

Challenges and Opportunities

In order to maintain public protections and make further progress, public health must improve its infrastructure, communicate its value to the public, be more effective in advocating for policies that affect health, and engage the wide variety of nongovernmental organizations that are so vital to carrying out its goals.

IMPROVING THE INFRASTRUCTURE

New Federal Resources; Declining State and Local Resources

At the federal level, there is some good news for **public health infrastructure**. The ACA authorized $15 billion dollars over 10 years for a Prevention and Public Health fund. In FY2010, $650 million is authorized, and the figure rises over time to $2 billion in FY2015 and thereafter (Trust for America's Health, 2010a). Funding for specific services, such as immunizations, is also secured. Better planning and coordination of prevention are mandated by the Act and through executive orders. For example, the White House has ordered coordination of childhood obesity prevention efforts across the USDA, CDC, National Institutes of Health, and Department of Education (White House, 2010). In addition, the federal stimulus fund allocated $500 million in FY2010 to a competitive grant program called *Communities Putting Prevention to Work*, which will fund state and local obesity and tobacco prevention programs.

Earlier in this decade, substantial new federal funding went to improve public health emergency preparedness. The anthrax attacks of 2001 vividly highlighted public health's shortfalls and led both the public and policy makers to pay renewed attention to it. With the possibility of additional biological, chemical, or radiological attacks fresh in mind, Congress appropriated much more funding to CDC and state health departments, enabling new hires, upgrades to the Health Alert Network, and improved informatics. The additional funding strengthened the overall public health infrastructure, in addition to fortifying the country against terrorism (Steib, 2004).

The bad news is at state and local levels, where resources and staff continue to stagnate or decline. Health departments have been hard-hit by the recession of 2009–2010, and the workforce is declining at the local level, according to the National Association of County and City Health Officials.

Training, Certification, and Accreditation

There has been considerable movement to upgrade the competence of individual public health workers. Schools of public health are vital to many of the country's public health functions. However, only a small percentage of health department employees have an advanced public health degree. The existing workforce needs to be upgraded through new continuing education programs, management academies, and certificate programs (Institute of Medicine, 2009). Some personnel, such as public health educators, have had national certification for many years. For others, certification is voluntary: the National Public Health Performance Standards Program (U.S. Centers for Disease Control and Prevention, 2004) gives guidance on the specific competencies needed for jobs in public health laboratories, informatics, and environmental health technology.

Public health agencies are not currently subject to national standards or reviewed by an external accrediting body. The accreditation of state and local governmental public health departments is therefore an important development (Public Health Accreditation Board, 2010). It provides benchmarks for quality improvement, establishes accountability for providing good services, strengthens the credibility of public health agencies, and, when health departments cannot meet accreditation standards, gives a basis to advocate for more resources.

NEW RESPONSIBILITIES FOR PUBLIC HEALTH

Since the 2001 anthrax attacks, public health agencies have faced the added responsibility of protecting the public against bioterrorism threats and other public health emergencies, such as pandemic influenza. Diseases spread much more quickly than they did in the past, because of international travel (e.g. influenza viruses), urban overcrowding and poverty (e.g., tuberculosis), climate change (e.g., cholera and malaria), and other reasons.

In particular, viruses can mutate quickly into new strains for which people have no immunity. Experts agree that another severe flu epidemic is not only inevitable, but also likely to happen soon. Three times during the 20th century, new flu strains have generated pandemics. For example, in 1918, a billion people worldwide were infected with a particularly dangerous influenza virus and 40 to 50 million of them died. In 1957, 2 million people died of flu and 1 million died in 1968 (Center for Infectious Disease Research & Policy, 2007).

Public health preparedness and response has improved considerably in recent years, including global surveillance networks, stockpiles of vaccines, and better communications to deal with outbreaks. Nations are now required to report unusual and serious outbreaks of disease to the World Health Organization within 24 hours.

The H1N1 flu in particular is of great concern, but public health systems' response to the threat in 2009 was exemplary, thanks to the new emphasis on emergency preparedness. Within a few weeks of first being detected in Mexico, the virus spread throughout the United States and many other countries. In June, the World Health Organization raised its pandemic alert to the highest level. Mexican authorities reported the outbreak of H1N1 8 days after they first started investigating pneumonia cases. The CDC was notified 4 days later. Federal, local, and state public health departments took unprecedented action to detect, track, and prevent H1N1's spread. DHHS declared a public health emergency, authorizing laboratory testing and the release of medications from the National Strategic Stockpile. State and local health departments stepped up their surveillance, laboratory specimen processing, and handling of medications from the National Stockpile. They handled critically important risk communications and intervened to prevent transmission at mass gatherings and school activities. Nevertheless, the virus spread faster than vaccine production: the U.S. government purchased 229 million vaccine doses, but they could not be available until after the second wave of infections had peaked. By April 2010, approximately 80 million Americans had been immunized against the virus. The rapid and comprehensive response to H1N1, although imperfect, shows tremendous national progress in preparing for disease outbreaks.

EFFECTIVE COMMUNICATION AND ADVOCACY

Public health needs to build a constituency that understands its value in order to create coalitions, gain allies to solve public health problems, and advocate effectively (Institute of Medicine, 2003). The general public does not understand what public health is, often supposing it refers solely to programs for the poor.

The public—and policy makers—react to specific problems and crises. They do not see the disease cases, injuries, disabilities, and deaths that have been prevented. And when an eroded infrastructure hinders crisis response—such as when the 2001 anthrax episode overwhelmed many public health laboratories or after Hurricane Katrina, when even such a basic function as handling the dead broke down—they do not understand why the problem is not solved quickly. Another reason for policy maker inattention may be that formally recognized public health programs have such small federal budgets compared to entitlement programs, such as Medicare and Medicaid, or the research program of the National Institutes of Health. With this in mind, how can public health develop an effective public constituency? One reason that policy makers and the public alike have become complacent about public health issues results from the field's success. Laws and systems are in place to keep our drinking water clean, to immunize our children, to deliver babies more safely, to provide food for the undernourished, and so on. As a result, we don't think about public health until one of these systems breaks down.

> *The public—and policy makers—react to specific problems and crises. They do not see the disease cases, injuries, disabilities, and deaths that have been prevented.*

Public health professionals are addressing the challenges of public relations in a variety of creative ways. Professional associations developed materials to explain public health in more engaging ways (National Association of County and City Health Officials, 2006). To improve communication about specific health risks and strategies, the CDC has developed *CDCynergy,* a computer-based tool to improve practitioners' communication about health risks, disease, and public health activities. Materials for improved communication are updated constantly at the CDC Web site (http://www.cdc.gov/healthmarketing/cdcynergy/), but the field still has a long way to go.

Public Health Flashpoints

Public health goals can sometimes conflict with other social or political agendas. The most prominent example in recent decades has been the prevention of AIDS. Because men who had sex with men and intravenous drug users were the first groups known to contract AIDS, policy support for its prevention was slow in coming, and many social conservatives expressed the belief that the people infected "deserved" AIDS (Shilts, 1987). The very methods of public health can conflict with other definitions of the public interest. For example, although using condoms is one of the few effective ways to prevent HIV/AIDS, social conservatives are unwilling to promote condom use because it appears to sanction sex outside of marriage. Likewise, they oppose needle exchange programs that prevent transmission by that route, in the erroneous belief that making needles available will encourage drug use. Similar objections have been raised regarding a new vaccine to prevent infection with the sexually transmitted human papilloma virus, which can cause cervical cancer. To be most effective, the vaccine should be administered to young women before they are sexually active and, again, social conservatives oppose it on the grounds that it would promote sexual activity.

Building and Maintaining Public Trust

Public health practitioners sometimes can be seen as authoritarian or paternalistic, especially when they stress science and technology ("what's good for you") while ignoring collaboration and democratic processes. This tendency weakens their connections to grassroots groups and local leadership. The last years of the 20th century heightened public awareness of the need for a new form of leadership in public health—one that engages people on their own terms, in order to engender trust and cooperation. For example, the populations most at risk of AIDS had no reason to trust authority figures and often did not seek medical care until it was too late. It was imperative for public health leadership to engage the grassroots leadership that was most trusted by the groups at risk and to approach people where they live and congregate, so that they learned about AIDS prevention through people they trusted and saw every day (Leviton & Guinan, 2003).

Similar challenges arose in the environmental movement. Over time, the EPA learned to work with communities affected by toxic contaminants. But in the early days, it did not listen to the public about their concerns, did not provide the information they needed, or gave them incomprehensible techno-babble that enraged community leaders (Leviton et al., 1997). The old bureaucratic ways of doing business were simply not effective when people had legitimate concerns.

The most difficult lesson for public health came from the Tuskegee Syphilis Experiment (Jones, 1993). In 1932, 600 poor African American men in Macon County, Alabama, unknowingly became syphilis research subjects, when the Public Health Service and the Tuskegee Institute began a study of the natural course of syphilis and offered the men free medical care. Of 600 subjects, 339 had syphilis but were left untreated for up to 40 years, even though a penicillin cure became available in 1947. As many as 100 of the men died of syphilis before a public outcry and a federal advisory panel's recommendations halted the study in 1972. Along with the Nuremberg Code on medical experiments, this episode led Congress to require a wide variety of new protections for human research subjects. In 1997, President Bill Clinton offered an official public apology to the Tuskegee Study's eight survivors and participants' families. However, public health—and the health care system more generally—have not fully regained African Americans' trust.

EFFECTIVE POLICY VOICES

The public health professional associations offer their memberships important tools to increase effectiveness in advocating for policies and resources at state and local levels. The Campaign for Public Health advocates for increases in the CDC budget, in particular.

The nonprofit organization, Trust for America's Health, is emerging as an especially vigorous and articulate champion. The Trust advocates passionately for attention to specific health problems—what Americans generally respond to—tying these issues to the need for a better public health infrastructure. Advocacy in public health generally has a twofold purpose. It can be aimed at strengthening the public health infrastructure through resources and reorganization, but it also can aim to achieve goals outside the formal agency structure. For example, advocacy led to increased taxes on cigarettes and bans on smoking in public places; now it is generating new state and local policies to increase the school physical education requirement, bring recess back into the school day, and require healthier offerings in school cafeterias (Trust for America's Health, 2010b).

A positive national development is the growing number of state-level public health institutes (PHIs). These institutes are outside state government and can accept private funds and implement ideas much more quickly than health departments can. PHIs also are more flexible than state bureaucracies. Institute staff can advocate vigorously for public health programs and funding, whereas state employees have limits. PHIs can sometimes offer a credible, neutral, third-party voice on issues and can convene all the interested parties to address a broad health problem and implement a multisector strategy. In general, health departments support PHIs and recognize their value.

Public health advocacy deals with a wider range of topics today than ever before. Because health is rooted in social conditions, the field has started using an approach called "health in all policies" (Puska & Stahl, 2010). In this approach, health advocates engage policy makers across various sectors to make sure that decisions will promote, or at least not adversely affect, health. For example, to prevent obesity, health advocates must engage departments of transportation (for walking- and biking-friendly streets), cities (for zoning of fast food, parks and recreation, locations of farmers' markets), schools (for recess and other physical activity opportunities and for healthy food at lunch), and industry (for healthy food offerings in restaurants, employee cafeterias, and grocery stores). A new approach to public health advocacy is to include **Health Impact Assessments** on any policy or program that might affect the public's health.

SHARED INTERESTS AND SHARED RESOURCES

Throughout this chapter, we have attempted to show the many ways in which a wide variety of organizations take on the public health role when they focus on populations (see Table 6.3). This approach means that other interests can be aligned with the public health mission. For example, walkable communities can appeal to both real estate developers and public health advocates. Across the nation, public health professionals are now working with city planners, police departments, real estate developers, and others, reframing suburban sprawl as an issue that has consequences for people's health. Likewise, employers and public health advocates alike see advantages to having health promotion and disease prevention programs in the workplace.

Local public health departments have always connected to grassroots leadership and other public services in order to solve collective problems. However, their leadership abilities for cross-sector collaboration are now being cultivated as never before, in what has become known as the **collaborative leadership approach**. For example, Colorado's data on health status were reported by race and ethnicity for the first time in 2001, leading residents to realize that the state's African Americans had an overall life expectancy 4 years shorter than whites. The state's Turning Point program began working with communities to build awareness of health disparities. Together, they advocated for a more diverse public health workforce and developed a Citizen's Advisory Commission on Minority Health. In 2004, Colorado formed an Office of Health Disparities within the state health department to continue work on this issue.

Collaborative leadership means understanding where public health shares common goals with other interest groups and building coalitions based on those common interests. In the same way, public health organizations are now participating more effectively in emergency preparedness and in health reform, because they can show where the public health interest is aligned with national defense and preparation for natural disasters, on the one hand, and health care quality and cost-containment, on the other. Through coalition-building at all levels, public health finally can leave the sidelines. Sometimes it must lead, and sometimes it must follow, but most often, we will find public health walking hand-in-hand with its many partners.

TABLE 6.3
Who's in Charge of What? Public Health Protection Every Day

Guidance and Education		
Public health issue	**Federal responsibility**	**Other responsibility**
Sleep	NIH, CDC, SAMHSA, OSHA (shift workers)	Popular press, medical care providers, schools
Nutrition	FDA, USDA, ODPHP	Schools, medical care, nutritionists and dieticians
Dental hygiene	CDC, NIH, Surgeon General	State and local health departments, schools, dental and medical care
Healthy weight	ODPHP, NIH, CDC	Popular press, medical care, state and local health departments, American Heart Association, AARP
Communicate risk of new infectious diseases	CDC, USDA, Homeland Security	State and local health departments, World Health Organization
Smoking	ODPHP, NIH, CDC	Popular press, medical care, state and local health departments, the courts, American Heart Association, American Lung Association
Physical activity	ODPHP, NIH, CDC	Popular press, medical care, state and local health departments, American Heart Association, AARP, urban planners, YMCA, YWCA, Sierra Club
Seat belts	ODPHP, CDC, NHTSA	State and local health departments, schools, medical care, popular press
Law and Regulation		
Fluoridation		State law, county and municipal codes
Drinking water	EPA, FEMA	State and local health departments, state and local departments of environment, municipal water authority/sanitary districts
Childhood immunization	DHHS regulation (standing orders to immunize)	State health codes (reportable disease) and immunization requirements
Food labeling, pure milk	FDA, EPA	State inspection programs (some)
Reproductive health—STD control		State health codes (reportable diseases)
Folic acid	FDA	
Seat belts		All state transportation laws
Car safety	NHTSA, other U.S. Dept. of Transportation programs	State laws
Safety at work	OSHA	State laws and agencies
Prevent or contain new infectious diseases	CDC, USDA, Homeland Security	State and local health departments
Services		
Nutrition	USDA, HHS (various)	State agencies, school districts, food pantries
Dental care	CMS, HRSA	State agencies, school districts, dentists
Immunization	CMS, HRSA	State agencies, local health departments, school districts, medical providers

(continued)

TABLE 6.3

Who's in Charge of What? Public Health Protection Every Day (*continued*)

Services		
Public health issue	**Federal responsibility**	**Other responsibility**
Reproductive health—STD control	CDC (training, guidance, lab oversight)	State and local health departments, medical care, family planning and other nonprofit organizations, medical care, pharmacies (condoms)
Folic acid	USDA (WIC)	State and local health departments, medical care, pharmacies
Healthy weight		Medical care, private and nonprofit organizations (e.g., Weight Watchers™)
Smoking	HHS (various)	American Cancer Society, American Heart Association, American Lung Association, state and local health departments, medical care, private organizations (SmokeEnders™), pharmacies (nicotine replacement)
Physical activity		Senior centers, American Heart Association, AARP, YMCA, YWCA, parks and recreation departments, Sierra Club
Prevent or contain new infectious diseases	HRSA, CDC, USDA	State and local health departments, state and local emergency management departments, World Health Organization, hospitals, American Red Cross

DISCUSSION QUESTIONS

1. What examples of public health and prevention can you identify in your daily life? How do you believe they have affected your health?
2. Pick two such examples from either your own life or the text; then go to the Internet and find out which federal laws and agencies, state laws and agencies, local health departments, nonprofit organizations, or city and county government units affect this aspect of your health. The more complete your answer, the better your answer is!
3. What is the difference between individual- and population-based prevention efforts? For population-based prevention, what is the difference between universal and targeted strategies?
4. What does a population focus take, in terms of planning, consensus building, and resources for implementation? In the case of auto safety belts? Heart attack prevention?
5. Why can't public health do more to achieve its goals? Name some of the political, legal, logistic, and resource challenges.
6. What should be left to the public sector to do, in order to achieve public health goals? Where could other health care delivery systems do more to help? Why?
7. Give some examples of the constituencies that public health will have to reach in order to implement its goals (a) in the case of environmental health and (b) in the case of HIV/AIDS.
8. Why do some public health problems pose "flashpoints" for conflict? What could be done about them? Give examples in the cases of HIV and other problems you think of.
9. How would you personally balance individual liberty, the common good, and social justice in public health? What would have to change to achieve this balance? Give specific examples in the area of public health that you are best acquainted with.

CASE STUDY

You are an analyst for a federal agency. Congress has ordered your agency to come up with policy options to find a cure for birth defects. You recognize that (a) birth defects have many causes, (b) some can be treated, (c) some can also be prevented, but (d) not all of them can be "cured." You analyze this issue using the problem-solving process outlined under Core Functions of Public Health.

Based on the information about spina bifida later in that section, you decide it should be the focus for policy making on birth defects. You decide to propose three options to Congress: more research on treatment of spina bifida, more health education for women about folic acid, and new regulations to increase the amount of folic acid in grain products. You may see additional options, so be sure to discuss them!

CASE STUDY QUESTIONS

1. For each option, what would you need to know to determine effectiveness? Cost-effectiveness?
2. What are the tradeoffs in each course of action?
3. Who would support this option, who would be opposed, and does it matter?
4. Is there a single best option? Why?

REFERENCES

Beitsch, L. M., Brooks, R. G., Menachemi, N., & Libbey, P. M. (2006). Public health at center stage: New roles, old props. *Health Affairs, 25*, 911–922.

Center for Infectious Disease Research & Policy. (2007). *Pandemic influenza*. Minneapolis, MN: Author. Retrieved July 28, 2010, from http://www.cidrap.umn.edu/cidrap/content/influenza/panflu/biofacts/panflu.html

Centers for Law and the Public's Health. (2008). Model laws. Retrieved July 18, 2010, from http://www.publichealthlaw.net/ModelLaws/index.php

Eng, T. R., & Butler, W. T. (1997). *The hidden epidemic: Confronting sexually transmitted diseases*. Washington, D.C.: National Academies Press.

Gebbie, K. M., & Turnock, B. J. (2006). The public health workforce, 2006: New challenges. *Health Affairs, 25*, 923–933.

Giang, T., Karpyn, A., Laurison, H. B., Hillier, A., & Perry, R. D. (2008). Closing the grocery gap in underserved areas: The creation of the Pennsylvania Fresh Food Financing Initiative. *Journal of Public Health Management and Practice, 14*, 272–279.

Gostin, L. (2000). *Public health law: Power, duty, restraint*. Berkeley, CA: University of California Press.

Green, L. W., & Kreuter, M. (1999). *Health promotion planning: An educational and ecological approach*. New York: McGraw-Hill.

Institute of Medicine. (2009). *HHS in the 21st century*. Washington, D.C.: National Academies Press, Chapter 5.

Institute of Medicine. (2003). *Who will keep the public healthy? Educating public health professionals for the 21st century*. Washington, D.C.: National Academies Press.

Institute of Medicine. (1988). *The future of public health* (pp. 39, 41). Washington, D.C.: National Academies Press.

Jones, J. H. (1993). *Bad blood: The Tuskegee Syphilis Experiment* (New and expanded edition). New York: Free Press.

Leviton, L. C., & Guinan, M. E. (2003). HIV prevention and the evaluation of public health programs. In R.O. Valdiserari (Ed.), *Dawning answers: How the HIV/AIDS epidemic has helped to strengthen public health.* Oxford, England: Oxford University Press.

Leviton, L. C., Needleman, C. E., & Shapiro, M. (1997). *Confronting public health risks: A decision maker's guide.* Thousand Oaks, CA: Sage.

Mission: Readiness. (2010). Too fat to fight: Retired military leaders want junk food out of America's schools. Washington, D.C.: author.

National Association of County and City Health Officials. (2006). *Shelter from the storm: Local public health faces Katrina.* Washington, D.C.: Author.

Public Health Accreditation Board. (2010). PHAB: Advancing public health performance. Alexandria, VA: Author. Retrieved July 21, 2010, from http://www.phaboard.org/

Puska, P., & Stahl, T. (2010). Health in all policies—The Finnish initiative: Background, principles, and current issues. *Annual Review of Public Health, 31*, 315–328.

Rosen, G. (1993). *A history of public health* (Expanded edition.). Baltimore, MD: Johns Hopkins University Press.

Shilts, R. (1987). *And the band played on: Politics, people and the AIDS epidemic.* New York: St. Martin's Press.

Sondik, E. J., Huang, D. T., Klein, R. J. & Satcher, D. (2010). Progress toward meeting the Healthy People 2010 goals and objectives. *Annual Review of Public Health, 31*, 271–281.

Steib, P. A. (2004). Federal funding key to public health preparedness. *ASTHO Report, 12*, 1, 5.

Trust for America's Health (2010a). Fact sheet: The affordable care act's new rules on preventive care. Retrieved July 19, 2010, from http://healthyamericans.org/assets/files/Reg.pdf

Trust for America's Health. (2010b). *F as in fat: How obesity policies are failing in America.* Retrieved on July 21, 2010, from http://healthyamericans.org/reports/obesity2010/

U.S., Department of Health and Human Services (DHHS). (2000). *Healthy People 2010: Understanding and improving health* (2nd ed.). Washington, D.C.: U.S. Government Printing Office. Stock Number 017-001-001-00-550-9.

U.S., DHHS, Agency for Healthcare Research and Quality. Preventive Services Task Force. (2009). *Guide to clinical preventive services.* Retrieved January 23, 2011, from http://www.ahrq.gov/clinic/pocketgd.htm

U.S., DHHS. Centers for Disease Control and Prevention. (2004). *The National Public Health Performance Standards Program.* Retrieved July 28, 2010, from http://www.cdc.gov/od/ocphp/nphpsp/index.htm

U.S., DHHS. Centers for Disease Control and Prevention. (1999). Achievements in public health, 1900–1999: Decline in deaths from heart disease and stroke—United States, 1900–1999. *Morbidity and Mortality Weekly Report, 48*, 649–656.

U.S., DHHS. Health Resources and Services Administration. (2005). *Public health workforce study.* Washington, D.C.: author. Retrieved July 19, 2010, from http://bhpr.hrsa.gov/healthworkforce/reports/publichealth/default.htm#exec

U.S., Department of Transportation. National Highway Traffic Safety Administration. (2010). *Crash Injury Research.* Retrieved July 28, 2010, from http://www.nhtsa.gov/CIREN

Wall, S. (1998). Transformations in public health systems. *Health Affairs, 17*, 64–80.

White House. (2010). *Solving the problem of childhood obesity within a generation: White House Task Force on Childhood Obesity report to the President.* Retrieved July 19, 2010, from http://www.nihb.org/docs/05112010/WH%20Task%20Force%20on%20Childhood%20%20Obesity%20Report%20to%20the%20President%20_%20May2010.pdf

7

HEALTH AND BEHAVIOR

C. Tracy Orleans and Elaine F. Cassidy

Health care professionals, who live in a world in which often heroic efforts are needed to save lives, can easily believe that medical care is the most important instrument for maintaining and assuring health. This chapter explains, however, that behavioral choices—how we live our lives—are the key instruments that determine Americans' health and well-being.

To some extent, the task of helping people adopt healthy lifestyles falls into the realm of behavioral psychology, public health, and sometimes social marketing. However, emerging theories of how to encourage healthy lifestyles include major roles for medical providers. Therefore, clinicians, health care payers, managers of provider organizations, and health care policy makers need to understand the dynamics of behavioral choices that affect health.

> *Social marketing strategies apply the concepts and tools of successful commercial marketing to the challenge of health behavior change.*

This chapter begins with a brief overview of the major behavioral risk factors that contribute to the growing burden of preventable chronic disease in the United States— tobacco use, alcohol abuse, sedentary lifestyle, unhealthy diet, and adult and childhood obesity and overweight.

It then describes the extraordinary progress that has been made over the past three decades to help adults modify these risk factors by intervening both at the individual level—with behavioral and clinical treatments that can be delivered in health care set- tings—and at the broader population level with public health environmental and policy changes that help to support and maintain healthy behavior. Theoretical advances (e.g., social learning theory, stage-based and social ecological models) have led to a clear under- standing of the need for broad-spectrum, multilevel ecological approaches, and new sci- ence-based clinical and community practice guidelines have developed to guide them.

Multifaceted efforts have been successful in encouraging clinicians to use proven health behavior change protocols in their interactions with patients. Many parallels can be drawn between what we have learned about ways to promote health through individual behavior change and what we have learned about improving health care quality through provider behavior change. Recent health reform legislation recognizes that the significant progress in both areas holds unprecedented potential for breakthrough improvements in national health status and health care quality.

Behavioral Risk Factors: Overview and National Goals

Acute and infectious diseases are no longer the major causes of death, disease, and disability in the United States. Today, chronic diseases—coronary heart disease, cancer, diabetes, and asthma—are the nation's leading causes of illness and death. Given the con- tinued aging of the population, both the prevalence and costs of chronic illness care will continue to rise. Yet, much of the growing burden of chronic disease is preventable.

More than a decade ago, McGinnis and Foege (1993) estimated that 50% of the mortality from the 10 leading causes of death could be attributed to personal behavior. A more recent analysis by Mokdad, Marks, Stroup, and Gerberding (2004) confirmed this estimate, finding that the four leading **behavioral risk factors**—tobacco use, alcohol abuse, sedentary lifestyle, and unhealthy diet—together accounted for more than 900,000 deaths in 2000. Moreover, research findings over the past two decades have established that modifying these risk factors leads to improved health and quality of life and to reduced health care costs and burden (Orleans, Ulmer, & Gruman, 2004).

Today, almost 90% of Americans report they have at least one of these risk factors, and 52% report two or more, with the highest prevalence of individual and multiple behavioral risks occurring in low income and racial and ethnic minority groups (Coups, Gaba, & Orleans, 2004). Given these statistics, it is not surprising that half of the leading health indicators tracked by *Healthy People 2010*—which sets forth the nation's primary objectives for promoting longer, healthier lives and eliminating **health disparities**—relate to healthy lifestyles. Although recent analysis suggests that our nation has an uneven record in achieving *Healthy People 2010* targets (see Chapter 6), more well-rounded improvements across multiple health indicators are needed in order to advance quality of life and reduce health disparities significantly (Koh, 2010). Selected indicators for tobacco use, alcohol abuse, physical activity, diet, and obesity are shown in Table 7.1.

TOBACCO USE

Tobacco use causes more preventable deaths and diseases than any other behavioral risk factor, including 443,000 premature deaths from several forms of cancer, heart, and lung disease, according to data on smoking rates collected by the U.S. Centers for Disease Control and Prevention (CDC). CDC estimates that tobacco use accounts for annual health care costs of $96 billion in addition to an estimated $97 billion in lost productivity costs.

Smoking represents the single most important modifiable cause of poor pregnancy outcomes, accounting for 20% of low birthweight deliveries, 8% of preterm births, and 5% of perinatal deaths. For infants and young children, parental smoking is linked to sudden infant death syndrome, respiratory illnesses, middle ear infections, and decreased lung function, with annual direct medical costs estimated at $4.6 billion. Quitting, even after 50 years of smoking, can produce significant improvements in health and less use of health care services.

Although the adult smoking prevalence rate decreased to 21% in 2008, smoking prevalence among adults remains well above the *Healthy People 2010* target of 12% (Koh, 2010; Piels, Lucas, and Ward, 2009). Nearly one in four adults still smokes, with the highest rates (33%) in low income populations. Rates of smoking during pregnancy also have dropped in the past decade, but in 2006, 12% of women reported that they smoked during pregnancy.

Each day, more than 3,000 children and teens become new smokers, 30% of whom will become addicted. Some 22% of high school students smoke cigarettes, and nearly 10 million Americans, mostly adolescent and young adult males, report using smokeless tobacco, which is linked to oral cancer, gum disease, and tooth loss. Finally, 27% of children age 6 and younger are exposed to harmful environmental tobacco smoke at home, and 37% of nonsmoking adults are exposed at home or in the workplace.

ALCOHOL USE AND MISUSE

People who abuse or misuse include those who are alcohol dependent as well as those whose drinking is risky (perhaps because they drive afterward) or harmful (perhaps because they suffer the effects of occasional binge drinking). About 5% of the U.S. adult population meets the criteria for alcoholism or alcohol dependence and another 20% engages in harmful or risky drinking—defined as drinking more than one drink per day or seven drinks per week for women, more than two drinks per day or 14 drinks per week for men, periodic binge drinking (five or more drinks on a single occasion), drinking and driving, or drinking during pregnancy.

TABLE 7.1

Selected *Healthy People 2010* Objectives: Behavioral Risk Factors

	Baseline[a] (%)	2010 Goals (%)
Tobacco Use		
Cigarette smoking		
• Adults (18 years and older)	24	12
• Adolescents (grades 9 through 12)	35	16
Exposure to secondhand smoke		
• Children (6 years and younger)	27	10
Alcohol Misuse/Risky Drinking		
• Proportion of adults who exceed guidelines for low-risk drinking	72 (women); 74 (men)	50
Binge drinking		
• Adults (18 years and older)	16.6	6
• Adolescents (12 to 17 years)	7.7	2
Deaths from alcohol-related auto crashes	5.9	4
Physical Activity		
Regular moderate physical activity		
• Adults (18 years and older)[b]	15	30
• Adolescents (grades 9 through 12)[c]	27	35
Vigorous physical activity (at least 3 days per week for 20 minutes)		
• Adults (18 years and older)	23	30
• Adolescents (grades 9 through 12)	65	85
Diet-and-Overweight (older than age 2)		
• Proportion of people eating at least two servings of fruit daily	28	75
• Proportion of people eating at least three servings of vegetables (at least one of which is dark green or orange) daily	3	50
• Proportion of people eating at least six servings of grain products (at least three being whole grains) daily	7	50
Overweight and obesity		
• Obesity among adults (aged 20 years and older)	23	15
• Overweight and obesity among children and adolescents (aged 6 to 19)	11	5

Note. [a]Baseline data extracted from sources between 1988 and 1999.
[b]At least 30 minutes per day.
[c]At least 30 minutes 5 or more days per week.
Source: U.S. Department of Health and Human Services. (2000). *Healthy People 2010: Understanding and improving health.* Washington, D.C.: Author.

In 2005, nearly half of all college students reported that they engaged in binge drinking—a rate well above the *Healthy People 2010* goal of 6% (Center for Science in the Public Interest, 2010). Alcohol misuse is most common in young adults, particularly among white and Native American men. Moderate levels of alcohol use in adults (below those defined as risky) have been linked to modest health benefits, such as lowered risk for heart disease.

Alcohol misuse is associated with approximately 100,000 U.S. deaths each year, including 60% to 90% of cirrhosis deaths, 40% to 50% of auto-related fatalities, and 16% to 67% of home and work injuries (McGinnis & Foege, 1993). The data are old, but the total annual costs of alcohol misuse in 1998—including costs related to health care, lost wages, premature death, and crime—were estimated at $185 million (U.S., National Institute on Alcohol Abuse and Alcoholism, 2001).

The health benefits of treating of alcohol dependence are well established, and the U.S. Preventive Services Task Force (USPSTF) found that brief behavior change interventions to modify risky drinking levels and practices produced positive health outcomes detectable 4 or more years later.

PHYSICAL ACTIVITY

The health risks associated with physical inactivity and sedentary lifestyle are numerous. They include heart disease, type 2 diabetes, stroke, hypertension, osteoarthritis, colon cancer, depression, and obesity (U.S. Preventive Services Task Force [PSTF], 2003a). Engagement in physical activity helps maintain healthy bones, muscles, joints, and weight and it is associated with positive psychological benefits. Physical activity has been shown to reduce feelings of anxiety and depression and promote feelings of well-being.

In 2008, nearly 67% of American adults reported that they did not engage in regular physical activity and 36% reported *no* physical activity whatsoever. Physical inactivity is even more common among adults from low income backgrounds. In 2008, 72% of adults from low income backgrounds reported that they never engaged in regular physical activity.

Although the societal costs of physical inactivity are difficult to quantify, CDC has estimated that nearly $95 billion (adjusted to 2009 dollars) would be saved if all inactive American adults were to become active. *Healthy People 2010* guidelines recommend that adults and adolescents engage in moderate physical activity (such as walking or biking) for at least 30 minutes at least 5 days a week and that they engage in vigorous physical activity that promotes the development and maintenance of cardiorespiratory fitness 3 or more days per week for 20 or more minutes per occasion.

As Table 7.1 shows, most American adults and adolescents do not follow these recommendations. The populations most at risk for inactivity include those with lower income and education levels, those living below the poverty line in all racial and ethnic groups, members of several racial/ethnic minority groups (e.g., African Americans, Hispanics), and those with disabilities.

DIET AND NUTRITION

In conjunction with sedentary lifestyle, unhealthy eating is linked to an estimated 400,000 deaths each year in the United States (Mokdad et al., 2004). Together, inactivity and unhealthy diet are associated with 25% to 30% of cardiovascular deaths, 30% to 35% of cancer deaths, and 50% to 80% of type 2 diabetes cases (McGinnis & Foege,

1993). They also have contributed to a surge in overweight and obesity that has reached epidemic proportions over the last 20 years, particularly within low income and minority populations.

> *Four of the 10 leading causes of death—coronary heart disease, some cancers, stroke, and type 2 diabetes—are associated with an unhealthy diet.*

Four of the 10 leading causes of death—coronary heart disease, some cancers, stroke, and type 2 diabetes—are associated with an unhealthy diet. The relationships between dietary patterns and health outcomes have been examined in a wide range of observational studies and randomized trials with patients at risk for diet-related chronic diseases. The majority of studies suggest that people consuming diets that are low in fat, saturated fat, trans-fatty acids, and cholesterol and high in fruits, vegetables, and whole grain products containing fiber have lower rates of morbidity and mortality from coronary artery disease and several forms of cancer (USPSTF, 2003b). Moreover, dietary change has been found to reduce risks for many chronic diseases, as well as for overweight and obesity.

Federal dietary guidelines for Americans age 2 and older recommend three to five daily servings of vegetables and vegetable juices, two or more daily servings of fruit, three daily servings of whole grain products, and three daily cups of nonfat or low-fat milk products, with no more than 30% of total calories from fat and 10% from saturated fat. Again, as Table 7.1 shows, enormous gaps exist between the recommended guidelines and actual diets for American children and adults. The diets of more than 80% of Americans, especially those in low income populations, do not meet these guidelines (USPSTF, 2003b).

OBESITY

As poor dietary habits and physical inactivity have become endemic, national obesity rates have soared. Nearly 70% of all American adults are overweight or obese—up from 12% just one decade ago. This trend is alarming, given the strong links between obesity and many chronic diseases. Total expenditures related to overweight- and obesity-related problems were estimated at nearly $110 billion, inflated to 2009 dollars (Finkelstein, Fiebelkorn, & Wang, 2003)—a number that will continue to increase until we have effective interventions to teach and reinforce healthy behavior. Even modest weight loss (e.g., 5% to 10% of body weight) over a period of 12 to 24 months can reduce these risks and prevent the onset of diabetes among adults with impaired glucose tolerance.

More alarming is the prevalence of overweight and obesity among children and adolescents (ages 6 to 19), which has increased significantly over the past two decades. Like adults, overweight youth are at risk for coronary heart disease, hypertension, certain cancers, and even type 2 diabetes early in life. The highest and fastest rising rates of childhood obesity are seen among children and adolescents of African American or Latino descent and children (particularly girls) from low income backgrounds— making efforts to reach these groups a public health priority (White House Task Force on Childhood Obesity, 2010).

Changing Health Behavior: Closing the Gap Between Recommended and Actual Health Lifestyle Practices

The landmark Institute of Medicine (IOM) report, *Health and Behavior,* published 30 years ago, was one of the first scientific documents to establish convincingly the links between behavioral risk factors and disease and to identify the basic biopsychosocial mechanisms underlying them. IOM recommended intensified social and behavioral science research to develop interventions that could help people change their unhealthy behavior and improve their health prospects. This section presents a broad overview of the research that has ensued—research that has attempted to close the gap between what we know and what we do when it comes to adopting healthy lifestyles.

A BRIEF HISTORY OF BEHAVIOR CHANGE INTERVENTIONS

Early behavior change efforts in the 1970s and 1980s relied primarily on public education campaigns and individually oriented health education interventions. They were guided by the health belief model and similar theories (the theory of reasoned action, the theory of planned behavior) that emphasized the cognitive and motivational influences on health behavior change. This type of intervention strategy sought to raise awareness of the harms of unhealthy behavior versus the benefits of behavior change (Glanz, Rimer, & Viswanath, 2008). These cognitive/decisional theories were based on a "rational man" model of human behavior change, with an underlying premise that people's intentions and motivations to engage in behavior strongly predict their actually doing so (i.e., "if you tell them, they will change"). Because raising health risk awareness and motivation was a primary goal, the doctor–patient relationship was seen as a unique and powerful context for effective health education.

In fact, both population-level and individual clinical health education efforts based on these theories achieved initial success. For instance, tens of thousands of smokers quit in response to the publication of the first U.S. Surgeon General's Report on Smoking and Health in 1964 and the multiple public education campaigns that followed. By the mid-1980s, most U.S. smokers said they wanted to quit and were trying to do so, mostly for health reasons.

By 2000, hundreds of studies had confirmed that even brief physician advice could be a powerful catalyst for health behavior change—boosting the number of patients who quit smoking for at least 24 hours or who made some changes in their diet and activity levels. But a growing body of research found these successes to be modest—the interventions were important and perhaps *necessary* for changing people's health knowledge, attitudes, and beliefs, as well as broader social norms, but *not sufficient* to produce lasting behavior change. And cumulative findings made it clear that people needed not only motivation but also new skills and supports to succeed in changing deeply ingrained health habits.

These findings spurred the development and testing of expanded multicomponent, cognitive-behavioral treatments designed not only to (a) raise perceptions of susceptibility to poor health outcomes and benefits of behavior change but also to (b) teach the skills required to replace ingrained unhealthy habits with healthy alternatives and to (c) help people make changes in their natural (home, work, social) environments that will aid them in successfully establishing and maintaining new behavior. **Social learning theory**, which emphasized interactions between internal and external environmental influences on behavior, provided the primary theoretical basis for this evolution and it remains the dominant model for effective cognitive-behavioral health behavior change interventions (Glanz et al., 2008).

Lifestyle change interventions derived from social learning theory combined education and skills development. They included techniques such as modeling and behavioral practice to help people learn not just why but *how* to change unhealthy habits. For instance, they taught effective **patient self-management** and behavior change skills, such as goal setting, self-monitoring, and stress management skills for people who had relied on smoking, eating, or drinking as coping tactics. They taught skills for reengineering the person's immediate environments by replacing environmental cues and supports for unhealthy behavior with new cues and supports for healthy ones (e.g., removing ashtrays, replacing unhealthy high-calorie foods with healthy alternatives, finding exercise buddies, and avoiding high-risk events, such as office parties at which risky drinking was expected).

Another principle was that problem solving should start with helping people set realistic, personal behavior change goals and go on to address the unique barriers and relapse temptations they face. The expectation was that setting and meeting achievable goals would lead to heightened self-efficacy and confidence in the ability to succeed. Finally, new social learning theory treatments taught patients to take a long-range perspective, viewing repeated attempts over time as part of a cumulative learning process rather than as signs of failure.

Effective multicomponent treatments were initially delivered and tested in multi-session, face-to-face group or individual clinic-based programs, typically offered in clinical or medical settings and usually led by highly trained (e.g., MD, PhD) professionals. Results were extremely encouraging, with substantial behavior change—for example, smoking quit rates as high as 40%—maintained 6 to 12 months posttreatment. However, participants were typically self-referred or recruited based on high readiness or motivation for change and thus represented a small fraction of those who could benefit.

And treatment costs were high. The next push was to distill core elements of this treatment approach into lower cost formats with much wider reach. These formats included paraprofessional led worksite clinics, self-help manuals and programs, and brief primary care counseling. Absolute treatment effects were smaller—for example, 20% long-term smoking quit rates—but potential population impacts were much greater: only 5% to 10% of smokers might ever attend intensive clinics, but a brief, effective tobacco intervention reaching the 70% of U.S. smokers who saw their primary care physicians each year would double the nation's annual quit rate.

Development of the **stages-of-change model** in the mid-1980s accelerated the shift from individual to population intervention models and has had a profound, lasting impact on the design and delivery of health behavior change programs. Studying how people went about changing on their own, Prochaska and DiClemente (1983) discovered that health behavior change was a multistage process:

- *Precontemplation:* not planning to change behavior; behavior is not seen as a problem.
- *Contemplation:* seriously planning to change behavior within the next 6 months, weighing the pros and cons, and building supports and confidence.
- *Preparation:* plans to change are imminent; small initial steps are taken.
- *Action:* active attempts are made to quit smoking, drink less, become more active, or change to a healthier diet and to sustain changes for up to 6 months.
- *Maintenance:* change is sustained beyond 6 months.
- *Relapse:* the individual returns to any earlier stage and begins to recycle through the earlier stages.

Based on these findings, different skills and knowledge and different types of treatment were recommended to help people in each stage—motivational and educational interventions were helpful to people in precontemplation and contemplation stages, and active cognitive-behavioral interventions were needed for those in preparation, action, and maintenance stages. Moreover, many population surveys found that, at any given time, the vast majority of people (80%) are in the precontemplation and contemplation stages, which helped to explain why so few enrolled in weight loss or quit smoking clinics, even when these were free and accessible.

The stages-of-change model has been successfully applied to each of the behavioral health risks covered in this chapter as well as to other risks (e.g., cancer screening adherence, sun protection). It also has been used to help people with multiple risk factors make progress in changing several at the same time.

Although research continues to examine stage-based differences in the processes of behavior change, the emergence of this model propelled a dramatic shift away from one-size-fits-all approaches to individualized, stage-tailored strategies that could be effectively applied to entire populations—in communities, worksites, and health care settings—assisting people at *all* stages of change, not just the motivated volunteers in action stages, but also those needing motivation and support to reach action stages. It stimulated the development and wider use of effective motivational interventions for clinical settings, especially motivational interviewing, which seeks to help people strengthen their determination to change behavior (Emmons & Rollnick, 2001).

Originating as they did in the study of successful self-change, stages-of-change models fueled a burgeoning movement toward low cost self-help tools and treatment formats. Some tools capitalized on computer-based and interactive communication technologies to design and deliver print materials, interactive video, Web-based, and telephone interventions geared to the individual's stage of change. These also addressed many other variables important for tailoring treatment methods and improving treatment outcomes—for example, degree of nicotine addiction, unique behavior change assets, barriers, and cultural norms.

A final force in the evolution from individual to population-based approaches was the emergence of **social marketing strategies**, which apply the concepts and tools of successful commercial marketing to the challenge of health behavior change. Basic marketing principles and methods—including market analysis, audience segmentation, a new focus on consumer wants and needs—played an especially important catalytic role in the development of culturally appropriate communication and intervention strategies for reaching underserved and high-risk, low income, and racial/ethnic minority populations for whom the prevalence of behavioral health risks is highest. For instance, one model program employed social marketing strategies to tailor a state-of-the-art smoking cessation intervention to the needs of African American smokers, using messages on black-format radio stations to promote culturally tailored quitline counseling and materials. Results included a higher quitline call rate and a higher quit rate among African Americans receiving the tailored versus a generic intervention.

Current efforts focus on building consumer demand for evidence-based health behavior change products and services and creating and harnessing the power of social network support for health behavior change (Christakis & Fowler, 2008) and using new media channels, such as the Internet, mobile devices, and social networking sites.

THE ROLE AND IMPACT OF PRIMARY CARE INTERVENTIONS

The progress in health behavior change research and treatment described previously set the stage for the development of brief, individually oriented, primary care health interventions that could be widely offered to all members of a practice, health plan, or patient population.

These efforts were based on a strong rationale for primary care interventions to address behavioral health risks. Over 80% of American adults report having a usual source of care, visiting their doctor's offices on average about three times each year. Patient surveys have repeatedly found that patients expect and value advice from their providers about diet, exercise, and substance use and are motivated to act on this advice (Woolf, 2008). And, most primary care providers describe health behavior change advice and counseling as an essential part of their role and responsibilities.

The unique extended relationship that is the hallmark of primary care provides multiple opportunities over time to address healthy behavior in a "string of pearls" approach, capitalizing both on teachable moments—for example, introducing physical activity or diet counseling when test results show elevated cholesterol levels—and a therapeutic alliance that often extends beyond the patient to include key family members. Moreover, there was growing evidence that the health benefits and cost effectiveness of evidence-based preventive health behavior change interventions rivaled and frequently surpassed those of remedial disease treatments (Maciosek et al., 2006; Woolf, 2008). This vision has prompted a tremendous amount of work to identify brief, effective interventions that can be integrated into routine practice.

In the *minimal contact* primary care counseling interventions that were distilled from the successful multicomponent models, the physician was seen as the initial catalyst for change, providing brief motivational advice, social support, and follow-up, with referral to other staff members or community resources for more intensive assistance. Stage-based and social marketing approaches held the potential to reach and assist entire populations of patients, including those not yet motivated for change and those in underserved and high-risk groups. Computer-based, patient-tailored, and population-targeted interventions provided new ways to reduce provider burden. And the emergence of managed care as the dominant health care model in the 1990s brought new incentives and demands for population-based preventive clinical services and more centralized systems for delivering them.

Progress in developing effective minimal contact, primary care interventions occurred first in the area of smoking cessation, culminating in the development of an evidence-based practice-friendly intervention model now known as the **5A's: Ask, Advise, Agree, Assist, Arrange Follow-up.** The 5A's model was developed through a review and meta-analysis of hundreds of controlled studies and has been widely promoted through government-approved **clinical practice guidelines**. The model was found to be effective when used by a variety of health care providers (physicians, nurses, dentists, dental hygienists), with as few as 2 to 3 minutes of in-office provider time.

The model starts with *asking* about tobacco use, leading to clear and personal *advice* to quit for smokers (or congratulations for quitters), and the offer of help. The *agree* step starts with assessing patient readiness to quit and goes on to establish a goal and quitting plan. For those not ready to quit, *assistance* includes a recommended motivational intervention; for those who are ready to quit, *assistance* combines brief face-to-face or telephone-based behavior-change counseling with FDA-approved pharmacotherapy, such as nicotine gum, patch, nasal spray or inhaler, bupropion hydrochloride (Zyban), varenicline (Chantix), or some combination, unless medically contraindicated (e.g., pregnancy).

Behavioral counseling was effective when provided through multiple formats—self-help materials *and* face-to-face or telephone counseling—and there is a clear dose-response relationship between the amount of counseling and quit rates. Effective follow-up *arrangements* include planned visits, calls, or contacts to reinforce progress, adjust the quitting plan to better meet individual needs, or refer for more intensive help. One-year quit rates for patients receiving these interventions are typically two to three times higher than the 5% to 7% quit rates among people who try quitting on their own. In fact, the Centers for Disease Control and Prevention (CDC) and Partnership for Prevention found the 5 A's intervention to be one of the most effective and cost effective of all evidence-based clinical preventive services (Maciosek et al., 2006).

The 5A's model has been formally adopted by the USPSTF as a unifying conceptual framework or guideline applicable to addressing *all* behavioral health risks, including risky drinking, physical activity, diet, and obesity. In most cases, the USPSTF found that counseling interventions could produce clinically meaningful, population-wide health improvements that were sustained for at least 6 to 12 months. Although there are many common elements, the specific intervention components and intensity of recommended strategies vary from behavior to behavior, as does their effectiveness with unselected versus high-risk patients. Primary care providers may intervene more forcefully with healthy patients when they are known to be at high risk for a particular chronic disease, and patients at high risk may feel more vulnerable and motivated to act on the advice and assistance they receive.

The first step is always to *assess* not only the relevant behavior (using a standard health risk appraisal or brief screening that can easily be administered in a busy practice setting), but also the individual factors that are helpful in tailoring the intervention, such as medical and physiologic factors, motives, barriers, patient's stage of change, social support, and cultural values.

Based on this information, ideally with reference to the patient's immediate health concerns and symptoms, the clinician provides brief, personalized *advice,* expressing confidence in the patient's ability to change and soliciting the patient's thoughts about the recommended changes.

The next critical step is to negotiate and *agree* on a collaboratively defined behavior-change goal and treatment plan, which commonly includes practical problem solving to *assist* the patient in addressing personal change barriers, building social support, developing a more supportive immediate social and physical environment, and securing adjunctive behavior change resources and pharmacologic aids, such as nicotine replacement. Adjunctive resources can include face-to-face or telephone counseling, tailored or generic self-help materials, and Web-based and other interactive tools that are tailored to a patient's gender, age, racial/ethnic or cultural group; health status or condition; stage of change; and other relevant variables. They can be used before, during, and after the office visit.

The final step is to *arrange* follow-up support and assistance, including referral to more intensive or customized help, or to online tools and supports to help the patient maintain behavior change (Cobb, Graham, & Abrams, 2010).

These new guidelines provided unprecedented scientific support for the USPSTF assertion that "the most effective interventions available to clinicians for reducing the incidence and severity of the leading causes of disease and disability in the United States are those that address patients' personal health practices" (1996, p. iv).

However, several important limitations and gaps remain. The greatest limitation is the lack of long-term maintenance (12 months or longer) following successful behavior change. This is not surprising, given that patients return to the environments that shaped and supported their unhealthy lifestyles and choices. Higher maintenance rates were achieved in clinic-based programs that offered extended booster or maintenance sessions, providing ongoing social support and behavior change assistance, or in those that helped patients create an enduring "therapeutic micro-environment" to shield them from unhealthy influences— for example, implementing an in-home smoking ban, arranging for the delivery of recommended diet foods, or arranging ongoing behavior change buddies.

Researchers and policy makers agree that current major research and evidence gaps are the result of too few studies that have developed and tested primary care interventions for children, adolescents, and underserved populations. Specifically:

- Although there is growing evidence for the power of social networks to motivate, assist, and support health behavior change, research has just begun to examine ways to create or harness such networks using social media
- Surprisingly, little still is known about how best to address multiple behavioral risk factors in the same individual or population—sequentially, simultaneously, or in an integrated way
- Little also is known about strategies for increasing the use and appeal of effective and increasingly accessible health behavior change interventions, such as free tobacco quitlines
- Despite growing evidence that effective and cost effective chronic illness care revolves around helping patients change the behavioral risks that cause or complicate their disease, formal evidence reviews and recommendations, such as those issued by the USPSTF, have focused mainly on primary prevention in healthy individuals

MULTILEVEL MODELS FOR POPULATION-BASED HEALTH BEHAVIOR CHANGE

The shift to population-based models of health promotion and disease prevention was prompted by several factors:

- The success of effective, brief, and intensive interventions based on social learning theory, which gave greater prominence to environmental factors in behavior
- The emergence of new stage-based and social marketing models for population-wide interventions
- The disappointing reach and long-term effectiveness of even the most successful cognitive-behavioral treatments

The lackluster performance of individual treatment approaches was especially apparent when contrasted with new evidence from public health research showing far-reaching and lasting health impacts from environmental and policy changes that eliminated the need for individual decision making. A prime example is the development of safer roads and more crashworthy automobiles, combined with shifts in laws and norms regarding seatbelt use and drinking and driving, which collectively produced a dramatic decline in auto-related deaths and injuries.

With the stage well set, the final push for a change in approach came in the 1990s with the development of **social ecological models** of health behavior. These models integrate behavioral science with clinical and public health approaches. They redefined what the targets of successful health interventions need to be—not just individuals but also the powerful social contexts in which they live and work. And they emphasized that a person's health behavior is affected by multiple levels of influence: interpersonal factors (e.g., physiologic factors, knowledge, skill, motivation), social factors (e.g., social-cultural norms, supports, and networks), organizational and community factors, broader environmental influences, and public policies.

Proponents of the ecological model recommended multilevel strategies that address all these levels of influence (Institute of Medicine, 2000; Koh, 2010). Specifically, they proposed that educational and clinical interventions to improve the motivation, skills, and supports for behavior change at the individual level (e.g., for permanently quitting

TABLE 7.2

The Population-Based Intervention Model

Downstream Interventions	Midstream Interventions	Upstream Interventions
Individual-level interventions aimed at those who possess a behavioral risk factor or suffer from risk-related disease. Emphasis is on changing rather than preventing risky behavior.	Population-level interventions that target defined populations in order to change and/or prevent behavioral risk factors. May involve mediation through important organizational channels or natural environments.	State and national public policy/ environmental interventions that aim to strengthen social norms and supports for healthy behavior and redirect unhealthy behavior.
• Group and individual counseling	• Worksite and community-based health promotion/ disease prevention programs	• National public education/ media campaigns
• Patient health education/ cognitive behavioral interventions	• Health plan-based primary-care screening/ intervention	• Economic incentives (e.g., excise taxes on tobacco products, reimbursement for effective primary care, diets, and extensive counseling)
• Self-help programs and tailored communications	• School-based youth prevention activities	• Policies reducing access to unhealthy products (e.g., pricing, access, labeling)
• Pharmacologic treatments	• Community-based interventions focused on defined at-risk populations	• Policies reducing the advertising and promotion of unhealthy products and behavior

Source: From McKinlay, J. B. (1995). The new public health approach to improving physical activity and autonomy in older populations. In E. Heikkinen (Ed.), *Preparation for aging,* New York: Plenum. pp. 87-103.

smoking or risky drinking, or adopting and maintaining healthier activity and eating patterns) would be more successful when policies and influences in the wider environment supported healthy behavior through, for example, clean indoor air laws and access to safe and attractive places to walk or bike and healthy, affordable food choices.

A strong, early proponent of the ecological approach to prevention, McKinlay (1995) proposed a template for more effective population health promotion strategies that linked individual-level, clinical health behavior change strategies with broader, population-level health promotion efforts, including upstream policy and environmental interventions.

The model McKinlay proposed (see Table 7.2) recommended interventions across a broad spectrum of factors, linking downstream individual clinical approaches with midstream interventions aimed at health plans, schools, worksites, and communities with upstream macro-level public policy and environmental interventions strong enough to subvert or redirect countervailing societal, economic, and industry forces. In essence, McKinlay was one of the first to argue that success in achieving lasting population-wide health behavior change required a "full court press."

In a review of the past three decades of progress in population health promotion, the Institute of Medicine's (2000) report recommended individual-level interventions aimed at those who possess a behavioral risk factor or suffer from risk-related disease. For these groups, the emphasis is on changing rather than preventing risky behavior. Population-level interventions that target defined populations in order to change and/or prevent behavioral risk factors may involve mediation through important organizational channels or natural environments. State and national public policy/environmental interventions aim to strengthen social norms and supports for healthy behavior and redirect unhealthy behavior.

> *"(I)t is unreasonable to expect that people will change their behavior easily when so many forces in the social, cultural and physical environment conspire against such change."—Institute of Medicine*

IOM used McKinlay's broad spectrum, multilevel model for describing the balance needed between the dominant clinical and individually oriented approaches to disease prevention, on one hand, and the population-level approaches addressing the generic social and behavioral factors linked to disease, injury, and disability, on the other. Observing that "it is unreasonable to expect that people will change their behavior easily when so many forces in the social, cultural and physical environment conspire against such change" (IOM, 2000, p. 2), the authors recommended population-based health promotion efforts that:

- Use multiple approaches (e.g., education, social support, laws, incentives, behavior change programs) and address multiple levels of influence simultaneously (i.e., individuals, families, communities, nations)
- Take account of the special needs of target groups (e.g., based on age, gender, race, ethnicity, and social class)
- Take the long view of health outcomes, because changes often take many years to become established
- Involve a variety of sectors in society that have not traditionally been associated with health promotion efforts, including law, business, education, social services, and the media

The last three decades of progress in national tobacco control, hailed by some as one of the greatest public health successes of the second half of the 20th century, is the example most often used to illustrate the power and promise of ecological approaches for health intervention.

Although major disparities in tobacco use and its addiction remain, regressive tobacco tax and price increases have proved especially effective in certain high-risk and underserved populations—including adolescents, pregnant women, and low income smokers. State telephone quitlines (1-800-QUIT-NOW) offering cost-free counseling and medication have greatly expanded the reach of evidence-based individual cessation treatments to traditionally underserved low income and minority populations.

Reflecting the growth in research evaluating the population impacts of midstream and upstream interventions for tobacco control, CDC's Task Force for Community Preventive Services was launched in1996 to conduct systematic reviews of **community-based and policy interventions** to change health behavior, similar to the reviews conducted by the USPSTF of "downstream" clinical preventive interventions (U.S., Centers for Disease Control and Prevention, 2005) Based on its review of evidence for 14 different tobacco control interventions, the CDC recommends

- Smoking bans and restrictions to reduce exposure to environmental tobacco smoke
- Tax and price increases and mass media campaigns to reduce the number of youth who start smoking and to promote cessation
- Telephone quitline support, as well as a number of health care system interventions, also to increase cessation

Similar ecological models have been described and proposed for each of the other major behavioral risk factors discussed in this chapter—risky drinking, physical activity, dietary behavior change, and obesity. And, in 2005, the CDC Community Preventive Services Task Force developed guidelines to promote better health among community members.

A great sense of urgency surrounds the need to identify evidence-based full-court press strategies that can halt the nation's current obesity epidemic, especially among children (Institute of Medicine, 2010; White House Task Force, 2010). The dramatic rise in the prevalence of overweight and obesity among youth and adults over the past several decades is primarily due to environmental and economic changes affecting behavior on both sides of the *energy balance equation*—that is, the amount of energy (calories) used versus the amount consumed.

The cumulative effects of technology—such as automobile-dependent transportation and more sedentary jobs—along with changes in lifestyles in typical suburban environments, which limit the places to which adults and children can walk, have reduced the amount of physical activity in everyday life.

At the same time, increased access to low-cost, sugar-laden, and high-fat foods and beverages; increased exposure to marketing for these unhealthy products, larger portion sizes, increased restaurant use, an exodus of grocery stores and other sources of fresh fruits and vegetables from cities to suburbs; and the rising cost of fresh produce relative to soda and snack foods have played a critical role in promoting excessive caloric intake, especially in low income and racial/ethnic minority populations.

Rapid progress is being made in understanding the environmental and policy factors that affect physical activity and in identifying promising multilevel, broad-spectrum interventions. The CDC Community Preventive Services Task Force reviewed research on interventions and found evidence for recommendations spanning the full McKinlay model. These include:

- *Downstream* health behavior change programs that increase social supports for physical activity and exercise (e.g., health care provider reminder systems plus provider education) and reducing out-of-pocket costs for effective cessation therapies
- *Midstream* requirements for school physical education classes that increase the time students spend in moderate or vigorous physical activity and "point of decision" prompts on elevators and escalators that encourage people to use nearby stairs
- *Upstream* efforts to create, or increase, access to safe, attractive, and convenient places for physical activity, along with informational outreach to change knowledge and attitudes about the benefits of and opportunities for physical activity

Again, there are pervasive racial/ethnic disparities in access to safe places to walk, bike, and play, which have sparked several studies of socio-economic differences in access to community sports areas, parks, swimming pools, beaches, and bike paths.

An additional set of CDC Task Force physical activity recommendations was issued in 2005, addressing transportation and land use policies, ranging from zoning guidelines to improved federal, state, and community projects for walking and bicycling. Together, these guidelines have provided a strong science-based blueprint for multisector efforts by professionals in public health, urban planning, transportation, parks and recreation, architecture, landscape design, public safety, and the mass media to close the gaps between recommended and actual physical activity levels for all U.S. children and adults.

As we learned from the success of tobacco control, highly credible scientific evidence can persuade policy makers and withstand the attacks of those whose interests are threatened. But the difficulty of implementing effective broad-spectrum approaches should not be underestimated. Powerful political opponents benefit from the sale, promotion, and marketing of unhealthy products. Other barriers include industry lobbying, limited public support for healthy public policies, and inadequate funding for and enforcement of effective policies and programs. For example, youth tobacco and alcohol access laws have been poorly enforced, the Tobacco Master Settlement Agreement funds have been used to reduce state budget deficits rather than for evidence-based tobacco control, and the farming of unhealthy crops continues to be subsidized.

Creating a favorable political climate requires advocacy in order to instigate broad public pressure and support for change, clear and well-communicated evidence of public demand and support for change, and evidence of the beneficial health and economic impact of proposed programs and policies.

With respect to high-risk populations and environments, systematic surveillance can increasingly monitor the prevalence of behavioral risk factors and related health-promoting programs, resources, and policies. Such surveillance systems, which already exist for tobacco control and are rapidly developing for physical activity, establish a national baseline that makes it possible to assess the effects of specific interventions and to evaluate important local, state, and national intervention efforts. Finally, although some events and political changes may create opportunities for rapid change, as did the Tobacco Master Settlement Agreement, a long-term view is essential. Most successful health promotion and social change efforts have required decades of hard work.

Changing Provider Behavior: Closing The Gap Between Best Practice And Usual Care

One of the most basic measures of national health care quality is the extent to which patients receive recommended, evidence-based care. Evidence-based guidelines exist for prevention-oriented primary care interventions related to behavioral risks, and putting these guidelines into practice has become an important objective for national health care **quality improvement** efforts.

A decade ago, the Institute of Medicine's (2001) report, *Crossing the Quality Chasm*, set forth a bold national agenda for improving health care quality across the full spectrum of care, from prevention to acute and chronic illness and palliative care, including health behavior change. A follow-up IOM report (2003) selected health behavior change interventions for tobacco and obesity as two of the top 20 priorities for national action. These reports and the reviews and recommendations issued over the past decade by the USPSTF and Community Preventive Services Task Force had a significant influence on the prevention and public health provisions of the Patient Protection and Affordable Care Act (health reform) enacted in 2010.

Despite strong evidence for behavioral prevention in primary care, there are gaps between recommended and actual care. A landmark study of the quality of outpatient health care found that U.S. adults, on average, receive about *half* the services recommended for people with their specific health problems and even less—only 18%—of the recommended lifestyle screening and counseling services (McGlynn et al., 2003). It is safe to say that most patients who could benefit from health behavior change counseling, especially those from low socioeconomic groups and with racial/ethnic minority backgrounds, are not receiving it. In most studies, patients receive only the first two of the 5 A's— *assessment* and *advice.*

- *Tobacco use:* Brief primary care tobacco use counseling has been ranked the single highest priority clinical preventive service that is received by fewer than half of the patients who need it. Yet, national data suggest that only 65% of current adult smokers report being asked about tobacco use and advised to quit, and many fewer report counseling or other effective treatments (e.g., one-on-one counseling, class or clinic, quitline, nicotine gum, nicotine patch, or prescription medication).
- *Alcohol use:* Only 10.5% of adults seen in primary care settings were screened for alcohol misuse and referred for treatment when alcohol-dependent (McGlynn et al., 2003).
- *Physical inactivity and unhealthy diet:* In a 1992 survey, 40% of internists and 30% of nurse practitioners reported routinely assessing the physical activity levels of their patients, but only about half of each group reported developing physical activity plans for them. Further, data from the 2005 National Health Interview Survey found that only 28% of adult received physician advice on physical activity.
- *Obesity:* CDC's 2005/06 National Ambulatory Medical Care Survey found that in 50% of visits by obese adults (body mass index [BMI] of 30 or greater) the complete height and weight data needed to screen for obesity was not obtained; in 70% of visits, obesity was not formally diagnosed; and 63% of obese patients received no counseling for diet, exercise, or weight reduction. Similarly, recent surveys of family practitioners (Sesseberg et al., 2010) and pediatricians (Klein et al., 2010) found that only about half of these primary care providers (45% and 52%, respectively) routinely assess BMI in children over age two.

Early efforts to improve provider adherence to recommended clinical practices mirrored early efforts to boost patient adherence to recommended health practices. These efforts employed individual provider-focused educational strategies, including educational materials and continuing medical education (CME) to change provider motivation, knowledge, attitudes, and self-efficacy. This was true for evidence-based clinical practice guidelines generally and for prevention and behavior change guidelines specifically. These efforts, like the parallel patient-focused efforts, achieved modest success.

Systematic evidence reviews conducted in the 1990s found that most educational approaches, including traditional CME, had limited impact; more interactive and skills-based educational efforts that used principles of adult learning and were consonant with the principles of social learning theory (including modeling by respected peer "opinion leaders") were somewhat more effective; and multicomponent interventions that addressed the multiple intrapersonal and environmental barriers to provider adherence, especially system barriers, were most effective.

The limited success of "if you tell them, they will change" provider education strategies drew critical attention to the many system-level barriers to adherence to evidence-based guidelines and recommendations, including the pressure of time (in the face of more urgent medical issues), inadequate office supports, a lack of provider and patient resources, and missing financial incentives.

Follow-up studies confirmed that clinician training was most effective when combined with efforts to create office supports to prompt, facilitate, and reward the delivery of preventive interventions, especially behavioral counseling, and that the most successful interventions were not one-size-fits-all, but tailored to the unique circumstances present in any particular office practice.

MULTILEVEL MODELS FOR IMPROVING DELIVERY OF EFFECTIVE HEALTH BEHAVIOR CHANGE INTERVENTIONS

Collectively, these findings led to a shift in understanding what the targets of interventions to change *provider* health care practices needed to be. Crabtree and colleagues (1998) introduced a "*practice ecology model*" emphasizing the need to address not just the behavior of individual providers, but also the powerful effects of the health care systems in which they practice.

They and other proponents of a broader view of health care improvement emphasized the need for *broad spectrum* strategies addressing multiple levels of influence: downstream intrapersonal/individual provider-level factors; midstream interpersonal/practice team, office micro-systems, and health plan influences; and upstream macro-level health care systems and policies (Goodwin et al., 2001).

Responding to the same evidence, the Institute of Medicine's (2001) *Crossing the Quality Chasm* report described the need for a new model for national health care quality improvement as follows: "The current care systems cannot do the job. Trying harder will not work. Changing systems of care will" (p. 4). The report went on to recommend a fundamental re-engineering of the nation's health care system—moving from a system designed primarily to support and pay for the delivery of reactive acute and remedial illness care to one that would support and pay for the proactive, preventive and behavioral care needed to manage and prevent chronic disease.

Several thorough reviews have identified effective systems supports and policy changes needed to improve the preventive care provided by clinicians (see Figure 7.1). Again, work in the area of tobacco led the way. The CDC reviewed research on the effectiveness of multiple interventions (e.g., provider training/feedback and organizational, administrative, and

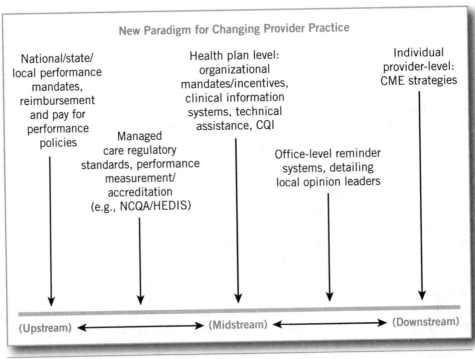

FIGURE 7.1
Comprehensive approach to changing provider practice.

reimbursement changes) to improve the delivery of primary care tobacco interventions. It recommended reducing patient co-payments for proven tobacco dependence treatment services and establishing reminder systems to help providers identify patients who use tobacco products and prompt them to implement the 5 A's (e.g., chart stickers, stamps including tobacco use as a "vital sign," medical record flow sheets, checklists). The CDC also recommended provider training because training plus office supports significantly improve the delivery of screening and counseling for unhealthy diet and risky drinking.

In response to these findings, it has been said that "an ounce of prevention takes a ton of office system change." Until recently, we lacked a coherent model for what this "ton of change" included. Filling this void, Wagner and colleagues reviewed the research on effective chronic illness care and prevention and devised a model for the multiple interlocking systems supports required for effective planned, proactive chronic illness care—the **chronic care model** (Wagner et al., 1996).

This model applies equally to the *prevention* as to the *treatment* of chronic disease, both of which require helping patients to change the behavioral risk factors that cause or complicate their illnesses. The chronic care model helped pave the way for the still-developing concept of the "medical home" as a means for reorganizing primary care practices to improve health outcomes and reduce health care costs and disparities.

The six key elements of the chronic care model can be implemented at the level of the office practice or the level of the larger health care delivery system. Each of the elements includes interventions that are planned rather than reactive, patient-centered and informed by individually relevant patient data, proactive, involve scheduled outreach and follow-up, and population-based—that is, focused on an entire panel of patients with a specific behavioral risk factor, disease, or condition and not just on individuals who seek care. Both prevention and treatment of chronic conditions require regular (nonsymptom-driven) screening and counseling for health behavior change, involve ongoing planned care with proactive follow-up, depend on active patient involvement in decision making and adherence, and require links to supportive community resources and services.

The chronic care model proved a helpful heuristic for describing an organization-wide initiative at Group Health Cooperative of Puget Sound that integrates screening and treatment for tobacco use with routine primary care. This successful plan applied all six model elements as follows:

- *Health care organization:* health plan leaders made reducing tobacco use their top prevention priority, provided financial and other incentives to providers (including hiring dedicated clinic counselors), and eliminated patient co-payments for counseling.
- *Clinical information systems* were used to create a registry of the tobacco users enrolled in the health plan, track their use of treatment resources and programs, and generate proactive telephone quitline calls for patients and feedback reports for providers.
- *Decision support tools* included extensive provider training, ongoing consultation, automated patient assessment and guideline algorithms, and reminder tools.
- *Practice redesign* and *self-management support* included self-help materials and a telephone quit line to deliver counseling and pharmacotherapy without burdening the provider.
- *Community resources and policies* included referral to community and worksite quit-smoking clinics and related healthy lifestyle change programs; focused on stress management, exercise, and weight loss; as well as support for worksite smoking cessation. And their efforts involved campaigns and smoking restrictions and expanded state funding for tobacco prevention and control programs.

This integrated "full-court press" approach dramatically reduced the prevalence of smoking among plan members, from 25% in 1985 to 15.5% in 1993, and led to substantial reductions in (former) smokers' inpatient and outpatient health services utilization (Glasgow et al., 2001).

The chronic care model has provided a unifying approach to health care quality improvement that cuts across different types of health behavior and chronic conditions with the promise of a more efficient, sustainable, and cost-effective approach to health care quality improvement. This is especially the case given the development of several successful continuous quality improvement (CQI) techniques for putting chronic care model–based system changes into place. Promising midstream CQI techniques have been used to design and test office system changes to find ways to eliminate the barriers there and to strengthen the supports for recommended care, often through a series of "rapid cycle" (plan-do-study-act) improvement efforts.

Successful preventive CQI interventions have been delivered through learning collaboratives involving multiple health care teams from different organizations that meet and work over a 12- to 18-month period with faculty experts in CQI techniques and in the type of care targeted for improvement (e.g., tobacco dependence, obesity, diabetes management). Individual practice-level, chronic care model–based improvements involve planning, implementing, evaluating, and refining changes in individual practices. These efforts have substantially increased the proportion of patients—including the most disadvantaged patients—who receive evidence-based preventive care and for whom individual behavior change plans were developed and implemented.

Effective individual practice consultation models for CQI with a focus on multiple risk behavior change were pioneered in the Step-Up (Study to Enhance Prevention by Understanding Practice) trial conducted by Goodwin and colleagues (2001). This randomized, controlled trial tested a brief practice-tailored approach to improving preventive service delivery, emphasizing improving rates of health habit counseling and the usage of effective community-based programs and supports for health behavior change.

Intervention practices received a one-day practice assessment, an initial practice-wide consultation, and several brief follow-up visits to assess and address practice-specific barriers. All interventions were delivered by a specially trained nurse facilitator who helped practices identify promising changes and presented a menu of tools for implementing them (e.g., reminder systems, flow sheets, patient education materials, clinical information systems), including a practice improvement manual. This brief CQI intervention resulted in significant improvements at 6 and 12 months that were maintained at a 24-month follow-up.

Improvements in behavioral counseling services were especially dramatic. The investigators attributed these lasting results to the maintenance of the practice and system changes that were made—changes that may have been easier to institutionalize because they were tailored to the unique characteristics of each practice.

The success of the Step-Up trial and similar chronic care model-based primary care practice redesign approaches inspired Robert Wood Johnson Foundation's Prescription for Health national program. This program funded 27 studies in primary care practice-based research networks to discover and test innovative ways of delivering 5A's interventions for two or more health behaviors: tobacco use, sedentary lifestyle, unhealthy diet, and/or risky drinking.

Projects in round 1 of the program demonstrated that practices could identify at-risk patients and motivate them to make changes. Round 2 projects built linkages between clinical practices and community resources to reduce provider burden and help patients sustain behavior changes. Each project required policy and environmental changes in the practice (e.g., reminder systems, patient registries, performance incentives) to facilitate delivery of evidence-based counseling and related treatments and to facilitate use of needed follow-up support from community resources, such as telephone quitlines. Results showed that primary care providers were able to deliver effective health behavior change interventions when working in supportive health care systems and practices.

In the long run, just as upstream macro-level societal and policy change is needed to sustain individual behavior change, upstream macro-level health system and policy change is needed to improve care in office practices and health plans. Such changes include quality performance measurement and public reporting; "pay-for-performance" initiatives that reward providers based on the quality of care they offer; and improved information technology to support care improvement.

> *Just as upstream macro-level societal and policy change is needed to sustain individual behavior change, upstream macro-level health system and policy change will be needed to support and improve care in office practices and health plans.*

Some research has found that providers were more likely to offer health behavior change counseling when a portion of their capitation payment depended on their doing so. And providers in physician organizations were found to be more likely to offer proven health promotion services if their performance measures were publicly reported, or they received public recognition or economic benefit, and they had greater clinical information technology capacity (McMenamin et al., 2004).

Conclusion

Changing health-related behavior represents a prime target for improving national health and health care. Never have we known more about the importance of addressing the lifestyle factors that pose the most serious threats to Americans' health, produce the greatest demands on our health system, and contribute most to health care costs. The growing burden of chronic disease, a national epidemic of obesity, and escalating health care costs—at a time when health care spending already is growing faster than the U.S. gross domestic product—make establishing a stronger preventive orientation in the nation's health care and public health systems an urgent priority.

Never have we known as much about how to motivate, support, and assist individuals to make lasting lifestyle changes or how to support and assist health care professionals to deliver evidence-based preventive care aimed at behavior change. The tremendous parallel gains made in what we have learned about how to achieve effective health promotion for individuals and health care quality improvement for providers have created unprecedented potential.

In the previous edition of this text, published in 2008, we concluded that the stage was set for breakthrough improvements in national health status and health care quality. But we recognized that realizing this potential depended on leadership and political will to translate the evidence for health behavior change and health care system change into practice and policy.

The landmark 2010 health care reform legislation affords just this kind of break-through potential. This bill places prevention at the heart of the efforts need to improve the nation's health and health care. Its prevention-oriented provisions include: full Medicaid and Medicare coverage for all preventive health services recommended by the U.S. Preventive Services Task Force, including those focused on health behavior change; funding for community-based prevention grants to implement programs and policy; environmental changes to improve nutrition, increase physical activity, reduce tobacco use and substance abuse, and to reduce health risk disparities; funding for childhood obesity community demonstration projects; and the establishment of a National Prevention, Health Promotion and Public Health Council to set and track goals and objectives for improving health through federally supported prevention, health promotion, and public health programs.

The law also requires funding for the continuation and greater coordination of the U.S. Preventive Services Task Force and CDC's Community Preventive Services Task Force. Combined, these efforts hold unprecedented potential to capitalize and build on the strong evidence for health-related behavior change created over the past three decades.

DISCUSSION QUESTIONS

1. Briefly describe the effects of personal health behavior (e.g., tobacco use, risky drinking, diet, and physical activity) on individual and population health status and health care costs in the United States.
2. How have health behavior change programs and interventions changed over the past 40 years?
3. Most clinical practice guidelines physicians use, in order to achieve effective behavioral interventions, are based on the "5 A's" model. Briefly describe this model, using tobacco cessation counseling as an example.
4. Describe the parallel shifts that have taken place in understanding what the essential targets need to be for successful interventions (a) to increase patients' adherence to recommended prevention-oriented health behavior and (b) to increase providers' use of recommended clinical preventive behavior change interventions.
5. With reference to McKinlay's population-based intervention model, outline possible coordinated "downstream," "midstream," and "upstream" strategies for one of the following: (a) curbing binge drinking on a college campus, (b) increasing smoking cessation and among pregnant smokers enrolled in a Medicaid managed care plan, or (c) increasing physical activity and healthy eating among middle school students in an urban center. Be sure to mention the different sectors that would need to be involved (e.g., public health, law enforcement, local business, school officials, policy makers, community planning, transportation, health plan leaders/providers, and so on).

CASE STUDY

You have just been hired as the director of strategic planning for a health plan that insures 30% of the residents in a metropolitan area of 500,000. Those insured by this health plan are employed mostly by large companies in the metropolitan area, and these companies pay for their employees' health insurance. The health plan leaders and the employers both recognize that their business model depends on their success in addressing behavioral risk factors that play a critical role in the prevention and management of chronic diseases, the containment of health care costs, and the enhancement of employee productivity.

In your new role, you are asked to create a comprehensive plan for addressing these behavioral risk factors—by improving both the clinical care provided and the plan's community-based efforts. Specifically, you want to develop strategies to reduce the levels of tobacco use, unhealthy diet, and physical inactivity.

CASE STUDY DISCUSSION

1. How would you go about preparing this plan?
2. What mix of interventions would you need to consider that might change enrollee behavior, provider behavior, and community policies and environments and maximize the cost-effectiveness of this plan?
3. Write a report to your manager that lays out the assumptions, model(s), and evidence-based strategies you will follow in developing this plan.

REFERENCES

Center for Science in the Public Interest. (2010). *Binge drinking on college campuses.* Retrieved July 15, 2010, from http://www.cspinet.org/booze/collfact1.htm

Christakis, N. A., & Fowler, J. H. (2008). The spread of obesity in a large social network over 32 years. *New England Journal of Medicine, 357,* 370–379.

Cobb, N. K., Graham, A. A., Abrams, D. A. (2010). Social network structure of a large online community for smoking cessation. *American Journal of Public Health, 100,* 1282–1289.

Coups, E. J., Gaba, A., & Orleans, C. T. (2004). Physician screening for multiple behavioral health risk factors. *American Journal of Preventive Medicine, 27,* 34–41.

Crabtree, B. F., Miller, W. L., Aita V. A., Flocke, S. A., & Stange, K. C. (1998). Primary care practice organization and preventive services delivery: A qualitative analysis. *Journal of Family Practice, 46,* 403-409.

Emmons, K. M., & Rollnick, S. (2001). Motivational interviewing in health care settings: Opportunities and limitations. *American Journal of Preventive Medicine, 20,* 68–74.

Finkelstein, E. A., Fiebelkorn, I. C., & Wang, G. (2003). National medical spending attributable to overweight and obesity: How much, and who's paying? Retrieved July 29, 2010, from http://content.healthaffairs.org/cgi/content/full/hlthaff.w3.219v1/DC1

Glanz, K., Rimer, B. K., & Viswanath, K. (2008). Theory, research, and practice in health behavior and health education. In *Health behavior and health education: Theory research and practice,* 4th ed. (pp. 23–41). San Francisco, CA: Jossey-Bass.

Glasgow, R. E., Orleans, C. T., Wagner, E. H., Curry, S., & Solberg, L. I. (2001). Does the Chronic Care Model serve also as a template for improving prevention? *Milbank Quarterly, 79,* 579–612.

Goodwin, M. A., Zyzanski, S. J., Zronek, S., Ruhe, M., Weyer, S. M., Konrad, N., et al. (2001). A clinical trial of tailored office systems for preventive service delivery: The Study to Enhance Prevention by Understanding Practice (STEP-UP). *American Journal of Preventive Medicine, 21,* 20–28.

Institute of Medicine. (2010). *Bridging the evidence gap in obesity prevention: A framework to inform decision making.* Washington, D.C.: National Academies Press.

Institute of Medicine. (2003). *Priority areas for national action: Transforming health care quality. Quality Chasm* series. K. Adams & J.M. Corrigan (Eds.). Washington, D.C.: National Academies Press.

Institute of Medicine. (2001). *Crossing the quality chasm: A new health system for the 21st century.* R. Briere (Ed.). Washington, D.C.: National Academy Press.

Institute of Medicine. (2000). *Promoting health: Intervention strategies from social and behavioral research.* Washington, D.C.: National Academy Press.

Klein, J. D., Sesselberg, T. S., Johnson, M. S., O'Connor, K. G., Cook, S., Coon, M., et al. (2010). Adoption of body mass index guidelines for screening and counseling in pediatric practice. *Pediatrics, 25,* 265–272.

Koh, H. K. (2010). A 2020 vision for Healthy People. *New England Journal of Medicine, 362,* 1653–1656.

Maciosek, M. V., Edwards, N. M., Coffield, A. B., Flottemesch, T. J., Nelson, W. W., Goodman, M. J., & Solberg, L. I. (2006). Priorities among effective clinical preventive services: Methods. *American Journal of Preventive Medicine, 31,* 90–96.

McGinnis, J. M., & Foege, W. H. (1993). Actual causes of death in the United States. *Journal of the American Medical Association, 270,* 2207–2212.

McGlynn, E. A., Asch, S. M., Adams, J., Keesey, J., Hicks, J., DeCristofaro, A., & Kerr, E. A. (2003). The quality of health care delivered to adults in the United States. *New England Journal of Medicine, 348,* 2635–2645.

McKinlay, J. B. (1995). The new public health approach to improving physical activity and autonomy in older populations. In E. Heikkinen, J. Kuusinen, & I. Ruoppila (Eds.), *Preparation for Aging.* New York: Plenum.

McMenamin, S. B., Schmittdiel, J., Halpin, H., Gillies, R., Rundall, T. G., & Shortell, S. M. (2004). Health promotion in physician organizations: Results from a national study. *American Journal of Preventive Medicine, 26,* 259–264.

Mokdad, A. H., Marks, J. H., Stroup, D. F., & Gerberding, J. L. (2004). Actual causes of death in the U.S., 2000. *Journal of the American Medical Association, 291,* 1238–1245.

Orleans, C. T., Ulmer, C., & Gruman, J. (2004). The role of behavioral factors inachieving national health outcomes. In R. G. Frank, A. Baum, & J. L. Wallander (Eds.), *Handbook of clinical health psychology: Vol. 3. Models and perspectives inhealth psychology.* Washington, DC: American Psychological Association.

Piels, J. R., Lucas, J. W., & Ward, B. W. (2009). Summary health statistics for U.S. adults: National Health Information Survey, 2008. *National Center for Health Statistics, 10(2).*

Prochaska, J. O., & DiClemente, C. C. (1983). Stages and processes of self-change of smoking: Towards an integrative model of change. *Journal of Consulting and Clinical Psychology, 51,* 390–395.

Sesselberg, T. S., Klein, J. D., O'Connor, K. G., Johnson, M. S. (2010). Screening and counseling for childhood obesity: results from a national survey. *American Board of Family Medicine, 23,* 334–342.

U.S., Department of Health and Human Services (DHHS). (2000). *Healthy People 2010: Understanding and improving health.* Washington, DC: Author.

U.S., DHHS, Centers for Disease Control and Prevention. (2005). Tobacco: Guide to community preventive services. Retrieved on July 29, 2010, from http://www. thecommunityguide.org/tobacco/index.html

U.S., DHHS, National Institute on Alcohol Abuse and Alcoholism. (2001). *Economic perspectives in alcoholism research: Alcohol Alert No. 51*. Washington, D.C.: Author.

U.S., DHHS, Preventive Services Task Force. (2003a). Behavioral counseling in primary care to promote a healthy diet: Recommendations and rationale. *American Journal of Preventive Medicine, 24*, 93.

U.S., DHHS, Preventive Services Task Force. (2003b). Screening for obesity in adults: Recommendations and rationale. *Annals of Internal Medicine, 139*, 930–932.

U.S., DHHS, Preventive Services Task Force. (1996). *Guide to clinical preventive services* (2nd ed.). Baltimore, MD: Williams & Wilkins.

Wagner, E. H., Austin, B. T., & Von Korff, M. (1996). Organizing care for patients with chronic illness. *Milbank Quarterly, 74*, 511–544.

White House Task Force on Childhood Obesity. (2010). *Report to the President: Solving the problem of childhood obesity within a generation*. Retrieved July 29, 2010, from http://www.letsmove.gov/obesitytaskforce.php

Woolf, S. H. (2008). The power of prevention and what it requires. *Journal of the American Medical Association, 299*, 2437–2439.

8

ACCESS TO CARE

John Billings, Joel C. Cantor, and Chelsea Clinton

KEY WORDS

underinsurance

noneconomic barriers

medicare

medicaid

cost-shifting

ambulatory care sensitive (ACS) conditions

quasi-economic barriers

employee retirement income security act
(ERISA)

Obama health care reform (ACA)

consolidated omnibus budget
reconciliation act (COBRA)

Clinton comprehensive reform

children's health insurance program (CHIP)

pay or play

individual mandate

safety-net providers

disproportionate share hospitals (DSH)

LEARNING OBJECTIVES

- Understand the nature of the access problem
- Understand the distinction between economic and noneconomic barriers to health care
- Understand the characteristics of the uninsured and the policy implications of those characteristics
- Understand how access barriers impinge on health
- Understand how access barriers affect the health care delivery system
- Understand the challenges for recently enacted national health care reform, particularly around reducing noneconomic and quasi-economic barriers to care

TOPICAL OUTLINE

- Economic barriers to care
- Noneconomic and quasi-economic barriers to care
- State and federal health care reforms
- The future: continuing and emerging issues

The U.S. health care system long has struggled to assure access to health care services for all Americans. In the 20th century, major steps forward included the growth of private, employer-based health insurance following World War II, the passage of the Medicare and Medicaid programs in 1965, and the growth of federal efforts in the 1970s to expand direct service programs, such as community health centers, for low-income patients, and the State Children's Health Insurance Program (SCHIP) in 1997.

TABLE 8.1

Characteristics of the U.S. Uninsured Population (in thousands), 2009

Characteristic	Total Population	Uninsured Population	% of all Uninsured	% Uninsured
Total U.S.	304,280	50,674	100.0	16.7
By age				
Under 18 years	75,040	7,513	14.8	10.0
18–24 Years	29,313	8,923	17.6	30.4
25–34 Years	41,085	11,963	23.6	29.1
35–44 Years	40,447	8,759	17.3	21.7
45–64 Years	79,782	12,840	25.3	16.1
65 Years and over	38,613	676	1.3	1.8
By race/ethnicity				
White, not hispanic	197,436	23,658	46.7	12.0
Black	38,624	8,102	16.0	21.0
Hispanic (any race)	48,901	15,820	31.2	32.4
Asian	14,011	2,409	4.8	17.2
By household income				
< $25,000	58,159	15,483	30.6	26.6
$25,000–$49,999	71,340	15,278	30.1	21.4
$50,000–$74,999	58,381	9,352	18.5	16.0
$75,000 and Over	116,400	10,561	20.8	9.1

Source: DeNavas-Walt, C., Proctor, B. D., & Smith, J. C. (2010). *Income, poverty, and health insurance coverage in the United States: 2009.* Report P60-238. U.S., Census Bureau, Current Population Reports, Consumer Income.

All of these developments helped improve access for many Americans, but, by 2009, 50.7 million Americans were uninsured, 16.7% of the total U.S. population (DeNavas-Walt, Proctor, & Smith, 2010).

In 2010, the landmark Patient Protection and Affordable Care Act (ACA) became law and is expected to lead to greatly expanded health insurance coverage; the Congressional Budget Office (CBO) estimates that the new law will decrease the number of uninsured in 2019 by 32 million, leaving 14 million nonelderly United States residents uninsured, including an estimated 30% of whom may be unauthorized immigrants. Of those Americans who will become insured over the next decade, an estimated 16 million will enter Medicaid and the Children's Health Insurance Program (CHIP, successor to SCHIP), with the balance purchasing coverage through new insurance exchanges or newly covered through their employers (U.S. Congress, CBO, 2010).

The potential health impact of lack of insurance on patients is well documented, as are the benefits of health insurance coverage. For instance, both children and adults with Medicaid or private insurance are more likely to have a usual source of care than people who are uninsured (Kaiser Family Foundation, 2010b). Having a large number of uninsured patients also has deleterious effects on the health care delivery system, as providers struggle to shift costs to other payers who can subsidize the expenses incurred by patients without coverage. Not surprisingly, proponents of the ACA often cited lack of insurance coverage and its consequences as key reasons to support the reform legislation.

> *Having a large number of uninsured patients also has deleterious effects on the health care delivery system, as providers struggle to shift costs to other payers who can subsidize the expenses incurred.*

However, access to care is not a one-dimensional problem. The **underinsurance** issue shows that insurance card alone does not eliminate barriers to access. First, there are issues of the extent and adequacy of coverage. Are outpatient services covered as well as inpatient care? Are prescription drugs included? Mental health and substance abuse services? Long-term care? Disease management services? And what about the levels of co-payments and deductibles? At least 61 million adult Americans are estimated to be *under*insured; their coverage is inadequate to assure financial access to care.

Then there's the other side of the coin. How adequate are the insurer's payments to providers? For example, Medicaid's pattern of low physician payment rates has discouraged physicians from participating in the program, thereby limiting where many Medicaid recipients can receive care. Similarly, managed care companies typically do not pay enough for mental health services, and agencies delivering these services lose money on every insured patient visit.

Even insured patients can face serious noneconomic barriers to care that have a dramatic effect on access, service utilization, and health outcomes. In most of the country, the delivery of care remains largely fragmented and uncoordinated (see Chapter 9), making it difficult for many insured Americans to arrange for and obtain the services they need efficiently. To the extent that the health care delivery system fails to respond to and accommodate differences in language, culture, religion, health care beliefs, care-seeking behavior, or educational levels, it creates additional impediments to access. Such **noneconomic barriers** are often worse for low income patients, leading to disproportionately high financial costs beyond those directly related to health care services. For example, obtaining timely doctor visits for a child may require that a parent take time off from work, forgo wages, arrange child care for siblings, or obtain transportation—all of which may be more difficult for families with limited resources or who are socially isolated.

These questions remain relevant even after passage of the ACA, particularly given the reliance of the reforms on expanding Medicaid and CHIP and the uncertainty around the insurance products that will ultimately be bought through state insurance exchanges.

This chapter examines the nature and extent of all of these barriers to care. In the first section, we explore economic barriers, including an overview of the characteristics of the uninsured, a discussion of problems in the extent and adequacy of coverage, and an examination of the consequences that lack of adequate insurance has for patients and providers. In the subsequent section, we describe noneconomic barriers and document their impact on health and health care. In the final section, we examine various reforms, discuss their potential significance and limitations, and explore future issues related to access.

Economic Barriers to Care

CHARACTERISTICS OF THE UNINSURED (PRE-REFORM)

Understanding the characteristics of the uninsured is important in understanding barriers to access and the challenges that ACA attempts to address. The level of uninsurance among the elderly is very low at 1.8% (DeNavas-Walt, Proctor, & Smith, 2010), reflecting the dramatic impact of the **Medicare** program, which provides almost universal coverage for Americans age 65 and over. Although the program has important limitations in coverage and noneconomic barriers exist for this population, Medicare has done much to make health care services accessible for older Americans.

Among the nonelderly, the highest rate of uninsurance is among young adults ages 18 to 34; in 2009, about 30% of this age group was uninsured. The higher rates in this age group reflect two important factors: their dependence on employer-based coverage for private insurance and the impact of the federal–state Medicaid program. When U.S. employers that historically have offered insurance stop providing coverage to their workers, or when an individual becomes unemployed, the risk of becoming uninsured increases enormously. The cost of individual coverage is prohibitive for most uninsured people, especially low income workers or the unemployed. Young adults have higher rates of unemployment, are more recent entrants to the workforce, and typically have lower wage jobs or work only part-time.

Young adults also often have difficulty establishing **Medicaid** eligibility, although eligibility rules vary among states. Medicaid eligibility currently is limited to low income individuals in certain age groups (children, the elderly) or who are blind/disabled, pregnant, single parents, or unemployed parents (in some states). Under ACA, eligibility will expand to include nearly everyone up to 133% of the federal poverty level ($24,352 for a family of 3 in 2010). This increased eligibility will enable coverage for employed parents and childless adults—groups that generally have not been eligible for Medicaid, regardless of income, although some states have provided coverage through state-financed programs for certain categories of adults (e.g., the "medically indigent"). The targeted nature of the Medicaid program also is reflected in the lower rates of uninsurance for children (who are categorically eligible through CHIP) and women (who are more likely to be single parents or may become eligible through pregnancy).

Most uninsured Americans work at least part-time. About 85% live in households where the family head has been employed during the past year. Accordingly, the problem of uninsurance is typically due to the failure of an employer to offer insurance or to the employees not enrolling in coverage that they are offered. In fact, as the proportion of Americans enrolled in employer-sponsored health insurance declined from 69% to 61% from 1999 to 2005, the uninsured proportion increased from 12% to 14% of the adult nonelderly population (The Commonwealth Fund, 2007).

Historically, the highest rates of uninsurance are among nonprofessional or managerial occupations in the retail, service, construction, and agricultural sectors, with much higher rates of uninsurance among small employers and the self-employed. In 2009, low wage earners (incomes less than 200% of the federal poverty level) represented more than half of the working uninsured and had rates of uninsurance more than six times greater than higher income workers. One 4-year study found that nearly 85 million Americans are without coverage for at least 1 month during a given year—more than double the number identified in studies reporting on a single point in time (Short & Graefe, 2003).

That same study showed that about 12% of people uninsured at some point during 1996 to 1999 were without coverage for the full 4 years. This suggests that for many people being uninsured was transitory, although for some it has been a long-term reality. In 2010, the uninsured are a heterogeneous lot, and no single public policy—short of universal insurance—is likely to address all of their coverage gaps, despite the ACA.

The rising cost of health care—and hence health insurance—has greatly outstripped both general inflation and workers' earnings (Figure 8.1), a trend that also has contributed to the rates of uninsurance and to the clamor for health care reform by the insured. Between 1999 and 2009, for example, employer-sponsored family health insurance plan premiums rose 131% on average nationally, whereas workers' earnings rose only 38%.

Rates of uninsurance also have historically differed markedly across states. For example, in Massachusetts, Iowa, Rhode Island, Minnesota, and Wisconsin, less than 9% of the population is uninsured, whereas in Texas and New Mexico, more than 20% is, according to the Census Bureau (Figure 8.2).

In addition to the categorical requirements noted here (children, the aged, people who are blind/disabled, etc.), states set minimum income standards for Medicaid eligibility. Historically, these standards were tied to welfare payment levels, again with considerable differences among states. Federal reforms in the 1990s broke this link and gave states more flexibility in setting eligibility standards. The ACA raises the floor for Medicaid income eligibility to 133% of the federal poverty level across all states by 2014 and preserves states' discretion to offer higher limits.

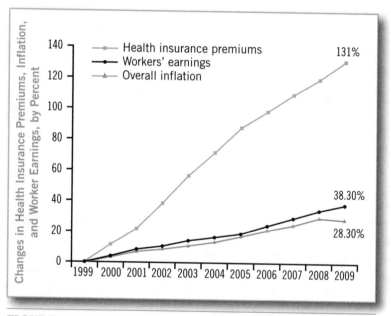

FIGURE 8.1

Changes in health insurance premiums and worker earnings, 1999–2009.
Source: Kaiser/HRET Survey of Employer-Sponsored Health Benefits, 1999–2009; Bureau of Labor Statistics, Consumer Price Index, U.S. City Average of Annual Inflation, 1999–2009; Bureau of Labor Statistics, Seasonally Adjusted Data from the Current Employment Statistics Survey, 1999–2009. This information was reprinted with permission from the Henry J. Kaiser Family Foundation, a nonprofit private operating foundation, based in Menlo Park, California, dedicated to producing and communicating the best possible analysis and information on health issues.

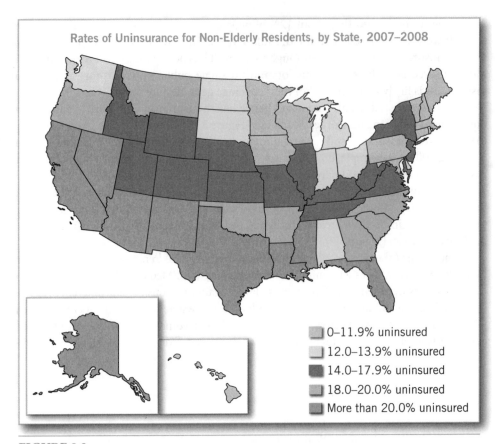

FIGURE 8.2

Rates of uninsurance for nonelderly residents, by state, 2007–2008.

Source: Kaiser Family Foundation. (2009). *The uninsured: A primer—key facts about Americans without health insurance.* Table 5. Retrieved June 12, 2010, from http://www.kff.org/uninsured/upload/7451-05.pdf. This information was reprinted with permission from the Henry J. Kaiser Family Foundation, a nonprofit private operating foundation, based in Menlo Park, California, dedicated to producing and communicating the best possible analysis and information on health issues.

A typical uninsured American might be a young adult in a low wage job, working for a small employer in the retail/services sector. Any realistic solution to the problem of uninsurance cannot depend on the uninsured themselves, more than half of whom earn less than 200% of the federal poverty level, or $36,620 for a family of three in 2009. Their employers mostly operate in the weakest sectors of the economy, and for them to offer insurance benefits would greatly increase their labor costs. No wonder that small business has been a long-standing vocal opponent of this type of requirement and that the recent reform legislation reflects many of their concerns. For instance, the ACA exempts employers with fewer than 50 employees from the legislation's stipulation that employers must provide health insurance coverage or pay a penalty if they choose not to do so. Part-time employees count toward the 50-employee minimum on a pro-rata basis based on hours worked.

Rather than using a "stick" to induce small employers to offer coverage, ACA offers "carrots." For the next 4 years, until the insurance exchanges are set up in 2014, businesses with 10 or fewer full-time-equivalent employees earning less than $25,000 a year each, on average, will be eligible for a tax credit of 35% of their health insurance costs. Businesses with between 11 and 25 workers and an average wage of up to $50,000 are eligible for partial credits.

Although the CBO estimates that 5 million more Americans post-ACA implementation will ultimately receive health insurance through their employers, concerns remain that many employees of small businesses will continue without employer-sponsored coverage. Small employers in the service and retail sectors are where much of the nation's job growth has occurred over the past decade, and many large employers increasingly rely on part-time workers, especially in the retail sector. It is not clear how the new reform will affect these industries or the choices they make around whom to employ and for how long.

In the pre-ACA world, questions about health insurance coverage and the uninsured dominated the access conversation. In the post-ACA world, at least for the foreseeable future, questions about to how to avoid underinsurance and how to respond to noneconomic and quasi-economic barriers to timely and effective care, as well as efforts to ensure quality and cost-conscience health care consumption, will likely dominate the access conversation.

UNDERINSURANCE AND OTHER LIMITATIONS OF COVERAGE

As noted previously, having an insurance card does not always assure financial or practical access to timely and effective care. For example, private insurance often excludes many services (including preventive and long-term care). Recent reform will not change this reality for many of the newly insured; for example, although long-term care will be included for many new Medicaid enrollees, coverage for those enrolling with private insurers will not include comprehensive long-term care.

Historically, most plans have exclusions or waiting periods for conditions present at the time of enrollment (preexisting conditions). These limits have affected people most in need of coverage and subjected them to substantial financial risk if they change jobs. The ACA immediately prohibits preexisting condition exclusions for children and, over time, will prohibit preexisting condition discrimination for employer-sponsored, individual market-purchased, and exchange-bought plans. The removal of the preexisting conditions barrier will undeniably expand access for many people who most urgently and chronically require health care. The recent legislation also removes, in 2014, lifetime limits on health care dollars available under any one plan.

Still, virtually all private insurance plans, even most managed care plans, require and will continue to require co-payments or deductibles that may discourage patients—especially lower income patients most sensitive to out-of-pocket costs—from seeking needed preventive care. One positive exception to this phenomenon will be "core preventive care services." As mandated by the ACA, commencing in 2013, cost sharing will disappear for Medicare, Medicaid, and private insurance plans for preventive care areas such as immunizations, prenatal services, and certain cancer screenings for high-risk individuals.

Although almost all Americans over age 65 have Medicare coverage, the program has substantial patient cost-sharing provisions and serious gaps in coverage that the recent reform did not repair. In 2010, the deductible is more than $1,100 for the first 60 days of hospital care and $135 annually for outpatient care (Part B). Once the deductible has been met, substantial co-payments (20%) are required in most cases.

Before 2006, Medicare provided virtually no coverage for outpatient prescription drugs, and the recent coverage expansion leaves large gaps for higher income patients (a $250 deductible, a 25% co-payment for the first $2,250 in drug costs, and no coverage at all for drug expenses between $2,250 and $5,100, as described in Chapter 3). This structure, otherwise known as the "donut hole," will remain in place through 2019. Starting in 2020, Medicare enrollees will pay the first $310 of drug costs out-of-pocket, 25% of their costs between $310 and $6,440, and then 5% of total costs that exceed $6,440. Even after these specific reforms come into play, older Americans, particularly those with chronic conditions, could still pay upward of $1,500 a year for prescription medicines. This is less than half of what many pay under the current system, but will remain a significant financial challenge for many low income older Americans.

Medicare also has substantial limits on coverage for long-term care (currently, only 2% of the elderly's nursing home costs are paid by Medicare). The Community Living Assistance Services and Supports (CLASS) Act, part of the recent health care reform, will make long-term care insurance available for the first time to all working Americans. Starting in 2011, all working adults will be automatically enrolled in this voluntary long-term care insurance program and will have to opt out if they do not want to participate. The program will be financed through a payroll deduction. Recent reforms also expanded long-term care options and funding for Medicaid. The legislation did not, however, provide for additional long-term care coverage or funding for current Medicare enrollees.

> *Medicare traditionally has paid less than half of elderly Americans'*
> *total costs of health care.*

As a result of these gaps, Medicare traditionally has paid less than half of elderly Americans' total costs of health care, and many people have purchased supplemental coverage for some of these expenses ("Medigap" plans), either directly or through their employer/retirement plan. Still, more than 20% of the elderly (35% of low income elderly) have no supplemental coverage and are exposed to serious financial risks and potentially substantial barriers to access.

Low income elderly Americans qualify for Medicaid, which is generally comprehensive, covering most services (including drugs and long-term care) with few restrictions or co-payments, although this varies dramatically from state to state. However, a great many providers don't participate in Medicaid, though this, too, varies across states. Although Medicaid payments to hospitals historically have been guaranteed at levels reasonably related to costs, payments to physicians are set by state administrative agencies that are facing staggering increases in program costs. Not surprisingly, payment levels for physicians and other noninstitutional providers have often been set well below rates paid by Medicare or private insurers. For example, until 2000, New York's Medicaid program would pay physicians $11 for an "intermediate office visit," an amount unchanged since 1985. The amount in 2010 is $27.50, still well below reimbursements from private payers.

In 2004 to 2005, more than 20% of physicians would not accept new Medicaid patients (Cunningham & May, 2006). Again, great variation exists across states. Medicaid also reimburses physicians more slowly than does Medicare—another reason why some physicians remain reluctant to participate in Medicaid.

Being uninsured has profound impacts on health and health care, particularly for people with chronic conditions such as asthma, diabetes, cellulitis, or chronic infections.

In one study, uninsured hospital patients were found to be substantially less likely to receive common diagnostic tests (colonoscopy, endoscopy, coronary arteriography, etc.) or costly surgical procedures (bypass surgery, joint replacement, eye surgery, etc.), even after controlling for socio-demographic and diagnostic case-mix factors (Hadley, Steinberg, & Feder, 1991). In other words, regardless of their condition or its seriousness, uninsured people were less likely to receive services that people with any type of insurance received.

Documenting the effect of having insurance on health status and on health outcomes is difficult, because people go on and off insurance periodically. Still, researchers have observed substantial differences between insured (especially privately insured) and uninsured groups. For example:

- Uninsured people are 2.9 times as likely to be diagnosed with late-stage breast cancer and twice as likely to be diagnosed with late-stage colorectal cancer than those with insurance (Halpern et al., 2008)
- Uninsured mothers begin prenatal care later and have fewer total visits (Braveman, Egerter, Bennett, & Showstack, 1991).
- Most dramatically, uninsured patients have higher overall mortality. In a national study conducted between 1971 and 1987, uninsured patients had a 25% greater risk of dying, even after adjusting for differences in socio-demographic characteristics, general health status, and health habits (Franks, Clancy, & Gold, 1993).

Although the cost of uninsurance and underinsurance is high in human terms, its serious impact on the health care delivery system affects all patients. First, distortions in utilization patterns can increase total costs. While uninsurance promotes underutilization, it also has the effect of steering uninsured patients to places and providers that must provide care, regardless of the patient's ability to pay—typically, hospital outpatient departments, emergency rooms, and community-based clinics. Costs in these settings, especially emergency departments, are high and increase the nation's overall health care spending. To the extent that an emergency visit is for a preventable condition or costs more than treatment in a primary care setting, these are avoidable costs.

These care patterns can also create financial disequilibrium. Providers serving large numbers of uninsured patients must somehow cover the costs of unreimbursed care. These same providers usually serve substantial numbers of Medicaid patients for whom costs of care often exceed reimbursement rates. These shortfalls can be cost-shifted to other payers (by raising charges sufficiently above actual costs to generate enough revenue to cover unreimbursed expenses), or providers can seek government or private subsidies. Although some states have established elaborate pooling systems to subsidize costs of uninsured patients (taxing some hospitals or insurers to support, or subsidize, hospitals with high burdens of uninsured patients) and many publicly operated providers receive direct subsidies, in most jurisdictions providers are dependent on the cost-shift.

Today's market forces make **cost-shifting** increasingly less viable. For example, managed care plans seek discounts from their provider network and, in some cases, encourage enrollees to use facilities with lower charges. The net result of these trends is that hospitals must further increase charges to a shrinking base of full-pay patients in order to cover rising, unreimbursed costs. The wholesale movement of Medicaid patients into managed care plans that has begun in most states will further undermine the financial stability of many providers. Given that millions of American residents will remain uninsured even after ACA's reforms are fully in place, these questions and concerns will remain relevant even after the size of the challenge has shrunk.

Ultimately, if hospitals close and safety-net providers fail, low income people's access to care may be seriously jeopardized because the providers most at risk of financial failure are the very ones that provide the most care to vulnerable people.

Noneconomic and Quasi-Economic Barriers to Care

MEDICAID COVERAGE DOESN'T ELIMINATE ALL BARRIERS

On some measures, patients with Medicaid coverage fare better than the uninsured, but not on many:

- Compared to uninsured children, children covered by Medicaid or CHIP are much more likely to have a usual source of care (96% vs. 68% for the uninsured) and to have had a doctor visit, and they are much less likely to have unmet health care needs (Kaiser Family Foundation, 2008).
- Medicaid recipients have fewer preventable hospitalizations than do uninsured patients, but almost 75% more than insured patients (Billings & Teicholz, 1990).
- Rates of late detection of breast cancer were only slightly higher for the uninsured than for Medicaid patients (Halpern et al., 2008).
- Pregnant women covered by Medicaid, like the uninsured, delayed prenatal care and had fewer prenatal care visit rates, compared to privately insured women (Braveman et al., 1991).

For such patients, Medicaid failed to eliminate the barriers to needed care. Low income and uninsured populations clearly face special problems in dealing with the complexities of our fragmented delivery system that create impediments to timely and effective care.

RACE/ETHNICITY

Large and persistent differences in health status, utilization, and outcomes among racial and ethnic groups are well documented. Americans who are black or Hispanic are less likely to have a usual source of primary care, they have fewer physician visits, they have higher rates of no or late prenatal care, they have lower rates of immunizations and screening tests, and they report worse health status. Large racial differences also have been documented in rates for infant mortality, low birthweight, late-stage cancer diagnosis, and mortality from all causes. Asian groups, which on some measures of health status do quite well, are more likely to be uninsured than the general population, have lower rates of regular cervical cancer screening, and higher rates of hepatitis B and liver cancer, for example.

In the United States, socioeconomic status and race/ethnicity are intertwined, and research has attributed many, but not all, racial/ethnic disparities in health care and health status to socioeconomic conditions. (High rates of liver problems in some Asian groups, for example, occur because hepatitis B is endemic in parts of China and Korea and pass from mother-to-child at birth. Lack of screening and immunization among immigrants allows the disease to perpetuate here.)

A growing body of research that attempts to control for socioeconomic and other factors suggests that minority status in and of itself is an important factor in health care utilization and outcomes. For example, after researchers adjusted for differences in insurance coverage, minority adolescents still were less likely to have a usual source of primary care, had fewer annual physician contacts, and had less continuity of care (Lieu, Newacheck, & McManus, 1993). Among children enrolled in managed care plans, minority children used fewer services, even after controlling for differences in health status (Riley et al., 1993).

In other research that adjusted for insurance coverage differences, African Americans with end-stage renal disease have been found to be only half as likely as whites to receive kidney transplants and, when they did, they had been on waiting lists significantly longer (Gaston, Ayres, Dooley, & Diethelm, 1993). Similarly, among patients with coronary artery disease, African American patients have fewer angiograms and coronary artery bypass surgeries, regardless of disease severity (Johnson et al., 1993).

Similar differences in rates for invasive cardiac procedures have been observed for Hispanic populations (Carlisle, Leake, Brook, & Shapiro, 1996). A study of patients visiting a trauma center emergency room with bone fractures found that non-Hispanic whites were more than twice as likely to receive pain medication than were Hispanic patients, even after accounting for differences in injury severity, pain assessment, insurance status, gender, and language (Todd, Lee, & Hoffman, 1994). Other studies have documented additional differences across Hispanic subgroups, with Mexican American, Puerto Rican, and Cuban American populations experiencing different rates of having no usual source of care, preventive care, and physician visits compared to non-Hispanic whites.

Large racial/ethnic disparities in utilization also occur among elderly Americans in the Medicare program. African American beneficiaries have fewer physician visits and receive less preventive care, such as influenza immunizations, than any other racial group. They also have lower rates for many diagnostic tests, surgical procedures (including surgeries like coronary bypass, prostatectomy, hysterectomy, orthopedic surgery, etc.), and other services (Gornick et al., 1996).

Of course, many potential explanations exist for these differences in utilization, outcomes, and health status. In research, controlling for factors such as socioeconomic status, education, disease incidence/prevalence, illness severity, resource availability, and insurance coverage can be extraordinarily difficult, and interpretation of these research findings must be tempered by recognition of these methodological limits. However, differences by race/ethnicity are substantial and persistent across numerous studies that use a variety of research designs. Even if race is the determining factor in these differences, we are left with many unknowns, although the possibility of overt or latent racial/cultural bias at all levels of the health care delivery system cannot be discounted. A landmark study in which a large sample of physicians were presented with computerized patient scenarios in which actors were interviewed about their hypothetical chest pain showed that race and gender were important independent determinants of physicians' decisions to refer patients for advanced diagnostic procedures. That study showed that referral rates for cardiac catheterization were lower for women and blacks (84.7% of each group) compared to white men (90.6%) (Schulman et al., 1999).

A landmark study . . . showed that race and gender were important independent determinants of physicians' decisions to refer patients for advanced diagnostic procedures.

There also are studies that provide evidence institutions exist in which racial disparities in both treatment and outcomes are smaller than the average. Veterans Administration (VA) hospitals are a notable such example. In fact, a recent study showed that, in some VA hospitals, African American veterans had better long-term outcomes than white veterans for certain high mortality conditions (Volpp et al., 2007). This was not always true. As recently as 1993, research demonstrated that white veterans were significantly more likely to receive coronary surgery than black veterans (Whittle, Conigliaro, Good, & Lofgren, 1993). Clearly, further research is required to explain the factors that contribute to or mediate any treatment bias and to identify how patient preferences (e.g., in weighing risks and benefits of medical interventions), care-seeking behavior, and attitudes toward the health care delivery system affect utilization and outcomes across populations.

Managed care may offer some hope of establishing a "medical home" or "patient-centered medical home" for all enrollees, but it may erect other barriers to appropriate care. In one national survey, African American, Asian, and Hispanic respondents with private coverage were up to twice as likely as their white counterparts to lack a usual source of care, but these differences were much smaller among members of managed care plans. Still, minority managed care members were much more likely to report dissatisfaction with their usual source of care, compared to minority members of traditional (nonmanaged care) health plans, whereas dissatisfaction among whites was low regardless of whether they were in managed care (Phillips, Mayer, & Aday, 2000).

CULTURE/ACCULTURATION/LANGUAGE

The effect of culture and acculturation on health care use and outcomes is still not well understood. It is hypothesized that cultural barriers may contribute to lower or less optimal utilization patterns by U.S. Hispanic and Asian immigrant populations. These barriers can involve a broad range of potential problems, including social isolation, distrust of Western medicine, unfamiliarity with the U.S. health care delivery system, differences in concepts of disease and illness, alternative care-seeking, perceptions of provider disrespect, fears about immigration status, or language difficulties.

Several studies have attempted to evaluate how increased acculturation tends to resolve these impediments to access. This research is limited by the difficulty of defining and assessing levels of acculturation. One of the better-designed studies suggests that language proficiency may be either the best indicator of acculturation or the most important component of these cultural factors in facilitating access. In that study, better language skills resulted in more use of preventive services such as physical exams, cancer screening, and dental checkups (Solis, Marks, Garcia, & Shelton, 1990).

Disparities have been observed for Pap smear and mammography screening rates among immigrant women. Even when data were adjusted for demographic factors including age and income, U.S.-born women (citizens) were significantly more likely to have screening tests than noncitizens (Echeverria & Carrasquillo, 2006).

Of course, acculturation itself may create new problems and new barriers. For example, many immigrant families have stable family structures, including strong intergenerational ties. To the extent that these relationships become more attenuated in urban America, it may become more difficult for families to cope with the requirements of managing a family member's serious health condition or chronic disease.

SEX AND GENDER

Little research has been conducted on sex-related barriers to health care, although differences in rates of procedures have been documented. For example, female end-stage renal disease patients are less likely than males to receive a kidney transplant (Held et al., 1988) or have cardiac surgery (Udvarhelyi et al., 1992). However, these differences were not associated with higher mortality rates for women (raising an important question about whether greater access to surgical care is always beneficial).

Again, further study is needed to determine whether gender-related patient preferences or attitudes toward surgery's risks and benefits help account for these differences. Three emerging lines of research underscore the potential seriousness of sex-related impediments to health care for women. First, women have been systematically excluded from clinical trials for new drugs and procedures (Cotton, 1990). The potential bias is obvious. To the extent that medical practice is based on findings of clinical trials, many practitioners may be reluctant to prescribe medications or recommend procedures that have not been fully tested for women. Accordingly, access to new drugs and technologies may be delayed and resource utilization patterns significantly affected. But the corollary also raises serious concerns: research generalized from gender-biased studies may not provide optimal guidance for care decisions.

A second body of research has begun to document how physicians' gender can affect practice patterns and the service utilization patterns of their patients. For example, one study of preventive care found that female patients of female physicians were more than twice as likely to receive cervical cancer screening tests (Pap smears) and 40% more likely to receive mammograms than patients of male physicians (Lurie et al., 1993). In another study, male and female doctors alike took more account of male patients' age and considered more age-related disease possibilities for men than for women (Adams et al., 2008). Again, the full impact of how differences in physician gender can influence the care provided to patients has not yet been determined.

Finally, many women do not have access to family planning, abortion counseling, or abortion services. There are explicit restrictions on use of federal funds for these services, which the recent health care reform legislation did not reverse. Insurance plans that will be marketed to individuals on state-based exchanges starting in 2014 will explicitly not include abortion services, as mandated by the ACA. Women can purchase separate abortion coverage if insurance companies choose to market those products. Barriers to these services are not only the lack of insurance coverage—many religiously affiliated providers simply do not offer them. In some states, providers, whether religiously affiliated or not, either have the option or are required to actively discourage women from seeking abortions. Moreover, the aggressive tactics of many antiabortion groups have deterred even providers who operate in states without such restrictions from offering these services and often have discouraged women from seeking them. Restricted access to reproductive services tends to affect low income patients disproportionately, because they are likely to have fewer alternatives, but the chilling politicization of abortion-related care affects access for all women.

EDUCATION

As with other indirect barriers to health care, it is difficult to isolate and quantify the effect of education on health care utilization and outcomes. Parental education deficits, however, are associated with lower levels of well-baby and other preventive services (Short

& Lefkowitz, 1992) and lower overall health care utilization by their children (Newacheck, 1992). Differences in education have been linked to lower rates of breast cancer screening, even after adjusting for a broad range of economic and socio-demographic factors (Lantz, Weigers, & House, 1997). In another study, Medicaid patients with limited education were found to be less likely to use preventive services, have greater difficulty following medical regimens, miss more appointments, and seek care later in the course of an illness (Weiss, 1994).

A growing body of research has begun to document the impact of functional health literacy—the ability to use reading, writing, and computational skills in typical, everyday patient situations, such as reading prescription labels, following diagnostic test instructions, or understanding treatment directions.

An estimated 40 million Americans are illiterate and another 50 million are marginally literate, results that did not statistically change between 1992 and 2003, the years the two most recent national surveys of literacy were conducted (Kirsch, Jungeblut, Jenkins, & Kolstad, 1993; U.S., National Center for Education Statistics, 2009). The 2003 survey found that more than 75 million American adults had below basic *health* literacy. Close to 30% of Americans older than 65 and close to half of Americans with below a high school education or equivalent lacked basic health literacy. Contributing to these problems are inadequate health education in schools, particularly at the middle school or early high school levels, and the lack of computer literacy, which might enable some self-education, particularly for older populations.

The potential literacy-related impediments to timely and effective care are serious. In a study conducted in two public hospitals, 42% of patients could not understand directions for taking medication on an empty stomach, 26% could not comprehend information on an appointment slip describing the scheduled follow-up visit, and more than 25% could not follow instructions for preparing for a gastrointestinal radiological exam. Overall, researchers determined that almost 30% of patients using the facilities had inadequate functional health literacy, and another 14% had only marginal levels (Williams et al., 1995).

RESOURCE AVAILABILITY/PERFORMANCE

The supply and distribution of health care resources has obvious implications for access. In remote rural areas, the absence of a primary care practitioner, an obstetrician/ gynecologist, a dentist, or even a hospital can have a serious impact on the ability of area residents to obtain timely care. In urban areas, supply issues are often more complex. There are huge, well-documented differences in physician supply across and within communities, with some central cities having serious shortages of practitioners. (See also Chapters 9 and 15.)

The issue for access, however, is the availability and capacity of providers, not the supply. Many large urban hospitals (and their associated medical office buildings) are located in or near lower income neighborhoods, but this proximity does not assure access. Although many hospital outpatient departments accept patients who cannot pay (or charge them on a sliding fee schedule), this is certainly not necessarily the case for the private-practice physicians clustered nearby.

Growing evidence suggests that changes in health system capacity, even in comparatively resource-rich areas, can be associated with measurable changes in access. Much of this evidence connects system capacity to gaps in use of medical services by racial/ethnic minorities. Mukamel and colleagues (2007), for example, linked a decline in the black–white disparity in heart surgery rates in New York to a rise in available cardiac surgeon capacity. Likewise, several studies have connected the successful diffusion of new medical technologies with reduced racial disparities (Stanley, DeLia, Cantor, 2007; Groeneveld, Heidenreich, & Garber, 2005; Ferris et al., 2006). Finally, a recent study of a policy reform in New Jersey allowing a doubling in the number of hospitals licensed to provide diagnostic coronary angiography, a critical test for heart disease, was associated with the elimination of a large black–white utilization disparity in this service (Cantor et al., 2009).

There are legitimate concerns that, as more people have insurance, service usage will increase, particularly in areas in which providers are already under stress. The ACA contains a number of provisions designed to address these anxieties. Among them, the ACA will increase, in 2011, the number of graduate medical education (i.e., medical residents) slots available to rural and underserved areas and provide states with grants for providers in rural and underserved urban areas. Additionally, after two decades in which no new medical schools were created, two new schools have opened in the past couple of years and four more have been granted accreditation, providing more potential primary care doctors and physicians broadly for underserved areas. However, increased capacity also presents serious risks of induced demand, especially if the new supply is not targeted at areas of greatest need (underserved urban and rural areas), contributing to further unwarranted variations in care that has been well documented (The Dartmouth Institute for Health Policy and Clinical Practice, 2007).

The ACA additionally increases Medicaid payments for primary care doctors (those practicing family medicine, general internal medicine, obstetrics and gynecology, and pediatrics) in hospital and private-practice settings to 100% of Medicare rates, but it does so only for 2013 and 2014. The finitude of this particular remedy, its restriction to primary care providers, and the expected return in 2015 to substantially lower Medicaid reimbursement rates raises concerns that, within a few years, many physicians may again be discouraged from participating in Medicaid.

Still, little is known about how the performance of the primary care delivery system affects access to care, including primary care itself. In part, to better understand the relationship between performance and access, the ACA requires enhanced collection of primary care and general medical care data for underserved rural, frontier, and urban populations, as well as data on race, ethnicity, gender, primary language, and disability status. Clearly, a highly efficient provider who can serve numerous patients can increase access. But, more important, providers also can organize their practices to reduce many indirect barriers to care discussed previously (e.g., eliminating language barriers, reducing wait times, developing a culturally sensitive environment, and developing more effective techniques to help chronic disease patients who have literacy problems).

> *Recently, patient satisfaction has become the focus of many health care delivery systems struggling to attract and maintain their middle class patient base.*

Recently, patient satisfaction has become the focus of many health care delivery systems struggling to attract and maintain their middle class patient base. These developments have spawned a mini-industry of researchers and consultants attempting to help providers become more responsive to patient needs and desires. A parallel effort should be targeted at understanding the indirect barriers to care for low income patients and helping safety-net providers adapt their delivery approach to these patients' needs. This is not yet on the horizon.

MORE ON THE IMPACT OF NONECONOMIC AND QUASI-ECONOMIC BARRIERS: PREVENTABLE/AVOIDABLE HOSPITALIZATIONS

As illustrated in many of the studies described previously, the impact of noneconomic and quasi-economic barriers on utilization patterns and health status can be substantial. A growing body of analysis, which began in the mid-1990s and produced unique, still-relevant data sets, has begun to explore how barriers to primary care services can result in increased use of other health care services, such as more costly hospital care (Table 8.2) (Billings, Zeitel, & Lukomnik, 1993; Billings, Anderson, & Newman, 1996; Bindman et al., 1995.)

This research is based on the simple premise that timely and effective primary care can usually (a) prevent the onset of an illness (e.g., congenital syphilis, pertussis, tetanus); (b) control a condition before it becomes more acute (e.g., ear infections in children, urinary tract infections, dehydration); and (c) manage a chronic disease or condition to help reduce the chances of a serious flare-up (e.g., asthma, diabetes, congestive heart disease, hypertension).

TABLE 8.2

Access Problems Reported by Patients Hospitalized for Ambulatory Care Sensitive Conditions

Access problem	Percentage Who Reported Problem		
	Ages 6 months–17 years	Ages 18–64 years	All ages
Not up to going	5.1	36.1	29.2
Too nervous or afraid	10.2	33.8	28.6
Unable to get free time to get care	8.1	27.2	22.9
Had to wait too long to get appointment	20.3	20.4	20.4
Problems with child care	32.8	14.3	18.2
Costs too much	13.8	18.1	17.2
Unable to keep medical appointment	7.4	20.2	17.1
Couldn't fill prescription	16.4	16.9	16.8
Transportation difficulties	19.3	15.8	16.5
Didn't know where to go to get care	8.6	13.8	12.7
Not sure provider would understand needs	22.4	9.1	12.2
Care not available when needed	11.3	12.1	12.0
Denied care	13.4	9.7	10.6
Didn't like usual place to get care	17.2	7.9	9.9
Lose pay/trouble getting off work	12.1	6.0	7.3
Language problem	1.8	4.7	4.3

Source: Billings, J., Mijanovich, T., & Blank, A. (1997). *Barriers to care for patients with preventable hospital admissions.* New York, NY: United Hospital Fund. Reprinted with permission.

To the extent that barriers exist for ambulatory care services, causing a patient to delay or be unable to obtain care, an illness or condition may deteriorate to the point that it cannot be controlled in an outpatient setting, and hospitalization becomes necessary.

Conditions that can be effectively managed on an outpatient basis are called **ambulatory care sensitive (ACS) conditions**. Researchers have documented huge differences in hospitalization rates for ACS conditions in different geographic regions. Areas with high ACS hospitalization rates, not surprisingly, also have more self-reported barriers to access than do areas with low ACS hospitalization rates (Bindman et al., 1995). Moreover, these differences are strongly associated with the area's average income; indeed, in some communities, more than 80% of the variation in admission rates among ZIP codes is explained by the percentage of low income residents (Figure 8.3). Admission rates for ACS conditions in low income areas are on average 2.5 to 3.5 times higher than in more affluent areas, and rates in some low income neighborhoods are as much as 20 times higher than in higher income areas of the same community (Billings & Weinick, 2003).

Of course, not all admissions for ACS conditions are preventable. However, the strong association between ACS admissions and the prevalence of poverty in a given geographic

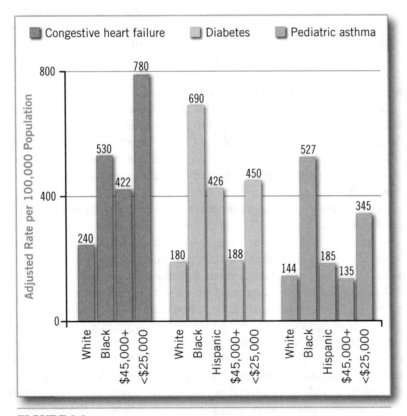

FIGURE 8.3

Hospital admissions for ambulatory care sensitive conditions by race/ethnicity.
Source: The Commonwealth Fund. (2006). *Why not the best? Results from a national scorecard on U.S. health system performance: Chartpack,* p. 41. Retrieved June 12, 2010, from http://www.commonwealthfund.org/Content/Publications/Fund-Reports/2006/ Sep/Why-Not-the-Best—Results-from-a-National-Scorecard-on-U-S—Health-System-Performance.aspx. Reprinted with permission.

area suggests significant local barriers to primary care. Insurance coverage is undoubtedly an important factor: differences in admission rates across urban areas in Canada, which has universal health insurance, are significantly smaller than in the United States. Lack of insurance coverage is nevertheless unlikely to be the sole or even the predominant cause for the disparities documented in U.S. urban areas, because the overwhelming majority of hospitalized low income patients had Medicaid coverage.

The impact of the noneconomic and quasi-economic barriers discussed previously is undoubtedly a substantial contributor to hospitalization rates for ACS conditions. Low income patients who have no regular source of care, who are dissatisfied with available providers (because of long wait times, language difficulties, or lack of cultural sensitivity) or who have difficulties arranging child care, getting off work, or simply coping with problems associated with illness are clearly at significant risk of delaying or not obtaining needed care until hospitalization is necessary, often even if they have Medicaid or access to a safety net provider.

The potential relationships among these noneconomic factors and access are illustrated by an analysis of ACS admission rates in Miami, Florida. Although, like most U.S. urban areas, Miami has significant concentrations of poor and minority residents, the difference in ACS admissions rates between low and high income areas is relatively small (about 1.6 times higher in low income areas), and the association between area ACS rates and income is weaker. This lack of a large income-related difference in ACS admission rates is particularly evident for ZIP codes where residents are mostly Cuban American. There, income did not affect hospitalization rates, but in other ZIP code areas the association between low income and high ACS hospitalization rates was comparable to that of other U.S. metropolitan areas (Billings, Anderson, & Newman, 1996).

These data suggest that noneconomic and **quasi-economic barriers** to care are not insurmountable. Further research is needed to sort out the influence of various factors, such as the family and social structure of the Cuban American population, their health status and care-seeking behavior, and the organization and performance of the primary care delivery system serving this population, which includes a substantial cadre of Cuban American physicians.

The extent and nature of indirect barriers to care are illustrated in a study of patients hospitalized for ACS conditions in New York City (Billings, Mijanovich, & Blank, 1997). In interviews after hospital admission and medical stabilization, 60.9% of low income patients reported that they had received no care prior to the admission, and another 17.4% had received care only in the emergency room. By contrast, among higher income patients, only 31.4% had received no prior care and 5.8% only emergency room care.

More than half of low income patients reported that they had delayed or not obtained needed care, compared with about one-fourth of higher income patients. The leading explanations for delay or failure to obtain care among low income patients were not directly related to the costs of care (the overwhelming majority had Medicaid coverage), but rather to a range of problems reflecting the difficulties encountered by low income patients and their families in their daily lives, as well as problems in negotiating the complexities of the health care delivery system. More than 25% of adult patients indicated they were "too nervous or afraid," "too busy with other things," or simply "not up to going," reflecting their serious ambivalence about the health care delivery system. Substantial numbers also reported difficulties arranging child care, problems with transportation, concern about having to wait too long, uncertainty about where to go, and apprehensions that providers wouldn't understand their needs.

Nonfinancial barriers to timely and effective care are substantial and serious. Clearly, successful access initiatives must go beyond simply providing an insurance card to the uninsured. Part of the solution must be to develop a health care delivery system that recognizes that low income people are struggling with many aspects of their lives, including their health care problems, and are less well-equipped from an educational or health literacy perspective to successfully deal with those challenges. Longer clinic hours, home visits, and special outreach for different populations may be essential aspects of quality care for these groups, along with more responsive social service, education, and other supportive programs.

State and Federal Health Care Reforms

STATE INITIATIVES TO IMPROVE ACCESS: INNOVATIONS AND LIMITATIONS

Although federal health reform struggled in the 1990s and dropped off the agenda in the decade prior to 2008, states took the initiative to drive access improvements, higher quality, and cost control. High voter interest in improving health care access, the troubling long-term decline in the number of people with employer-sponsored health coverage, and discord and delay in Washington over how to proceed with reform stimulated debate and action in many states. As states emerged from their late-1990s fiscal slump, a few took up the mantle of comprehensive reform (Burton, Friedenzohn, & Martinez-Vidal, 2007). Three New England states, in particular, enacted bold new near-universal coverage strategies for their populations and several have taken significant incremental steps toward that goal.

Maine was the among the first wave of states to tackle comprehensive health reform with its 1993 Dirigo Health plan (*Dirigo*, the Maine state motto, is Latin for "I lead") (Rosenthal & Pernice, 2004). Dirigo Health is a voluntary plan that offers new insurance products with sliding-scale state premium subsidies for people below three times the federal poverty rate. Part of the Dirigo coverage expansion is funded by Medicaid (including with federal dollars), and some of the financing comes from employers and individuals. A controversial component of the Dirigo plan reduces payments to health care providers as more people gain coverage under the plan. The rationale is that, with most people insured, providers will experience less bad debt and charity care. Dirigo also includes significant quality improvement and cost-control features that policy makers hope will improve the cost effectiveness and affordability of care over time. In the early phases of Dirigo's implementation, voluntary enrollment was slower than projected, but there is still an opportunity for Maine to meet its goal of affordable coverage for all.

In 2006, Massachusetts and Vermont followed Maine with ambitious strategies, each targeting coverage of at least 95% of state residents. Like Maine's, these states' plans are multifaceted and complex. Two strategies are at the center of the Massachusetts plan: a law requiring nearly every person in the state to have coverage and a new program for individuals and small-employer groups to purchase affordable coverage, foreshadowing the key coverage strategies of the ACA.

The individual mandate—the boldest and most attention-getting part of the Massachusetts plan—was supported by both conservatives (including then-governor and later Republican presidential candidate, Mitt Romney) and liberals (including long-time national health insurance advocate, the late Democratic Senator Edward M. Kennedy).

To make coverage affordable, Massachusetts subsidizes individuals in families whose income is less than three times the federal poverty rate, using a blend of federal and state funds. The plan also requires employers with more than 10 workers to contribute to coverage. Residents who violate the individual mandate will face increasing financial penalties over time, and employers who do not meet requirements to contribute to employee coverage also could face penalties. (The individual mandate is one aspect of the ACA that, as of October 2010, is facing legal challenge in the states.)

The second innovation in the Massachusetts plan is a new purchasing pool called the Commonwealth Health Insurance Connector. People eligible for state subsidies obtain their plans through the Connector and it serves as a source of affordable coverage for other individuals and small businesses. The Connector also provides a vehicle for workers to use pretax dollars to buy coverage, and employers are required to offer this option. These so-called Section 125 plans (named for the governing provision in the federal internal revenue code) save workers roughly 25% on their premiums, because these payments are not taxed like other forms of income.

By late 2008, Massachusetts had reduced the number of uninsured substantially—2.6% of state residents were uninsured versus 10.4% in 2006 (Long, Cook, and Stockley, 2008). Yet, 200,000 state residents remained uninsured and health care costs had risen more than the national average, by 8 to 10 percentage points a year.

Vermont's Catamount Health plan, like the Maine and Massachusetts plans, provides a subsidized insurance product for residents below three times the federal poverty line. It also requires employers to contribute to coverage for workers or pay an assessment. Federal Medicaid matching dollars play a role in financing the Vermont plan, as does an increase in the state tobacco tax. A key feature of the Vermont plan is a concerted program to promote better management of chronic illnesses, such as diabetes and heart disease. These conditions often lead to expensive hospital care when not well controlled through lifestyle changes, adherence to prescription drug regimens, and strong ambulatory care management.

To obtain approval for use of federal Medicaid dollars to fund the plan, Vermont has made the bet that chronic disease management and other plan features will control future health costs. Under a federal Global Commitment to Health Medicaid waiver, the federal government has given the state more flexibility in how it uses its dollars, in exchange for a cap on future federal Medicaid expenditure growth. It is too early to tell whether Vermont has made a wise bet, but implementation of Catamount Health is under way, with full implementation targeted for 2010.

The reforms in Maine, Massachusetts, and Vermont have important elements in common. All three states started with the advantage of having low uninsured rates compared to other states and comparatively robust employer health insurance sectors. All three programs use subsidies to help pay premiums for families whose household income is less than three times the federal poverty rate—well above Medicaid and CHIP eligibility thresholds in most states. Each of the states brought new revenue to the table, and all three found ways to bring in new federal funding through Medicaid. The political culture of New England also may have played a role in bringing these plans to fruition, although, notably, these reforms all had bipartisan support, and in some cases, bipartisan leadership.

Although states have provided a hot-bed of innovation, only a handful has made any progress in significantly expanding coverage.

These initiatives also illustrate the limitations of reform at the state level. Although states have provided a hot-bed of innovation, only a handful has made any progress in significantly expanding coverage. In some important ways, the reform deck is stacked against them. First, unlike the federal government, states are required to balance their budgets, so periods of economic downturn threaten the financial sustainability of expensive programs. Economic downturns not only limit tax revenues available to pay for the programs and subsidies, but they simultaneously increase demand for those subsidies as more people lose jobs and private coverage. Second, employer financing of coverage—a common source of revenue for state reforms—is constrained for two reasons. Imposing employer mandates and taxes works against states' economic development efforts to recruit and retain jobs within their boundaries, and federal law (the **Employee Retirement Income Security Act [ERISA]**) restricts the degree to which states can regulate and tax employers' benefit plans. Finally, it is no accident that many of the states that have moved ahead with the boldest coverage reforms had comparatively low uninsured rates and high per-capita incomes. In fact, the states with the biggest access challenges are those with the least capacity to pay for new plans. This fact alone limits the degree to which the U.S. access problem can be solved by state-level reforms. Still, these efforts provided a partial blueprint for the federal health reform debate that began during the presidential election campaign of 2008.

AT THE FEDERAL LEVEL: THE LONG AND TORTUOUS PATH TO REFORM

The history of federal health care reform, from the creation of Medicaid and Medicare through amendments to the Social Security Act in 1965, until the recent passage of **President Obama's historic ACA** is largely a chronicle of failed overhauls and somewhat successful incremental expansions in coverage. Senator Ted Kennedy and President Nixon failed to reach a compromise on national health care reform in the early 1970s, and President Clinton failed to pass comprehensive health care reform in the early 1990s.

In the early 1980s, a series of significant Medicaid expansions occurred via the "backdoor" of Medicaid waivers, which increased coverage for children with disabilities, pregnant women, and children who met certain need thresholds. In 1986, Congress enacted the Emergency Medical Treatment and Active Labor Act (EMTALA), requiring hospitals participating in Medicare—effectively all U.S. hospitals—to admit all people to their emergency rooms, regardless of ability to pay. Also in 1986, as part of the **Consolidated Omnibus Budget Reconciliation Act (COBRA)**, employees gained the right to maintain their health plan coverage up to 18 months after losing a job.

In 1996, after the failure of the **Clinton comprehensive reform** effort in 1994, Congress passed and President Clinton signed the Health Insurance Portability and Accountability Act (HIPAA), marking one of the first consensus incremental reforms following the failure of the Clinton plan. HIPAA assured greater continuity of insurance coverage when a worker changes jobs—an important issue for the middle class, but one affecting the 45 million uninsured only marginally.

The 1995 to 1997 federal budget debates focused primarily on how much savings could be extracted from Medicare and Medicaid. In fact, the Balanced Budget Act of 1997 included Medicare and Medicaid reductions of almost $140 billion (mostly from reduced payments to providers, many of which were never enacted). But the Balanced Budget Act also introduced one of the largest incremental expansions in access since Medicare and Medicaid—the **State Children's Health Insurance Program (SCHIP, now CHIP)**. The new law included $40 billion over 10 years for SCHIP to provide coverage for many of the country's estimated

10 million uninsured children. SCHIP supported state action and, unlike Medicare and Medicaid, capped the federal government's financial liability for expanded coverage, making it more acceptable to conservatives. Funds were to be distributed to states based on the number of low income, uninsured children in their population, adjusting for differences in wages and the costs of health care.

As SCHIP matured, states encountered challenges in sustaining their progress. Federal SCHIP spending limits and state budgetary constraints led some states to freeze SCHIP enrollments and others to tighten eligibility rules. In recent years, states have faced gaps between their SCHIP spending and federal allotments. In 2005, more than half of the states exceeded their federal funding allotment by 10% or more, causing stress on state budgets and pressure to limit SCHIP enrollment and reduce program benefits, as well as pressure on the federal government to fill those gaps (Lambrew, 2007).

In 2007, Congress passed two different versions of a bill to reauthorize SCHIP. Despite bipartisan support and advocates' pointing to SCHIP's many accomplishments—more than 6 million children covered, lower rates of unmet health needs, and improved health outcomes—President Bush vetoed the bill twice. SCHIP received temporary extensions in 2007 and 2008 and, in 2009 Congress passed and President Obama signed a reauthorization and expansion of CHIP. At that time, CBO estimates asserted that, thanks to CHIP funding, 4.1 million children would be reached who otherwise would have been uninsured in 2013.

The Bush administration presided over another historically significant incremental expansion of the federal role in health care financing: the Medicare Prescription Drug, Improvement, and Modernization Act of 2003. The law established a program, referred to as Medicare Part D, that, beginning January 1, 2006, for the first time provided Medicare beneficiaries with outpatient prescription drug coverage.

Of the 47 million Medicare beneficiaries who are eligible for Medicare Part D, approximately 27.7 million have enrolled; overall 90% of eligible Medicare beneficiaries have some type of drug coverage, either through Part D, stand-alone drug plans, retiree benefits, and so on. Before Part D went into effect, Medicare was responsible for about 7% of drug costs paid by government (Medicare, Medicaid, and other public programs); in 2008, it was responsible for 60% of those costs (Kaiser Family Foundation, 2010c).

Both the successes and failures of these incremental approaches in expanding coverage set the stage for the hard-fought, but ultimately successful passage of President Obama's health care reform in March 2010. The ACA dramatically expands coverage while leveraging preexisting programs, most notably Medicaid (Kaiser Family Foundation, 2010a). Key provisions of ACA include:

- A substantial expansion of Medicaid, raising the floor for eligibility to 133% of the poverty level across all states and including, for the first time, coverage for childless adults
- **"Pay or play"** provisions for employers with 51 or more employees, with fines for those who do not provide coverage
- An **"individual mandate"** provision for adults, who must obtain coverage or pay a fine of $695 annually or 2.5% of household income, whichever is greater
- State-based exchanges where individuals (and ultimately employers) can obtain subsidized coverage for individuals and families with incomes up to 400% of the federal poverty level
- Insurance reforms mandating guaranteed issue, regulating premium rating, and prohibiting restrictions on coverage for preexisting conditions and lifetime limits on coverage

- Allowing adults up to age 26, regardless of student status, to be covered under their parents' health insurance plan

Given these and other provisions, CBO estimates that the number of uninsured will drop by 32 million by 2019 and that the ACA will cost a net $938 billion over 10 years.

The Future: Continuing and Emerging Issues

Passage of ACA is a landmark event in the history of U.S. health care. Of course, there is much uncertainty about its impact on the nation's health and the health care system, and much will be dependent on how it is implemented and the results of the various studies, demonstration projects, and pilot programs included in its provisions. However, there are several issues that will be critical and how they will be resolved will have an important effect on access to care.

First, rising health costs create barriers to patients without coverage (the 14 to 16 million who will not be covered even when ACA is fully implemented), as well as for insured patients who face higher premiums, higher co-pays, and higher costs for uncovered services. National health reform did not directly address the issue of health costs that continue to grow more rapidly than other sectors and the economy as a whole. Cost containment provisions of ACA are limited to a range of experiments and demonstrations on payment policy reforms (such as bundled payments or promotion of accountable care organizations; see Chapter 9), promotion of health information technology (Chapter 16), and support for research to identify the effective (and perhaps less costly) treatment modalities (Chapter 13).

> *. . . the (health reform) legislation has no immediate effect on the underlying structural factors that drive health care costs.*

Although much of the coverage expansion is financed by reductions in expected future payment increases to Medicare providers, the legislation has no immediate effect on the underlying structural factors that drive health care costs. Most providers continue to be paid on a fee-for-service basis, with strong incentives to maximize the units of service provided. More services mean more revenue and the ACA mandates coverage of more services than ever before. For example, prenatal care and delivery services must be covered by insurance companies that sell their products through the state-based exchanges. Moreover, because of the uncertainties inherent in much of medical care and the absence of evidence on comparative effectiveness for many alternative treatment approaches, the criteria for need are not well defined and the risks of provider-induced demand are substantial.

These circumstances are exacerbated by the classic conditions of market failure in health care: insured patients are largely insulated from the costs of care (except for co-payments and deductibles) and there remains substantial asymmetry of information between doctors and their patients. And all of this is in the context of a fragmented health care delivery "system," where a lack of integration means that (a) each segment of the "system" is working to maximize its revenue, (b) there is lack of information-sharing among components (despite the promise of electronic health records), and (c) there are often failures at handoff points between components (such as at hospital discharge where meaningful planning for care in the community is the exception to the rule). ACA includes strategies that have the potential to ultimately move the needle on these forces in the long-run, but its prospects for doing so are uncertain at best.

Another likely critical emerging issue is the plight of **"safety-net" providers** that serve patients regardless of their ability to pay. Although coverage expansion will reduce the number of uninsured patients treated by safety net providers, 5% to 8% of the nation's population will remain uninsured, including large numbers of unauthorized immigrants. The coverage expansion is partially financed by reductions in the extra payments Medicaid and Medicare provide to hospitals having large numbers of uninsured and Medicaid patients. Many of these **disproportionate share hospitals (DSH)** worry that reimbursements for newly covered patients will not offset reductions in DSH payments. Moreover, the care needs of many of those currently uninsured who will be covered by ACA are complex and often require more intensive and longer-term social, translation, and other services not adequately reimbursed.

The ability of safety net providers, already in precarious financial circumstances, to absorb these costs will remain a serious issue. With the post-ACA uninsured population consisting largely of unauthorized immigrants, it may not be politically feasible to advocate continued, much less increased, funding for safety-net providers.

Health reform also does little to address directly the noneconomic barriers to care. There are provisions for enhanced federal collection and reporting of data on race, ethnicity, sex, primary language, and disability status, and the Secretary of Health and Human Services is required to analyze and monitor these data to document trends in disparities. Recommendations as to how providers or insurers ought to respond to these data are scarce in the current legislation. Again, financially healthy providers would be able to use these data to tailor and expand their services for vulnerable population segments and, ultimately, reduce disparities, whereas financially challenged institutions are likely encounter greater difficulties.

In another limitation, the current health reform does not significantly change incentives around prevention and health promotion for providers, patients, or insurers. Although it expands federal support for preventive services within Medicare, adds coverage for Medicaid enrollees' immunizations, and permits employers to offer rewards to employees who participate in their insurer's wellness programs, it does not attempt to significantly move the health care system from its current orientation toward treatment.

Chronic diseases account for 70% of deaths annually (U.S., Centers for Disease Control and Prevention, 2009) and for 75% of annual health care dollars spent. These costs are borne disproportionally by public payers—Medicare, Medicaid, and soon-to-be-insured populations. The recent health reform is a lost opportunity to more strongly link payment incentives and programs to help people acquire the very tools to stay healthy and avoid the common risk factors for chronic diseases.

Finally, large numbers of children and adults are eligible but not enrolled in existing CHIP and Medicaid programs. ACA will make even more Americans eligible for publicly supported health care, especially under Medicaid. Overcoming barriers to enrollment—excess paperwork, frequent reenrollment requirements, language problems, limited outreach efforts, etc.—will be essential in order to achieve the expected benefits of expanded coverage.

The ACA is an historic effort to enable millions of Americans to get into the health care system, but providing *effective* access to a well-designed care system will remain challenging for years to come.

DISCUSSION QUESTIONS

1. Who are the currently uninsured, and what does this tell us about the nature of the problem that national health reform has tried to address in your state and more broadly?
2. Even after full implementation of national health reform, there will remain 14 to 16 million uninsured in the United States. Who are these remaining uninsured, and what are the financial and other implications of their lack of coverage for your state?
3. Who is responsible for reducing noneconomic and quasi-economic barriers to timely and effective health care? What are the different responsibilities of local, state and federal governments currently and after the full implementation of national health reform?
4. How will ACA change noneconomic and quasi-economic barriers to access? In what ways will health reform increase and decrease these barriers?
5. What are the costs of barriers to access, and who bears these costs?

CASE STUDY

You are the governor of a midsized industrial state. You have just read this chapter and have decided that you want to take on the noneconomic and quasi-economic barriers to access. How would you proceed?

CASE STUDY DISCUSSION

1. How would you staff the effort?
2. Who are the stakeholders?
3. How would you obtain their input but limit inappropriate influence?
4. Which of the various barriers are likely the most important to overcome in your state? A weak safety net? Poor provider performance? Cultural or language barriers? Education?
5. What is the realistic range of solutions/reforms that might be considered?
6. What is the likelihood of meaningful reform and over what time frame?

REFERENCES

Adams A., Buckingham, C. D., Lindenmeyer, A., McKinlay, J. B., Link, C., Marceau, L., & Arber, S. (2008). The influence of patient and doctor gender on diagnosing coronary heart disease. *Sociology of Health and Illness, 30,* 1–18.

Billings, J., Anderson, G., & Newman, L. (1996). Recent findings on preventable hospitalizations. *Health Affairs, 15,* 239–249.

Billings, J., Mijanovich, T., & Blank, A. (1997). *Barriers to care for patients with preventable hospital admissions.* New York: United Hospital Fund.

Billings, J., & Teicholz, N. (1990). Uninsured patients in the District of Columbia. *Health Affairs, 9,* 158–165.

Billings, J., & Weinick, R. M. (2003). *Monitoring the health care safety net: A data book for metropolitan areas.* AHRQ Pub No. 03-0025. Rockville, MD: Agency for Health Care Research and Quality.

Billings, J., Zeitel, L., & Lukomnik, J. (1993). Impact of socioeconomic status on hospital use in New York City. *Health Affairs, 12,* 162–173.

Bindman, A. B., Grumbach, K., Osmond, D., Komaromy, M., Vranizan, K., Lurie, N., Billings, J., & Stewart, A. (1995). Preventable hospitalizations and access to health care. *Journal of the American Medical Association, 274,* 305–311.

Braveman, P. A., Egerter, S., Bennett, T., & Showstack, J. (1991). Differences in hospital resource allocation among sick newborns according to insurance coverage. *Journal of the American Medical Association, 266,* 3300–3308.

Burton, A., Friedenzohn, I., & Martinez-Vidal, E. (2007). *State strategies to expand health insurance coverage: Trends and lessons for policymakers.* New York, NY: Commonwealth Fund Commission on a High Performance Health System.

Cantor, J. C., DeLia, D., Tiedemann, A., Stanley, A., & Kronebusch, K. (2009). Reducing racial disparities in coronary angiography. *Health Affairs, 28,* 1521–1531.

Carlisle, D. M., Leake, B. D., Brook, R. H., & Shapiro, M. F. (1996). The effect of race and ethnicity on the use of selected health care procedures: A comparison of south central Los Angeles and the remainder of Los Angeles County. *Journal of Health Care for the Poor and Underserved, 7,* 308–322.

The Commonwealth Fund. (2007). *The future of employer-sponsored health insurance charts.* Retrieved June 11, 2010, from http://www.commonwealthfund.org/Maps-and-Data/ChartCart/View-All.aspx?chartcategory=The+Future+of+Employer+Sponsored+Health+Insurance

Cotton, P. (1990). Examples abound of gaps in medical knowledge because of groups excluded from scientific study. *Journal of the American Medical Association, 263,* 1051–1055.

Cunningham, P. J., & May, J. H. (2006). *Medicaid patients increasingly concentrated among physicians.* Tracking Report No. 16. Washington, D.C.: Center for Studying Health System Change.

The Dartmouth Institute for Health Policy and Clinical Practice. 2007. *Supply-sensitive care.* Retrieved June 12, 2010, from http://www.dartmouthatlas.org/keyissues/issue.aspx?con=2937

DeNavas-Walt, C., Proctor, B. D., & Smith, J. C. (2010). *Income, poverty, and health insurance coverage in the United States: 2009.* Report P60-238. U.S., Census Bureau, Current Population Reports, Consumer Income. Retrieved October 16, 2010, from http://www.census.gov/prod/2010pubs/p60-238.pdf

Echeverria, S. E., & Carrasquillo, O. (2006). The roles of citizenship status, acculturation, and health insurance in breast and cervical screening among immigrant women. *Medical Care, 44,* 788–792.

Ferris, T. G., Kuhlthau, K., Ausiello, J., Perrin, J., & Kahn, R. (2006) Are minority children the last to benefit from a new technology? Technology diffusion and inhaled corticosteriods [*sic*] for asthma. *Medical Care, 44,* 81–86.

Franks, P., Clancy, C. M., & Gold, M. R. (1993). Health insurance and mortality: Evidence from a national cohort. *Journal of the American Medical Association, 270,* 737–741.

Gaston, R. S., Ayres, I., Dooley, L. G., & Diethelm, A. G. (1993). Racial equity in renal transplantation: The disparate impact of HLA-based allocation. *Journal of the American Medical Association, 270,* 1352–1356.

Gornick, M. E., Eggers, P. W., Reilly, T. W., Mentnech, R. M., Fitterman, L. K., Kucken, L. E., & Vladeck, B. C. (1996). Effects of race and income on mortality and use of services among Medicare beneficiaries. *New England Journal of Medicine, 335,* 791–799.

Groeneveld, P. W., Heidenreich, P. A., & Garber, A. M. (2005). Trends in implantable cardioverter-defibrillator racial disparity: The importance of geography. *Journal of the American College of Cardiology, 45,* 72–78.

Hadley, J., Steinberg, E. P., & Feder, J. (1991). Comparison of uninsured and privately insured hospital patients: Conditions on admission, resource use, and outcome. *Journal of the American Medical Association, 265,* 374–379.

Halpern, M. T., Ward, E. M., Pavluck A. L., Schrag, N. M., Bian, J., & Chen, A. Y. (2008). Association of insurance status and ethnicity with cancer stage at diagnosis for 12 cancer sites: a retrospective analysis. *The Lancet Oncology, 9,* 222–231.

Held, P. J., Pauly, M. V., Bovbjerg, R. R., Newmann, J., & Salvatierra, Jr., O. (1988). Access to kidney transplantation: Has the United States eliminated income and racial differences? *Archives of Internal Medicine, 148,* 2594–2600.

Johnson, P. A., Lee, T. H., Cook, E. F., Rouan, G. W., & Goldman, L. (1993). Effect of race on the presentation and management of patients with acute chest pain. *Annals of Internal Medicine, 118,* 593–601.

Kaiser Family Foundation. (2010a). *Explaining the basics of health care reform.* Retrieved June 11, 2010, from http://www.kff.org/healthreform/basics.cfm#explaininghealth carereformseries

Kaiser Family Foundation. (2010b). *Medicaid beneficiaries and access to care.* Retrieved June 11, 2010, from http://www.kff.org/medicaid/upload/8000-02.pdf

Kaiser Family Foundation. (2010c). *Prescription drug trends.* Retrieved June 11, 2010, from http://www.kff.org/rxdrugs/3057.cfm

Kaiser Family Foundation. (2008). Children's access to care by health insurance status. (slide) Retrieved June 12, 2010, from http://facts.kff.org/chart.aspx?ch=485

Kirsch, I., Jungeblut, A., Jenkins, L., & Kolstad, A. (1993). Adult literacy in America: A first look at the results of the National Adult Literacy Survey. Washington, D.C.: National Center for Education Statistics, U.S. Department of Education.

Lambrew, J. M. (2007). The State Children's Health Insurance Program: Past, present, and future. New York, NY: Commonwealth Fund Commission on a High Performance Health System.

Lantz, P. M., Weigers, M. E., & House, J. S. (1997). Education and income differentials in breast cancer and cervical cancer screening. *Medical Care, 35,* 219–236.

Lieu, T. A., Newacheck, P. W., & McManus, M. A. (1993). Race, ethnicity, and access to ambulatory care among U.S. adolescents. *American Journal of Public Health, 83,* 960–965.

Long, S. K., Cook, A., & Stockley, K. (2008). *Health insurance coverage in Massachusetts: Estimates from the 2008 Massachusetts Health Insurance Survey.* (PowerPoint Presentation). Massachusetts Division of Health Care Finance and Policy. Retrieved June 11, 2010, from http://www.mass.gov/Eeohhs2/docs/dhcfp/r/pubs/08/hh_survey_08.ppt

Lurie, N., Slater, J., McGovern, P., Ekstrum, J., Quam, L., & Margolis, K. (1993). Preventive care for women—Does the sex of the physician matter? *New England Journal of Medicine, 329,* 478–482.

Mukamel, D. B., Weimer, D. L., Buchmueller, T. C., Ladd, H., & Mushlin, A. I. (2007). Changes in racial disparities in access to coronary artery bypass grafting surgery between the late 1990s and early 2000s. *Medical Care, 45,* 664–671.

Newacheck, P. W. (1992). Characteristics of children with high and low usage of physician services. *Medical Care, 30,* 30–42.

Phillips, K. A., Mayer, M. L., & Aday, L. (2000). Barriers to care among racial/ethnic groups under managed care. *Health Affairs, 19,* 65–75.

Riley, A. W., Finney, J. W., Mellits, E. D., Starfield, B., Kidwell, S., Ouaskey, S., et al. (1993). Determinants of children's health care use: an investigation of psychosocial factors. *Medical Care, 31,* 767–783.

Rosenthal, J., & Pernice, C. (2004). Dirigo Health Reform Act: Addressing health care costs, quality, and access in Maine. Portland, ME: National Academy for State Health Policy.

Schulman, K. A., Berlin, J. A., Harless, W., Kerner, J. F., Sistrunk, S., Gersh, B. J., et al. (1999). The effect of race and sex on physicians' recommendations for cardiac catheterization. *New England Journal of Medicine, 340,* 618–626.

Short, P. F., & Graefe, D. R. (2003). Battery-powered health insurance? Stability in coverage of the uninsured. *Health Affairs, 22,* 244–255.

Short, P. F., & Lefkowitz, D.C. (1992). Encouraging preventive services for low-income children: The effect of expanding Medicaid. *Medical Care, 30,* 766–780.

Solis, J. M., Marks, G., Garcia, M., & Shelton, D. (1990). Acculturation, access to care, and use of preventive services by Hispanics: Findings from HHANES 1982–1984. *American Journal of Public Health, 80* (Suppl.), 11–19.

Stanley, A., DeLia, D. & Cantor, J. C. (2007). Racial disparity and technology diffusion: The case of cardioverter defibrillator implants, 1996–2001. *Journal of the National Medical Association, 99,* 201–207.

Todd, K. H., Lee, T., & Hoffman, J. R. (1994). The effect of ethnicity on physician estimates of pain severity in patients with isolated extremity trauma. *Journal of the American Medical Association, 271,* 925–928.

Udvarhelyi, I. S., Gatsonis, C., Epstein, A. M., Pashos, C. L., Newhouse, J. P., & McNeil, B. J. (1992). Acute myocardial infarction in the Medicare population. *Journal of the American Medical Association, 268,* 2530–2536.

U.S., Centers for Disease Control. (2009). Chronic disease prevention and health promotion. Retrieved May 27, 2010, from http://www.cdc.gov/chronicdisease/overview/index.htm

U.S. Congress, Congressional Budget Office. (2010). H.R. 4872, Reconciliation Act of 2010 (Final Health Care Legislation). Retrieved June 11, 2010, from http://www.cbo.gov/doc.cfm?index=11379&zzz=40593

U.S., Department of Education, National Center for Education Statistics (2009). *National assessment of adult literacy.* Retrieved June 11, 2010, from http://nces.ed.gov/naal/kf_demographics.asp

Volpp, K. G., Stone, R., Lave, J. R., Jha, A. K., Pauly, M., Klusaritz, H., et al. (2007) Is thirty-day hospital mortality really lower for black veterans compared with white veterans? *Health Services Research, 42,* 1613–1631.

Weiss, B. D., Blanchard, J. S., McGee, D. L., Hart, G., Warren, B., Burgoon, M., & Smith, K. J. (1994). Illiteracy among Medicaid recipients and its relationship to health care costs. *Journal of Health Care for the Poor and Underserved, 5,* 99–111.

Whittle, J., Conigliaro, J., Good, C. B., & Lofgren, R. P. (1993). Racial differences in the use of invasive cardiovascular procedures in the department of Veterans Affairs Medical System. *New England Journal of Medicine, 329,* 621–627.

Williams, M. V., Parker, R. M., Baker, D. W., Parikh, N. S., Pitkin, K., Coates, W. D., & Nurss, J. R. (1995). Inadequate functional health literacy among patients at two public hospitals. *Journal of the American Medical Association, 274,* 1677–1682.

Medical Care Delivery

The topics chosen for Part III provide the reader with an introduction to medical care delivery. Carol Caronna and Michael Ong describe in Chapter 9 the major components of the medical care system, focusing on doctors and the settings they practice in: hospitals, ambulatory and emergency care centers, nursing homes, home care agencies, and other facilities. They also discuss how and why the care they provide is not adequately coordinated.

In Chapter 10, Doug McCarthy describes a different approach to medical care delivery on which many hopes are pinned: delivery models that take an integrative approach, rather than treating patient ailments in a piecemeal, uncoordinated way. Such approaches appear to provide better care at lower cost and are particularly attractive, given rising rates of chronic diseases and increasing numbers of older Americans with multiple chronic conditions.

Quality of care should be the primary goal of medical care in every setting. In the last decade, Americans have increasingly realized that our medical care system falls far short when it comes to providing high-quality care and that there are many opportunities to improve medical care outcomes. In Chapter 11, Carolyn Clancy and Bob Lloyd explore the most robust quality measurement and improvement strategies.

Increasingly important to all stakeholders is the value of medical services rendered. This concept encompasses more than the costs of a particular service; it addresses the question of "what did the patient (and the taxpayer) get out of it?" The value calculation is somewhat similar to a cost-benefit analysis, although "value" stresses benefits to patients, if any, whereas cost-benefit analysis focuses on benefits for those making the investment (i.e., bearing the costs). In Chapter 12, Herb White discusses the current and future prospects for getting better value for the money we spend on medical care.

"Rationing" is an unpopular word in the lexicon of health care politics. However, some observers say that medical care is rationed now, primarily based on patients' ability to pay—either through insurance or out-of-pocket. Health reform is in part intended to produce a more equitable system, by expanding health insurance coverage. In Chapter 13, Amir Satvat and Jessica Leight focus on initiatives in the United States and other countries to measure the comparative effectiveness—and, in some countries, the costs—of various medical tests, drugs, and other treatments, as a means of directing health care dollars to where they will do the most good for individual patients.

9

ORGANIZATION OF MEDICAL CARE

Carol A. Caronna and Michael K. Ong

KEY WORDS

ambulatory care	specialty care
acute care	uncompensated care
chronic care	chronic care model
long-term care	patient-centered medical home
end-of-life care	accountable care organization (ACO)
palliative care	bundled payment
primary care	

LEARNING OBJECTIVES

- Describe key components and characteristics of U.S. medical care delivery
- Describe critical issues facing the current delivery system
- Describe approaches to improve the organization of U.S. medical care
- Describe barriers preventing change in the delivery system

TOPICAL OUTLINE

- Basic framework of medical care delivery
- Characteristics of the medical care field
- Critical issues facing the delivery system
- Pathways to better organized care
- Barriers to change

The organization of U.S. medical care is complex and multifaceted. The field includes a diverse array of medical practitioners and organizations with different ownership types and goals. Numerous external factors influence the design and management of medical care, including the policies and practices of health insurance plans and other payers; laws, regulations, and accreditation standards; and patients themselves. In addition, the state of medical knowledge constantly changes. Research leads to better understandings of the nature of disease and pathways of effective treatment, while improved technologies enable new diagnostic and treatment procedures.

This complexity creates a medical care system that has been described as fragmented, disorganized, inefficient, and even chaotic (Bohmer, 2009; Devers & Berenson, 2009; Lee & Mongan, 2009). For some lucky Americans, the disjointed medical care system poses no problems. People with relatively few health issues, generous health insurance coverage, and a regular primary care provider might see the system as acceptable and even ideal. But for many others—often the ones who need medical care most—the system can be frustrating and even dangerous. Patients with several conditions, especially chronic ones, are likely to receive conflicting treatment plans from different specialists and prescriptions for drugs that adversely interact. Patients with low health literacy can be overwhelmed and bewildered by complex instructions, making treatment plans difficult to follow. And, for uninsured patients, most of the medical care system is simply out-of-reach.

> *For many Americans—often the ones who need medical care most—the U.S. health care system can be frustrating and even dangerous.*

The goal of this chapter is to provide an overview of current aspects of the U.S. health care delivery system that impede its safety, quality, and efficiency. The first section of the chapter provides a basic introduction to the system's framework. The second section describes the system's key limitations, including its diversification and fragmentation, and how these limitations create disjointed and poorly coordinated care for the average patient (Fisher, Staiger, Bynum, & Gottlieb, 2007). The third section addresses pathways to improved medical care proposed by policy makers, academics, and practitioners, and the final section describes barriers to change that must be overcome in order to better coordinate medical care in the 21st century.

Basic Framework of Medical Care Delivery

All medical care, from a simple flu shot to an intricate organ transplant, takes place within a large and complex delivery system with multiple levels and stakeholders, and affected by many external (and internal) influences, described in this section of the chapter.

PATIENTS

At an individual level, how patients interact with the medical delivery system depends on their insurance coverage (the type of coverage and whether they are insured at all), their medical history (diagnoses, medications, relationships with providers, and so forth), and their medical need. Depending on their conditions, patients may require a number of different types of care. One major distinction is between **ambulatory care** (outpatient services, requiring no overnight stay) and *inpatient care* (hospitalization).

Types of care also are classified by medical need: **acute care** (treatment of medical conditions of recent onset), **chronic care** (treatment of a *chronic condition*: any illness or impairment expected to last a year or longer that limits what one can do, or requires ongoing medical care), **long-term care** (a range of supportive, rehabilitative, nursing, and palliative services provided to people—young and old—whose capacity to perform daily activities is restricted due to chronic disease or disability), **end-of-life care** (care given to patients in their final stages of life, including symptom, pain, and medication management), or **palliative care** (a comprehensive type of care, addressing physical and mental health issues, spirituality, and family care).

HEALTH CARE PRACTITIONERS

Health care practitioners include physicians and surgeons, nurses, a wide variety of therapists and technicians, and supporting staff, such as health aides. Practitioners help shape the delivery system by applying their professional training, knowledge, and beliefs to the care of individual patients. Physicians in particular provide specialized care based on their training. *Generalist physicians* (general internists, family practitioners, pediatricians, and in some cases gynecologists/obstetricians) typically provide **primary care**: "integrated, accessible care services by clinicians who are accountable for addressing a large majority of personal health care needs, developing a sustained partnership with patients, and practicing in the context of family and community" (Institute of Medicine, 1996, p.1). *Specialist physicians* have received additional training in a specific area of expertise (e.g., endocrinology, pediatric cardiology) and provide **specialty care**.

PROVIDER ORGANIZATIONS

Provider organizations range from doctor's offices and general hospitals to more specialized organizations, such as ambulatory surgery facilities, eye-and-ear hospitals, and hospices. Pharmacies and medical laboratories provide ancillary services. Currently, the United States has about 5,000 community and general hospitals and 4,600 emergency departments (American Hospital Association, 2010a) (see Chapter 14 for information on hospitals' diverse structures and organization). Growing numbers of ambulatory surgery centers provide surgery on an outpatient basis; in 2008, there were about 6,300 Medicare-approved ambulatory surgical centers in the United States, compared to 4,600 in 2003. Other large categories of providers include 5,000 renal dialysis treatment centers, 9,800 home health agencies, 15,000 nursing homes, and 4,900 hospice organizations (MedPAC, 2009).

INSURERS AND PAYERS

In the United States, health insurance is linked to employment and individuals are responsible for obtaining their own insurance. In the 1960s, the introduction of Medicare and Medicaid provided federal- and state-funded health insurance for Americans who lacked an employment relationship—namely, the elderly and the poor. In the late 1990s, the federal government expanded need-based public coverage to American children through the Children's Health Insurance Program (CHIP). The payment mechanisms adopted by health insurers and payers greatly influence provider organizations' and practitioners' incentives, strategies, and structures. These include fee-for-service reimbursement, capitated payment plans, pay-for-performance approaches, and the establishment of networks of contract providers who provide services at discounted fees (see Chapters 2 and 3 for more information on health care policy and financing).

LAW, REGULATION, AND POLICY

Federal, state, and local governments influence the delivery system by establishing practice and licensing laws, funding research and practitioner training, providing insurance for certain populations, and setting policy agendas. The federal government in particular has the ability to create sweeping change in the health care field, such as the 1965 Social Security

Amendments establishing Medicare and Medicaid. Currently, the extent of major change created by the Patient Protection and Affordable Care Act of 2010 (ACA) will become clearer as various provisions of the Act are initiated over the next decade. The Act, in part, mandates individual insurance coverage by 2014, prohibits denial of coverage based on preexisting conditions, and creates health insurance exchanges open to the general public (see Chapter 2). At the federal level, the entities that have the most influence on the health care delivery system are congregated within the U.S. Department of Health and Human Services (DHHS).

ACCREDITATION

Accreditation agencies, such as The Joint Commission and the National Committee for Quality Assurance, create standards for medical care, construct measurements of quality, and determine which organizations meet their standards. Provider organizations seek accreditation in order to prove that they meet the standards of legitimate and appropriate medical practice, which can be critical for receiving reimbursement and contracts from insurance companies. For example, in order to be reimbursed for services to patients with public insurance (Medicare, Medicaid, and CHIP), providers must meet certain conditions of coverage and participation. One way they can demonstrate compliance with these requirements is to be accredited by agencies approved by the Centers for Medicare and Medicaid Services. Accreditation agencies also accredit, certify, and recognize insurers, health plans, treatment programs, and practitioners.

MEDICAL KNOWLEDGE

"Since World War II, U.S. federal and corporate funding for research has grown rapidly, leading to not just new drugs and technologies but also an explosion in medical knowledge" (Lee & Mongan, 2009, p. 10). As this knowledge has become more comprehensive and detailed, the medical field has witnessed a proliferation of treatment choices and protocols. Better scientific understanding of many medical problems has encouraged attempts to standardize methods for diagnosis and treatment. In the 1990s, the movement to create clinical guidelines using evidence-based medicine encouraged practitioners around the country to treat a specific illness or injury with the same treatment protocol. These expectations have changed the relationship between clinicians and the organizations in which they practice (Bohmer, 2009)—hospitals, health systems, and insurers have all taken a larger role in setting expectations for patient care and outcomes.

TECHNOLOGY

The current state of information technology in health care ranges from the lowest to the highest levels (see Chapter 16). In the last decade, the use of complex imaging techniques—magnetic resonance imaging (MRI), functional MRIs (fMRIs), computerized tomography (CT) scanning, and positron emission tomography (PET) scans—has increased dramatically in both clinicians' offices and emergency departments. In medical research, more robust information technology has made it easier to analyze the large amounts of data needed to create tailored medical treatments for specific populations. Another use of information technology—electronic medical records (EMRs) and interconnected health information technology systems—has developed more slowly in the United States; in some physicians' offices, paper files of handwritten medical records share space with high-tech diagnostic equipment.

In some physicians' offices, paper files of handwritten medical records share space with high-tech diagnostic equipment.

The fragmented organization of U.S. medical care across many providers, generally practicing care in their own way, both facilitates and constrains the processes by which patients' health problems are solved (Bohmer, 2009). At the micro level, every patient–practitioner encounter is influenced by the patient's insurance, medical history, and medical need, as well as the practitioner's training, knowledge, beliefs, and preferences with respect to treatment strategies. In addition, every encounter is framed, at the macro level, by the reimbursement structures of insurers and payers; policy, law, and accreditation standards; and the state of medical knowledge and technology.

The degree to which these components interact to create a safe, effective, high-quality delivery system depends on the coordination among multiple stakeholders and participants, the consistency between the different levels and parts of the system, and the extent of systematic planning and oversight. In its current state, the U.S. health care system lacks the necessary coordination and intentional design required to consistently deliver effective and efficient care to all patients. The next section identifies some of the most critical shortcomings of our current system and their impact on patient care.

Characteristics of the Medical Care Field

Americans made almost a billion visits (994,321,000) to doctors' offices in 2007—about 3.4 visits per person (U.S., DHHS, 2010a)—and spent more than $2.3 trillion on health care in 2008. The United States ranks number one among other developed countries in terms of medical costs and expenditures. It spends the highest share of its gross domestic product on medical care, it has the highest per capita health expenditures, and it has the highest out-of-pocket expenditures in absolute terms (American College of Physicians, 2008; see Chapter 2).

Yet, Americans' health is no better than the health of those in other countries and, in some cases, is worse. For example, a 2005 Commonwealth Fund study of six countries (the United States, Canada, Germany, the United Kingdom, Australia, and New Zealand), found the United States ranked last on three important indicators of healthy lives. Compared to the other countries, the United States had the shortest life expectancy, the highest rates of mortality and infant mortality, and the highest proportion of adults with activity limitations related to medical conditions.

Much of the blame for this combination of high costs and suboptimal care is attributed to the way the U.S. delivery system is organized—and disorganized. In its current state, the delivery system is *complex, diversified, fragmented,* and *stratified.* These four characteristics create "disjointed and poorly coordinated care . . . as [patients] move across settings and among providers: more frequent and flawed care transitions, failure at communication, and errors" (Fisher et al., 2007, p. w55). This section explains each of these characteristics and why it has negative effects on patient care—all critical issues facing the U.S. delivery system. In addition, this section briefly examines how other developed countries have addressed the same issues, resulting in improved health outcomes.

SOURCES OF COMPLEXITY

Medical Knowledge

Medical knowledge has improved to the point that

> *(t)here is, quite simply, too much to know . . . take one of the most mundane problems in medicine: the simple urinary tract infection. A generation ago, there were perhaps two to three options for treating these infections; today there are dozens. . .(W)hen physicians in their fifties and sixties went to medical school, there was one test for diagnosing pulmonary embolism; there are now at least five tests that are commonly used, in a wide array of combinations. . .there are too many issues and too many drugs, and not enough time to learn about them (Lee & Mongan, 2009, pp. 14–15).*

Insurance Plans

The rules of health insurers, including those of Medicare and Medicaid, vary markedly, and the multiple providers and multiple types of plans create a bewildering assortment of relationships between practitioners and insurers (e.g., in-network, out-of-network), negotiated rates and payment systems, quality standards and pay-for-performance incentives, and levels of physician accountability (e.g., to individual patients or to a population).

Patient Population: Prescription Drugs

During 2003–2006, 47% of Americans used at least one prescription drug, and 21% used three or more. In 1988–1994, these same percentages were 39% and 12% (U.S., DHHS, 2010a). Among the population over age 65, 50% take five or more medications, not including over-the-counter and alternative medications (Bohmer, 2009).

Patient Population: Chronic Conditions

In 2010, 133 million Americans had chronic conditions—such as hypertension, diabetes, asthma, and heart disease—with this number expected to grow to 171 million by 2030 (Robert Wood Johnson Foundation, 2010). In 2006, 90.7% of Americans over age 65 had at least one chronic condition, and 73.1% had two or more (see Figure 9.1). Chronic conditions also create activity limitations for 69 million adults over the age of 18.

Not all chronic conditions have the same impact on individuals—they vary considerably in how much they limit what one can do and the type of ongoing care required. Each patient's mix of acute and/or chronic conditions, diet and exercise, sleep habits, risk-taking behavior, preventive behavior, medications, and inherent strengths and weaknesses creates a relatively unique profile of "health" and need for health care services.

TYPES OF DIVERSIFICATION

Specialist vs. Generalist Practitioners

Over the last 60 years, the percentage of physicians who practice general primary care has declined from about 59% in 1949 to 39% in 2007. In 2003, only 27% of third-year internal medical residents planned to practice general medicine, compared to 1998 when 54% did (Lee & Mongan, 2009). Young doctors' professional choices are driven by debt incurred from medical school, projected salaries of different specialties (generalist physicians earn up to $100,000 less per year than do specialists), and expectations of workload.

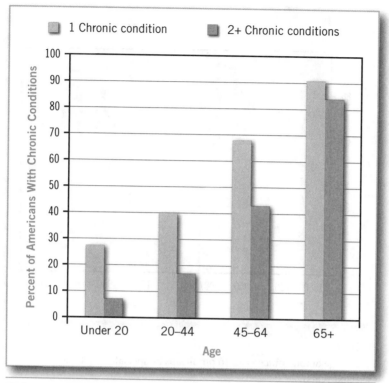

FIGURE 9.1

Percentage of Americans with one or more chronic conditions, by age, 2006.
Source: U.S., Agency for Healthcare Quality and Research, Medical Expenditure
Panel Survey, 2006.

Some studies estimate a primary care doctor with a panel of 2,500 patients would
need to work 18 hours a day to provide all necessary care to all patients (Lee & Mongan,
2009). As a consequence of the growing proportion of specialist physicians, the percentage
of physician visits provided by generalists has declined. In 1980, 33.8% of physician visits
were to specialists and 66.2% to generalists, whereas in 2007, 42.6% of visits were to specialists and 57.4% to general practitioners (U.S., DHHS, 2010a). Figure 9.2 shows that this
trend is even more pronounced for patients over age 65—almost 60% of physician visits in
this age group were to specialists in 2007.

"Superspecialization"

As medical knowledge has become more complex and specific, specialties have branched
into "superspecialties": "at many academic medical centers . . . cardiologists are divided into
experts on arrhythmia, heart failure, coronary disease, or prevention. Oncologists . . . concentrate
on just one [type of cancer]—lymphoma experts do not see myeloma patients, and myeloma
experts do not see Hodgkin's disease patients, and so on" (Lee & Mongan, 2009, p. 11).

New Types of Provider Organizations

Fifty years ago, many services performed in ambulatory settings today were available only
in hospitals. The first free-standing kidney dialysis center, ambulatory surgery center, hospice, and federally funded community health center were founded in the 1960s and 1970s.
In recent years, specialized provider organizations have experienced significant growth,

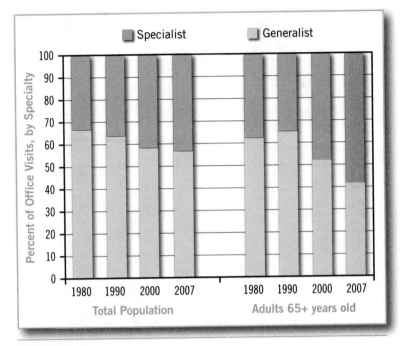

FIGURE 9.2

Percentage of total office visits to physicians by specialty, 1980–2007
(selected years).
Source: U.S., Department of Health and Human Services (DHHS), Centers for Disease
Control and Prevention, National Center for Health Statistics. (2010a). *Health, United
States, 2009*, Table 92. Retrieved June 1, 2010, from http://www.cdc.gov/nchs/hus.htm

including ambulatory care centers, long-term care facilities, and chronic disease management services. This growth has changed practice patterns. For example, in 2007, 62.7% of all surgeries were performed on an outpatient (ambulatory) basis, compared to 1980, when only 16.4% of surgeries were ambulatory. Health insurers' efforts to reduce patients' use of expensive acute care facilities, especially hospitals, are one driver of this diversification.

Insurance Plans and Reimbursement Strategies

Many different types of insurance plans exist, including traditional fee-for-service insurance, preferred provider organizations, health maintenance organizations, point-of-service plans, and high-deductible health plans with a savings option. Reimbursement strategies include fee-for-service reimbursement, prospective payment, pay-for-performance, and capitation (see Chapter 3). Insured Americans could have one or more different sources of coverage: employer-sponsored health plans, private insurance made by direct purchase, Medicare (either fee-for-service or a managed care plan), Medicaid, CHIP, or coverage through the military or the Veterans Health Administration.

SOURCES OF FRAGMENTATION

Physician Silos

Specialization has created rigid "silos," in which the various specialists train, research, teach, and practice independently from one another. Stores of knowledge are sequestered

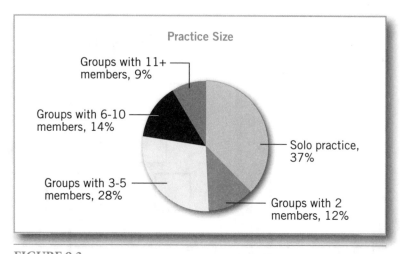

FIGURE 9.3

Distribution of office-based physicians, 2005–2006.
Source: Adapted from Pham, H. H., Schrag, D., O'Malley, A. S., Wu, B., & Bach, P. B. (2007). Care patterns in Medicare and their implications for pay for performance. *New England Journal of Medicine, 356,* 1130-1139.

within each specialty, rather than integrated across the physician population. The predominance of small physician practices creates an additional kind of silo—one in which a patient's medical information is kept within the practice, inaccessible to outside providers. Most physicians practice medicine by themselves (37% in 2005–2006) or in small groups of two to five doctors (40%) (American Hospital Association, 2010b) (see Figure 9.3). Small practices are reinforced by a professional culture that rewards physician autonomy and does not require or reward skills in negotiation and conflict resolution, even though these skills might be of great value to patients.

> *Stores of knowledge are sequestered within each medical specialty, rather than integrated across the physician population.*

Underdeveloped Health Information Technology (IT)

Practitioners lack the information technology (IT) infrastructure necessary to connect to other practices and collaborate with other physicians, hospitals, and other organizational providers. If providers have IT at all they use independent, site-based information systems (see Chapter 16).

Lack of Care Coordination

Each year, the typical Medicare beneficiary, as illustrated in Figure 9.4, sees two different primary care doctors and five different specialists, in four different settings. Beneficiaries with multiple chronic conditions see three different primary care doctors and eight different specialists across seven different settings (American Hospital Association, 2010b). At present, no medical provider bears the responsibility for coordinating the care and treatments provided by these multiple practitioners.

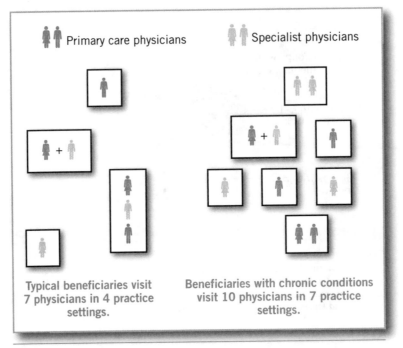

FIGURE 9.4

Average number of physicians and practice settings that Medicare beneficiaries visit each year.

Source: American Hospital Association. (2010). *Clinical integration—The key to real reform.* Retrieved June 1, 2010, from http://www.aha.org/aha/trendwatch/2010/10feb-clinicinteg.pdf. Reprinted with permission.

For a primary care provider, coordinating patient care across practitioners would take considerable time and resources. A Robert Wood Johnson Foundation-funded study (2009) found that for every 100 Medicare patients served by a primary care physician, that doctor would have to communicate with 99 physicians in 53 practices in order to coordinate patient care; for patients with chronic conditions, the physician would have to communicate with 134 physicians in 62 practices. For a typical primary care physician treating Medicare patients, this would require reaching out to 229 physicians across 117 practices, most of whom are not electronically connected or in regular communication with one another. Lack of coordination also occurs when patients are transferred from one type of care facility to another, such as from a hospital to an inpatient rehabilitation center. These kinds of transitions, which are encouraged by insurers and payers in order to reduce costs, further the tendency for an individual's health care to be overseen by multiple individuals and organizations. The result: "most patients and physicians have come to *expect* chaos when patients leave the hospital" (Lee & Mongan, 2009, p. 131, italics in original).

Lack of Incentives to Coordinate Care

Insurers reimburse practitioners for discrete services, such as office visits and tests, but rarely provide payment for time spent communicating with other providers, answering patients' e-mail inquiries, or investing in health IT. Insurance plans independently reimburse each provider involved in a patient's care, so there is no financial incentive to communicate and coordinate treatment. Some reimbursement strategies even discourage coordination—under fee-for-service reimbursement, physicians reimbursed for hospital visits may want to keep their patients hospitalized, whereas hospitals having incentives to reduce lengths-of-stay may want to discharge patients quickly (Lee & Mongan, 2009).

Focus on Acute Care

It seems logical that the focus of the delivery system would depend on the prevalence of particular illnesses, the state of medical technology, and the availability of treatment. So, for example, in the early 1900s, U.S. medical care emphasized treating infectious diseases, such as tuberculosis and influenza. And, after World War II, the medical system shifted focus to the treatment of acute illnesses, such as trauma and heart attacks, and use of improved surgical techniques. In fact, the field prioritizes acute care to this day.

However, advances in medical technology and improved life expectancy have increased the need for chronic and long-term care. Yet, the emphasis on acute care persists, reinforced by fee-for-service reimbursement, which treats each office visit, test, and treatment as an individual unit. In addition, patients change physicians fairly frequently, which creates disincentives for practitioners to plan for patients' long-term health and invest in developing the relationships that would improve care coordination.

TYPES OF STRATIFICATION

Uninsured Americans

In 2009, 16.7% or approximately 50.7 million people in the United States had no health insurance. Rates of uninsurance were higher for those with incomes of $25,000 or less (27% uninsured), Hispanics (32%), and blacks (21%) (see Table 8.1). In 2007, about 9% of Americans did not obtain needed medical care because of its costs—20% of the uninsured, but only 3% of the insured. In addition, in 2007, only 13.5% of people with insurance did not have an ambulatory care visit, compared to 37.4% of the uninsured. Overall, Americans without health insurance "have less access to effective clinical services including preventive care and, if sick or injured, are more likely to suffer poorer health outcomes, greater limitations in quality of life, and premature death" (Institute of Medicine, 2009, p. 49).

Uncompensated Care

In the United States, some provider organizations bear a greater burden than others for **uncompensated care**—that is, the care they provide people who cannot pay for it, either through insurance or out-of-pocket. These organizations include the nation's approximately 400 teaching hospitals and more than 100 public hospitals. Members of the National Association of Public Hospitals and Health Systems, who constitute only 2% of the nation's hospitals, provide one-quarter of all uncompensated care; costs for uncompensated care in public hospitals increased more than 10% in 2009 due to the economic recession and averaged more than $2.3 million per member hospital (National Association of Public Hospitals and Health Systems, 2010).

The uninsured, underinsured, and other vulnerable populations often seek care at hospital emergency departments (EDs), because they have no source of regular primary care. Emergency departments face enormous financial pressure (Institute of Medicine, 2006). In 2007, 25% of EDs reported being "at capacity," 22% reported being *over* capacity at some point during the year, and over one-third reported diverting ambulances to other hospitals due to overcrowding and a lack of resources (American Hospital Association, 2010a). The nation's supply of 1,200 federally supported community health centers, which have 7,500 delivery sites, serve more than 20 million Americans in poverty-stricken rural areas and inner cities. But these health centers alone cannot provide enough care for the nation's needy (National Association of Community Health Centers, 2009).

Critical Issues Facing the Delivery System

A number of critical issues stem from the complexity, diversification, fragmentation, and stratification of the U.S. health care field just described. These issues are even more pronounced when compared to the situation in other developed countries.

SHORTAGE OF PRIMARY CARE PROVIDERS

Currently, the United States faces a shortage of generalists combined with an increasing demand for primary care (New England Healthcare Institute, 2010) (see also Chapter 15). The American Academy of Family Physicians projects a shortfall of 40,000 family physicians by 2020, in part because of the aging population (American Academy of Family Physicians, 2010). This shortage is a critical issue, because research in other countries, as well as within the United States, clearly demonstrates that higher proportions of primary care practitioners relative to specialists are associated with a number of desirable outcomes. In the United Kingdom, these outcomes include decreased mortality rates, reduced health disparities between blacks and whites, and lower total costs of health services. In Costa Rica and Cuba, a higher proportion of primary care providers has produced lower infant mortality rates; in Spain, lower hospital admission rates; and, in Brazil, higher self-reported health (Starfield, Shi, & Macinko, 2005).

In the United States, state-level variations in the proportion of generalists versus specialists also are associated with varying health outcomes. As the proportion of specialists in a state increases, the state experiences higher overall age-adjusted mortality; higher mortality rates for heart disease and cancer; more low birth-weight births and neonatal deaths; and Medicare patients undergo more surgery and other procedures and generate higher costs (Starfield, Shi, Grover, & Macinko, 2005). Increasing the proportion of primary care providers relative to specialists could be accomplished with increased national control over medical training. For example, a number of countries, including Australia, Canada, France, Germany, and Japan, pay for medical school, which gives the federal government the ability to direct a larger proportion of medical students into primary care (American College of Physicians, 2008). Another possible solution is to provide specialized training for general practitioners, as done in the United Kingdom, which lessens the need for specialists.

UNCOORDINATED CARE

The lack of care coordination in the U.S. delivery system has serious consequences for patients.

> *Consider the case of Mary, an 86-year-old Medicare beneficiary with diabetes, coronary heart disease, asthma, and hypertension, who is in the initial stages of Alzheimer's disease. She sees at least six doctors and numerous other health care practitioners who treat these various conditions. However, because her doctors and other providers*

rarely, if ever, communicate with one another, each one will develop a treatment protocol for Mary without knowing what the others are doing. As a result, she will have duplicate tests, unnecessary and redundant work-ups, advice from one clinician that contradicts the advice of another, preventable hospitalizations and nursing home stays, and other services that increase health spending and lower the quality of care for Mary. At least one time during the year she is likely to arrive at the pharmacy only to be told that the prescription she is trying to fill could cause an adverse drug reaction with other medications she is taking. This situation would be time-consuming, expensive, and frustrating for any patient, but in Mary's case, her decreasing mental function will make this lack of coordination potentially life-threatening.

In a number of other countries, primary care practitioners are given financial incentives for coordinating care. For example, in Denmark primary care providers receive a capitated payment for coordinating the care of each patient. This payment covers services such as communicating with other practitioners, answering patients' e-mails, tracking the need for preventive care, and so forth. Office visits, tests, treatments, and the like are reimbursed separately (American College of Physicians, 2008). Without incentives, primary care providers are much less likely to have the time and resources to provide this level of coordination, lack of which critically reduces the quality and safety of patient care.

> *Without incentives, primary care providers are much less likely to have the time and resources to provide the necessary level of care coordination, lack of which critically reduces the quality and safety of patient care.*

UNDERDEVELOPED HEALTH INFORMATION TECHNOLOGY

Developed countries with better health outcomes, such as lower infant mortality, longer life expectancy, and lower proportions of adults with activity limitations, have much higher rates than the United States of electronic medical records (EMRs) and integrated health IT systems. In Australia, New Zealand, the United Kingdom, and the Netherlands, 79% to 100% of physicians use EMRs. Many developed countries, such as Canada, Germany, the UK, and Australia, started major health IT policy initiatives in the 1990s, which places the United States 4 to 13 years behind in health IT development (Anderson, Frogner, Johns, & Reinhardt, 2006).

ACCESS, COST, AND THE UNINSURED

In the United States, Americans of lower socioeconomic status have less access to primary care, but this is not the case in Western Europe. In countries that provide or mandate universal coverage, all residents have at least some form of basic health insurance (see Chapter 4). Given the clear connections between insurance coverage and health outcomes, it should come as no surprise that the United States ranks lower than other developed countries on numerous measurements of healthy lives. In addition, some developed countries subsidize co-payments for health services for lower income individuals in order to provide access to care without financial barriers. (Provisions of the recently enacted health reform law will require Americans to have health insurance, but provide tax credits so that low income individuals can afford it.)

UNMET MEDICAL NEEDS OF THE CHRONICALLY ILL

Treating chronic conditions is costly: in 2005, 91% of all U.S. health care expenses were spent on chronic care, as were 99% of home health care and 97% of prescription drug expenses (American Hospital Association, 2010a). Because of a lack of care coordination, patients with chronic conditions can experience costly inefficiencies such as duplicate diagnostic testing, potential harm from drug interactions, and confusion from conflicting care plans resulting in lower rates of compliance. A number of other countries have better chronic care outcomes than the United States, using strategies such as requiring patients to register with a primary care practitioner, providing same-day and after-hours appointments, making medical help lines easily accessible, using EMRs to prompt patients for follow-up and preventive care, and including nurses on primary care teams (Schoen et al., 2009). Given the great expense of treating chronic illnesses, reducing costs is a critical issue, but an even greater concern is providing safer, higher quality care for the millions of Americans with chronic illnesses.

Pathways to Better Organized Care

How can U.S. medical care be better designed and coordinated, and who is responsible for making improvements? In such a complex system, who and/or what should be changed—patient behavior and choice of provider? Physicians' practice patterns, beliefs, and training? The structure and types of provider organizations? Laws, policies, and regulations? Accreditation standards? Technology and infrastructure? Where would one begin? The difficulty of resolving all these thorny problems at once is symbolized by the Patient Protection and Affordable Care Act of 2010 (ACA), which authorized a number of pilot and demonstration projects to test various ideas about reorganizing care delivery, instead of creating sweeping transformations of the field. In the same vein, rather than try to resolve all these thorny problems at once, the ACA punted and instead authorized a number of pilot and demonstration projects to test various ideas about reorganizing care delivery in different locales and patient care settings, in order to gather evidence about which strategies most warrant wider replication.

Meanwhile, a number of practitioners, researchers, and policy makers have proposed models of better coordinated and integrated care. These models place the responsibility for change on practitioners, health plans, and, to some extent, health information systems. This section will describe four models, from the most all-encompassing to the least complex. Each of these models should be considered hypothetical, as each requires levels of coordination that have yet to be developed among different providers and institutions in the U.S. delivery system.

THE CHRONIC CARE MODEL

The **chronic care model** developed by Edward Wagner and his colleagues at Group Health of Puget Sound recommends extensive improvements to the U.S. health care system that could lead to better care for people with chronic conditions (Bonomi, Wagner, Glasgow,

& Von Korff, 2002). They propose that the overall health system should be organized to be proactive and focused on keeping people as healthy as possible, instead of just reacting when people are injured or sick. The health care delivery system design should integrate chronic care guidelines into reminders, feedback, and standing orders for practitioners, in order to make them more evident as clinical decisions are made.

Keeping providers focused on maintaining health rather than restoring it requires a combination of case management, aggressive follow-up, and ensuring that information is relayed to patients in ways that are compatible with their culture and background. Community programs can play an important supporting role. Nutrition and exercise classes at senior centers, for example, can reinforce healthy behavior and provide opportunities for socialization.

In addition to system design, managing chronic care effectively requires access to information not only on individual patients, but on populations as well. A comprehensive clinical information system helps providers issue timely reminders about needed services and allows for an individual patient's health care data to be followed easily and effectively. Population-level data can point to groups needing additional attention and help monitor the performance of particular providers and, thereby, support quality improvement efforts. Access to these data allows providers to develop evidence-based guidelines for their practices and to share them with their patients, so that they can understand the principles underlying their care.

A crucial aspect of the chronic care model is the patient's own self-management. Patients who take care of themselves properly can minimize complications, symptoms, and disabilities. Engendering a sense of personal responsibility for health outcomes encourages people to assume a central role in their own care. Using established programs to provide basic information, emotional support, and strategies for living with chronic conditions is an important part of self-management support. Care decisions must be based on clearly established guidelines rooted in clinical research, and these guidelines need to be explained to people so they can make fully informed choices.

The chronic care model emphasizes that patients who are informed about their conditions and who assume an active role in managing their care—working in tandem with providers who are prepared and supported with time and resources at their disposal— are likely to have more productive health care interactions and better health outcomes (Bonomi et al., 2002). For example, acute episodes for people with diabetes or asthma decrease when engaged patients work closely with proactive providers. These patient–physician interactions are not restricted to face-to-face encounters, but may be telephone conferences, group visits, or e-mail exchanges.

PATIENT-CENTERED MEDICAL HOMES

A **patient-centered medical home** is a physician-directed medical practice with a team of providers in which each patient has an ongoing relationship with a personal physician. The personal physician coordinates the patient's acute care, preventive care, chronic care, and end-of-life care, across and within accessible health care providers in the patient's community. This coordination provides "primary care that emphasizes timely access to medical services, enhanced communication between patients and their health care team, coordination and continuity of care, and an intensive focus on quality and safety" (Improving Chronic Illness Care, 2010).

In order to create a medical home, a physician practice would need to be able to "monitor their patients' medical histories; work with patients over time, not just during office visits; follow up with patients and other providers; manage populations, not just individuals, using evidence-based care; encourage better health habits and the self-management of medical conditions; and avoid medical errors" (Lee & Mongan, 2009, p. 139). The potential for medical homes to improve health outcomes is shown in the case of Rita, a 57-year-old patient with diabetes:

> *Rita, who was diagnosed with diabetes 3 years ago at age 54, was told by her doctor to lose weight, exercise, and return to his office in 3 months, advice she promptly ignored. When her condition suddenly worsened, she was referred to [a medical home] where she worked with a multidisciplinary team to develop a care plan. The team includes a doctor, nurse, dietician, and diabetes educator, all of whom meet with her regularly about her care plan, her medications, and keeping her blood sugar under control. The team not only meets with Rita, but with each other to discuss Rita's care and coordinate next steps. Over the next year, Rita lost 24 pounds, began walking 3 miles per day, and has her blood sugar under control (U.S., DHHS, 2010b).*

ACCOUNTABLE CARE ORGANIZATIONS

A different strategy for better coordinating medical care is the **accountable care organization (ACO)** (Fisher et al., 2007; Rittenhouse, Shortell, & Fisher, 2009) (see Chapter 8). An ACO attempts to reconcile two contrasting aspects of the U.S. health care system: the physician organizations most capable of coordinating care are traditional health maintenance organizations (HMOs) and multispecialty group practices, but the majority of U.S. physicians practice by themselves or in single-specialty groups. The basic idea of an ACO is to create an entity consisting of "a local health care organization and a related set of providers (at a minimum, primary care physicians, specialists, and hospitalists) that can be held accountable for the cost and quality of care delivered to a defined population" (Devers & Berenson, 2009, p. 1). Some existing provider organizations already fit the definition of an ACO, such as Kaiser Permanente and other traditional HMOs, large multispecialty group practices, and Physician-Hospital Organizations (Shortell & Casalino, 2008). But how could the majority of physicians, who choose not to practice in these types of organizations, be convinced to coordinate care with other providers and be held accountable for populations of patients?

One strategy for developing more ACOs would capitalize on existing relationships and connections between patients, practitioners, and provider organizations in local areas. For example, in a particular location, an ACO called "General" would be a virtual organization centered on General Hospital and its "extended medical staff"; that is, all the doctors who practice at General Hospital and all the doctors who have patients admitted to General Hospital. The physicians of General ACO would be expected to accept a degree of responsibility for all the patients in the local delivery system (defined as patients who have been admitted to General Hospital in the last year, and patients of physicians who practice primarily at General Hospital). The ACO would coordinate across a continuum of care for these patients and receive capitated payments that would require prospective budget planning. The physicians and health care organizations would not be employed by the ACO or formally integrated, but would be expected to work together as a unit.

The changes to the delivery system necessary to achieve the promise of ACOs are substantial. Physicians in particular would have to accept responsibility for the quality of care and overall costs of delivering care to a defined population of patients. In addition, without incentives for specialists to work with primary care providers, an ACO might not place enough emphasis on primary care (Rittenhouse, Shortell, & Fisher, 2009). In addition, patients would need incentives to choose ACOs as their care providers (Shortell & Casalino, 2008).

BUNDLED PAYMENTS

A simpler method of coordinating care might be **bundled payments**, or case rates, which would pay providers for an individual's episode of care instead of the individual treatments provided. A bundled payment could span multiple providers and settings, which would create incentives for practitioners and providers to communicate and coordinate their care plan, as illustrated in the case of Antonio.

> *Antonio, age 78, had hip replacement surgery covered by Medicare's typical fee-for-service reimbursement policy. Medicare made a series of payments to a number of different service providers, including his hospital, his surgeon, the rehabilitation facility Antonio stayed in after hospital discharge, and the physical therapy provider he used. Because each provider was paid separately, there was no incentive for the hospital to coordinate with Antonio's surgeon, or the surgeon to coordinate with the physical therapist, in terms of planning the most efficient, most cost-effective strategy for the surgery and recovery. If Antonio's Medicare coverage employed a bundled payment approach, all of his providers would have needed to collaborate, in order to distribute shares of the payment; presumably, these connections would create incentives for them to work together proactively to coordinate care as well as to avoid unnecessary or duplicative costs.*

Bundled payments would not require a set of providers to be part of the same organization and would not specify how the care should be coordinated, but it would provide a financial incentive and peer pressure to do so effectively. Bundled payments could be used for both acute and chronic care management.

OVERALL ASSESSMENT

How would each of these models improve patient care for a specific individual? Take Mary, the 86-year-old Medicare beneficiary described previously who has the most complex situation. Under the chronic care model, Mary would find a delivery system that allows her to participate in decisions about her care. She would know her various clinicians, and they would openly communicate with her and with each other. The community in which she lives would be supportive of her and her caregivers' needs. In a patient-centered medical home, Mary would receive continuous and coordinated care, with one physician knowledgeable about all her practitioners' diagnoses and treatments. Membership in an ACO might provide Mary with an experience similar to a patient-centered medical home, depending on its structure. At the very least, an ACO would create an affiliation between her practitioners (if they all practice in the same local area) that might encourage improved communication and planning. Bundled payments, although less comprehensive, again would encourage her various providers to communicate with each other while allocating reimbursement monies for a particular episode of treatment.

Although all four models could improve care for patients, they address only some of the crucial issues facing the U.S. delivery system. All four attempt to ameliorate the lack of coordination between and across practitioners and provider organizations. The chronic care model and the patient-centered medical home directly address unmet medical needs for the chronically ill. However, none of the models would relieve the shortage of primary care providers or increase access to care for the uninsured and other vulnerable populations. In addition, although each of the models would be aided by improved health IT, none of them specifically recommend strategies for improving the nation's health IT infrastructure. A larger question looming over each model is how costly would its implementation be and who would be responsible for financing the recommended changes.

Barriers to Change

Although new models of medical care organization are promising, they face significant challenges. Despite health care reform, many additional system changes are needed. Such changes relate to revising provider payment policies, encouraging wider use of health information technology (new incentives for adoption are described in Chapter 16), care management process redesign and improvements, professional cultural changes from individual practice to teamwork and patient-centered approaches, as well as stronger managerial and physician leadership. This section provides a brief overview of some of these issues.

TEAM-BASED MEDICAL PRACTICE

A potential solution to fragmentation is to alter the dynamics between health care providers and create a team-oriented or collaborative approach to care. Collaborative care approaches range from co-location of services within offices, such as psychologists in primary care offices to help integrate mental and physical health, to multidisciplinary teams, such as those used in the Programs for All-Inclusive Care for the Elderly, which bring together health providers—physicians, social workers, physical and occupational therapists, nurses, and others, as needed—to focus on individual patients (U.S., DHHS, 2010b).

In team-based approaches, a critical focus is care management. Further development of the role of professional care managers and reorienting other health provider perspectives into a team approach that works with a care manager, however, is a sizable future challenge, particularly for physicians. The culture of professional medicine and the training of future physicians must drastically alter in order to create practitioners who value teamwork and collaboration over setting their own individual standards and maintaining personal independence. In addition, physicians will need to learn how to work more effectively with health care professionals from other disciplines.

> *The culture of professional medicine and the training of future physicians must drastically alter in order to create practitioners who value teamwork and collaboration over setting their own individual standards and maintaining personal independence.*

PAYMENT STRUCTURES

Critical for achieving integrated medical care are new methods of insuring patients and reimbursing providers. In the current system, fee-for-service payments that pay substantially more for specialists' services discourage trainees from entering primary care. Coordinated care models cannot be implemented if the workforce best suited for coordinating care is already overburdened. In addition, fee-for-service payments do not encourage collaborative work; rather, they reward providers for each additional treatment. In order to encourage communication among providers, health plans would need to reimburse practitioners for time spent coordinating care, including answering patients' e-mail, and consulting and meeting with other providers. Finally, the multiplicity of insurers—public and private—offer different incentives for providers to collaborate. Unless all insurers offer similar incentives, clinical integration is less feasible and the higher costs it may entail, less attractive.

LEGAL BARRIERS

Clinical coordination and integration not only would require a changed physician culture and payment structure, but also the elimination of legal barriers. In order for medical practitioners to collaborate about a patient's care, they would need legal authority to negotiate contracts and share patient information. A number of federal and state statutes work against physician collaboration (American Hospital Association, 2010b). For example, the Sherman Antitrust Act of 1890, which began as an attempt to prevent price-fixing, prohibits joint negotiations by providers. Federal anti-kickback laws, passed in 1972, make it illegal to reward practitioners for making referrals of Medicare and Medicaid patients. A series of laws passed in the late 1980s and 1990s, known collectively as the Stark Laws, make it illegal for a physician to refer a Medicare patient to a provider organization in which the referring physician holds a financial stake. Although each of these—and other—laws is specific in its prohibitions, the overall set of laws creates a legal framework in which collaboration risks being seen as collusion.

INFORMATION TECHNOLOGY

Increased collaboration and coordination require that communications occur quickly and reliably between providers, as well as between providers and patients. Health information technology provides potential solutions for these problems, but also faces significant hurdles for implementation. Health care reform has created strong financial incentives for implementation of electronic health records that have "meaningful use." However, implementation requires sizable upfront costs to medical care providers, due to the complexity of health care information. According to one estimate, a system of electronic medical records would cost $10,000 per year per doctor in a practice, with the start-up costs two to five times higher (Lee & Mongan, 2009).

Sizable savings from using health information technology can be accrued by large health care systems (such as the VA Health Care System). However, small physician practices still predominate, making the implementation difficult and the payoff for these providers potentially low. No wonder, then, that in 2007, large medical groups with 11 or more physicians were more likely to use EMRs (74.3%) than were solo practitioners (20.6%) (Hing & Hsiao, 2010). Privacy issues pose another challenge, and may prevent sharing information among different systems or providers.

In a problematic development, mental health providers have been exempted from electronic health records requirements, in order to minimize risks to patient confidentiality. This will perpetuate the longstanding lack of integration of physical and mental health treatment and prevent appropriate coordination of care.

Furthermore, there are significant barriers to integrating health information across different EMR systems which remain to be resolved.

PATIENT ACTIVATION

To date, health care has been practiced *upon* patients, rather than *with* patients (Bohmer, 2009). This approach may have been more appropriate when it was difficult for patients to acquire knowledge about health and medicine. However, information asymmetries between patients and providers have been lessened by the improved availability and accessibility of health information via the Internet and generally rising educational levels. Still, health literacy varies greatly among Americans and engaging patients fully in their health care will be a continuing challenge.

In addition, patient empowerment—giving the patient the responsibility of self-administering treatment, assessing its effectiveness, monitoring symptoms, and participating in medical decision-making—is more effective for some diseases (such as diabetes) than others. Having patients become active participants in their own care is one strategy to stem the further fragmentation of medical care, and the patient-centered approach was supported in recent health care reform legislation. But whether patient activation will lead to improved health outcomes and system efficiency remains to be seen.

Conclusion

The U.S. health care system is complex, diverse, fragmented, and stratified. Unlike in other developed countries, the United States has no single entity that systematically and intentionally organizes the delivery system. Therefore the field's various components and influencers—patients, practitioners, provider organizations, insurers and payers, law and policy, accreditation, knowledge, and technology—develop and evolve relatively independently from one another, resulting in disjointed and poorly coordinated patient care. In its current state, improvement in health care safety, cost-effectiveness, accessibility, and quality would require change of multiple entities at multiple levels.

Creating better communication between practitioners and provider organizations would not be as simple as installing integrated health IT and reimbursing physicians for phone calls. The professional identity of physicians would have to change from being autonomous practitioners (well exemplified by the term "solo practice") to members of teams. Likewise, improving the management of chronic illnesses would be aided by EMRs and better communication between providers, but also would require a reorientation of the field from acute to chronic and preventive care.

Improving access to care for millions of Americans is a pressing national priority, as reflected by the terms of the Patient Protection and Affordable Care Act of 2010, but without addressing the nation's shortage of primary care providers, there will be no one to serve the newly insured. Incentives for change most likely would need to come from both the public sector through law, regulation, and policy, and the private sector through accreditation and health plans. But it is difficult to regulate and accredit another important component of the delivery system—patients' personal responsibility for their health and the health of their families, including their diet and exercise, preventive health behavior, and understanding of and compliance with medical treatments.

As the experiences of other developed countries make clear, however, the United States must create opportunities for more intentional design and strategic management of its health care system. Without intervention, it is bound to perpetuate its inefficiencies and grow even more complex and unwieldy, resulting in more costly, less safe, and lower quality health care for all.

DISCUSSION QUESTIONS

1. Explain how each of the following factors influences the patient–physician relationship: insurance, medical knowledge, technology, accreditation, and regulation.
2. What are the main sources of complexity in the U.S. medical care field? What factors contribute to its diversification? In what ways is the field fragmented? How is it stratified? How do each of these characteristics—complexity, diversification, fragmentation, stratification—influence patient care and health?
3. How have other Western countries addressed issues of fragmentation and stratification? How do their strategies influence patient care and health?
4. Summarize the main similarities and differences between the four pathways to better care (the chronic care model, the patient-centered medical home, accountable care organizations, and bundled payments).
5. What factors prevent the U.S. medical care field from becoming more coordinated and less stratified?
6. Imagine you are a Washington lobbyist. What would your main messages regarding changes needed in the health system (if any), if you worked for an association representing generalist physicians? What if you worked on behalf of Medicare patients? Nonprofit community hospitals? The insurance industry? The chronically ill? Community health clinics that serve poor and vulnerable populations? How would your messages be similar or different, and why?
7. Choose three critical issues facing the U.S. health care system and rank order them in terms of their *impact* on patient health. Explain your ranking.
8. Choose three critical issues facing the U.S. health care system and rank order them in terms of the *availability of solutions*. Explain your ranking.
9. Why do you think U.S. insurance companies do not reimburse practitioners for time spent coordinating patients' care (e.g., calling other practitioners, answering e-mail, etc.)?
10. The current U.S. medical care field has an acute care focus. Could current structures of the field sustain a focus on chronic and preventive care? If so, how? If not, what aspects of the field would need to change in order to accommodate this changed focus?

CASE STUDIES

For each of the case studies here, identify the source(s) of inefficiency and reduced quality of care. Then, discuss what changes to the medical care delivery system could have improved the patient's outcome.

Raymond, Age 78

Raymond, a 78-year-old man living in a motel, is found lying on the floor of his room, semi-conscious, by a housekeeper. The motel manager calls 9-1-1, and Raymond is taken to the closest emergency room, where he lies on a gurney in the hallway for

6 hours before he is examined by a physician. Because it is unclear what is wrong with him and he cannot speak coherently, the physician admits him to the hospital for observation. Later, when it is determined that he had suffered a stroke, he is discharged to an inpatient rehabilitation facility that has no knowledge of his medical history, including his current medications for hypertension and high cholesterol. He dies there several weeks later.

Tanya, Age 7

Tanya, a 7-year-old girl who suffers from chronic asthma, is hospitalized when her asthma exacerbates a case of pneumonia. Although her pediatrician and pediatric asthma specialist are members of the same medical group, they recommend conflicting medications and treatments. Decisions about how to treat Tanya are made by the pediatric ward nurses, shift-by-shift. Her parents cannot understand why her treatment in the hospital is so confusing and uncertain. After a week in as an inpatient, Tanya returns to school where she is kept indoors at recess and the lunch period due to the fragile state of her lungs. Months later, her parents find out from the pediatrician that, in addition to the pneumonia, Tanya had a collapsed lung, and the pediatrician and asthma specialist disagreed about how to treat it.

Margaret, Age 58

Margaret, a 58-year-old woman, begins to experience tremors. She has difficulty keeping her head and hands from shaking. These physical movements cause her to panic and worry endlessly about the state of her health. Her primary care physician orders blood tests, a CT scan, and an MRI, which reveal a slight case of anemia but are otherwise normal. Over a series of months, he sends her to a hematologist, an endocrinologist, and a neurologist, each of whom evaluates one specific aspect of her symptoms and does not communicate any findings or test results to the other doctors. Finally, after exhausting every possible physical cause of the tremors, Margaret's doctor refers her to a psychiatrist, who immediately diagnoses her with generalized anxiety disorder and prescribes a commonly used antianxiety medication. Within weeks, Margaret's condition greatly improves.

REFERENCES

American Academy of Family Physicians. (2010). *Family physician workforce reform: Recommendations of the American Academy of Family Physicians.* (AAFP Reprint No. 305b). Retrieved June 1, 2010, from http://www.aafp.org/online/en/home/policy/policies/w/workforce.html

American College of Physicians. (2008). Achieving a high-performance health care system with universal access: What the United States can learn from other countries. *Annals of Internal Medicine, 148,* 55–75.

American Hospital Association. (2010a). *Chartbook. Trends affecting hospitals and health Systems.* Retrieved June 1, 2010, from http://www.aha.org/aha/research-and-trends/chartbook/index.html

American Hospital Association. (2010b). *Clinical integration—The key to real reform.* Retrieved June 1, 2010, from http://www.aha.org/aha/trendwatch/2010/10feb-clinicinteg.pdf

Anderson, G. F., Frogner, B. K., Johns, R. A., & Reinhardt, U. E. (2006). Health care spending and use of information technology in OECD countries. *Health Affairs, 25,* 819–831.

Bohmer, R. M. J. (2009). *Designing care: Aligning the nature and management of health care.* Boston, MA: Harvard Business Press.

Bonomi, A. E., Wagner, E. H., Glasgow, R., & Von Korff, M. (2002). Assessment of chronic illness care: A practical tool for quality improvement. *Health Services Research, 37,* 791–820.

Devers, K., & Berenson, R. (2009). Can accountable care organizations improve the value of health care by solving the cost and quality quandaries? (Series: *Timely Analysis of Immediate Health Policy Issues*). Washington, D.C.: Urban Institute. Retrieved June 1, 2010, from http://www.urban.org/url.cfm?ID=411975

Fisher, E. S., Staiger, D. O., Bynum, J. P. W., & Gottlieb, D. J. (2007). Creating accountable care organizations: The extended hospital medical staff. *Health Affairs, 26,* w44–w57.

Hing, E., & Hsiao, C. J. (2010). Electronic medical record use by office-based physicians and their practices: United States, 2007 (*National Health Statistics Reports,* no. 23). Hyattsville, MS: National Center for Health Statistics. Retrieved from http://www.cdc.gov/nchs/data/nhsr/nhsr023.pdf

Improving Chronic Illness Care. (2010). *Patient-centered medical home.* Retrieved June 1, 2010, from http://improvingchroniccare.org/index.php?p=Patient-Centered_Medical_Home&s=224

Institute of Medicine. (2009). *America's uninsured crisis: Consequences for health and health care.* Washington, D.C.: National Academies Press.

Institute of Medicine. (2006). *Emergency medical services at the crossroads.* Washington, D.C.: National Academies Press.

Institute of Medicine. (1996). *Primary care: America's health in a new era.* Washington, D.C.: National Academy Press.

Lee, T. H., & Mongan, J. J. (2009). *Chaos and organization in health care.* Cambridge, MA: The MIT Press.

MedPAC. (2009). *A data book: Healthcare spending and the Medicare program.* Retrieved June 1, 2010, from http://www.medpac.gov/documents/jun09databookentirereport.pdf

National Association of Community Health Centers. (2009). *Fact sheet: America's health centers.* Retrieved June 1, 2010, from http://www.nachc.com/client/documents/America's_%20Health_Centers_updated_11_09.pdf

National Association of Public Hospitals and Health Systems. (2010). *Safety net health systems: An essential resource during the economic recession.* Retrieved June 1, 2010, from http://www.naph.org/Main-Menu-Category/Publications/Economic-Recession-Research-Brief.aspx

New England Healthcare Institute. (2010). *Rethinking primary care: A framework for the future.* Retrieved June 1, 2010, from http://www.nehi.net/publications/45/remaking_primary_care_a_framework_for_the_future

Rittenhouse, D. R., Shortell, S. M., & Fisher, E. S. (2009). *Primary care and accountable care—two essential elements of delivery system reform.* Retrieved from http://healthcarereform.nejm.org/?p=2205&query=TOC

Robert Wood Johnson Foundation. (2009). *Scope of care coordination daunting for physicians treating Medicare patients.* Retrieved June 1, 2010, from http://www.rwjf.org/qualityequality/product.jsp?id=38949

Robert Wood Johnson Foundation. (2010). *Making health systems work for people with chronic conditions.* Retrieved June 1, 2010, from http://www.rwjf.org/pioneer/product.jsp?id=59588

Schoen, C., Osborn, R., How, S. K. H., Doty, M. M., & Peugh, J. (2009). In chronic condition: Experiences of patients with complex health care needs, in eight countries, 2008. *Health Affairs, 28*, w1–w16.

Shortell, S. M., & Casalino, L. P. (2008). Health care reform requires accountable care systems. *Journal of the American Medical Association, 300*, 95–97.

Starfield, B., Shi, L., & Macinko, J. (2005). Contribution of primary care to health systems and health. *Milbank Quarterly, 83*, 457–502.

Starfield, B., Shi, L., Grover, A., & Macinko, J. (2005). The effects of specialist supply on populations' health: Assessing the evidence. *Health Affairs*, w5–97 to 5–107.

U.S., Department of Health and Human Services (DHHS), Centers for Disease Control and Prevention, National Center for Health Statistics. (2010a). *Health, United States, 2009* (with special feature on medical technology). Retrieved June 1, 2010, from http://www.cdc.gov/nchs/hus.htm

U.S., DHHS, Centers for Medicare and Medicaid Services. (2010b). *Quick Facts about Programs of All-inclusive Care for the Elderly (PACE)*. Retrieved June 1, 2010, from http://www.medicare.gov/publications/pubs/pdf/11341.pdf

10

INTEGRATIVE MODELS AND PERFORMANCE

Douglas McCarthy

Early in the last century, experts began noting the benefits of organized forms of health care delivery, such as the Mayo Clinic's multispecialty group practice in Minnesota. In 1933, the Committee on the Costs of Medical Care recommended that "[m]edical service should be more largely furnished by groups of physicians and related practitioners, so organized as to maintain high standards of care and to retain the personal relations between patients and physician" (Falk, Rorem, & Ring, 1933). Despite their reputation for innovation and excellence, Mayo and other models of integrated care have remained exceptional in American health care, which has long been characterized as a "cottage industry" of solo and small physician practices paid on a fee-for-service basis. Yet concern has been growing that traditional care is too often fragmented, uncoordinated, and inefficient, leading to undesirable patient experiences, suboptimal outcomes, and unnecessarily high costs (Schoen, How, Weinbaum, Craig, & Davis, 2006).

Enactment of federal health care reform legislation makes it timely to reconsider recent expert recommendations for greater organization of health care delivery. The Commonwealth Fund Commission on a High Performance Health System (2007), for example, called for the United States to "embark on the organization and delivery of health care services to end the fragmentation, waste, and complexity that currently exist. Physicians and other care providers should be rewarded, through financial and non-financial incentives, to band together into traditional or virtual organizations that can provide the support needed to physicians and other providers to practice 21st century medicine." Similar calls have come from the Institute of Medicine (2001) and the Medicare Payment Advisory Commission (2009).

To illustrate the potential of organized care delivery, the Commonwealth Fund has sponsored an ongoing series of case studies of leading health care delivery organizations located across the United States (Figure 10.1) that have been recognized for higher levels of performance (McCarthy & Mueller, 2009).[1] This chapter briefly describes their scope, highlights how they are exhibiting the six attributes of an "ideal health care delivery system" identified by the Commission, and synthesizes key lessons from their experience.

We use the term **organized health care delivery** to mean that *care providers have established relationships and mechanisms for communicating and working to coordinate patient care across health conditions, services, and care settings over time.* Such relationships and mechanisms may include any or all of the care system redesign imperatives identified by the Institute of Medicine (2001): the development of effective teams, redesign of care processes, effective use of information technologies, management of knowledge and skills, and use of performance and outcome measurement for continuous quality improvement and accountability. It may also include payment mechanisms for sharing risk that foster greater accountability for clinical and financial outcomes over the continuum of care.

The Structure of Integration

The case study sites represent diverse types of organizations that range from fully **integrated delivery systems (IDSs)** that provide a full scope of health care services and insurance coverage to **multispecialty physician group practices (MSGPs)** to looser networks of physicians. They can be categorized into four broadly defined models of organized health care delivery based on the general nature of their clinical and financial integration (Table 10.1). We describe each of these models with examples to help illustrate various organizational types. There are many variations within these models—no two

---

[1]Case study organizations were selected by experts through a ranking process. Candidate sites were identified from the professional literature, performance benchmarking data, and expert recommendations. Information was gathered from interviews with organization leaders, internal material provided by the sites, and external sources.

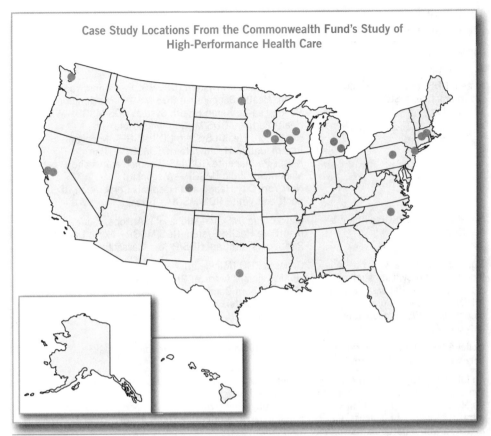

FIGURE 10.1
Case study locations from the Commonwealth Fund's study of high-performance health care.

organizations are alike, nor do these represent all possible types. Some organizational structures straddle categories. For example, many of the IDSs include a MSGP at their core, whereas others are affiliated with physicians through a **physician-hospital organization (PHO)**. Even when organizations appear to have similar components, they may differ greatly in configuration.

MODEL 1: IDS OR MSGP, WITH A HEALTH PLAN

Including the health insurance function in an integrated delivery system provides flexibility, aligned incentives, and expertise in organizing to deliver high-value care. Just one system—Kaiser Permanente—has retained a "closed" model in which affiliated physicians and facilities exclusively serve patients who are members of its health plan. All others are "open" systems that serve patients both within and outside their health plans, or are mixed-model health plans that include both an integrated medical group and independent physicians in private practice. Only a core set of patients receives both care and coverage from the integrated system in these hybrid organizations. Two examples follow.

Kaiser Permanente (KP), founded in 1945, is the largest not-for-profit IDS and group-model **health maintenance organization (HMO)** in the United States, integrating care and

TABLE 10.1
Models of Organized Health Care Delivery

Models	Case Study Sites and Principal Locations
Model 1: integrated delivery system (IDS) or multispecialty group practice (MSGP) with a health plan	Denver Health (IDS—Colorado) Geisinger Health System (IDS/MSGP—Pennsylvania) Group Health Cooperative (IDS/MSGP—Washington state) Gundersen-Lutheran Health System (IDS/MSGP—Wisconsin) HealthPartners (IDS/MSGP—Minnesota) Henry Ford Health System (IDS/MSGP—Michigan) Intermountain Healthcare (IDS/MSGP—Utah) Kaiser Permanente (IDS/MSGP—nine states and D.C.) Marshfield Clinic (MSGP—Wisconsin) New York City Health and Hospitals Corporation (IDS) Scott and White (IDS/MSGP—Texas)
Model 2: IDS or MSGP without a health plan	Mayo Clinic (MSGP—Minnesota, Arizona, Florida) MeritCare Health System (IDS/MSGP—North Dakota) Partners HealthCare (IDS/PHO—Massachusetts)
Model 3: private network of independent providers, such as a physician-hospital organization (PHO), independent practice association (IPA) or cooperative network	Genesys PHO (Michigan) Hill Physicians Medical Group (IPA—California) Mount Auburn Cambridge Independent Practice Association (Massachusetts) North Dakota Rural Cooperative Networks
Model 4: government-facilitated network of independent providers	Community Care of North Carolina

An **IDS** is a group of health care organizations that collectively provides a full range of health-related services in a coordinated fashion to those using the system.

An **MSGP** employs primary and specialty care physicians who share common governance, infrastructure, and finances, refer patients for services offered within the group, and are typically affiliated with a particular hospital or hospitals.

PHOs and **IPAs** organize independent providers to contract with one or more health plans for the purpose of providing health care services to a defined population; PHOs do so through a partnership between a hospital and all or some of its affiliated physicians; IPAs may contract with hospitals in various ways.

Source: Adapted in part from Shih, A., Davis, K., Schoenbaum, S. C., Gauthier, A., Nuzum, R., & McCarthy, D. (2008). *Organizing the U.S. health care delivery system for high performance.* New York: The Commonwealth Fund.

coverage for 8.6 million members in eight regions. KP comprises three separate yet interdependent entities that exist in a "partnership of equals" through exclusive contracts built on common vision, joint decision making, and aligned incentives: Kaiser Foundation Health Plan, Kaiser Foundation Hospitals, and the Permanente Medical Groups.

Kaiser Foundation Health Plan contracts with purchasers (individuals, employer groups, and government programs) to finance a full range of health care services for its members. Kaiser Foundation Hospitals arranges inpatient, extended, and home health care for Kaiser members in owned and contracted facilities. It operates 35 medical centers in three states, offering both inpatient and outpatient services, and it has 431 outpatient medical offices across all regions.

The Permanente Medical Groups are locally governed professional corporations or partnerships that work in Kaiser facilities and accept **capitation** payment (a predetermined payment **per-member-per-month**) from Kaiser Foundation Health Plans to provide medical care exclusively for Kaiser members. Working in cooperation with health plan and facility managers, the more than 14,000 Permanente physicians take responsibility for clinical care, quality improvement, resource management, and the design and operation of the care delivery system in their region.

Geisinger Health System, founded in 1915, is a physician-led, not-for-profit IDS serving an area of 2.6 million people in rural northeastern and central Pennsylvania. The Geisinger Medical Group employs some 765 physicians who practice at Geisinger-owned hospitals and clinics and in non-Geisinger hospitals in the region. About 200 of these physicians provide primary care in 40 community practice clinics; other physicians provide specialty care, predominantly from three large hubs.

Major facilities include two acute-care hospitals (the Geisinger Medical Center in Danville is staffed exclusively by Geisinger physicians, whereas the hospital in Wilkes-Barre is staffed by both Geisinger and non-Geisinger physicians), ambulatory surgery centers, specialty hospitals, and a drug and alcohol treatment center. About 30% of Geisinger patients are enrolled in the Geisinger Health Plan, a network-model HMO. About half of the health plan's 230,000 members have a Geisinger primary care physician. The health plan also contracts with 28,000 independent health care providers, including 90 community hospitals in the region.

MODEL 2: IDS OR MSGP, WITHOUT A HEALTH PLAN

Organizations in this model contract with or accept payment from multiple insurers. Some partner with one or more insurers to better align financial incentives to support mutual objectives for care system redesign, aided by their infrastructure.

Mayo Clinic is the world's first and largest MSGP. From its roots in a 19th-century family medical practice, Mayo by the 1920s had developed the key attributes that distinguish it today: private, not-for-profit status, a salaried staff, and a mission to "provide the best care to every patient every day through integrated clinical practice, education, and research."

More than 3,700 Mayo Clinic physicians and researchers representing nearly every medical discipline provide inpatient and outpatient care to more than 500,000 patients each year in four hospitals and outpatient facilities on three major campuses located in Rochester, Minnesota; Scottsdale, Arizona; and Jacksonville, Florida. Mayo Health System is an affiliated network of hospitals, clinics, and physicians serving 70 communities in the upper Midwest. The nonprofit Mayo Foundation owns the facilities and other assets. There are five affiliated schools of biomedical education.

Partners HealthCare, founded in 1994, is a loosely integrated, nonprofit organized delivery system serving more than 1.5 million patients in greater Boston and eastern Massachusetts. The system includes two founding academic medical centers (Brigham and Women's Hospital and Massachusetts General Hospital), community and specialty hospitals, community health centers, a physician network, home health and hospice care, and rehabilitation and skilled nursing facilities. Partners is a major site for medical research and is a principal teaching affiliate of Harvard Medical School.

Partners Community Healthcare, Inc., contracts with and provides management services to more than 1,000 primary care physicians and 3,500 specialists. The network is organized into regional service organizations (RSOs) ranging from a 10-physician group practice to a PHO of more than 250 physicians. Within each RSO, physicians coordinate care for their patients and share financial risk against system-wide **pay-for-performance** goals negotiated with a large insurer.

MODEL 3: PRIVATE NETWORKS OF INDEPENDENT PROVIDERS

This model includes PHOs and **independent practice associations (IPAs)** that organize independent providers to deliver health care services under contract to one or more insurers. It also includes cooperatives among providers who join together to share and coordinate services. These entities may provide infrastructure services (e.g., performance improvement and information technology) and care management under delegated authority from health plans.

Hill Physicians Medical Group, founded in 1984, is a northern California IPA that contracts with health plans to provide care to more than 300,000 patients enrolled in commercial HMOs, Medicare advantage plans, and Medi-Cal, California's Medicaid program. Hill contracts with approximately 3,500 independent providers, including some 900 primary care physicians in 450 practices, 30 hospitals, and 15 urgent care centers. A subset of 230 physician-shareholders elect a governing board, which contracts with a management services organization for day-to-day operations.

Hill is paid on a capitated basis (fixed payment per-member per-month) by health plans and reimburses physicians on a fee-for-service basis plus bonuses (funded internally and in part by participation in purchasers' pay-for-performance programs) for meeting performance goals including service utilization, clinical quality, and use of information technology. On average, Hill patients account for about 40% of participating physicians' entire patient base, although some physicians exclusively treat Hill patients.

Genesys PHO is a physician-led organization that negotiates risk-based managed care contracts and participates in pay-for-performance programs with health plans on behalf of the Genesys Regional Medical Center (GRMC) and a network of 150 community-based primary care physicians who practice in medical groups in a five-county service area around Flint, Michigan. GRMC is a component of Genesys Health System, a nonprofit IDS that provides a continuum of medical care in mid-Michigan. PHO physicians refer patients almost exclusively to GRMC for inpatient care and to a closed panel of 354 contracted medical specialists (who receive most of their referrals from the PHO) and a few hospital-employed specialists. The PHO handles physician credentialing, as well as utilization and care management functions delegated to it by health plans.

The Genesys Integrated Group Practice (GIGP), a so-called "group practice without walls," makes up the core of physicians participating in the Genesys PHO. It includes 81 shareholder primary care physicians in private practices ranging in size from one to six physicians who cooperate to meet quality and utilization goals. GIGP also owns and operates three diagnostic centers and three after-hours clinics.

Rural North Dakota health care providers have established cooperative arrangements to provide local access to quality care by sharing scarce resources such as a mobile magnetic resonance imaging service, expertise such as grant development for community health centers, infrastructure such as a rural tele-pharmacy network, and service delivery such as rural mental health services provided by clinical nurse specialists. Some programs are developed under grants and are then operationalized over time.

Small critical access hospitals act as "health care central" for rural communities, providing emergency, inpatient, skilled nursing, and home care from a single location. West River Health Services, for example, coordinates a continuum of care across a large rural area of North Dakota through a multidisciplinary group of 15 physicians who support midlevel practitioners in satellite clinics in local communities.

MODEL 4: GOVERNMENT-FACILITATED NETWORKS OF INDEPENDENT PROVIDERS

In this model, government takes an active role in organizing independent providers, usually to create a delivery system for Medicaid beneficiaries. They may develop care coordination networks, provide information technology infrastructure, perform care management, or deliver other services characteristic of an organized delivery system.

Community Care of North Carolina (CCNC), founded in 1998, is a public–private partnership between the state and 14 nonprofit community-based care networks that comprise essential local providers including hospitals, primary care physicians, and county health and social services departments. The local networks provide key components of a primary care "medical home" (defined later) and locally led care management and quality improvement initiatives to meet statewide goals for access, cost, and quality of care for almost 1 million low income children and adults enrolled in Medicaid and the Children's Health Insurance Program. The state provides resources, information, and technical support, such as performance measurement and benchmarking. The state supplements physician fee-for-service reimbursement with a per-member per-month (PMPM) fee for participation in CCNC and pays the community networks a PMPM fee to cover the cost of staff (e.g., network and medical directors and care managers) to support care management and network administration.

Attributes of Organized Health Care Delivery

The structure of an organized delivery system may be thought of as the framework on which its attributes or functional capabilities can be built, which in turn influences its performance and outcomes. The full array of case study organizations demonstrate six attributes of an ideal health care delivery system (Table 10.2) identified by the Commonwealth Fund Commission on a High Performance Health Care System (Shih et al., 2008). Each of these attributes is discussed below using examples from the case studies.

TABLE 10.2

Six Attributes of an Ideal Health Care Delivery System

1. **Easy access to appropriate care:** Patients have easy access to appropriate care and information at all hours, there are multiple points of entry to the system, and providers are culturally competent and responsive to patients' needs.

2. **Information continuity:** Patients' clinically relevant information is available to all providers at the point of care and to patients through electronic health record (EHR) systems.

3. **Care coordination and transitions:** Patient care is coordinated among multiple providers, and transitions across care settings are actively managed.

4. **Peer review and teamwork for high-value care:** Providers (including nurses and other members of care teams) both within and across settings have accountability to each other, review each other's work, and collaborate to reliably deliver high-quality, high-value care.

5. **Continuous innovation:** The system is continuously innovating and learning in order to improve the quality, value, and patients' experiences of health care delivery.

6. **System accountability:** There is clear accountability for the total care of patients.

Source: Adapted from Shih, A., Davis, K., Schoenbaum, S. C., Gauthier, A., Nuzum, R., & McCarthy, D. (2008). *Organizing the U.S. health care delivery system for high performance.* New York: The Commonwealth Fund.

EASY ACCESS TO APPROPRIATE CARE

Patients who receive care in a setting that is well organized and offers appropriate access to providers (e.g., in a medical home) are more likely to get the care they need, receive reminders for preventive screenings, and report better management of chronic conditions than are patients who do not receive regular care in such settings (Beal, Doty, Hernandez, Shea, & Davis, 2007). Many of the study sites have reengineered their work processes to reduce waiting times for appointments by offering same- or next-day access to primary care and after-hours alternatives (e.g., nurse call lines and urgent care centers) to emergency department (ED) care. Some also offer patients the option of joining group visits, which provide peer support for making lifestyle changes and adhering to self-care routines. Co-location of multispecialty services in a single facility further promotes convenient access to care.

Prepaid care has encouraged Kaiser Permanente and Group Health Cooperative to use telephone visits and secure electronic messaging and Henry Ford Health System to offer patients Web-enabled electronic visits. These often are convenient alternatives to face-to-face encounters for patients with nonurgent needs and an efficient means for physicians and the care team to reach out to patients in need of follow-up. Several sites use **telehealth** technologies for routine home monitoring of patients with chronic conditions. The Marshfield Clinic has been a leader in developing a telehealth network to provide remote consultations and pharmacy services for patients in rural Wisconsin.

Large delivery systems or smaller systems linked through virtual networks or shared services agreements have the resources to develop culturally sensitive programs for diverse patient populations.

Large delivery systems or smaller systems linked through virtual networks or shared services agreements have the resources to develop culturally sensitive programs for diverse patient populations. For example, several of Kaiser Permanente's California medical centers offer culture-specific patient-care modules (Chinese, Spanish/Latino, and Vietnamese). These modules allow patients to communicate in their native language with a bilingual care team oriented to their cultural norms, which can be critical to providing effective treatment. HealthPartners in Minnesota has eliminated most disparities in the receipt of preventive care by instilling equity as a principle to be achieved through a consistent care process, including asking patients to voluntarily provide information on race, country of origin, and language at registration, so that services can be customized to meet individual needs.

INFORMATION CONTINUITY

Many study sites have been leaders in implementing **electronic health record (EHR)** systems that support coordination of care by making patient information available across providers and settings, promote the delivery of evidence-based care with decision support and patient education tools, and reduce duplication of services because laboratory and imaging tests results are available when needed. Most have instituted electronic prescribing, in order to reduce medication errors by eliminating illegible handwriting, enable the reconciliation of medication lists as patients move across care settings, and warn physicians of drug allergies and potential harmful drug interactions.

EHRs figure prominently in improving access to appropriate care. For example, advice nurses at the Marshfield Clinic can use the clinic's EHR to view a patient's treatment plan when speaking to the patient on the telephone and add a record of the call to the EHR for the patient's primary care physician to review and follow up as needed. Some organized delivery systems operate walk-in convenience clinics, located in retail outlets, that are linked to the system's EHR to help preserve continuity of care. Telehealth consultations linked to a common EHR at both the transmitting and receiving sites create a powerful combination for delivering virtual care that can equal the quality of face-to-face encounters.

Many systems offer patients the use of a Web portal linked to the EHR to promote knowledge, convenience, and engagement in their care. Some have created Web portals that allow authorized community physicians to view records of their own patients or to make electronic referrals into the system and receive the results of those referrals. Several are collaborating with other stakeholders to create regional networks for electronic information exchange. For example, New York City's Health and Hospitals Corporation gave "smart cards" with embedded medical histories to patients in its Queens network and installed electronic card readers in every hospital ED in Queens. This assures that providers have access to the information they need to treat patients in an emergency.

Some organizations developed their own EHR systems to meet local needs, whereas others purchased vendor-developed systems but enhanced them to realize their full potential. In these instances, the involvement of physicians in system development or vendor selection was essential to success. The investment in these systems was made directly by the delivery system or, as in the case of Partners HealthCare, funded in part by a pay-for-performance program negotiated with a payer. Henry Ford Health System attributed $14 million in cost savings to a regional electronic prescribing system linked to retail pharmacies that it developed in collaboration with purchasers. Intermountain Healthcare's leaders observed that the organization did not realize the full value of its investment in clinical information systems until the EHR became a key enabler of a broader clinical improvement strategy (described later).

Case Example: Instituting Electronic Health Records at Kaiser Permanente

Building on more than 40 years of experience with information technology, KP and its physicians in 2003 launched a $4 billion health information system called KP HealthConnect designed to electronically connect member-patients to their health care team, to their personal health information, and to relevant medical knowledge to promote integrated care. The EHR at the heart of this system links KP facilities nationwide, provides a longitudinal record of member encounters across clinical settings, and contains laboratory, medication, and imaging data. Other key features include:

- Electronic prescribing and test-ordering with decision support tools such as medication safety alerts, preventive care reminders, and online clinical guidelines
- Patient-panel management tools such as disease registries that help the care team identify, track, and conduct outreach or follow-up with patients having chronic conditions
- Electronic referrals that directly schedule patient appointments with specialist physicians
- Patient registration, performance monitoring, and analytic and reporting capabilities.

With the encouragement of physicians and staff, more than one-third of health plan members nationwide are using a Web portal to view their history of physician visits and preventive care reminders, schedule appointments, refill prescriptions, and send secure electronic messages to their care team or pharmacist. Online laboratory test results—the most popular online function—include links to a knowledge base of information on what test results mean and self-care strategies. Members can complete an online health risk assessment, receive customized feedback on behavioral interventions, participate in health behavior change programs, and choose whether to send results to KP HealthConnect to facilitate communication with their physician.

Although EHRs require more of physicians' time than paper records, they create efficiencies for the care team or organization as a whole while improving patient care. Use of the EHR and online portal is also having positive effects on utilization of services and patient engagement. For example, KP's Hawai`i region experienced a 26% decrease in its physician visit rate following implementation of KP HealthConnect, while overall patient contacts increased, due primarily to a large increase in scheduled telephone visits facilitated by the EHR (Chen, Garrido, Chock, Okawa, & Liang, 2009).

Case Example: Creating Incentives for EHR Adoption at Partners HealthCare

A 5-year pay-for-performance contract between Partners and Blue Cross Blue Shield of Massachusetts created incentives, first, for the adoption of EHRs by physicians, and second, for the use of an EHR to evaluate outcomes and identify patients in need of better management. To speed progress, the Partners board required that affiliated primary care groups adopt one of two preferred EHRs as a condition of participation in the network: either a Partners-developed EHR (known as the longitudinal medical record) or a certified third-party vendor system. Adoption among Partners' community-based primary care physicians increased from 9% in 2003 to 100% in 2009. In comparison, only 17% of office-based physicians surveyed nationally in 2008 reported using an EHR with at least basic functionality (DesRoches et al., 2008).

CARE COORDINATION AND TRANSITIONS

The study sites have developed mechanisms for care coordination to reduce the potential for frustrating patient experiences and poor outcomes, as patients attempt to navigate across different providers and settings. At the Mayo Clinic, for example, all patients are assigned a coordinating physician to ensure that they have an appropriate care plan, that all ancillary services and consultations are scheduled in a timely fashion, and that they receive clear communication throughout and at the conclusion of an episode of care.

An organized delivery system can provide a supportive environment for developing the primary care **"medical home"** concept, which aims to make patient care more accessible, continuous, comprehensive, patient-centered, and coordinated.[2] This often entails:

- A team-based, population-health management approach that stratifies patients according to their health risks and needs and leverages physician time

---

[2]A primary care medical home can be defined as a physician practice or clinic that offers patients enhanced access to primary care, employs a clinical team to efficiently coordinate patients' care, actively engages patients in their care, uses decision-support tools and measures performance to improve care, and receives enhanced payment to support these efforts.

- Enhanced roles for clinical support staff—midlevel practitioners (nurse practitioners or physician assistants), and care managers (trained nurses, social workers, or pharmacists)—to support patients in need of preventive care, disease or medication management, transitional care, and self-care education and
- Integrated mental health and primary care, in order to identify and appropriately treat or refer patients with co-occurring physical and mental illnesses.

Several sites find that routine care management activities are more effective when embedded in or closely linked to primary care teams, often through innovative funding arrangements. For example, MeritCare Health System collaborated with Blue Cross Blue Shield of North Dakota to develop a chronic disease management program that linked diabetes patients to a nurse care manager in their primary care clinic, with positive clinical and financial results. Geisinger Health Plan pays for nurse care managers located in Geisinger clinics and in community primary care practices as part of an advanced medical home program that has reduced hospitalizations and medical costs.

In loosely organized systems, teamwork takes the form of establishing interpersonal rapport as well as agreed-upon protocols and objectives to link centrally located care managers to primary care sites. Referring patients to centralized care managers appears to work well for delivering standardized services, such as anticoagulation medication management for high-risk patients—especially when such patients make up only a small number of any one physician's practice or when such services benefit from linkage to specialty care.

Case Example: Modeling the Primary Care Medical Home at Group Health Cooperative (GHC)

One of the nation's first HMOs, GHC has evolved into a mixed-model health plan in which two-thirds of members receive care from an integrated multispecialty group practice whereas the other third receives care from contracted community providers. In recent years, as GHC pushed to improve its competitiveness in the marketplace, it began to see unintended consequences of a "production-oriented" approach to primary care in the integrated medical group: swollen patient panels (averaging 2,300 patients per physician), increasing specialty care referrals, rising costs of hospital and emergency care, and signs of burnout in its workforce.

In response to these challenges, GHC in 2007 began a pilot project to define and test a medical home model at a primary care clinic in a Seattle suburb (Table 10.3). Although many elements of the medical home were already in place at GHC, the pilot intensified them to promote proactive care planning and patient engagement. Key interventions included using the EHR to identify and address patient care needs, expanding and enhancing the roles of the care team to reduce panel size (to about 1,800 patients per physician), planning work during daily team huddles, and using phone calls and secure electronic messaging as alternatives to personal visits when appropriate. The care team and their roles are:

- Medical assistants support pre-visit planning and post-visit communication
- Clinical pharmacists provide advice to the care team and educate patients
- Licensed practical nurses answer patient calls, conduct telephone outreach, and follow up with patients after unplanned visits to an emergency department
- Registered nurses provide intensive, short-term disease management for patients with uncontrolled chronic illnesses, and transitional care after hospitalizations
- Midlevel professionals see patients for same-day acute-care needs and follow-up chronic care visits
- Primary care physicians spend extended time with patients with chronic conditions

TABLE 10.3

Core Principles of a Medical Home at Group Health Cooperative (Washington state)

1. The relationship between the personal care physician and the patient is the core of all that we do. The entire delivery system and the organization will align to promote and sustain this relationship.

2. The personal care physician will be a leader of the clinical team, responsible for coordination and integration of services, and together with patients will create collaborative care plans.

3. Continuous healing relationships will be proactive and will encompass all aspects of health and illness. Patients will be actively informed about their care and will be encouraged to participate in all its aspects.

4. Access will be centered on patients' needs, will be available by various modes 24/7, and will maximize the use of technology.

5. Our clinical and business systems are aligned to achieve the most efficient, satisfying, and effective patient experiences.

Source: McCarthy, D., Mueller, K., & Tillmann, I. (2009). *Group Health Cooperative: Reinventing primary care by connecting patients with a medical home.* Retrieved October 16, 2010, from http://www.commonwealthfund.org/Content/Publications/Case-Studies/2009/Jul/Group-Health-Cooperative-Reinventing-Primary-Care-by-Connecting-Patients-with-a-Medical-Home.aspx.

Relative to comparison care sites, the medical home pilot site demonstrated better outcomes 21 to 24 months after implementation. There were significant improvements in measures of patient experience and clinical quality, reduced provider burnout, 29% fewer ED and urgent care visits, 6% fewer hospitalizations, and a trend toward lower overall costs of care (Reid et al., 2010). GHC's leaders report that these improvements, now being spread to all its integrated primary care sites, are making the organization a more attractive place to work.

Case Example: Patient-Panel Management at Kaiser Permanente of Northern California

A population-health approach builds on a strong primary care system as the most efficient way to interact with most patients most of the time, while recognizing that some patients who have—or who are at risk for developing—chronic diseases need additional support and specialty care to achieve the best outcomes. Patients are stratified into three levels of care:

1. Primary care with self-care support for the 65% to 80% of patients whose conditions are generally responsive to lifestyle changes and medications
2. Assistive care management for the 20% to 30% of patients whose diseases are not under control at level one
3. Intensive case management and specialty care for the 1% to 5% of patients with advanced disease and either complex comorbidities or frailty

Focusing on the entire spectrum of prevention for cardiac care management has contributed to multiple improvements in the Northern California region, such as a 25% decline in the adult smoking rate, increased use of therapies to control risk factors for cardiovascular disease, a doubling in blood pressure control among patients with hypertension, and substantial reductions in hospitalization rates for cardiovascular conditions and in heart disease deaths.

Case Example: Coordinated Care for High-Cost Patients at Partners HealthCare

Massachusetts General Hospital and its affiliated community physicians in the Massachusetts General PHO are participating in a Medicare demonstration project that initially enrolled about 2,500 of their highest risk Medicare beneficiaries—those with one or more serious chronic conditions and costs in the top 3% to 5% of patients. Each high-risk patient was assigned a practice-based nurse care manager trained in collaborative health coaching and charged with seeing that all elements in the care plan are executed, including psychosocial and medication adherence assessments, health care proxies and advance directives, community-based supports, and access to providers.

Care managers use the shared EHR to coordinate care with physicians. Although most patient contact is by telephone, location in the physician practice enables care managers to engage in occasional face-to-face patient meetings that help establish rapport and to form working relationships with the care team that enhance communication and care planning. A consulting psychiatrist provides evaluation services for patients with a major psychiatric diagnosis. Patients may receive home visits and home telemonitoring when needed. When a patient visits the ED, his or her physician receives a pager alert, which enables proactive intervention to help avoid unnecessary hospital admissions. When patients are hospitalized, care managers ensure they receive three key interventions at discharge to help avoid readmissions: (1) education on how to recognize signs of deteriorating health and a plan of action to prevent unnecessary ED visits, (2) scheduling of a follow-up appointment, and (3) a follow-up call by a pharmacist within 3 to 4 days to review medications and adjust them as needed.

The hospital receives a monthly fee for each beneficiary participating in the program, which covers administrative and care management costs. And, it is at financial risk for meeting a cost-savings target to Medicare (one of only a few care management demonstration programs to do so through reductions in hospitalizations and ED visits). Physicians rate the program highly, and many report that it saves them time. The program is now being extended to additional patient populations and Partners hospitals.

Case Example: Integrated Behavioral Health Care at Intermountain Healthcare

Concern that resources were not being used effectively to treat patients with mental health conditions led a multidisciplinary group of leaders at Intermountain Healthcare—a large IDS serving Utah and Idaho—to design an evidence-based, team-oriented mental health integration program to improve family-centered care and outcomes in primary care clinics. The program defines collaborative roles to enhance communication and coordination among team members including primary care physicians, mental health specialists, care managers, and support staff. Team members receive standardized training and tools (e.g., screening assessment, depression registry) to enhance their confidence and ability to identify and treat mental illnesses in the context of other chronic health conditions and to engage patients and their families in a treatment partnership tailored to individual needs. Clinic-based generalist care managers (nurses and social workers) support the team and assist patients and families to obtain needed services and engage in self-care and peer-support activities to promote recovery and wellness.

Among patients treated for depression, results include improved detection of depression, optimized service use, and lower overall treatment costs, accompanied by increased physician productivity and greater satisfaction among patients, physicians, and clinic staff. The program was cost-neutral after accounting for the administrative cost of the intervention (Reiss-Brennan, Briot, Savitz, Cannon, & Staheli, 2010).

PEER REVIEW AND TEAMWORK FOR HIGH-VALUE CARE

The study sites are typically characterized by a culture of group responsibility and shared commitment to quality care, evidenced in multiple ways. The performance improvement infrastructure frequently consists of interdisciplinary teams of clinical experts who collaborate to develop and spread evidence-based guidelines and standard care processes, often by embedding them in the EHR. Although MSGPs such as the Mayo Clinic have a formal peer review process, they emphasize the value of informal peer review facilitated by shared medical records in which clinicians can give one another feedback that promotes ongoing group accountability for clinical excellence. All sites have a robust measurement infrastructure that enables routine monitoring and feedback of system and provider performance, sometimes in identifiable or "unblinded" manner within a group or department to strengthen peer accountability. Physicians also may serve as "clinical champions" to identify and promote best practices and lead internal quality improvement collaborations.

Physicians are typically involved in decision making in these organizations through formal leadership roles, often in partnerships or "dyads" with administrative leaders, to help ensure consideration of clinical and patient perspectives. Organizations develop consensus and momentum for change through physician involvement in committees or work groups to complement vertical management structures. For example, many of participating physicians in the Genesys PHO and the Hill Physicians Medical Group (IPA) serve on committees to provide leadership and guidance on programs to improve coordination, quality, and efficiency of care.

Case Example: Governance at the Mayo Clinic

The Mayo Clinic is physician-led at all levels and operates through committees and a shared governance philosophy in which physician leaders work with administrative partners in a horizontal, consensus-driven structure. For example, site-based clinical practice committees are responsible for quality of care including dissemination of expert-developed clinical protocols. A system-wide clinical practice advisory group reconciles protocols across sites and is responsible to the board of governors for overall system quality. Although the committee process may take longer to reach consensus than would a traditional "top-down" management structure, it speeds and increases the odds of successful implementation of decisions because physician buy-in has already been achieved.

Case Example: Teamwork in a Loosely Organized Network

Within Community Care of North Carolina (CCNC), a committee of network clinical directors from across the state meets regularly to identify objectives for improvement and best practice models and to create system-wide quality measures and initiatives. Regional medical management committees and quality improvement planning groups implement initiatives locally. Local clinical directors work with peers in the community to support and encourage quality improvement efforts. Participating physicians receive comparative performance profiles (compiled by the CCNC central office) that provide feedback on progress and help motivate improvement on network initiatives.

CONTINUOUS INNOVATION AND ORGANIZATIONAL LEARNING

The case studies found widespread evidence of innovation and continuous improvement. Organized delivery systems take advantage of their scale and infrastructure to improve health care quality and value. The Mayo Clinic, for example, is building an electronic learning system to spread medical knowledge system-wide, supplementing existing methods such as "grand rounds," online curricula, and an in-house clinical journal in support of its philosophy that "no one is as smart as all of us."

> *Organized delivery systems take advantage of their scale and infrastructure to improve health care quality and value.*

Without an organizing entity, physicians and hospitals could certainly engage in collaborative improvement projects and take advantage of external resources such as Medicare Quality Improvement Organization programs, but they may lack the expertise, economies of scale, shared resources and incentives that come from working in a large, well-organized system.

Among the various improvement methods in use, many leaders are enthusiastic about the ability of "lean" techniques (borrowed from the manufacturing industry) to bring together frontline staff to design process improvements, minimize waste, and determine measures by which their performance will be evaluated. They find that clinicians are more amenable to the idea of standardizing their work processes when they see that it avoids "wasted" time and frees them to spend more time on clinically oriented tasks with or for their patients. DenverHealth has used such techniques to conduct nearly 100 rapid-cycle improvement projects to redesign strategic "value streams" thereby realizing almost $50 million in reduced costs or increased revenue during the first 5 years of this ongoing effort.

Case Example: Clinical Integration at Intermountain Healthcare

In 1988, Intermountain initiated a quality improvement training course, based on principles espoused by W. Edwards Deming, known as the Advanced Training Program (ATP). (In ATP, all participants undertake a focused improvement project that measures clinical and financial outcomes, and all senior administrators are required to participate and complete a project.) An analysis of Intermountain's early experience with the program found that 65 clinical projects originating from the ATP were associated with approximately $30 million in cost savings.

The process and structure for deploying projects developed during the ATP became known as clinical integration, an overarching strategy that focuses on improving value in key work processes. The program is built on three pillars: integrated management information systems, an integrated clinical and operations management structure, and integrated incentives. Multidisciplinary clinical development teams guide quality improvement activities within nine priority clinical programs ("service lines"), such as primary care and cardiovascular care. Care process models support physicians with evidence-based protocols, decision-support tools, and patient educational materials.

Activities taken to scale include a feedback component for providers that illustrates gaps to motivate improvement, forges collegial bonds for sharing improvement strategies, and "makes it easy to do it right." Examples of this approach include the mental health integration model in primary care (described previously), and the design of a discharge medication program for cardiac patients that led to improved medication compliance and reductions in hospital readmissions and mortality. Through these and other means, Intermountain achieves substantially lower than average use and costs of care for Medicare beneficiaries (Wennberg, Fisher, Goodman, & Skinner, 2008).

Geisinger's leaders believe that the organization can simultaneously improve quality, satisfaction, and efficiency only by redesigning and reengineering how care is delivered. The organization typically begins its efforts by targeting Geisinger patients insured by the Geisinger Health Plan, in whose treatment clinical and financial responsibilities intersect. Once a model is proven, the innovation may be expanded to encompass additional patients or groups. Its "innovation architecture" includes the following components (Paulus, Davis, & Steele, 2008):

- Convening teams of diverse stakeholders to identify the best care model for enhancing value in the prevention and treatment of disease
- Setting targets for care model redesign based on factors such as impact on populations and cost, variation in outcomes, interest among physicians, and gaps in performance
- Developing a clinical business case for the redesign including identifying efficiency and quality goals and developing a road map of needed changes and linkages in processes, analytic support, and financial and nonfinancial incentives
- Applying a variety of improvement approaches, including borrowing and adapting approaches that have worked in previous initiatives
- Culling promising innovations for expansion

ProvenCare is Geisinger's portfolio of evidence-based quality and efficiency programs addressing both acute and chronic conditions. Clinical workgroups redesign care processes to deliver reliably a coordinated bundle of evidence-based (or consensus-based) best practices. These are "hardwired" into the EHR through templates, order sets, and reminders. The process may include a "patient compact" to convey the expectation that patients should be active partners in their own care. For health plan members having certain surgical procedures, Geisinger charges a flat fee (a packaged or **bundled price**) that includes preoperative care, surgery, and 90 days of follow-up treatment (at a Geisinger facility) including treatment of any related complications. Pricing the bundle at a discount creates an incentive for efficiency and, in effect, offers a warranty against complications. Results for heart bypass surgery, the original ProvenCare product, include improved clinical and financial outcomes (Casale, Paulus, & Selna, 2007).

SYSTEM ACCOUNTABILITY

Typically, in the current fragmented U.S. health care system, no single physician or entity is accountable for the total care of a patient, but only for the portion of care that individual provider directly delivers. Perverse payment incentives mean that hospitals stand to lose revenue when they work to improve transitional care and reduce readmissions. Without accountability for total care, it is easy to ignore the need for care coordination and care transitions, which means patients "fall through the cracks." And, physicians and hospitals are rewarded for focusing on high-cost, intensive medical interventions rather than higher value, preventive medicine and the management of chronic illnesses. (The recently enacted federal health care reform law includes a number of demonstration and pilot programs that may begin to address these gaps, as described later in the chapter.)

Although some study sites assign an accountable physician or an accountable practice (e.g., medical home) for a patient, it may be more appropriate to say that each of the delivery systems as a whole assumed accountability for the patient or member. This arrangement is most explicit when a patient is covered by a health plan owned by an IDS, which creates clear financial, as well as clinical, accountability for patients' total care. However, study organizations also assumed responsibility for patients covered by third-party payers, as reflected in their efforts to coordinate care and manage care transitions—sometimes as part of pay-for-performance initiatives that allowed them to develop programs and tools that can benefit all their patients.

Case Example: Population-Based Care at the Genesys PHO

Two central values that guided the Genesys PHO—consistent care for all patients regardless of their type of insurance and a commitment to improving the health of the community—laid the foundation for its population-based focus. Operating under a strategic vision crafted by community members, leaders at Genesys Health System have willingly forgone some hospital revenue by working with physicians in the PHO to improve the health of patients through better ambulatory care management. For example, the hospital helps fund a "health navigators" program that supports physicians in motivating patients to engage in health behavior change. They believe that by lowering admissions, the system lowers its costs, which attracts payers and patients to the extent that they are focused on better value. At the same time, the health system is not willing to shrink its hospital bed capacity (beyond a previous "right-sizing" that consolidated several hospitals into one regional medical center), because it supports education and research activities that are attractive to a high-quality medical staff. The solution, from the health system's perspective, is to attract more patients by collaborating with affiliated physicians in its PHO to increase the overall primary care patient population base.

Cross-Cutting Themes: The "Methods" of Organized Delivery

Across the study sites, several overarching themes stand out that are important to understanding how providers successfully organize care for higher performance.

VALUES-DRIVEN LEADERSHIP, GOVERNANCE, AND ORGANIZATIONAL CULTURE

Organizational and physician leaders appear to motivate the achievement of higher performance among peers and the general workforce by inculcating a mission and culture that appeal to common values, such as patient welfare, professional pride, and shared responsibility for quality and outcomes. This kind of environment can make organized delivery systems an attractive place for physicians to work. Sites are often physician-led or run in close partnership between administrators and physicians, a collaborative approach that puts patient care on an equal footing with finance and operations. Leaders balance a focus on values with management discipline by setting clear and ambitious goals, communicating with and enlisting the workforce in carrying out a strategic vision, and marshalling resources to support implementation of agreed-upon strategies.

INTERDISCIPLINARY TEAMWORK

Teamwork takes many forms and is a key mechanism in the coordination of care. For example, it facilitates the orchestration of the functions of extended primary care and care management teams (which may include physicians, nurses, pharmacists, psychologists, social workers, and medical assistants), and can bring together experts from across medical and administrative disciplines to develop standardized and evidence-based care processes, thereby fostering continuous improvement.

INTEGRATION

In general, greater integration makes it possible for a system to better understand and design programs to meet the comprehensive needs of a population so as to improve the quality and efficiency of care. Case study organizations are taking multiple paths to integrating care, bringing together providers and services across disciplines and settings to focus on particular conditions or care episodes (e.g., diabetes, cancer, cardiac surgery). They also may do this across time and types of care, such as using every patient contact as an opportunity to schedule needed preventive care. A common EHR and other electronic linkages appear to be an important enabling tool for integrating and coordinating care as patients move across these systems.

Fully integrated systems, such as Kaiser Permanente, find that owning hospitals and co-locating services in medical centers promotes tighter care coordination and efficiency. Likewise, critical-access hospitals in North Dakota often serve as "one-stop shops" for integrating inpatient and outpatient care for rural communities. Other systems, such as Group Health Cooperative, find that excess hospital bed capacity in its market makes it more efficient to contract and coordinate with independent hospitals for inpatient care, which frees GHC to focus expertise on ambulatory care delivery. Although some multi-specialty group practices, such as the Marshfield Clinic, report challenges in coordinating care with independent hospitals, these have not deterred their physicians from adopting a population-based approach to patient care.

Simply owning the pieces of a system is not enough, however. The experience of organizations such as Henry Ford Health System that have made financial turnarounds indicates that organized delivery systems must actively pursue the opportunities for integration inherent in their model, in order to achieve the desired internal alignment, coordination, and synergy between parts of the system. This entails realizing efficiencies ranging from eliminating redundant layers of administration to cross-marketing and in-sourcing services to avoid "leakage" of revenues outside the IDS—in short, taking advantage of the organization's core strengths.

ALIGNED INCENTIVES

Alignment occurs at the organizational level by integrating care and coverage and/or by setting budgets centrally, so that services can be organized in ways that make the most sense operationally and clinically. For example, some IDSs subsidize primary care services from other operations in recognition that effective primary care delivery contributes to a more efficient system overall. Delivery systems that include health plans have financial incentives to provide care coordination and care transition services. To the extent that overall costs are reduced because of fewer ED visits or hospitalizations, these programs offer a positive return on investment. In other cases, provider organizations are collaborating with payers and purchasers to participate in incentive programs and create payment reforms that help fund care management activities, a process facilitated by a prepared infrastructure.

Delivery systems that include health plans have financial incentives to provide care coordination and care transition services.

Following an evolution in the market that has demanded choice of provider, several integrated systems with health plans "opened" their networks to contract with community physicians and accept payers other than their own health plan, thereby shifting their orientation away from an exclusive reliance on prepaid practice. These organizations have adapted by developing performance information and incentives to help overcome the limitations of fee-for-service payment. Several of these "hybrid" organizations report an advantage from being able to influence other providers in the community who practice in their facilities or who contract with their health plans, and of creating a spirit of "competitive excellence" within their organization as they seek the loyalty of patients who have a choice of provider.

At the physician level, the compensation method is aligned with the organization's objectives, values, and market environment. Some entities, such as the Mayo Clinic, believe that salaried physicians—free of fee-for-service incentives—are motivated intrinsically by professional and organizational culture to do their best for patients. Other organizations see a positive role for extrinsic rewards, including financial incentives, which may include productivity-based pay or bonuses for meeting quality and service goals.

MUTUAL ACCOUNTABILITY

At its best, multispecialty group practice fosters a cohesive group culture that helps to minimize "turf battles" between disciplines and departments; instead, physicians work together and with other staff to achieve common goals based on common values. Working as part of a self-governing physician group appears to involve a trade-off in which physicians sacrifice some individual autonomy for the benefits of group practice, such as the expertise and resources to jointly determine best practice protocols. Groups that are accountable for both financial and clinical outcomes under capitated payment find that it protects their clinical freedom from outside micromanagement. In some areas, such as North Dakota and Minnesota, this theme takes the form of a spirit of collaboration among different organizations with similar interests that jointly pursue common objectives. In the words of one observer, "Everyone is in the same boat, pulling together."

TRANSPARENCY

Supporting a culture of accountability, case study organizations engage in rigorous performance measurement, reporting, and recognition—both internally at the unit and individual level to promote peer accountability and externally at the organizational level to demonstrate the value of their efforts to purchasers, patients, and other stakeholders. As one leader noted, transparency fosters honesty, awareness, and commitment to improvement throughout the workforce.

Accountability is further reinforced by public performance reporting in a competitive marketplace. This is especially true in places such as California, where purchasers have structured the market to reward plans that deliver higher value. For example,

Kaiser Permanente long enjoyed a price advantage in the California market due to the integrated financial and clinical principles underlying its model, but its competitors learned to achieve similar gains in part by emulating its strategies. Financial losses in the late 1990s and the advent of public performance reporting, reinforced by unblinded internal performance feedback within the medical group, energized the organization to demonstrate the potential of its model by making a stronger push for innovation and quality.

The Value of Organized Delivery

Commonly reported results of the initiatives and programs documented in the case studies included:

- Improved clinical quality of care and control of chronic diseases
- Increased patient satisfaction, shorter waiting times
- Reduced hospitalizations, emergency visits, and prescription drug expenses (McCarthy & Mueller, 2009).

Some of their achievements may represent the first rewards of a process that will require continuing innovation and effort to sustain a trajectory of improvement and to broaden its reach across all areas of performance. Organizational culture and what one leader calls "pride of purpose" appear to be key factors propelling excellent organizations to sustain such efforts over time. Although some institutions such as Mayo Clinic have been developing their culture over decades, in others cases leaders describe how managers can engage the workforce to inculcate the behavior and attitudes that shape a culture aimed toward higher performance, especially as it relates to keeping patients safe from harm (McCarthy & Blumenthal, 2005).

> *Organizational culture and what one leader calls "pride of purpose"*
> *appear to be key factors propelling excellent organizations to*
> *sustain such efforts over time.*

A recent review of the health services literature found that "more organized systems generally perform better than less organized systems on measures of clinical quality, show promise for reducing health care costs, and have a mixed record in terms of patients' experiences" (Shih et al., 2008). Similarly, in comparison to external benchmarking data, the study organizations generally performed more highly on clinical quality than on patient satisfaction metrics, although, in recent years, several have made strides in improving the patient experience. Not all the sites did equally well across all dimensions of performance, however, and better comparative data are needed to assess their ability to control the per-capita costs of care. Although their models of care delivery work well most of the time, the case studies also documented instances when they failed to live up to their promise. Nevertheless, their overall experience and achievements suggest that a greater degree of organization will be essential to improving the value of American health care.

Realizing the Potential

The case studies illustrate that there are many ways of achieving more organized delivery of health care, yet there are common themes. These factors suggest that in seeking to develop or foster organized delivery systems, managers and policy makers should adopt a flexible approach that takes into account not only what is most effective but also what is most feasible in a local context and environment, and that they should focus on building a guiding vision, integrative capabilities, and supportive organizational culture as much as the structural components of an organization.

More physicians are moving to employment relationships with hospitals—a trend that might be harnessed to realize the fuller advantages of an employed group practice model (Minott, Helms, Luft, Guterman, & Weil, 2010). Intermountain Healthcare's relatively recent experience creating an integrated medical group from scratch shows that it is possible to do so in a matter of years, not decades, if the process is managed well. It found that a medical group recruited from community physicians with a "collaborative bent" and built around core values and a common work ethic "self-selects" its members over time and becomes a stable unit with a shared culture. By emphasizing value creation based on quality and service, rather than on productivity alone, Intermountain allowed physicians the opportunity to develop an internally motivated pride for achieving excellence both clinically and financially.

In other circumstances, physicians, hospitals, and other providers may find that it makes sense to develop alternative ways to organize and integrate care through independent private practices, although they may or may not enjoy all the levers for integration available to employed physician groups. The Genesys PHO in metropolitan Flint, Michigan, built and sustained a partnership between its hospital and a virtual "group practice without walls" in which physicians in private practice developed peer accountability for achieving quality and efficiency goals.

Primary care physicians are thus involved in determining appropriate guidelines for clinical care and specialty referral and negotiating with insurers to obtain delegated authority for medical management under a capitated payment structure. This ensures that physicians are not overruled by an outside managed care organization nor micro-managed by hospital administrators. This clinical and operational autonomy, together with a respectful relationship with the hospital that treats the physicians as true partners, appears to have given the Genesys PHO an endurance that was often lacking in other efforts to establish PHOs. The Mount Auburn Cambridge Independent Practice Association, in metropolitan Boston, has achieved similar success in partnering with a local hospital through joint-risk contracting with HMOs.

Market and reimbursement incentives as currently structured do not fully support organized delivery systems in "doing the right thing" for their patients. For example, a review of the literature found that only a few economic integration strategies motivating hospitals and physicians to work together, such as bundled payments for episodes of care, were linked with clinical integration strategies aimed at lowering costs and improving quality of care (Burns & Muller, 2008). Likewise, an analysis of the financial impact of integration strategies by 36 large hospital systems found that integration with an insurance function, but not with physicians or other hospitals, was rewarded financially during the 1990s (Burns, Grimm, & Nicholson, 2005). These findings indicate that external factors can influence the motivations for undertaking integration, the form that integration will take, and the success it can achieve.

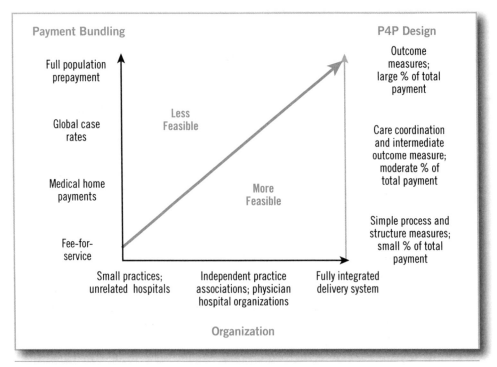

FIGURE 10.2

Model of organization and payment methods.

Source: The Commonwealth Fund. (2009). *The path to a high performance U.S. health system: A 2020 vision and the policies to pave the way.* New York: Author. Reprinted with permission.

Hence, the prospects for stimulating greater organization and integration of care in the United States depend in large part on changes in the policy and macro-environment, such as aligning financial incentives; making changes to the regulatory, professional, and educational environments; and developing supportive infrastructure for higher performance (Shih et al., 2008). The relationship between organization and payment methods is depicted in Figure 10.2.

The figure shows that, as the delivery system becomes more organized (e.g., going from unrelated hospitals and small practices toward IDSs), more bundled payment methods and robust pay-for-performance programs are not only more feasible, they become more desirable. Bundled payment methods reward care coordination and efficiency, which more organized delivery systems should be able to achieve. In addition, with greater organization, it would be possible to increase the percent of total reimbursement subject to pay-for-performance programs, and to focus these programs on clinical outcomes measures. Not only would this create incentives for high performance, but it also would counterbalance the risk that bundled payments would lead providers to deliver too few services. By contrast, it is not feasible to implement these payment methods at the small provider level (Shih et al., 2008).

Recent federal health reform legislation includes provisions to foster greater organization of care through various payment and delivery system reforms, pilots, and demonstration programs, as well as a new Center for Medicare and Medicaid Innovation charged with testing models to improve quality while reducing costs (Guterman, Davis, Stremikis,

& Drake, 2010). For example, beginning in 2012, Medicare reimbursement rates will be reduced for hospitals with high ("excess") rates of readmissions for certain conditions.

A Medicare shared savings program will provide incentives for newly designated **accountable care organizations (ACOs)**, such as those described in this chapter, to achieve cost-savings from coordinated care. Experts propose a tiered pathway for ACO evolution and qualification that would reward performance based on the degree of financial risk assumed by the ACO (McClellan, McKethan, Lewis, Roski, & Fisher, 2010; Shortell, Casalino, & Fisher, 2010). Participants in the new ACO program can learn from the experience of the recent Medicare Physician Group Practice Demonstration, which found that achieving both quality and efficiency goals required redesigning care processes and strengthening relationships between physicians and hospitals to improve transitions in care (Trisolini, Aggarwal, & Leung, 2008).

Going forward, additional work will be needed to rapidly spread successful pilots and support change at the ground level. For example, a recent study of efforts to create ACOs in Vermont found that "most small and medium-sized communities and care systems will need state and/or national support for defining a common financial framework for all payers, supporting the development and expansion of primary care medical homes, information technology support, technical support, and training and start-up funding" (Hester, Lewis, & McKethan, 2010). According to leaders, physicians are increasingly attracted to organized care settings and can be motivated to take part in and lead ACOs if they see that new arrangements offer a way to provide better care, sustain patients' loyalty, and maintain control over their own destiny.

Delivery system reforms to stimulate greater organization of care generally enjoy the support of both consumers and health system leaders (How, Shih, Lau, & Schoen, 2008; Stremikis, Guterman, & Davis, 2009). Health system leaders see that impending demographic shifts and fiscal constraints create an urgent need to creatively bring these approaches to scale (Dentzer, 2010). Patients also may play a role in bringing about change as they demand greater responsiveness and convenience from the care system, such as the ability to communicate electronically with their care team, and as they make use of performance information to choose their care providers. The public availability of such comparative data—especially as it focuses on system-level outcomes—can enable purchasers and policy makers to calibrate better policies and motivate providers to respond for the sake of professional pride and reputation.

Conclusion

Although there are significant challenges to realizing the full potential of organized health care delivery systems, those profiled here add to a growing body of research demonstrating that their models are feasible in diverse settings across the country (Shortell, Gillies, Anderson, Erickson, & Mitchell, 2000). Their experience demonstrates how higher performance can be attained through convenient access to appropriate care, information continuity, patient engagement, care coordination, team-oriented care delivery, and continuous innovation and learning. Realizing these attributes in turn requires the cultivation of values-based leadership, interdisciplinary teamwork, and aligned incentives (both at the organizational and provider level) supported by accountability for and transparency of results. Adapting and spreading these approaches more widely would help assure that more Americans can benefit from receiving care that is designed and delivered to provide a higher level of performance.

DISCUSSION QUESTIONS

1. Think about an episode of health care that you received, or that someone you know received. Describe how that care experience would have differed had it been delivered in accordance with the six attributes of an ideal health system (Table 10.2).

2. Do you think the kind of organizations described in the case examples provide an ideal way for patients to receive care? Why or why not? Does one organizational model appeal to you more than others? Which model do you think would be most effective overall in improving health care quality, access, and efficiency? Are any models missing from these examples?

3. With which of the following statements do you agree most? (1) It's best to keep health care simple so that it stays personal. (2) Modern medicine is so complex that it requires a certain sophistication to manage well. Describe what you think is the right balance between "systemness" and responsiveness and how you would seek that balance as a leader.

4. How could a physician group or an affiliation of independent physicians apply the lessons offered by the case examples to create an organized system of care?

5. How important is coordinated care given the state of health care today? Are there other ways for patients to get the care they need without involving a health care professional to help coordinate it for them? What kinds of patients are more or less likely to benefit from care coordination? How might care coordination evolve in the future?

6. Why do you think that many of the case study organizations consider EHRs an essential tool in their ability to coordinate care? Are there any drawbacks that EHRs may pose? Is there anything the health care industry could learn from the way that other industries or sectors use information technology to improve operations or services?

7. In what ways might leaders go about shaping the culture of an organization (the attitudes and behaviors that characterize the way things get done) to improve performance?

8. Describe how innovations in health care can be either cost-increasing or cost-decreasing. Are there ways that organizations or policy makers can ensure that they tend toward the latter?

9. What behavior is each of the following methods of paying for health care likely to reward, and in what circumstances would each be more or less appropriate: (1) salary with or without a bonus; (2) a fee for each service or unit of work rendered (fee-for-service or productivity-based pay); (3) a bundled payment for a complete episode of care (e.g., preoperative to postoperative care for surgery); and (4) fixed payment for all care needed in a given time period (capitation)?

CASE STUDY

General Hospital is a (hypothetical) 150-bed, not-for-profit, acute-care community hospital located in the center of a mid-size U.S. city. Although it employs a few doctors, such as a radiologist and pathologist, its medical staff consists of independent community physicians. Until recently, it enjoyed a loyal patient base and modest but stable operating margins. Within the past several years, however, a number of challenges have threatened its survival. The local economy, which was dependent on the manufacturing industry, has been in decline and losing jobs, although a new high-tech industrial park is under development. The hospital's margins are being squeezed as the burden of uncompensated care has risen along with the proportion of patients who are uninsured.

The local population is aging more rapidly than the U.S. as a whole and suffers from proportionately greater disease burdens owing to unhealthy lifestyles. This did not pose a problem for the hospital under traditional fee-for-service reimbursement that paid for each admission. However, under the new federal health reform law, the Medicare program will begin reducing reimbursement rates for hospitals that have high rates of readmissions. General Hospital's chief financial officer calculates that the hospital will suffer a substantial financial penalty if it doesn't measurably reduce its readmission rate, especially if commercial insurers begin to mimic Medicare's payment policy.

General's main competitor in the region, Progressive Hospital, undertook a diversification strategy leading it to purchase a home health care agency, a skilled nursing facility, and a few of the area's leading physician practices. It also jointly owns an ambulatory surgery center with community surgeons. Progressive advertises itself as an integrated health system offering patients a full continuum of care, and it negotiated a pay-for-performance program with a local insurer that rewards it for meeting certain quality and outcome goals. General Hospital has talked to the insurer about participating in the program, but is unable to do so without a way to work more closely with physicians and post-acute care providers who would determine its success.

General Hospital's CFO has recommended that the hospital explore becoming an accountable care organization (ACO) to qualify for incentives under Medicare's new shared-savings program. He recently attended a conference where other CFOs talked about the benefits of employing doctors to create better alignment with the hospital. At the same time, several independent primary care physicians in the community are in discussions to organize a "group practice without walls" or an independent practice association (IPA) to support their transformation—and qualify for enhanced reimbursement—as medical homes. It is also known that they are considering partnering with one of the hospitals to qualify as an ACO, which will require better care coordination and information exchange with the hospital.

Assume you are General Hospital's CEO. The hospital's board of trustees has asked you to present recommendations for the hospital's future, including whether and how the hospital will meet the challenge of becoming an ACO. They are particularly concerned that the hospital should balance its nonprofit mission to improve the health of the community with the imperative to assure its financial viability.

CASE STUDY DISCUSSION

Using the case examples from the chapter, develop a strategy that you think will best position the hospital for the future. Describe the rationale for your chosen strategy and outline how you would implement your recommended course of action.

REFERENCES

Beal, A., Doty, M. M., Hernandez, S. E., Shea, K. K., & Davis, K. (2007). *Closing the divide: How medical homes promote equity in health care.* New York: The Commonwealth Fund.

Burns, L. R., Gimm, G., & Nicholson, S. (2005). The financial performance of integrated health organizations. *Journal of Healthcare Management, 50,* 191–211.

Burns, L. R., & Muller, R. W. (2008). Hospital-physician collaboration: Landscape of economic integration and impact on clinical integration. *Milbank Quarterly, 86,* 375–434.

Casale, A. S., Paulus, R. A., & Selna, M. J. (2007). A provider-driven pay-for-performance program for acute episodic cardiac surgical care. *Annals of Surgery, 246,* 270–280.

Chen, C., Garrido, T., Chock, D., Okawa, G., & Liang, L. (2009). The Kaiser Permanente electronic health record: Transforming and streamlining modalities of care. *Health Affairs, 28,* 323–333.

Commonwealth Fund Commission on a High Performance Health System (2007). *A high performance health system for the United States: An ambitious agenda for the next president.* New York: The Commonwealth Fund.

Dentzer, S. (2010). Geisinger chief Glenn Steele: Seizing health reform's potential to build a superior system. *Health Affairs, 29,* 1200–1207.

DesRoches, C. M., Campbell, E. G., Rao, S. R., Donelan, K., Ferris, T. G., Jha, A., Kaushal, R., et al. (2008). Electronic health records in ambulatory care: A national survey of physicians. *New England Journal of Medicine, 359,* 50–60.

Falk, I. S., Rorem, C. R., & Ring, M. D. (1933). *The costs of medical care: A summary of investigations on the economic aspects of the prevention and care of illness.* Chicago, IL: University of Chicago Press.

Guterman, S., Davis, K., Stremikis, K., & Drake, H. (2010). Innovation in Medicare and Medicaid will be central to health reform's success. *Health Affairs, 29,* 1188–1193.

Hester, J., Lewis, J., & McKethan, A. (2010). *The Vermont accountable care organization pilot: A community health system to control total medical costs and improve population health.* New York: The Commonwealth Fund.

How, S. K. H., Shih, A., Lau, J., & Schoen, C. (2008). *Public views on U.S. health system organization: A call for new directions.* New York: The Commonwealth Fund.

Institute of Medicine (2001). *Crossing the quality chasm: A new health system for the 21st century.* Washington, D.C.: National Academy Press.

McCarthy, D., & Blumenthal, D. (2006). Stories from the sharp end: Case studies in safety improvement. *Milbank Quarterly, 84,* 165–200.

McCarthy, D., & Mueller, K. (2009). *Organizing for higher performance: Case studies of organized delivery systems. Series overview, findings, and methods.* New York: The Commonwealth Fund.

McClellan, M., McKethan, A. N., Lewis, J. L., Roski J., & Fisher, E. S. (2010). A national strategy to put accountable care into practice. *Health Affairs, 29,* 982–990.

Medicare Payment Advisory Commission (2009). Accountable care organizations. In: *Report to the Congress: Improving incentives in the Medicare program.* Washington, D.C.: Author.

Minott, J., Helms, D., Luft, H., Guterman, S., & Weil, H. (2010). *The group employed model as a foundation for health delivery reform.* New York: The Commonwealth Fund.

Paulus, R. A., Davis, K., & Steele, G. D. (2008). Continuous innovation in health care: Implications of the Geisinger experience. *Health Affairs, 27,* 1235–1245.

Reid, R. J., Coleman, K., Johnson, E. A., Fishman, P. A., Hsu, C., Soman, M. P., et al. (2010). The Group Health medical home at year two: Cost savings, higher patient satisfaction, and less burnout for providers. *Health Affairs, 29,* 835–843.

Reiss-Brennan, B., Briot, P., Savitz, L. A., Cannon, W., & Staheli, R. (2010). Cost and quality impact of Intermountain's mental health integration program. *Journal of Healthcare Management, 55,* 97–113.

Schoen, C., How, S. K. H., Weinbaum, I., Craig, J. E., Jr., & Davis, K. (2006). *Public views on shaping the future of the U.S. health system.* New York: The Commonwealth Fund.

Shih, A., Davis, K., Schoenbaum, S. C., Gauthier, A., Nuzum, R., & McCarthy, D. (2008). *Organizing the U.S. health care delivery system for high performance.* New York: The Commonwealth Fund.

Shortell, S. M., Casalino, L. P., & Fisher, E. (2010). *Advancing national health reform: Implementing accountable care organizations.* Policy Brief. University of California, Berkeley, School of Law: Berkeley Center on Health, Economic & Family Security.

Shortell, S. M., Gillies, R. R., Anderson, D. A., Erickson, K. M., & Mitchell, J. B. (2000). *Remaking health care in America: The evolution of organized delivery systems,* 2nd ed. San Francisco, CA: Jossey-Bass.

Stremikis, K., Guterman, S., & Davis, K. (2009). *Health care opinion leaders' views on slowing the growth of health care costs.* New York: The Commonwealth Fund.

Trisolini, M., Aggarwal, J., & Leung, M. (2008). *The Medicare physician group practice demonstration: Lessons learned on improving quality and efficiency in health care.* New York: The Commonwealth Fund.

Wennberg, J. E., Fisher, E. S., Goodman, D. C., & Skinner, J. S. (2008). *Tracking the care of patients with severe chronic illness: The Dartmouth Atlas of Health Care 2008.* Hanover, NH: The Dartmouth Institute for Health Care Policy & Clinical Practice.

11

HIGH QUALITY HEALTH CARE

Carolyn Clancy and Robert Lloyd

KEY WORDS

outcomes

structure

process

performance measurement

quality measurement journey (QMJ)

statistical process control

value-based purchasing

pay-for-performance

LEARNING OBJECTIVES

- Learn what quality care is and how it is defined
- Understand how well the United States is doing in providing high quality care
- Understand how quality is measured
- Learn how quality measures are applied in practice to guide improvements in care
- Identify promising initiatives to improve care and future directions in health care

TOPICAL OUTLINE

- Defining quality
- Quality matters: How are we doing?
- Measuring quality
- Practicing quality measurement in health care
- The quality measurement journey
- Promising initiatives
- Future directions
- Core competencies for health administrators

P AC is a 24-year-old law student and avid soccer player. Before starting his last year of law school, PAC's right knee gives out while playing soccer. He visits an orthopedist who tells him he needs surgery for his torn anterior cruciate ligament. He contacts his physician aunt with an urgent question: where should he have the surgery done?

Historically, most people assumed that this question could be answered with a list of surgeons in a particular area, with some consideration for convenience. In other words, the assumption was that the combination of well-trained health care professionals, clean facilities, and location in this country represented a virtual guarantee of superb care.

Today, people can search a variety of Web sites and other sources to learn what the injury is, how it is treated, and possibly which physicians and facilities provide high-quality care for that particular medical problem. Along the way, they will see frequent advertisements by providers, all proclaiming to be the best. After investing considerable time, they may or may not find precisely what they need and will then turn to friends, family and "people like me."

As a result of numerous studies, prestigious reports, and media accounts, Americans now know that high-quality, safe care is not automatic. The past 20 years have been marked by widespread efforts to assess and improve health care quality. Most recently, the 2010 Patient Protection and Affordable Care Act (ACA) and the 2009 American Recovery and Reinvestment Act both accelerated this momentum with multiple provisions focused on a path to high-quality, affordable health care.

This chapter describes the current state of health care quality; reviews selected efforts to conceptualize, measure, and improve quality; describes how measures are used to guide improvements in care; addresses promising initiatives to improve care; and describes how the health care landscape will evolve in the coming years.

Defining Quality

Quality was defined by the Institute of Medicine as "the degree to which health services for individuals and populations increase the likelihood of desired health outcomes and are consistent with current professional knowledge" (Lohr & Schroeder, 1990). Implicitly this definition covers both individuals and patient groups, including those who seek care and those who do not. Further, the definition was intended to focus on **outcomes** or end results important to individuals and to recognize that medical knowledge evolves. A frequently used shorthand definition is "the right care for the right patient at the right time."

Quality was initially described by Avedis Donabedian (1988) as consisting of three important dimensions: structure, process, and outcomes. **Structure** refers to facilities and health care professionals providing care, process to the set of services provided, and outcomes to the end results that people experience and care about. Donabedian consistently emphasized that these three dimensions are clearly interrelated, but that little is known about their causal linkages. The earliest efforts to assure quality focused on structure, for example, urging hospitals to update their equipment and check the credentials and training of all health care workers.

Numerous studies examining the **process** and outcomes of care demonstrated substantial variations in clinical practice, itself an indicator of questionable quality, and resulted in a movement to develop better methods for determining the relationship between care processes and outcomes, including the establishment of the Agency for Health Care Policy and Research in 1989, now the Agency for Healthcare Research and Quality (AHRQ). These efforts also revealed the existence of underuse, overuse, and misuse of services, as well as the substantial time lapse for new scientific findings to be translated into practice—a problem that persists to this day.

One notable example of the latter concerns the use of medications known as beta blockers to reduce mortality among patients who have had a heart attack. In 2007, the National Committee for Quality Assurance, the private-sector organization that accredits health plans, found that this recommended practice had become so widespread that they no longer included the percentage of patients with a heart attack who received a beta blocker (absent a reason not to use that medication such as an allergy) in their scoring of health plan performance. However, the study documenting a 40% reduction in mortality due to use of beta blockers had been published 25 years previously (Lee, 2007). In short, biomedical scientific advances do not lead automatically to their reliable application in patient care.

Quality Matters: How Are We Doing?

As examples of continuing shortfalls in quality, a landmark study found that Americans receive recommended care 55% of the time, a result that shocked many physicians, health care leaders, and the public; patients with high blood pressure received approximately 64% of recommended services, even though poorly controlled blood pressure contributes to more than 68,000 preventable deaths annually (McGlynn et al., 2003); health care-associated infections, largely preventable, result in an estimated 99,000 deaths per year; and largely preventable harms occur in 13.7% of Medicare patients hospitalized in a given year.

> *Variations in clinical practice mean that too often the care provided is more strongly related to zip code than to patient need or preference.*

In addition, variations in clinical practice mean that too often the care provided is more strongly related to zip code than to patient need or preference. AHRQ's annual reports on quality and disparities have demonstrated annual improvements in quality that are statistically significant, but the net impact is modest (U.S., Department of Health and Human Services, AHRQ, 2009). Disparities associated with individuals' race, sex, ethnicity, income, education, and other factors are pervasive and usually associated with poor care quality. In short, the return on investment for substantial health care expenditures is far less than desired.

Of course, advances in biomedical science have resulted in life-saving treatments for diseases that once resulted in death at an early age. For example, mortality from cardiovascular disease has declined substantially in the past few decades due to:

- Better treatments for high blood pressure, cholesterol, and other cardiovascular risk factors;
- A substantial decrease in the proportion of Americans who smoke; and
- Enhancements in care provided to those experiencing an acute event, such as a heart attack or stroke.

Such achievements have led to dramatic improvements in longevity (a gain of approximately 30 years in the 20th century), but also mean that the greatest threat to health is now chronic illness. For these conditions U.S. health care quality urgently needs improvement.

Public reporting of quality measures for health plans, hospitals, nursing homes, and other settings has consistently been associated with improved performance. However, those improvements are most dramatic for services under the direct control of a clinician or health care organization, such as ordering the right tests for patients with diabetes or heart disease. Control of cholesterol, diabetes, and related aspects of care (e.g., through use of screening tests for these problems) have been far slower to improve, as have aspects that depend on patients' lifestyle changes to support disease prevention and treatment efforts (see Chapter 7).

Measuring Quality

Since the late 1980s, measuring quality has focused on assessing clinical performance. Process measures are commonly expressed as a percentage of eligible patients who received a specific clinical service—for example, patients with a heart attack who received a beta blocker or the proportion of women who received timely screening for breast and cervical cancer.

Ideally, process measures derive from strong evidence that a specific service results in an improved outcome. Many would much prefer to measure outcomes such as mortality, ability to function, or relief from symptoms. However, these are more challenging to assess because of the time required to observe patients and because outcomes may be influenced by nonmedical factors, such as education, and clinical factors, such as coexisting illnesses. For example, an important difference in outcomes between two hospitals would help PAC select where to have his surgery, but that information doesn't help the poorer-performing hospital learn how to improve processes of care that could improve patient outcomes. Thus, a combination of both process and outcome measures is likely ideal. (Selection and application of measures are discussed later in this chapter.)

An important and relatively new dimension of quality measurement is the voice of the individual patient. Quality of care has become synonymous with patient-centered care. Although there is consensus that the purpose of quality assessment is improving patient care, a more recent development is the incorporation of patients' assessments of care into overall quality assessment. Today patients can and do reliably report on their experience of care through standardized surveys, which include questions about communication, relief of pain, understanding of illness and treatments, as well as care satisfaction.

In addition, patients can provide valuable information regarding end results or outcomes that are known only to them, such as symptoms from illness or treatments, ability to conduct usual activities, and mental well-being. This last dimension is particularly important for individuals with chronic illnesses for whom laboratory and other tests may provide little insight about whether the person is functioning and feeling better as a result of treatment.

DATA SOURCES

The major currency of health care is information and communication. Every encounter involves information collection—from insurance type to countless test results—yet the information is not easily shared by the multiple providers involved in a patient's care. PAC was advised to hand-carry his X rays to the surgeon, because it is often not feasible for relevant information to follow the individual, due to technological and other barriers. Indeed, most physicians effectively "fly blind," with little if any information about how their practices compare to their peers', and limited capacity to identify quickly all patients in their practice with a specific condition or treatment. Important clinical details are most often recorded on paper, whereas billing is almost universally electronic.

Major data sources for quality assessment include billing data, which are ubiquitous but have limited clinical detail (e.g., which knee PAC injured); medical charts, which are more detailed, but expensive and laborious to review; and patient surveys. Provisions in the American Recovery and Reinvestment Act that require broad adoption of electronic health records that can be shared among providers should make the task of data collection easier and enable more timely feedback to providers to accelerate improvements in care where needed (see Chapter 16).

Fundamentally, at the front lines of care delivery, the process of measurement itself remains very much a work in progress. The heterogeneity of the U.S. health care system means that most hospitals experience separate demands for information on quality from states, public payers, private-sector payers, accreditors, and others. Advances in measurement science have enhanced our capacity to assess dimensions of care and identify opportunities for improvement. For example, various tools, such as AHRQ's *State Snapshots*, allow care providers to compare their quality scores with other providers in their region or state and allow states to compare themselves on numerous quality measures with other states (AHRQ, 2010). Overall, coordination of priorities for quality measurement among multiple payers will be required.

Measurement of care is the first practical step toward improving care. But determining what to measure and how to measure are critical for gathering the right information necessary to improve processes of care and positively transform care delivery in health care organizations.

Practicing Quality Measurement in Health Care

As a group, human beings are fascinated with measuring things. This fascination starts at an early age. We give children in the first grade a ruler and tell them to go home and measure the length of the kitchen table, the height of their parents, or the size of their television. They do this with great enthusiasm and usually go beyond the basic instructions and start to measure things not on the teacher's list. As we grow older, we usually remain fascinated with measuring things, especially if they are important to us. Golfers, runners, bowlers, and cyclists, for example, frequently keep meticulous records on the events in which they have participated or in matching improvements they try against previous results. But (and this is a big BUT), when we ask people to measure things they are not interested in or which they feel will be used against them, they have an entirely different perspective on the measurement act.

This mixed attitude toward measurement is played out every day in health care organizations. Not too long ago, measurement of health care processes and outcomes was not a dominant focus within the industry. For example, if you went to see your family doctor back in the 1950s, 1960s, or even the early 1970s, you would most likely end your visit by saying something like this: "Thank you very much doctor. How much do I owe you?"

Today things have changed a great deal. It is not uncommon for a doctor to have a patient ask, "Where did you get your medical degree? How many times have you done this procedure? What is the infection rate associated with this procedure? Will this medicine help me to live longer? Have you had a malpractice claim filed against you recently?" Then, if patients are really actively involved in their own health care delivery, they will probably pull out a piece of paper and inform the doctor, "This is what I found on the Internet last night, and here is what I think is wrong with me."

One of the authors (Lloyd) went through this very scenario last year. He needed to have a total hip replacement. So what did he do? He selected several orthopedic surgical groups in the Chicago area, set up appointments, then proceeded to use the World Health Organization (WHO) surgical checklist to see how well each group actively followed the recommended steps in the checklist prior to surgery. He then asked the surgeons to show him the data they have for infection rates, revisions, length of stay in the hospital, deep vein thrombosis events for the procedure, and its total costs.

The group he finally picked answered the majority of the questions in a manner accept-able to him. But several of the surgeons gave him very strange looks and one even asked, "Why are you asking me all these questions?" Obviously, that surgeon was not selected to do his hip replacement. In many ways, the health care industry has been experiencing the classic Bob Dylan line, ". . . the times they are a-changin.'"

Although our perspectives on measurement and the availability of data in the health care sector have changed dramatically, we still have a long way to go to catch up with other industries. For example, if you are interested in buying a new car, within a few min-utes, you can find out on the Internet which cars have the longest time on the road, the fewest repairs, and the best results when engaged in a 40-mile-per-hour crash. In con-trast, if patients want to know which surgeon or hospital is the "best" to go to for a heart bypass operation, a laminectomy, or fertility treatment, or which one has the best record on infection control or patient-centered care, where do they turn?

The problem is that, unlike rating and ranking of cars, **performance measures** for doctors, hospitals, clinics, home care providers, long-term care facilities, or patient outcomes are much more complicated. First, the inputs to the health care system (i.e., the patients, their physiologi-cal characteristics, and their health problems) all vary. Unlike the wiring systems for a Saab 95, which are all identical, the wiring systems (i.e., the nervous systems) of patients differ.

Patients in the same category (e.g., 62-year-old white males who live in Chicago) are all quite different, unlike all cars of the same model, which are the same. Thus, measurement of the performance of a Saab 95 is a relatively straightforward and easy task. This also allows us to predict the reliability and future performance of the car (e.g., rate of repairs, longevity, and safety). On the other hand, measuring the performance, reliability, and characteristics of 62-year-old white males who live in Chicago and predicting their future performance is quite another matter.

The second factor that makes measuring and assessing health care performance challenging is the fact that there is considerable variation in the theories and processes that drive the delivery of care. Clinicians have different theories as to why certain medical conditions arise and different approaches to treating medical conditions. Hospitals and clinics have different processes and procedures for allowing patients into their systems. Once the patient is in the system, different departments and units have different steps that they follow in delivering care, day-to-day. In short, the health care industry has considerably more variation than auto manufacturers would tolerate, not only in the inputs it must deal with, but also in the processes that have been established to deliver service to its customers.

Given these challenges, is it really possible to measure the quality, performance, and reliability of health care? The simple answer is yes. But to be even moderately successful at such assessments, individuals and organizations need a roadmap to guide their quality measurement journey.

The Quality Measurement Journey

The **quality measurement journey (QMJ)** consists of two major segments: (1) planning your journey (i.e., determining the aim or purpose of your measurement efforts) and (2) the execution of your journey (i.e., the technical steps and milestones along the way). The remainder of this section provides details on measurement aims and methods, the two key aspects of the QMJ.

WHY ARE YOU MEASURING?

Many health care professionals approach measurement as if it were a singular event that is done the same way every time someone says, "We need some data." Rarely is there a dialogue prior to collecting data that focuses on a very simple question, "Why are you measuring?"

> *The three faces of performance measurement are: improvement, accountability, and research.*

Solberg, Mosser, and McDonald (1997) provide an extremely useful framework for thinking about why you are measuring. They highlight what they call the three faces of performance measurement: improvement, accountability, and research. In health care we regularly engage in and use all three approaches to performance measurement. The challenge is to be aware of the similarities and differences of the three approaches and then to be clear about which approach is most appropriate to help answer the questions you are addressing. The authors highlight this idea by concluding, "We are increasingly realizing not only how critical measurement is to the quality improvement we seek but also how counterproductive it can be to mix measurement for accountability or research with measurement for improvement" (Solberg et al., 1997, p. 135).

When we mix the aims and methods of the three aspects of performance measurement, we run the risk of not only sending mixed messages to those who work in the organization about the purpose of measurement, but also increase the probability that the conclusions we draw from the data may in fact be incorrect. Table 11.1 provides a summary of the overall aim and methods associated with each of the three approaches to measurement. Several points related to the aim of measurement, data collection practices, and determining whether the data demonstrate a significant change need to be highlighted.

Measurement Aims

The aim of each approach is fundamentally different. *Improvement* is pursued in order to enhance the performance of a process or produce more desirable outcomes. This is usually done by improving the efficiency or effectiveness of process performance or by eliminating defects. For example, reducing the wait time to see a doctor, improving the efficiency of the laboratory test turnaround time process, or reducing hospital-acquired infections are all aims of quality improvement (QI). QI aims usually consist of two parts. First, the aim must identify "how good" the improvement team wants to be (e.g., to increase patient satisfaction score by 25%). The second aim is to specify "by when" (e.g., by the end of the year). By establishing how good/by when aim statements, the QI team is laying out the context for improvement.

The measurement aim from the *accountability* perspective is based on a simple yes/no question, "Are you better now than when we last looked at you?" This type of question is asked by external groups (e.g., governmental bodies, accrediting organizations, health care purchasing and insurance groups, or business coalitions) as well as internal groups (e.g., governing boards of health care organizations and the senior management team). The aim is to make comparisons and pass judgment on the performance of the individuals or organizations being evaluated. For example, when a governmental body or a state rates and ranks hospitals in a particular state or region, the theory is that those at the bottom

TABLE 11.1

Aim and Methods Associated with Improvement, Accountability, and Research Measurement

Aspect	Improvement	Accountability	Research
Measurement aim	Improvement of care (efficiency and effectiveness research)	Comparison, choice, judgment, incentives	Build and test theories; develop new knowledge (efficacy research)
Measurement methods	Tests are observable to those making the improvements and to interested parties	No tests; focus is on evaluating current performance against past performance	Tests are blinded or controlled by using experimental and quasi-experimental designs; reduce confounding factors
Bias	Identify bias and stratify observations or accept a consistent bias over time	Adjust to bias by using severity or risk adjustment methods	Design to eliminate bias and/or control for it
Sample size	"Just enough" data; small sequential samples; monthly or more recent data	Obtain 100% of available, relevant data usually by years or quarters	"Just in case" data (get large databases "just in case" additional questions are asked later)
Flexibility of hypothesis	Hypotheses are flexible; they will be revised as learning takes place	No hypothesis (there is a simple question: Are you better now than the last time we looked at you?)	Fixed hypothesis (the null hypothesis is the basis for deciding whether differences are detected)
Testing strategy	Sequential testing	No tests	One large test or compare performance time 1 with time 2
Determining if the data demonstrate a significant change	Use statistical process control methods	No improvement focus; a percent change might be computed to see whether time 1 differs from time 2	Statistical tests of significance (t-test, F-test, chi-square) applied against the null hypothesis (p values)
Confidentiality of the data	Data used only by those involved with improvement; patient data are protected	Data are made available for public consumption and review	Research subjects' identities protected; institutional review board review frequently required

of the ranking will be motivated to get better. Incentives or bonuses are often offered as inducements to motivate better performance.

Research aims are different from both improvement and accountability aims. The primary aim of academic research is to test existing theories, develop new theories, and build knowledge. Unlike improvement measurement, research measurement is usually not focused on solving everyday problems or even applying the new knowledge gained to improve current conditions.

Understanding how the aims of these three approaches to measurement vary is a critical issue. They all have utility and are useful for the advancement of the health care industry. But they set up different assumptions and pathways for the measurement act to follow.

HOW ARE YOU MEASURING?

Measurement Methods

When you scan the entries under the measurement methods section in Table 11.1, you will start to understand why Solberg and his colleagues wrote how "... counterproductive it can be to mix measurement for accountability or research with measurement for improvement." Sample size and determining if the data demonstrate a significant change deserve special attention. The sample sizes collected for both accountability and research usually consist of large data sets (e.g., thousands of observations or patient records) that are collected over relatively long periods of time (e.g., quarters or years).

In some instances the data will not even be sample-based, but instead will be data collected on a population (e.g., all Medicare patients seen by a hospital during the year 2010). This approach to data collection can be referred to as "just in case" data. This means that to measure for accountability and research you may have to answer additional questions that you had not even thought about when the study was first conceived. So what do you do? You collect even more data than you initially thought you would need "just in case" someone asks you to do more analysis down the road. In academic circles, another motivating factor in building just-in-case data sets is to be better prepared to respond to editorial inquiries when you are trying to get your research published.

Improvement sample sizes, on the other hand, are relatively small and are collected as close to real time as possible (e.g., record the turnaround time for five laboratory tests during each day shift Monday through Friday). This type of data collection can be characterized as "just enough" data. The idea here is that: (1) you want to get data as close to real time as possible in order to understand variations in the process and (2) the people collecting the data (namely health care professionals who are delivering care to patients) are not full-time data collection specialists like you find in accountability and research settings. Their primary job is caring for patients, not collecting data.

Data collection plans must be practical, efficient, and not a burden. However, collecting data on a daily or even hourly basis in small doses can provide as rich a data base for statistical analysis as you will find when large data sets are obtained. Deming characterized these different approaches to measurement and data collection as reflecting enumerative and analytic studies (Deming, 1975).

Determining whether the data demonstrate a significant change is another method identified in Table 11.1 that serves as a major point of demarcation among the three faces of performance measurement. When data are analyzed for accountability purposes, descriptive statistics (i.e., the mean, median, and standard deviation) are frequently used to provide comparative parameters. Percent change calculations (e.g., this year's performance compared to last year's performance) are also a common part of accountability data analysis. Rank-order distributions are usually developed at some point so that the people, units, or organizations can be arrayed from the "best" to "worst" performers. The rank-order distribution may also be divided into quartiles or deciles to further stratify the performance.

Researchers approach data analysis with a little more complexity and with statistical methods that are more robust than merely computing percent-change statistics. Descriptive statistics provide a starting point for most research. Measures of central tendency (mean, median, and mode) and measures of dispersion (minimum, maximum, range, and standard deviation) allow researchers to evaluate the overall characteristics of the data they have collected and, if the data represent a sample, determine whether the sample is reasonably representative of the population from which it was drawn. Once the descriptive statistics are assessed, however, the researchers will usually move on to apply a wide variety of inductive statistical methods.

Classic works by statisticians such as Johnson and Jackson (1959) and Blalock (1960) have guided the application of descriptive and inductive statistical methods to social and biological issues for decades. The classic approach is to establish the null hypothesis (H_o), select a statistical test (e.g., t-test, chi square, F-ratios), establish a significance level that seems appropriate for the hypotheses being tested (e.g., .01 or .05 level of significance), run the analysis, and then decide whether you have sufficient statistical grounds to reject or fail to reject the null hypothesis.

(Note that the term "fail to reject" is the proper phrase to use when determining the outcome of a null hypothesis test. It is not synonymous with "accept" the null hypothesis, which many people incorrectly state. Henkel [1976] provides a very nice explanation of how and why these terms are used.)

In addition to statistical tests of significance, a variety of multivariate statistical methods enable researchers to make causal inferences (Blalock, 1971), test the relationships among many variables (Kerlinger & Pedhazur, 1973; Hu, 1973; Namboodiri, Carter, & Blalock, 1975) or find underlying concepts that are hiding in large amounts of data (Harman, 1976).

Finally, consider the primary statistical approach used in quality improvement to determine whether the data demonstrate a significant change—**statistical process control** (SPC) methods. SPC has a long and rich history that dates back to the early 1920s when Walter Shewhart outlined the basic concepts and procedures to the management team at Western Electric. To this day, his ideas and methods serve as the foundation for modern industrial quality control (Shewhart, 1931, 1939).

Shewhart was keenly interested in understanding the variation in a process over time. The run chart and the Shewhart chart (sometimes called a control chart) are the two SPC tools that enable the QI researcher to determine whether the process reflects what Shewhart classified as controlled (common cause) and uncontrolled (special cause) variation (Lloyd, 2004; Carey & Lloyd, 2001; Carey, 2003; Provost & Murray, 2007; Wheeler, 1995). Basically, *common cause variation* reflects regular, natural, or ordinary fluctuations in the data. It affects all the outcomes of a process and is referred to as stable or "in control" variation. In describing common cause variation, Shewhart said, "A phenomenon will be said to be controlled when, through the use of past experience, we can predict, at least within (statistical) limits, how the phenomenon may be expected to vary in the future" (Shewhart, 1931).

Special cause variation, by contrast, arises from irregular or unnatural causes that are not inherent in a process. Special cause variation affects some, but not necessarily all of a process's outcomes. When special causes are present, a process is considered "out of control" and unstable.

The key points to remember about variation are as follows: (1) variation exists in all that we do, (2) processes that exhibit common or chance causes of variation are predictable within statistical limits, (3) special causes of variation can be identified and eliminated, (4) only processes that exhibit common cause variation can be improved, and (5) attempting to improve processes that contain special causes will *increase* variation and waste resources.

Let's consider the example of patient falls to gain insights about common and special causes of variation. Suppose that you are the manager of the Patient Safety Department at Community General Hospital. Each month you report data on patient falls, which have averaged 26 per month for the past 2 years. Some months are higher than this average whereas other months, of course, are lower. Staff has become used to the fact that "on the average, we'll have about 26 falls a month." When the falls data are repeatedly presented at management meetings, the general opinion is that "this is the way things are here at Community General."

But at a recent Patient Safety Council meeting, someone points out that, over the past 4 months, there has been a constant increase in the number of falls. The Council chair claims this is an unacceptable trend and asks for an explanation. You are at a loss in terms of explaining the increase because you do not know whether the observed variation is just part of the random variation you have seen over the past 2 years, or if something is going on that signals a true statistical trend. So, what do you do? Do you bite your tongue and agree with the Council chair, because you do not want to question her authority? Do you contend that the data are flawed and that you really need several more months to see whether this is a verifiable upward trend?

What you *should* do is to create a run or control chart and determine whether the process is exhibiting common or special causes of variation. If it is truly an upward trend the statistical rules for special cause will verify it. Only after using SPC methods can you determine whether the process is performing differently than it has over the past 2 years.

In addition to the run and Shewhart charts, QI teams will also rely on planned experimentation (also known as design of experiments) to analyze multiple variables simultaneously, in order to determine direct and indirect effects of the variables on an outcome, as well as explore possible interactions among the variables (Moen, Nolan, & Provost, 1999).

In summary, health care professionals who think that all measurement is alike in terms of its aim and methods are making a critical error. The growing demand for health care data and results requires that health care workers at all levels in the organization (1) know their data better than anyone else and (2) are very clear about why and how they are measuring. Claiming you are engaged in QI, for example, while using methods more appropriate for accountability or research will not only waste time and effort, but will most likely lead to incorrect decisions.

Milestones in the Quality Measurement Journey

The remainder of this chapter assumes that the reader is interested in QI as the primary reason for measuring performance. The milestones in the QMJ are outlined in Lloyd (2004) and summarized in Figure 11.1. Figure 11.2 provides an example of how this journey is initiated and completed.

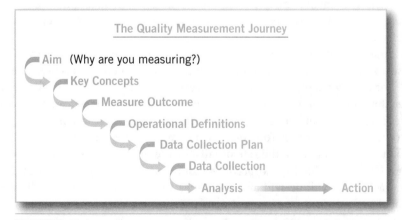

FIGURE 11.1

Milestones in the quality measurement journey.
Source: Lloyd, R. (2004). *Quality health care: A guide to developing and using indicators.*
Sudbury, Mass.: Jones & Bartlett Learning.

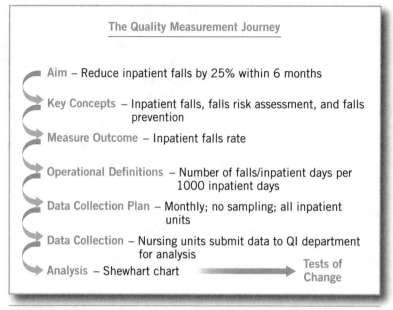

FIGURE 11.2

Example of the milestones in the quality measurement journey.
Source: Lloyd, R. (2004). *Quality health care: A guide to developing and using indicators.*
Sudbury, Mass.: Jones & Bartlett Learning.

> *Concepts are ideas in search of a measure.*

We have already discussed the first milestone, *establishing an aim*. Let's say that Hospital A has been plagued by a rash of patient falls in the past year. Its aim is to reduce inpatient falls by 25% within 6 months (Figure 11.2). The key concepts of interest to the improvement team include inpatient falls, falls risk assessment, and falls prevention. But these concepts are ideas or abstractions, they are not measures. Concepts are ideas in search of a measure.

An improvement team needs to build skills, therefore, in moving from concepts to measures (i.e., ways to quantify a concept in terms of a count, a score, a percentage, or rate). For each concept, the options for measuring need to be discussed. For example, consider the concept of a patient fall shown in Figure 11.2. How can this concept be measured? You could merely count the number of patients who fell during a defined period of time, say a month. You could also compute a percent of inpatients who fall, perhaps by age or diagnosis, the rate of falls, or the number of days that have gone by without a fall. Being able to *link specific measures with a concept* is a critical early step in your QMJ. More will be said about the measurement options in the discussion on operational definitions.

Once you have selected specific measures, you must *develop operational definitions* for each measure. Without a well developed operational definition, the measures will remain vague and data collection will be confusing, if not incorrect. An operational definition is a description, in quantifiable terms, of what to measure and the steps to follow to measure it consistently. A good operational definition, according to Lloyd (2004, p. 72):

- Gives communicable meaning to a concept
- Is clear and unambiguous
- Specifies the measurement method and equipment needed to capture the data, and
- Identifies criteria when necessary.

In Figure 11.2, the outcome measure is the inpatient fall rate. A good operational definition for this measure will specify two components: (1) what is (and is not) an inpatient fall and (2) what you mean by a rate? First, what constitutes an inpatient fall? On the surface, this appears to be a rather straightforward event to define. You find someone on the floor, you call it a fall. But all falls are not the same. There are falls without injuries, falls with injuries, partial falls, and assisted falls (Lloyd, 2004). You have to determine which type(s) to include in your definition.

Next you need to define what you mean by a rate. Note that a rate is not the same as a percentage. Although a rate and a percentage both have a numerator and a denominator, they are very different measures. A percentage, or proportion, is determining the number of observations in a defined sample or population that have a certain characteristic. For example, a percent of inpatient falls would be calculated by defining a numerator (the number of patients who fell once or more during their stay) and then defining the denominator (the total number of inpatients during a defined period of time). A percentage is a binomial metric based on a simple question: "While this patient was with us did he/she fall once or more?" It is a simple yes or no answer.

The denominator is all patients in the population of interest and the numerator is the number of patients from this population who fell once or more during their hospitalization. But note the qualifier when calculating a percentage of falls: *once or more*. A percentage does not capture the fact that a patient could fall more than once. If you use a percentage of falls as your measure, you are assuming that the patients who fall once are the same as patients who fall a half-dozen times during their stay. Most health care professionals would predict, however, that falling six times is a more serious outcome than falling once. This is where rates come into play.

A rate also consists of a numerator and a denominator, but they are two different sets of numbers. In this case, a falls rate is defined as the total number of inpatient falls (including multiple falls by the same patient) divided by the total number of inpatient days for the month. We now have falls over days which produces an inpatient falls rate (e.g., 3.2 falls per 1000 inpatient days). A percentage, by contrast, might provide a result that indicated that 13% of the patients fell (once or more) while they were in your hospital.

The clarity of your measures and the ability to draw valid conclusions from your data all start with being clear about the measure and then developing good operational definitions. A worksheet for developing clear operational definitions is provided in Figure 11.3.

Once you have identified measures and developed operational definitions you will be at the *data collection* milestone. This is a road marker that many people either overlook or find is a major pothole in the journey. There is an assumption that someone will collect the data, verify it, and then organize it so that it can be analyzed. Data do not magically pop out of a computer or into reports, however, unless there is a very clear plan defining the

Operational Definition Worksheet ©

Team name:

_____

Date: _____   Contact person: _____

WHAT <u>PROCESS</u> DID YOU SELECT?

WHAT <u>SPECIFIC MEASURE</u> DID YOU SELECT FOR THIS PROCESS?

OPERATIONAL DEFINITION
Define the specific components of this measure. Specify the numerator and denominator if it is a percent or a rate. If it is an average, identify the calculation for deriving the average. Include any special equipment needed to capture the data. If it is a score (such as a patient satisfaction score), describe how the score is derived. When a measure reflects concepts such as accuracy, complete, timely, or an error, describe the criteria to be used to determine "accuracy."

DATA COLLECTION PLAN
Who is responsible for actually collecting the data?
How often will the data be collected? (e.g., hourly, daily, weekly or monthly?)
What are the data sources (be specific)?
What is to be included or excluded (e.g., only inpatients are to be included in this measure or only stat lab request should be tracked).
How will these data be collected?
Manually _____ From a log _____ From an automated system _____
Are these data:
       Attributes data? _____   or   Variables data? _____

BASELINE MEASUREMENT
What is the actual baseline number? _____
What time period was used to collect the baseline? _____

TARGET(S) OR GOAL(S) FOR THIS MEASURE
Do you have target(s) or goal(s) for this measure?
Yes ___ No ___

Specify the **External** target(s) or Goal(s) (specify the number, rate or volume, etc., as well as the source of the target/goal.)

Specify the **Internal** targets(s) or Goals (specify the number, rate or volume, etc., as well as the source of the target/goal.)

FIGURE 11.3

Operational definition worksheet©.
Source: Lloyd, R. (2004). *Quality health care: A guide to developing and using indicators.* Sudbury, Mass.: Jones & Bartlett Learning.

tasks that need to be accomplished. Key questions (Carey & Lloyd, 2001, pp. 28–38) that you need to address before you hit this milestone include:

- How often and for how long will you collect data? Every day? Once a week? Will it be collected every shift or just during the day shift?
- Will you employ sampling? If so, what sampling design do you propose? Will you use probability or nonprobability sampling methods?
- Will you conduct a pilot study before collecting data on a large scale?
- How will you collect the data? Will it be a manual process or can you get the data from an automated system? If it is to be a manual process, who will actually be assigned to go out and gather the data?
- Will this data collection effort have any negative impacts on patients, staff, or the families of patients? Will you need to get approval from the institutional review board before you collect the data?
- How will the data be coded, edited, verified, and analyzed? Is staff in the various departments expected to gather, organize, analyze, and interpret their data, or will a centralized analytics group do all this for them?
- How will the data be used and who will have access to the raw data and the results?

After assembling the relevant data you reach the *analysis* milestone. As was mentioned previously, SPC methods provide the foundation for the analysis of QI data. The two primary statistical tools are the run chart and Shewhart charts. Both charts provide a graphic display of data over time. For health care professionals, though, this format should provide a natural referent. Telemetry read-outs of electroencephalograms and electrocardiograms are essential plots of data over time. When health care professionals are shown SPC charts, they usually find them easy to use and a logical way to look at variations in processes.

A run chart is shown in Figure 11.4. The data are plotted in chronological order. The unit of time (day, week, or month) is displayed on the horizontal or x axis, whereas the measure of interest is plotted on the vertical or y axis. The median of the data set is plotted as the center line, then run chart rules are used to determine whether the data reflect random or nonrandom patterns (Lloyd, 2004; Provost & Murray, 2007; Carey, 2003.).

Although there is only one way to make a run chart and you can place any type of data on it (e.g., counts, percentages, rates, scores, time), there are many different types of Shewhart, or control, chart. Figure 11.5 shows the basic elements of a Shewhart chart. Just like a run chart, the unit of time is displayed on the horizontal axis and the measure of interest is placed on the vertical axis. The data points are plotted and connected by a line, but unlike a run chart, the *mean* is plotted as the center line, rather than the median. When the mean replaces the median, we now can analyze the variation from data point to data point and compute what are known as the upper and lower control limits. Another set of statistical rules is then used to determine whether the data reflect common or special causes of variation.

If you have never been acquainted with run and Shewhart charts, this may seem a little confusing. You may find yourself asking, "Why do we use a median on one chart and the mean on another? What are these rules you keep talking about? How do the control limits fit into the picture? What is the difference between common and special causes of variation?"

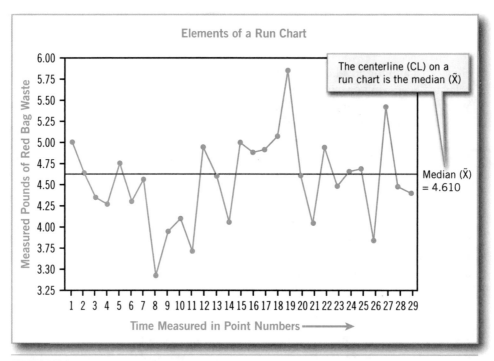

FIGURE 11.4
Elements of a run chart.
Source: Lloyd, R., and the Institute for Healthcare Improvement.

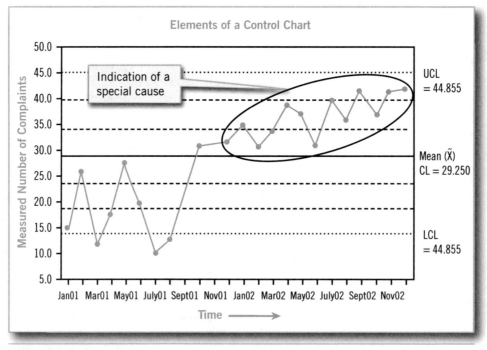

FIGURE 11.5
Elements of a Shewhart chart.
Source: Lloyd, R., and the Institute for Healthcare Improvement.

These are all very legitimate questions and ones that almost every person asks when first exposed to SPC methods. We do not have sufficient room in this chapter to go into detail on the SPC methods, the various formulas used to create the charts, and the decision rules. But the reader is encouraged to study the references offered at the end of this chapter for guidance in the development and use of these essential statistical tools.

> *Managers must demonstrate skill in turning data into information for decision making.*

The final milestone in the QMJ is actually the most important. It is the milestone where you stop and take a moment to link *the measurement milestones to an improvement strategy.* This is the point at which you need to demonstrate skill in turning data into information for decision making. Data without a context or plan for action give the QI team a false sense of accomplishment.

It is not until you identify ideas that you believe can improve the performance of a care process that the QMJ becomes complete. All too often, health care managers and leaders see data as the beginning *and* end of the journey. They rely too heavily on the technical aspects of measurement and not enough on its interpretative and learning aspects. Data merely allow us to set the direction of our improvement journey, not define its completion.

The sequence for improvement is shown in Figure 11.6. Note that although data are used throughout this sequence, the primary objective is to start with small tests of new ideas, build on the success and failures of these tests, and move to testing under different

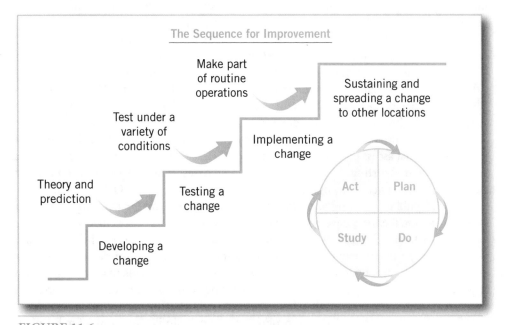

FIGURE 11.6

The sequence for improvement.
Source: Lloyd, R., and the Institute for Healthcare Improvement.

conditions to determine how robust and reliable the new ideas are. When sufficient testing has been accomplished, it is time to implement the new ideas and make them a permanent part of the daily work in the pilot or demonstration area(s). Once implementation has been successful, it is time to turn your attention to sustaining the gains that have been realized and then start to make plans to spread the improved practices to other locations.

Promising Initiatives

Numerous initiatives in policy, health information technology, and clinical strategies promise to improve the quality and safety of care. Public reporting of patient outcomes by hospitals and other care facilities and financial incentives for quality care (so-called "pay for performance") are policy initiatives already raising the quality bar.

Rapid growth in health care expenditures, coupled with accumulating evidence of suboptimal care quality, has prompted multiple initiatives to promote transparency about care quality through public reporting, initially on a voluntary basis by private-sector payers and in recent years by public payers as well. Starting in 2003, federal law has offered financial incentives for such reporting by hospitals, with an enthusiastic increase in the proportion of participating hospitals, which is now close to 100%. Proponents of a market-based system place a high premium on the importance of this information to consumers' selection of health insurance plans, hospitals, and other care sites.

Evidence to support the usefulness to consumers of making these data available has proved somewhat elusive, possibly due to a poor fit between available metrics and what consumers consider important. However, several studies have documented that public reporting motivates providers to improve, which is itself an important result. Numerous initiatives now provide information on quality of care for individual hospitals, nursing homes, end-stage renal disease facilities, and health plans.

Examples include Medicare's Hospital and Nursing Home Compare Web sites (http://www.hospitalcompare.hhs.gov/ and http://www.medicare.gov/nhcompare), the Leapfrog Group's hospital comparisons Web site (http://www.leapfroggroup.org/cp), the Dartmouth Atlas on regional variations developed by the Dartmouth Institute for Health Policy and Clinical Practice (http://www.dartmouthatlas.org), and AHRQ's State Snapshots (http://statesnapshots.ahrq.gov/snaps09/index.jsp).

Consumers also can find out what patients thought of a given care site by looking at valid surveys that assess patients' perspectives of their care, which are now part of hospital and health plan reporting. See AHRQ's Consumer Assessment of Health Care Providers and Systems surveys (www.cahps.ahrq.gov/content/cahpsOverview/OVER_Intro.asp).

Beyond public reporting and what some have termed *pay for reporting*, numerous local and regional efforts have attempted to link achievement of specified levels of care quality with financial incentives, known as **pay for performance**. In these programs, physicians or practices may be paid incentives for conducting recommended screening tests for a certain proportion of all patients or subgroups of patients (e.g., diabetics) who require specific screening tests. To date these have been the province of major employers, concerned that poor quality itself is further exacerbating health expenditure increases.

The ACA directs the Medicare program to launch similar programs for hospitals, referred to in the Act as **value-based purchasing**, and to explore similar approaches for other settings. These programs hope to counter the fundamental inflationary nature of fee-for-service reimbursement, which rewards the volume of services provided, by implementing initiatives that explicitly reward quality and value.

For example, in today's payment world, where fee-for-service remains the predominant mode of payment, dramatic improvements in chronic illness care, such as regular blood glucose screening and eye and foot checks for patients with diabetes, would result in substantial savings by reducing the need for frequent outpatient visits and avoidable hospitalizations. The negative effect on revenue for clinicians and hospitals, however, would be equally dramatic.

To date, the incentives offered in pay-for-performance programs are relatively modest. Nonetheless, there is broad consensus that a transition to a system that explicitly recognizes and rewards high-quality, safe care rather than the amount of care is highly desirable. The Center for Medicare and Medicaid Services already has taken the bold step of refusing to reimburse hospitals for the care of infections that could have been prevented with quality care. In fact, the ACA includes numerous provisions directing Medicare and Medicaid to support innovative demonstrations and pilot studies to accelerate movement in this direction.

Transparency and financial incentives command substantial attention and scrutiny in academic and policy circles. However, other levers also are important. Two promising developments are professional incentives that link efforts to improve quality with continuing medical education for health care professionals as well as maintenance of specialty board certification for physicians.

Broad adoption of electronic health records and other health information technology applications also promise to improve data collection and add value to those providing direct care. One project under development is the delivery of state-of-the-art research evidence on a particular disease directly to a doctor's handheld computer to aid clinical decisions—a far cry from the 25 years it took for evidence of beta blockers' value in reducing heart attacks to become everyday practice. Doctors can already access drug information and alerts this way.

Other clinical tools, such as checklists for physicians to reduce life-threatening infections in intensive care units and guides to improve teamwork among operating room staff, are already markedly improving care quality and safety.

Continued measurement of quality and safety, which directs the course of quality improvement, along with enhanced information technology and other tools, promises to robustly improve the quality of health care in the United States over the next decade. However, it will require a concerted and collaborative effort by all stakeholders.

Future Directions

So what does all this mean for students today? What will the health system, particularly the hospital component, look like in the next 5 to 10 years? And, how do these trends affect the quest for higher quality care?

Care will be patient focused. Health care providers will collaborate with increasingly more informed patients in decisions about their care, considering alternative treatments and outcomes important to the patient. Patients will look up publicly reported hospital and physician quality scores to decide where to seek care. Hospitals are also being designed via human factors engineering (evidence-based design) to be more "healing," with more space for family, plants, light, etc. and to reduce environmental contributors to errors.

Care may be better coordinated. This may be accomplished via use of a "medical home" for each patient, through Accountable Care Organizations or other new arrangements (see Chapters 8, 9, and 10) and electronic medical records that can be accessed by a patient's primary care doctor, specialists, and other health care providers (see Chapter 16). The hospital discharge process also will be redesigned with use of a discharge coordinator to ensure patients take the proper medications and have the right follow-up upon discharge, so they don't fall through the cracks and require readmission.

Health information technology will transform care. Clinicians can already receive drug alerts and clinical decision support on handheld computers. However, they will soon be able to incorporate clinical guidelines on a particular disease with patient-specific data to make clinical decisions for individual patients. In fact, the Recovery Act allows for bonuses for physicians and hospitals that meaningfully use electronic health records (see Chapter 16). It is also phasing in Medicare payment penalties by 2014 for hospitals and physicians *not* using electronic health records.

Health information technology will make telemedicine more available for underserved areas. Use of tele-psychiatry for Iraq War veterans suffering from posttraumatic stress disorder who live in rural areas already has shown some success. Tele-radiology has transformed the capacity of small hospitals to perform sophisticated imaging and receive rapid results from a radiologist who may be located across the country. Finally, a growing number of patients will be able to e-mail their clinicians for advice, will get alerts from their clinician about needed tests or test results, and will be able to be monitored electronically.

Prevention and chronic disease management will be a focus. More system alerts will enable physicians to remind patients to obtain recommended tests and patients to share their progress on weight management or other lifestyle modifications. With the aging population in particular, more focus will be on chronic disease management. In many cases, so-called complex patients with multiple conditions can be followed by a disease management team that may consist of a physician, nurse, dietitian, care coordinator, and other professionals. As more research is done on specific ethnic and other populations, care will be increasingly tailored to those groups.

Patient safety will become even more important. With the rise in drug-resistant, often deadly infections, such as methicillin-resistant *Staphyloccus aureus* (MRSA), infection control continues to be a problem in hospitals, ambulatory surgical units, kidney dialysis centers, and other facilities. Safeguards against these health care-associated infections, such as surgical checklists, team protocols, and other infection control procedures, will eventually become part of everyday life in hospitals and other facilities. The goal is to promote health care safety with a team that collaborates to report systemic safety problems rather than blaming individuals. Malpractice liability laws may change to reflect the "systems component" of medical errors, instead of attributing them solely to human error.

Quality care will be rewarded. New financial incentives put in place by the ACA will reward health care providers for care quality and safety. Rather than reward them for the volume of services used, as in fee-for-service system, the new law encourages coordinated care via bundled payments. Multiple providers are reimbursed a single sum of money for all services related to an episode of care—for example, surgery, hospitalization, and post-hospital care for coronary artery bypass graft surgery. The goal is to reward clinicians for providing care that keeps the patient healthier and prevents hospital readmissions. Public report cards for hospitals and other care providers will continue to provide incentives for quality care and to inform consumers.

Core Competencies for Health Administrators

Until very recently, assessing and improving quality of care has not necessarily been at the top of the priority list for administrators. Yet the bottom line for all health care facilities increasingly will include an explicit focus on care quality—quality that is transparent and verifiable, rather than reputed. Required expertise for health care administrators will be a solid grounding in quantitative assessments of both quality and the impact of interventions and programs to improve quality (Lloyd, 2010).

Addressing near-term challenges specified by the ACA—including preventing health care-associated infections, avoidable hospital readmissions, and avoidable patient harms—will require a new vision for understanding how individual health care facilities relate to others in the community or region.

For example, policies that promote decreased payments for higher-than-average readmission rates will motivate hospitals to work with community partners in very different ways to address the cause of the poor performance, be it due to limited primary care capacity, limited after-hours care, poor health literacy among patients in the community, or other causes. Similarly, the Act's provisions to promote health (i.e., addressing the upstream causes of disease and illness) will also blur the traditional hospital boundaries. The hospital administrator's job will no longer be confined to the hospital walls. In the future, part of the job will include working with community partners, perhaps via health education and disease prevention programs.

In short, a focus on improving quality and safety cannot be outsourced to the quality department; rather, it will become a strategic imperative for every department of organizations that succeed and thrive. At this time we are much better at measuring quality and safety than improving it.

Success in the years ahead will depend on the ability of administrators to implement and continuously enhance environments that promote excellence in response to individual patient needs and preferences, promote effective teamwork, and celebrate efforts to identify innovations that make the right thing the easy thing to do. In short, today's status quo will be unrecognizable in a few short years, as health care delivery responds to public and policy incentives for superb care, closely linked with broad efforts to promote health and reduce the need for high-intensity services. The public should expect no less.

DISCUSSION QUESTIONS

1. What challenges do we face in developing consistent and comprehensive process and outcome measures for doctors and health care institutions?
2. Explain the differences between proportions, percentages, and rates.
3. Describe the key issues that need to be resolved before you start to collect data.
4. Why is using statistical process control methods (SPC) the preferred approach to analyzing data for quality improvement? Name the two primary SPC tools and describe the key elements of each.
5. Describe the sequence for improvement (i.e., testing, implementing, and diffusing) and why it is so important to link any quality-related measurement effort to these improvement strategies.

CASE STUDY

You are the CEO of a 200-bed community hospital and have heard that Medicare hospital payments will continue to be trimmed for patients who experience harms considered to be largely preventable, such as blood clots, surgical infections, ventilator-associated pneumonias, and others. You want to make sure that your hospital prevents all possible avoidable harms to patients.

Your assistant summarizes the issues for you: denied payments focus exclusively on additional care required to treat the injury (e.g., when a second procedure is required to retrieve a surgical instrument). To date, the denied payments are for hospital care only, but some analysts have recommended that the same policy be applied to physician payments.

One measure your hospital already has taken is to require that all workers who interact with patients wash their hands, in order to prevent hospital-acquired infections. Although this would seem a simple and obvious initiative, it has met with limited success. In response to additional queries, you learn that the hospital's patient safety department does not track the kinds of events for which it may be financially penalized.

You also learn that the Affordable Care Act will affect hospital payment in another way: trimming reimbursements for potentially avoidable hospital readmissions. Your hospital serves an older population and many patients currently have multiple admissions for acute exacerbations of chronic illnesses, such as congestive heart failure and diabetes. In the future, these multiple admissions may be very costly.

Your hospital's margin last year was razor thin; the combination of the economic downturn and any decreased reimbursements could result in closure.

CASE STUDY QUESTIONS

1. Who on your senior team should lead this effort?
2. Who else should be involved?
3. What precisely are you charging the team to do?
4. Who will help communicate this effort to all front line staff?
5. What kinds of systems need to be created to track progress?
6. What external resources could be utilized?

REFERENCES

Blalock, H. (1960). *Social statistics*. New York: McGraw-Hill Book Company.

Blalock, H. (1971). *Causal models in the social sciences*. Chicago, IL: Aldine Publishing Company.

Carey, R. (2003). *Improving health care with control charts*. Milwaukee, WI: ASQ Quality Press.

Carey, R., & Lloyd, R. (2001). *Measuring quality improvement in health care: A guide to statistical process control applications*. Milwaukee, WI: ASQ Quality Press.

Deming, W. E. (1975). On probability as a basis for action. *The American Statistician, 29*, 146–152.

Donabedian, A. (1988). The quality of care. How can it be assessed? *Journal of the American Medical Association, 260*, 1743–1748.

Harman, H. (1976). *Modern factor analysis* (3rd ed.). Chicago, IL: The University of Chicago Press.

Henkel, R. (1976). *Test of significance. Sage series in quantitative applications in the social sciences.* Beverly Hills, CA: Sage Publications.

Hu, T. (1973). *Econometrics: An introductory analysis.* Baltimore, MD: University Park Press.

Johnson, P., & Jackson, R. (1959). *Modern statistical methods: Descriptive and inductive.* Chicago, IL: Rand McNally & Company.

Kerlinger, F., & Pedhazur, E. (1973). *Multiple regression in behavioral research.* New York: Holt, Rinehart and Winston, Inc.

Lee, T. H. (2007). Eulogy for a quality measure. *New England Journal of Medicine, 357*, 1175–1157.

Lloyd, R. (2004). *Quality health care: A guide to developing and using indicators.* Sudbury, MA: Jones and Bartlett Publishers, Inc.

Lloyd, R. (2010). Helping leaders to blink correctly: Part I and part II. *Health Care Executive*, May/June (Part I) and July/August (Part II). Available at: http://www.ache.org

Lohr, K. N., & Schroeder, S. A. (1990). A strategy for quality assurance in Medicare. *New England Journal of Medicine, 322*, 707–712.

McGlynn, E. A., Asch, S. M., Adams, J., Keesey, J., Hicks, J., DeCristofaro, A., et al. (2003). The quality of health care delivered to adults in the United States. *New England Journal of Medicine, 348*, 2635–2645.

Moen, R., Nolan, T., & Provost, L. (1999). *Quality improvement through planned experimentation* (2nd ed.). New York: McGraw-Hill.

Namboodiri, N., Carter, L., & Blalock, H. (1975). *Applied multivariate analysis and experimental designs.* New York: McGraw-Hill.

Provost, L., & Murray, S. (2007). *The data guide.* Austin, TX: Associates in Process Improvement and Corporate Transformation Concepts.

Shewhart, W. (1931). *Economic control of quality of manufactured product.* New York: D. Van Nostrand; reprinted by The American Society for Quality, Milwaukee, WI (1980).

Shewhart, W. (1939). *Statistical method from the viewpoint of quality.* Washington, D.C.: Graduate School, Department of Agriculture; reprinted by Dover, New York (1986).

Solberg, L., Mosser, G., & McDonald, S. (1997). The three faces of performance measurement: Improvement, accountability and research. *Journal on Quality Improvement, 23*, 135–147.

U.S., DHHS, Agency for Healthcare Research and Quality. (2009). *National healthcare quality report and national healthcare disparities report.* (AHRQ Publication No. 10-0004). Rockville, Md.: Author. Retrieved September 13, 2010, from http://www.ahrq.gov/qual/qrdr09.htm

U.S., Department of Health and Human Services (DHHS), Agency for Healthcare Research and Quality. (2010). *State snapshots.* Retrieved September 13, 2010, from http://statesnapshots.ahrq.gov/snaps09/index.jsp

Wheeler, D. (1995). *Advanced topics in statistical process control.* Knoxville, TN: SPC Press, Inc.

12

HEALTH CARE COSTS AND VALUE

Herbert P. White

KEY WORDS

gross domestic product (GDP)
rationing
per-member, per-month (PMPM)
center of excellence (COE)
value-based purchasing (VBP)

program of all-inclusive care for the elderly
(PACE)
formulary
cost shifting
moral hazard

LEARNING OBJECTIVES

- Understand reasons for the growth in health care costs over the past 50 years and expected growth into the future
- Explain the concept of value, as created by health care services
- Learn about the conflicts in the health care delivery system that hinder greater effectiveness
- Discuss some potential approaches to constraining growth in health care expenditures
- Analyze whether current federal health care reforms are likely to be successful

TOPICAL OUTLINE

- The value of medical spending
- What is cost, anyway?
- Third-party payers
- Employers
- Providers
- Suppliers
- Role of the individual

This chapter begins by describing the "problem" of cost escalation or, better yet, achieving cost effectiveness in the U.S. health care system. Inherent in that statement—and in most recent discussions about health care reform—is the assumption that there is a problem. If so, what do we know about the growth of health care costs over time?

From 1960 to 2008, annual national health care spending rose from $27 billion to $2.3 trillion. Over that period, the U.S. population rose from 186 million to 304 million, and the **gross domestic product (GDP)** rose from $527 billion to $14.4 trillion. Clearly, health care spending grew at a much faster rate during this period than did population. In fact, per capita spending on health care rose from $148 per person in 1960 to $7,681 per person in 2008 (1960 per capita spending would be $918 if adjusted to 2008 dollars).

Health spending also grew faster than the GDP. Throughout the period from 1960 to 2008, the annual percentage increase in the GDP was always less than the percentage increase in health care expenditures. In 1960, health care spending accounted for 5.1% of GDP and by 2008 it had risen to 16.2%, the highest level of health care spending of any country in the world (see Chapter 4). This means that although the GDP was increasing, creating a much bigger national economic pie, health care spending was an ever-larger slice of that pie. It also means that less of the pie is available for spending on all other goods and services.

Federal estimates are that U.S. health care spending will more than double between 2004 and 2014, and by 2015 will consume 20% of the GDP (Borger et al., 2006). The rate of cost increases varies substantially across different parts of the sector. For example, in 2008, health care costs increased 4.4% overall. That year's spending increases for hospital and physician services (4.5% and 5.0%, respectively) were not substantially different from the overall rate. Meanwhile, investment in research rose only 2.6%, but spending on home health care services rose 9.0% (Hartman et al., 2010).

Were current trends in U.S. health care spending to continue indefinitely, health care eventually would squeeze out all other spending. But that is clearly impossible. So, at what point do Americans draw the line—choosing to spend less on health care and more on other priorities, such as economic development, housing, education, and infrastructure? U.S. leaders indeed are beginning to look seriously for ways to curtail the growth in health care expenditures. The question now is whether we, as a society, can find more cost-effective and acceptable means to maintain the current level of health care services, provide greater access to these services, and improve their quality.

Health care spending differences across U.S. states and local regions are almost as great as those between the United States and other countries (see Chapter 1A, Figure 1A.4). Would it even be feasible for a national program to control health care spending in a way that takes into account these differences? The U.S. average per capita expenditure in 2004 (as this book went to press, CMS was analyzing 2009 data) was $5,263. However, in Arizona the average spent per capita was $4,103—78% of the national average—and in Washington., D.C., it was $8,295 which is 157% of the national average. What drives a state like California to have below-average health care spending of $4,638 per person and Vermont to have above-average spending of $6,069 (Kaiser Family Foundation, 2010b)? It is often said, and clearly true, that all health care is local. Any resolution to rising health care spending that also increases the efficiency and quality of care will need to be flexible, allowing each community to adopt models that can accommodate its unique dynamics.

So, let's start to answer the question, what do we know about the growth of health care costs over time? We know that they have grown substantially. We know that they have increased faster than either the population or the GDP. And we know that, if unchecked, health care spending will consume an ever-larger percentage of the nation's

GDP, squeezing out other spending. Because most economists and policy makers view this last possibility with concern, health care cost containment has been and continues to be an important national issue.

The Value of Medical Spending

The first question is, how do health care expenditures add value? Repairing a damaged knee so a person may easily walk and be unencumbered in his or her work has value. But is there a difference in the value when the person is 40 years old as opposed to 70? What if the surgery did not improve the ability to work but did improve the person's tennis game, is the value any different?

Health economists have used various methods to measure value created by health care. One common measure is called quality adjusted life years (QALY) (see also Chapter 13). There are two factors whose product results in the QALY: These factors are (a) a measure of the patient's quality of life on a scale where 0.0 is essentially death and 1.0 is perfect health, and (b) the number of years the treatment will extend the person's life (explained further in Chapter 13). The value of a given treatment would be the treatment's cost divided by the QALY, giving an annualized figure.

Even with value measures such as QALYs, controlling spending means either becoming vastly more efficient in providing health care services or placing limits on the health care services provided. If we were to place limits on the service provided, how should we allocate health care resources, and who should make such decisions? These are difficult questions and begin to broach the subject of **rationing** health care—that is, limiting the consumption of health care services to those situations that add the greatest value. Rationing or setting treatment priorities is a politically tricky subject and runs counter to the unfettered demand for services that has characterized the U.S. health care system to date.

A study performed in the United Kingdom of the public's opinion on rationing health care highlighted the difficulty in deciding to treat some and not others (King & Maynard, 1999). The first series of questions addressed the funding of health services. Survey respondents preferred unlimited funding, in order to avoid rationing. They also preferred "sin" taxes on items such as tobacco and alcohol as a means to provide the funding. When asked who should set treatment priorities, 75% of respondents indicated that physicians should, 24% indicated the general public, 22% indicated health service managers, 20% indicated nurses, and 12% indicated politicians (people could choose multiple answers). Respondents also desired objective and fair decision making based on improving quality of life and not inflexible criteria such as age.

However, in a review of 15 studies from eight countries, Daniel Strech and colleagues (2008) found physicians less willing to make rationing decisions. They observed:

> *With regard to the scarcity of health care resources, physicians acknowledge that they no longer can ignore the cost impact of their decisions, but they would prefer measures that increase efficiency rather then withhold beneficial care (i.e. ration). This is certainly not very surprising as these cost-containment strategies do not involve conflict with the physicians' traditional ethical commitment to the best interest of the individual patient.*

This creates a dilemma for health policy makers. The answer, at least in the short run, is to identify areas where the health care community can improve the cost effectiveness of health care services, thereby controlling costs while not limiting the level of health care services provided (see Chapter 13).

What Is Cost, Anyway?

The answer to this question depends on whose shoes you're standing in. When this question is posed to economists, cost is measured in large aggregate terms, reflecting all cash flowing through a city's, state's, or country's health care system. This is what has been discussed so far in this chapter. But as we delve into those very complex health systems the concept of cost and value varies dramatically. This chapter examines the perspectives on costs of five general categories of people:

1. *Third-party payers,* defined as any entity paying on behalf of a patient (the first party) or a provider or supplier (the second party). Third-party payers may be private (insurance companies) or public (state and federal health coverage programs, including Medicare and Medicaid).
2. *Employers,* who pay for some or all of the health care coverage for their employees as a fringe benefit.
3. *Providers* defined as any party or entity that provides health care services to patients.
4. *Suppliers* defined broadly as any entity that supplies a product either directly or indirectly to patients.
5. *Individuals* are not only patients currently seeking treatment, but also people who may become patients in the future.

As you will see, there are direct conflicts in the incentives of each of these groups. Although each believes that it contributes to the health of the greater community in a cost effective manner, each has a different **value proposition**. The revenue generated by one is often the cost to another, and the actions of one often directly impact the economics of another.

> *Patients pay little out-of-pocket for their own care and may have, at best, a dim understanding of its costs, have few incentives to question the likely benefit of services being offered, and cannot serve as an effective brake on over-spending.*

Hospitals and other *providers* seek to provide high quality, timely care needed to cure the patient's illness or remediate an injury. *Payers* attempt to manage the amount of services they pay for, as well as the prices they pay for those services, in order to improve their financial position and be able to price their premiums competitively. *Employers* try to provide an attractive *and* cost-competitive benefit package. All of these groups have, and continue to refine, quality measures to help improve the effectiveness of the health care provided. *Patients* want fast and convenient access to quality care. Patients pay little out-of-pocket for their own care and may have, at best, a dim understanding of its costs, have few incentives to question the likely benefit of services being offered, and cannot serve as an effective brake on over-spending.

Third-Party Payers

Payers identify a set of services for which they will cover a set population for a certain premium. Health maintenance organization (HMO) payers refer to their beneficiaries as "members" and non-HMO payers refer to their beneficiaries as "lives." Put most simply, payers track their performance based on a variety of actuarially derived ratios relative to size of their enrollment. Numerous ratios have been developed to address each aspect of a payer's revenues and expenses, for example:

- Overall medical cost **per-member** ("per life") **per-month (PMPM)**, which is the total medical cost to the payer divided by the number of "member months." Member months are the summation of the number of months members have been enrolled in a plan during the year.
- Cost PMPM divided by the premium revenue PMPM, called the medical loss ratio (MLR), is the percentage of the insurer's revenue consumed by medical costs. If an insurer's MLR is 80%, then 80% of the insurer's premium revenue is being used for medical costs, and the remaining 20% is available for administrative costs and the insurer's profit.
- "Units of service PMPM" are calculated for selected activities, such as physician visits or prescriptions filled—all on a PMPM basis.
- "Units of service per thousand members (lives)," commonly referred to as simply "*x* per thousand." These figures may be calculated for such services as inpatient hospital days, prescriptions, or hospital discharges—all expressed as "per thousand."

Payers actively manage their performance, but how deeply they invade the provision of care varies depending on their products and competition in the marketplace. Payers adjust their coverage and negotiate rates with providers so they may set actuarially sound and competitive premiums. Payers may take various approaches to containing the cost of the coverage that they provide.

A gap for payers is that decisions for patient care are made at the clinician-patient level. Although there are some very successful HMOs that have bridged that gap, such as Geisinger Health Plan, Fallon Community Health Plan, and Kaiser Permanente, and have saved substantial amounts as a result, most payers need to more effectively influence care management at the clinician-patient level. Measures payers have taken to contain the level and growth of health care spending are described in succeeding sections.

ESTABLISHING LIMITED NETWORKS

Insurance Models

HMOs, preferred provider networks (PPOs), and similar insurance models may seek to create a network of providers willing to perform their services at less than their "standard" fee. Under a limited network plan, members are assured of coverage only at selected providers and may face significant costs if they use providers outside the network. Although this approach has been successful in some locales, in many markets the covered members and their employers want access to virtually every provider in the market. Employers become involved because they don't want to limit their potential for recruiting new employees who may prefer one provider over another.

An example of this situation was the 2001 negotiations between Partners HealthCare System, the provider, and Tufts Health Plan, the insurer, in Boston (Strunk, Devers, & Hurley, 2001). Partners proposed a 29.7% increase to the payment rates it would receive from Tufts over 3 years. Tufts proposed a 9.9% increase over the same period. The negotiations went on for 3 months, and both sides announced they would terminate their agreement. However, the desire by employers, patients, and physicians to have access to Partners forced Tufts to return to the bargaining table and settle on a significant rate increase. This example shows that insurers like Tufts earn their income from the number of members or lives they insure and usually must provide a wide network to compete for them.

Centers of Excellence

Although limiting the overall size of the network is generally not promising, with respect to specific tertiary and quaternary services, payers have successfully limited the number of providers whose services they cover. To do so, they have created **centers of excellence (COEs)**, selecting participating providers based on quality indicators. Why does this work better than limiting the network for all services? Fewer patients will require these services, the cost of the services tends to be very high, and severely ill patients will more readily select providers based on quality than convenience. These three conditions engender greater cooperation from patients and a strong argument—quality—for selecting one provider over another.

The most common COEs provide organ transplant services. The federal Centers for Medicare and Medicaid Services (CMS) has established COE programs for all transplant services and certifies programs based on minimum volume levels, complication rates, and survival rates. Providers not certified by CMS may not be paid for providing services to Medicare and Medicaid recipients. Many commercial plans have COEs for transplant services that "shadow" the Medicare qualifications and have similar networks of providers. Others plans take a more aggressive stance, requiring even higher volume and quality thresholds and negotiating rates well below those charged patients not covered by a COE agreement. COEs have been designed for open heart surgery, major joint replacement, and major spine surgery, too, as an effective means to control costs by funneling expensive, clinically intensive procedures to providers who achieve better outcomes at lower cost.

The COE approach does raise a question regarding the ability for a new program to meet growing market demand. For example, if a hospital is located in a growing market that has a need for heart transplant services and all payers enforce COE programs, how would the hospital reach the required volume of transplants and related quality indicators to qualify for COE heart transplant programs? The hospital may be able to reach agreement for exceptions with a few payers; however, it will be required to provide the service without payment before it can break into the limited network of COE facilities.

Tiered Networks

In addition to COE programs, some payers are experimenting with tiered networks. Under a tiered program, members are encouraged, through lower deductibles and co-pays, to use a core group of providers. Members may use a second or even a third tier of providers if they are willing to pay the higher out-of-pocket costs of doing so. Tiers are often determined based on quality and cost factors.

There are situations where tiered networks are formed by health systems that want to encourage the use of their facilities by their own employees and key employers in their community. For tiered networks to be successful they need to provide reasonably acceptable access to providers in the first tier so the employees will feel confident that they will receive convenient and timely treatment. If two hospitals exist in the same community, one reasonably could be designated as tier one and the other as tier two. But if the second hospital is well outside the community, it would be very difficult to designate the more local hospital as a second- or third-tier provider.

QUALITY INCENTIVE PROGRAMS

Medicare has developed two quality-based programs called Hospital Quality Initiatives (HQI) and Hospital Acquired Conditions (HAC). HQI was initiated in 2003 with the goal of equipping patients with hospital quality measures so that they may make informed decisions about their care. The program also had a goal of transparency that would encourage hospitals to improve quality of care.

The program started with 10 measures in 2004 and will have 46 measures by 2011. Each is evidence-based and may include the timing of a key procedure, such as how rapidly a patient with an acute myocardial infarction (heart attack) receives a procedure to restore blood flow, or it may be as simple whether such a patient is counseled about quitting smoking before being discharged from the hospital. The incentive Medicare provides—possibly better described as its penalty—is a reduction to the annual rate increase for any hospital that fails to supply its HQI data. As of 2009, 99% of all U.S. hospitals have supplied their HQI data and, according to CMS officials, its Hospital Compare Web site has more than 1 million page views per month (Simmons, 2010).

The HAC program was initiated in 2005 and is designed to eliminate specific problems created within the hospital environment. The current list is:

- Foreign object retained after surgery
- Surgical site infection
- Air embolism
- Blood incompatibility
- Stages III and IV pressure ulcers
- Falls and trauma
- Manifestations of poor glycemic (blood sugar) control
- Catheter-associated urinary tract infection
- Catheter-associated vascular infection
- Deep vein thrombosis (blood clot) or pulmonary embolism (blood clot or other material that blocks the lung's main artery)

The problems on the list occur because of medical error or inadequate or improper care. To encourage hospitals to reduce the incidence of these secondary problems, Medicare will not pay for the additional care they require, above and beyond patients' primary diagnoses. Medicare is further moving down the path of providing hospitals with incentives for improved quality with **value-based purchasing (VBP)**. Under VBP, Medicare will redistribute inpatient diagnosis related group (DRG) payments to better performing hospitals and reduce inpatient DRG payments for the lowest performing hospitals.

Commercial payers are instituting quality initiatives similar to those of Medicare. These have had varying success depending on the market and provider. Hindering greater progress are factors such as: providers' mistrust of payers, the complexity of programs, and the difficulty of maintaining multiple quality programs with different measures for different payers. Some payers have taken to shadowing the Medicare quality programs, so that measures are consistent across them.

CONTRACTS AND RATE NEGOTIATIONS

Over the years both payers and providers have become very sophisticated in their negotiation of agreements and rates. Often they will create large databases and spend months analyzing claims data in preparation for a negotiation. Sophisticated payers will attempt to identify the provider's actual cost to provide care utilizing Medicare cost reports, claims data, and publicly available information. Payers will protect themselves by limiting rate increases for services with potentially high growth. For example, a payer may be willing to offer a larger rate increase for heart bypass surgery, knowing that those surgeries are likely to decline in volume, but it may be reluctant to increase reimbursement for outpatient percutaneous transluminal coronary angioplasty (PTCA), knowing this service is likely to grow rapidly. Providers, naturally, will want to take the exact opposite approach.

The opportunity exists within payer agreements to incorporate quality measures and continuous improvement programs, with the payer and provider sharing in savings. This can be an attractive option; however, the short-term nature of payer agreements leaves both the parties cautious. It is difficult to pursue changes that can dramatically impact revenues and expenses under an agreement that may have only a 3-year time horizon.

END-OF-LIFE AND DISEASE MANAGEMENT PROGRAMS

Health care costs typically are concentrated in a small group of insured individuals. Not surprisingly, the last year of a person's life (when they are sickest) is often that person's most expensive health care year. In a 2001 study by CMS—the payer most often covering a person's last year of life—beneficiaries who died represented only 5.6% of all beneficiaries, but consumed 28.8% of CMS resources (Calfo, Smith, & Zezza, undated). Many studies of different types have shown that much of this care is unwanted, unneeded, and of little patient benefit.

By focusing programs on serving this population better, through eliminating unwanted and unnecessary (futile) services, there is the potential to not only improve the quality of life for the dying, but also to leverage considerable savings in this high-cost category. If Medicare saved, say 10%, on this small group, it would save 2.88% in its overall spending—or, some $14.4 billion.

What are some of the programs that Medicare has created to improve options for people nearing the end of life? One is reimbursement for hospice providers that have developed specific lower cost palliative care programs in the final stage of a person's life. For patients to enter hospice programs, their physician must certify that they have 6 months or less to live and patients must agree to follow the hospice protocols.

CMS also has adopted the successful **Program of All-Inclusive Care for the Elderly (PACE)** that provides support services, such as home health, and other services to beneficiaries in their homes, in combination with adult day services, as an alternative to nursing home care. In a 1998 report prepared for CMS, participants in PACE programs were found to have a lower probability of hospital admissions, fewer hospital days, and improved quality of life over the long term (Chatterji, Burstein, Kidder, & White, 1998).

Disease management programs employ a similar approach, in which payers identify specific groups of patients or members with chronic diseases that similarly generate disproportionately high ongoing costs and whose complex care is difficult to manage. The core disease management conditions are diabetes, asthma, congestive heart failure, coronary artery disease, and chronic obstructive pulmonary disease.

> *A 2006 study of 120 of the 150 largest payers in the United States found that, on average, 20% of their covered members had at least one serious chronic condition, and this population consumed 55% of payers' medical costs.*

In its 2006 study of 120 of the 150 largest payers in the United States, the Boston Consulting Group found that, on average, 20% of their covered members had at least one of these chronic conditions, and this population consumed 55% of payers' medical costs (Matheson, Wilkins, & Psacharopoulos, 2006). Similar to the need for improvements in care at the end of life, a 10% savings in this relatively small group of members would yield a 5.5% savings in the overall payer cost—some $68 billion if achieved by U.S. private payers. Disease management programs vary, but the common thread is the identification of members with specific high-cost medical conditions, designing programs to help improve self-care (appropriate frequency of check-ups, clinical instructions that are easy to follow), and developing and refining effective clinical protocols.

PRESCRIPTION DRUGS

The cost of prescription drugs increased from $2.7 billion in 1960 to $234.1 billion in 2008. Although this is a substantial rise, it represented 9% of health care expenditures in 1960 compared to 10% in 2008, an increase only slightly more than that for overall health care expenditures. Prescription drugs have the promise of improving a patient's clinical condition and reducing the potential for requiring additional expensive health care services, such as surgery.

Nonetheless, better management of prescription drug costs is an opportunity to manage a large segment of overall health care expenditures. Payers may take several complementary approaches. Typically, they define the prescription drugs they will pay for on a **formulary** (essentially a listing of the drugs they will cover). Payers actively manage their formularies and may exclude high-cost drugs if equally effective, lower cost products are readily available. They also will encourage the use of lower cost generic drugs through education of clinicians and requiring lower deductibles for generics. A more aggressive approach, being used increasingly often, is the use of a precertification process for high-cost drugs. Through this process the payer confirms with prescribing physicians that the planned use of the drug is appropriate and discusses alternatives with them.

In addition, payers routinely analyze prescribing trends to identify covered members who may be abusing their benefit and physicians who write costly prescriptions that could be targeted for education efforts or incentives to reduce prescription costs.

Employers

Although one may expect employers—as the purchasers of health care benefits—to be actively engaged in quality and other activities to reduce costs, many are not. Most see health care costs simply paying a premium to insurers, not that the size of the premium depends on the quantity—and quality—of services ultimately delivered. Employers understand that insurers may be imposing some cost-saving and quality improvement approaches—and insurers may offer them cost-saving approaches such as HMO plans, limited networks, or wellness and disease management programs—but employers rarely have the infrastructure to effectively pursue and implement such initiatives themselves. Employers instead focus on identifying the lowest premium and richest benefit package that they believe is competitive in their employment market.

The Employer Health Benefits Annual Survey published by the Kaiser Family Foundation and the Health Research & Educational Trust (2010) shows that almost three-fourths of employers who offer health benefits offer their employees at least one wellness program. It may be a wellness newsletter, a healthy living Web site, or access to a fitness center. About 11% offer health risk assessments, a useful tool to improve health status by encouraging healthier employee behavior. A health risk assessment allows employees to identify personal health risks and decide whether to pursue wellness, disease management, and other programs.

A more prevalent approach, one that is easy to pursue and has immediate results, is to shift insurance costs to employees. The Kaiser/HRET study (2010c) said that in the 2010 survey

> *30% of employers responded they reduced the scope of health benefits or increased cost sharing, and 23% said that they increased the share of the premium a worker has to pay. Among large firms (200 or more workers), 38% reported reducing the scope of benefits or increasing cost sharing, up from 22% in 2009, while 36% reported increasing their workers' premium share, up from 22% in 2009.*

Corporate benefits directors commonly report that they have found savings in the firm's health care benefits, discovering only later that much of the savings was nothing more than shifting the burden to the employees—usually without a comprehensive plan to use the shift as an incentive to reduce the overall health care costs or improve quality.

What hinders employers from becoming advocates for better quality, lower cost health care? First, in order to pursue such an initiative the employer needs to make an upfront investment that may pay off over a number of years. For the same reason, insurers may under-invest in health promotion, because, given the turnover of employees and insurance plans, some other entity will be the one to reap the benefits, decades later. Second, such an investment requires the employer to be large enough to have the economies of scale to generate a substantial return. Finally, the employer must take the perspective that the upfront cost is not just additional overhead, but rather a worthwhile long-term investment whose benefit will be lower future health care premiums. Many employers cannot rationalize the potential future return and may choose to invest instead in sales and production where they may produce a larger, more immediate, and more certain return.

Providers

Providers are at the opposite side of the health care cost equation from payers. Whereas a payer sees individuals as members for whom they are responsible for a set of health care expenditures over a set period of time, a provider sees individuals as patients needing their services to treat a disease or injury and to prevent new problems over an indeterminate period of time. Clinical decisions that greatly affect costs are made in the provider community, yet many providers make decisions without full consideration of the effect on the overall costs of care. Providers see themselves as diagnosing, treating, and curing problems, not as fiscal watchdogs.

> *Providers are faced with a Byzantine array of often conflicting rules and requirements from their state's Department of Health, Medicare, Medicaid, other payers, and, in certain cases, local city governments.*

What's more, providers are faced with a Byzantine array of often conflicting rules and requirements from their state's Department of Health, Medicare, Medicaid, other payers, and, in certain cases, local city governments. Changing the behavior and practices of providers to improve their cost effectiveness and quality for an overall population requires alignment of incentives and flexibility of many different parties—payers, providers, regulators, and suppliers, among others—to implement change, standardize forms and procedures, and so on.

REVENUE AND REIMBURSEMENT

Let's begin with how providers are reimbursed. Although most of us are paid a specific wage or salary for the work we perform, and although retailers generally set fixed prices for their products, providers may receive dramatically different reimbursement from payers for the exact same service. Medicaid programs, for example, vary from state to state, resulting in dramatically different payment rates. Private insurers' plans vary, too. At the lower level, the reimbursement may not even cover the cost of care.

This lack of standards in reimbursement can provide conflicting incentives or jeopardize access to care. Many doctors either won't accept insurance at all or won't accept certain insurance companies—their patients must pay cash for their visits and get back what they can from the insurer. Recently, a group of Texas doctors has threatened to stop serving Medicaid patients, because they believe reimbursements are too low.

A study by the American Hospital Association (2009) showed that, on average, U.S. hospitals recover only 91% of their costs under Medicare and 89% of their costs under Medicaid. Physicians have an even more precarious situation. Similar to hospitals, physician Medicare rates are considered to be below cost and often form a base from which physicians will negotiate a multiplier for commercial plans, which means that a physician will accept Medicare but seek a commercial (private insurance) rate that is a multiple of Medicare.

For Medicaid, physicians suffer a greater reimbursement gap than hospitals do. And, across the United States, a 2008 study showed that the average Medicaid reimbursement was only about three-quarters of that provided by Medicare (Zuckerman, Williams, & Stockley, 2009). This is one area that the 2010 health reform law hopes to fix, most notably by increasing reimbursement rates for primary care and reducing interstate program variations (Kaiser Family Foundation, 2010a).

REDUCING EXPOSURE TO POORLY PAYING PAYERS

Providers use a number of tactics to compensate for disparities in reimbursement rates. They may choose to limit the volume of Medicare and Medicaid patients. The first and most obvious way to accomplish this is to locate in an area with where poorly paying insurers (and poor people) do not exist in any large numbers. Obviously this is not an option for a large hospital located in an area with a high concentration of Medicaid recipients, although some do eventually relocate to a more suburban location when time comes to replace the hospital.

Another means is to indirectly limit access. For example, it is not uncommon to find an inner city specialist operating at a hospital but not caring for patients who enter through the hospital's emergency department, where a large number of patients with stingy insurance seek care. A hospital may limit the size of its emergency room or eliminate certain services, such as obstetrics, to reduce the number of Medicaid patients. There is an old adage "no money, no mission." Providers with an overwhelming number of uninsured and inadequately insured patients may see such service cuts as a matter of survival. Others may simply see the cutbacks as a means to maximize gains, in order to fund other missions, such as education and research.

A more common strategy to offset the losses incurred by treating Medicare and Medicaid patients is **cost shifting**. With cost shifting, the provider shifts costs not covered by Medicare and Medicaid to other payers, by requiring higher reimbursement rates from them. This has been a long-standing and effective means of covering Medicare and Medicaid shortfalls. However, as the burden on other payers has grown, they have balked, and cost shifting has become less feasible. The declining ability to cost-shift has pressured providers to find new ways deliver care more cost effectively, limit services, or, in some extreme cases, to close their doors. The 160-year-old St. Vincent's Hospital in Manhattan is a well-publicized recent casualty of intractable financial problems.

BUDGETING AND MANAGING PROVIDER COSTS

To understand opportunities to contain costs and provide care more effectively requires an understanding of how providers establish their budgets and yearly financial plans. There are two aspects of this. The first is the development of individual clinical department budgets. The second is commonly referred to as "care management."

Clinical departments encompass areas in the hospital—such as radiology where X rays will be performed or the hospital's operating rooms or a particular unit of the hospital providing nursing care for cancer patients—where specific procedures or tests are done. Staff of these departments may be unaware of what is planned for the patient during the hospital stay or, for an outpatient, the course of treatment. They pay attention only to the specific test or procedure that they were requested to provide. These hospital areas may have state-of-the-art equipment and highly trained staff, but they are production areas of a hospital. Although "production" may have an industrial undertone, in truth, the clinical departments do need to provide a high-quality and cost-effective service. As in any production process, when developing their annual budgets and managing their day-to-day business, managers in these areas will consider the throughput, resources per unit produced, and the cost of those resources.

How do clinical area managers develop their annual budget? Providers will establish a measure of the expected volume of patients that will be served over the next year and multiply it by a cost factor, per unit of volume, often referred to as a cost driver. Let's take a nursing floor in a hospital as an example. Working with the hospital management and its physicians, the nurse manager will estimate the average number of patients the nursing unit is projected to care for each day and multiply that by calendar days to establish the total number of patient days. The nurse manager will then multiply the patient days by a cost driver, which in this case would be the number of nursing hours the unit should average per patient day. The product of this simple formula provides the total budgeted hours for the year. Multiplying this by nurses' average hourly wage rate will establish the nursing salary budget for the unit. As patient volume increases or decreases through the year, the nurse manager will adjust the nursing unit's staffing, so that the actual nursing hours stay close to the budgeted amount.

You may ask, how do nurse managers establish the number of hours per day for their budget? A number of factors are involved, including the acuity of the typical patients served by that specific nursing unit, benchmark comparisons to similar nursing units in peer institutions, the layout of the nursing unit, and sometimes state staffing regulations. Similar volume and cost driver measures are used in budgeting for all clinical areas in a hospital— from the emergency department to the laboratory to the operating rooms. This approach allows personnel to manage and be held accountable for the activity that takes place within their departments. If volume is above budget, the manager will know how many more hours to schedule for that day. Conversely, if the volume is below budget, then the manager knows how many hours to remove from the schedule. Large shifts in volume become the charge of the hospital's chief executive officer, who may need to make difficult decisions such as closing entire nursing units and curtailing programs to quickly and dramatically reduce costs.

This system works well from the department manager's perspective. How does it contribute to cost-effective care overall? Is something missing? It does enable department managers to provide a unit of service cost effectively. And it does allow the hospital to set performance measures that hold managers accountable for their department's financial performance. But it does not provide any assurance that the number of units of service—patient days, X rays, and other services consumed by the patient—are themselves cost-effective. This leads us to the second area of managing costs, care management.

CARE MANAGEMENT

The clinical departments in a hospital are individual areas of production, whereas care management looks at the costs incurred by a patient while being treated by all hospital services. This may involve the total days that the patient is in the hospital, the number of laboratory tests received, or complications the patient may have suffered. Care management analyzes the services consumed by each patient and the benchmarking of those services against industry standards. To conduct that analysis requires information systems that accumulate the relevant data and provide analytic tools, staff teams that understand how to analyze the data, benchmark comparisons, and clinical teams that may harness the information to effect changes in the clinical management of patients.

OUTSOURCING AND SHARED SERVICES

Many activities are carried out by health care organizations that might be less expensive if performed by outside contractors. Traditionally, the most common of these were food services, laundry, housekeeping, and facilities maintenance. Larger health systems will create a shared services unit to perform financial reporting, payroll, accounts payable, billing and collections, and information systems, as a means to secure more consistent and cost-effective processes. With the development of health information technology applications, more and more organizations are finding effective means to outsource large components of their services to third parties.

With the development of health information technology applications, more and more organizations are finding effective means to outsource large components of their services to third parties.

Today, even certain clinical services are being outsourced. Improvements in bandwidth now permit digital X rays to be transmitted to radiologists in other parts of the United States or in countries such as India. Remote radiologists will read the digital X ray and provide their reports electronically. Outsourcing is moving ever deeper into the clinical environment with centrally located intensive care physicians, often in large academic centers, using video conferencing to provide consultations and monitor intensive care unit patients for several hospitals.

SUPPLY CHAIN

Supplies, capital equipment, service agreements, and inventory costs are areas where hospitals and other providers can find substantial savings. These may come from several areas. Providers may seek to improve logistics, which is the transportation, storage, and final delivery of a product from the manufacturer to the point where it is actually used. Although not readily understood, reducing storage requirements or inventory provides cost savings and will often free up precious space for clinical needs. Just-in-time delivery of parts or products has become a hallmark of efficient enterprises from Toyota to Walmart.

Group purchasing by several facilities and narrowing the number of similar products used by clinicians allows facilities to negotiate lower prices from their vendors and thereby reduce the cost of their supplies. Supply chain savings require arrangements with group purchasing organizations, sophisticated supply chain information systems and engagement of physicians and other clinical staff who have a significant influence on specifications and use of supplies and capital equipment.

MANAGING THE PRODUCT AND REVENUE CYCLE

Focusing on high-volume, specialized services allows fixed costs to be shared among a greater number of patients, lowering the cost per patient. This is especially important in areas that require technological depth in the clinical staff, equipment, and information systems. Specializing in a specific service also provides a learning environment in which providers may explore new techniques and care management protocols that reduce costs and improve quality. Managers may also consider culling out low-volume services where they may not reach cost efficiencies and quality standards. Historically, the elimination of low-volume services has been politically difficult, especially for hospitals that are the sole providers in their community. However, as cost pressures mount, this is one area that managers will need to consider.

The process of collecting patient revenues is complex and prone to errors on the part of both provider and payer. Providers have invested substantial resources in information systems to collect and validate clinical and financial information, in order to accurately, efficiently, and quickly collect their revenues. The revenue cycle begins with the accurate capture of patients' demographic information and the services provided to them. This includes the appropriate coding of patient diagnosis and procedures performed. Coding is derived from clinicians' documentation and requires clinician engagement to be accurate. Leaving out one seeming small diagnostic descriptor can have a significant impact on the ultimate reimbursement the provider receives. Revenue cycle improvements can reduce the resources needed to collect revenues and, more importantly, can be a means to increase the revenues collected for services provided.

CLINICIAN ENGAGEMENT

Clinicians direct patient care and, therefore, the consumption of patient care resources. Most often, the direction clinicians set for patient care commits the resources of others, too—payers, hospitals, and other service providers. To improve the costs and care, institutional providers need to engage physicians in some portions of the decision process. Hospitals and other institutions must recognize and strive to harness the strength of their clinicians and their natural competitiveness. Clinicians compete vigorously to attend the best universities and colleges, achieve the highest grades, score the highest on their entrance exams, and achieve a high ranking in residency placements. Clinicians are swayed by facts and will make evidenced-based decisions.

Another approach is to share the savings achieved with the physicians, essentially giving them an incentive for working with the hospital to achieve cost savings. Although this would seem relatively simple, a hospital's ability to effect change using physician incentives can be limited by current regulations. The two regulations that have a direct impact are the Anti-Kickback Statute (Sec. 1128B. 42 U.S.C. 1320a–7b) and Stark Law ([42 U.S.C.S. §1395nn]). These were implemented to address very real concerns that a hospital might "pay" physicians to refer patients to its facility. There are provisions in these two laws that permit a sharing of savings from specific projects; however, the provisions are so narrow and the risk of penalty so great that few hospitals pursue this strategy.

Suppliers

Suppliers are those companies that provide medical supplies, devices, equipment, and pharmaceuticals to the health care industry. Most often these companies are selling products to providers in a very competitive environment. On one hand, they seek to find breakthrough technology that can provide a new technological leap that substantially improves outcomes of patient treatment. In return for developing this new technology or drug, the supplier will be able to maintain exclusive rights to market and sell it during the years that it has patent or copyright protection. On the other hand, when the product's patent or copyright expires, the supplier will likely have to drop the product's price in order to compete in an open market.

Suppliers may develop new technology that can have a significant benefit to improving the quality and costs of care. For example the digitization of X rays and other diagnostic images has allowed faster throughput, more flexibility for reading results, and has made the results accessible remotely on almost any Internet-based device.

At times, a new technology may promise improved patient outcomes but have a negative financial impact on the hospital. An example is robotic surgery. This development is popular in clinical research and even in the public media. However, the cost of robotic surgery can be significantly greater than that of traditional surgery. A surgical robot costs approximately $1.2 million and requires annual maintenance costing $100,000. A robot is bulky, often requiring substantial renovation of operating rooms so that surgical teams can safely incorporate it in their procedures.

In a 2004 study of the costs of alternative prostate surgery techniques, robotic surgery required less time in the operating room and a shorter length of hospital stay than did traditional open surgery; however, the robotic surgery's per-case costs were $7,126 higher (Lotan, Cadeddu, & Gettman, 2004). The cost differential was attributed to the purchase and maintenance of the robot and related equipment costs. In addition, physicians using robotic surgery will have a learning curve of approximately 12 months to master the technique. During this learning period, the physician is likely to treat fewer patients and collect less revenue. Despite this, hospitals have found themselves in a situation where physicians and patients are attracted to facilities offering robotic surgery.

New technology in its earliest stages is usually more expensive than traditional methods, but often becomes more cost effective as it evolves. Suppliers can play a role in adding value, by ensuring their products are correctly implemented and the desired results achieved through, for example:

- Educating providers regarding the new product's potential to improve quality and be cost effective
- Being the bridge between providers and payers to advocate for higher payments for technologies that promise savings due to lower utilization and complication rates
- Creating supply chain alternatives that lower the provider's inventory, logistics demands, and purchase price
- Assisting providers to implement new tools and treatments

Suppliers should engage with providers to ensure the appropriate utilization of their products and to identify needs for new products that the supplier might develop.

Role of the Individual

I have saved the best for last. The individual is you. What is our perception of cost and value? Most of us see cost as purely that which we have to pay out of our pocket. That would include the co-pay that may come out of our paycheck or possibly a premium that a student or self-employed individual might pay an insurer for some level of health care coverage. It would include the deductible we may have to pay when we receive a health care service covered by our health plan, and it would include those services we need that are not covered by our health plan.

For most individuals, we see only small fragments of the overall cost of our health care. Often the portion we see is not clear and often it may be misleading. For example, we may hear that a hospital will charge $1 for an aspirin. What is rarely understood is that the hospital charge is its list price, not unlike an automobile manufacturer's list price. However, the hospital may collect only a tiny fraction of that amount or may collect nothing at all.

Being so far removed from understanding and feeling the impact of our health care costs—the actual payments made to providers and suppliers—brings us to the **moral hazard** argument. That is, that individuals removed from the financial risk of a certain activity will change their behavior to take on more of that risk. Although usually applied to insurance, let's consider the case of two freshmen, one on an unlimited food plan and the other on a 19-meal per week plan. Which is more likely to consume more food and gain more weight?

The same concept applies to health care consumption. Those individuals with very good insurance, who have few limits and low co-payments, will tend to consume more health care services than those with poor insurance and high co-pays. For example, it is not uncommon to find patients with low co-pays visiting a high-cost emergency room for services that could be effectively provided in a physician's office. Because price is removed from the decision making process, patients will go to an emergency room where there is prompt treatment, even though it may cost several times as much as a physician office visit.

How can individuals make the health care system more inefficient? Take the simple situation of a physician office visit. A person calls and makes an appointment. The physician will pay for a reminder to be mailed a few days before or even have a service call the day before to remind the patient of their impending appointment. However, even with reminders, patients fail to appear ("no shows"). No shows plague the industry, but from the patients' perspective missing an appointment usually has no impact. In one large physician group practice, for every 100 patients scheduled for appointments, 40 did not show up or canceled. Because physician offices seek to be efficient, they typically schedule more patients than can possibly be seen to counter the effect of no shows. The disadvantage is that this practice can create significant back-ups on a day when more patients than expected appear for their appointments.

When it comes to quality, how do individuals measure quality? For primary and secondary care we usually value immediate access. Individuals are not likely to quibble about the quality of care when in need of an antibiotic to fight a simple infection. For this level of service, it may make no difference to us whether we are helped by a nurse practitioner in a pharmacy-based walk-in center or a full clinical team in an emergency room. When we end up in a hospital we look at our surroundings—is the hospital clean, do we have a private room, are the staff nice? For routine hospital care, we are as likely to be influenced by appearances and marketing as anything else.

Higher end tertiary and quaternary services to treat conditions that could result in death or significant disability sharpens our attention on quality. We are more likely to do the research, even if it is based solely on the advice of family and physicians we trust.

Lastly, what do we value in health care? Scientists have quantified the value of health care by measuring its impact on productive years, life expectancy, and other measures. Is that what we value, or is there more to it? Is a knee surgery necessary today so that I can continue to play tennis, or is knee surgery something that should be delayed until it becomes an impediment to performing my job? If we lived in a country with long wait times for knee surgery, would we be willing to travel to a foreign country and pay for the surgery ourselves, if our insurer didn't cover it?

Do individuals have the ability to influence the cost of care? As individuals, we are in a great position to help control the cost of care, if we truly desired to. First we could manage our health much more closely. We could stop unhealthy behavior like smoking, overeating, and too little exercise. We could better manage any chronic conditions we have like diabetes or high blood pressure. We could also insist on better support for managing our health from employers, payers, providers, and retailers, including the local food store or restaurant. And, we could ask questions: Is this test really needed? Is there a generic version of this drug? Are the X rays you're ordering going to change the treatment plan and, if not, can we skip them? What can I do to stay healthy?

Conclusion

For decades, U.S. health care spending has grown faster than the country's overall economy, consuming an ever increasing share of GDP each year. This may be partially explained by our view toward health care access. If left unchecked, health care spending will continue to consume an ever increasing portion of GDP. The United States has the highest health care expenditures per capita in the world, but within the U.S. borders spending on health care is remarkably uneven. There is as much variability in spending among states as there is among countries.

Although the growth of health care spending is recognized as a problem by most observers, different segments of the health care system view costs and value very differently. The cost reductions achieved by a payer may very likely be revenue reductions to a hospital, making such changes confrontational at best. Clinicians have some of the greatest control over the costs of health care, but most often act independently, disconnected from the value propositions of payers, other providers, and even patients. Suppliers have their own value proposition that tends to focus on new technology and innovative treatments as opposed to the overall cost of the care provided to the overall population.

Improvements in cost effectiveness are taking place even in the face of these conflicting perspectives on cost and value. But, in order to achieve even greater leaps in cost effectiveness and quality, a concordance among perspectives is needed. Incentives must be designed that can align the economic goals of the health care segments and distribute overall savings equitably among the affected segments. In the achievement of savings, there will be displacement—either a reduction in size or the complete elimination—of certain health care organizations. To effect these necessary changes, transitional plans must be available to allow these organizations (and their employees) to transition to more productive activities. Although this sounds simple on paper, the health care system is a complex and easily broken system made up of hundreds of thousands of entities, with 306 million constituents—that is, every one of us. Moving toward a better-aligned system for health care in the United States cannot be accomplished overnight. It will require incremental steps, learning and adjusting every step of the way.

DISCUSSION QUESTIONS

1. Is it ethical to limit access to patients covered by poorly paying insurers? As a hospital administrator, how would you approach a situation where you needed to limit losses created by treating patients with no insurance or poorly paying insurance who arrive in your emergency room?
2. Does every facility need to have a surgical robot? Does it benefit the supplier to limit the number of surgical robots sold, in order to maximize utilization per robot? Would the market benefit if the supply of surgical robots were restricted?
3. As an employer, how would you establish co-pays and deductibles to encourage more efficient use of health care services? What other actions could you envision that would encourage employees to improve their use of health care services?
4. Since health care tends to be local, as a policy maker what would you do to encourage the larger community—retailers, restaurants, employers, schools, religious institutions, payers, and providers—to improve the health of the community? For these initiatives should the government play a role or should they be sponsored by other entities?

CASE STUDY

Certificate of need (CON) legislation was designed to control costs by limiting the approval of new construction and new health care services based on demand for those services. By limiting supply, the CON would allow efficient development of the health care infrastructure. The first CON legislation was enacted in New York state in 1964. Other states enacted various forms of CON legislation and, in 1974, the Nixon administration supported federal legislation calling for all 50 states to enact CON laws. This mandate stood for 13 years until it was repealed in 1987. Today 36 states retain their CON laws.

Without CON legislation, the health care environment becomes a free market with open competition and decision making about expanding services that are not directly related to the demand for them. For example, Pennsylvania's CON legislation sunset in 1996. With the market freed from CON supply and demand controls, the state saw significant changes in health care services.

A case in point is open heart surgery—a highly profitable service, which often supports many of a hospital's money-losing services that are, nonetheless, part of its mission. With the lifting of CON controls, from 1996–1997 to 2007–2008, Pennsylvania experienced a 25% increase in the number of hospitals providing open heart surgery, even though the number of procedures across the state declined 37% during that period. The result was that the average annual volume per hospital declined 49%, from 653 to 300. At the same time, it is well documented that facilities performing a higher volume of complex surgeries have better patient outcomes and that it can be dangerous to have such services in facilities that do too few of them.

This change resulted not only in less efficient use of clinical facilities, cardiothoracic surgeons, and highly skilled surgical teams, but also resulted in a change in the landscape of health care. The Philadelphia five-county region experienced similar changes, which contributed to the closure of three urban teaching hospitals: Medical College of Pennsylvania, Graduate Hospital, and Episcopal Hospital.

CASE STUDY DISCUSSION

1. Why would so many open heart programs be launched, in the face of a declining market?
2. Were the new programs justified?
3. What would you do to rationalize the number of programs in an open and free market? If you were the governor of Pennsylvania, what issues would you consider in returning to a CON-based health care environment?

REFERENCES

American Hospital Association. (2009). Underpayment by Medicare and Medicaid. *Fact Sheet*. Retrieved September 13, 2010, from http://www.aha.org/aha/content/2009/pdf/09medicunderpayment.pdf

Borger, C., Smith, S., Truffer, C., Keehan, S., Sisko, A., Poisal, J., & Clemens, M. K. (2006). Health spending projections through 2015: Changes on the horizon. *Health Affairs, 25*, w61–w73.

Calfo, S., Smith, J., & Zezza, M. (Undated). Last year of life study. Centers for Medicare and Medicaid Services, Office of the Actuary. Retrieved September 13, 2010, from http://www.cms.gov/ActuarialStudies/downloads/Last_Year_of_Life.pdf

Chatterji, P., Burstein, N. R., Kidder, D., & White, A. (1998). *Evaluation of the program of All-Inclusive Care for the Elderly (PACE) demonstration: The Impact of PACE on participant outcomes.* Cambridge, MA: Abt Associates.

Hartman, M., Martin, A., Nuccio, O., Catlin, A., & the National Health Expenditure Accounts Team. (2010). Health spending growth at a historic low in 2008. *Health Affairs, 29*, 147–155.

The Kaiser Family Foundation. (2010a). Health reform issues: Key issues about state financing and Medicaid. *Focus on Health Reform.* Retrieved September 13, 2010, from http://www.kff.org/healthreform/upload/8005-02.pdf

The Kaiser Family Foundation. (2010b). *State health facts.* Health spending per capita. Retrieved June 1, 2010, from http://www.statehealthfacts.org

The Kaiser Family Foundation and Health Research & Educational Trust. (2010c). *Employer health benefits—2009 Annual Survey.* Retrieved September 13, 2010, from http://ehbs.kff.org/

King, D., & Maynard, A. (1999). Public opinion and rationing in the United Kingdom. *Health Policy, 50*, 39–53.

Lotan, Y., Cadeddu, J. A., & Gettman, M. T. (2004). The new economics of radical prostatectomy: Cost comparison of open, laparoscopic and robot assisted techniques. *Journal of Urology, 172*, 1431–1435.

Matheson, D., Wilkins, A., & Psacharopoulos, D. (2006). *Realizing the promise of disease management: Payer trends and opportunities in the United States.* Boston, MA: The Boston Consulting Group.

Simmons, J. (2010). Outpatient, readmission data added to hospital compare site. *Health-Leaders Media,* July 9, 2010.

Strech, D., Persad, G., Marckmann, G., & Danis, M. (2008). Are physicians willing to ration health care? Conflicting findings in a systematic review of survey research. *Health Policy, 90*, 113–124.

Strunk, B. C., Devers, K., & Hurley, R. E. (2001). Health plan-provider showdowns on the rise. *Issue Brief No. 40.* Washington, D.C.: Center for Studying Health System Change.

Zuckerman, S., Williams, A. F., & Stockley, K. E. (2009). Trends in Medicaid physician fees, 2003–2008. *Health Affairs, 28*, w510–w519.

13

COMPARATIVE EFFECTIVENESS

Amir Satvat and Jessica Leight

KEY WORDS

variations in care
comparative effectiveness research (CER)
CER system
national institute for health and clinical
   excellence—U.K. (NICE)

quality adjusted life years (QALY)
formulary
agency for healthcare research and
   quality—U.S. (AHRQ)

LEARNING OBJECTIVES

- Learn the purpose, function, and mechanisms of comparative effectiveness systems
- Understand how comparative effectiveness functions in other countries today
- Consider a blueprint for comparative effectiveness based on international experiences
- Understand the key issues in the debate about implementing comparative effectiveness in the U.S. health care system
- Construct an ideal "amalgam" system for comparative effectiveness

TOPICAL OUTLINE

- What comparative effectiveness is all about
- Comparative effectiveness program models
- Benefits of comparative effectiveness systems
- Public and private comparative effectiveness systems
- The U.S. debate on comparative effectiveness systems
- Comparative effectiveness systems: guidelines for design

What Comparative Effectiveness Is All About

Over recent decades, as health systems have grown in complexity and scope and as health technology has developed at a staggering rate, developed country health systems have faced two principal challenges: maintaining and standardizing quality and controlling costs. A well-functioning health system must first ensure that effective new interventions are identified and used for the patients who will receive the most benefit from them. At the same time, unwarranted or unproductive **variations in care** for patients with the same characteristics should be eliminated. As important, costs must be controlled by, among other measures, ensuring that the abundance of highly expensive and complex procedures and pharmaceuticals now available are used only when they provide measurable improvements in outcomes for patients.

Comparative effectiveness research (CER) has shown itself to be a key tool employed by health systems in achieving these goals—namely, identifying the best and most cost-effective interventions and standardizing their use. At its core, CER is simply the comparison of two or more health care interventions in which technologies, products, or procedures are evaluated against each other and against conventional standards of care. CER uses the highest standards of clinical evidence to examine how well a health care treatment or other type of intervention works under real-world conditions, weighing both quantitative and qualitative metrics, such as longevity improvement, quality of life years gained, and intervention costs. In the United States, this type of analysis is commonly performed in many academic settings, as well as by industry and quasi-governmental bodies.

However, CER has a much more important role in many other developed countries' health systems—those of the UK, France, Germany, and Australia, among others—in which it is used to generate guidelines for care and reimbursement that are binding on the many players within the health system. A supervisory body synthesizes the available information on different treatments and uses it to standardize recommendations for treatment and to approve payment. Although the primary goal is to improve health outcomes (and avoid exposing patients to the risks inherent in almost any treatment, even ineffective ones), the presumption is that eliminating unnecessary and ineffective services also will control costs. Using CER findings is the principal mechanism by which otherwise highly controversial decisions pitting access to therapies against their costs can be resolved based on scientific, not political, criteria.

A **CER system** is a mechanism for synthesizing research about different medical interventions and translating it into guidelines for or restrictions on the use of different types of therapies, in an attempt to maximize good outcomes for patients. As medical service providers are under increasing pressure to be accountable for the quality of care they provide, the use of best-evidence standards will become increasingly important.

This chapter begins by outlining various models for a CER system and the type of guidelines or restrictions that can be employed in order to standardize high-quality care and control costs. The subsequent section provides a number of case studies of countries using various types of CER systems and how they operate. The final sections provide an overview of the CER debate in the United States and guidelines for designing a CER system.

Comparative Effectiveness Program Models

Information about the relative efficacy of different therapies is, of itself, not sufficient to shape the operations of a health system. In order to ensure that the most effective therapies are employed, health systems use various mechanisms to disseminate CER findings and use them to develop binding policies that affect providers, patients, and insurers. This section provides an overview of those tools and their operations.

MODELS WITHIN THE HEALTH CARE SECTOR

Restrictions on the Introduction and Dissemination of Technology
Over the past four decades, health care technology's implementation and purchasing costs have grown at an astonishing pace. The U.S. Congressional Budget Office estimates that real health care expenditures per person increased sixfold between 1965 and 2005. Half of

that increase was attributable to technological improvements (U.S. Congress, 2008). At the same time, a dramatic gap in technology utilization has opened between the United States and other industrialized countries.

Health policy experts generally agree that the much higher utilization of technology in the United States is driven by both an upstream over-proliferation of medical equipment and devices purchased and placed within hospitals and medical practices, a downstream overuse of equipment after it is bought, and a fee-for-service system that creates incentives for overuse.

These purchases have contributed to a "medical arms race," as providers cater to patient needs (and demands) by obtaining the latest, fastest, and, almost always, costliest versions of new technology in their care centers. In key cost areas such as open heart surgery, cardiac catheterization, radiation therapy, and magnetic resonance imaging, an oversupply of equipment results in considerable idle time.

This phenomenon stands in contrast to the experience of countries like Canada, where high-tech equipment is more scarce and experiences a higher workload. Medical specialists utilizing this equipment also are used more productively there. As a result, the United States had in 2004 19.5 magnetic resonance imaging (MRI) units per million population, compared with 4.6 units per million in Canada, and 29.5 computerized tomography (CT) scanners per million population, compared to 10.3 in Canada (Canadian Institute for Health Information, 2005).

These trends are driven not only by lower equipment availability in other countries, but also by variations in the culture of medical practice. In other countries, physicians may be more concerned about overusing equipment or unnecessarily relying on equipment for patient treatment. Preventing overuse of existing equipment is a separate downstream problem for reimbursement policy, but the correct start in appropriately allocating government support for capital expenditures would be to evaluate existing equipment capacity in a geographic area.

Coordinated planning of hospital capital expenditures and major equipment purchases is a key element in a CER system that prioritizes the most effective interventions, rather than merely the most technologically intensive ones. Limitations on the availability of expensive technology also have the potential to eliminate the pressure on physicians and hospitals to overuse high-tech equipment in order to recoup its cost, a phenomenon that can result in needlessly invasive procedures that carry higher risks for patients.

In the United States, state certificate-of-need (CON) laws require health care facilities to receive approval from a state health planning agency before launching major capital projects, including opening a new facility, expanding an existing one, or purchasing costly equipment. Thirty-six states currently have such laws. However, there is no consensus on whether these laws have been effective in controlling costs. Opponents argue that CON laws may actually increase costs by minimizing competition and allowing existing facilities to raise their prices (National Conference of State Legislators, 2010).

Restrictions on Choice of Treatment and Procedures

The most visible effort to restrict physician treatment choices is the United Kingdom's **National Institute for Health and Clinical Excellence (NICE)**. In the UK, the central government sets a budget for National Health Service (NHS) expenditures every year, based on estimated health care needs of the population. The government must then decide how to allocate these funds.

The first step under this system is for the government to estimate the effectiveness of health treatments using a **quality adjusted life years (QALY)** method. For example, consider a treatment for cancer that costs £40,000 and allows a patient to live an extra 3 months, with those months adjusted according to the quality of life the patient can expect during this period. Such a treatment would cost £160,000 per quality adjusted life year (£40,000 × 4).

The NHS sets guidelines on cost per QALY for every health medical treatment and procedure. Currently, the guideline for the maximum acceptable cost is between £20,000 and £30,000 ($30,000 and $45,000) per QALY (Towse, 2009). If NICE rules that a therapy is too expensive relative to its benefits, the NHS will not pay for it.

> *A common misconception is that, in the UK, patients who are sick or need emergency care are denied services or left to die.*

A common misconception is that, in the UK, patients who are sick or need emergency care are denied services or left to die. NICE allows exemptions for life-threatening situations, as long as supervising physicians agree that there is the potential for an improvement in patient outcomes. In addition, if they can afford it, patients can pay out-of-pocket for expensive therapies that are not paid for by the government under NICE guidelines.

Restrictions on Sites of Care

Provision of services, particularly those with high technological intensity, may be confined to inpatient settings. As a result, patient waiting times for such services can be lengthy if facilities are overstretched. Waiting times could be reduced substantially by encouraging wealthier patients to use private, fee-based services, which would lessen care delays for patients who must rely on government services (Employee Benefit Research Institute [EBRI], 1993).

Restrictions on Choices of Provider

Provider restrictions can be enforced through varied mechanisms, usually centered on fee schedules or a gatekeeper structure, in which primary physicians must provide patients with a referral before they can see other specialists. In the UK, patients enroll with a general practitioner gatekeeper, similar to American health maintenance organization (HMO) plans, in which a physician serves as a first point of contact and determines specialist referrals. Or, provider choice may be restricted to more "thrifty" care givers by providing only partial reimbursement for treatments from doctors other than salaried hospital physicians unless patients have a referral from a general practitioner (EBRI, 1993).

MODELS OUTSIDE HEALTH CARE

Examples of CER models in other sectors of the economy are scant, largely because there are few other sectors where core operations have the same degree of scientific complexity and the enormous range of costs, inputs, and outcomes as those that characterize medical care. In the case of energy, there is an academic literature examining the relative cost effectiveness of different forms of energy generation (Rogner, Sharma, & Jalal, 2008), but there is no policy system by which various countries implement and enforce these findings that is analogous to how CER is used in health care. In addition, the energy literature seeks to answer a much simpler question: namely, the nature of the most cost-effective method for generating energy.

At the international level, the International Atomic Energy Agency (IAEA) also provides some programming to assist member states in assessing different strategies for sustainable energy development and their impact on economic, energy, and environmental goals (IAEA, 2001). Such assessment is voluntary, however, and, in the United States, the relative safety of nuclear energy remains a controversial question not convincingly addressed by any systematic government-initiated system of research and evaluation such as CER provides. In fact, following the most recent major energy initiative of the George W. Bush administration, there were widespread accusations that policy was driven by special interests and not by any considerations of efficiency, economic benefit, or safety (Grunwald & Eilperin, 2005), suggesting that a true system of comparative effectiveness evaluation in energy is still a distant goal.

Benefits of Comparative Effectiveness Systems

QUALITY IMPROVEMENT

The Institute of Medicine in its 2009 report, *Initial National Priorities for Comparative Effectiveness Research*, states that "comparative effectiveness research provides an opportunity to improve the quality and outcomes of health care by providing more and better information to support decisions by the public, patients, caregivers, clinicians, purchasers and policy makers" (p. 29). This clearly places quality improvement as a central objective of a CER system.

A number of major examples illustrate how CER served to establish the relative benefits of different approaches to different clinical situations:

- CER established that surgery to reduce lung capacity was more effective than drug treatment for patients with certain types of emphysema, but not for others. As a result, doctors can identify patients who would not benefit from surgery, treat them with drug therapy, and avoid the enormous risks to the patient associated with an unnecessary invasive procedure.
- CER found that neither angioplasty nor stents performs better than drug therapy and lifestyle change in treating patients with stable coronary artery disease. This again enables doctors and their patients to obtain the most effective therapy while minimizing unnecessary and painful procedures (Bernstein, 2009).
- CER established that patients who receive antibiotics in the 2 hours prior to surgery have half the risk of developing infection compared to patients who received antibiotics after surgery. This again enables hospitals and physicians to uniformly offer the therapy known to achieve the best patient outcome (Bernstein, 2009).
- CER of treatments for hemophilia identified the treatment that works best, providing health systems with the information needed to prescribe the correct treatment uniformly (Next Generation Pharmaceutical, 2010).

Clearly, however, information is only part of the solution. In order for CER to have an impact on patient outcomes, it must be widely disseminated to health care practitioners, and practitioners and health facilities must incorporate recommended best practices into their treatment standards and daily practice. In Europe, Canada, and Australia, this process is controlled by government bodies that use CER to generate guidelines binding on health care practitioners. In the United States, by contrast, decisions about how to respond to CER findings are in the hands of private bodies. Both of these systems are described in more detail subsequently.

COST SAVINGS

The second important benefit of CER systems is their impact on health care costs. More specifically, using CER enables health systems to control costs without compromising patient outcomes. Of course, implementing a CER system is costly in and of itself. Within a federal system, these costs usually vary from $100 million to $300 million per fiscal year (U.S. Congress, 2007). Accordingly, quantifying the potential savings in a CER system is of central importance.

The preeminent research on unwarranted treatment variations and potential savings in health care comes from Dr. John Wennberg and colleagues, authors of the *Dartmouth Atlas*, which compares data on the utilization of services, patient outcomes, and health care costs for the 50 states and more than 300 smaller regions. Wennberg's classic research compared treatment variations and costs between physicians and hospitals in New Haven versus Boston. He found that per capita expenditures in Boston were more than double those in New Haven (Wennberg, 1984), despite similar population demographics and sites of care (largely university hospitals).

Hospital expenditures in Boston were $300 million higher in FY1982 than they would have been if Boston had the same usage rates as New Haven. This excess expenditure was largely due to more frequent hospital admissions for conditions where hospitalization is not automatic. (Discharge rates were similar for conditions where there is a strong agreement about the need for hospitalization.) Despite the greater likelihood of hospitalization in Boston, mortality rates in the two cities were virtually identical, suggesting that New Haven's lower hospital utilization had no adverse impact on mortality (Wennberg, Freeman, Shelton, & Bubolz, 1989).

Similar studies have been replicated many times across other regions and treatment categories, consistently illustrating wide variations in medical practices and expenditures. These illustrations of practice variations, many showing unjustified cost differences of 100% or more from one geographic region to another, suggest the clear and immense potential benefits of a well-implemented CER system.

In the previous example involving Boston and New Haven, if research about the comparative benefits of hospitalization for certain conditions had been compiled and applied in both cities, it could have dramatically lowered hospitalizations in Boston without negatively affecting patient outcomes. The results would have been substantial savings for the health system.

Public and Private Comparative Effectiveness Systems

The next step in this analysis is to evaluate models for the implementation of CER findings at a system-wide level. Public systems in the UK (NICE), France (Haute Autorité de Santé [HAS]),

Germany (Institut für Qualität und Wirtschaftlichkeit im Gesundheitswesen [IQWiG]), and Australia (Pharmaceutical Benefits Advisory Committee [PBAC]) will be considered, followed by an analysis of private systems, represented by academic medical centers, employers/health plans and third-party data aggregators. The goal is to evaluate how such systems are structured and to what extent they have delivered on their stated goals and, perhaps more important, on goals of interest to other health systems.

PUBLIC COMPARATIVE EFFECTIVENESS SYSTEMS

United Kingdom

NICE is the UK's entity for CER, housed within NHS, the government's health plan. NICE's primary goals are to improve health outcomes, reduce practice variation, and diffuse information about new technologies and their effectiveness. In fact, "the government's explicit objective was for NICE to target additional funding toward good value innovation rather than to cut costs" (Chalkidou, 2009).

NICE suggests clinical guidelines for treatment; conducts performance assessments for drugs, devices, and diagnostic tests; and provides guidance on surgical and invasive diagnostic procedures. Information is distributed electronically to clinicians and hospital leaders and to industry, professional, and patient groups. Alerts and an annual conference are also provided, and consultant networks are available to those with questions about guidelines. This extensive system of information dissemination is intended to live up to NICE's goals of openness and transparency (Chalkidou, 2009).

NICE's structure for evaluating research gives preference to high-quality primary research, rather than emphasizing the quantity of research on a particular question. Studies are primarily single technology appraisals (STAs), which evaluate a new product or method in comparison to a placebo, without a review of efficacy relative to other established treatments in a combined trial.

NICE is a consumer, and not a producer, of CER information and evidence. Although the organization does offer guidance on topics for research and standard-setting, it does not self-fund or perform evaluations. NICE selects areas in which it develops suggested standards and makes recommendations on treatments, but final decision making lies with NHS's secretary of State for Health, who can overrule NICE recommendations, topic selection, or coverage decisions. Following the secretary's final approval, NICE standards are the basis for NHS reimbursement; services that are not approved can be obtained privately, but NHS will not pay for them.

National responses to NICE guidelines have been speedy and widespread, with hospitals showing 85% to 95% adherence. Unwarranted variation in treatments has decreased meaningfully. Also, NICE has greatly increased public awareness of the importance and existence of effectiveness-based standards for health care. NICE had an approximately $70 million annual budget in 2009, expected to rise to more than $180 million in the next few years. In addition, implementing NICE guidelines costs some £1.5 billion per year (Chalkidou, 2009).

France

The comparative effectiveness program in France is based in the HAS, an independent, public organization with financial autonomy and a government-appointed board. Although operating in concert with government agencies and the French National Health System, the organization functions as a third party. HAS's primary goals are to provide integrated evaluation data across disciplines using robust methodologies, to create widespread diffusion of information, and to include all medical stakeholders in its decision processes (Rochaix & Xerri, 2009).

HAS supervises the review and approval of drugs, devices, and procedures on behalf of the Ministry for Health and Social Security. Unlike NICE, HAS directly conducts its own research, making both STAs and multiple technology appraisals (MTAs). The breadth and importance of these studies is greater in France than in England, given that they must be completed before a drug, device, or procedure can be added to the list of approved benefits or receive funding. Also, MTAs are much more comprehensive than STAs, because the former compare new treatments to existing therapies, as well as to a placebo, offering an in-depth assessment of the health value of treatments beyond their initial intended purpose. MTAs have a greater impact on public health standards than do STAs and are focused on realistic coverage and delivery in target populations.

HAS's full-time staff numbers 400, plus it has available 734 surveyors and 3,000 external consultants to help conduct its studies. Opinions and recommendations are forwarded to the Ministry for Health and Social Security, which decides whether to reimburse products and the extent to which its policy decisions are circulated (Rochaix & Xerri, 2009).

National responses to HAS guidelines have been strong: 95% of HAS's positive recommendations regarding reimbursement have been followed by the Ministry. Also, close to 90% of HAS's recommendations to stop reimbursing medications deemed to have insufficient benefit have been accepted. In calculating total program costs, HAS received €66 million in funding for 2008. These funds do not come directly from the government, but rather are collected from a tax on pharmaceutical company advertising and from France's health insurance fund (Rochaix & Xerri, 2009). A robust calculation of adoption costs has not been completed for HAS.

Germany

The CER system in Germany is centered around the IQWiG, created by the government in 2004 to act as an advisory body that would provide evidence-based evaluations of the costs and benefits of pharmaceuticals and medical services, using international standards. Coverage decisions based on these recommendations are then made by the Federal Joint Committee, including members from all major stakeholders in the health system. These decisions are binding on sickness funds in the statutory health insurance (SHI) system and on providers. Given that 90% of Germans are enrolled in the SHI system, the recommendations of the IQWiG are extremely influential in determining standards of care in the German health care system (Nasser & Sawicki, 2009).

The primary focus of the IQWiG and the Joint Committee is setting guidelines for reimbursement by the SHI funds, rather than care provision per se. SHI funds are required by law to reimburse any services that are necessary for diagnosis or curing a disease, preventing its deterioration, or alleviating its symptoms. Effective treatments cannot be excluded from coverage on the basis of cost, but cost-effectiveness analysis can be used to set a maximum reimbursement for a given treatment. Thus the goal of IQWiG is to examine whether a treatment meets the criteria of necessity, considering impacts in relation to alternative treatments or no treatment at all, and it assesses benefit and harms in terms of patient-relevant medical outcomes. More recently, a working paper on cost-benefit evaluation suggests that cost-effectiveness studies should become standard in each therapeutic area (Nasser & Sawicki, 2009).

The IQWiG receives requests for reimbursement determinations for pharmaceuticals and medical services through a number of channels. In the case of pharmaceuticals, drugs approved for marketing are immediately reimbursable with stated exceptions (over-the-counter drugs and lifestyle drugs), unless the Federal Joint Committee requests an assessment. The committee itself or any of the associations represented there, as well as patient advocacy and self-help groups and the Ministry of Health, can request the evaluation of a drug. The Joint Committee will then use the IQWiG's evaluation to develop a directive that is binding.

Similarly, the Joint Committee makes only negative determinations regarding inpatient medical services. For non-hospital-based services, however, new procedures or technologies are not automatically reimbursable and may be covered only if the Joint Committee has approved their use. If evidence of a service's benefits is incomplete, the Joint Committee can propose a conditional coverage scheme to enable the collection of more data.

Because the Joint Committee exerts control only in barring pharmaceuticals and hospital services, Germany has higher prices for drugs and more new drugs available than many other European countries. And, it can be controversial to withdraw reimbursement approval for a drug after-the-fact (Nasser & Sawicki, 2009).

The IQWiG is not charged with developing guidelines for medical practice. Providers may still prescribe excluded drugs or treatments if patients themselves will pay the full cost, or they may request exceptions to the nonreimbursement rule. In addition, a recent court decision mandated that SHI's cover the physician's recommended treatment for a life-threatening disease, if the chance of success is not remote, and there is no other treatment choice. The narrow focus of the IQWiG on reimbursement limits its role in promoting standards of high-quality care across the health system (Nasser & Sawicki, 2009).

Australia

The most prominent mechanism for the use of CER in Australia is the PBAC, which uses it to make decisions about the inclusion or exclusion of drugs in Australia's national **formulary** (the list of prescription drugs that a health plan will pay for). Australia's Pharmaceutical Benefits Scheme (PBS) was established in 1948 and subsidizes approximately 80% of all prescriptions dispensed there (Lopert, 2009).

The PBS was the first national pharmaceutical reimbursement program to use an explicit consideration of comparative effectiveness in coverage decisions. A drug that has received marketing approval based on its efficacy, safety, and quality can be dispensed with a private prescription; however, to be covered under the PBS, it must meet the additional criterion of cost-effectiveness. The PBAC analyzes submissions for the listing of new medicines on the formulary, taking into account their effectiveness and costs compared with other drugs. Drugs that are more costly than other available treatments will be included on the formulary only if they provide a significant increase in effectiveness or reduction in toxicity.

The goal of introducing the PBAC was not explicitly to contain costs, and the PBS has no cap on its appropriations. The goal is rather to ensure that the national formulary reflects "value for money." Recommendations of the PBAC are advisory opinions for the Minister of Health, who makes the final decision; however, the minister may not add a medicine to the formulary without a positive recommendation from the committee (Lopert, 2009).

The PBAC does not commission CER itself, but is a consumer of such research as identified and presented by the applicant manufacturer. Reviews of applications are then undertaken by academic institutions contracted to perform such analyses. Generally, evidence from head-to-head randomized controlled trials is favored. The PBAC considers a number of factors in decisions, and although the committee chair has indicated that a cost-effectiveness ratio above A$50,000 (Australian dollars) per QALY is high, this ratio is not the only factor. Other information relevant to the decision is clinical need and the availability of alternative treatments, the degree of uncertainty in the estimate of cost effectiveness, potential total cost, and affordability in the absence of a subsidy. The committee also can recommend restricted use for only certain therapeutic purposes, or payment only with prior authorization (Lopert, 2009).

The PBS retains strong public support, despite some controversial recommendations. Generally, it has been found to perform well in balancing equity and efficiency in the approval of drugs. As more advanced and expensive end-of-life treatments become available, the PBS increasingly relies on careful restrictions on the use of certain therapies to ensure they are reserved for situations when their use is cost effective. Ultimately, more detailed guidelines on standards of care that go beyond a simple formulary may be required in order to ensure that the PBS system remains both affordable and effective in expanding access to new therapies.

Public Reaction to National Systems of Comparative Effectiveness

Clearly, a successful CER system must be sustained by public support and particularly the endorsement of its goals by providers, insurers, and patients. Enforcing comparative effectiveness guidelines in the face of opposition or skepticism would be extremely difficult and costly. In general, the public CER systems described here have been extremely successful in winning stakeholder approval.

> *The UK's NICE program has generated significant public support by limiting unwarranted variations in practice and increasing the speed of diffusion of new, high value-for-money treatments.*

NICE has generated significant public support by limiting unwarranted variations in practice and increasing the speed of diffusion of new, high value-for-money treatments across the NHS. However, there also have been delays in adoption of comparative effectiveness decisions on treatments, due to challenges in completing multiple comparisons of different treatments (Chalkidou, 2009). In 2008, NICE tackled some of the trial delay and approval process problems by launching a formal program for engaging with the medical technologies industry during phase II and III trials. This helps NICE make sure that the trial is designed to produce the information needed for decision making—especially with regard to outcome measures, types of costs, and appropriate comparators.

In France, HAS receives strong public support in regulating products and practices. The most common criticism is that it exerts too much control over the country's corporate and scientific players. However, HAS will sometimes allow for upward payment adjustments in cases of insufficient reimbursement. Some French physicians and scientists are concerned that the high impact of HAS opinions on decision makers can lead to hasty abandonment of unapproved treatments, despite their long-term promise (Rochaix & Xerri, 2009).

The IQWiG is praised by most Germans for regulating pharmaceuticals and nonpharmaceutical medical services. However, many wish more preliminary evaluation was completed before treatments are authorized. Frequently, not enough time is spent on raising public awareness regarding which treatments are approved and why. Finally, IQWiG often needs more money for clinical trials and lacks access to unpublished studies on treatments (Nasser & Sawicki, 2009).

PBAC has strong public support from Australians and is believed to perform well with respect to assuring equity, efficiency, quality, and acceptability. A 2005 study comparing the Australian pharmaceuticals industry and commercial environment to those of the United States, United Kingdom, Germany, Japan, India, and Singapore gave Australia the second-highest ranking behind Singapore. The study's authors lauded the country for its industry skills, regulations, and best practices. Still, advanced therapies in Australia can cost as much as those in the United States, particularly in the case of biologics, a burden on Australian pocketbooks that citizens often protest (Lopert, 2009).

PRIVATE MODELS FOR COMPARATIVE EFFECTIVENESS RESEARCH

Academic Medical Centers

Academic medical centers (AMCs)—which are partnerships between medical (and often nursing and other health professions) schools and affiliated hospitals—currently perform most CER in the United States. Funding for this activity generally comes from the National Institutes of Health (NIH), private donations, and relationships with pharmaceutical companies. Stakeholders within AMCs determine the focus of this research; for example, surgeons may focus on innovations in and effectiveness of the medical devices they currently use. AMC researchers distribute their findings internally and may publish them in academic journals or disseminate them via conferences and interorganization collaboration. However, the development of such research is haphazard, and sharing is fragmented and limited.

AMCs' scope of activities is generally confined to their local area and, as a result, they are not direct competitors with each other outside of their geographic region. Accordingly, sharing CER results across the country generally will not affect competition among hospitals. For this reason, there is an increasing trend for hospitals to recognize the benefits of implementing the CER results, including possible improvements in patient outcomes, accountability, and efficiency gains. However, without a broader system to organize and synthesize such research, its impact on the health system will inevitably be limited.

Large Private Employers

In America, some large private employers, such as Pitney Bowes, have been motivated to leverage learning from CER in an attempt to reduce employee health costs. Large employers generally evaluate a medical procedure's effectiveness by mining large databases containing their employees' health care claims experience or by performing meta-analyses of existing CER findings (Wilensky, 2006).

Employers are likely to evaluate procedures with high expected cost or volume and use several methods to evaluate the effectiveness of a course of treatment. Sometimes these methods include QALY, although private industry uses various nonstandardized data formats. Employers may not have strong incentives to share the results of their research with other firms, especially competitors, and distribution of information remains largely internal (Ohio Department of Insurance, 2010).

Private CER systems are believed to be effective in improving health care outcomes, but the impact is largely undocumented. However, when it comes to cost reduction, these systems are better able to quantify efficiency gains compared to their public counterparts, given their more manageable scale. The savings achieved by some of these organizations, such as Pitney Bowes, are well known and indicate the potential for major bends in long-term cost curves.

Private Health Systems

A number of private health systems have also implemented comparative effectiveness-based guidelines in their own practices. For example, the Mayo Clinic used CER results to generate a standard protocol for administering warfarin, a blood-thinning medication that is the most commonly prescribed anticoagulant drug in North America. They succeeded in reducing the number of incidences of both overdosages of warfarin and blood clots, thus diminishing extra days of hospitalization that otherwise would result from a mis-dosage. In this case, standardization of care based on CER both improved care and reduced costs (Bernstein, 2009).

Another private health system that has successfully implemented CER is Intermountain Healthcare in Utah. Intermountain researchers examined the impact of early induction of births (prior to 39 weeks of pregnancy) on the rate of newborns' admissions to neonatal intensive care units (NICU). They found that babies born earlier were more likely to need intensive care services. As a result, Intermountain developed a protocol that required physicians to justify any induction of labor prior to 39 weeks. This resulted in several improvements: fewer Caesarean sections, less time spent in labor, and fewer NICU admissions. All of these changes also saved Intermountain $10 million a year.

Similarly large benefits were seen from the implementation of a checklist to standardize care for cardiac disease, in accordance with clinical guidelines, which reduced deaths by 23%, and created an annual savings of $3.5 million (Bernstein, 2009). These are major examples of how private health systems can both produce and implement CER, yielding major benefits in both quality of care and cost savings.

Data Aggregators

A few large private companies, such as Milliman and McKesson, aggregate clinical effectiveness research and prevailing clinical wisdom into clinical guidelines. The guidelines generally focus on accepted courses of treatment for specific conditions, such as hypertension. Data aggregators then sell their guidelines to hospital systems and insurers, who use them to set practice standards, particularly for procedures associated with Medicare pay-for-performance reimbursements. Clinical guidelines are moving away from multi-volume hard-copy formats to Internet or software systems that are more interactive and flexible. Although useful as an informational resource, such clinical guidelines are clearly not binding on decisions by providers or payers and thus have limited influence in the overall operation of the health system.

The U.S. Debate on Comparative Effectiveness Systems

The recent U.S. health care reform debate largely ignored a significant missing piece in our health system: the absence of any formal mechanism to evaluate different treatments and ensure that patients receive only those shown to have a clinically significant, positive impact on outcomes. This absence is substantially responsible for the high variability in amount and kinds of treatment for a given condition, for many of the quality problems observed in U.S. health care, and for its skyrocketing costs. Nonetheless, the American population remains largely hostile to the implementation of any CER system.

In a March 2009 survey by the Harvard School of Public Health and National Public Radio, almost 60% of respondents said that medical treatments should be reimbursed even if they are higher cost or less effective than other treatments. In the same poll, only 10% of respondents said they greatly trusted a panel of medical experts or even NIH to decide which tests or treatments should be reimbursed by government programs. Only half of the respondents said they would trust nonbinding recommendations made by a panel of medical experts to be valid and useful in guiding health care reimbursement decisions (National Public Radio & others, 2009).

This survey and similar opinion polls conducted in 2009 and 2010 suggest that Americans fundamentally distrust government decision making with respect to issues of health care. Many politicians and policy makers believe these biases stem from fundamental misunderstandings of the goals and potential benefits of the CER approach. To combat this resistance, several U.S. government agencies and independent task forces have attempted to show the benefits of CER through a combination of proof-of-concept pilot programs and international collaborations.

THE AMERICAN RECOVERY AND REINVESTMENT ACT: NIH AND AHRQ

In 2009, President Obama signed the American Recovery and Reinvestment Act (ARRA), providing $1.1 billion in funding for projects related to CER. The bill established the Federal Coordinating Council for Comparative Effectiveness Research (FCC-CER), which comprises representatives of 15 different federal agencies. ARRA required that at least half of the representatives be physicians or people with clinical expertise. The newly created FCC-CER was tasked with a number of priorities: reducing duplication of efforts, encouraging coordinated and complementary uses of resources, coordinating related health services research, and making recommendations to Congress and the administration on CER infrastructure requirements. However, ARRA specified that the FCC-CER could not determine coverage, reimbursement, or other policies of public or private payers.

Some $300 million of the appropriation was funneled directly to the **Agency for Healthcare Research and Quality (AHRQ)** to continue its Effective Health Care program. This research program includes "horizon scanning, evidence gap identification, evidence synthesis, evidence generation, dissemination and translation, and research training and career development." Another $400 million was to be allocated at the discretion of the secretary of the Department of Health and Human Services, but managed by AHRQ. And, another $400 million was directed to NIH, which developed a grant program offering funding for initiatives that will substantially advance CER by improving analytical techniques, building new infrastructure for conducting CER, and establishing information systems to share the progress and results of such research.

The goal of these pilot programs is to provide a foundation for CER in the United States and to begin to demonstrate its relevance and usefulness. The hope is that once the role and relevance of this type of research in improving health systems operations is more widely understood, a more comprehensive system can be developed.

INTERNATIONAL PROGRAMS

CER funding within ARRA strongly encouraged the FCC-CER to learn more about CER systems in other countries and to consider establishing a global health information-sharing network, but such a network has not yet been established.

Comparative Effectiveness Systems: Guidelines for Design

Analysis of public and private CER systems suggests that the best model for placement and funding of such an organization would be through a semipublic agency. This agency could be an attached quasi-governmental entity that would promote objectivity while also preserving independence from formal governmental agency structures or political pressure (Wilensky, 2009). Although additional funding could be requested from governmental insurance and self-paying patients, the French model of using corporate taxes to provide supplementary funding is promising and would likely win public approval.

With regard to the focus of its recommendations, a new U.S. CER system would have the greatest impact by limiting its scope to a relatively narrow set of medical issues, rather than attempting to examine them all. In fact, the ARRA included funding for the Institute of Medicine to seek stakeholder input on national priorities for CER, with the resultant report to be used to guide spending the $400 million allocated to the secretary (Institute of Medicine, 2009).

The UK system (NICE) has been highly effective in making and implementing recommendations on drugs and devices, and a U.S. system could emulate this focus, at least initially. More important, however, any CER agency should follow France's HAS model in funding its own clinical research, in order to ensure consistency of recommendations, rather than just assessing previous studies.

> *Knowledge distribution is widely cited as a significant challenge in creating an effective comparative effectiveness research system.*

From the outset, a U.S. CER system should attempt to provide a better sense of how well various tests and treatments work across racial, ethnic, cultural, age, and other defined groups—essential in a diverse country such as the United States. This need may make it more difficult to depend on MTA trials, which require a longer lead time than STA studies and are more difficult to execute across multiple population subgroups.

Knowledge distribution is widely cited as a significant challenge in creating an effective CER system. Government channels should be employed to disseminate information in a uniform and accessible way, and, in any U.S. program, government should be responsible for increasing awareness of CER's benefits (Wilensky, 2009).

Finally, new CER systems should follow the French/English model in which directives generated by the CER organization and approved by other relevant officials become part of reimbursement policy. This is clearly more challenging in a multipayer system, such as that in the United States, in contrast to the single-payer systems dominant in Western Europe, but the leverage provided by Medicare and Medicaid, especially with respect to hospitals, would serve as a starting point for more widespread adoption.

Even an ideally designed comparative effectiveness system would face several potential implementation and operational hurdles. First, a CER system may curb progress in technological innovation. Drug and device makers may fear that their new and expensive products will lose out to older, cheaper therapies judged equally effective. This may dampen incentives for innovation and result in fewer new drugs being developed and a slower pace in improvement in patient outcomes. There is, however, no concrete evidence that such a slowdown has occurred in countries that use CER systems. In fact, recent research indicates that the European drug industry is becoming more productive than the U.S. industry, despite robust CER systems there (Chalkidou, 2010).

Second, cost savings are still unproven in public CER programs. Total health care costs have been steadily increasing across Europe, and savings from CER are difficult to quantify, even in France, where the capacity to convert large MTA trials into societal health policy is most highly developed (Rochaix & Xerri, 2009).

Conclusion

The evidence surrounding existing CER systems suggests that the potential net impact of these initiatives makes them an essential addition to health care systems in a variety of settings. Health systems in England and France, countries that have taken the lead in CER implementation, have seen notable benefits in terms of: reduced treatment variations, increased diffusion speed for cost-effective treatments, improvements in public health, incremental cost reduction through the elimination of unproven treatments, and reductions in wasted effort.

These systems incorporate CER not only by performing trials and evaluating treatment options, but also by rapidly analyzing and dispersing the information gained from trials, revising national treatment standards, and generating timely buy-in from providers and other key health players.

Designing a realistically implementable CER system in the United States or any of the other countries currently lacking these systems will clearly require adapting successful elements of existing approaches to the unique characteristics of a given nation's health system. The goal will be to establish a system that replicates the strongest elements of models successful in other countries while winning the widest possible public acceptability. New research also is needed, including: more detailed econometric studies on the impact of CER on research and development spending, compiling additional data on health care cost trends in countries with different CER systems, and further qualitative and quantitative illustrations of the improvements in health outcomes that CER can generate.

Any health system faces the same challenges of balancing the three core elements of U.S. health policy making: access, cost, and quality. CER is not a silver bullet, but its implementation is essential to health system reform and has the potential to improve access to services and raise the quality of care while also controlling costs.

These opportunities for health system improvement are particularly important as the industrialized countries confront the strains of greater demands on their health systems and skyrocketing health care expenditures. CER systems created using a new, ideal template could be a major step in the reform of health systems around the world.

DISCUSSION QUESTIONS

1. What are the benefits and costs of comparative effectiveness knowledge for a society?
2. Do the benefits of using a comparative effectiveness approach outweigh the costs of withholding health services from certain members of the population?
3. Does a comparative effectiveness program actually save money for the health care system?

4. Why has the U.S. health care system not yet implemented a comparative effectiveness effort?
5. What parties stand to gain or lose from the introduction of comparative effectiveness in the United States?
6. Are the countries that have already implemented comparative effectiveness programs benefitting from their decisions and, if so, in what ways?
7. Which agencies should evaluate the comparative effectiveness of different health care services and in what ways?
8. Who should distribute findings of comparative effectiveness research and in what ways?
9. What products or treatments should be subject to comparative effectiveness evaluations?
10. Who should fund a national comparative effectiveness program?

CASE STUDY

The United States, the United Kingdom, and Canada vary in the ways they limit women's access to screening mammograms. Surprisingly, this is not due to differing clinical guidelines offered by experts in each country, which overall are quite similar (basically, that the average woman should receive a mammogram once every 2 years from age 50 to age 70 or 75).

The CER programs in Canada and Britain can recommend that their government health programs pay for screening mammograms only according to the biennial guidelines, whereas, in the United States, *annual* screening mammograms are covered for women with Medicare, Medicaid, and most private insurance.

Canada and Britain limit mammogram screenings based on a metric of dollar costs to QALYs. The benefits of a given therapy in terms of an extended life span are estimated and the extra years lived are adjusted according to the quality of life the patient can expect. The cost of each additional year lived can then be calculated. Within those countries, medical products and treatments that cost more than £20,000 to £30,000 for each quality adjusted year of life are generally not paid for by the NHS. This ceiling is used as the principal—but not sole—guidance in approving most medical products and treatments (Rawlins & Culyer, 2004). The goal of this guideline is to avoid spending government money on treatments that offer only very minimal improvements in life span and quality of life, and to focus spending on treatments that are known to be effective relative to their cost.

The major public objection to CER systems is that they can be used to limit patients' access to services they want and their physicians recommend. Many people believe that limiting services will lead to worse health outcomes, though research performed here in the United States has shown exactly the opposite (Wennberg et al., 1989). CER skeptics argue that patient outcomes are better in the United

States, citing higher rates of cancer survival and lower cancer mortality, compared to Britain and Canada. This is partially true. Breast cancer mortality is only 1% higher in Canada than in the United States, although it is 21% higher in Britain (Mettlin, 2009). Many people believe these differences are driven by more limited access to diagnostic services, longer waiting times, and government refusals to fund certain types of care.

In fact, 47% of Canadian breast cancer patients do wait longer than the government-recommended 4 weeks for the beginning of radiation treatment (Priest, 2006), whereas in the UK, less than 1% of breast cancer patients waited longer than 4 months, as of late 2006. Meanwhile, the United States is not immune to this problem. A study of breast cancer patients in California found that the median wait time for low income patients was comparable to that in Canada; worse, some low income patients never received treatment at all (Gorey, Luginaah, Holowaty, Fung, & Hamm, 2009).

Concerns about NICE's recommendations leading to decreased access to specific treatments do not acknowledge the exemptions NICE can provide for high-risk patients. A UK physician who deems that a patient is truly at high risk for breast cancer can request an exemption from NICE guidelines that will allow her to obtain a mammogram. NICE recommends yearly MRI scans and exemptions if a patient carries the faulty TP53, BRCA1, or BRCA2 breast cancer genes. This holds true even if the patient is as young as 20, or if the patient is as young as 30 and is believed to have an 8% or higher chance of developing breast cancer in the next 10 years (NICE, 2006).

Finally, opponents of CER in the UK and Canada worry that their governments' reimbursement limits encourage health technology companies to offer their newest products and services first to the United States and other countries that are willing to "full-pay" for treatments. This claim has not been convincingly proven or denied.

CASE STUDY DISCUSSION

1. Does a CER program lead to system-wide health care cost reductions through reduced utilization? How might such a program improve the quality of care?
2. Are the British and Canadian governments best serving the public interest in limiting public insurance payments for mammograms based on clinical guidelines and cost-per-QALY metrics?
3. Are the limitations that the British and Canadian governments enforce on mammogram utilization too stringent? Are U.S. policies not stringent enough? What, if any, policies on limiting mammogram utilization should be adopted?
4. Would CER programs inevitably stifle the availability and implementation of health care innovations in a country? Why or why not?

REFERENCES

Bernstein, J. (2009). *The facts about comparative effectiveness: How studying which treatments work can improve care and reduce costs.* Denver, CO: CoPIRG Foundation.

Canadian Institute for Health Information (CIHI). (2005). *Medical imaging in Canada.* Ottawa: The Institute.

Chalkidou, K. (2010). The (possible) impact of comparative effectiveness research on pharmaceutical industry decision making. *Clinical Pharmacology and Therapeutics, 87,* 264–266.

Chalkidou, K. (2009). *Comparative effectiveness review within the U.K.'s National Institute for Health and Clinical Excellence.* New York, NY: The Commonwealth Fund.

Employee Benefit Research Institute. (1993). *Making choices: Rationing in the U.S. health system.* Issue Brief No. 136. Washington, D.C.: Author.

Gorey, K. M., Luginaah, I. N., Holowaty, E. J., Fung, K. Y., & Hamm, C. (2009). Wait times for surgical and adjuvant radiation treatment of breast cancer in Canada and the United States: greater socioeconomic inequity in America. *Clinical and Investigative Medicine, 32,* 239–249.

Grunwald, M., & Eilperin, J. (2005). "Energy bill raises fears about pollution, fraud." *Washington Post,* July 30.

Institute of Medicine. (2009). *Initial national priorities for comparative effectiveness research.* Washington, D.C.: National Academies Press.

International Atomic Energy Agency. (2001). *Annual report: Comparative assessment for sustainable energy development.* Vienna, Austria: Author.

Lopert, R. (2009). *Evidence-based decision-making within Australia's pharmaceutical benefits scheme.* Issue Brief. New York, NY: The Commonwealth Fund.

Mettlin, C. (2009). Global breast cancer mortality statistics. *CA: A Cancer Journal for Clinicians, 49,* 138–144.

Nasser, M., & Sawicki, P. (2009). *Institute for quality and efficiency in health care: Germany.* Issue Brief. New York, NY: The Commonwealth Fund.

National Conference of State Legislators. (2010). Certificate of need: State health laws and programs. Retrieved July 6, 2010, from http://www.ncsl.org/IssuesResearch/Health/CONCertificateofNeedStateLaws/tabid/14373/Default.aspx

National Institute for Health and Clinical Excellence (NICE). (2006). *Understanding NICE guidance.* Retrieved May 12, 2010, from http://www.nice.org.uk/nicemedia/pdf/CG041PublicInfoCorrected.pdf

National Public Radio, Kaiser Family Foundation, & Harvard School of Public Health. (2009). *The public and the health care delivery system.* Retrieved May 12, 2010, from http://www.kff.org/kaiserpolls/posr042209pkg.cfm

Next Generation Pharmaceuticals. (2010). Leveraging opportunities in comparative effectiveness research. Retrieved July 6, 2010, from http://www.ngpharma.eu.com/article/Leveraging-opportunities-in—comparative-effectiveness-research/

Ohio Department of Insurance. (2010). *How to appeal a health coverage decision made by your insurer.* Retrieved May 12, 2010, from http://www.insurance.ohio.gov/Consumer/Publications/IROHealthAppealsTipSheet.pdf

Priest, L. (2006). Vow broken on cancer waiting times. *The Globe and Mail, (Toronto),* November 21.

Rawlins, M., & Culyer, A. J. (2004). National Institute for Clinical Excellence and its value judgments. *British Medical Journal, 329,* 224–227.

Rochaix, L., & Xerri, B. (2009). *National authority for health: France.* Issue Brief. New York, NY: The Commonwealth Fund.

Rogner, H., Sharma, D., & Jalal, A. I. (2008). Nuclear power versus fossil-fuel power with CO_2 capture and storage: a comparative analysis. *International Journal of Energy Sector Management, 2,* 181–196.

Towse, A. (2009). Should NICE's cost threshold be raised? Yes. *British Medical Journal, 338,* 268–269.

U.S. Congress. (2008). *Technological change and the growth of health care spending.* Washington, D.C.: Congressional Budget Office.

U.S. Congress. (2007). *Research on the comparative effectiveness of medical treatments: Issues and options for an expanded federal role.* Washington, D.C.: Congressional Budget Office.

Wennberg, J. E. (1984). Dealing with medical practice variations: a proposal for action. *Health Affairs, 3,* 6–32.

Wennberg, J. E., Freeman J. L., Shelton, R. M., & Bubolz, T. A. (1989). Hospital use and mortality among Medicare beneficiaries in Boston and New Haven. *New England Journal of Medicine, 331,* 1168–1173.

Wilensky, G. (2009). The policies and politics of creating a comparative clinical effectiveness research center. *Health Affairs, 2,* 719–729.

Wilensky, G. (2006). Developing a center for comparative effectiveness research. *Health Affairs, 25,* 573–585.

Support for Medical Care Delivery

IV

Numerous topics would fit comfortably under the Support for Medical Care Delivery rubric. Additional chapter candidates for this section included law, financial management, and human resources management. The three topics selected are vital supports for effective medical care delivery and yet often are not dealt with adequately.

Tony Kovner in Chapter 14 discusses governance, management, and accountability, issues often taken for granted or perceived negatively by clinicians working in medical care organizations. For example, Kovner has heard explicit and implicit statements such as "all administrators think about is money (and they get paid too much)," and "what do trustees do anyway other than meddle and raise money (and not enough of it)?" Yet, it is commonly acknowledged that the weakness of nonprofit organizations, relative to for-profit and governmental organizations, is that they lack formal accountability either to voters or shareholders. Kovner discusses the current situation and these and other issues.

Workforce issues are presented by Richard Scheffler and Joanne Spetz in Chapter 15. Key issues include disconnects between new demands for vital primary care professionals—especially physicians—and their dwindling numbers. Reasons for the shortages and the challenges in addressing it are discussed, including the possibility of advanced practice nurses filling some of the large gap.

Information technology is changing rapidly as everyone with a smartphone knows. The United States lags behind other nations in its implementation of communications technology in health care and, in the United States, the health care sector lags behind other business sectors. Facilitating implementation of electronic medical records is a high priority under health reform, as it is expected to both enable quality of care improvements and reduce costs. Standardization, confidentiality and security, and interoperability among different systems (e.g., hospital–doctor's office–pharmacy) are important, persistent challenges. Use of equipment with electronic communication capability for preventing, treating, and monitoring patient care is increasing, yet there is no consensus currently on how to pay for many of these services. In Chapter 16, Roger Kropf presents these issues and challenges.

14

GOVERNANCE, MANAGEMENT, AND ACCOUNTABILITY

Anthony R. Kovner

KEY WORDS

governance

management

accountability

ownership

organizational performance

stakeholders

evidence-based management (EBMgmt)

LEARNING OBJECTIVES

- Understand the limits of health care organization accountability for performance
- Learn metrics for measuring organizational performance
- Learn how managers contribute to organizational performance
- Identify and frame issues of health care organization governance and management

TOPICAL OUTLINE

- Key processes and stakeholders
- Governance vs. management
- Current governance issues
- Basic managerial functions and successful managers
- Current management issues

Key Processes and Stakeholders

This chapter describes the processes of governing and managing thousands of health care organizations (HCOs) in the United States. Put simply, **governance** is the process organizations use to make important decisions, such as about mission, goals, budget, capital financing, mergers, and quality improvement. The people who make up the organization's **management** are the agents of the governing board and are held accountable for achieving organizational objectives. **Accountability** means being answerable—usually to important stakeholders—for decisions that affect organizational performance.

Whether one is discussing for-profit, nonprofit, or public (government) HCOs, all are accountable to specific sets of stakeholders: regulators and accrediting bodies, payers and financiers, clinicians and other employees, and local community leaders and donors, patients, members, and taxpayers. Public HCOs are, in addition, accountable to elected officials, and for-profit HCOs to shareholders. Central to this discussion of HCOs is the governance of nonprofit HCOs, including hospitals, because of their size, diversity, complex ownership, and centrality to the American health care system.

Governance is how important decisions are made in organizations. Who makes specific decisions varies across organizations and within a single organization. For example, one set of persons makes decisions regarding financing of a new hospital; a different set evaluates the quality of care; and yet a third set decides who should be hired as, say, the new vice president for human resources. Organizational bylaws define who governs or controls the organization. Commonly in a nonprofit organization, this is the board of trustees or directors.

GOVERNANCE, OWNERSHIP, AND MANAGEMENT

"Who governs?" as used here, it means "who controls organizational decision making?" Boards may be subject to ultimate control by remote owners, who can appoint the board, as in the case of hospitals owned by the Catholic Church, or they may be controlled by the shareholders who elect them. Important governance decisions may be reserved to the owners. For example, the Catholic Church, as owner, has decided that its hospitals will not perform abortions; it also makes decisions regarding mergers.

HCO **owners** include physicians, cooperatives, governments, religious organizations, investors, employers, unions, and philanthropists. These different ownership groups have varying goals and, as a result, their governing boards' goals may vary, too—from finding jobs for their members (unions), to achieving a return on investment (financiers), to being reelected (government politicians).

WHAT BOARDS DO

Board members are not employees of the organization on whose board they serve and many may have limited experience in making important HCO decisions. Yet, as a whole, the board must exercise the duties of care (acting as prudent persons), obedience (to the mission of the organization), and loyalty (have no conflicts of interest), as they carry out their roles.

> *Fundamentally, board members' decisions must serve their HCO's mission, so the board of a nonprofit nursing home should not invest in a race track.*

Board members cannot be found liable for bad business decisions, as long as it is shown that a hypothetical "prudent board member" could have made the same decisions in the same situation. Fundamentally, board members' decisions must serve their HCO's mission, so the board of a nonprofit nursing home should not invest in a race track. They also must be attuned to potential conflicts of interest. For example, when a board is considering a banking relationship, a board member who manages a local bank must disclose that interest and be absent from the discussion.

Little is known about the relationship between what nonprofit boards do and organizational performance. Most organizations have no formal accountability mechanisms for their boards. Board members elect themselves and they may or may not have limited terms of office. According to Bowen (2008), nonprofit boards should serve eight principal functions:

1. *Select, encourage, advise, evaluate, compensate, and, if need be, replace the CEO.* This is probably the most important function of the governing board.
2. *Discuss, review, and approve strategic directions.* In many organizations, strategy is primarily developed by management, but the board commonly reviews and approves strategy changes.
3. *Monitor performance.* Not all performance is measurable (e.g., how does one measure "tender loving care?"), and not all organizations set objectives whose outcome is measurable. (Common performance indicators that *are* measurable include infection rates, waiting time, profit-and-loss, market share, and, for hospitals, length of stay). Increasingly, hospital boards have become involved in reviewing quality metrics and discussing ways to improve them.
4. *Ensure that the organization operates responsibly as well as effectively.* This may involve acting to improve the health of a defined population by helping other community organizations achieve their goals.
5. *Act on specific policy recommendations and mobilize support for decisions taken.* Often this function is exercised within the frame of choosing capital investments and measuring their short- and long-term costs and returns.
6. *Provide a buffer for the president or CEO—"take some of the heat."* A board chair who is greatly respected in the community can help the CEO implement unpopular decisions, such as closing a money-losing service or recruiting new physicians to the community.
7. *Ensure that the necessary resources will be available to pursue strategies and achieve objectives.* All HCO boards have primary responsibilities for fundraising. This is especially true for capital projects.
8. *Nominate suitable candidates for election to the board and establish and carry out an effective system of board governance.* Often the nominating committee of the board is responsible for the board's internal evaluation of governance and for evaluating current board members who are being considered for additional terms.

Boards of smaller HCOs often take on the task of developing and updating organizational strategy. Whether or not most boards in larger HCOs actually develop strategy and adapt it to changing environments, strategy affects the mission of the HCO, and boards of directors are guardians of the mission. In that sense, organizational strategy is a concern of every board member.

Governance vs. Management

The board of directors selects the HCO's chief executive officer (CEO), who generally selects the other managers. The board delegates decision making to these managers, reserving the power to subsequently review or overturn management decisions. Managers are viewed as agents of the board and they work full-time. By contrast, most nonprofit board members are not paid, and many have full-time jobs elsewhere. Managers may spend a full day a week—or even more—working with board members and keeping lines of communication open.

Traditionally, the trustee role (governance) has been defined as policy making, whereas management's role has been defined as policy implementation. This dichotomy is often not relevant in practice, nor should it be. The distinction is perhaps better made between who makes important and less important decisions. Too intense board involvement in less important decisions is deemed micromanagement, and it is a common defect of ineffective boards. After all, the board has hired a professional manager. Rather than continuing to try to do the CEO's work (especially when board members disagree among themselves), the board should consider hiring a new manager whom they will not view as needing such close supervision. (In emergency situations, of course, such as the death of the CEO, the board may need to step in and make detailed decisions until a replacement is hired.)

Some management experts recommend that managers not have a governance role. They believe that a manager's participation on a board of directors is overreaching or a conflict of interest because managers function as agents of the board. Other management experts argue that CEOs *should* share in governance, as they have the skills and experience to participate effectively, and this is in fact the case in many HCOs. Many CEOs not only serve on their HCO's board, where they participate in decision making and nominate members, but also they often chair the board and serve as president of the corporation. In some smaller, nonprofit HCOs, the owners are founders, who are both board members and full-time staff. As these HCOs grow, they commonly experience problems in governance, if the founders do not possess the skills and experience to lead a much larger HCO effectively.

LINKING BOARD ROLES TO ORGANIZATIONAL PERFORMANCE

Accountability cannot be achieved in the absence of measurable objectives, developed by an organization's leadership. The objectives should be shared with key stakeholders, and progress toward them reported regularly. They may use a variety of strategies to achieve the objectives and their strategies may change over time, but the bedrock of accountability is having transparent, measurable objectives. The process of governance-by-objectives has not been the reality for many HCOs and, in many cases, still is not.

Historically, many HCOs have not been accountable for **organizational performance** and have not regularly reported on performance to external **stakeholders**, such as regulators, payers, and accrediting bodies, or to internal stakeholders, such as clinical staff, other employees, patients, and members. In the current environment, when Americans have seen so many reports about unnecessary deaths in hospitals and the often poor quality of care, as well as ill-conceived actions of large, trusted organizations, it may be hard to believe that, for many years, people simply took for granted that hospitals and other clinical entities were providing quality care. Evidence to the contrary came to light only rarely, when providers were successfully sued for malpractice, lost their accreditation, or developed a poor word-of-mouth reputation among patients and others in the community.

Measuring a nonprofit HCO's performance can be tricky. One might assume that among its goals would be improving the health of a given population by providing quality care at reasonable cost. But, if other organizations also serve the same population, how can the board assess its organization's contribution? How does it define "quality of care" or even "health"? Does this goal mean treating everyone who comes for care regardless of whether they will or can pay? What is "reasonable cost"? If a group practice provides care for a lower price than its competitors, but one that is much higher than that of group practices in another state or in another country, is that "reasonable"? Nonprofit boards regularly struggle with such difficult questions.

Board members who believe the board as a whole is not adequately monitoring organizational performance have several alternatives:

1. They can do nothing, either because they assume performance is probably satisfactory or because the rest of the leadership does not perceive any serious problem
2. They can raise the issue, with supporting data in hand, with the whole board
3. They can ask the CEO and board chair to survey other board members to see whether they share these concerns
4. They can attempt to engage the members of an appropriate board committee (some boards have governance committees) to examine issues involving audit, finance, or quality
5. They can offer their resignation

Board members must make sure they are satisfied with management explanations regarding current performance, problems and issues, best practices, and performance relative to industry standards or local or industry competitors. Board members should ask questions until they get acceptable answers or, if the answers are not satisfactory, until they are presented with an appropriate plan for remediation. The board is the conscience of the organization and the body ultimately accountable for protecting and achieving the HCO's mission.

Current Governance Issues

In an era of health reform, HCOs have been subject to criticism of varying degrees about a number of issues. Some are pervasive issues in the health system and some are specific to individual communities. One of the most common complaints, backed up by a wealth of data, is that our nation's HCOs provide care that is uncoordinated, too often of poor quality, and uniformly too expensive, especially relative to HCOs in other developed countries. U.S. managers, clinicians, and other health care workers are highly paid, but our HCOs do not provide the access to care and quality of services—or the positive health care outcomes—common elsewhere.

How should the governing bodies of HCOs respond to these fundamental issues? How should they measure organizational performance? Who is really in charge of improving population health, and how do individual HCOs fit in? And, what aspects of organizational performance do and should boards seek to measure?

Experts disagree about what boards should actually measure. It is fine to say that organizations should "specify measurable organizational objectives," but how does the board actually determine what objectives they want to achieve, how they should be measured, and at what levels of performance?

Currently, some HCOs use their mission statement as a starting point for establishing measurable objectives. Most HCOs do not include improving health of a given population as part of their mission. Assuming that, in a given region, some residents will be members/ patients of the HCO and some will not, what is the HCO's responsibility for improving population health? The board may agree that the HCO can work to improve the health of the local population, but organizations typically (and understandably) focus on the care they themselves provide, not with the care patients obtain before and afterward, which may be from sources not affiliated with the HCO. And, they focus on the results of care for patients who come to them, not the ones who seek care elsewhere.

Perhaps all board members can agree that their organization should specify measurable objectives to answer these essential questions: "which services do we provide, to whom, at what cost, and of what quality?" The difficult question here may be "which services?" How should the organization decide this basic question? It may not be that complicated to determine what services are needed by a particular population, only whether the HCO can or should make the investment. For example, a scattered population of ranchers might want—and need—its small rural hospital to provide orthopedic services for occasional catastrophic injuries, but the specialty equipment, physicians, and care arrangements necessary to do so may be beyond the hospital's means. Or, an urban hospital may decide to close its emergency room, in order to reduce the influx of low- and no-pay patients who rely on emergency care.

The board also should examine how its array, quality, and delivery of services are evaluated relative to those provided by other local organizations or as compared with the HCO's own best practice historically.

Finally, the board should evaluate the support its HCO gives to other community organizations, such as schools and social service organizations, serving the same population with the same goal of improving population health.

Our question—"which services do we provide, to whom, at what cost, and of what quality?"—is made more difficult to answer because HCO data systems have been developed largely to suit payers, accrediting bodies, and regulators, rather than managers. For example, hospital managers typically cannot easily figure out for a particular disease, say heart disease, what services have been provided to which patients at what cost, and certainly they find it near impossible to assess the value of those services in terms of improving the outcomes for a particular patient, much less for a population. One place boards clearly should focus is on developing and implementing new management data systems better aligned with their HCO's strategic priorities.

THE LOCUS OF GOVERNANCE

In small HCOs serving relatively few people, whether decision making occurs at the national, state/regional, or local level is usually not critical. Whether the organization survives or fails usually does not have significant impact on a large population (although every local community wants to keep its hospital). But for large HCOs—particularly those that are the sole provider in a region—where decisions are made can be vitally important. When a large health system decides to close one of its major facilities, losing convenient access can affect a great many community residents. Similarly, hospital prices are significant when a hospital has a geographic monopoly. If a hospital chain dominated by facilities in wealthier suburban communities sets high rates for *all* its hospitals, including those serving low income communities, those residents will have more limited access. If a hospital system concludes that one of its rural hospitals is financially untenable and decides to close it, local residents will have to turn to a hospital that might be an hour or more distant.

The difficulty in legislating national solutions to our health care delivery problems—that is, taking decision making power out of the hands of local owners—is that HCOs are so varied in size, mission, services offered, and market characteristics that the unintended consequences of such global interventions are impossible to accurately predict. At the same time, legislators, voters, and patients want HCOs to provide accessible care of high quality at reasonable prices, and most believe that government has at least some role in bringing about such outcomes.

ACHIEVING COORDINATED CARE

Improving the *coordination of care* is often seen as one of the best ways to improve quality of care and, at the same time, reduce costs. But, even on the relatively narrow issue of improving care coordination, reasonable people differ as to what government—or even large HCOs—should do to achieve this. For example, electronic medical records (EMRs) are usually put forward as one "solution" to coordination, but increasing experience with EMRs raises questions as to whether they are sufficient to reduce fragmentation, who will or should pay for them, how to make them interoperable, and how to assure security and confidentiality of patient data. Fundamentally, Americans are not interested in investments in coordinating care until they themselves need treatment or try to arrange care for a loved one with multiple complex chronic conditions.

> *Americans are not interested in investments in coordinating care until they themselves need treatment or try to arrange care for a loved one with multiple complex chronic conditions.*

The issue can be expressed as the extent to which it is desirable for government to encourage coordinated care by making it easier for people to hook up with one organization or system offering more-or-less comprehensive services. There are strong arguments for the government to do so. Many analysts make the following assumptions: First, if government pays for health insurance for a broad array of benefits, then government has some responsibility for monitoring how the money is spent; second, fragmentation of care is an urgent problem for many Americans, and it often results in duplication of costly services and less proactive, preventive, and other care that would improve outcomes. Of course, if government and other payers would reimburse this coordination, more of it would occur.

The desirability of greater coordination is embodied through the policy initiatives encouraging a "medical home" and "accountable" HCOs. The recent health reform legislation provides funding for demonstrations and evaluation of these models. Implementation issues include: (1) how individuals and families are assigned to or choose accountable HCOs, (2) how various sets of reimbursable services are organized and paid for, such as after-hours and weekend primary care, and (3) how to fund the research and changes in workforce composition and training necessary in order to carry out any reconfiguration.

MANAGEMENT

What do HCO managers really do? For that matter, what should they do? What makes managers successful, or not? How are they hired and fired? How much power do they have relative to physicians? How much value do they add to the work of the HCO? These are some of the fundamental questions that stakeholders ask about management work.

Managers do what they are supposed to do, what they are asked to do, what they want to do, and what they can do. Managers, other than nursing home administrators in some states, are not licensed. What they do day-to-day varies by the behavior, interests, skills, and experiences they bring to the HCO, the priorities of those who hire them, and the HCO's size, history, environment, and complexity.

Managerial roles in HCOs differ from those in other sectors for several reasons. First, the purpose of an HCO is more complex—whether this is to provide services, teach clinicians, conduct research, improve the health of a community, or some combination of these.

Second, measurable objectives associated with any of these purposes are more difficult to agree on than generating a return on investment or increasing a product's market share. For example, it is an academic medical center's responsibility to teach future clinicians, but how many people in which disciplines need to be taught which specific skill sets, and how are learning outcomes to be assessed by whom? Within these questions are imbedded sub-questions such as how training should be paid for and by whom, where training should take place, and how it should be organized.

Third, the HCO environment operates in too many "silos" with minimal cross-communication. For example, many hospitals profess the goal of more coordinated, "patient-centered" care, but that is rarely achieved, even though increasing evidence shows that patient outcomes improve markedly when clinicians from different disciplines coordinate their services around the needs of the patient. Thus, managers who seek to improve the quality of care are likely to emphasize the need for more effective teamwork. However, working across medical specialties or across disciplines such as medicine and nursing, flies in the face of entrenched traditions of professional independence. Working across agencies (hospital – rehabilitation services – home health) is even more problematic.

Basic Managerial Functions and Successful Managers

According to Longest (1990), basic managerial functions include:

- *Planning:* determination of goals and objectives
- *Organizing:* structuring resources—people, dollars, services, equipment—to accomplish the work required to meet the objectives
- *Directing:* the stimulation of members of the organization to meet the objectives
- *Coordinating:* the conscious effort of assembling and synchronizing diverse activities and participants so that they work toward the attainment of objectives
- *Controlling:* comparing actual results with objectives to enable mid-course corrections and provide a measure of success or failure

Simply put, managers have to rally large numbers of people who are diverse in interests, professional identities, skills, and loyalties, to work together to achieve HCO goals. Often these people cannot be simply commanded to work together, especially if they work in different departments of a large HCO.

Goleman (1998) suggests that the most effective leaders have a high degree of what he calls "emotional intelligence," which he believes is more important than technical skills and IQ for managerial jobs at all levels. The five components of emotional intelligence are: self-awareness, self-regulation (e.g. the ability to think before acting), motivation, empathy, and social skills.

Even though, as noted previously, successful managers vary a great deal in their backgrounds, experiences, personal styles, and extent of formal training, researchers have tried to unravel the specific underlying factors that lead to successful managerial performance. Boyatzis (1995) has developed a model that describes three sets of managerial competencies:

1. Primarily "people skills": efficiency orientation, planning, initiative, attention to detail, self-control, flexibility, empathy, persuasiveness, networking, negotiating, self-confidence, group management, developing others, and oral communication.
2. Use of concepts, systems thinking, pattern recognition, theory building, technology, quantitative analysis, and social objectivity
3. Written communication and analytical reasoning

In addition to these underlying competencies, there must be a good fit between a candidate's managerial skills and experience and the attributes required in a specific organizational position. This seems self-evident until one tries to understand what really are the required skills and experiences that managers need. Further, the needs of a particular job change over time, so that one set of skills and experience may be important early in an HCO's history, and a different set may be more useful when the HCO grows rapidly, merges, broadens services, or reaches steady-state.

Managers can be successful with various kinds of formal training, including no formal training at all. Some CEOs of large HCOs have MBAs or MDs, and many do not. CEOs are almost always hired by a board of directors and, in the best case, the board will have developed (or approved) specific measurable objectives for the HCO and will support the CEO's efforts to achieve them. New CEOs do not have an unfettered hand, however, because the means they choose to achieve the objectives must be acceptable to powerful stakeholders, especially physicians. When managers are CEOs of large for-profit companies in the health sector, such as pharmaceutical or insurance firms, their expected behavior and requirements are similar to those of other large industrial and service firms.

For many years, a special characteristic of U.S. acute care hospitals has been the strong influence that attending physicians have on hospital policy and practice. These doctors are not hospital employees, yet many of them view the hospital as an extension of their private office practice. A hospital medical staff, which includes the attending physicians, has its own bylaws and makes rules and regulations that affect the physicians who practice there, such as the procedures to follow when a patient is admitted or dies. The hospital's governing board must approve these bylaws and acts as a trustee of patient and community interests. The power of attending physicians—essentially, independent contractors—in hospital decision making varies greatly. In general, it has lessened in the last 15 years, especially in hospitals such as academic medical centers, which are dominated by salaried physicians.

THE VALUE MANAGERS CONTRIBUTE TO HCO PERFORMANCE

In the United States, more than 250,000 persons are employed in the broad category of HCO managers. The work they do ranges widely, from managing accounts receivable in a group practice to marketing a nursing home, to buying space for a surgical practice, to managing labor relations in a neighborhood health center. Staff specialists also do "managerial" work, often requiring data analysis. Staff specialists include internal consultants in a hospital, marketing analysts in a consulting company, strategic planners in a health system, and physician chairs of medical staff committees dealing with medical credentials or quality improvement.

In theory, HCO goals are more effectively and efficiently accomplished because of the contributions of managers, although one can easily think of situations in which hiring an additional manager (not to mention an ineffective manager) adds to costs, decreases quality, or decreases access to care, say, by preventing HCOs from hiring additional clinicians.

But managerial efforts can do more to support clinical services or provide patient care than would hiring another doctor. A clear example is hiring an additional manager within the fundraising department. Such a manager may bring in sufficient funds to enable the hiring of 10 new clinicians. A more subtle example is the work that internal consultants can do to reduce process variation by taking out unnecessary steps or reducing duplicative work. This is work clinicians haven't been trained to do and asking them to perform process analysis would decrease the time they can spend taking care of patients.

Some observers say that managers (not only HCO managers) are "hired to be fired," much like the managers of professional sport teams. Managers may be easier to fire than key physicians, just as baseball managers are easier to fire than star sluggers or strikeout pitchers. Yet, like team managers, HCO managers contribute significantly to the success of their organizations. To make appropriate hiring, firing, and compensation decisions boards must have and use appropriate metrics related to measurable objectives agreed to by all parties in advance. When this is not the case and HCO financial performance suffers, managers are often scapegoated for poor results.

Current Management Issues

Current challenges for improving management performance are:

- Focusing accountability for results and improving transparency of decision making
- Investing appropriately in management training and development
- Investing in research to improve management practice

FOCUSING ACCOUNTABILITY FOR RESULTS

What results are managers accountable for and how do they achieve these results? In driving performance, what difference does the manager make? Traditionally, in for-profit organizations, the mission is clear—it is to generate return on investment—and board members (who are often shareholders) measure performance in those terms. If the management team's performance is inadequate, shareholders sell their shares or fire their managers. Commonly, in takeovers or mergers whole management departments are eliminated or reduced substantially.

> *A basic flaw with the not-for-profit form is the lack of accountability of governing boards to any outside body, such as legislatures or stockholders.*

Not-for-profit HCOs operate between the extremes of typically stable government agencies, where managers enjoy a great deal of job security, and the more volatile for-profit entities. A basic flaw with the not-for-profit form is the lack of accountability of governing boards to any outside body, such as legislatures or stockholders. The potential problems this raises are compounded by the difficulty in specifying the outputs of HCOs in general, conflicting goals, and frequent lack of agreement among board members as to the HCO's mission—the driving force behind most nonprofit organizations' existence—or even the purpose of the governing board. For example, if the mission is to care for people who are poor and cannot pay fully for services, some board members may believe the mission puts the organization in financial jeopardy.

All HCOs encounter accountability problems, inasmuch as even the terms "health" and "health care" are open to interpretation. How would an external observer recognize that one nursing home or group practice produces better health outcomes than another? How do regulators measure adequate performance of managed care plans with respect to improving the health of covered populations? Little is known about how HCOs specify their goals and devise performance metrics related to the most important measure: health care outcome. HCO performance is usually measured in terms of improving shorter term results, such as low rates of hospital acquired infections and readmissions, low staff turnover, low waiting times in the emergency department, greater fundraising, and higher market share and name recognition. Although such measures are widespread, little is known about how the HCO leadership makes important decisions and the part that these types of evidence play in those decisions.

INVEST IN MANAGEMENT TRAINING AND DEVELOPMENT

Management training programs are needed both to prepare entry-level HCO managers and to develop managers in their initial positions. Formal management education is not always required for many management positions and the need for it varies by the individual and type of position desired. What is required are the competencies, such as those described by Boyatzis, that can be acquired through learning on and off the job. However, many employers have a bias toward hiring managers with formal undergraduate and graduate-level management education or requiring them to obtain such education after being hired.

Students who choose health care management as a career can reasonably start on this educational path in the junior year of college. Arguments for not pursuing management education until graduate school relate to the opportunity costs of not pursuing education in other areas—such as government, biology, languages, or the arts—that would presumably make the individual a more well-rounded person, a more effective citizen, or, in the case of social sciences and quantitative methods, a better manager.

As of 2010, there is much discussion among educators regarding appropriate graduate school curricula in management, a topic usually debated in terms either of content covered or competencies required. Arguments can be made for inclusion of broad content areas: statistics, microeconomics, management and financial management, health economics, management information systems, reducing process variation, human resources management, and ethics, among others. And arguments can be made for development of certain competencies: written, verbal and interpersonal communications skills, statistical analysis and application, financial and market analysis, quality improvement, managing and leading work in organizations, improving population health, and career management.

But scant evidence correlates successful coursework in these competencies and succeeding at various management positions. Experts disagree as to whether all these competencies should be required for all management positions. That is, should a manager of a community advocacy program need the same core education as a manager of information systems? Or, how skillful do managers need to be at public speaking or quantitative analysis?

The educational process should not stop after entering a management position. First, a new manager requires formal orientation into the new organization. After that, formal educational programs (not necessarily degree programs) should be tied to the organization's performance appraisal system. In other words, they should be geared to helping new managers achieve what the HCO most wants them to achieve.

As part of a well-designed performance appraisal system, managers and their supervisors should periodically review the skills and experiences required to perform the current job better or prepare for the next position. Employers should pay for this developmental education as part of their compensation and human resources policies. The development program should be monitored, in order to assure that it is actually helping managers achieve their goals—for example, did the manager learn more effective ways to search for evidence or apply quantitative skills?

Leaders of many nonprofit organizations argue that, because they are nonprofit, they should not spend money on management development. The same argument can, of course, be made for not employing any managers at all, not to mention lowering their salaries to the lowest that acceptable candidates would accept. Clearly the management challenges all HCOs face today are severe. One could argue that, because nonprofits are, in a sense, "community organizations," they require the best-trained leaders in order to return to the community the maximum benefit.

INVESTING IN MANAGEMENT RESEARCH

Management decisions should be made based on the best evidence available, just as clinical decisions should be. Hundreds of millions of dollars have been spent on evidence-based medical research in order to identify and promote medical treatments that result in positive, predictable, cost-effective outcomes for patients. There is a parallel research discipline in health care that supports **evidence-based management (EBMgmt)**, but unfortunately, well-designed management research in HCOs is sparse compared to clinical research. It does not begin to produce the array of research results available to guide managers in other industries, such as banking or management consulting.

EBMgmt has been defined as "the systematic application of the *best available evidence* to the evaluation of management strategies for improving organizational performance" (Hsu et al., 2006), and management has a lot to learn from participation in it. Steps in the evidence-based management process include: translating a specific management challenge into research question(s), acquiring relevant research findings and other evidence, assessing the validity, quality and applicability of the evidence, and presenting evidence in a way that it will be useful in the decision making process.

Here are just a few examples of the important questions HCO management research could address:

- How should the hospital organize emergency services to reduce patient waiting times?
- How can schools train and organize health care clinicians—doctors, nurses, mental health professionals, social workers, and others—to work more effectively in teams?
- How can large HCOs assess and improve results from investments in management development?

Deciding whether to invest in research is similar to deciding whether to invest in management development. Namely, do such expenditures require HCO funds that would otherwise be better spent on patient care, in both the short and long term? Large HCOs often assume that management research is "not their responsibility" and should be funded by government or philanthropic organizations. However, because HCOs are prime beneficiaries of such research, one can argue persuasively that they should fund it, as do industries outside of health care. Indeed, finding out how to improve systems to benefit patients, staff, and the community should be part of every HCO's ongoing quality improvement program.

Managers who do not follow the precepts of evidence-based decision making often fail to investigate a full range of evidence related to some planned decision or innovation, nor do they search the literature or the Web effectively for already established "best practices." Too many HCO leaders are not aware of EBMgmt research methods, and there are too few incentives for managers to take what may appear to be a more time-consuming approach, although, time and again, adequate analysis at the outset saves costly false starts or misguided policy.

HCOs are more likely to use EBMgmt when the incentives are strong. This may be when there are favorable external conditions, such as when insurers pay for better performance, when an HCO has a hard-wired questioning culture rather than a strictly hierarchical decision making process, when it has a focused accountability structure linked to the quality and timeliness of decision making, and when managers participate in management research.

Conclusion

HCO boards and managers are increasingly accountable for their organizations' performance. They may perceive the requirements of accrediting agencies, regulators, and payers as limits on their autonomy, but in most cases, these requirements have been developed in an effort to assure access, quality of care, and cost control.

Accountability has several key dimensions: accountability "for what," "to whom," and "by what means?" In the best of all free market worlds, the market would decide accountability. Patients would choose services from providers who they believe "give them the most value"—charge the lowest price for acceptable service quality, or provide the highest quality for an acceptable price.

Health economists generally agree that the free market has serious limitations when it comes to health care. First, patients may not have a choice of providers, as there may be insufficient providers in a given specialty in their geographic area. Or, their insurer may limit their choice. Patients may not be able to decide in an informed way as to what amount and kinds of care are appropriate or high-quality, particularly in complicated medical situations. (Although, when give a clear and full explanation of their choices, patients often choose less costly, more conservative treatment approaches.) Because insurers are paying for care, physicians rarely see the need to explain to patients the costs of alternative treatments, medications, or other services, and patients do not ask.

Few more-or-less local HCOs are accountable in any formal way for improving the health of their local populations. Accountability to patients is typically limited to not doing them any harm and for services they pay for out-of-pocket. Because patients are rarely organized (except, occasionally, by disease groups), they can do little collectively to hold HCOs accountable for harmful practices.

Governance and management are vital elements affecting HCO performance. Organizational performance suffers if those who govern and manage HCOs cannot agree and specify in measurable terms what services the HCO will provide, how much it will charge, and whom it will serve.

Critics of current HCO governance and management must first understand the rules under which most HCOs operate. Many HCOs are struggling for financial survival and face relentless demands to improve the quality of care. Many have difficulty in recruiting and retaining key staff—doctors, nurses, pharmacists, and technicians. Many HCOs experience competitive pressure to offer the most technologically sophisticated—and costly to install, operate, and staff—equipment and services. This situation is a far cry from a more positive set of ground rules, under which HCOs would be held accountable for their contribution to improving the health of a population and to providing care of the highest quality, at a reasonable cost.

DISCUSSION QUESTIONS

1. What are some of the ways to measure performance of HCOs?
2. What are the advantages and disadvantages of the different forms of ownership of HCOs—public, nonprofit, and for-profit?
3. What skills and experience are required to own and manage HCOs?
4. Who should be in charge of HCOs, and how should they be trained?
5. What mechanisms of accountability are most effective for nonprofit HCOs?

CASE STUDY

What follows is a summary of Montefiore Medical Center's 2009–2010 strategic plan:

- *Mission:* To heal, to teach, to discover, and to advance the health of the communities we serve.
- *Vision:* To be a premier academic medical center that transforms health and enriches lives.
- *Values:* Humanity, innovation, teamwork, diversity, and equity.
- *Strategic Goals:*
  - Advance our partnership with Albert Einstein College of Medicine
  - Create notable centers of excellence in heart care, cancer care, and the Children's Hospital
  - Build specialty care broadly
  - Develop a seamless delivery system with superior access, quality, safety, and patient satisfaction
  - Maximize the impact of our community service
- *Organizational Goals:*
  - Create a culture of high performance, motivation, and fulfillment
  - Sustain strong financial health
  - Invest in state-of-the art facilities and technology
  - Build an aligned and interconnected organization
  - Foster supportive partnerships and alliances.

CASE STUDY QUESTIONS

Given the above statements of fundamental purpose,

1. How should organizational performance at Montefiore be measured?
2. Why don't all HCOs have strategic goals like Montefiore's?
3. What contributions could Montefiore's governing board make toward accomplishing the strategic goals?
4. What contributions should the management team make?
5. How is Montefiore accountable to its various stakeholders for organizational performance?

REFERENCES

Bowen, W.G. (2008). *The board book*. New York, NY: W.W. Norton & Co., Inc.

Boyatzis, R. E. (1995). Cornerstones of change: building the path to self-directed learning. In: R. E. Boyatzis, S. S. Cowen, D. A. Kolb, et al. (Eds.), *Innovation in professional education* (pp. 50–94). San Francisco, CA: Jossey-Bass.

Goleman, D. (1998). What makes a leader. *Harvard Business Review, 76*(6), 93–102.

Hsu, J. L., Arroyo, I., Graetz, E., et al. (2006). Methods for developing actionable evidence for consumers of health services research (match study): A report from organizational decision-maker discussion groups & a toolbox for making informed decisions. Contract No. 290-00-0015, Task Order No. 13. Rockville MD: U.S. Agency for Healthcare Research and Quality.

Longest, B. B. (1990). *Management practices for the health professional* (4th ed.). Norwalk, CT: Appleton & Lange.

15

HEALTH WORKFORCE

Richard Scheffler and Joanne Spetz

KEY WORDS

patient protection and affordable
  care act (ACA)
health insurance
primary care

nurse practitioners
physician assistants
scope of practice
advanced practice nurses

LEARNING OBJECTIVES

- Consider the impact of health reform on the health workforce
- Understand the structure of the health workforce labor market and its policy implications
- Learn about the critical nature of primary care
- Understand why the market may not produce the required supply of primary care doctors
- Learn why shortages of registered nurses can be persistent
- Consider ways in which advanced practice nurses can help address primary care shortages

TOPICAL OUTLINE

- Health care reform and the health care workforce
- Physician health workforce
- The crucial nature of primary care
- The supply of nurses and nurse practitioners

The supply of health care workers is perhaps the most important component of the health care system, because the delivery of health care services is dependent on the availability of skilled professionals who can provide needed care and supporting services. Knowing when we have an adequate supply of these professionals and the techniques used to make this judgment are the focus of this chapter. It will examine the supply of physicians, with a special focus on primary care physicians, then examine the supply of nurses and nurse practitioners. The policies, licensing, and training of people in these two major professional groups differ significantly. Understanding the structure of the market and policy implications of this structure will be key objectives of this chapter.

Why do we as a society care if we have the "right" supply of health care workers? The answer seems almost obvious: we need them to deliver health care and allow our health system to function efficiently. But what is the result if we have too few? Some individuals will have reduced access to health services—longer distances to travel to see a doctor or a longer wait time for an appointment, for example. And, those without adequate health insurance or the ability to pay will be less likely to receive the care they need.

What if we have too many health care workers, especially doctors? Is this a bad thing? It can be. The resources and cost of training a doctor would be wasted if the doctor's skills and services are underused. Even more serious could be the problem that doctors may provide services that are unnecessary in order to generate desired income. This has been called supplier-induced demand.

So how do we know when we have too many or too few health care workers? One way is to use a market model—namely, the tools of supply and demand.

Figure 15.1 shows the classic market situation. The supply of doctors in this example is a direct function of wages or income. Higher income increases the supply of doctors in the long run. The demand for doctors declines as their income increases because the price of their services increases. This makes sense in a market situation. At point E (equilibrium), the market is in balance: the wage is at a level where the supply of health care workers equals the demand for workers.

To put these numbers in perspective, assume there are 900,000 doctors in the United States, earning an average of $200,000 at the market equilibrium (E). What if income were lower than $200,000—say, $180,000? At this level, the demand for doctors (Y) is higher than the supply (X), which gives us a shortage of 100,000 (X–Y) doctors. If the market is working, the excess demand for doctors will lead to an increase in their income and, when it reaches $200,000, the shortage will be eliminated.

That's the basic market model. But most health policy experts understand that the market for doctors does not function as described in the market model

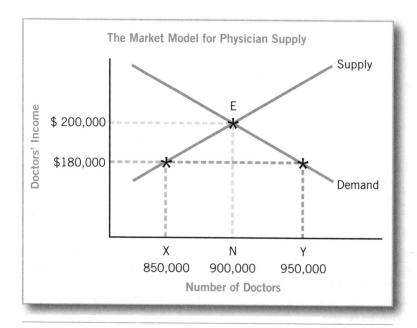

FIGURE 15.1
The market model for physician supply.
Note. E = Equilibrium.

(Scheffler, 2008). Consumers and patients have much of their health care paid by insurers or the government. The price of a doctor's time has little or, in some cases, no effect on them and thus demand for services is not readily affected by changes in that price. On the supply side, doctors must complete many years of medical school and residency before they can practice, so supply cannot easily adjust in the short run. For these reasons, the classic market may not be a good way to judge when we have too many or too few physicians.

Another approach to estimating the requisite supply would be to base it on a population's needs—the average number of heart disease patients requiring cardiologists, the average number of bone disease and injury cases requiring orthopedic care, for example. The needs-based approach makes intuitive sense, but requires many judgments and assumptions. What is the "required" level of cesarean deliveries, for example? This depends on the number of women having babies and the judgment of doctors, which vary widely across the United States (Baicker, Buckles, & Chandra, 2006). We also need to know how productive the obstetric surgeons are. How many cesarean deliveries do they do per day or week? This approach ignores the cost of the treatment and the earnings of doctors (Scheffler, Liu, Kinfu, & Dal Poz, 2008).

WHAT IS AN "ADEQUATE" SUPPLY OF PHYSICIANS?

There are multiple definitions of an "adequate" supply of physicians. According to the federal government (U.S., Department of Health and Human Services [DHHS], Health Resources and Services Administration [HRSA], Bureau of Health Professions [BHP], 2008), "An adequate physician supply could be defined as having the right number of physicians, with the right skills, in the right place, at the right time. The adequacy of supply, therefore, has specialty, geographic, and time dimensions."

Another definition comes from Ehrenberg and Smith (1991):

Labor shortages are sometimes characterized by a tendency to define a shortage in terms that are independent of demand. According to our definition a shortage exists if, at the prevailing wage rate for a given occupation, demand exceeds supply. Frequently, however, actual demand is ignored and a shortage is defined with reference to what someone thinks society 'needs' (p. 55).

A definition of the optimal supply of health workers that combines the concepts of need and the market would say it is the number needed to deliver the care necessary to maximize the health of a population, given the resources spent in the health care industry.

Health Care Reform and the Health Care Workforce

The **Patient Protection and Affordable Care Act (ACA),** enacted March 23, 2010, is landmark legislation. The last wholesale reform of the U.S. health care system was the introduction of the Medicare and Medicaid programs in 1965, which provided government-sponsored health insurance for elderly, disabled, and low income Americans. Between 1965 and 2010, no federal health care reform was of similar magnitude.

Under the ACA, an estimated 35 million Americans, about two-thirds of the uninsured, will gain **health insurance** coverage over the next 4 years (see Chapters 2 and 3). The impact of health reform on the supply of health care workers is a key public policy concern. More individuals with insurance will increase the demand for doctors and other health workers. Will the supply be adequate to meet this new demand?

Providing people with health care insurance, which expands their access to health care (an increase in demand), will also place pressure on the health care system to provide more services and, thus, could increase costs. In order to ensure that the ACA is successful, costs must not be allowed to skyrocket, despite this pressure.

The remainder of this chapter focuses on the issue of the health workforce and the implications of the passage of the ACA.

Physician Health Workforce

There are different views about whether we have an overall shortage of doctors, but there is general recognition that there is an inadequate supply of **primary care** providers, including physicians. This shortage is a major obstacle to providing adequate and cost-effective care to a greater number of Americans, as intended by the ACA. Why is this the case? We begin by documenting the decrease in primary care over the last few decades and highlight the barriers to choosing a primary care career. There are multiple factors, but clearly one of them is primary care physicians' lower earnings, compared to specialist physicians (see also Chapter 9). We will also discuss some of the policy initiatives in the ACA that are intended to increase the delivery of primary care and its efficiency.

> *The shortage of primary care clinicians is as a major obstacle to providing adequate and cost-effective care to a greater number of Americans, as intended by health reform legislation.*

SUPPLY OF PHYSICIANS

The number of physicians in the United States has grown consistently over the last 50 years. As shown in Table 15.1, the number of active physicians increased from 1.27 to 2.57 per 1000 population from 1949 to 2007, more than a 200% increase. At the same time, the total number of primary care specialists (i.e., general and family physicians, obstetrician-gynecologists, and general pediatricians) increased from 0.75 to 1.01 per 1000 population, only a 35% increase. In 1960 and 1970, primary care specialists actually declined followed by an increase in 1980, 1990, and 2000.

Clearly, growth in the total number of doctors is largely being affected by growth in specialties other than general primary care. Among the primary care specialties, the lowest—the general practice/family medicine—category has experienced the greatest decrease, some of which may have been picked up by an increase in general internal medicine. So, whereas about 60% of all active physicians were in general practice 60 years ago, only about 40% are in recent years (U.S., DHHS, National Center for Health Statistics [NCHS], 2010).

TABLE 15.1

Number of U.S. Doctors of Medicine, per 1000 population, 1949–2007

	1949	1960	1970	1980	1990	2000	2007
Active doctors of medicine	1.27	1.38	1.53	1.83	2.20	2.46	2.57
% Change		8.2%	9.8%	16.5%	16.8%	10.6%	4.5%
General primary care specialists	0.75	0.70	0.66	0.75	0.86	0.98	1.01
% Change		−7.0%	−5.8%	12.3%	12.2%	12.0%	3.1%

Note. 1949 data calculated with 1950 population; the most recent physician data available are from 2007. *Sources:* U.S., Department of Health & Human Services. (2009). *Health, United States - 2009;* U.S. Census, population data.

According to Margolius and Bodenheimer (2010), "the gap between the supply of primary care physicians and the demand for primary care continues to grow. Primary care practices must find a way to increase their patient capacity without sacrificing quality of care or adding more work to already overburdened physicians." This is key to the success of the health system, because primary care doctors are—or should be—the gateway to our health system.

The Crucial Nature of Primary Care

WHY PRIMARY CARE IS IMPORTANT

Grundy and colleagues (2010) explain that "a multi-stakeholder movement for primary care renewal and reform has emerged in the United States, out of recognition that the achievement of an efficient, effective, and sustainable health system requires a vibrant primary care sector."

There are three major reasons why primary care is so important. First, primary care is ideally the first point of access to the health care system and, again ideally, the primary care physician or nurse practitioner coordinates the advice and treatment plans of various specialists. A primary care health professional also can work closely with the patient and the patient's family to engage them in activities to improve health.

Second, evidence suggests that increasing the number of primary care doctors will not only improve access to care and quality of care, but will also reduce its costs. Primary care can be a cost-reduction strategy because, if patients use primary care physicians, they (1) may avoid unnecessary and costly specialist services and (2) will avoid duplicate tests and procedures that better coordinated care enables. As a result, "despite contentious debate over the new national health care reform law, there is an emerging consensus that strengthening primary care will improve health outcomes and restrain the growth of health care spending" (Friedberg, Hussey, & Schneider, 2010).

Third, primary care physicians are vital in achieving better quality of care. Primary doctors coordinate patients' health care needs and, as a result, obtain better health outcomes. Lack of primary doctors can delay patients' access to appropriate services.

BARRIERS TO PRIMARY CARE

There are numerous barriers to expanding the supply of primary care physicians. One has to do with income. Although physician incomes have generally increased in the last several decades, general/family practitioners' income increased by only 0.8% from 1983 to

2006, and that increase was concentrated in the years from 1983 to 1993. That period was followed by a stagnant change from 1993 to 2002–03, followed by an abrupt and continuing decrease.

In addition to low and declining levels of pay, the primary care specialty has a fairly low status in medicine. Furthermore, there has been inadequate training support from the government or other organizations that might provide incentives for students to pursue primary care careers.

One might ask why general/family practitioners are paid so poorly compared to specialists. In 2006, a general/family practice physician was paid $145,000, on average, compared to $351,000 for a radiologist. Are the generalist's lower fees the result of market forces? Again, the answer is no. Reimbursement rates are established annually by the Center for Medicare and Medicaid Services (CMS) using the "resource-based relative value scale" methodology (RBRVS), which inherently gives more weight to specialists. The RBRVS method establishes the relative value of each service physicians provide based on three components: the amount of physician work that goes into the service, the practice expense associated with the service, and the professional liability expense associated with provision of the service.

The "physician work" component, which represents 52% of the total value assigned to each service, takes into account the time it takes to perform the service, the technical skill and physical effort required, the mental effort and judgment necessary, and stress due to the potential risk to the patient. The relative value of each service is further adjusted by a factor that takes into account geographic differences in costs of maintaining a practice. (Expenses are higher in Manhattan than Indianapolis, for example.)

Much of a primary care physician's time is spent in relatively low-cost (but vitally important to patients) activities like counseling, health education, and coordination of care. These activities have been consistently undervalued in the RBRVS system.

Other payers are influenced by the payments and fees that CMS sets. The ACA emphasizes the need to shift care from specialists to primary care practitioners (PCPs), and has included several provisions to make primary practice more attractive.

INCREASING THE NUMBER OF PRIMARY CARE PHYSICIANS

According to the Association of American Medical Colleges' Center for Workforce Studies (2010), four major elements in the ACA are intended to help address the shortage of PCPs:

1. A 10% bonus payment for primary care services provided by family physicians, general internists, geriatricians, and pediatricians
2. An increase in Medicaid payments for primary care services performed by PCPs to 100% of the Medicare rate in 2013 and 2014
3. Grants to develop or expand primary care residency programs
4. Seventy-five percent of Medicare graduate medical education (GME) positions must be reserved for primary care or general surgery

Another solution would be to increase our use of international medical graduates (IMGs). In 1985, IMGs were about 21% of the nation's total supply of doctors. By 2007, they were more than 25% (U.S., DHHS, NCHS, 2010). These are doctors from other countries who receive their basic medical training outside the United States, but come here for residency training. Typically, they establish practices in the United States and many practice in primary care. This approach raises some significant ethical issues, given the shortage of qualified physicians in many nations.

Yet a third option is discussed in the following section of this chapter.

The Supply of Nurses and Nurse Practitioners

HEALTH WORKFORCE ISSUES FOR NURSES AND NURSE PRACTITIONERS

Licensed nurses constitute the single largest occupation in the health care industry (U.S., DHHS, NCHS, 2010). Licensed nurses—registered nurses (RNs), licensed practical nurses (LPNs), licensed vocational nurses (LVNs), and nurses in advanced practice such as nurse practitioners (NPs)—work in a variety of health care settings, including hospitals, homes, schools, clinics, physicians' offices, long-term care facilities, and public health agencies. Nurses play a critical role in the provision of health care because their scope of practice places them in direct contact with patients in most health care environments.

Since the late 1990s, attention has focused on the nursing profession due to a crippling shortage of RNs working in hospitals in the United States and many other countries (Buerhaus & Staiger, 1999). At the same time, recognition of the importance of nursing care to ensuring that patients are safe and have good health care outcomes has increased. How to ensure adequate hospital nurse staffing during a time of shortage has been a widespread challenge and has led to policy efforts to both increase nurse supply and mandate minimum staffing levels in health care facilities.

> *The shortage of primary care physicians has led health care leaders to consider whether other types of health professions can help close the gap.*

More recently, the shortage of primary care physicians has led health care leaders to consider whether other types of health professions can help close the gap. This has become even more important with the passage of the ACA because the expansion of health insurance will increase demand for health care services—and there may not be enough primary care physicians to meet it.

Principally, leaders look to whether nurses with advanced education in the delivery of primary care services—especially **nurse practitioners**—can be deployed more effectively. Nurse practitioner education prepares these professionals to work independently, even though there are barriers to their doing so, as discussed later.

Physician assistants also can play a role in delivering primary care services, although their education and professional standards generally involve working under the direction of a physician, rather than as independent practitioners. There are more than 74,000 physician assistant positions in the United States, so these professionals contribute much to the health care workforce.

LICENSED NURSES, SHORTAGES, AND QUALITY OF CARE

Several types of licensed nurses are involved in the assessment, treatment, and monitoring of patients' diseases and conditions, as well as in patient education and other patient care activities.

RNs comprise the largest group of health care workers in the United States, with nearly 2.6 million employed in nursing positions (U.S., DHHS, HRSA, BHP, 2010). RNs obtain their licenses after completing an associate degree, baccalaureate, or diploma nursing program and passing an examination approved by their state's nursing board.

The legal scope of practice of RNs (**"scope of practice"** is established by state licensing boards and indicates which specific services a licensed health professional is legally allowed to perform) includes assessment of patients, development of care plans, providing intravenous and other medications, administering blood products, and provision of other complex therapies and treatments. As a result of this broad scope of practice, RNs are employed in a wide variety of clinical environments, including those in which patients are severely ill.

LPNs—called licensed vocational nurses (LVNs) in Texas and California—have a narrower scope of practice, which, again, varies across states. They obtain their licenses after completing a 1- or 2-year program at a community college, adult educational program, or private vocational school and passing an examination. In most states, an LPN's scope of practice includes provision of basic hygienic and nursing care, measurement of vital signs, performance of prescribed medical treatments, administration of prescribed medications, and performance of nonmedicated intravenous therapy and blood withdrawal (U.S. Department of Labor, 2010). About 720,000 LPNs and LVNs are employed in the United States, with the majority working in nursing homes and hospitals (U.S., DHHS, NCHS, 2010).

Some RNs continue their education to enter one or more **advanced areas of practice**. In 2008, more than 250,000 RNs have become nurse practitioners, nurse midwives, nurse anesthetists, and clinical nurse specialists. The majority were nurse practitioners (NPs), accounting for 63%. Nurse practitioner education is at the graduate level, although, in the past, many NP education programs conferred a certificate, rather than a degree. NP education prepares students to work in one or more areas of patient care, including family care, pediatrics, geriatrics, adult health, women's health, psychiatry, neonatology, and acute hospital care. NPs are educated to practice independently, although the degree to which they can practice without physician collaboration or supervision differs across states (Dower, O'Neil, and Christian, 2007).

NURSING SHORTAGES

Reports of nursing shortages, especially in U.S. hospitals, have arisen periodically over the past 60 years; there was a shortage reported in the late 1980s and early 1990s, which vanished by the mid-1990s, to be replaced by concerns about an oversupply. Of course, in a normal market, shortages would not last long because wages and income would adjust, so that supply would rise and demand would drop.

However, the nurse market is not "normal," and shortages can be persistent: wages don't rapidly change, supply increases slowly due to the profession's lengthy education requirements, and demand does not easily decline. RN demand is affected by regulations that prevent health care providers from reducing their nurse staffing, including minimum staffing laws and the standards of certification organizations.

Many employers of nurses face limited revenues because their services are reimbursed by government programs and their private revenues are determined by preexisting contracts. Thus, employers cannot easily absorb increased labor costs and they find it difficult to increase wages, even though they cannot reduce their utilization of nurses.

Because RN labor markets do not follow the standard market model, policy makers have reason to intervene when shortages arise. For example, in 2002, California's governor, Gray

Davis, dedicated $60 million to programs to increase the supply of RNs, and his successor, Arnold Schwarzenegger, further expanded funding for nurse education later that decade.

QUALITY OF NURSING CARE

As the most recent hospital nurse shortage emerged, there also was substantial debate about the relationship between staffing reductions that had occurred in the 1990s in acute care hospitals and the quality of patient care (Wunderlich, Sloan, & Davis, 1996). Although nurses are important to ensuring patient safety, it does not necessarily follow that health care organizations should always employ more nurses. Nurse staffing is expensive and the money used to pay nurses also could be used to improve infection control programs, purchase new diagnostic or treatment equipment, or invest in a number of other options that might improve patient care.

In a normal market, the ideal level of nurse staffing would be reached when the marginal cost of nurses equals the marginal benefit of their work. However, as we know, health care markets are not normal! A central problem for hospitals and other health care providers is that they are not paid according to the quality of care they provide and thus they do not have an incentive to increase quality or to hire more nurses to achieve it. Of course, hospitals that are very poor quality often are penalized in the market but, in general, a hospital that provides adequate care receives as much revenue as a hospital that provides excellent care.

In response, some federal and state policy makers have implemented programs designed to improve the quality of care, often through increased nurse staffing. Two strategies can be used: strict regulations for nurse staffing and financial incentives. California has taken the former approach. In 1999, it passed the first U.S. legislation mandating minimum staffing levels for RNs and LVNs working in hospitals. In May 2009, federal legislation was introduced in the Senate (S.1031) by Barbara Boxer (D-CA), largely based on California's regulations. Other states have implemented less stringent regulations, requiring that hospitals have staffing systems based on the severity of illness of their patients.

Financial incentives to improve quality are being used by Medicare and some private insurance companies. Health care providers either are penalized for poor quality care or receive additional payments for excellent care. Because nurses are identified as important contributors to quality, hospitals have a financial incentive to increase nurse staffing to reach quality goals. Because these payment-based strategies that reward quality are fairly new, little is known about whether financial incentives have been successful in improving quality or whether nurse staffing has increased as a result of performance-based payment systems.

NURSE PRACTITIONERS, PRIMARY CARE, AND THE ACA

The expansion of health insurance that will occur as a result of the ACA will increase demand for health care services. The Act's cost projections rely in part on the assumption that cost-effective improvements in population health can be best achieved by providing better access to primary care services (U.S., Government Accountability Office, 2008; MedPAC, 2008).

However, the shortage of primary care physicians has raised concerns that there may not be enough providers to meet primary care needs. Researchers have found that up to 75% of primary care services could be provided by advanced practice registered nurses and physician assistants (PAs) (Sullivan-Marx, 2008), and numerous studies have demonstrated that nurse practitioners provide high-quality patient care with outcomes as good as for patients seen by physicians (Laurant et al., 2004). But, a number of barriers prevent full utilization of nurse practitioners, as well as PAs and other advanced practice RNs.

BARRIERS TO FULL UTILIZATION OF NURSE PRACTITIONERS

The main factor limiting the ability of nurse practitioners to be fully engaged in the delivery of primary care is that the legal scope of practice of NPs is too restrictive in some states. Only 11 states permit NPs to practice independently, without physician involvement (Figure 15.2). The majority of states—27 in 2007—require NPs to practice in collaboration with a physician. The specific definition of "collaboration" varies, but usually requires written protocols for NP practice.

In addition, some physician and health care employer organizations restrict NP practice more than others, and thus the implementation of the collaboration requirements can be strict or liberal. In 10 states, NPs must be supervised by physicians. In all states, NPs may prescribe medications, but most require some degree of physician involvement,

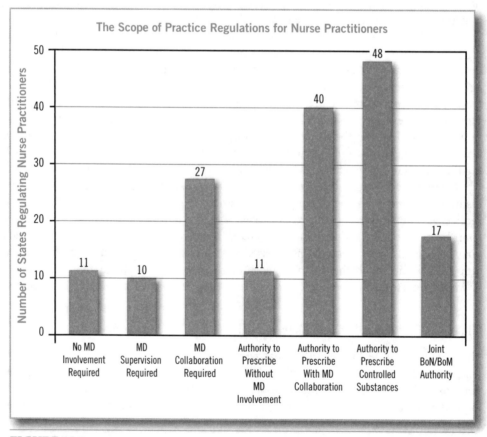

FIGURE 15.2

Scope of practice regulations for nurse practitioners.
Source: Adapted by the author (Spetz) from: Dower, C., O'Neil, E., & Christian, S. (2007). Overview of nurse practitioner scopes of practice in the United States. Retrieved July 20, 2010 from http://www.futurehealth. ucsf.edu/Public/Publications-and-Resources/Content.aspx?topic=Overview_of_Nurse_Practitioner_Scopes_ of_Practice_in_the_United_States

ranging from limited formularies to restrictions on the quantity of a drug that can be pre-scribed, such as 72-hour or 30-day supplies.

Rules regarding the reimbursement of NP services also can limit their utilization. A variety of state and federal policies and regulations control the payments made for NP services. Medicare limits NP payment to 85% of the physician payment, although some NP services are billed directly through the supervising or collaborating physician at the full rate. State Medicaid programs vary in their reimbursement rules. Private insurance companies can establish their own reimbursement policies and, in some states, they are permitted to refuse to reimburse NPs directly. There are few studies on the impacts of these varying payment policies on the ability of NPs to provide health services, but it is likely that changes in reimbursement policies could provide incentives for more efficient use of these providers in the delivery of primary care.

Some nurse practitioners do not work in the field of primary care. In 2008, about 30% of employed NPs did not have the job title of "nurse practitioner" (U.S., DHHS, 2010). Some NPs work in management and others work in specialty care or acute care. There are a number of reasons NPs may work outside their traditional roles, including limitations to their scope of practice, difficulties receiving reimbursement for primary care services, and differences in pay between hospitals and non-hospital employers. In some areas, NPs may earn higher incomes working as hospital managers than as primary care providers (Scheffler, 2008).

IMPROVING NURSE PRACTITIONER UTILIZATION

When health professionals cannot practice to the full extent of their competence, there are negative effects on health care costs, access, and quality. Restrictions on NP practice and reimbursement do not serve the public well, even though these restrictions are often justified as necessary to protect public welfare.

Many analysts recommend that current trends toward expanded scope of practice of NPs—to the maximum level of their education and competence—should continue (Dower et al., 2007). Moreover, efforts should be made to reduce variations in scope of practice laws across states because these differences inhibit NPs from moving to locales where their care may be the most needed.

The reimbursement of NPs for their services needs to be examined carefully. One of the reasons that NPs can deliver services cost efficiently is that their educational require-ments are less onerous than those of physicians and their incomes are correspondingly lower. Increasing NP payment to match physicians' may not be the most efficient policy, because doing so might shift demand toward physicians and reduce NP utilization further. But, NP reimbursements should be sufficient to ensure that NPs can afford to work in primary care. Increasing reimbursement for primary care services would likely increase the supply of both primary care physicians and NPs. Changes in payment programs to support interprofessional, team-oriented practice have the potential to enhance the ability of all primary care providers to meet health care needs.

Conclusion

The demand for health care workers is affected by factors that determine demand for medical care. Because patients usually do not directly pay for health care, the demand for care is not sensitive to its price. Thus, the classic market model of demand does not apply well to health care. Health care policy changes, such as the 2010 ACA, can have significant effects on the demand for health workers, particularly increasing demand for primary care health workers. Primary care is important to improving population health and improving the efficiency of the health care system.

At the same time, the supply of health care workers also does not clearly match a market model. Health worker supply is constrained by licensing requirements, limited education spaces, and scope of practice regulations. Shortages of registered nurses have occurred cyclically for decades due to these characteristics, with a protracted shortage lasting throughout the early 2000s.

The availability of primary care physicians is further limited because primary care is reimbursed less than other specialty medical services. In the midst of a primary care physician shortage, attention has turned to the potential for other highly skilled professionals, including nurse practitioners and physician assistants, to help meet primary care needs. These professionals face barriers to their ability to provide care to their fullest knowledge, including restrictions on the scope of their practice, limited reimbursements, and higher earnings in other areas of work.

The principles discussed here can be applied to other health workforce issues. For example, there has been concern that the delivery of health care would improve if there were more minorities in the health professions. Increasing compensation to minority health professionals would increase their supply, perhaps through loan repayment or other grants. Another approach would be to reduce the cost of education for minorities, such as through scholarships, which would increase the return on investment in education and spur an increase in supply.

Strategies to increase the productivity of doctors in order to encourage better quality can also be developed. Financial incentives that reward providing high-quality care, such as bonus payments for achieving performance targets, can increase quality. Investments that reduce the effort required to increase quality—such as effective computerized patient health records, development of skills in cultural competence, and interprofessional teams—can achieve the same goal. Programs to support quality improvement can also be subsidized by the government or nonprofit organizations.

Concerns about shortages of geriatricians and nurses with specialization in geriatrics also can be considered within the framework presented in this chapter. Why do nurses and physicians not choose these specialties? Is it because they pay poorly? Is it because the work is more difficult and thus requires higher earnings to compensate for a more challenging job? Reimbursement of services provided by geriatric specialists, and subsidies for education, can help to address these problems.

Policy makers and health care leaders can consider many policies to address primary care workforce shortages and ensure that health care workers are able to provide care at the maximum possible capacity. Changes to reimbursement policies, addressing scope of practice limitations, and ensuring adequate educational capacity are among the key policies that can ensure that the ACA is implemented effectively.

DISCUSSION QUESTIONS

1. How do we know when we have too many or too few doctors, nurses, or other health professionals?
2. What determines the supply of doctors and nurses?

3. How will health reform impact the health care workforce?
4. Why is primary care so important?
5. With the global shortage of doctors, especially in less developed countries, is relying on international medical graduates an ethical solution to U.S. primary care shortages?
6. To what extent can nurses substitute for doctors?
7. Why are incomes of primary care doctors lower than incomes for specialists?
8. How can reimbursement policy improve the supply of primary care?

CASE STUDIES

CASE STUDY #1

According to the article "How to fix the doctor shortage," by D. G. Kirch, published in the *Wall Street Journal* on January 5, 2010, "the United States will face a shortage of more than 125,000 physicians in the next 15 years . . . [and] . . . at least 16,000 more primary care physicians are needed today."

A decade ago, the story reports, new patients had to wait an average of 8 days to see a family or general practitioner. The author cites criticisms of the U.S. health care workforce for lacking sufficient primary care, and notes the widespread opinion that this situation is directly related to poor reimbursement. "The physician shortage is, in part, a result of expectations in the 1990s that managed care and primary care would greatly drive down the need for physicians, particularly specialists. However, these expectations fell short against the rising needs of an aging, growing population. . ." (Kirch, 2010).

Others have argued that there is no shortage of physicians and, rather, that the problem lies in the uneven distribution of physicians between rural and urban areas. Still others blame government policies that drive physicians out of the health care field and say, therefore, that government should not be counted on for the solution to the problem. Now, with health reform, whether there is an overall shortage or not, there definitely needs to be a different mix of doctors, particularly, more doctors who are trained in primary care.

CASE STUDY #1 DISCUSSION

1. Is there a shortage of physicians overall, or only in key areas? If the latter, what policies might encourage more physicians to enter important fields like primary care and geriatrics?
2. What are the key barriers to increasing the number of primary care physicians?
3. What policies might be used to address these issues?

CASE STUDY #2

In July 2010, *PRNewswire* published an announcement by U. S. Department of Health and Human Services Secretary Kathleen Sebelius of $15 million in federal funding for the operation of 10 nurse-managed health centers. The centers would be used in the education and training of nurse practitioners. Such centers are staffed by nurse practitioners and provide comprehensive primary health care services to residents of medically underserved communities.

Advanced preparation of nurse practitioners, which takes place at the graduate level (Master's, post-masters, and doctoral degrees) employs a strong curriculum, which adds to the knowledge and skills of practicing professional nurses. These programs of study prepare fully accountable clinicians to provide care for a range of conditions and severity of illnesses.

However, physicians groups are not necessarily supportive. For example, the American College of Physicians published a position paper in 2009 that included the following:

Position 1: Physicians and nurse practitioners complete training with different levels of knowledge, skills, and abilities that while not equivalent, are complementary. As trained health care professionals, physicians and nurse practitioners share a commitment to providing high-quality care. However, physicians are often the most appropriate health care professional for many patients.

Position 4: In the patient-centered medical home (PCMH) model, care for patients is best served by a multidisciplinary team where the clinical team is led by a physician.

CASE STUDY #2 DISCUSSION

1. What types of patients would benefit most from a physician? From a nurse practitioner?
2. Why is there a shortage of primary care providers? Why is this shortage more severe in some regions?
3. What types of barriers and difficulties exist for nurse practitioner-led practices? Will the new grant program help solve any of these barriers?

REFERENCES

Association of American Medical Colleges' Center for Workforce Studies. (2010). *Health Care Reform and the Health Workforce: Workforce Provisions included in the Patient Protection and Affordable Care Act, P.L.111–148 (HR 3590).* Retrieved July 20, 2010, from http://www.aamc.org/workforce/healthcarereformleg.pdf

American College of Physicians. (2009). *Nurse practitioners in primary care.* Philadelphia, PA: Author.

Baicker, K., Buckles, K. S., & Chandra, A. (2006). Geographic variation in the appropriate use of cesarean delivery. *Health Affairs, 25,* w355–w367.

Buerhaus, P. I., & Staiger, D. O. (1999). Trouble in the nurse labor market? Recent trends and future outlook. *Health Affairs, 18,* 214–222.

Dower, C., O'Neil, E., & Christian, S. (2007). Overview of nurse practitioner scopes of practice in the United States. Retrieved July 20, 2010 from http://www.futurehealth.ucsf.edu/Public/Publications-and-Resources/Content.aspx?topic=Overview_of_Nurse_Practitioner_Scopes_of_Practice_in_the_United_States

Ehrenberg, R., & Smith, R. (1991). *Modern labor economics, 4th edition*. New York, NY: HarperCollins Publishers, Inc.

Friedberg, M. W., Hussey, P. S., & Schneider, E. C. (2010). Primary care: A critical review of the evidence on quality and costs of health care. *Health Affairs, 29*, 766–772.

Grundy, P., Hagan, K. R., Hansen, J. C., & Grumbach, K. (2010). The multi-stakeholder movement for primary care renewal and reform. *Health Affairs, 29*, 791–798.

Kirch, D. G. (2010, January 5). How to fix the doctor shortage. *Wall Street Journal*. Retrieved July 20, 2010 from http://online.wsj.com/article/SB1000142405274870348 3604574630321885059520.html

Laurant M., Reeves D., Hermens R., Braspenning J., Grol R., & Sibbald B. (2004). Substitution of doctors by nurses in primary care. *Cochrane Database of Systematic Reviews*, Issue 4. Art. No.: CD001271.

Margolius, D., & Bodenheimer, T. (2010). Transforming primary care: From past practice to the practice of the future. *Health Affairs, 29*, 779–784.

Medicare Payment Advisory Commission (MedPAC). (2008). Promoting the use of primary care. Chapter 2 in *Report to the Congress: Reforming the Delivery System*. Washington, D.C.: Author.

PRNewswire. (2010, July 6). $15 Million in funding announced for nurse practitioner-led clinics. Retrieved July 20, 2010, from http://www.prnewswire.com/news-releases/15-million-in-funding-announced-for-nurse-practitioner-led-clinics-97853529.html

Scheffler, R. M. (2008). *Is there a doctor in the house? Market signals and tomorrow's supply of doctors*. Palo Alto, CA: Stanford University Press.

Scheffler, R. M., Liu, J. X., Kinfu, Y., & Dal Poz, M. R. (2008). Forecasting the global shortages of physicians: An economic- and needs-based approach. *The Bulletin of the World Health Organization, 86*, 516–523.

Sullivan-Marx, E. (2008). Lessons learned from advanced practice nursing payment. *Policy, Politics, & Nursing Practice, 9*, 121–126.

U.S., Department of Health and Human Services (DHHS), Health Resources and Services Administration (HRSA), Bureau of Health Professions (BHP). (2008). *The physician workforce: Projections and research into current issues affecting supply and demand*. Retrieved July 20, 2010, from ftp://ftp.hrsa.gov/bhpr/workforce/physicianworkforce.pdf

U.S., DHHS, HRSA, BHP. (2010). *The registered nurse population: Initial findings from the 2008 National Sample Survey of Registered Nurses*. Retrieved July 20, 2010, from http://bhpr.hrsa.gov/healthworkforce/rnsurvey/

U.S., DHHS, National Center for Health Statistics. (2010). *Health, United States, 2009: With special feature on medical technology*. Retrieved July 20, 2010, from http://www.cdc.gov/nchs/data/hus/hus09.pdf

U.S., Department of Labor. (2010). Licensed practical and licensed vocational nurses. *Occupational Outlook Handbook, 2010-11 Edition*. Washington D.C.: United States Department of Labor.

U.S., Government Accountability Office (GAO). (2008). Primary care professionals—Recent supply trends, projections, and valuation of services. Testimony Before the Committee on Health, Education, Labor, and Pensions, U.S. Senate. *GAO-08-472T*.

Wunderlich, G. S., Sloan, F. A., & Davis, C. K. (Eds.). (1996). *Nursing staff in hospitals and nursing homes: Is it adequate?* Washington, D.C.: National Academy Press.

16

HEALTH INFORMATION TECHNOLOGY

Roger Kropf

KEY WORDS

computerized physician order entry (CPOE)
clinical quality
electronic health record (EHR)
american recovery and reinvestment act
    (ARRA)
health information technology (HIT)
health information technology for economic
    and clinical health (HITECH)
"meaningful use"
health information exchanges (HIE)

health insurance portability and
    accountability act (HIPAA)
clinical decision support
regional health information organizations (RHIO)
return on investment (ROI)
radio-frequency identification (RFID)
authorization
authentication
encryption

LEARNING OBJECTIVES

- Identify why collecting and using information is important to patients, clinicians, and payers
- Describe the support and involvement of the federal government in the implementation of information technology in hospitals and physician offices
- Illustrate how information technology can help improve the quality of medical care
- Show how technology can increase patient satisfaction
- Provide examples of how information technology can help reduce or control the increase in health care costs
- Describe some of the issues that face providers and some of the options for dealing with them

TOPICAL OUTLINE

- Why managing information is important in health care
- How the federal government is involved in HIT implementation
- Improving clinical quality through HIT
- Improving health care service quality through HIT
- Opportunities for controlling health care costs
- Current issues

Why Managing Information Is Important in Health Care

Enormous advances in medical knowledge, technology, and the training of health care professionals have been made in the last 100 years. We know more and have better tools for preventing, finding, and curing disease. Yet the way in which information is managed in most health care organizations hasn't changed nearly as much. Most physicians, nurses, and other clinicians still write on pieces of paper which are then filed. When information is needed, someone goes and finds that paper and brings it to the clinician. If a bank operated that way, tellers would be writing checking account balances in a ledger, which would have to be retrieved every time someone wanted money.

In 2009, only 1.5% of U.S. hospitals had a comprehensive electronic records system (i.e., present in all clinical units) and an additional 7.6% had a basic system (i.e., present in at least one clinical unit). **Computerized physician order entry (CPOE)** for medications has been implemented in only 17% of hospitals. Larger hospitals, those located in urban areas, and teaching hospitals were more likely to have electronic records systems (Jha et al., 2009). In 2008, 4% of physicians reported having an extensive, fully functional electronic records system, and 13% reported having a basic system (DesRoches et al., 2008).

Health care organizations have fallen behind other organizations in managing information. What makes this a serious concern for all of us is that medical knowledge saves lives and errors cost lives. We examine why managing information is important for the patient, the provider, and the employers and insurers who pay for health care.

IMPROVING CLINICAL QUALITY

Walk into a hospital and go to one of the floors. For a particular patient there are dozens if not hundreds of pages in the medical chart, including reports of laboratory tests, orders for drugs, and notes written by nurses and doctors. Paper records may lead to errors, some with serious or fatal consequences. Some of the handwriting is hard to read. It's left up to the nurse or physician to decide how to interpret new information that is arriving and to find the information they need. A clinician in another department who is treating the patient has no access to the entire record.

In contrast, medical records stored in a computer appear as easy-to-read text or graphics. When information arrives that requires action, the nurse or physician can be automatically alerted. The information can be searched. Clinicians in different places can all view the information they need to see.

This is only one application of information technology that offers the potential to improve the **clinical quality** of care. For the patient, it can mean shorter hospital stays and fewer physician visits, a faster recovery, and fewer complications due to errors. For the physician, the technology can save time and support better decisions. For the payer— the employer, the insurance company, or government—the result can be lower medical expenses. Despite the benefits, technologies such as the computer-stored or **electronic health record (EHR)** exist in a minority of U.S. hospitals and physician offices. Some of the reasons are examined later and include both the cost of the technology and uncertainty about its effects on productivity of physicians.

IMPROVING PATIENT SATISFACTION AND ACCESS TO CARE

A patient who visits a physician's office and the radiology and laboratory departments of a hospital is very likely to be asked for the same information (name, Social Security number, etc.) three times. It would be hard to name another service in the United States that requires such redundant (and boring) requests for information.

> *The ways in which health care organizations fail to use information technology to serve patients grow more obvious all the time.*

The ways in which health care organizations fail to use information technology to serve patients grow more obvious all the time. I can track the progress of a package from FedEx or UPS hour by hour, but I have absolutely no idea where my blood test is once I've left a doctor's office. I can order movie tickets on the Internet, but have to wait on hold for a receptionist when I call to make an appointment with a doctor.

Improving patient satisfaction through information technology should be easy. We are increasingly using the technology in our everyday lives. There's nothing to invent, yet many health care organizations haven't adopted technology that has become common-place for other services.

The problem goes beyond patient satisfaction. Technology can make it much easier for patients to communicate with providers. A patient who has a question about a medication may now have to make multiple phone calls to contact a physician. This information could be provided by e-mail or by accessing information on a Web site. Patients may not know whom to contact to provide a service they feel that they need, whereas that information could be made available on the Internet. Technology affects access to care as well as patient satisfaction.

CONTROLLING COSTS

Chronic conditions like asthma have to be managed. Patients must be educated on how to monitor their conditions and to take appropriate actions. Information technology can help by facilitating the monitoring of patients and delivering information to them. There are devices that asthma patients can breathe into and then attach to a phone line to transmit the data to a clinician, who can provide advice on when to begin taking medication. Expensive visits to the emergency room are avoided. Personalized Web sites can provide access to tests and records that can help an emergency room physician diagnose a condition faster and avoid complications that lead to longer hospital stays. E-mail can be used to send messages from clinicians and to forward health education materials that permit chronically ill patients to manage their diseases and avoid acute episodes that lead to expensive hospital stays.

Information technology can also be used to improve efficiency. Scheduling software can track the use of operating rooms and surgical equipment to assure that both are available when needed and neither is underutilized. Inventory management systems can control the use of drugs and other supplies.

The benefits for the patient are lower health care expenses as a result of avoiding more expensive or unnecessary treatment. Payers can avoid medical expenses normally reimbursed by insurance. To the extent that hospitals have signed agreements to assume the financial risk of providing care, they can also benefit. Physicians can benefit from technologies that improve the efficiency of care and save their time.

Although the financial impact of technologies to improve clinical quality and patient satisfaction may be hard to measure, a range of information technologies is available with the proven ability to control costs. Yet they have not been widely adopted by hospitals and physicians.

How the Federal Government Is Involved in HIT Implementation

A 2009 survey revealed that among hospitals without electronic records systems, the most commonly cited barriers to acquisition were inadequate capital for purchase (74%), concerns about maintenance costs (44%), resistance on the part of physicians (36%), unclear return on investment (32%), and lack of availability of staff with adequate expertise in information technology (30%). Hospitals that had adopted electronic records systems were less likely to cite these concerns (except for physicians' resistance) as major barriers to adoption (Jha et al. 2009)

Other barriers that have been cited are the technical and logistic challenges involved in installing, maintaining, and updating EHRs, and consumers' and physicians' concerns about the privacy and security of electronic health information (Blumenthal, 2009).

In a 2008 survey of physicians who did not have access to an electronic records system, the most commonly cited barriers to adoption were capital costs (66%), not finding a system that met their needs (54%), uncertainty about their return on the investment (50%), and concern that a system would become obsolete (44%). Physicians with electronic health records tended to highlight the same barriers but less frequently than did nonadopters (DesRoches et al., 2008).

All of these concerns are addressed in provisions of the 2009 **American Recovery and Reinvestment Act (ARRA)**. ARRA marked the end of the debate over whether the federal government should invest significant funds to promote information technology (IT) implementation in hospitals and physician offices. It included a $19 billion program to promote the adoption and use of **health information technology (HIT)** and especially EHRs. The HIT components of the stimulus package, the **Health Information Technology for Economic and Clinical Health (HITECH) Act** offered payments for the "meaningful use" of a "certified" EHR.

"The provisions of the HITECH Act are best understood not as investments in technology per se but as efforts to improve the health of Americans and the performance of their health care system" (Blumenthal, 2010). The concern of the Obama administration and Congress was that federal money should lead to quality improvements, not just in an individual hospital or physician office, but in the community.

The U.S. Department of Health and Human Services (DHHS) defined **meaningful use** carefully so as to further five health care goals: "improving the quality, safety, and efficiency of care while reducing disparities; engaging patients and families in their care; promoting public and population health; improving care coordination; and promoting the privacy and security of EHRs" (Blumenthal, 2010). "Meaningful use" includes more than the use of IT to record and retrieve information (potentially reducing errors from causes such as illegible handwriting). Hospitals and physicians would also have to be able to exchange information and report information on the quality of the services they provide.

To address the lack of infrastructure for the exchange of health information, the federal government is channeling more than $560 million in HITECH Act monies to state governments to lead the development of exchange capabilities within and across their jurisdictions (Blumenthal, 2010). **Health information exchanges (HIEs)** at the regional and state levels would provide the infrastructure for exchanging information, including standards for how data should be created, agreements among participants, and the required computer resources.

HITECH offered a total of $17 billion in payments to hospitals and physicians in the form of increases in Medicare payments. Hospitals and physicians would have to meet "stage one" standards for meaningful use and begin using a certified EHR, in order to receive these payments, starting in 2011.

Physicians can receive as much as $18,000 in additional Medicare payments in the first year if they adopt a certified EHR in 2011 or 2012, at least $15,000 if they adopt in 2013, and somewhat less if they do so in 2014. Incentives end in 2016. "Thus, physicians demonstrating meaningful use starting in 2011 could collect $44,000 over 5 years" (Blumenthal, 2009). Meanwhile, hospitals demonstrating meaningful use of EHRs in 2011 will earn a one-time bonus payment of $2 million, plus an add-on to their Medicare payments.

"HITECH also threatens financial penalties to spur adoption. Physicians who are not using certified EHRs meaningfully by 2015 will lose 1% of their Medicare fees, then 2% in 2016, and 3% in 2017" (Blumenthal, 2009). Hospitals face penalties beginning in 2015 in the form of cuts in their annual reimbursement updates under the diagnosis related group system.

Receiving HITECH funds offers a number of challenges to hospitals and physicians. They have to find the money to invest in order to be paid later. (A program available to physicians serving a high proportion of Medicaid patients does offer a partial advance payment.) Hospitals and physicians who do not have an EHR (or were using an outdated one) have to locate a certified EHR and implement it to meet the meaningful use criteria by 2011. They—and their vendors alike—are expected to face a shortage of trained staff, especially those with both clinical and information technology experience.

To assist, the federal government offered contracts to community colleges that would create short-term certificate programs to train HIT workers. Five universities were given contracts for the development of curricula for the colleges to use.

Nine universities received grants totaling $32 million to train professionals for specialized HIT roles. Most trainees in these programs will complete intensive courses of study in 12 months or less and receive a university-issued certificate of advanced training. Other trainees supported by these grants will study toward masters' degrees.

The government has committed almost $650 million under the HITECH Act to the creation of a network of up to 70 regional HIT extension centers. Focusing initially on primary care providers in small practices, these centers will offer advice on which EHR systems to purchase and then assist physicians and hospitals in becoming meaningful EHR users (Blumenthal, 2010).

A Beacon Communities program was established to designate communities capable of collecting evidence of the positive effects of the use of HIT. Grants for $220 million were signed with 15 nonprofit organizations or government entities to build and strengthen HIT infrastructure and health information exchange capabilities.

Strategic Health IT Advanced Research Projects (SHARP) awards totaling $60 million were provided to four advanced research institutions ($15 million each) to focus on solving current and future challenges that represent barriers to adoption and meaningful use of HIT.

Physician and hospital concerns and uncertainty about which products to buy were addressed in the establishment of certification requirements and federal designation of organizations that would certify that products meet those requirements.

HITECH strengthens protections for the confidentiality of health care information as well. It extends the privacy and security regulations of the **Health Insurance**

Portability and Accountability Act (HIPAA) to health information vendors not previously covered by the law, including businesses such as Google and Microsoft, when they partner with health care providers to create personal health records for patients. It requires health care organizations to notify patients promptly when personal health data have been compromised, and it limits the commercial use of such information (Blumenthal, 2009).

Federal HIT investments are intended to improve the quality of health care while stimulating efficiencies in how care is provided. These were aspirations, not certainties. Critics argued that only limited improvement would result and suggested the possibility of negative quality outcomes, that patient privacy might be compromised, that little reduction in the cost of health care was likely. In any case, they argued, hospitals would not be able to implement EHRs effectively within the federal timetable. In particular, they worried that physicians would ignore the subsidy because of their concern about a loss of productivity and the complexity of introducing an EHR, especially in small practices.

Who is right will be known only as the provisions of HITECH are implemented over the next few years. The remainder of this chapter explores the possibility of positive change while describing in greater detail the challenges ahead.

Improving Clinical Quality Through HIT

WHERE ARE WE? CURRENT ISSUES AND PROBLEMS

Institute of Medicine (IOM) reports in 1999 and 2001 focused attention on how the quality of medical care could be improved by the adoption of information technology. In *Using Information Technology* the IOM stated that "much of the potential of IT to improve quality is predicated on the automation of at least some types of clinical data." They discussed four of the barriers to this automation: privacy concerns, the need for standards, financial requirements, and human factor issues. The first two were partially addressed by Congress through passage of HIPAA, which set standards for maintaining the security and privacy of personal health information and for information required for transmitting insurance claims. HITECH has provisions that address all four concerns.

The human factor issues include the highly variable IT-related knowledge and experience of the health care workforce and varying receptivity to learning and acquiring these skills. Disruptions in patient care result in lost revenues for many clinicians. HIT may alter the clinician and patient relationship, which may be threatening to clinicians—for example, when patients can use the Internet to find data on their performance compared to that of other clinicians.

Many technologies have been shown to improve clinical quality and outcomes. Some of them are described in the next few pages. The number of providers that use them is small and has grown slowly since the publication of the IOM's 1999 report. How to accelerate adoption is a major issue for all payers.

TECHNOLOGIES FOR CLINICAL QUALITY IMPROVEMENT

Shortliffe and Perreault (1990) have categorized the role of computers in **clinical decision support** as tools for information management, tools for focusing attention, and tools for patient-specific consultation. Each category offers the opportunity to improve how care is provided. Systems that manage information can gather and display relevant information about the patient; systems that focus attention can alert the clinician to conditions that should be dealt with, such as abnormal lab values; and those that provide consultation or advice use patient-specific data and the latest information or judgments about appropriate care. The advice might be what antibiotic to use, taking into account patient allergies, age, and other relevant factors. Just by moving from hand-written records to computer entry, errors resulting from legibility could be eliminated and data made available to anyone with on-line access.

Reducing Medication Errors

Unlike paper ordering, computerized physician order entry (CPOE) systems allow for interaction between the clinician and information stored in the computer. A study of pre- scriptions written by health care providers at 12 community practices in the Hudson Valley region of New York compared the number and severity of prescription errors between 15 health care providers who adopted e-prescribing and 15 who continued to write prescrip- tions by hand. The study found that those using an electronic system to write prescriptions were seven times less likely to make errors than those writing prescriptions by hand. The providers who adopted e-prescribing used a commercial, stand-alone system that pro- vides dosing recommendations and checks for drug-allergy interactions, drug-drug inter- actions, and duplicate drugs. After one year, the percentage of errors dropped from 42.5% to 6.6% for the providers using the electronic system (Kaushal, Kern, Barrón, Quaresimo, & Abramson, 2010).

Studies in hospitals have also shown a reduction in errors when CPOE is used (Kaushal, Shojania, & Bates, 2003), but at least until recently, fewer than 5% of hospitals had the technology to allow physicians to entry orders directly into the computer (Cutler, Feldman, & Horwitz, 2005; Jha et al., 2009). CPOE systems have been shown to reduce the incidence of serious medication errors by as much as 55% (Bates et al., 1998). A medica- tion error may nevertheless occur if the patient has received medications from a number of physicians, and that information may not be available to the prescriber. A physician may order an inappropriate prescription. This is a particular problem during the transi- tion to and from a hospital. It is rare for Americans to have a single medical record that covers all contacts with health care providers.

The creation of a data repository for an entire system of hospitals and physicians, or the sharing of information among providers in a community, would help resolve this problem.

Adherence to Clinical Guidelines and Protocols

Clinical guidelines and protocols can be offered to physicians as part of a CPOE system. When an order is entered, the physician can be reminded that a particular test or pro- cedure is suggested by a guideline. For example one study showed that tools improved clinician compliance with National Asthma Education Prevention Program guidelines (Bell et al., 2010).

The physician can be asked to provide a written justification for not following the guideline or even be asked to seek approval from a department head or medical director for ordering a test or drug not deemed necessary or appropriate. The absence of an order can be noted and a reminder or alert sent to the physician or nurse. For example, if the medication order log doesn't show that aspirin has been ordered upon discharge for a patient who has suffered a heart attack, a reminder can be sent (Dexter et al., 2001).

> *Storing patient records in a computer opens up a number of possibilities for improving their availability and accuracy.*

Availability and Accuracy of Patient Records

Storing patient records in a computer opens up a number of possibilities for improving their availability and accuracy. Whereas a paper record is available in only one location, computerized patient records can be accessed from multiple locations in the same building or another state. Clinicians can consult with each other on the care of the patient.

With the development of Internet tools and standards (including browsers such as Firefox and Internet Explorer), it has became possible to offer access to patient records to anyone by giving them a password or other method of identification and authorization. "Web-enabled" systems are offered by health care software vendors to allow such access. Patient records can also be made available to patients, who can then examine and verify medical information.

If clerks enter data from hand-written documents into a computer, the accuracy of that data could be worse than the paper record. A trained nurse will interpret a physician's handwriting or call to verify questionable information. Clerks type what they believe they see. The great advance in accuracy from computerized records comes when clinicians enter the information themselves or it is automatically sent from a lab or other equipment through a connection called an interface. Equipment manufacturers now offer such interfaces. Getting clinicians to enter information directly is more difficult because it involves a change in the location and method of data entry. The technologies to assist in data entry include wireless systems that connect the clinician to the computer from a patient room or hallway and devices such as personal digital assistants (PDAs) and tablet computers.

Regardless of whether a clerk, nurse, or physician is entering data, computer systems can check whether data are missing and whether they are logical given what is known about the patient. This can be as simple as checking the date of a lab test and rejecting one that precedes the date of a hospital patient's admission. Or it could be a more complex check that rejects a procedure inconsistent with other information, such as diagnosis. Such "edit checks" are important for receiving payment from an insurance company, which will run similar checks and reject claims with illogical data, delaying payment.

Patients usually see physicians and hospitals whose computer systems aren't linked. Efforts are now being made within hospital systems and even communities to provide such information either through connections between computer systems or "data repositories" that can be accessed by all providers.

Increasing awareness of the importance of having access to all the medical records for a patient has led to substantial federal support under the HITECH act for the development of HIEs and **regional health information organizations (RHIOs).** Such organizations have developed in many communities (eHealth Initiative, 2009). As an example, the Indiana Network for Patient Care (INPC) includes information from the state's five major hospital systems (15 separate hospitals), the county and state public health departments, and Indiana Medicaid. It provides cross-institutional access to physicians in emergency rooms and hospitals. The network includes and delivers laboratory, radiology, dictation, and other documents to a majority of Indianapolis office practices (McDonald et al., 2005).

Access to Knowledge

Presenting information when it is needed is one type of "decision support," and information technology is available that can assist the clinician. The National Library of Medicine's Medline or PubMed (http://www.ncbi.nlm.nih.gov/pubmed/), allow clinicians to search for and retrieve journal articles. (See also the National Center for Biotechnology Information Web site, www.ncbi.nlm.nih.gov). However, it is up to the clinician to extract the information that would be useful for a particular decision.

PDAs and smart phones have become popular devices for providing specific information when clinicians need it. Software such as ePocrates (www.epocrates.com) allows physicians to access drug information that is constantly updated, unlike a book on the shelf.

Such information is not specific to the institution where the clinician practices. Guidelines or protocols for specific institutions nevertheless can be made available using computer systems in a hospital or physician practice. Such knowledge can be provided passively or actively. In passive systems, the clinician asks for knowledge or advice. In active systems, the knowledge is presented to the clinician when a problem or diagnosis is entered or when a test, procedure, or medication is ordered. This information could include citations from the latest medical journals. These are sometimes referred to as "evidence-based systems," because the information comes from evidence obtained through clinical research.

If the clinician is using a computer linked to the facility's system, information from the medical record can be used to tailor the information that is provided. For example, if a patient is allergic to penicillin, information on only appropriate antibiotics can be provided. Data in a clinical data repository can be analyzed and presented, such as the effectiveness of different antibiotics in treating specific types of infections seen in the hospital (Evans et al., 1998).

Computer systems can therefore greatly improve access to knowledge by presenting knowledge at the point of care and using data stored in clinical systems.

Improving Health Care Service Quality Through HIT

A comparison of the experience of a bank customer and a patient who visits a physician's office suggests the extent to which health care providers have fallen behind in adopting information technology. Banks allow the retrieval of most information and many transactions using an automated teller. Many transactions that don't involve a physical object such as cash or checks can be carried out online using a secure Internet site. Customers can utilize inter-bank networks to carry out transactions at a different bank, even in foreign countries. Most patients can do very little using a computer. They cannot retrieve information, make a request for services, such as the renewal of a prescription, or communicate with anyone in the physician's office. Records from a physician's office can't be accessed even by emergency room physicians in a nearby hospital.

If the health system used the technology now commonly available for other services (e.g., database access via the Internet), information would be available to consumers and providers at any time. Patients would not have to wait on hold during a telephone call to obtain their blood test results, nor would physicians have to wait for a letter or fax to receive the results of consultations they requested. Our current paper-based system for moving information results in delays that affect both patient satisfaction and the quality of care.

There are a number of explanations for why health care providers have not implemented technologies that are commonplace in banking, retail sales, and other consumer services. Often cited is the lack of money. HIT competes with technologies for diagnosis and treatment—technologies that are both expensive and constantly emerging. Faced with the choice of acquiring an improved magnetic resonance imaging (MRI) scanner or patient access to medical records, the choice is often the former. Philosophical differences concerning access to information may also inhibit adoption. Although no bank employee will deny that customers should have access to their bank records, health care providers differ in their opinions on whether full access by a patient to medical records is important, even though HIPAA makes that a patient right. There are differing opinions on whether patients can appropriately interpret the information without a physician's guidance.

In the absence of a strong consensus for full and easy access, there is less incentive for the information system investments that are needed. Patient expectations may be another barrier. Patients may have no expectation of easy access to information and don't consider this an important factor in choosing a physician. A bank that failed to provide 24-hour, 7-day access to cash and information would quickly not have customers. A physician's office or hospital that offers no online information can still be full.

To understand what expectations patients can and should have, we need to describe the available technologies. How could information technology improve both patient satisfaction and access to services?

TECHNOLOGIES FOR IMPROVING SERVICE QUALITY

Improving Access to Information and Services

Web sites are the most obvious way to provide online information. But personalization and two-way interaction can also be provided that allows patients to customize the information they receive and actually carry out transactions, such as appointment scheduling.

My HealtheVet (MHV) (www.myhealth.va.gov) is a personal Web site offered by the U.S. Department of Veterans Affairs (VA) to veterans. It provides access to health information, links to federal and VA benefits and resources, a personal health journal, and VA prescription refill ordering. The personal health journal includes the opportunity for veterans to track their health status by recording blood pressure, cholesterol, and so on, in a section called Track Health. A personal information section contains the veteran's registration profile and emergency contacts. Care-related health records, such as treatment locations and health care providers, is in a section called Get Care.

Both Microsoft HealthVault (http://www.healthvault.com/) and Google Health (https://www.google.com/health) have been developed as similar personal health records (PHRs). A problem with previous efforts was the need for patients to enter all of the data. Both companies have sought agreements with prominent health care organization that would allow updating of the PHR by the health care organization. For an example, see CareGroup's PatientSite, which offers access to both products and a demonstration (https://www.patientsite.org).

Online Communication With Clinicians

Once a visit to a physician is over, most patients rely on the telephone for further communication with the doctor's office. This is, at best, indirect and often frustrating. Patients are put on hold or asked to leave a message for a busy physician who will call back (one hopes). Calls may be returned when the patient is not available, leading to "telephone tag" that frustrates both parties.

Phone calls and voicemail are no longer the only option for communication between physicians and patients. E-mail applications include RelayHealth (www.relayhealth.com) and iHealth by Medfusion (http://medfusion.net/ihealth/).

Vendors of hospital and physician information systems are offering applications that allow access to medical information and the use of e-mail to communicate between clinicians, too. Examples are Elysium Clinical Messaging (www.axolotl.com/products.html) and EpicWeb (www.epic.com/).

E-mail offers the same advantages in health care as in business and personal communication. It allows each party to communicate when they are available in legible text. It avoids inconvenient interruptions and provides better documentation. It also has disadvantages, some of which are specific to health care. Communication is not direct, so the provider can't engage in a question and answer conversation. The patient may leave out important information, and the patient can't follow up with additional questions without sending another message. Regular e-mail is not secure, so messages could be intercepted. Physicians are concerned about a possible flood of messages, which they are not paid to respond to, and the legal and ethical implications of communicating with patients via e-mail.

E-mail systems have been developed that address some of these concerns. The assumption that e-mail must be direct communication with the physician isn't necessarily true. As in telephone communication, a process can be developed that routes appropriate messages to the appropriate person based on physician preferences. The practice support staff plays a greater role in triaging incoming requests, routing them to the appropriate staff member or physician and tracking all messages to be sure they are attended to in a reasonable time.

Managing Waiting Time

Edward Hospital in Naperville, Illinois, is advertising in the community the availability of current emergency department wait times via text messages, telephone, or its Web site. The wait times are the average time from when patients check in and are triaged to the time they are placed in a room where treatment begins. The times are updated every 15 minutes (Goedert, 2010).

St. Jude Children's Research Hospital in Memphis implemented a centralized scheduling system that allows one scheduler to make all the appointments for a patient. St. Jude's vision was to "integrate orders with scheduling without multiple phone calls to provide patient-centered schedules." The amount of time children had to wait was reduced and the number of appointments that could be made in a single day was increased, resulting in less travel (Shepherd & Dotson, 2002).

Opportunities for Controlling Health Care Costs

WHERE ARE WE? CURRENT ISSUES AND PROBLEMS

The lack of money to invest in information technology is often cited by providers as the reason for their slow adoption, despite the potential for improving clinical and service quality. The **return on investment (ROI)** is said to be low or nonexistent. There is evidence that some information technologies do lower costs, but those savings are not always delivered to the organization that has to incur the expense of purchasing, implementing, and maintaining them.

There is evidence that some information technologies do lower costs, but those savings are not always delivered to the organization that has to incur the expense of purchasing, implementing, and maintaining them.

To illustrate, if a hospital spends $500,000 on a system to reduce medication errors that uses bar codes, the result may be a shorter length of stay for patients. But if the hospital is being paid an all-inclusive per diem rate by the insurer, it receives less revenue, because the patient is hospitalized fewer days. The savings accrue to the insurer. Although bar codes may save nurses' time in administering medications, the likely result will be that nurses spend more time on other tasks—it is unlikely that nursing staff (and the costs thereof) will be reduced. The hospital may also incur lower litigation expenses related medication errors. That estimate is difficult to make and merely speculative. Lower malpractice premiums might also represent a savings, but not all insurers offer such reductions.

This leads to a discussion in professional magazines of how ROI comprises "soft" savings (those that are uncertain or difficult-to-estimate in dollars) versus "hard" savings (those that are certain and can be measured in dollars). The former would include improved clinical decision making resulting in improved patient outcomes. The latter would include a reduction in the cost of paper and film. Many of the technologies we've discussed have obvious soft savings (e.g., improvements in patient satisfaction), but the hard savings are difficult to document. And, again, the savings may not accrue to the provider who bears the cost of HIT implementation.

DISEASE MANAGEMENT

There are three categories of disease management tools. Predictive modeling applies sophisticated mathematical models and analysis to identify patients whose medical conditions or health status are most likely to lead to significant medical costs (therefore leading providers to more closely manage these patients to prevent hospitalizations and thereby reduce the overall costs associated with their care). Patient registries are primarily database tools used to track and manage patients with certain diseases so that clinical interventions are completed as required and patients are kept healthier through preventive care. Patient-focused disease management tools can include a wide range of devices that patients use to help monitor and manage their own health remotely, by connecting them from home to the physician's office (McDonald, Turisco, & Drazen, 2003).

A variety of devices is available to link patients in their homes to clinicians. One such patient-focused tool is Health Buddy, a device placed in the home and connected to a telephone line. Patients can be prompted to carry out and report specific activities that are important for health maintenance and improvement (http://bit.ly/dxoMGr). This can include taking medications. A report is sent directly to the clinician who can evaluate the results for many patients without an office visit. The system also can prompt the clinician to make contact with a patient who hasn't used the device or carried out a particular action.

The Wound Technology Network (WTN), a Hollywood, Florida-based network of physicians, is using wireless services and mobile devices to provide better care to chronic wound patients. The WTN is using wireless technology to equip clinical staff across south Florida and southern California with smart mobile devices. Physicians can teleconference with wound experts at WTN to better diagnose wounds and administer appropriate treatment (Hardy, 2009).

EFFICIENT USE OF RESOURCES

There is a significant cost when expensive resources are not used. An operation that is delayed because a microscope isn't available or because an instrument is broken or missing costs hospitals and physicians revenue while staff costs are still incurred. When patients do not appear for an appointment, the result is lost revenue. All of these problems can be handled by scheduling systems that not only record the day and time of a procedure, but can verify that the needed resources are available. They can also prompt staff to call patients in advance to remind them of the visit. Some systems will even call the patient and provide a reminder using a physician's own voice.

Mercy Heart Hospital in Des Moines, Iowa, implemented a real-time inventory management system. The hospital installed **radio-frequency identification (RFID)** enabled cabinets in the hospital to store and track all products. Each product box is tagged with a passive RFID tag and registered in the database. The intelligent cabinets have built-in RFID antennas that read tagged items on the shelves every 20 minutes and feed the data to the database. Because the cabinets automatically read all the tags numerous times daily, the system has a near-real-time count of inventory levels, which continually change whenever an item is removed or put into the intelligent cabinets. Target inventory levels were reduced by 25%, for a dollar savings of almost $400,000 annually. For example, the use of the bulk buy calculator has saved the department almost $300,000 in preparing the right shopping list based on accurate usage data. The hospital also achieved a 40% reduction in waste from expired products (Wilson, 2009).

Current Issues

Health care organizations are far behind those in other parts of the economy in the use of information management technology. Why? There isn't just one reason. The cost of technology, the perceived lack of information on the benefits, a lack of standardization that makes implementation costly and difficult, resistance by clinicians, and concerns about security and patient confidentiality are all frequently mentioned as obstacles. Each of these factors and possible solutions is discussed below.

COST OF TECHNOLOGY

As mentioned previously, IT competes with technology for diagnosis and treatment, such as MRI scanners. It competes with salary increases for nurses, renovation and construction of facilities, and other proposed uses of funds. Today, these requests come at a time when many hospitals are concerned about the impact of the health care reform bills passed in 2010, which may result in lower reimbursement rates, possibly balanced by reduced expenses for uninsured and indigent care. Many of the provisions will be implemented after 2014, signaling a lengthy period of uncertainty, but federal regulations require the "meaningful use" of a certified EMR by 2011, in order to receive all of the money offered under the HITECH provisions of the ARRA. That money will come in the form of increases in Medicare payments after EMR implementation, so hospitals and physicians will have to find the funds to move forward as soon as possible.

The low level of IT investment to date has worsened the problem for hospitals and physicians. A bank that has made recent investments in computers can consider only the cost of new software and training in deciding whether to install a new system. A hospital that doesn't have computers at all nursing stations or computer cables connecting them will have to bear the cost of a basic IT infrastructure before considering acquisition of an EHR system. Similarly, a physician's office with one computer in the business manager's office faces significant hardware and staff training costs before implementing an EHR.

The cost of hardware and software does not reflect the full cost of implementing information technology. Staff must be trained and become proficient. Physicians are concerned about a reduction in their own productivity and consequent revenue losses while EHRs are being implemented. Hospitals are aware that computerizing inefficient processes will not reduce costs or improve quality. But redesigning underlying processes—for example, how medications are ordered and delivered—will cost money either for consultants or internal staff time, at least in the short term.

Still, some health systems are recognizing that major benefits could result if their hospitals, outpatient facilities, and physicians could exchange information and have allocated large sums of money to make that happen.

WINNING CLINICIAN ACCEPTANCE AND SUPPORT

Indifference or hostility on the part of physicians and nurses to clinical information systems is often attributed to age, prior training, or organizational culture. The most experienced and powerful clinicians were trained without this technology, so they may be concerned about their ability to use it and believe it may affect their independence—for example, by advising them on what care to provide. Using technology such as CPOE is said to take more time and reduce efficiency (Poon et al., 2004).

Much has been written on how health care organizations should respond to these concerns. Physician involvement in an HIT project is critical (Austin, Klasko, & Leaver, 2009). New roles for clinicians—as champions and active participants in IT development strategies—have been proposed.

A physician or nurse "champion" helps an IT project gain credibility with the clinical staff (Poon et al., 2004). A person who is an influential (but not necessarily the most knowledgeable) clinician who could offer support after learning about IT's benefits. Champions would be included on committees involved in product selection and implementation. Or, hospitals can create a full- or part-time paid position for a physician and nurse who would provide advice to managers and a voice for clinicians within the IT team. They could be recruited from clinicians who have a strong interest in the technology, and they would be offered opportunities for learning. The Association of Medical Directors of Information Systems (www.amdis.org) is an organization for physicians who have such a formal title and role.

Fine-tuning the process of implementation is also advocated. Pilot tests allow the documentation of positive results and the identification of problems. The pace of implementation needs to be monitored to assure that it is neither too fast or too slow. Careful training is advocated, as well as constant personal support. The systems themselves need to be customized to the needs of clinicians (Poon et al., 2004).

Much can be done to help clinicians accept and use HIT. Success isn't guaranteed, because the technology is still perceived as increasing the time to provide care, and some physicians believe it lowers rather than increases quality.

ASSURING THE CONFIDENTIALITY OF PATIENT INFORMATION

It's not surprising that the continual flow of stories about computer viruses and hackers would make everyone concerned about the confidentiality of medical information stored in computers. And, stories about data breaches appear with distressing regularity. Very often, these occur when staff take data home with them and their storage media or laptop computers are stolen or lost. As required by the HITECH Act, the Office for Civil Rights in the Department of Health and Human Services has launched a Web page (http://bit.ly/ampvbu) listing covered entities that have reported breaches of unsecured protected health information, each of which has affected more than 500 individuals.

Americans are also worried that they might lose their health insurance coverage or have their job opportunities limited because of information in their medical record. Yet many people do their banking online, use their credit cards to make purchases on the Internet, and are aware that their personal information is being held by a wide variety of public and private organizations. Less well-known is the extent to which medical information on paper is not secure. Physicians and nurses not involved in specific patients' care can look at their hospital charts. Staff who do billing in hospitals and physician offices have access to patients' medical information, as do workers in insurance companies.

Yet, the current flow of stories about unauthorized access to digitized records puts the burden of proof on those who advocate them. How can patient information be kept secure and private?

> *The privacy and security of digitized medical information depends as much on people as on technology.*

We need to recognize that the privacy and security of digitized medical information depends as much on people as on technology. A hospital can require the use of passwords to access files, but if a medical resident gives that password to another resident while taking a break, security and privacy have been compromised. This is also true when a physician working at home accesses patient records while others are in the room and able to view the screen. Clearly stated procedures, training on those procedures, and monitoring and enforcement are critically important.

Equally important is the use of specific technology for assuring privacy and security. This includes technology for **"authorization"**—that is, determining who has access. Unlike paper files, access to specific elements of the medical record in a computer can be restricted on a "need to know" basis. A clerk arranging for transportation to the radiology department needs to know the patient's name and room number, but not their diagnoses. A food service worker in the cafeteria should have no access to the record at all.

Technology is also available for **"authentication"**—that is verifying the identity of people who attempt to access information. A common procedure requires the user to "know something and have something." They must know a password and user name, but also possess a key or special card encoded with information on a magnetic strip or in a computer chip. The voluntary or involuntary sharing of passwords and user names is then less of a threat to confidentiality. There is growing interest in devices that use fingerprints, the iris of the eye, and facial images to authenticate identity. The International Biometric Group (www.biometricgroup.com/) tests such devices.

Although it may seem that storing medical information in a computer makes it easier to access, it also makes it easier to determine who looked at a record inappropriately. Computer systems with "audit trails" record the identity of each person who looks at a medical record. Employee education and a schedule of penalties help to deter inappropriate access.

Access to the information system outside of the health care facility raises many security issues that need to be addressed. Flash drives that allow the storage of gigabytes of information can be protected with passwords. **Encryption** (storing information in a format that requires a password *and* special software to read) can be used for both flash drives and laptops.

Protecting the confidentiality of patient information, therefore, requires a combination of people and technology. Either alone is insufficient. Health care organizations risk significant financial risks and damage to their reputations if they fail to take aggressive preventive action.

Conclusion

Information technology that can improve the quality of health care, increase patient satisfaction, and help control costs is available, but it is used by a small minority of U.S. hospitals and physicians. The obstacles are real, but large sums of money are being invested in HIT by the federal government, with the expectation that both improvements in health and some control over rising health care costs will result. An important unresolved issue is whether physicians will implement the technology and cope with the practice changes that are required. Hospitals also face the challenge of finding sufficient staff to implement the technology and helping clinicians adapt to new ways of working.

DISCUSSION QUESTIONS

1. Why do you think the health care industry has invested less in information technology than the banking industry?
2. Who do you think should pay for improvements in HIT?
3. What role should the federal government pay in stimulating the adoption of information technology?
4. What role should insurance companies and employers play in increasing the use of information technology in health care? Should they contribute financially?
5. Name one or two technologies that can both improve the quality of care and increase patient satisfaction.
6. Should patients be allowed to control who sees their medical information? How should this be accomplished?
7. What can be done to insure the privacy and security of patient information?
8. What are the causes of physician resistance to CPOE? What can hospitals do to reduce it?

CASE STUDY

Phil Jones is the CEO of a 200-bed hospital in the Midwest. His hospital is currently using IT to assist in billing and managing the purchase and use of medical supplies. Individual electronic systems have been implemented in the pharmacy, laboratories, and radiology department. He is aware that money from the federal government will become available beginning in 2011 for hospitals that can demonstrate "meaningful use" of a certified EHR and that penalties will be applied beginning in 2015 for hospitals that fail to meet this standard. The hospital's physicians have made it clear that they will not accept any EHR which requires that they spend additional time doing their work. However, every study that Phil has read says that physicians will need to spend more time, at least in the beginning. They will also need to invest time helping the hospital select a system and advising on how to customize it before it is implemented. In conversations with his CIO and hospital board of directors, Phil has developed a number of options to overcome this hurdle:

- Hire a physician to work as chief medical information officer to engage with the physicians and do some of the work in selection and implementation of an EHR system. Questions regarding this approach include: should the position be filled by a current physician or someone from another hospital with experience in IT? Should he or she be full-time or practice medicine part-time? Will the medical staff respect someone who has stopped practicing?
- Pay physicians during the first few months to attend training sessions, vendor presentations, and other meetings.
- Hire additional doctors to work as temporary backup for the current physicians.
- Train nurses to serve as "super-users" of the new EHR system and assist nurses and doctors in its use. And, here, should these be younger nurses who may be more comfortable with technology or older nurses who might command the respect of their peers?

The board has made it clear that the hospital cannot afford all of these measures. But it says that the hospital should not, under any circumstances, fail to receive the federal stimulus funds, starting in 2011. As the next board meeting approached, Phil begins drafting his recommendation.

CASE STUDY DISCUSSION

1. List the concerns of physicians as they learn about the hospital's impending adoption of an EHR. Which are the most important and must be addressed?
2. Should the hospital pay the physicians to participate in a process that will improve patient care?
3. What should the nursing staff's role be in the selection and implementation of the EHR?

REFERENCES

Austin, G., Klasko, S., & Leaver, W. (2009). The art of health IT transformation. White Paper from the National Center for Healthcare Leadership. Retrieved April 21, 2010, from http://www.nchl.org/Documents/Ctrl_Hyperlink/doccopy4770_uid11172009427102.pdf

Bates, D. W., Leape, L. L., Cullen, D. J., Laird, N., Petersen, L. A., Teich, J.M., et al. (1998). Effect of computerized physician order entry and a team intervention on prevention of serious medication errors. *Journal of the American Medical Association, 280,* 1311–1316.

Bell, L. M., Grundmeier, R., Localio, R., Zorc, J., Fiks, A. G., Zhang, X., et al. (2010). Electronic health record-based decision support to improve asthma care: A cluster-randomized trial. *Pediatrics, 125,* e770–e777.

Blumenthal, D. (2009). Stimulating the adoption of health information technology. *New England Journal of Medicine, 360,* 1477–1499.

Blumenthal, D. (2010). Launching HITECH. *New England Journal of Medicine, 362,* 382–385.

Cutler, D., Feldman, N., & Horwitz, J. (2005). U.S. adoption of computerized physician order entry systems. *Health Affairs, 24,* 1654–1663.

DesRoches, C., Campbell, E. G., Rao, S. R., Donelan, K., Ferris, T. G., Jha, A, et al. (2008). Electronic health records in ambulatory care — a national survey of physicians. *New England Journal of Medicine, 359,* 50–60.

Dexter, P., Perkins, S., Overhage, M. O., Maharry, K., Kohler, R. B., & McDonald, C. J. (2001). A computerized reminder system to increase the use of preventive care for hospitalized patients. *New England Journal of Medicine, 345,* 965–970.

eHealth Initiative. (2009). Migrating toward meaningful use: The state of health information exchange, a report based on the results of the eHealth initiative's 2009 Sixth Annual Survey of Health Information Exchange. Retrieved May 5, 2010, from http://www.ehealthinitiative.org/HIESurvey/

Evans, R. S., Pestotnik, S. L., Classen, D. C., Clemmer, T. P., Weaver, L. K., Orme, J. F., et al. (1998). A computer-assisted management program for antibiotics and other infective agents. *New England Journal of Medicine, 338,* 232–238.

Goedert, J. (2010, March 9). Hospital: Check our ER wait times. *HDM Breaking News.* Retrieved May 4, 2010, from http://www.healthdatamanagement.com/news/er_wait_time_text_phone_consumer-39919-1.html

Hardy, K. (2009, November 20). Physicians network uses wireless IT to improve home-based care. *Healthcare IT News.* Retrieved May 5, 2010, from http://www.health care-itnews.com/news/physicians-network-uses-wireless-it-improve-home-based-care

Institute of Medicine. (2000). *To err is human: Building a safer health system.* Washington, D.C.: National Academy Press.

Institute of Medicine. (2001). *Crossing the quality chasm: A new health system for the 21st century.* Washington, D.C.: National Academy Press.

Jha, A., DesRoches, C. M., Campbell, E. G., Konelan, K., Rao, S. R., Ferris, T. G., et al. (2009). Use of electronic health records in U.S. hospitals. *New England Journal of Medicine, 360,* 1628–1638.

Kaushal, R., Kern, L. M., Barrón, Y., Quaresimo, J., & Abramson, E. L. (2010). Electronic prescribing improves medication safety in community-based office practices. *Journal of General Internal Medicine, 25,* 530–536.

Kaushal, R., Shojania, K. G., & Bates, D. W. (2003). Effects of computerized physician order entry and clinical decision support systems on medication safety: A systematic review. *Archives of Internal Medicine, 163,* 1409–1416.

McDonald, C., Overhage, J. M., Barnes, M., Schadow, M., Blevins, L, Dexter, P. R., Mamlin, B., & the INPC Management Committee. (2005). The Indiana Network for patient care: A working local health information infrastructure. *Health Affairs, 24,* 1214–1220.

McDonald, K., Turisco, F., & Drazen, E. (2003). *Advanced technologies to lower health care costs and improve quality.* Massachusetts Technology Collaborative. Retrieved May 19, 2010, from www.masstech.org/ehealth/STATFinal9_24.pdf

Poon, E. G., Blumenthal, D., Jaggi, T., Honour, M., Bates, D. W., & Kaushal, R. (2004). Overcoming barriers to adopting and implementing computerized physician order entry systems in U.S. hospitals. *Health Affairs, 23,* 184–190.

Shepherd, G., & Dotson, P. (2002). The design and implementation of an integrated scheduling application. In *Proceedings of the 2002 Annual HIMSS Conference.* Chicago, IL: HIMSS.

Shortliffe, E. H., & Perreault, E. (1990). *Medical informatics: Computer applications in health care* (pp. 469, 475–480). Reading, MA: Addison-Wesley.

Wilson, L. (2009). Patient safety improvements through real-time inventory management. Retrieved May 5, 2010, from http://www.himss.org/storiesofsuccess/docs/tier1/MercyHeartHospital.pdf

The Future of Health Care Delivery

V

17

THE FUTURE OF HEALTH CARE DELIVERY IN THE UNITED STATES

James R. Knickman and Anthony R. Kovner

LEARNING OBJECTIVES
- Explain the rationale for futures planning
- Describe approaches to planning and forecasting
- Analyze factors that drive change in the health system
- Predict changes likely to occur in the health system

TOPICAL OUTLINE
- Definitions and approaches to forecasting
- Key drivers of change
- New five-year trend forecast

Forecasting is a hazardous business because the future is so affected by unknowns. One could not predict the 9/11 disaster or how the reaction to this terrorist attack would shape American life in the past 10 years. In health care, many experts have predicted for years that universal health insurance was "just around the corner," but when the 2010 health reform law actually happened, in some ways it seemed quite surprising.

A concern about change preoccupies most Americans. All stakeholders in health care—taxpayers, patients, providers, suppliers, employers, and government officials—suggest changes and respond to change proposals. Sometimes they seek to make change occur, whereas at other times they block it. Managing the change process is a key part of most high-level careers in the health sector.

Strategic decisions about change can have very long-lasting impacts. For example, installation of a new regional information system or building a new children's hospital can affect the delivery of care for decades—and freezing wages during World War II gave rise to a tremendous increase in employer-based health insurance, because adding benefits was a way of increasing compensation without increasing wages. Without this wage freeze, health insurance in 2007 might have been based on citizenship, rather than employment status.

What impact do forecasts have on those of us who work in health care? Can we work together to achieve a positive forecast or forestall a dismal one? We suggest that forecasts can be made in a way that helps us plan for the future. Forecasters can tell us, for example, how much insurance coverage for all children would cost, using different assumptions, and how increased coverage is likely to affect access to care and utilization of services. Of course, "the experts" don't always agree on such matters, because their analyses are inevitably based on less-than-perfect information and some amount of uncertainty and judgment. But, collectively, they may suggest a reasonable range of futures.

Forecasts should not dictate actual policy choices, however, which must take into account not just analysis, but also values. The citizenry, not just the experts, must decide whether we want universal coverage or electronic medical records and how much of our spending should be on priorities outside of the health sector—achieving energy independence or improving public education, for example.

Definitions and Approaches to Forecasting

Exercises in forecasting have a range of practical values. Most important, forecasting is a crucial step in strategic planning. Deciding where to focus attention depends on a sense of future trends and prospects. What new services must be designed? How large should a new hospital be? How many elderly will use Medicare services 20 years from now? Questions such as these guide current actions and some approach to forecasting is crucial in order to provide tentative answers to these questions.

"History is a vast early warning system."

Forecasting requires us to look at history. It often starts with a look at patterns of past trends to make predictions about future ones. In this sense, as Norman Cousins said, "history is a vast early warning system." Studying historical events and trends is what helps us create new solutions to current problems. Epidemiologists, for example, use patterns of past behavior to sort out what types of behavior, environmental factors, and interventions are associated with good and bad health outcomes. This type of analysis then leads to ideas for how to achieve improvements. Most social scientists use the same basic approach in studying how the health system works and how it can be improved.

Finally, forecasting gives us a reference point that we can use in the future to assess our past logic. Reexamining earlier forecasts allows us to sharpen our analytic abilities, to make forecasts more accurate, and to link causes to effects. For example, what would cause Americans to use less medical care per capita on an age-adjusted basis? Would it take increased cost-sharing? Or price competition based on clinical outcomes? Or increased electronic communication between physicians and patients? Or single payer national health insurance? What would be the intended and unintended consequences of using less medical care per capita? Lower employment of physicians or higher physician charges? Under any likely scenario, would Americans use less medical care, as long as new technology and drugs keep producing better outcomes? In 2008, we wrote the following in an earlier edition of this text:

> *Imagine the future: competition in health care is based primarily on quality of service—that is, the results a set of providers obtain for patients with a specific medical condition, such as heart attack, hip or spine operation, or diabetes. The price*

of their services is known in advance, and patients receive a single bill for all services related to their medical condition. Everyone has basic insurance. All Americans have their own health record on a wallet-sized card, and all providers can access this record when the patient shows up for care. To graduate from high school, children must demonstrate that they understand how their body works and how to keep it healthy, and all prospective parents are paid to attend child-rearing classes.

Although this seemed a bit far-fetched just a few years ago, many of these ideas are slowly working their way into our current health system.

In 2012, a scenario such as the following may seem as unlikely as our 2008 scenario:
Virtually all physicians in 2012 work on salary within organized health systems, rather than in small private practices. The focus of the entire health system is on population health: a set of providers, including physicians, nurse practitioners, physician assistants, and hospitals receive a fixed sum to maintain the health of a defined population that generally includes between 50,000 and 100,000 people. The number of hospitals has shrunk significantly, but well-run clinics offer wide ranges of prevention services and primary care. Technology makes it possible for people to have most procedures, such as surgeries and diagnostic tests, performed right in the clinics. Sometimes they involve telehealth approaches that involve medical experts many miles away. The changes in incentives and the organization of care have lowered expenditure increases in health care from about 2 or 3 percentage points more than the annual increase in the overall economy to the same rate as general economic growth.

Will the future really look like this? When, if ever? In truth, it may be easier to specify the forces shaping the nation's future health care than the specific results of those forces. In the preceding 16 chapters, authors have examined many of these forces, as they explored key aspects of the health system. Understanding the present and being knowledgeable about the past are first steps in making relevant forecasts and adapting to predicted change: "If you don't know where you are going, you might end up somewhere else."

FORECASTING METHODS

Forecasting methods vary. Economists have developed highly quantitative forecasting approaches. They analyze past data to predict future economic events. Often they collect time-series data on a set of economic variables, then develop theories about how each variable influences the others, then test these theories with data from the past, and finally estimate how the variables will change events in the future, based on the estimated relationships established. This approach works only when extensive empirical data are available, and it most useful for short-term forecasts.

The Delphi method, a more qualitative approach to forecasting, systematically obtains expert opinions, with an end goal of achieving consensus. Delphi administrators poll experts about their forecasts in three or four rounds of questionnaires. After each round, results are tabulated and disseminated to the group. The group completes a Delphi when it reaches a convergence of opinion. Of course, if rounds go on too long, consensus can evaporate as contrarians move away from the consensus. The Delphi method overcomes geographic barriers that plague many consensus-building exercises. Its flexibility allows it to apply to health and medicine as easily as to war and weapons, and to all levels of decision making. Reliability, as well as the work required, increases as the number of rounds and experts increases. Poor questionnaire design also can degrade the method's usefulness.

A third, less scientific approach to forecasting is to rely on nationally recognized leaders in a field to apply their experience about the past and dynamics of the present to make predictions about the future. This is the approach often used in the popular media, where forecasting is common, and it is the one we use in this chapter, drawing on the wide literature contributed by experts analyzing the present to predict the future and present our interpretation and inferences of what current patterns in the health care system suggest for the future. Our analysis is shaped by our vantage points, working full-time at a health care philanthropy and a major university, and part-time on boards of hospitals and health systems in the greater New York City area.

Key Drivers of Change

As the second decade of 21st century began, there were clearly large changes on the health care horizon and substantial challenges facing both the health system and the U.S. economy. In 2010, the economic downturn that began in 2008 was still constraining the general economy and the health care economy alike. And, the ambitious health reform law passed in 2010 awaited the difficult task of implementation. Our prediction is that four key forces will shape change in the health system over this decade:

1. The circumstances of health reform implementation
2. The path of the current economic challenges
3. The ability of the health system to improve quality and slow expenditure growth
4. The obesity epidemic and other behavior-related health conditions

The Patient Protection and Affordable Care Act of 2010 (health reform) was difficult to pass, as described in Chapter 2, but it will perhaps be an even bigger challenge to implement its provisions over the next decade. The long road to implementing health reform will be a key driver of change because the health system that emerges may very well be different than the one we have now. The dynamics of implementation—with major impacts on how dollars flow through the system and with ambitious efforts to encourage "system reform" along with insurance coverage expansions—should preoccupy government, insurers, and other payers (employers and individuals) over the next decade.

Designing a system of subsidized private insurance where the subsidy varies depending on a family's current income is a difficult task. It also will be a challenge to actually set up the insurance "exchanges" that will link consumers to the approved policies that can be purchased. And, for many states, the new law will lead to a huge expansion of the number of individuals who are eligible for free health insurance through state Medicaid programs.

States are the main players in the reform implementation task, with the federal government also playing a significant role. Insurance companies will be affected by the insurance exchanges and by fundamental changes in the regulation of newly mandated insurance rules. Successful implementation depends on how effectively state governments can establish the complex organizational and financial infrastructures that need to be in place and operating by 2014. This challenge comes at a time when most state governments are experiencing large decreases in tax revenues and shrinkage of staffing in their health and insurance agencies. To be successful, state governments need to learn from one another and actively engage consumers and insurance companies in the design and implementation of the exchanges.

> *Ever-expanding health care expenditures would make the subsidies and Medicaid expansions that are the core of the reform law unsustainable.*

The other ingredient to successful implementation of the reform law is addressing the cost containment challenge. Ever-expanding health care expenditures would make the subsidies and Medicaid expansions that are the core of the reform law unsustainable. The hope is that the waste in the health care system can be eliminated through reforms in how providers are paid and how care is organized.

The outcomes of the 2010 and 2012 federal elections also will have big impacts on what actually emerges from the health reform law. Republicans have denounced the new law that was voted in by a Democratic president and a House and Senate controlled by Democrats. The Republicans have now expanded their numbers in the House and Senate and statehouses around the country; if they win the presidency in 2012, the law could be changed, scaled back, or even abolished. Thus, implementation needs to happen in a quite uncertain political environment. Further, as of this writing, two states have enacted or are considering legislation exempting their residents from the provision of the new law mandating that individuals have coverage; such laws have not been tested in the courts yet but, even if they are rejected, could delay and confuse the implementation process.

Consumers will end up being a key driver of how health reform implementation plays out. Will consumers purchase insurance policies as mandated by the new law? Or, will a large number choose to pay the tax penalty that occurs if they refuse? Will there be a dramatic consumer backlash to the mandates that leads Congress to reconsider them? Consumer response will determine whether the estimated 32 million extra people that are projected to get coverage actually are enrolled in insurance by 2015.

THE PATH OF THE CURRENT ECONOMIC CHALLENGES

A major force that will shape the future of health care in coming years is the economic downturn that started in 2008. If America emerges from the downturn early in the decade, health care will see the pressures of the 2008 to 2010 period slowly subside. But if economic growth remains very slow, then state governments will continue to cut the rates they pay for Medicaid services, employers will continue to reduce the comprehensiveness of insurance policies and they will pass along more and more costs (in the form of co-payments, higher deductibles, and premium-sharing) to employees.

A constrained economy will particularly affect federal government policy toward the Medicare program. Even if the economy returns to normal growth patterns, Medicare payments cannot grow as quickly as they have been, because the tax revenues that pay for Medicare will not support such growth, under any economic scenario. Similarly, if the economy continues to grow slowly, then the brakes on Medicare payments will need to be much more substantial than if economic growth is average or above average. Continued cuts in Medicare and Medicaid growth rates—and in the rates private insurers pay— would force providers to find more efficient ways to deliver health care and to allocate scarce health care resources (see Chapter 13).

Many system reform implications inherent in the 2010 health reform law were not fully funded by the initial legislation. A slow economy would decrease the likelihood that Congress ever will fund tests of some system reform options. A slow economy also may strengthen the influence of the legislators who oppose the current law, who may push for less ambitious coverage expansions.

THE ABILITY OF THE HEALTH SYSTEM TO IMPROVE QUALITY AND SLOW EXPENDITURE GROWTH

The past 10 years have seen amazing progress on a range of organizational improvement innovations. The result has been the development of new management and financing ideas, tests of them on a demonstration basis at selected providers or in selected communities, and a popularization of them throughout the industry. This is progress, but far short of widespread adoption. These ideas could become key drivers of change over the next decade if they begin to become the norm, rather than the exception, and if they work as well when implemented wide-scale.

Electronic medical records are perhaps the most obvious example of a management tool that has come of age (see Chapter 16). Affordable, easy-to-use systems are available for almost every type of provider. When electronic records are used, providers make fewer mistakes and have more command of the needs and history of the problems their patients face. Electronic records will drive change if the current push to persuade most if not all physicians to use them is successful. And, they will become key drivers of quality if systems are interoperable, enabling easy sharing across providers, so that when patients go from one part of the health system to another, their medical histories follow them.

New approaches to primary care, such as the medical or health home and the chronic care model, also could drive quality of care if they are widely implemented. Both approaches emphasize continuity of care and the availability of a team of health care providers (doctors, nurse practitioners, case managers, community health workers, and others) to make sure that people receive the care they need efficiently and consistently (see Chapters 8 and 9). Both models also emphasize the importance of patient "self management" by working to make patients part of their own care team.

Finally, quality might improve under an array of new attempts to change the way providers are reimbursed. Although Americans seem to have rejected the health management organization (HMO) concept that relies on capitation of payments (i.e., one annual payment to a provider and the agreement that a patient will use only the HMO's providers), new 21st century versions of paying providers for an episode of care or a time-defined period of care are reemerging.

The general push for these new payment approaches is the recognition that somebody needs to be responsible for a population's "health" rather than just having responsibility for treating illnesses once somebody becomes "unhealthy." Ideas like medical or health homes, accountable care organizations, and bundled payments all represent new approaches for changing the incentives and responsibilities of providers to maintain the health of their patients and to use as few resources as possible when an illness or medical problem arises. If these payment reforms take hold, they could drive the way physicians, hospitals, and other providers relate to one another and to their patients.

THE OBESITY EPIDEMIC AND OTHER BEHAVIOR-RELATED HEALTH CONDITIONS

In essence, the way we live our lives creates most of the need for health care in America. The vast majority of health care costs are driven not by random health problems that arise over a lifetime, but by health problems that relate to lifestyle choices we make: overuse of alcohol and other drugs, tobacco use, careless driving or non-use of seatbelts, inactivity, and poor eating habits (see Chapter 5).

The most dramatic behavioral challenge ravaging our country right now is the obesity epidemic. The number of people who are overweight has increased dramatically, and we have yet to find a national, community, or self management strategy that seems to be systematically effective in helping people control their weight (see Chapter 7).

Obesity is a key driver of the health care system because it greatly increases the risk for acquiring many high-cost diseases, most notably diabetes and heart disease, but also many other conditions, including asthma and orthopedic problems. The growing incidence of these diseases is a major driver of health care costs. Obesity also increases the costs of providing care: hospitals have had to purchase sturdier equipment and furniture, install wider doorways, and lose staff time to back injuries from handling overweight patients. Perhaps no single change would have more impact on health costs and the well-being of individuals than coming up with an effective strategy to reduce weight across the population.

Greater understanding of the problem and some promising ideas have emerged in recent years, but no plan has been made for a wide-scale effort that would make a significant difference. We now well understand the role of eating and regular exercise in weight control. We recognize that working with children—through schools and sports programs—is where obesity prevention needs to begin. And, we now recognize that part of the issue is about individual motivation, but perhaps even more important is to make our communities more food and exercise-friendly. Too many neighborhoods lack access to affordable, healthy food and to safe places to exercise regularly (see Chapter 7).

The recognition of the importance of healthy behavior choices and of the dramatic impacts of obesity on population health could be a key driver of public health and prevention activities over the next decade. Will we begin to invest in healthier communities? Will we develop effective strategies to combat obesity? Will we develop medical innovations (whether surgeries or prescription drugs or other interventions) that will help people reduce these health risks?

MAJOR TRENDS OVER THE NEXT FIVE YEARS

In 2008, Knickman and Kovner made four predictions about the coming years:

1. That the federal government would act to expand health insurance if more middle class Americans began to fear losing coverage
2. That cost containment efforts would begin more intensively
3. That health care providers would focus more on managing chronic diseases
4. That providers would become more customer friendly, transparent, and accountable

These forecasts proved relatively accurate. A huge economic recession affected the middle class and one result was an ambitious federal law to expand insurance coverage. Cost containment has become a major focus, although efforts to rein them in are so far ineffective.

Transparency (ratings of providers, quality data online), accountability (movement to pay providers for episodes of care, or bundling), and customer service have improved. And, innovative approaches to managing chronic illness have spread widely in the past 5 years, in the form of primary care medical homes and disease management protocols.

New Five-Year Trend Forecast

Our predictions for the following 4 or 5 years have evolved from the previous list, although at least one remains. Our key predictions about changes in health care now are:

1. The 2010 health care reform law will evolve considerably over the next 5 years
2. Growth in health care costs will slow
3. A two- or three-tier health system will continue to develop
4. Electronic medical records will finally be implemented widely
5. More resources will finally move into primary care, public health, and prevention
6. The number of hospital beds will shrink

THE HEALTH CARE REFORM LAW WILL CHANGE CONTINUALLY OVER THE NEXT FIVE YEARS

Conceivably, a new Congress or president could successfully push for a repeal of the health reform law, but more likely the political process will work to continually change aspects of the law. Republicans—if in control—will attempt to shrink the scope of reform and reduce its costs. Democrats—if in control—will attempt to expand the modest system reform provisions included in the original bill.

> *Republicans—if in control—will attempt to shrink the scope of reform and reduce its costs. Democrats—if in control—will attempt to expand the modest system reform provisions included in the original bill.*

The process of continual change and shaping is what happened after the Social Security Act was passed in 1935 and after Medicare and Medicaid were enacted in 1965. Over the intervening years, these programs have experienced substantial legislative changes—many of which were enacted even before the programs became operational.

The political process will react to what Americans like about the law and what they find overdone. The entire idea of an individual mandate and of the modest employer mandates will surely be debated, as people grow to understand that even subsidized insurance will require substantial financial burdens for American families. And, the effort to make health system changes to improve quality and slow expenditure growth will generate additional amendments.

GROWTH IN HEALTH CARE COSTS WILL SLOW

Although America can technically afford continued rapid growth in health care costs for decades, we believe that over the next 5 or 10 years, effective strategies for cost containment will finally appear. Slowed growth in health care expenditures will happen either directly—through a range of payment and systems reforms—or it will happen indirectly, by pushing higher and higher insurance premium shares, as well as larger and larger consumer-paid co-payments, leading people to use less health care. One way or the other, employers definitely will limit the growth in the costs they pay. This trend has already begun. If consumers have to pay more for health care or for insurance premiums, they will begin to use fewer health care services and will choose less comprehensive insurance policies—perhaps at best a short-term strategy for individuals and the system alike.

Preferably, ideas like accountable care organizations and medical homes and incentive reimbursement systems will take hold and offer health system restructuring that reduces the costs of health care. Three choices will emerge and the third one will happen if neither of the first two do:

1. Efficiency of the system could improve through better management and better reimbursement approaches
2. Capitation may return, which, in effect, asks providers to ration care
3. Deductibles, coinsurance, and exclusions could increase, which, in effect, asks consumers to self-ration

A TWO- OR THREE-TIER HEALTH SYSTEM WILL CONTINUE TO DEVELOP

The downside of successful efforts to reduce health care expenditures may be that we will begin to have two or three tiers of health care service delivery. The wealthy can buy their way out of any approaches that limit choice or restrict access to what is judged more convenient and perhaps higher quality care. A second tier could develop that serves the rest of the population that has health insurance, and perhaps yet a third tier could act as a bare bones safety net for the uninsured. To date, Americans have disapproved of a multi-tiered health care system (although one could effectively argue that it exists nevertheless). The politics of this explicit or implicit choice could be complex.

Multi-tiered systems could vary by what types of expensive new technologies are covered by insurance. We already have wrestled quietly with rationing issues like who should be eligible for arguably discretionary services, such as reproductive health care, bariatric surgery, and pharmaceuticals that aid sexual performance. But the future could include a much longer and debatable list of such services, including genetic therapies that affect the odds of certain illnesses (like Alzheimer's disease), interventions that enhance the quality of everyday life, or drugs that increase a child's height, intellectual performance, and other desired characteristics.

ELECTRONIC MEDICAL RECORDS WILL FINALLY BE IMPLEMENTED WIDELY

The promise of electronic medical records has been present for a long time, but the next 5 years may finally be the era of wide-scale, successful implementation. The ambitious federal stimulus programs that are providing incentives for hospitals and physician practices serving large numbers of Medicare or Medicaid patients to adopt electronic records will fuel implementation (see Chapter 16).

Electronic records could have an impact on health care costs. But, more likely, they will drive improvements in the quality of care. Better information and "meaningful use" of this information can let providers know systematically when they are not having good outcomes for their patients. This type of information generally pushes providers to improve their quality of care.

The full promise of electronic medical records, however, will emerge only when they become "interoperable" or easily shared across providers that touch a given patient. Sharing information can markedly decrease resource use (e.g., duplicative diagnostic tests; prescribing of redundant or conflicting drugs) and improve the ability of providers to manage care effectively. Such records also can empower patients to participate actively in the management of their medical conditions. At the same time, the sector should seek better hardware, software, and humanware solutions to the as-yet unsolved problems of privacy and confidentiality of patient medical records.

MORE RESOURCES WILL MOVE INTO PRIMARY CARE AND PREVENTION

We believe the case has been made that our health system under-allocates resources to primary care and to the entire health and public health enterprise of keeping people healthy and slowing the progression of diseases such as diabetes and coronary heart disease (see Chapters 5, 8, and 9). Emerging delivery models such as medical homes and accountable care organizations could change the flow of resources from inpatient care to primary, community-based care and to the public health activities focused on prevention.

The medical home approach pays reimbursement incentives to organizations that can meet the full range of primary care and prevention needs of a population of patients and that have good systems in place to manage chronic diseases, including referrals to specialists only when necessary. Accountable care organizations take responsibility for the health of a defined population and receive some form of capitated payments or partially capitated payments for this responsibility. The new models of primary care use teams of health professionals, with highly skilled nurse practitioners and physician assistants playing much more extensive roles in managing health and engaging patients in self-management of their chronic diseases.

The movement toward more extensive primary care capacity must be accompanied by changes in the health care workforce (see Chapter 15). Medical education will be challenged to prepare physicians better for work in primary care settings and for work as part of a team. The education of other members of the clinical team also must be strengthened. Educational programs in specific disciplines will learn how to work better with one another to foster the team concept. And, we think the importance of management research to learn how teams can work best to produce good health outcomes will become more and more obvious (see Chapter 14).

THE NUMBER OF HOSPITAL BEDS WILL SHRINK

The corollary to better, more extensive primary care is a reduction in the demand for traditional hospital beds. But, the hospital industry will need help to shrink at the margins in a way that does not threaten its viability. Crude, across-the-board cuts in payment rates only lead to decreased staffing and lower quality of care. Two key approaches can help hospitals survive in the coming years. First, we need to reimburse hospitals so that each type of patient care can result in payments that closely approximate actual costs. The current reimbursement approaches tend to create a very small number of "profit centers" in hospitals (often heart surgeries and other high-tech interventions), whereas most types of patient care result in losses. Better approaches for measuring the relative costs of hospital care across types of patients need to be put in place.

A second key approach to helping hospitals in a shrinking industry is to close or merge some hospitals. Having every hospital survive, but become smaller, does not result in substantial cost savings. Robust market dynamics don't exist that would allow us to let the "hidden hand" of competition lead to the natural closing of the *right* hospitals. This is an area where old-fashioned health planning needs to play a role.

In the past, when hospital beds were in oversupply, hospitals rarely closed, because government usually would intervene to help them survive. The current economic environment makes such interventions less and less likely. Closings—always controversial in a local area—likely will happen, but they can be done responsibly, so that the closure does not threaten the capacity of a community's health system to meet residents' inpatient needs.

Conclusion

This textbook began with a list of the key stakeholders that shape the U.S. health system: consumers and taxpayers, direct providers of care, for-profit companies in sectors such as pharmaceuticals and insurance, organizations that pay for or regulate health care, and the government, both in its roles as a payer and regulator.

Clearly, whether the predictions we made come to pass will be shaped by this range of stakeholders. The power that each stakeholder group wields waxes and wanes over time, but each will play a contributing role.

As we conclude this textbook, we want to emphasize that, in each of the stakeholder groups are *individual leaders* who are essential actors for positive change. America's complex health care system needs new generations of creative, practical, and compassionate leaders to manage every aspect of the system; to study, analyze, and understand how the system works; and to develop smart public policy. Although the sector faces challenges, it is a vibrant and essential component of our economy—an enterprise that helps people in need each and every day. We hope that the many authors who have contributed to this joint enterprise help stimulate and motivate this next generation.

DISCUSSION QUESTIONS

1. Why is it difficult to forecast the impact of trends on the future of health care delivery in the United States?
2. What are some of the common forecasting methods used?
3. What forces do the chapter authors believe will be the principal drivers of changes in health care delivery in the next 5 years?
4. What major trends affecting health care delivery will be important in the next 5 years?

CASE STUDIES

CASE STUDY #1

You have taken an analyst's position at the federal Department of Health and Human Services and have been asked to write a short position paper summarizing the positive impact of health reform and the implementation difficulties that need to be addressed.

CASE STUDY DISCUSSION

1. Thinking ahead a year or two, and given what you know about health care reform from the various chapters of this text, what do you anticipate may be the two most significant positive impacts of health reform and what are likely to be its two most serious problems?

2. Again, drawing on information throughout the text, what are some of your best ideas to improve quality and contain costs going forward?

CASE STUDY #2

You have an analyst's position in the Department of Health and Human Services. The 2010 health reform law is expected to increase insurance coverage for a significant number of Americans. But many problems in the health care system remain unresolved. Write a 1-page memorandum to your new supervisor describing what you believe are the most important of these, saying why they are important and suggesting how they might be approached.

This is the same challenge you were presented in Chapter 1. Please consider how your responses then have been reinforced or changed by what you have learned in the intervening chapters and discussion.

APPENDIX
MAJOR PROVISIONS OF THE PATIENT PROTECTION AND AFFORDABLE CARE ACT OF 2010

The following summary of the new health reform law was reprinted with permission from the Henry J. Kaiser Family Foundation, a nonprofit private operating foundation, based in Menlo Park, California, dedicated to producing and communicating the best possible analysis and information on health issues.

The Foundation makes available an up-to-date Implementation Timeline, which is an interactive tool designed to explain how and when the provisions of the health reform law will be implemented. This tool is available at http://healthreform.kff.org/timeline.aspx

FOCUS *on* Health Reform

THE HENRY J.
KAISER
FAMILY
FOUNDATION

SUMMARY OF NEW HEALTH REFORM LAW

On March 23, 2010, President Obama signed comprehensive health reform, the Patient Protection and Affordable Care Act, into law. The following summary of the new law, and changes made to the law by subsequent legislation, focuses on provisions to expand coverage, control health care costs, and improve health care delivery system.

	Patient Protection and Affordable Care Act (P.L. 111-148)
Overall approach to expanding access to coverage	Require most U.S. citizens and legal residents to have health insurance. Create state-based American Health Benefit Exchanges through which individuals can purchase coverage, with premium and cost-sharing credits available to individuals/families with income between 133-400% of the federal poverty level (the poverty level is $18,310 for a family of three in 2009) and create separate Exchanges through which small businesses can purchase coverage. Require employers to pay penalties for employees who receive tax credits for health insurance through an Exchange, with exceptions for small employers. Impose new regulations on health plans in the Exchanges and in the individual and small group markets. Expand Medicaid to 133% of the federal poverty level.

INDIVIDUAL MANDATE

Requirement to have coverage	• Require U.S. citizens and legal residents to have qualifying health coverage. Those without coverage pay a tax penalty of the greater of $695 per year up to a maximum of three times that amount ($2,085) per family or 2.5% of household income. The penalty will be phased-in according to the following schedule: $95 in 2014, $325 in 2015, and $695 in 2016 for the flat fee or 1.0% of taxable income in 2014, 2.0% of taxable income in 2015, and 2.5% of taxable income in 2016. Beginning after 2016, the penalty will be increased annually by the cost-of-living adjustment. Exemptions will be granted for financial hardship, religious objections, American Indians, those without coverage for less than three months, undocumented immigrants, incarcerated individuals, those for whom the lowest cost plan option exceeds 8% of an individual's income, and those with incomes below the tax filing threshold (in 2009 the threshold for taxpayers under age 65 was $9,350 for singles and $18,700 for couples).

EMPLOYER REQUIREMENTS

Requirement to offer coverage	• Assess employers with more than 50 employees that do not offer coverage and have at least one full-time employee who receives a premium tax credit a fee of $2,000 per full-time employee, excluding the first 30 employees from the assessment. Employers with more than 50 employees that offer coverage but have at least one full-time employee receiving a premium tax credit, will pay the lesser of $3,000 for each employee receiving a premium credit or $2,000 for each full-time employee. (Effective January 1, 2014) • Exempt employers with 50 or fewer employees from any of the above penalties. • Require employers that offer coverage to their employees to provide a free choice voucher to employees with incomes less than 400% FPL whose share of the premium exceeds 8% but is less than 9.8% of their income and who choose to enroll in a plan in the Exchange. The voucher amount is equal to what the employer would have paid to provide coverage to the employee under the employer's plan and will be used to offset the premium costs for the plan in which the employee is enrolled. Employers providing free choice vouchers will not be subject to penalties for employees that receive premium credits in the Exchange. (Effective January 1, 2014)
Other requirements	• Require employers with more than 200 employees to automatically enroll employees into health insurance plans offered by the employer. Employees may opt out of coverage.

EXPANSION OF PUBLIC PROGRAMS

Treatment of Medicaid	• Expand Medicaid to all individuals under age 65 (children, pregnant women, parents, and adults without dependent children) with incomes up to 133% FPL based on modified adjusted gross income (as under current law and in the House and Senate-passed bills undocumented immigrants are not eligible for Medicaid). All newly eligible adults will be guaranteed a benchmark benefit package that at least provides the essential health benefits. To finance the coverage for the newly eligible (those who were not previously eligible for a full benchmark benefit package or who were eligible for a capped program but were not enrolled), states will receive 100% federal funding for 2014 through 2016, 95% federal financing in 2017, 94% federal financing in 2018, 93% federal financing in 2019, and 90% federal financing for 2020 and subsequent years. States that have already expanded eligibility to adults with incomes up to 100% FPL will receive a phased-in increase in the federal medical assistance percentage (FMAP) for non-pregnant childless adults so that by 2019 they receive the same federal financing as other states (93% in 2019 and 90% in 2020 and later). States have the option to expand Medicaid eligibility to childless adults beginning on April 1, 2010, but will receive their regular FMAP until 2014. In addition, increase Medicaid payments in fee-for-service and managed care for primary care services provided by primary care doctors (family medicine, general internal medicine or pediatric medicine) to 100% of the Medicare payment rates for 2013 and 2014. States will receive 100% federal financing for the increased payment rates. (Effective January 1, 2014)

Patient Protection and Affordable Care Act (P.L. 111-148)	

EXPANSION OF PUBLIC PROGRAMS (continued)

Treatment of CHIP	• Require states to maintain current income eligibility levels for children in Medicaid and the Children's Health Insurance Program (CHIP) until 2019 and extend funding for CHIP through 2015. CHIP benefit package and cost-sharing rules will continue as under current law. Beginning in 2015, states will receive a 23 percentage point increase in the CHIP match rate up to a cap of 100%. CHIP-eligible children who are unable to enroll in the program due to enrollment caps will be eligible for tax credits in the state Exchanges.

PREMIUM AND COST-SHARING SUBSIDIES TO INDIVIDUALS

Eligibility	• Limit availability of premium credits and cost-sharing subsidies through the Exchanges to U.S. citizens and legal immigrants who meet income limits. Employees who are offered coverage by an employer are not eligible for premium credits unless the employer plan does not have an actuarial value of at least 60% or if the employee share of the premium exceeds 9.5% of income. Legal immigrants who are barred from enrolling in Medicaid during their first five years in the U.S. will be eligible for premium credits.
Premium Credits	• Provide refundable and advanceable premium credits to eligible individuals and families with incomes between 133-400% FPL to purchase insurance through the Exchanges. The premium credits will be tied to the second lowest cost silver plan in the area and will be set on a sliding scale such that the premium contributions are limited to the following percentages of income for specified income levels: Up to 133% FPL: 2% of income 133-150% FPL: 3 – 4% of income 150-200% FPL: 4 – 6.3% of income 200-250% FPL: 6.3 – 8.05% of income 250-300% FPL: 8.05 – 9.5% of income 300-400% FPL: 9.5% of income • Increase the premium contributions for those receiving subsidies annually to reflect the excess of the premium growth over the rate of income growth for 2014-2018. Beginning in 2019, further adjust the premium contributions to reflect the excess of premium growth over CPI if aggregate premiums and cost sharing subsidies exceed .54% of GDP • Provisions related to the premium and cost-sharing subsidies are effective January 1, 2014.
Cost-sharing subsidies	• Provide cost-sharing subsidies to eligible individuals and families. The cost-sharing credits reduce the cost-sharing amounts and annual cost-sharing limits and have the effect of increasing the actuarial value of the basic benefit plan to the following percentages of the full value of the plan for the specified income level: 100-150% FPL: 94% 150-200% FPL: 87% 200-250% FPL: 73% 250-400% FPL: 70%
Verification	• Require verification of both income and citizenship status in determining eligibility for the federal premium credits.
Subsidies and abortion coverage	• Ensure that federal premium or cost-sharing subsidies are not used to purchase coverage for abortion if coverage extends beyond saving the life of the woman or cases of rape or incest (Hyde amendment). If an individual who receives federal assistance purchases coverage in a plan that chooses to cover abortion services beyond those for which federal funds are permitted, those federal subsidy funds (for premiums or cost-sharing) must not be used for the purchase of the abortion coverage and must be segregated from private premium payments or state funds.

PREMIUM SUBSIDIES TO EMPLOYERS

Small business tax credits	• Provide small employers with no more than 25 employees and average annual wages of less than $50,000 that purchase health insurance for employees with a tax credit. – *Phase I:* For tax years 2010 through 2013, provide a tax credit of up to 35% of the employer's contribution toward the employee's health insurance premium if the employer contributes at least 50% of the total premium cost or 50% of a benchmark premium. The full credit will be available to employers with 10 or fewer employees and average annual wages of less than $25,000. The credit phases-out as firm size and average wage increases. Tax-exempt small businesses meeting these requirements are eligible for tax credits of up to 25% of the employer's contribution toward the employee's health insurance premium. – *Phase II:* For tax years 2014 and later, for eligible small businesses that purchase coverage through the state Exchange, provide a tax credit of up to 50% of the employer's contribution toward the employee's health insurance premium if the employer contributes at least 50% of the total premium cost. The credit will be available for two years. The full credit will be available to employers with 10 or fewer employees and average annual wages of less than $25,000. The credit phases-out as firm size and average wage increases. Tax-exempt small businesses meeting these requirements are eligible for tax credits of up to 35% of the employer's contribution toward the employee's health insurance premium.
Reinsurance program	• Create a temporary reinsurance program for employers providing health insurance coverage to retirees over age 55 who are not eligible for Medicare. Program will reimburse employers or insurers for 80% of retiree claims between $15,000 and $90,000. Payments from the reinsurance program will be used to lower the costs for enrollees in the employer plan. Appropriate $5 billion to finance the program. (Effective 90 days following enactment through January 1, 2014)

Patient Protection and Affordable Care Act (P.L. 111-148)

TAX CHANGES RELATED TO HEALTH INSURANCE OR FINANCING HEALTH REFORM

Tax changes related to health insurance	• Impose a tax on individuals without qualifying coverage of the greater of $695 per year up to a maximum of three times that amount or 2.5% of household income to be phased-in beginning in 2014. • Exclude the costs for over-the-counter drugs not prescribed by a doctor from being reimbursed through an HRA or health FSA and from being reimbursed on a tax-free basis through an HSA or Archer Medical Savings Account. (Effective January 1, 2011) • Increase the tax on distributions from a health savings account or an Archer MSA that are not used for qualified medical expenses to 20% (from 10% for HSAs and from 15% for Archer MSAs) of the disbursed amount. (Effective January 1, 2011) • Limit the amount of contributions to a flexible spending account for medical expenses to $2,500 per year increased annually by the cost of living adjustment. (Effective January 1, 2013) • Increase the threshold for the itemized deduction for unreimbursed medical expenses from 7.5% of adjusted gross income to 10% of adjusted gross income for regular tax purposes; waive the increase for individuals age 65 and older for tax years 2013 through 2016. (Effective January 1, 2013) • Increase the Medicare Part A (hospital insurance) tax rate on wages by 0.9% (from 1.45% to 2.35%) on earnings over $200,000 for individual taxpayers and $250,000 for married couples filing jointly and impose a 3.8% tax on unearned income for higher-income taxpayers (thresholds are not indexed). (Effective January 1, 2013) • Impose an excise tax on insurers of employer-sponsored health plans with aggregate values that exceed $10,200 for individual coverage and $27,500 for family coverage (these threshold values will be indexed to the consumer price index for urban consumers (CPI-U) for years beginning in 2020). The threshold amounts will be increased for retired individuals age 55 and older who are not eligible for Medicare and for employees engaged in high-risk professions by $1,650 for individual coverage and $3,450 for family coverage. The threshold amounts may be adjusted upwards if health care costs rise more than expected prior to implementation of the tax in 2018. The threshold amounts will be increased for firms that may have higher health care costs because of the age or gender of their workers. The tax is equal to 40% of the value of the plan that exceeds the threshold amounts and is imposed on the issuer of the health insurance policy, which in the case of a self-insured plan is the plan administrator or, in some cases, the employer. The aggregate value of the health insurance plan includes reimbursements under a flexible spending account for medical expenses (health FSA) or health reimbursement arrangement (HRA), employer contributions to a health savings account (HSA), and coverage for supplementary health insurance coverage, excluding dental and vision coverage. (Effective January 1, 2018) • Eliminate the tax deduction for employers who receive Medicare Part D retiree drug subsidy payments. (Effective January 1, 2013)

Tax changes related to financing health reform	• Impose new annual fees on the pharmaceutical manufacturing sector, according to the following schedule:
	  – $2.8 billion in 2012-2013;
	  – $3.0 billion in 2014-2016;
	  – $4.0 billion in 2017;
	  – $4.1 billion in 2018; and
	  – $2.8 billion in 2019 and later.
	• Impose an annual fee on the health insurance sector, according to the following schedule:
	  – $8 billion in 2014;
	  – $11.3 billion in 2015-2016;
	  – $13.9 billion in 2017;
	  – $14.3 billion in 2018
	  – For subsequent years, the fee shall be the amount from the previous year increased by the rate of premium growth.
	For non-profit insurers, only 50% of net premiums are taken into account in calculating the fee. Exemptions granted for non-profit plans that receive more than 80% of their income from government programs targeting low-income or elderly populations, or people with disabilities, and voluntary employees' beneficiary associations (VEBAs) not established by an employer. (Effective January 1, 2014)
	• Impose an excise tax of 2.3% on the sale of any taxable medical device. (Effective for sales after December 31, 2012)
	• Limit the deductibility of executive and employee compensation to $500,000 per applicable individual for health insurance providers. (Effective January 1, 2009)
	• Impose a tax of 10% on the amount paid for indoor tanning services. (Effective July 1, 2010)
	• Exclude unprocessed fuels from the definition of cellulosic biofuel for purposes of applying the cellulosic biofuel producer credit. (Effective January 1, 2010)
	• Clarify application of the economic substance doctrine and increase penalties for underpayments attributable to a transaction lacking economic substance. (Effective upon enactment)

HEALTH INSURANCE EXCHANGES

Creation and structure of health insurance exchanges	• Create state-based American Health Benefit Exchanges and Small Business Health Options Program (SHOP) Exchanges, administered by a governmental agency or non-profit organization, through which individuals and small businesses with up to 100 employees can purchase qualified coverage. Permit states to allow businesses with more than 100 employees to purchase coverage in the SHOP Exchange beginning in 2017. States may form regional Exchanges or allow more than one Exchange to operate in a state as long as each Exchange serves a distinct geographic area. (Funding available to states to establish Exchanges within one year of enactment and until January 1, 2015)

HEALTH INSURANCE EXCHANGES (continued)

Eligibility to purchase in the exchanges	• Restrict access to coverage through the Exchanges to U.S. citizens and legal immigrants who are not incarcerated.
Public plan option	• Require the Office of Personnel Management to contract with insurers to offer at least two multi-state plans in each Exchange. At least one plan must be offered by a non-profit entity and at least one plan must not provide coverage for abortions beyond those permitted by federal law. Each multi-state plan must be licensed in each state and must meet the qualifications of a qualified health plan. If a state has lower age rating requirements than 3:1, the state may require multi-state plans to meet the more protective age rating rules. These multi-state plans will be offered separately from the Federal Employees Health Benefit Program and will have a separate risk pool.
Consumer Operated and Oriented Plan (CO-OP)	• Create the Consumer Operated and Oriented Plan (CO-OP) program to foster the creation of non-profit, member-run health insurance companies in all 50 states and District of Columbia to offer quali-fied health plans. To be eligible to receive funds, an organization must not be an existing health insurer or sponsored by a state or local government, substantially all of its activities must consist of the issuance of qualified health benefit plans in each state in which it is licensed, governance of the organization must be subject to a majority vote of its members, must operate with a strong consumer focus, and any profits must be used to lower premiums, improve benefits, or improve the quality of health care delivered to its members. (Appropriate $6 billion to finance the program and award loans and grants to establish CO-OPs by July 1, 2013)
Benefit tiers	• Create four benefit categories of plans plus a separate catastrophic plan to be offered through the Exchange, and in the individual and small group markets: – *Bronze plan* represents minimum creditable coverage and provides the essential health benefits, cover 60% of the benefit costs of the plan, with an out-of-pocket limit equal to the Health Savings Account (HSA) current law limit ($5,950 for individuals and $11,900 for families in 2010); – *Silver plan* provides the essential health benefits, covers 70% of the benefit costs of the plan, with the HSA out-of-pocket limits; – *Gold plan* provides the essential health benefits, covers 80% of the benefit costs of the plan, with the HSA out-of-pocket limits; – *Platinum plan* provides the essential health benefits, covers 90% of the benefit costs of the plan, with the HSA out-of-pocket limits; – *Catastrophic plan* available to those up to age 30 or to those who are exempt from the mandate to purchase coverage and provides catastrophic coverage only with the coverage level set at the HSA current law levels except that prevention benefits and coverage for three primary care visits would be exempt from the deductible. This plan is only available in the individual market. • Reduce the out-of-pocket limits for those with incomes up to 400% FPL to the following levels: – 100-200% FPL: one-third of the HSA limits ($1,983/individual and $3,967/family); – 200-300% FPL: one-half of the HSA limits ($2,975/individual and $5,950/family); – 300-400% FPL: two-thirds of the HSA limits ($3,987/individual and $7,973/family). These out-of-pocket reductions are applied within the actuarial limits of the plan and will not increase the actuarial value of the plan.
Insurance market and rating rules	• Require guarantee issue and renewability and allow rating variation based only on age (limited to 3 to 1 ratio), premium rating area, family composition, and tobacco use (limited to 1.5. to 1 ratio) in the individual and the small group market and the Exchange. • Require risk adjustment in the individual and small group markets and in the Exchange. (Effective January 1, 2014)
Qualifications of participating health plans	• Require qualified health plans participating in the Exchange to meet marketing requirements, have adequate provider networks, contract with essential community providers, contract with navigators to conduct outreach and enrollment assistance, be accredited with respect to performance on quality measures, use a uniform enrollment form and standard format to present plan information. • Require qualified health plans to report information on claims payment policies, enrollment, disen-rollment, number of claims denied, cost-sharing requirements, out-of-network policies, and enrollee rights in plain language.
Requirements of the exchanges	• Require the Exchanges to maintain a call center for customer service, and establish procedures for enrolling individuals and businesses and for determining eligibility for tax credits. Require states to develop a single form for applying for state health subsidy programs that can be filed online, in person, by mail or by phone. Permit Exchanges to contract with state Medicaid agencies to determine eligibility for tax credits in the Exchanges. • Require Exchanges to submit financial reports to the Secretary and comply with oversight investiga-tions including a GAO study on the operation and administration of Exchanges.
Basic health plan	• Permit states the option to create a Basic Health Plan for uninsured individuals with incomes between 133-200% FPL who would otherwise be eligible to receive premium subsidies in the Exchange. States opting to provide this coverage will contract with one or more standard plans to provide at least the essential health benefits and must ensure that eligible individuals do not pay more in premiums than they would have paid in the Exchange and that the cost-sharing require-ments do not exceed those of the platinum plan for enrollees with income less than 150% FPL or the gold plan for all other enrollees. States will receive 95% of the funds that would have been paid as federal premium and cost-sharing subsidies for eligible individuals to establish the Basic Health Plan. Individuals with incomes between 133-200% FPL in states creating Basic Health Plans will not be eligible for subsidies in the Exchanges.

Patient Protection and Affordable Care Act (P.L. 111-148)

HEALTH INSURANCE EXCHANGES (continued)

Abortion coverage	• Permit states to prohibit plans participating in the Exchange from providing coverage for abortions. • Require plans that choose to offer coverage for abortions beyond those for which federal funds are permitted (to save the life of the woman and in cases of rape or incest) in states that allow such coverage to create allocation accounts for segregating premium payments for coverage of abortion services from premium payments for coverage for all other services to ensure that no federal premium or cost-sharing subsidies are used to pay for the abortion coverage. Plans must also estimate the actuarial value of covering abortions by taking into account the cost of the abortion benefit (valued at no less than $1 per enrollee per month) and cannot take into account any savings that might be reaped as a result of the abortions. Prohibit plans participating in the Exchanges from discriminating against any provider because of an unwillingness to provide, pay for, provide coverage of, or refer for abortions.
Effective dates	• Unless otherwise noted, provisions relating to the American Health Benefit Exchanges are effective January 1, 2014.

BENEFIT DESIGN

Essential benefits package	• Create an essential health benefits package that provides a comprehensive set of services, covers at least 60% of the actuarial value of the covered benefits, limits annual cost-sharing to the current law HSA limits ($5,950/individual and $11,900/family in 2010), and is not more extensive than the typical employer plan. Require the Secretary to define and annually update the benefit package through a transparent and public process. (Effective January 1, 2014) • Require all qualified health benefits plans, including those offered through the Exchanges and those offered in the individual and small group markets outside the Exchanges, except grandfathered individual and employer-sponsored plans, to offer at least the essential health benefits package. (Effective January 1, 2014)
Abortion coverage	• Prohibit abortion coverage from being required as part of the essential health benefits package. (Effective January 1, 2014)

CHANGES TO PRIVATE INSURANCE

Temporary high-risk pool	• Establish a temporary national high-risk pool to provide health coverage to individuals with pre-existing medical conditions. U.S. citizens and legal immigrants who have a pre-existing medical condition and who have been uninsured for at least six months will be eligible to enroll in the high-risk pool and receive subsidized premiums. Premiums for the pool will be established for a standard population and may vary by no more than 4 to 1 due to age; maximum cost-sharing will be limited to the current law HSA limit ($5,950/individual and $11,900/family in 2010). Appropriate $5 billion to finance the program. (Effective within 90 days of enactment until January 1, 2014)
Medical loss ratio and premium rate reviews	• Require health plans to report the proportion of premium dollars spent on clinical services, quality, and other costs and provide rebates to consumers for the amount of the premium spent on clinical services and quality that is less than 85% for plans in the large group market and 80% for plans in the individual and small group markets. (Requirement to report medical loss ratio effective plan year 2010; requirement to provide rebates effective January 1, 2011) • Establish a process for reviewing increases in health plan premiums and require plans to justify increases. Require states to report on trends in premium increases and recommend whether certain plan should be excluded from the Exchange based on unjustified premium increases. Provide grants to states to support efforts to review and approve premium increases. (Effective beginning plan year 2010)
Administrative simplification	• Adopt standards for financial and administrative transactions to promote administrative simplification. (Effective dates vary)
Dependent coverage	• Provide dependent coverage for children up to age 26 for all individual and group policies. (Effective six months following enactment)
Insurance market rules	• Prohibit individual and group health plans from placing lifetime limits on the dollar value of coverage and prohibit insurers from rescinding coverage except in cases of fraud. Prohibit pre-existing condition exclusions for children. (Effective six months following enactment) Beginning in January 2014, prohibit individual and group health plans from placing annual limits on the dollar value of coverage. Prior to January 2014, plans may only impose annual limits on coverage as determined by the Secretary. • Grandfather existing individual and group plans with respect to new benefit standards, but require these grandfathered plans to extend dependent coverage to adult children up to age 26, prohibit rescissions of coverage, and eliminate waiting periods for coverage of greater than 90 days. Require grandfathered group plans to eliminate lifetime limits on coverage and beginning in 2014, eliminate annual limits on coverage. Prior to 2014, grandfathered group plans may only impose annual limits as determined by the Secretary. Require grandfathered group plans to eliminate pre-existing condition exclusions for children within six months of enactment and by 2014 for adults. (Effective six months following enactment, except where otherwise specified) • Impose the same insurance market regulations relating to guarantee issue, premium rating, and prohibitions on pre-existing condition exclusions in the individual market, in the Exchange, and in the small group market. (See new rating and market rules in Creation of insurance pooling mechanism.) (Effective January 1, 2014)

Patient Protection and Affordable Care Act (P.L. 111-148)

CHANGES TO PRIVATE INSURANCE (continued)

Insurance market rules (continued)	• Require all new policies (except stand-alone dental, vision, and long-term care insurance plans), including those offered through the Exchanges and those offered outside of the Exchanges, to comply with one of the four benefit categories. Existing individual and employer-sponsored plans do not have to meet the new benefit standards. (See description of benefit categories in Creation of insurance pooling mechanism.) (Effective January 1, 2014) • Limit deductibles for health plans in the small group market to $2,000 for individuals and $4,000 for families unless contributions are offered that offset deductible amounts above these limits. This deductible limit will not affect the actuarial value of any plans. (Effective January 1, 2014) • Limit any waiting periods for coverage to 90 days. (Effective January 1, 2014) • Create a temporary reinsurance program to collect payments from health insurers in the individual and group markets to provide payments to plans in the individual market that cover high-risk individuals. Finance the reinsurance program through mandatory contributions by health insurers totaling $25 billion over three years. (Effective January 1, 2014 through December 2016) • Allow states the option of merging the individual and small group markets. (Effective January 1, 2014)
Consumer protections	• Establish an internet website to help residents identify health coverage options (effective July 1, 2010) and develop a standard format for presenting information on coverage options (effective 60 days following enactment). • Develop standards for insurers to use in providing information on benefits and coverage. (Standards developed within 12 months following enactment; insurer must comply with standards within 24 months following enactment)
Health care choice compacts and national plans	• Permit states to form health care choice compacts and allow insurers to sell policies in any state participating in the compact. Insurers selling policies through a compact would only be subject to the laws and regulations of the state where the policy is written or issued, except for rules pertaining to market conduct, unfair trade practices, network adequacy, and consumer protections. Compacts may only be approved if it is determined that the compact will provide coverage that is at least as comprehensive and affordable as coverage provided through the state Exchanges. (Regulations issued by July 1, 2013, compacts may not take effect before January 1, 2016)
Health insurance administration	• Establish the Health Insurance Reform Implementation Fund within the Department of Health and Human Services and allocate $1 billion to implement health reform policies.

STATE ROLE

State role	• Create an American Health Benefit Exchange and a Small Business Health Options Program (SHOP) Exchange for individuals and small businesses and provide oversight of health plans with regard to the new insurance market regulations, consumer protections, rate reviews, solvency, reserve fund requirements, premium taxes, and to define rating areas. • Enroll newly eligible Medicaid beneficiaries into the Medicaid program no later than January 2014 (states have the option to expand enrollment beginning in 2011), coordinate enrollment with the new Exchanges, and implement other specified changes to the Medicaid program. Maintain current Medicaid and CHIP eligibility levels for children until 2019 and maintain current Medicaid eligibility levels for adults until the Exchange is fully operational. A state will be exempt from the maintenance of effort requirement for non-disabled adults with incomes above 133% FPL for any year from January 2011 through December 31, 2013 if the state certifies that it is experiencing a budget deficit or will experience a deficit in the following year. • Establish an office of health insurance consumer assistance or an ombudsman program to serve as an advocate for people with private coverage in the individual and small group markets. (Federal grants available beginning fiscal year 2010) • Permit states to create a Basic Health Plan for uninsured individuals with incomes between 133% and 200% FPL in lieu of these individuals receiving premium subsidies to purchase coverage in the Exchanges. (Effective January 1, 2014) Permit states to obtain a five-year waiver of certain new health insurance requirements if the state can demonstrate that it provides health coverage to all residents that is at least as comprehensive as the coverage required under an Exchange plan and that the state plan does not increase the federal budget deficit. (Effective January 1, 2017)

COST CONTAINMENT

Administrative simplification	• Simplify health insurance administration by adopting a single set of operating rules for eligibility verification and claims status (rules adopted July 1, 2011; effective January 1, 2013), electronic funds transfers and health care payment and remittance (rules adopted July 1, 2012; effective January 1, 2014), and health claims or equivalent encounter information, enrollment and disenrollment in a health plan, health plan premium payments, and referral certification and authorization (rules adopted July 1, 2014; effective January 1, 2016). Health plans must document compliance with these standards or face a penalty of no more than $1 per covered life. (Effective April 1, 2014)

Patient Protection and Affordable Care Act (P.L. 111-148)

COST CONTAINMENT (continued)

Medicare	• Restructure payments to Medicare Advantage (MA) plans by setting payments to different percentages of Medicare fee-for-service (FFS) rates, with higher payments for areas with low FFS rates and lower payments (95% of FFS) for areas with high FFS rates. Phase-in revised payments over 3 years beginning in 2011, for plans in most areas, with payments phased-in over longer periods (4 years and 6 years) for plans in other areas. Provide bonuses to plans receiving 4 or more stars, based on the current 5-star quality rating system for Medicare Advantage plans, beginning in 2012; qualifying plans in qualifying areas receive double bonuses. Modify rebate system with rebates allocated based on a plan's quality rating. Phase-in adjustments to plan payments for coding practices related to the health status of enrollees, with adjustments equaling 5.7% by 2019. Cap total payments, including bonuses, at current payment levels. Require Medicare Advantage plans to remit partial payments to the Secretary if the plan has a medical loss ratio of less than 85%, beginning 2014. Require the Secretary to suspend plan enrollment for 3 years if the medical loss ratio is less than 85% for 2 consecutive years and to terminate the plan contract if the medical loss ratio is less than 85% for 5 consecutive years.
	• Reduce annual market basket updates for inpatient hospital, home health, skilled nursing facility, hospice and other Medicare providers, and adjust for productivity. (Effective dates vary)
	• Freeze the threshold for income-related Medicare Part B premiums for 2011 through 2019, and reduce the Medicare Part D premium subsidy for those with incomes above $85,000/individual and $170,000/couple. (Effective January 1, 2011)
	• Establish an Independent Payment Advisory Board comprised of 15 members to submit legislative proposals containing recommendations to reduce the per capita rate of growth in Medicare spending if spending exceeds a target growth rate. Beginning April 2013, require the Chief Actuary of CMS to project whether Medicare per capita spending exceeds the average of CPI-U and CPI-M, based on a five year period ending that year. If so, beginning January 15, 2014, the Board will submit recommendations to achieve reductions in Medicare spending. Beginning January 2018, the target is modified such that the board submits recommendations if Medicare per capita spending exceeds GDP per capita plus one percent. The Board will submit proposals to the President and Congress for immediate consideration. The Board is prohibited from submitting proposals that would ration care, increase revenues or change benefits, eligibility or Medicare beneficiary cost sharing (including Parts A and B premiums), or would result in a change in the beneficiary premium percentage or low-income subsidies under Part D. Hospitals and hospices (through 2019) and clinical labs (for one year) will not be subject to cost reductions proposed by the Board. The Board must also submit recommendations every other year to slow the growth in national health expenditures while preserving quality of care by January 1, 2015.
	• Reduce Medicare Disproportionate Share Hospital (DSH) payments initially by 75% and subsequently increase payments based on the percent of the population uninsured and the amount of uncompensated care provided (Effective fiscal year 2014)
	• Eliminate the Medicare Improvement Fund. (Effective upon enactment)
	• Allow providers organized as accountable care organizations (ACOs) that voluntarily meet quality thresholds to share in the cost savings they achieve for the Medicare program. To qualify as an ACO, organizations must agree to be accountable for the overall care of their Medicare beneficiaries, have adequate participation of primary care physicians, define processes to promote evidence-based medicine, report on quality and costs, and coordinate care. (Shared savings program established January 1, 2012)
	• Create an Innovation Center within the Centers for Medicare and Medicaid Services to test, evaluate, and expand in Medicare, Medicaid, and CHIP different payment structures and methodologies to reduce program expenditures while maintaining or improving quality of care. Payment reform models that improve quality and reduce the rate of cost growth could be expanded throughout the Medicare, Medicaid, and CHIP programs. (Effective January 1, 2011)
	• Reduce Medicare payments that would otherwise be made to hospitals by specified percentages to account for excess (preventable) hospital readmissions. (Effective October 1, 2012)
	• Reduce Medicare payments to certain hospitals for hospital-acquired conditions by 1%. (Effective fiscal year 2015)
Medicaid	• Increase the Medicaid drug rebate percentage for brand name drugs to 23.1 (except the rebate for clotting factors and drugs approved exclusively for pediatric use increases to 17.1%); increase the Medicaid rebate for non-innovator, multiple source drugs to 13% of average manufacturer price. (Effective January 1, 2010) Extend the drug rebate to Medicaid managed care plans. (Effective upon enactment)
	• Reduce aggregate Medicaid DSH allotments by $.5 billion in 2014, $.6 billion in 2015, $.6 billion in 2016, $1.8 billion in 2017, $5 billion in 2018, $5.6 billion in 2019, and $4 billion in 2020. Require the Secretary to develop a methodology to distribute the DSH reductions in a manner that imposes the largest reduction in DSH allotments for states with the lowest percentage of uninsured or those that do not target DSH payments, imposes smaller reductions for low-DSH states, and accounts for DSH allotments used for 1115 waivers. (Effective October 1, 2011)
	• Prohibit federal payments to states for Medicaid services related to health care acquired conditions. (Effective July 1, 2011)
Prescription drugs	• Authorize the Food and Drug Administration to approve generic versions of biologic drugs and grant biologics manufacturers 12 years of exclusive use before generics can be developed. (Effective upon enactment)

Patient Protection and Affordable Care Act (P.L. 111-148)

COST CONTAINMENT (continued)

Waste, fraud, and abuse	• Reduce waste, fraud, and abuse in public programs by allowing provider screening, enhanced oversight periods for new providers and suppliers, including a 90-day period of enhanced oversight for initial claims of DME suppliers, and enrollment moratoria in areas identified as being at elevated risk of fraud in all public programs, and by requiring Medicare and Medicaid program providers and suppliers to establish compliance programs. Develop a database to capture and share data across federal and state programs, increase penalties for submitting false claims, strengthen standards for community mental health centers and increase funding for anti-fraud activities. (Effective dates vary)

IMPROVING QUALITY/HEALTH SYSTEM PERFORMANCE

Comparative effectiveness research	• Support comparative effectiveness research by establishing a non-profit Patient-Centered Outcomes Research Institute to identify research priorities and conduct research that compares the clinical effectiveness of medical treatments. The Institute will be overseen by an appointed multi-stakeholder Board of Governors and will be assisted by expert advisory panels. Findings from comparative effectiveness research may not be construed as mandates, guidelines, or recommendations for payment, coverage, or treatment or used to deny coverage. (Funding available beginning fiscal year 2010) Terminate the Federal Coordinating Council for Comparative Effectiveness Research that was founded under the American Recovery and Reinvestment Act. (Effective upon enactment)
Medical malpractice	• Award five-year demonstration grants to states to develop, implement, and evaluate alternatives to current tort litigations. Preference will be given to states that have developed alternatives in consultation with relevant stakeholders and that have proposals that are likely to enhance patient safety by reducing medical errors and adverse events and are likely to improve access to liability insurance. (Funding appropriated for five years beginning in fiscal year 2011)
Medicare	• Establish a national Medicare pilot program to develop and evaluate paying a bundled payment for acute, inpatient hospital services, physician services, outpatient hospital services, and post-acute care services for an episode of care that begins three days prior to a hospitalization and spans 30 days following discharge. If the pilot program achieves stated goals of improving or not reducing quality and reducing spending, develop a plan for expanding the pilot program. (Establish pilot program by January 1, 2013; expand program, if appropriate, by January 1, 2016) • Create the Independence at Home demonstration program to provide high-need Medicare beneficiaries with primary care services in their home and allow participating teams of health professionals to share in any savings if they reduce preventable hospitalizations, prevent hospital readmissions, improve health outcomes, improve the efficiency of care, reduce the cost of health care services, and achieve patient satisfaction. (Effective January 1, 2012) • Establish a hospital value-based purchasing program in Medicare to pay hospitals based on performance on quality measures and extend the Medicare physician quality reporting initiative beyond 2010. (Effective October 1, 2012) Develop plans to implement value-based purchasing programs for skilled nursing facilities, home health agencies, and ambulatory surgical centers. (Reports to Congress due January 1, 2011)
Dual eligibles	• Improve care coordination for dual eligibles by creating a new office within the Centers for Medicare and Medicaid services, the Federal Coordinated Health Care Office, to more effectively integrate Medicare and Medicaid benefits and improve coordination between the federal government and states in order to improve access to and quality of care and services for dual eligibles. (Effective March 1, 2010)
Medicaid	• Create a new Medicaid state plan option to permit Medicaid enrollees with at least two chronic conditions, one condition and risk of developing another, or at least one serious and persistent mental health condition to designate a provider as a health home. Provide states taking up the option with 90% FMAP for two years. (Effective January 1, 2011) • Create new demonstration projects in Medicaid to pay bundled payments for episodes of care that include hospitalizations (effective January 1, 2012 through December 31, 2016); to make global capitated payments to safety net hospital systems (effective fiscal years 2010 through 2012); to allow pediatric medical providers organized as accountable care organizations to share in cost-savings (effective January 1, 2012 through December 31, 2016); and to provide Medicaid payments to institutions of mental disease for adult enrollees who require stabilization of an emergency condition (effective October 1, 2011 through December 31, 2015). • Expand the role of the Medicaid and CHIP Payment and Access Commission to include assessments of adult services (including those dually eligible for Medicare and Medicaid). ($11 million in additional funds appropriated for fiscal year 2010)
Primary care	• Increase Medicaid payments in fee-for-service and managed care for primary care services provided by primary care doctors (family medicine, general internal medicine or pediatric medicine) to 100% of the Medicare payment rates for 2013 and 2014. States will receive 100% federal financing for the increased payment rates. (Effective January 1, 2013) • Provide a 10% bonus payment to primary care physicians in Medicare from 2011 through 2015. (Effective for five years beginning January 1, 2011)

Patient Protection and Affordable Care Act (P.L. 111–148)

IMPROVING QUALITY/HEALTH SYSTEM PERFORMANCE (continued)

National quality strategy	• Develop a national quality improvement strategy that includes priorities to improve the delivery of health care services, patient health outcomes, and population health. Create processes for the development of quality measures involving input from multiple stakeholders and for selecting quality measures to be used in reporting to and payment under federal health programs. (National strategy due to Congress by January 1, 2011) • Establish the Community-based Collaborative Care Network Program to support consortiums of health care providers to coordinate and integrate health care services, for low-income uninsured and underinsured populations. (Funds appropriated for five years beginning in FY 2011)
Financial disclosure	• Require disclosure of financial relationships between health entities, including physicians, hospitals, pharmacists, other providers, and manufacturers and distributors of covered drugs, devices, biologicals, and medical supplies. (Report due to Congress April 1, 2013)
Disparities	• Require enhanced collection and reporting of data on race, ethnicity, sex, primary language, disability status, and for underserved rural and frontier populations. Also require collection of access and treatment data for people with disabilities. Require the Secretary to analyze the data to monitor trends in disparities. (Effective two years following enactment)

PREVENTION/WELLNESS

National strategy	• Establish the National Prevention, Health Promotion and Public Health Council to coordinate federal prevention, wellness, and public health activities. Develop a national strategy to improve the nation's health. (Strategy due one year following enactment) Create a Prevention and Public Health Fund to expand and sustain funding for prevention and public health programs. (Initial appropriation in fiscal year 2010) Create task forces on Preventive Services and Community Preventive Services to develop, update, and disseminate evidenced-based recommendations on the use of clinical and community prevention services. (Effective upon enactment) • Establish a Prevention and Public Health Fund for prevention, wellness, and public health activities including prevention research and health screenings, the Education and Outreach Campaign for preventive benefits, and immunization programs. Appropriate $7 billion in funding for fiscal years 2010 through 2015 and $2 billion for each fiscal year after 2015. (Effective fiscal year 2010) • Establish a grant program to support the delivery of evidence-based and community-based prevention and wellness services aimed at strengthening prevention activities, reducing chronic disease rates and addressing health disparities, especially in rural and frontier areas. (Funds appropriated for five years beginning in FY 2010)
Coverage of preventive services	• Improve prevention by covering only proven preventive services and eliminating cost-sharing for preventive services in Medicare and Medicaid. (Effective January 1, 2011) For states that provide Medicaid coverage for and remove cost-sharing for preventive services recommended by the US Preventive Services Task Force and recommended immunizations, provide a one percentage point increase in the FMAP for these services. Increase Medicare payments for certain preventive services to 100% of actual charges or fee schedule rates. (Effective January 1, 2011) • Provide Medicare beneficiaries access to a comprehensive health risk assessment and creation of a personalized prevention plan. (Health risk assessment model developed within 18 months following enactment) Provide incentives to Medicare and Medicaid beneficiaries to complete behavior modification programs. (Effective January 1, 2011 or when program criteria is developed, whichever is first) Require Medicaid coverage for tobacco cessation services for pregnant women. (Effective October 1, 2010) • Require qualified health plans to provide at a minimum coverage without cost-sharing for preventive services rated A or B by the U.S. Preventive Services Task Force, recommended immunizations, preventive care for infants, children, and adolescents, and additional preventive care and screenings for women. (Effective six months following enactment)
Wellness programs	• Provide grants for up to five years to small employers that establish wellness programs. (Funds appropriated for five years beginning in fiscal year 2011) • Provide technical assistance and other resources to evaluate employer-based wellness programs. Conduct a national worksite health policies and programs survey to assess employer-based health policies and programs. (Conduct study within two years following enactment) • Permit employers to offer employees rewards—in the form of premium discounts, waivers of cost-sharing requirements, or benefits that would otherwise not be provided—of up to 30% of the cost of coverage for participating in a wellness program and meeting certain health-related standards. Employers must offer an alternative standard for individuals for whom it is unreasonably difficult or inadvisable to meet the standard. The reward limit may be increased to 50% of the cost of coverage if deemed appropriate. (Effective January 1, 2014) Establish 10-state pilot programs by July 2014 to permit participating states to apply similar rewards for participating in wellness programs in the individual market and expand demonstrations in 2017 if effective. Require a report on the effectiveness and impact of wellness programs. (Report due three years following enactment)
Nutritional information	• Require chain restaurants and food sold from vending machines to disclose the nutritional content of each item. (Proposed regulations issued within one year of enactment)

Patient Protection and Affordable Care Act (P.L. 111-148)	
LONG-TERM CARE	
CLASS Act	• Establish a national, voluntary insurance program for purchasing community living assistance services and supports (CLASS program). Following a five-year vesting period, the program will provide individuals with functional limitations a cash benefit of not less than an average of $50 per day to purchase non-medical services and supports necessary to maintain community residence. The program is financed through voluntary payroll deductions: all working adults will be automatically enrolled in the program, unless they choose to opt-out. (Effective January 1, 2011)
Medicaid	• Extend the Medicaid Money Follows the Person Rebalancing Demonstration program through September 2016 (effective 30 days following enactment) and allocate $10 million per year for five years to continue the Aging and Disability Resource Center initiatives (funds appropriated for fiscal years 2010 through 2014). • Provide states with new options for offering home and community-based services through a Medicaid state plan rather than through a waiver for individuals with incomes up to 300% of the maximum SSI payment and who have a higher level of need and permit states to extend full Medicaid benefits to individual receiving home and community-based services under a state plan. (Effective October 1, 2010) • Establish the Community First Choice Option in Medicaid to provide community-based attendant supports and services to individuals with disabilities who require an institutional level of care. Provide states with an enhanced federal matching rate of an additional six percentage points for reimbursable expenses in the program. Sunset the option after five years. (Effective October 1, 2011) • Create the State Balancing Incentive Program to provide enhanced federal matching payments to eligible states to increase the proportion of non-institutionally-based long-term care services. Selected states will be eligible for FMAP increases for medical assistance expenditures for non-institutionally-based long-term services and supports. (Effective October 1, 2011 through September 30, 2015)
Skilled nursing facility requirements	• Require skilled nursing facilities under Medicare and nursing facilities under Medicaid to disclose information regarding ownership, accountability requirements, and expenditures. Publish standardized information on nursing facilities to a website so Medicare enrollees can compare the facilities. (Effective dates vary)
OTHER INVESTMENTS	

Medicare	• Make improvements to the Medicare program:
	  – Provide a $250 rebate to Medicare beneficiaries who reach the Part D coverage gap in 2010 (Effective January 1, 2010);
	  – Phase down gradually the beneficiary coinsurance rate in the Medicare Part D coverage gap from 100% to 25% by 2020:
	    • For brand-name drugs, require pharmaceutical manufacturers to provide a 50% discount on prescriptions filled in the Medicare Part D coverage gap beginning in 2011, in addition to federal subsidies of 25% of the brand-name drug cost by 2020 (phased in beginning in 2013)
	    • For generic drugs, provide federal subsidies of 75% of the generic drug cost by 2020 for prescriptions filled in the Medicare Part D coverage gap (phased in beginning in 2011); Between 2014 and 2019, reduce the out-of-pocket amount that qualifies an enrollee for catastrophic coverage;
	  – Make Part D cost-sharing for full-benefit dual eligible beneficiaries receiving home and community-based care services equal to the cost-sharing for those who receive institutional care (Effective no earlier than January 1, 2012);
	  – Expand Medicare coverage to individuals who have been exposed to environmental health hazards from living in an area subject to an emergency declaration made as of June 17, 2009 and have developed certain health conditions as a result (Effective upon enactment);
	  – Provide a 10% bonus payment to primary care physicians and to general surgeons practicing in health professional shortage areas, from 2011 through 2015; and
	  – Provide payments totaling $400 million in fiscal years 2011 and 2012 to qualifying hospitals in counties with the lowest quartile Medicare spending; and
	  – Prohibit Medicare Advantage plans from imposing higher cost-sharing requirements for some Medicare covered benefits than is required under the traditional fee-for-service program. (Effective January 1, 2011)

Workforce	• Improve workforce training and development:
	  – Establish a multi-stakeholder Workforce Advisory Committee to develop a national workforce strategy. (Appointments made by September 30, 2010)
	  – Increase the number of Graduate Medical Education (GME) training positions by redistributing currently unused slots, with priorities given to primary care and general surgery and to states with the lowest resident physician-to-population ratios (effective July 1, 2011); increase flexibility in laws and regulations that govern GME funding to promote training in outpatient settings (effective July 1, 2010); and ensure the availability of residency programs in rural and underserved areas. Establish Teaching Health Centers, defined as community-based, ambulatory patient care centers, including federally qualified health centers and other federally-funded health centers that are eligible for Medicare payments for the expenses associated with operating primary care residency programs. (Initial appropriation in fiscal year 2010)

Patient Protection and Affordable Care Act (P.L. 111-148)	
OTHER INVESTMENTS (continued)	
Workforce (continued)	– Increase workforce supply and support training of health professionals through scholarships and loans; support primary care training and capacity building; provide state grants to providers in medically underserved areas; train and recruit providers to serve in rural areas; establish a public health workforce loan repayment program; provide medical residents with training in preventive medicine and public health; promote training of a diverse workforce; and promote cultural competence training of health care professionals. (Effective dates vary) Support the development of interdisciplinary mental and behavioral health training programs (effective fiscal year 2010) and establish a training program for oral health professionals. (Funds appropriated for six years beginning in fiscal year 2010) – Address the projected shortage of nurses and retention of nurses by increasing the capacity for education, supporting training programs, providing loan repayment and retention grants, and creating a career ladder to nursing. (Initial appropriation in fiscal year 2010) Provide grants for up to three years to employ and provide training to family nurse practitioners who provide primary care in federally qualified health centers and nurse-managed health clinics. (Funds appropriated for five years beginning in fiscal year 2011) – Support the development of training programs that focus on primary care models such as medical homes, team management of chronic disease, and those that integrate physical and mental health services. (Funds appropriated for five years beginning in fiscal year 2010)
Community health centers and school-based health centers	• Improve access to care by increasing funding by $11 billion for community health centers and the National Health Service Corps over five years (effective fiscal year 2011); establishing new programs to support school-based health centers (effective fiscal year 2010) and nurse-managed health clinics (effective fiscal year 2010).
Trauma care	• Establish a new trauma center program to strengthen emergency department and trauma center capacity. Fund research on emergency medicine, including pediatric emergency medical research, and develop demonstration programs to design, implement, and evaluate innovative models for emergency care systems. (Funds appropriated beginning in fiscal year 2011)
Public health and disaster preparedness	• Establish a commissioned Regular Corps and a Ready Reserve Corps for service in time of a national emergency. (Funds appropriated for five years beginning in fiscal year 2010)
Requirements for non-profit hospitals	• Impose additional requirements on non-profit hospitals to conduct a community needs assessment every three years and adopt an implementation strategy to meet the identified needs, adopt and widely publicize a financial assistance policy that indicates whether free or discounted care is available and how to apply for the assistance, limit charges to patients who qualify for financial assistance to the amount generally billed to insured patients, and make reasonable attempts to determine eligibility for financial assistance before undertaking extraordinary collection actions. Impose a tax of $50,000 per year for failure to meet these requirements. (Effective for taxable years following enactment)
American Indians	• Reauthorize and amend the Indian Health Care Improvement Act. (Effective upon enactment)
FINANCING	
Coverage and financing	The Congressional Budget Office (CBO) estimates the new health reform law will provide coverage to an additional 32 million when fully implemented in 2019 through a combination of the newly created Exchanges and the Medicaid expansion. CBO estimates the cost of the coverage components of the new law to be $938 billion over ten years. These costs are financed through a combination of savings from Medicare and Medicaid and new taxes and fees, including an excise tax on high-cost insurance, which CBO estimates will raise $32 billion over ten years. CBO also estimates that the health reform law will reduce the deficit by $124 billion over ten years.
Sources of information	www.democraticleader.house.gov/

This publication (#8061) is available on the Kaiser Family Foundation's website at www.kff.org

THE HENRY J. KAISER FAMILY FOUNDATION   www.kff.org
Headquarters: 2400 Sand Hill Road   Menlo Park, CA 94025   650.854.9400   Fax: 650.854.4800
Washington Offices and Barbara Jordan Conference Center: 1330 G Street, NW   Washington, DC 20005   202.347.5270   Fax: 202.347.5274

GLOSSARY

access: An individual's ability to obtain medical services on a timely and financially acceptable basis. Factors determining ease of access also include availability of health care facilities and transportation to them and reasonable hours of operation.

accountable care organizations (ACOs): Encouraged under ACA to develop legal agreements among hospitals, primary care providers, specialists, and other providers that align their incentives to promote quality care and control costs.

accreditation: A decision made by a recognized organization that an institution substantially meets appropriate standards.

activities of daily living (ADLs): Tasks required for a person's normal functioning.

acute care: Medical care of a limited duration, provided in a hospital or outpatient setting, to treat an injury or short-term illness.

advanced practice nurse: Registered nurse, such as a clinical nurse specialist, nurse practitioner, nurse anesthetist, or nurse midwife, with a master's or doctoral degree concentrating on a specific area of practice.

adverse selection: Occurs when a population characteristic, such as age, increases health services utilization and costs above the capitation rate.

alliance: Organizational relationship for specific purposes.

ambulatory care: Health care services that patients receive when they aren't an inpatient or home in bed.

ambulatory care sensitive conditions: Conditions for which patients are hospitalized that could have been handled on an outpatient basis.

appropriate care: Care for which expected health benefits exceed negative consequences.

assisted living: Services provided to individuals who need assistance with activities of daily living.

attending physicians: Doctors who have "privileges" to use a particular hospital for inpatient care of their patients.

average daily census: The average number of patients counted in a health care institution, usually calculated over a 1-year period.

Several of these definitions have been adapted from terms defined in *Healthcare Acronyms & Terms for Boards and Medical Leaders*, published by the Governance Institute, 6333 Greenwich Drive, Suite 200, San Diego, CA 92122, June 2004.

behavioral risk factor: An element of personal behavior—such as unbalanced nutrition, use of tobacco products, leading a sedentary lifestyle, or the abuse of alcohol—that leads to an increased risk of developing one or more diseases or negative health conditions.

benchmark: The best known value for a specific measure, from any source.

beneficiary: Any person, either a subscriber or a dependent, eligible for service under a health plan contract.

benefits: Specific areas of plan coverage, such as outpatient visits, hospitalizations, or prescription drugs, that make up the range of medical services marketed under a health plan.

biotechnology: The application of a technology such as computer science, mechanical engineering, economics, or electronic imaging to the prevention, diagnosis, evaluation, treatment, or management of a disease or negative health condition.

bundled payment: A new approach to payment where the payer provides the physician and hospital a fixed amount for an episode of care or for a time period of care, in the case of a patient with a chronic condition.

capitation: A payment method in which a physician or hospital is paid a fixed amount per-patient per-year, regardless of the volume or cost of services each patient requires.

carrier: An insurer; an underwriter of risk that is engaged in providing, paying for, or reimbursing all or part of the cost of health services under group insurance policies or contracts, medical or hospital services agreements, membership or subscription contracts, or similar arrangements in exchange for premiums or other periodic charges.

case management: Often utilized as part of a managed care system; practitioner (a "gatekeeper") makes decisions regarding the type and volume of services to which the patient may have access.

case manager: An individual who coordinates and oversees other health care workers in finding the most effective methods of caring for specific patients and arranges for necessary services.

catastrophic coverage: A type of insurance that pays for high-cost health care, usually associated with injuries and chronic conditions, such as cancer and AIDS.

census: In the United States, refers to the count of members of the national population and their demographic characteristics undertaken by the U.S. Census Bureau every 10 years; in the health care delivery system specifically, refers to the number of patients in a hospital or other health care institution at any one time.

Centers for Medicare & Medicaid Services (CMS): Administers Medicare, Medicaid, and the Children's Health Insurance Program (CHIP). Formerly called the Health Care Financing Administration (HCFA).

certificates of need: Approval for major new services and construction or renovation of hospitals or related facilities, as issued by states.

charity care: Care given to needy patients without expectation of payment.

chronic care: Treatment or rehabilitative health services provided to individuals on a long-term basis (more than 30 days), in both inpatient and ambulatory settings.

chronic care model: Organizing care to be proactive and focused on keeping people as healthy as possible, instead of performing reactively when people are injured or sick. A critical aspect is the focus on patient self-management.

clinical nurse practitioner: Nurse with extra training who accepts additional clinical responsibility for medical diagnosis or treatment.

clinical trials: The testing on patients in a clinical setting of a diagnostic, preventive, or therapeutic intervention, using a study design that will provide for a valid estimation of safety and efficiency.

closed panel: A managed care plan that contracts with physicians on an exclusive basis for services and does not allow those physicians to see patients who are members of another managed care organization.

coinsurance: An insurance provision that limits the amount of plan coverage to a certain percentage, commonly 80%. Any additional costs are paid out-of-pocket by members.

community hospital: A hospital offering short-term general and other special services, owned by a corporation or agency other than the federal government.

community rating: The rating system by which a plan or an indemnity carrier uses the total experience of the subscribers or members within a given geographic area or "community" to determine a reimbursement rate that is common for all groups, regardless of the individual claims experience of any one group.

comparative effectiveness research: Studies that compare two or more health care technologies, products, or services against each other or against the conventional standard of care. Interventions are also compared for their costs relative to their benefits.

competency: The combination of knowledge, skills, personal characteristics, and individual and social behavior needed to perform a job effectively.

complementary and alternative medicine: Diagnostic and treatment interventions that fall outside the realm of state-licensed medical practice as it is defined by the privilege to use certain restricted diagnostic regimens, prescribe drugs, and practice surgery. Such disciplines include chiropractic, acupuncture, homeopathy, herbal medicine, naturopathy, and therapeutic touch.

comprehensive coverage: A health insurance system that pays for a broad range of services.

Consolidated Omnibus Budget Reconciliation Act of 1985 (COBRA): Federal law (P.L. 99–272) that requires all employer-sponsored health plans to offer certain employees and their families the opportunity to continue, at their personal expense, health insurance coverage under their group plan for up to 18, 24, or 36 months, depending on the qualifying event, after their coverage normally would have ceased (e.g., due to the death or retirement of the employee, divorce or legal separation, resignation or termination of employment, or bankruptcy of the employer).

continuous quality improvement (CQI): A systematic approach to improve processes of health care, such as admission to the hospital or delivery of patient medications.

co-payment: A specified amount that an insured individual must pay for a specified service or procedure (e.g., $8 for an office visit).

cost-sharing: A provision that requires individuals to cover some part of their medical expenses (i.e., co-payments, coinsurance, deductibles).

cost-shifting: Passing the excess costs of care for one group onto another group. For example, if the rate one group of health plan enrollees pays for services is less than the actual cost of those services, the difference can be made up through higher-than-cost charges to another group.

credentialing: The most common use of the term refers to obtaining and reviewing the documentation of professional providers.

critical pathway: The mapping out of day-to-day recommendations for patient care based on best practices and scientific evidence.

data: In health, an event, condition, or disease occurrence that is counted. In health services, an episode of care, costs of care, expenditures, quantification of human resources and facilities and their characteristics, and the like.

deductible: The amount insured individuals must pay out-of-pocket, usually annually on a calendar-year basis, before insurance will begin to cover their health care costs.

defined contribution plan: Benefits plan that gives employees a certain amount of total compensation to allocate among various benefits, rather than providing employees with the specific benefits, such as hospitalization coverage.

demographic characteristics: Such characteristics of an individual or population group (averages in the latter case) as age, sex, marital status, ethnicity, geographic location, occupation, and income.

denominator: For health care, the total number of people among whom numerator items are being counted.

diagnosis related groups (DRGs): Groups of inpatient discharges with final diagnoses that are similar clinically and in resource consumption; used as a basis of payment by the Medicare program and, as a result, widely accepted by others.

discharge planning: A part of the patient management guidelines and the nursing care plan that identifies the expected discharge date and coordinates the various services necessary to achieve the target.

disproportionate share hospital (DSH): A hospital that provides a large amount (or disproportionate share) of uncompensated care and/or care to Medicaid and low income Medicare beneficiaries.

electronic health records (EHRs): Electronic patient information available across providers and setting. Kaiser-Permanente, for example, can electronically connect patients to their health care team, to their personal health information, and to relevant medical knowledge to promote integrated care.

Emergency Medical Treatment and Labor Act (EMTALA): A portion of the COBRA law setting forth requirements for hospitals participating in Medicare to provide emergency care so that patients who cannot pay are not "dumped" to other hospitals.

Employee Retirement Income Security Act (ERISA): A 1974 federal law (P.L. 93–406) that set the standards of disclosure for employee benefit plans to ensure workers the right to at least part of their pensions. The law governs most private pensions and other employee benefits and overrides all state laws that concern employee benefits, including health benefits; therefore, ERISA preempts state laws in their application to self-funded, private employer-sponsored health insurance plans.

encounter: A patient visit to a provider. The term often refers to visits to providers by patients in capitated health plans.

enrollment: The process by which an individual and family become subscriber(s) for coverage in a health plan. This may be done either through an actual signing up of the individual, or through a collective bargaining agreement, or the employer's conditions of employment. A result is that the health plan is aware of its entire population of eligible beneficiaries. As a usual practice, individuals must notify the health plan of any changes in family status that affect the enrollment of dependents.

entitlements: Government benefits (e.g., Medicare, Medicaid, Social Security, food stamps) that are provided automatically to all qualified individuals, and are therefore part of mandatory spending programs.

evidence-based medicine (EBM): That portion of medical practice, estimated at much less than 50%, that is based on established scientific findings.

experience rating: A method used to determine the cost of health insurance premiums, whereby the cost is based on the previous amount a certain group (e.g., all the employees of a particular business) for medical services.

Federal Employee Health Benefits Program (FEHBP): The health plans made available to federal employees as part of their employment benefits.

fee-for-service: A billing system in which a health care provider charges a patient a set amount for each individual service provided.

fee schedule: A listing of accepted fees or established allowances for specified medical procedures, as used in health plans; it usually represents the maximum amounts the program will pay for the specified service.

fixed costs: Costs that do not change or vary with fluctuations in enrollment or in utilization of services.

formulary: A listing of drugs prepared by, for example, a hospital or a managed care company, that a drug plan will pay for.

for-profit hospitals: Those owned by private corporations that declare dividends or otherwise distribute profits to individuals, also called investor-owned; many are also community hospitals.

full-time equivalent (FTE): Refers to the number of hours employees must work to be regarded as full-time; thus two half-time employees, each working 20 hours a week, may equal one full-time equivalent.

gatekeeper: A health care practitioner who makes decisions regarding the type and volume of services to which a patient may have access; generally used by health maintenance organizations (HMOs) to control unnecessary utilization of services.

generic drug: A therapeutic drug, originally protected by a patent, the chemical composition of which meets the standards for that drug set by the Food and Drug Administration, usually manufactured by a different company than the branded drug.

governance: The activity of an organization that monitors the outside environment, selects appropriate alternatives, and negotiates the implementation of these alternatives with others inside and outside the organization.

governing board: A group of individuals who, under state law, own an organization, regardless of whether they can obtain any financial advantage through such ownership.

graduate medical education: The education and training of physicians beyond the 4 years of medical school, in positions that may be termed internships, residencies, fellowships, postgraduate years 1, 2, 3, and so on. Although one can enter medical school with only an undergraduate degree, in the United States, the 4 years of medical school leading to the MD or DO (doctor of osteopathy) degrees are customarily referred to as "undergraduate medical education."

group model: An HMO that contracts with a medical group for the provision of health care services. The relationship between the HMO and the medical group is generally very close, although there are wide variations in the relative independence of the group from the HMO; a form of closed panel health plan.

group practice: Three or more physicians who deliver patient care, make joint use of equipment and personnel, and divide income by a prearranged formula.

health care delivery: The provision of preventive, treatment, or rehabilitative health services, from short-term to long-term, to individuals as well as groups of people, by individual practitioners, institutions, or public health agencies.

health care providers: Professional health service workers—physicians, dentists, psychologists—who are licensed to practice independently of any other health service worker; hospitals and other institutions offering health care services.

health care workforce: All of the people, professional and nonprofessional alike, who work in the health care services industry.

Health Insurance Portability and Accountability Act of 1996 (HIPAA): Key provisions of this federal law improve health coverage for workers and their families when they change or lose jobs and establish privacy standards for medical information, overseen by the Department of Health and Human Services Office of Civil Rights.

health maintenance organization (HMO): A managed care company that organizes and provides health care for its enrollees for a fixed prepaid premium.

Health Plan Employer Data and Information Set (HEDIS): A standard set of performance measures of the quality and performance of health plans, sponsored by the National Committee for Quality Assurance (NCQA).

health promotion (personal): Personal health promotion is the science and art of helping people change their lifestyles to move toward a state of optimal health. Optimal health is defined as a balance of physical, emotional, social, spiritual, and intellectual health.

health systems: Organizations that operate multiple service units under single ownership.

Healthy People 2020: Formal goals and objectives for the nation's health status, updated every 10 years by the federal government.

home health care: Health services provided in an individual's home.

hospice care: Programs that operate in different settings to provide palliative care and comprehensive support services to dying patients, as well as counseling and bereavement support for their family members. Hospice care is reimbursable under Medicare and many state Medicaid programs, as well as by private insurers.

hospitalists: Physicians, usually hospital employees, who practice only in acute care settings to provide inpatient care otherwise provided by attending physicians.

hospitalization: The admission of a patient to a hospital.

hospitalization coverage: A type of insurance coverage for most inpatient hospital costs (e.g., room and board), diagnostic and therapeutic services, care for emergency illnesses or injuries, laboratory and X ray services, and certain other specified procedures.

human genome: The human genetic code, involving billions of base pairs in the DNA sequence of 26,000 to 40,000 genes in the 23 human chromosomes.

incidence: The number of new events, disease cases, or conditions counted in a defined population during a defined period of time.

indemnity insurance: Benefits paid in a predetermined amount in the event of a covered loss; differs from reimbursement, which provides benefits based on actual expenses incurred.

There are fewer restrictions on what a doctor may charge and what an insurer may pay for a treatment, and generally there are also fewer restrictions on a patient's ability to access specialty services.

independent practice association (IPA): Association of independent physicians formed as a separate legal entity for contracting purposes with health plans. Physicians see fee-for-service patients as well as those enrolled.

infant mortality: The death of a child born alive before 1 year of age.

information technology: Electronic systems for communicating information. Health care organizations want information technology that is accessible—with privacy safeguards—to multiple users within an organization.

insurance exchanges: New entities that will be established under the ACA, insurance exchanges offer private insurance policies with premium rates subsidized by federal dollars. They can be offered at various levels and in various ways, usually by states.

integrated delivery system (IDS): A group of health care organizations that collectively provides a full range of health-related services in a coordinated fashion to those using the system.

integration, horizontal: Affiliations among providers of the same type (e.g., a hospital forming relationships with other hospitals).

integration, vertical: Affiliations among providers of different types (e.g., a hospital, clinic, and nursing home forming an affiliation).

international medical school graduate: A U.S. citizen or noncitizen physician who has graduated from a medical school not located in the United States that is also not accredited by the U.S. medical school accrediting body, the Liaison Committee on Medical Education.

investor-owned hospital: A hospital owned by one or more private parties or a corporation for the purpose of generating a profitable return on investment.

The Joint Commission: Formerly the Joint Commission on Accreditation of Healthcare Organizations (JCAHO), The Joint Commission is a national organization of representatives of health care providers: American College of Physicians, American College of Surgeons, American Hospital Association, American Medical Association, and consumer representatives. The Joint Commission inspects and accredits the quality of operations for hospitals and other health care organizations.

length of stay: Days billed for a period of hospitalization.

licensure: A system established by a given state recognizing the achievement of a defined level of education, experience, and examination performance, which qualifies the person or organization meeting those standards to work or operate in a defined area of practice, which is prohibited to any person or organization that has not met those standards.

life expectancy: The predicted average number of years of life remaining for a person at a given age.

long-term care: A general term for a range of services provided to chronically ill, physically disabled, or mentally disabled patients in a nursing home or receiving long-term home health care.

loss ratio: A term used to describe the amount of money spent on health care. An insurance company with a loss ratio of 0.85, for instance, spends 85 cents of every premium dollar on health care and the remaining 15 cents on administrative costs, such as marketing and profits.

managed care: A system of health care delivery that influences or controls utilization of services and costs of services. The degree of influence depends on the model used. For example, a preferred provider organization (PPO) charges patients lower rates if they use the providers in its preferred network. HMOs, on the other hand, may choose not to reimburse for health services received from providers with whom the HMO does not contract.

mandated benefits: Benefits that a health plan is required to provide by law. This term generally refers to benefits above and beyond routine insurance-type benefits and it generally applies at the state level (where there is high variability). Common examples include in vitro fertilization, defined days of inpatient mental health or substance abuse treatment, and other special condition treatments. Self-funded plans are exempt from mandated benefits under the Employee Retirement Income Security Act (ERISA).

Medicaid: A joint federal/state program of health care coverage for low income individuals, under Title XIX of the federal Social Security Act. States set benefits and eligibility requirements and administer the program. Medicaid is the major source of payment for nursing home care of the elderly.

medical home: A physician-directed medical practice with a team of providers in which each patient has an ongoing relationship with a personal physician, who coordinates care.

medical savings account: Accounts similar to individual retirement accounts (IRAs) into which employers and employees can make tax-deferred contributions and from which employees may withdraw funds to pay covered health care expenses.

medically indigent: Those who do not have and cannot afford medical insurance coverage yet who are not eligible financially for Medicaid.

Medicare: A federal entitlement program of medical and health care coverage for the elderly and disabled and people with end-stage renal disease, governed by Title XVIII of the federal Social Security Act and consisting of several parts: Part A for institutional and home care; Part B for physician care; a managed care component (informally called Part C); and Part D, covering prescription drugs.

Medicare Prescription Drug, Improvement, and Modernization Act (MMA): Federal law signed in 2004 that offers a discount card at a nominal fee to Medicare beneficiaries for drugs and a prescription drug benefit that started in 2006 for those on Medicare who enroll and pay a premium.

medigap: Also known as Medicare supplemental insurance, a type of private insurance coverage that may be purchased by an individual enrolled in Medicare to cover certain needed services that are not covered by Medicare Parts A or B (i.e., "gaps").

morbidity: An episode of sickness, as defined by a health professional. A morbidity rate is the number of such episodes occurring in a given population during a given period of time.

mortality: A death. A mortality rate is the number of deaths—either the crude rate, which is all deaths, or a specific rate, which is number of deaths by, for example, a specific cause, at a specific location, or within a specific age group—occurring during a given period of time.

multi-specialty group practice (MSGP): An MSGP employs primary and specialty care physicians who share common governance, infrastructure, and finances; refer patients for services offered within the group; and are typically affiliated with a particular hospital or hospitals.

natality: A live birth. The natality rate is the number of live births occurring in a given population during a given period of time.

national health insurance: A system for paying for one or more categories of health care services that is organized on a nationwide basis, established by and usually operated by a government agency.

National Health Service (NHS): Refers to a comprehensive, government-funded and operated system, such as that found in Great Britain.

National Institute for Health and Clinical Excellence (NICE): Housed within the UK's National Health Service, NICE is an organization supporting comparative effectiveness research as a way to improve health outcomes, reduce unwarranted practice variation, and diffuse information about new technologies and their effectiveness.

network: An arrangement of several delivery points (i.e., medical group practices affiliated with a managed care organization); an arrangement of HMOs (either autonomous and separate legal entities or subsidiaries of a larger corporation) using one common insuring mechanism such as BlueCross BlueShield; a broker organization (health plan) that arranges with physician groups, carriers, payer agencies, consumer groups, and others for services provided to enrollees.

nonprofit or not-for-profit plan: A term applied to a prepaid health plan under which no part of the net earnings accrues, or may lawfully accrue, to the benefit of any private shareholder or individual. An organization that has received 501(c)(3) or 501(c)(4) designation by the Internal Revenue Service.

nurse practitioner (NP): Registered nurses who have been trained at the master's level in providing primary care services, expanded health care evaluations and decision making, and can write prescriptions, either independently or under a physician's supervision, depending on state law.

office visit: A formal, face-to-face contact between a physician and a patient in a health center, office, or hospital outpatient department.

open enrollment period: A requirement that all possible customers for a particular health insurance policy be accepted and, once accepted, they cannot be terminated by the insurer due to claims experience.

outcomes: Measures of treatments and effectiveness in terms of access, quality, and cost.

outlier: Under a DRG system of payment, additional per diem payments are made to hospitals for cases requiring extraordinary stays. Such cases are referred to as long-stay outliers.

Patient Protection and Affordable Care Act of 2010 (ACA): The 2010 health reform act, which will extend health insurance coverage to more than 32 million Americans and prevents insurance companies from denying coverage due to preexisting medical conditions.

per diem payment: Reimbursement rates that are paid to providers for each day of services provided to a patient, based on the patient's illness or condition.

physician assistant (PA): A specially trained and licensed worker who performs certain medical procedures under the supervision of a physician. Physician assistants are usually not registered nurses.

point-of-service plan (POS): A managed care plan that offers enrollees the option of receiving services from participating or nonparticipating providers. The benefits package is designed to encourage the use of participating providers through higher deductibles or only partial reimbursement for services provided by nonparticipating providers.

policy: Guidelines adopted by organizations and governments that promote constrained decision making and action and limit subsequent choices.

preexisting condition: A physical and/or mental condition of an insured that first manifests itself prior to issuance of a policy or that exists prior to issuance and for which treatment was received.

preferred provider organization (PPO): A limited group (panel) of providers (doctors and/or hospitals) who agree to provide health care to subscribers for a negotiated and usually discounted fee and who agree to utilization review.

premium: A periodic payment required to keep an insurance policy in force.

prepayment: A method of providing, in advance, for the cost of predetermined benefits for a population group through regular periodic payments in the form of premiums, dues, or contributions, including contributions that are made to a health and welfare fund by employers on behalf of their employees and payments to managed care organizations made by federal agencies for people who are Medicare eligible.

prescription: An order, usually made in writing, from a licensed physician or an authorized designee to a pharmacy, directing the latter to dispense a given drug, with written instructions for its use.

prevalence: The total number of events, disease cases, or conditions existing in a defined population, counted during a defined period of time or at a given point in time (known as point-prevalence).

primary care: The general health care that people receive on a routine basis that is not associated with an acute or chronic illness or disability and may be provided by a physician, nurse practitioner, or physician assistant.

primary care practitioners: Doctors in family practice, general internal medicine, obstetrics/gynecology, or pediatrics; nurse practitioners and midwives; and may also include psychiatrists and emergency care physicians.

privileges: Rights granted annually to physicians and affiliate staff members to perform specified kinds of care in the hospital.

public hospital: A hospital operated by a government agency. In the United States, the most common are the federal Veterans Health Administration hospitals (restricted to certain categories of veterans), state mental hospitals, and county and city general hospitals.

quality assurance: A formal set of activities to measure the quality of services provided; these may also include corrective measures.

quality of care: Measurement of the quality of health care provided to individuals or groups of patients, against a previously defined standard.

rates, crude and specific: A rate is a measure of some event, disease, or condition occurring in members of a defined population divided by the total number in that population. For crude rates, the whole population is the denominator. A specific rate defines the denominator by one or more demographic characteristics.

registered nurse (RN): A nurse who is a graduate of an approved education program leading to a diploma, an associate degree, or a bachelor's degree who also has met the requirements of experience and exam passage to be licensed in a given state.

reinsurance: Insurance purchased by a health plan to protect it against extremely high-cost cases.

reserves: A fiscal method of withholding a certain percentage of premiums to provide a fund for committed but undelivered health care and such uncertainties as higher hospital utilization levels than expected, overutilization of referrals, and catastrophes.

resource-based relative value scale (RBRVS): As of January 1, 1992, Medicare payments are based on a resource-based relative value scale (which replaced the former "usual, customary and reasonable" charge mechanism) for fee-for-service providers participating in the Medicare program. The objective is for physician fees to reflect the relative value of work performed, their practice expense, and malpractice insurance costs.

risk: Any chance of loss, or the possibility that revenues of the health plan will not be sufficient to cover expenditures incurred in the delivery of contractual services.

risk contract: A contract to provide services to beneficiaries under which the health plan receives a fixed monthly payment for enrolled members and then must provide all services on an at-risk basis.

risk management: Identification, evaluation, and corrective action against organizational behavior that would otherwise result in financial loss or legal liability.

Sarbanes-Oxley Act (SOA): The 2002 federal legislation that affects corporate governance, financial disclosure, and the practice of public accounting.

self-insurance: A program for providing group insurance with benefits financed entirely through the internal means of the policyholder, in place of purchasing coverage from commercial carriers. By self-insuring, firms avoid paying state taxes on premiums and are largely exempt from state-imposed mandates.

skilled nursing facility (SNF): Facility providing care for patients who no longer require treatment in the hospital but who do require 24-hour medical care or rehabilitation services.

socialized medicine: Usually an epithet used by opponents of any type of national government involvement in either the financing or operation of a national health care delivery system, regardless of whether such a government could be defined as socialist.

solo practice: Individual practice of medicine by a physician who does not practice in a group or does not share personnel, facilities, or equipment with three or more physicians.

staff model: An HMO that employs providers who see members in their own facilities. A form of closed-panel HMO.

stakeholders: Persons with an interest in the performance of an organization. Examples of hospital stakeholders are physicians and nurses, payers, managers, patients, and government.

Stark legislation: Federal laws (named after their sponsor, California Rep. Fortney "Pete" Stark) that place limits on physicians' referring patients to facilities in which they have a financial interest.

strategic planning: A process reviewing the mission, environmental surveillance, and previous planning decisions used to establish major goals and nonrecurring resource allocation decisions of an organization.

surveillance: Ongoing observation of a population for rapid and accurate detection of events, conditions, or emerging diseases.

teaching hospital: A hospital in which undergraduate and/or graduate medical education takes place.

tertiary care: Medical care or procedures that are performed by specialized physicians and teams in specially equipped hospitals. Advanced cancer care, burn treatment, and advanced surgeries are examples of tertiary care. Quaternary care is even more highly specialized, rarely used, and sometimes experimental.

third-party administrator: An organization that acts as an intermediary between the provider and consumer of care but does not insure care.

underwriting: Bearing the risk for something (i.e., a policy is underwritten by an insurance company); also the analysis that is done for a group to determine whether it should be offered coverage.

uninsured: In the United States, a person who has no third-party source of payment for health care services.

universal health insurance: A national health insurance system that provides for comprehensive coverage for all permanent residents of a country.

utilization: Quantity of services used by patients, such as hospital days, physician visits, or prescriptions.

utilization review: A system for measuring and evaluating the how physicians utilize services for their patients, against established standards.

vital statistics: Numbers and rates for births, deaths, abortions, fetal deaths, fertility, life expectancy, marriages, and divorces.

volunteers: People who are not paid for giving their time and service to a health care organization, their only compensation being personal satisfaction.

wraparound plan: Insurance or health plan coverage for co-payments and deductibles that are not covered under a member's basic plan, such as Medicare.

INDEX

Note. f refers to a figure; *t* refers to a table.